THE OLD WEST

TRAVEL · HISTORIC · AMERICA

First Edition

Fodor's Travel Publications
New York | Toronto | London | Sydney | Auckland
www.fodors.com

Fodor's Travel Historic America: The Old West

Senior Editor: Constance Jones

Contributors

Editors: Emmanuelle Morgen, Amanda Theunissen, William Travis
Writers: Jean Arthur (Montana), Cheryl Murfin Bond (Oregon), Kate Boyes (Utah), Geoff Carter (Washington), Deke Castleman (Nevada), Lisa Church (Utah), Andrew Collins (New Mexico), Lori Cumpston (Colorado), Lisa Dunford (Texas), Foss Farrar (Oklahoma), Karen Gibson (Oklahoma), Tom Griffith (South Dakota), Marilyn Haddrill (New Mexico, Texas), Lisa Hamilton (California), Candice Helseth (North Dakota), Eric Lucas (Washington), Diana Lambdin Meyer (Nebraska), Carrie Miner (Arizona), Cynthia Mines (Kansas), Janet Moore (Texas), Candy Moulton (Introduction, Idaho, Wyoming), June Naylor (Texas), Susan S. Novak (Kansas), Reed Parsell (California), Patrick Regan (Colorado), Holly Smith (Oregon), John Andrew Vlahides (California), Bob and Gloria Willis (Arizona), Bobbi Zane (California)
Design: Tina Malaney
Maps: Rebecca Baer, Robert Blake, David Lindroth, Todd Pasini
Production/Manufacturing: Colleen Ziemba
Cover Photos: Log cabins and wagons in ghost town, Cody, Wyoming, Kevin R. Morris/Corbis; Miner of Clear Creek near Idaho Springs, L.C. McClure/Denver Public Library, Western History Collection (Call# MCC-367)

First Edition

ISBN 1–4000–1232–5

ISSN 1541–3225

Important Tip
Although all prices, opening times, and other details in this book are based on information supplied to us at press time, changes occur all the time in the travel world, and Fodor's cannot accept responsibility for facts that become outdated or for inadvertent errors or omissions. So **always confirm information when it matters,** especially if you're making a detour to visit a specific place.

Special Sales
Fodor's Travel Publications are available at special discounts for bulk purchases for sales promotions or premiums. Special editions, including personalized covers, excerpts of existing guides, and corporate imprints, can be created in large quantities for special needs. For more information, contact your local bookseller or write to Special Markets, Fodor's Travel Publications, 1745 Broadway, New York, NY 10019. Inquiries for Canada should be directed to your local Canadian bookseller or sent to Random House of Canada, Ltd., Marketing Department, 2775 Matheson Boulevard East, Mississauga, Ontario L4W 4P7. Inquiries from the United Kingdom should be sent to Fodor's Travel Publications, 20 Vauxhall Bridge Road, London SW1V 2SA, England.

PRINTED IN THE UNITED STATES OF AMERICA

10 9 8 7 6 5 4 3 2 1

CONTENTS

TRAVELING THROUGH HISTORY

From the beginning, America has been a land of travelers—settlers on the move on foot and horseback, in sailing ships, wagon trains, canal barges, railroad cars, and pack-coaches—and there has never been a better time than now to partake of that tradition. There is a grand excitement in going to the very sites where the nation's character was formed and actually setting foot in momentous places you've until now only read about. When you're there you discover new things about the country's past, in the process deepening your understanding of America's historic events.

If you want to get to know what the United States is all about, nothing beats visiting the places where the nation's life story unfolded. When you stroll the streets of heritage-rich towns, gaze across battlefields where destiny was determined, and enter rooms where history was made, you travel back in time. Before your eyes, the past sheds its dusty mantle and becomes new again, a fresh and even thrilling experience for you to relive. You imagine you can see pioneers heading west, watch colonists going about their business, hear the militia practicing its maneuvers, and smell the powdery ink on the latest broadsheet. Whether you are a great-grandparent who's heard (and perhaps told) the story over and over, or a third-grader who's finding out about it for the very first time, a trip into the past can leave you with a whole new perspective on the people and events that made America what it is today.

And what about that third-grader (or sixth-grader or tenth-grader)? Even if your kids yawn their way through their history homework, a field trip to a place they've learned about in school is almost guaranteed not to bore them. Leave behind the textbook and head for the trail, and what they've read about immediately becomes real. Take the lesson out of the classroom and into the cabin, and suddenly even the most reluctant students can't resist the urge to join in. When you're face-to-face with the America of long ago, history bursts to life before your eyes, in illuminating and often unexpected ways. It makes for an unforgettable vacation.

LET US HEAR FROM YOU

Keeping a travel guide fresh and up-to-date is a big job, and we welcome any and all comments. We'd love to have your thoughts on places we've listed, and we're interested in hearing about your own special finds. Our guides are thoroughly updated for each new edition, and we're always adding new information, so your feedback is vital. Contact us via e-mail in care of editors@fodors.com (specifying the name of the book on the subject line) or via snail mail in care of *Travel Historic America: The Old West,* at Fodor's, 1745 Broadway, New York, NY 10019. We look forward to hearing from you. And in the meantime, have a wonderful trip.

HOW TO USE THIS GUIDE

▼▼▼

Travel Historic America: The Old West contains everything you need to know in order to plan and enjoy your trip into the American past. For a family on summer vacation, a retiree traveling the country by RV, a college student on break, or simply anyone who wants to be immersed in our country's history up-close and in-person, the book that you hold in your hands is a great tool. With it as your guide you can tour an old silver mine, examine pioneer artifacts in a museum, or grab a bite in a bullet-scarred saloon. Whatever your interests, this book will help you make the story of America part of your personal history.

WHAT'S INSIDE

For each of the 17 states that was part of the Old West, you will find information on the cities, villages, and ghost towns where you can still glimpse the American frontier. *Travel Historic America: The Old West* includes as many authentically historic towns, attractions, events, restaurants, and lodgings as space allows, focusing on delivering to you the kind of in-depth, expert knowledge that you won't get anywhere else. The guide opens with an introduction to that uniquely American time and place in history known as the Old West; the text is accompanied by a time line that highlights the pivotal moments of the story. A map of the region shows the cities and highways of today as well as the old trails of the past. Also marked on the map are the routes of the regional driving tours described in the introduction; these itineraries take you deep into the past as you travel from state to state.

In alphabetical order by state name, the chapters contain everything you need to know to plan a fun and fulfilling Old West vacation. Whether you are trying to decide which part of the Old West to explore or have already chosen a destination, the opening sections of the state chapters can answer your questions. A brief historical overview of the state, accompanied by a time line of events, opens each chapter. On a state map are marked the towns listed within the chapter, plus major roads and landmarks, and the routes of the state driving tours.

The driving tours mapped out for each state are an excellent trip-planning tool. To help you customize your trip according to your interests, the driving tours trace themes—pioneer trails, ranching empires, Indian wars, etc.—in the early history of the state. Each is an efficient yet adventurous itinerary for a road trip, complete with recommendations on which routes to take for a great drive, interesting places to stop along the way, and historic places to eat and sleep. The towns visited on the driving tours, along with the many other communities of historical interest included in the guide, are listed in alphabetical order within the chapters. As you peruse the town listings you will also come across boxes filled with fascinating anecdotes and legends that will enrich your Old West experience.

The final chapter of the guide, "Resources," directs you to a wealth of sources for further information on the history of the Old West and contacts who can help you plan your trip. There are both general sources, which can inform you about the Old West as a whole, and state-specific sources, which can tell you what you need to know about the state you plan to visit. Organizations listed under "Historical and Tourism Organizations" specialize in supplying information, while those under "History Tours and Packages" can set you up on a pre-planned trip or can customize a guided itinerary for you. Under "Further Reading" are the kind of solidly researched yet enjoyably readable books that can put you in the mood for your Old West adventure months ahead of time—or prolong the excitement for months afterward.

At the back of the book is a geographical directory of towns by region. Use this directory to cross-reference listed towns with others that are nearby. In the alphabetical index that follows the geographical directory you can look up the people, places, and events that are described in the guide.

Where to Find It Town by Town

▼▼▼

It's easy to find the city you are looking for in *Travel Historic America: The Old West,* because the towns within each state are listed alphabetically.

TOWN LISTINGS, A TO Z
A brief description of each town summarizes its place in history and its character today. Some of the towns included in the guide played an important role in history, whereas others represent towns typical of the period. You can get more information before you visit by contacting the organizations—chambers of commerce, visitor bureaus, historical associations, and the like—listed below the town introduction.

ATTRACTIONS AND EVENTS
From farmsteads and historic homes to heritage festivals and battle reenactments, the historically oriented things you can see and do in and around each town are all here, and it's all true to history. You won't find hokey theme parks or bogus roadside attractions in these pages: every destination listed is of genuine historical significance. You'll learn about museums, walking tours, hands-on activities, state and national parks, theatrical performances, narrated van trips, and annual events. Note that attractions in smaller nearby towns are sometimes listed under larger towns, and that when a town is of interest in its entirety but is too small to have its own heading, it may appear as an attraction under a larger town.

HISTORIC DINING AND LODGING
In this section you will find reviews of dining and lodging options of historical interest in and near the town. Not every town has such accommodations, but those that do are worth considering as a stopover for lunch, dinner, or a night's sleep. These distinctive restaurants, hotels, inns, B&Bs, and watering holes have been selected for their combination of authenticity and quality. Some of these properties have served the public continuously; others have been restored after years of disuse, or converted from other uses, with meticulous respect for history. Furnishings may be antiques or reproductions and food may be old-fashioned or updated, but your overall experience will be transporting, allowing you to remain immersed in the past even when your day of touring is done. Of course, every review provides all the practical information you will need, such as phone numbers, prices, and the policies (such as seasonal closings and whether credit cards are accepted) of each property.

CONQUERING A CONTINENT

owboys, covered wagons, explorers, frontier forts, mountain men, gold mines: These are probably the kinds of images that come to mind when you think of the Old West. Of course, there was an even older West, before any of those things appeared in the western half of what is today the United States. Peoples of diverse linguistic and cultural heritage made their homes on the wide and sweeping prairies and plains, in the rugged mountains, and amid the seemingly impenetrable deserts as long as 10,000 years ago. The arrival in these lands of Europeans and Anglo-Americans in the 16th through 19th centuries set in motion a collision of very different worlds, a clash that was often violent and deadly. Yet Native Americans and newcomers had something in common: Both groups were always on the move, seeking opportunity and a better life in the American West.

The West's history as a destination for emigrants started with the prehistoric arrival of its first settlers, the ancestors of the Native American tribes. Travel remained a way of life for thousands of years, as most Indians were hunters and gatherers who moved seasonally from place to place in order to find food. They also developed extensive trade networks to exchange goods and information with their far-flung neighbors. In some areas, agriculture took hold and sophisticated Native American civilizations arose, some of them establishing permanent or semi-permanent settlements. But in the vast American West, relatively small numbers of people were spread out thinly over a large area. To people arriving from densely populated Europe and the burgeoning eastern parts of North America, the West seemed all but uninhabited. It is with the arrival of the first of these Euro-Americans that the story of the Old West begins.

EXPLORERS AND MOUNTAIN MEN

The first European explorers—Spanish conquistadores and priests—set foot in the American West in the 16th century. While on an expedition to Florida with Pánfilo de Narváez in 1527, Cabeza de Vaca and some others were separated from the main group. Using makeshift boats they made their way west across the Gulf of Mexico, eventually landing on an island (likely Galveston Island), where they were captured by native people. Early in 1535, Cabeza de Vaca and three other survivors escaped to the mainland and trekked across a portion of what is now the southwestern U.S. before entering Mexico and eventually returning to Spain in 1537.

De Vaca wrote of his adventure, describing among other things the villages of the Zuñi Indians, which he said lay in an area of great wealth. The legend of the Seven Cities of Cibola fanned the flames of the Spanish imagination, which had long been fueled by dreams of New World gold. Other Spanish explorers made their way to the Southwest in search of the precious metal. In 1539 Hernando de Soto landed in Florida along with some 600 explorers, marched north along the Gulf Coast, and traveled throughout the Southwest in search of Cibola. Finding no gold, his men seized the native people's grain and burned their villages; de Soto died on the disastrous journey. Francisco Vásquez de Coronado set out in 1541 to find Cibola, making it to the Grand Canyon and into present-day Kansas and Oklahoma. But he didn't find any gold, either, so he returned to Mexico.

The early Spanish expeditions made two important marks upon the West: They were the first to introduce European diseases, and they were the first to bring the horse to North America. Native Americans had no immunity to many European ailments, and thousands died simply by meeting up with the strangers. Other tribes benefited from contact with the Spanish, acquiring horses that improved their standard of living. Before Indians had horses, they traveled on foot, carrying their possessions or packing them onto small drags, called *travois*, that were pulled by dogs. But after they obtained horses, the Indians could carry more goods on larger travois, and eventually on two-wheeled carts or even wagons. Some Indians became proficient riders who could travel long distances to hunt and to trade. Equipped with the horse, Native Americans traveled traditional migrational and trade routes and charted new ones—the first roads across the American West. Now tribes with horses could trade throughout the region; Southwest tribes like the Zuñis traded turquoise and salt for buffalo hides taken by Plains Indians like the Arapaho and Lakota. Some Indians used their new mobility for other purposes, raiding the territory of other tribes.

Though the Spaniards never found the fabled gold of Cibola, they developed trade routes and settlements in the West. Along the California coast they built a series of Catholic missions, and farther inland they founded Santa Fe, New Mexico, in 1607. Spanish settlers began to tap into the wealth of natural resources in the Southwest. President Thomas Jefferson had these unexploited riches of the rest of the West in mind when he made a deal with France to purchase the Louisiana Territory in 1803. For pennies an acre, Jefferson more than doubled the land mass of the young United States of America. To explore the vast territory, he recruited his personal secretary, Meriwether Lewis, and an able military man, William Clark, to head up an expedition. The Corps of Discovery, as the group led by Lewis and Clark became known, spent two years poling and pulling a keelboat up the Missouri River, crossing the Bitterroot Range on horseback and foot, and then shivering and nearly starving in a winter camp on the shores of the Pacific Ocean. They endured incredible hardship only to find there was no easy water route to the Pacific, but they lost only one man. Along the way, the explorers identified dozens of new species of plants and animals, and they found that there were abundant numbers of beaver living in the cold mountain streams.

By the time of the Lewis and Clark expedition, the French and British were already trapping beaver in the West, particularly north of the Medicine Line (as the U.S./Canadian border was called). Now the Americans wanted to take advantage of the riches in their new back yard. John Colter, who traveled with Lewis and Clark, didn't even make it back to St. Louis with the expedition. Instead he turned around and joined Manuel Lisa in exploratory and trapping expeditions. In the winter of 1807–08 Colter spent time in the region that became Grand Teton and Yellowstone national parks; he is believed to be the first white man ever to see that area. Over the next 15 years, other trappers made their way west. Traders established posts where these mountain men could barter pelts or plews (as they called beaver hides) for goods like bullets and rifles, frying pans, cloth, or blankets.

On the Pacific Coast, the Astorians (a party funded by fur magnate John Jacob Astor) established a post. When some of them headed east in 1812, they followed a network of Indian trails, finding a low pass through the Rocky Mountains, which they named South Pass, before continuing on to the Missouri River. The route they took would become the major highway to the West, traveled by fur-trade caravans, missionaries, and eventually by some 500,000 emigrants on their way to Oregon and California. In the Southwest, trade between the United States and Mexico picked up in 1821, when Mexico won its independence from Spain and shed Spanish restrictions on commerce with Americans. William Becknell pioneered the Santa Fe Trail from Franklin, Missouri, across present-day Kansas, Colorado, and New Mexico to Santa Fe. Other American traders poured onto the trail to grab a share of the newly opened market.

In 1822 William Ashley revolutionized the fur trade, advertising for 100 young men to go west and trap beaver in the mountains. Answering the initial call were such men as Thomas Fitzpatrick, William Sublette, James Bridger, and Kit Carson. Three years later Ashley made his first delivery of trade goods to the mountains, meeting with his trappers at a site on the BlacksFork of the Green River in present-day Wyoming. In return for the goods that they needed, the mountain men gave Ashley the pelts they had brought in. That first rendezvous was small, but in subsequent years the annual rendezvous grew into a big party, where hundreds of mountain men and Indians gathered at a predesignated spot to exchange goods with each other and with the trading caravans that brought new supplies. Always held in mid-summer, the rendezvous took place each year until 1843. By that time the streams were nearly trapped out, and the demand for beaver had dwindled as fashion changed.

PIONEERS AND PROSPECTORS

The idea of western expansion had by now taken hold of the American imagination. In 1836, the westward journey of two intrepid missionary women made it clear that not only men, but also women (and therefore families), could cross the continent. Eliza Spalding and Narcissa Whitman accompanied their husbands and a fur caravan to that year's mountain-man rendezvous, then continued on to Oregon, where they established the Whitman Mission.

As Anglo-American interest and activity in the West grew, Indian tribes found themselves increasingly on the move. Federal authorities started forcing Native Americans to leave their homelands, pushing them out of the way of white settlement. Many of the tribes were sent to Indian Territory, the area of present-day Oklahoma; because of the concentration of Indians there, it soon became known as the Nations. In 1838, under removal orders approved by President Andrew Jackson, the so-called Five Civilized Tribes (the Creek, Choctaw, Cherokee, Chickasaw, and Seminole) were forced to move. Hundreds of them died along the Trail of Tears on their way to Indian Territory.

Led by John Bidwell and John Bartleson, the first dedicated emigrant party journeyed to California in 1841. They had to abandon their wagons along the way, but they did reach the West Coast. More Americans turned their eyes toward the frontier, and the push west began in earnest in 1843 as emigrants flooded onto the Oregon Trail. Mormon leader Brigham Young did not take the Oregon Trail when he led his followers west from Nauvoo, Illinois, in 1846 to escape persecution and seek a new home. The party made its exodus in late winter and early spring, struggling through mud, snow, and rain to reach the Missouri River by summer. There, Young faced a delicate situation. The area west of the Missouri was Indian land, occupied by the Omaha, Oto, and other tribes; the emigrants had no right to cross the river and make a camp, even though they would undoubtedly be safer there, away from the persecution they'd endured in the East. The solution to Young's problem came in the form of the Mexican-American War.

In the mid-1820s Steven Austin had led settlers into Texas, and by 1836 they had declared their independence from Mexico and become the Republic of Texas. Seeking protection from Mexico, the Lone Star Republic immediately requested annexation to the United States. Although Congress did not want Mexico to take back the large Texas territory, it delayed voting on annexation. Texas and Mexico skirmished on and off, and in 1845 Mexico broke off diplomatic relations with the United States. Hoping to further the expansion of the United States, President James Polk sent troops to Texas to defend its border with Mexico. On May 11, 1846, Polk declared war on Mexico. A month later and 1,500 mi from Texas, John Charles Fremont stuck a flag in the ground and claimed California for the United States. Polk was now in a bit of a quandary. Troops under the command of Commodore Robert Stockton were headed toward California by ship, but Polk realized he must also send troops overland through the Southwest. He ordered Colonel Stephen Watts Kearny to march on Santa Fe with the Army of the West, but he knew Kearny didn't have a full fighting force.

So, James Polk needed more troops for the Army of the West and Brigham Young needed a way to cross the Missouri. The two men struck a simple deal: Young would raise a battalion of men to serve with Kearny, and Polk would negotiate on Young's behalf with the tribes west of the Missouri. The Mormon Battalion had 500 men plus some camp followers when it struck out for the Southwest. Polk persuaded the Indians to allow Young and his remaining followers—most of whom were the families of the troops in the Mormon Battalion—to cross the river and set up a camp on its western banks. The Mormon Battalion marched with Kearny's Army of the West, taking Santa Fe without firing a shot and continuing on to California, but their families had a much rougher time of it. In the fall and winter of 1846–47, Winter Quarters, as the Mormons called their outpost on the Missouri, became a death camp where dozens and dozens of people died from cholera and other diseases. In the spring of 1847, Young led the survivors overland to Utah, forging the Mormon Trail. Over the next 20 years thousands of Mormons traveled to Utah on the trail. Among them were 10 companies of immigrants from abroad, who made the trek on foot, pushing and pulling handcarts.

Some of the men who served with the Mormon Battalion were in California when gold was discovered at Sutter's Mill near San Francisco in January, 1848. That discovery set off the gold rush of 1849, which added to the stream of emigrants flowing westward. The 1850s were a busy decade along the Oregon, Mormon, California, and Santa Fe trails. Most folks, whether prospectors or settlers, passed right over the Great Plains, which had so far been written off as the Great American Desert, heading straight for the West Coast. Their passage was not without conflict, however. In 1854, when Lieutenant John Grattan and his military command confronted Lakota Indians over the death of a cow, the Indians killed the soldiers in the first such conflict along the Oregon Trail. But when a party of Cherokee emigrants found gold on Cherry Creek on the east slope of the Rockies in 1858, the news set off a new stampede to the West. In what became known as the Pikes Peak Gold Rush, the goal was only half as far from the Missouri River as was California.

Argonauts raced west once again, traveling the well-established Oregon-California road from Missouri River towns across to Fort Kearny in present-day central Nebraska, and then following the Platte and South Platte rivers to the diggings. Of course, some wanted to find a quicker way, so they headed across Kansas and Colorado up the Smoky Hill River. This route, named the Smoky Hill Trail, was commonly called the Starvation Trail because so many of the men who followed it starved to death before reaching their destination. But with more mineral discoveries elsewhere, miners flocked to diggings in present-day Idaho and Montana, to strikes in Nevada, and eventually even to Wyoming, where a late-era gold boom occurred at South Pass City in 1868.

ABOLITIONISTS AND HOMESTEADERS

As far from the eastern states as it was, and as busy with gold rushes and settlement, the West was not immune to the tensions that led up to the Civil War, nor to the bloodshed of the war itself. The Underground Railroad operated along the Missouri River, allowing escaped slaves to make their way west. Seeking statehood in the 1850s, Nebraska and Kansas became the focus of a national debate over the "free" or "slave" status of new states. The debate erupted in violence, especially in Kansas, which as a result earned the name Bleeding Kansas. As forces on both sides of the conflict hoped to persuade western territories and states to side with

OLD WEST TIME LINE

1535–41 Spaniards explore the West.

1804–06 Lewis and Clark lead the Corps of Discovery on an exploration of the Louisiana Purchase territories.

1821 Mexico wins its independence from Spain. Travel starts over the Santa Fe Trail.

1834 Indian Territory is created in what will become Oklahoma.

1838 Cherokee Indians travel to Indian Territory over the Trail of Tears.

1836 Declaring its independence from Mexico, the Republic of Texas organizes a provisional government and requests annexation to the United States.

1841 John Bidwell and John Bartleson take the first emigrants overland to California.

1843 Major migration begins on the Oregon Trail.

1845 Texas is admitted to the United States as a state, on December 29.

1846 The Mexican-American War commences. When it ends in 1848 the United States has gained the New Mexico, Arizona, and California regions.

1847 Cayuse Indians attack the Whitman Mission in Oregon on November 29, killing men, women, and children and taking others captive. Brigham Young blazes the Mormon Trail to Utah.

1848 Workers find gold at Sutter's Mill in California. Oregon Territory is created on August 14.

1849 Thousands of argonauts make their way to the West Coast on the California Trail.

1850 California becomes a state and New Mexico becomes a territory on September 9. Utah becomes a territory.

1851 Some 10,000 Indians gather at Fort Laramie in Wyoming for a treaty conference that establishes tribal regions and allows non-native roads across Indian land.

1853 Washington becomes a territory on February 8.

1854 Kansas and Nebraska become territories on May 30.

1859 Oregon becomes a state on February 14.

1860 The Pony Express begins its 18 months of mail-delivery service between St. Joseph, Missouri, and Sacramento, California.

1861 Kansas becomes a state on January 21, Colorado becomes a territory on February 28, and Nevada and Dakota become territories on March 2. The Civil War begins and Texas secedes from the Union on February 1. The first western battles of the war occur at Fort Bliss near El Paso on July 3 and 4.

1862 The most significant western Civil War battle takes place in March, at Glorietta Pass in New Mexico. President Abraham Lincoln signs the Pacific Railway Act, leading to construction of the Transcontinental Railroad. The Homestead Act becomes law, enabling thousands of people to claim land in the West.

1863 Arizona becomes a territory on February 24 and Idaho a territory on March 4.

1864 Montana becomes a territory on May 24 and Nevada becomes a state on October 31. Kit Carson forces Navajo Indians to make the Long Walk in New Mexico. Col. John Chivington leads the Sand Creek Massacre.

1865 The Civil War ends on April 9.

1867 Nebraska becomes a state on March 1. Cowboys begin trailing cattle from Texas to railheads and open range in Kansas and Nebraska.

1868 A treaty with Northern Plains Tribes is negotiated at Fort Laramie, ending Red Cloud's War. Wyoming becomes a territory on July 25. The Transcontinental Railroad is completed at Promontory, Utah, on May 10.

1870 Texas is readmitted to the Union on March 30.

1876 Lieutenant Colonel George Armstrong Custer and members of the Seventh Cavalry die in battle with the Lakota and Cheyenne at Little Bighorn. Colorado becomes a state on August 1.

1881 Hunkpapa Sioux leader Sitting Bull surrenders at Fort Buford in Dakota Territory, and Apache leader Geronimo surrenders in Arizona.

1886–87 Severe winter storms kill thousands of head of cattle from Montana to Texas.

1889 Indian Territory is opened to non-Indian settlement on April 22. Its western half becomes Oklahoma Territory. Dakota Territory separates and becomes the states of North Dakota and South Dakota on November 2. Montana becomes a state on November 8 and Washington becomes a state on November 11.

1890 Idaho becomes a state on July 3 and Wyoming becomes a state on July 10. The massacre of Indians at Wounded Knee in South Dakota is the last major conflict of the Indian Wars.

1896 Utah becomes a state on January 4.

1907 Oklahoma Territory and the remainder of Indian Territory are combined and become the state of Oklahoma on November 16.

1912 New Mexico becomes a state on January 6 and Arizona becomes a state on February 12.

them, there was great demand for rapid communication between East and West. To meet this demand the Pony Express was created. The Pony Boys could carry a letter between St. Joseph, Missouri, and Sacramento, California in ten days, riding hard in legs of 20 mi. At the station at the end of each leg they'd get a fresh horse, and would be replaced by relief riders after a few hours in the saddle. It operated for only 18 months (April 1860–October 1861), but the Pony Express met the need for fast mail service with a style and energy that still capture the imagination today.

When the Civil War broke out, Texas and portions of New Mexico quickly sided with the Confederates, other western states and territories took up the Union banner, and still others sat squarely on the fence. Most of the fighting took place east of the Mississippi River, but the West saw a few Civil War battles, some as far west as Arizona. The most important western battle, known as the Gettysburg of the West, occurred just east of Santa Fe in March 1862. Confederate forces were marching north from Texas, intent on capturing Fort Union and moving into Colorado, where they hoped to take control of the gold mines. At Glorietta Pass, the Confederates ran into Union forces commanded by Colonel John Chivington. When the smoke of the hard-fought battle cleared, the Confederates realized they were whipped, in part because Chivington had destroyed their supplies. They retreated to Texas, where the final battle of the Civil War took place, the troops unaware that the war was already over.

Following the Civil War, homesteading changed the American West more profoundly than any other phenomenon either before or since. In 1862, President Abraham Lincoln signed into law the Homestead Act. There had been similar earlier legislation, but the Homestead Act expanded opportunities for non-native settlement of the West by allowing people to claim 160 acres of land under its basic provisions, and even more land under special conditions. Men and women, black and white, the homesteaders came from all parts of the eastern United States. Others immigrated from European countries, bringing with them their customs and cultures, their own traditions, and their native languages. The West took on a melting-pot atmosphere, with Germans settling in Texas, ex-slaves in Kansas, and Scandinavians in North Dakota and Montana.

Stage and freight lines served even remote areas of the West, but to travel from east to west emigrants still had to rely on wagon trains. With so many people settling in the West, the time had come to build a railroad to link the nation. Railroad companies had conducted surveys of possible routes, in the south across Texas and Arizona, in the north across the Dakotas and Montana to Oregon, and in the central part of the country through Kansas and Colorado. But the Pacific Railway Act, signed by President Lincoln in 1862, decreed that the Transcontinental Railroad was to follow a path similar to that taken by so many emigrants for so many years. The railroad would strike west from Omaha, Nebraska along the Platte River, then continue along the Overland Trail across southern Wyoming to Sacramento, California. Two crews would build two rail lines—one headed west from Omaha, the other headed east from Sacramento—that would meet up to form a single line. Starting from the East were the crews of the Union Pacific Railway Company, primarily Irish immigrants supported by Germans, Civil War veterans, Mormons, and even a few Indians. Beginning in California were the crews of the Central Pacific Railway Company, mostly Chinese immigrants. The Central Pacific faced the task of crossing the Sierra Nevada and the Nevada desert, fighting altitude and the elements.

The great Pacific Railway brought the nation together on May 10, 1869, at Promontory, Utah, where officials from both rail companies drove the final, ceremonial golden spike. The completion of the railroad spelled the end of major overland emigrant travel by wagon train, though of course many people continued to use wagons as they moved from place to place. Cities sprang up at station stops along the rail line, and feeder railroads branched out from the main route. Formerly remote areas could now be reached with relative ease, and Euro-American culture and institutions began to thrive throughout the West.

INDIANS AND SOLDIERS

In order to open more of the West for white settlement, the United States stepped up efforts to clear the land of Native Americans. The government broke treaties made with various tribes in earlier years, and the military campaign known as the Indian Wars started to escalate. One of the broken treaties had been made in 1851, when the tribes of present-day Wyoming and Nebraska had agreed to allow white travelers to use roads—primarily the Oregon-California-Mormon route—across their lands. In exchange, the United States set aside the Powder River Basin for the Lakotas, Cheyennes, and Crows; no roads were to traverse that region. But gold-seekers started traveling through the area in 1863 on a route called the Bozeman Trail. The trail struck north from the Oregon-California-Mormon Trail to cross the Powder River Basin, skirt the east face of the Bighorn Mountains, follow the Yellowstone River toward the settlement of Bozeman, and continue on to Virginia City, Montana. Bitterly opposed to the trail, the Indians regularly attacked wagon trains, driving off livestock and killing anyone they could. Ignoring the treaty of 1851, the U.S. Army established three posts to provide protection to whites using the Bozeman Trail: Fort Reno, Fort Phil Kearny, and Fort C. F. Smith.

Elsewhere, the U.S. Army committed out-and-out atrocities. In 1864 Kit Carson rounded up Navajo Indians and forced them to march 300 mi to Bosque Redondo Reservation in New Mexico, where they were held prisoner. Their journey became known as the Long Walk. That year, the Sand Creek Massacre in Colorado left scores of peaceful Plains Indians dead. Miners and Indians had been skirmishing in the area, and a group of Cheyenne and Arapaho led by Chief Black Kettle had camped along Sand Creek in southeastern Colorado, believing they were under the protection of nearby military troops. But early on the morning of November 29, 1864, Colonel Chivington of Civil War fame led a force called the Colorado 100-Day Volunteers in an attack on the camp. The troops killed more than a hundred of the Indians, including many women and children. The massacre shocked most of the country. Chivington was condemned for the action, and the Indians prepared for retaliation.

In the wake of such incidents, 1865 became known as the Bloody Year on the Plains, as fighting broke out all across the northern and southern prairie. Led by Chief Red Cloud, Indians attacked the Bozeman Trail forts almost incessantly. After two years of constant harassment and several bloody engagements (including the December 21, 1866, battle that resulted in the deaths of Lieutenant William J. Fetterman and his entire troop of 80 soldiers near Fort Phil Kearny), the Indians won what had come to be called Red Cloud's War. New treaties were negotiated at Fort Laramie in 1868, the army abandoned the three hated posts, and the Indians immediately burned them.

There was a period of uneasy truce after the closing of the Bozeman Trail forts, but then Lieutenant Colonel George Armstrong Custer rode onto the scene in 1874. Even though the area had been set aside for the Indians by the 1868 treaty, Custer led a military reconnaissance of the Black Hills, a place considered sacred by the Lakotas and the Cheyennes. His men discovered gold, and prospectors rushed to the area. In what became known as Crazy Horse's War, the Indians fought to keep the whites off their land. The war culminated in the annihilation of Custer and part of the Seventh Cavalry at the Battle of the Little Bighorn on June 25, 1876, and with the retaliatory destruction of Indian camps that fall and winter. Though the Indians won the big battle at Little Bighorn, they ultimately lost Crazy Horse's War and were forced onto reservations.

In 1877 the Nez Perce Indians, ordered out of their Wallowa Valley homeland, fled across Idaho, into Wyoming, and through Montana. They hoped to find refuge with Chief Sitting Bull, who had moved to Canada after Little Bighorn, but they did not make it that far. In October, about 40 mi south of the Medicine Line, soldiers finally caught up to the Nez Perce, captured their horses, and forced Chief Joseph to surrender in order to save his people. Weary of war, he surrendered with the words, "I will fight no more forever." Joseph was sent to jail, and later to a small reservation in Indian Country; he never returned to the Wallowa Valley.

In the Southwest, the Apache of Arizona held out against white domination as long as any tribe. Under the leadership of Cochise and later Geronimo, they eluded authorities in both Mexico and the United States until 1881, when Geronimo finally surrendered. Geronimo was moved from his beloved homeland to a prison camp in Florida and eventually to a reservation in Oklahoma. The same year Geronimo surrendered, Sitting Bull finally turned himself in to American authorities, at Fort Buford in western North Dakota. The final battle of the Indian wars played out nine years later, a few days after Sitting Bull was killed. On a cold, wintry day in late December 1890, the Seventh Cavalry attacked a Lakota camp at a place called Wounded Knee in South Dakota, killing men, women, and children in a brutal massacre.

COWBOYS AND OUTLAWS

While the Indian Wars raged, the last of the western bonanzas boomed and went bust, creating the West's most enduring character: the cowboy. The Cattle Kingdom, as it was called, started with Civil War veterans returning home to Texas. Cattle had been trailed from Texas and Arkansas clear to California in the 1850s, by Cherokee Indians and others traveling the Cherokee Trail across Colorado and Wyoming. But that was a minor operation compared to the big Texas cattle drives of the 1870s. After the war, thousands of head of cattle roamed wild in the mesquite thickets of Texas, and the former soldiers knew there was great demand for beef in the East. The Texans began rounding up the longhorns and driving them north to railheads in Kansas, at Abilene, Dodge City, and later Ogallala. There they sold the cattle, which were loaded onto rail cars for shipment to other parts of the country. Other drives took livestock to stock ranches in Kansas and Nebraska, or through Colorado and Wyoming to the open ranges of Montana. Huge ranching enterprises were born, and cattle streamed along the Goodnight-Loving, Texas, Western, and other trails.

The era of the cattle drives lasted less than 20 years. By the mid-1880s the northern ranges were overstocked with cattle. Relying as always on the abundance of the open range, the owners (many of them wealthy English or Scottish aristocrats who had taken up ranching as an adventure) didn't harvest any hay for winter feed. The Cattle Kingdom fell quickly and horribly in a winter that became known from Montana to Texas as the Great Die-Up. In the winter of 1886–87 snows and frigid temperatures pummeled the land, and free-ranging cattle drifted into gullies and against newly placed fences, where they died by the thousands.

The western cattle industry was never the same after that terrible winter, and it was further weakened by competition for valuable range land. One competitor was the sheep-ranching industry. Sheep were being moved into Rocky Mountain states like Montana, Wyoming, and Colorado from places such as Oregon and California. Cattlemen believed that sheep ruined the range, and they fought to keep the "range maggots" out of prime grazing land. They drew lines, which came to be called deadlines, over which sheep were not to move. Vigorously protecting the land they wanted for their cattle, ranchers killed sheepherders and sheep. In a practice known as rimrocking, cowboys drove herds of sheep over cliffs to their deaths. They sometimes shot dozens of sheep and left them lying on the ground.

Cattlemen faced another challenge as well, in the form of homesteading. They were accustomed to letting their herds graze wide areas without regard for land ownership, but now homesteaders were breaking up the range by filing claims. These claims often lay along creeks and rivers, where the settlers had access to water for their livestock and for the irrigation of hay and other crops. Homesteaders put up fences to protect their property, blocking customary cattle routes as well as access to water. The feud between rancher and homesteader culminated in the Johnson County Invasion (sometimes called the Johnson County War), when gunmen from Texas and Idaho joined prominent Wyoming cattlemen to search out specific men whom they intended to kill or run off the range. The invaders found two of the men in a cabin and killed them, but before they could track down the rest of the men on their list, word spread and homesteaders rose up in defense. Pinned down, the cattlemen appealed to President Benjamin Harrison for aid. Harrison eventually sent troops to the area to take the cattlemen into custody. Charges were filed against them, but their case never went to trial.

The range wars were far from over. Likely the most infamous incident of the conflict occurred in the Iron Mountain country of Wyoming in July 1901. A 14-year-old sheepman's son, Willie Nickell, was ambushed and killed on his family ranch. The man arrested, tried, and hanged for the deed was Tom Horn. He was a range detective, a man hired by ranchers to patrol their lands and keep homesteaders and sheepmen away. His job was to scare people, or to kill them, and he certainly did a little of both before swinging from a hangman's rope in Cheyenne in 1902. Folks in Wyoming, however, still argue about whether or not Horn really pulled the trigger on Willie Nickell.

In 1890 historian Frederick Jackson Turner declared that there was no more frontier in the American West, but he clearly jumped the gun by at least a decade. Not only were cattlemen taking the law into their own hands, but bandits like Butch Cassidy, the Sundance Kid (Harry Longabaugh), Elzy Lay, and Kid Curry carried on the outlaw traditions founded by such men as Billy the Kid, John Wesley Hardin, Frank and Jesse James, Cole Younger, and the Daltons. They robbed trains and raced away with the money, taking refuge in isolated spots like the Hole-in-the-Wall country of Wyoming or Browns Park in Colorado and Utah. Eventually, lawmen rounded up most of the bad guys and clapped them in jail, though a few escaped. Butch and Sundance fled to South America.

By the turn of the 20th century, as the old-time outlaws disappeared, settlement had overspread much of the West. The region had been divided into territories that had eventually become states, and some cities had modern amenities like street lamps, and in some cases even electricity. Towns large and small had theaters and opera houses, schools and churches. The trails of the Indians and the emigrants became highways, graded and eventually paved; wagons and horses were replaced by the newfangled horseless carriages. The West didn't seem quite so wild any more, but it still retained some of its Old West flavor. People from other places began to see it as an interesting place to visit. They came to Wolf, Wyoming, to spend their nights in rough log cabins and their days riding horses on the Eaton Ranch, the first

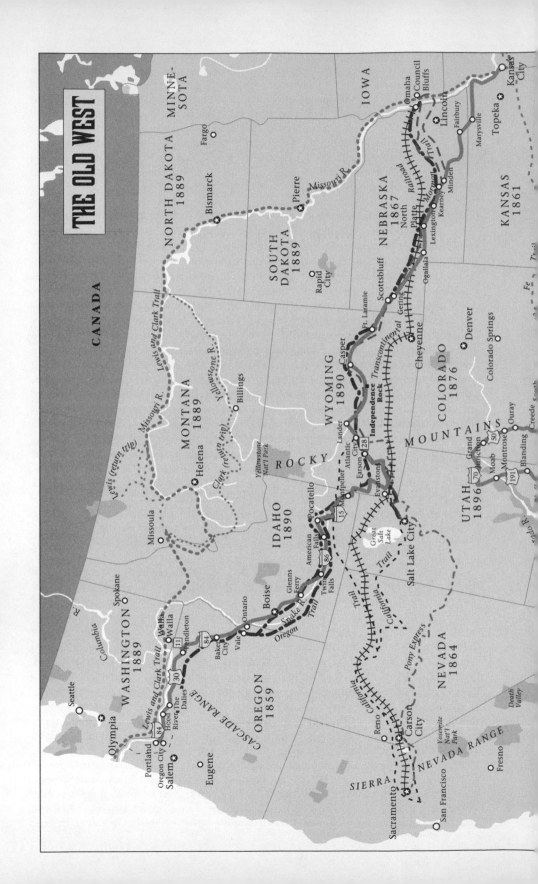

THE OLD WEST

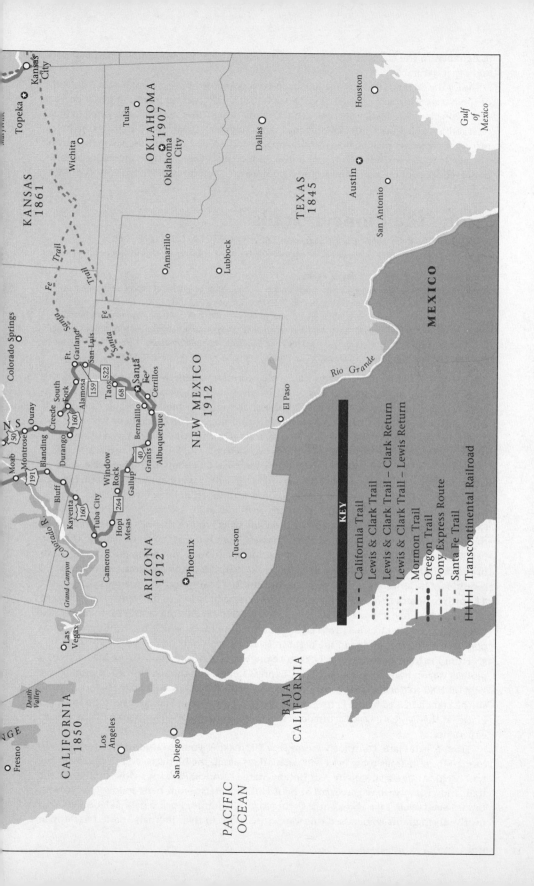

PACIFIC
OCEAN

Fresno ○

VGE

CALIFORNIA
1850

Death
Valley

Los ○
Angeles

San Diego ○

Las ○
Vegas

Grand Canyon

Colorado R.

Cameron ○

Tuba City

Kayenta ○
160

Bluff ○

Blanding

Moab ○
191

N S

50

Montrose ○

Ouray ○

Creede ○

South
Fork

Durango ○

160

Hopi
Mesas

264

Window
Rock

Gallup ○

40

Grants ○

Colorado Springs

Ft.
Garland ○

San Luis

Alamosa ○

159

522

Taos ○

68

Bernalillo ○

Albuquerque ○

Santa Fe

Cerrillos

Santa Fe Trail

Santa Fe Trail

NEW MEXICO
1912

El Paso ○

Rio Grande

MEXICO

Phoenix ✪

ARIZONA
1912

Tucson ○

BAJA
CALIFORNIA

Colorado Springs

KANSAS
1861

Topeka ✪

Kansas ○
City

Wichita ○

Tulsa ○

OKLAHOMA
1907

Oklahoma ✪
City

Amarillo ○

Lubbock ○

Dallas ○

TEXAS
1845

Austin ✪

San Antonio ○

Houston ○

Gulf
of
Mexico

KEY

- - - California Trail
····· Lewis & Clark Trail
····· Lewis & Clark Trail – Clark Return
····· Lewis & Clark Trail – Lewis Return
——— Mormon Trail
●●● Oregon Trail
—·—· Pony Express Route
—··— Santa Fe Trail
┝┿┥ Transcontinental Railroad

dude ranch in the country. They also visited Yellowstone, the world's first national park, and other natural wonders.

As for the original settlers of the American West, Wounded Knee did not herald the demise of the Native American. Indeed, though some tribes that had been around when de Vaca first stepped foot in Texas were now extinct, many other tribes survived. Relegated to bleak reservations and forced into schools meant to "civilize" them, the Indians nonetheless managed to preserve their traditions and languages. Indeed, on the Hopi Reservation in Arizona life has changed very little over the centuries. In such places, and in state and national parks, preserved Spanish missions, and restored boomtowns, you can still glimpse the Old West.

Along the Pioneer Trails
A DRIVING TOUR FROM MARYSVILLE, KANSAS, TO OREGON CITY, OREGON

▼▼

Distance: About 2,000 mi   **Time:** 2 weeks
Breaks: Some of the towns suggested as overnight stops offer dining or lodging of exceptional historical interest, such as Dancing Leaf Earth Lodge in North Platte, Nebraska; Hotel Higgins in Casper, Wyoming; and J. J. Shaw House in Boise, Idaho. In other spots, such as Atlantic City and Evanston, Wyoming, and Pendleton, Oregon, you can bed down in a rustic frontier ranch, a lavish boomtown mansion, or a Wild West brothel. Towns without historic properties of note—Kearney and Gering-Scottsbluff, Nebraska; Lander, Wyoming; American Falls and Twin Falls, Idaho; and Oregon City, Oregon—can put you up in simple comfort.

Emigrants who followed the Oregon-California-Mormon trails in the 1800s passed along this route when the land all around was virtually empty of man-made comforts and conveniences. When they stopped for the night, they had to make camp, find water (if there was any), gather wood or buffalo dung for the fire, and hope for fresh game or berries to eat. Their trip, generally by wagon train, took five or six months, but yours—driven in air-conditioned (or heated) comfort—will take about two weeks.

Begin your tour about 150 mi northwest of **Kansas City,** Kansas, in **Marysville,** Kansas, where the Oregon Trail crosses the Blue River. Marysville was also on the St. Joseph Road of the California Trail and served as a Pony Express station. From here, travel west on U.S. 36, then turn north on Route 15 and cross into Nebraska at Rock Creek Station just south of **Fairbury.** Here you will be able to see the indelible wheel ruts of the wagons that went west, though they are partially obscured by tall grasses. From Fairbury, travel west along U.S. 136 to Hebron; then turn north on U.S. 81 to Fairmont and turn west again on U.S. 6 to Hastings. Continue on west to **Minden** to view Harold Warp's incredible collection of nearly two centuries of transportation history. Then continue to the west on U.S. 6 before taking Route 44 north to **Kearney,** site of the fort by the same name (it is spelled differently), constructed in 1847 and the first important way station for westward-bound emigrants. Visit the re-created fort; then cross I–80 to the Great Platte River Road Archway, which has exhibits on transportation in the region. Spend the night in Kearney.

From Kearney, head west on I–80 to **Lexington,** site of the Plum Creek Massacre of a pioneer wagon train. Stop in at the Pony Express station and the Sod House Museum. Drive west on I–80 to **North Platte,** where you can visit Buffalo Bill Ranch State Historical Park, site of a ranch owned by the Pony Express rider and showman. You can overnight in North Platte, at the Dancing Leaf Earth Lodge if you are looking for an authentic Plains Indian experience.

From North Platte continue west on U.S. 30, making your way along the Oregon-California-Mormon Trails route (you will see markers along the highway, and in places on the trail itself). At **Ogallala,** stop by Ash Hollow State Historical Park for a close-up look at the trail, and visit a cowboy graveyard at Boot Hill Cemetery. From here, follow U.S. 26 west toward **Scottsbluff.** Take a break near Gering to visit Chimney Rock, a natural landmark that nearly all emigrants who passed this way wrote about in their journals and letters. Stop at the museum at Scotts Bluff National Monument, and if you have the time, take a side trip to Roubidoux Pass or spend a few days on a wagon train in the area. You can overnight in the Gering-Scottsbluff area.

When you are ready to head west again, take U.S. 20/26 into Wyoming, to **Fort Laramie.** This fort started as a fur-trading post and became a military post to protect travelers on the trail. It was the most important trail stop for most emigrants because they could get supplies, perhaps exchange weak or ill animals for new stock, and rest for a few days. Near Fort Laramie you can see trail sites at Register Cliff and near Guernsey. Make your way to I–25 and follow it to **Casper,** where you will spend the night. Stop in at the National Historic Trails Interpretive Center, which tells the story of the trails that crossed this area, and pick up emigrant trail maps. Also plan to visit Fort Caspar.

In the morning travel west once again, this time taking Route 220 to Independence Rock. Walk around the base of Independence Rock, or climb on the granite outcrop and view signatures carved by trail travelers. Nearby is the Handcart Ranch, whose visitor center relates the story of the Mormon emigrants who walked west pushing and pulling handcarts. Turn north on U.S. 287, following the Sweetwater River valley just as the pioneers did. The trail zigzags the highway, so if you watch for white markers you can see it. You can drive to **Lander** or turn west on Route 28 to **Atlantic City;** spend the night in either town. Just about on the Continental Divide, South Pass City State Historic Site near Atlantic City commemorates the birth of woman suffrage in the United States: In December 1869, Wyoming was the first state to grant women the right to vote.

Back on the trail, head to South Pass, the low pass through which all early overland emigrants crossed. From this point for the next hundred or so miles, you are in the vicinity of the most visible remaining sections of the Oregon-California-Mormon trails. Continue on Route 28 to the west. It parallels some trail segments; east and west of **Farson** you can visit a number of sites such as Parting of the Ways, Simpsons Hollow, and the Lombard Ferry, all of which have interpretive signs to make them more visible. After you cross the Green River, turn to the south on Route 372, to I–80; then head west to **Evanston,** stopping at Fort Bridger State Historic Site along the way. It is about 500 mi from Fort Laramie to Fort Bridger, and you can drive it in three days; the emigrants took about a month to cover the same distance on the trails. Spend the night in Evanston.

Head north in the morning on U.S. 189 to its junction with U.S. 30 and follow that road west to **Montpelier,** Idaho. Here, visit the the National Oregon-California Trail Center, situated right on a popular emigrant campsite. Then continue west on U.S. 30 and north on I–15 to Fort Hall Indian Reservation, near **American Falls.** Started as a fur-trading post, by the time the emigrants were traveling the route, Fort Hall was another supply station for them. You can see a replica of the fort and stop in at the Shoshone-Bannock Tribal Museum. Ten miles west of American Falls is Massacre Rocks State Park, with an informative visitor center. You can spend the night in American Falls, or drive the 95 mi west on I–86 and I–84 to Twin Falls, where there are more lodging choices.

As you resume your trip, continue west to **Glenns Ferry.** Stop at Three Island Crossing State Park, a place where emigrants had to make a dangerous river crossing. The trail continues on and you should as well, to **Boise.** The Idaho state capital is a great place to learn about Old West Idaho, at places such as the Idaho State Historical Museum and the Basque Museum and Cultural Center, which traces the history of this important frontier ethnic group. Boise also makes a fine overnight stop, where you can try some Basque food and sleep at an historic B&B.

In the morning, cross the state border on I–84 into Oregon and stop in Vale. Take the time to see the Oregon Trail Murals and visit the Stone House Museum, which was once a way station for travelers on the trail. Move on along I–84 to **Baker City,** site of the Oregon Trail National Interpretive Center and the Oregon Trail Regional Museum. You can take a break from the trail to visit the several mining ghost towns in the area. As you proceed west on I–84 you will follow the route the emigrants took as they ascended the Blue Mountains and made their way along the Columbia River. Plan to spend a night in **Pendleton.** Oregon Trail Interpretive Park is here, as well as a number of other interesting Old West sights, such as the Pendleton Underground, a subterranean labyrinth of gambling rooms, opium dens, and Chinese laborers' quarters. In the evening, check into a former stagecoach stop or brothel.

Take a side trip in the morning to **Walla Walla,** Washington, north of Pendleton on Route 11. Here you will find the Whitman Mission National Historic Site, well worth the 80-mi round-trip detour. Walk the ground just as Narcissa Whitman did when she made her way west in 1836, one of the first two white women to travel across the country. Return to I–84/ U.S. 30 west and make your way to **The Dalles,** Oregon, on a bend of the Columbia River. Stop in at the Wasco County Courthouse, whose museum has exhibits related to the Oregon Trail, and at the Fort Dalles Museum, which houses artifacts of the pioneer era.

The last leg of your tour is an easy drive through the Willamette Valley to **Oregon City,** where many pioneers finished their journey. Among the sites you can visit here are the End of the Oregon Trail Interpretive Center, identified by its three large covered wagons. Numerous museums, such as the Museum of the Oregon Territory, and historic farms and homes, such as the McLoughlin House National Historic Site, can easily fill a day. From Oregon City it is just a 20-mi hop on I–205 north and I–84 west to Portland.

Four Corners Country

A DRIVING TOUR IN NEW MEXICO, COLORADO, UTAH, AND ARIZONA

▼▼

Distance: About 1,300 mi   **Time:** 10–12 days

Breaks: Each of the main towns on this tour has ample dining and lodging. Albuquerque, Santa Fe, and Taos, New Mexico, offer everything from humble motels to four-star hotels and restaurants, while Creede and Durango, Colorado, have colorful Old West accommodations. In Grand Junction, Colorado; Moab, Utah; and Gallup, New Mexico, you will find the variety typical of well-traveled but less-distinctive western towns, but facilities on the Navajo Reservation in Kayenta and Window Rock, Arizona, are more limited.

Old mining camps, traditional trading posts, and Indian reservations are all a part of Four Corners country, so called because it is the only place in the country where four states (Arizona, Colorado, New Mexico, and Utah) meet at one point. At the actual meeting point there's nothing much to see but a marker, but the surrounding lands were the scene of colorful Old West history.

Start in **Albuquerque,** New Mexico, by far the largest city on the tour. Take a full day to absorb the charm and heritage of Old Town and to visit the Indian Pueblo Cultural Center. Plan to enjoy dinner in a historic restaurant and spend the night.

When you head for **Santa Fe** in the morning travel north from Albuquerque on I–25, stopping at Coronado State Monument in Bernalillo if you have the time. Another way to reach Santa Fe is via the Turquoise Trail (Route 14), a slower but more scenic route that passes through funky small towns like **Cerrillos** and Golden. However you get there, spend at least 24 hours in Santa Fe, where you will see reminders of Spanish colonialism and Pueblo Indian culture everywhere you look. Established in 1607, Santa Fe was the capital of the Spanish colony of New Mexico and is now the state capital, and it was also the western terminus of the Santa Fe Trail. Among the don't-miss sights are the Palace of the Governors, St. Francis Cathedral, Loretto Chapel, and San Miguel Mission. Stay here for at least one night.

To get from Santa Fe to **Taos,** drive north on U.S. 285. Within a few miles you can choose between two routes for the rest of your journey: The High Road follows Route 503 to County Road 98 to Route 76 northeast, then Route 75 east to Route 518 north. The drive through the rolling foothills and tiny valleys of the Sangre de Cristos, dotted with orchards, pueblos, and picturesque villages, is stunning. The Low Road, Route 68, travels upstream along the Rio Grande through a verdant valley into a rocky canyon and finally onto the high plateau where Taos stands. Scenic in its own right, the Low Road is faster than the High Road. Taos

Pueblo, 2 mi north of Taos Plaza, is the most famous sight around town, but the Kit Carson Home and Museum, San Francisco de Asís Church, and other spots make sticking around Taos for a full day well worth your while. Taos is also a good place to overnight.

Colorado is but a few miles north of Taos via Route 522/159, which will take you to San Luis, the oldest incorporated town in Colorado. Take a walk around; then drive another 16 mi north to Fort Garland, where you can stop in the museum that traces the history of Colorado's first military post. From here, head west on U.S. 160, passing through **Alamosa** on your way to the San Juan mining country. At South Fork, turn north off U.S. 160 onto Route 149 for a trip to **Creede,** one of the wildest of the silver-rush boomtowns. Spend the afternoon taking a mine tour, visiting the museums, and driving past abandoned mining camps. Have dinner at the Creede Hotel and Restaurant, and spend the night.

Returning to U.S. 160, head west over the Continental Divide on Wolf Creek Pass on your way to **Durango,** a place that caused Will Rogers to wisecrack, "It's out of the way and glad of it." It's easy to spend an entire day in the city's historic district, which is filled with superlative Victorian-era buildings, but you might prefer to take the eight-hour round-trip journey on the Durango & Silverton Narrow Gauge Railway, deep into the heart of Colorado's mining country. In any case, Durango is a good place to overnight, perhaps after a drink at the Diamond Belle saloon in the Strater Hotel.

In the morning, drive north from Durango on U.S. 550 to **Ouray,** which has its own historic district and mining tours, then on to **Montrose,** where you can learn about Chief Ouray at the Ute Indian Museum. North of Montrose via U.S. 50 you will reach **Grand Junction,** where you can get an overview of the area at the Museum of Western Colorado and, if you like, venture into the Little Bookcliffs Wild Horse Range to glimpse the descendants of the animals that changed the West. There are many motels and hotels here in which to grab a night's sleep.

Your next day starts with a drive west on I–70 and south on U.S. 191 to **Moab,** Utah. At the Daughters of the Utah Pioneers Meeting Hall you can learn about the early Mormon settlers, and in Arches National Park you can visit the Wolfe Ranch. Moab is the best place to dine and lodge in the area.

Another morning drive, this one south on U.S. 191, brings you to **Blanding,** where you can stop in at the the Nations of the Four Corners Cultural Center. A few miles farther south, take the historic walking tour of **Bluff**; then cross into Arizona and the Navajo Indian Reservation. Spend the afternoon in Monument Valley taking in the massive red rock formations that are among the most famous images of the Old West. As you travel across the Navajo Nation, forget about your watch and take things as they come, easing into the slower pace of reservation life. **Kayenta,** location of the Navajo Cultural Center, is a good place to overnight.

Head southwest from Kayenta on U.S. 160 to **Tuba City,** then south on U.S. 89 to pick up a sack lunch at Cameron Trading Post. Then drive east on Route 264 and spend the day visiting the **Hopi Mesas,** where life goes on much as it did before the first Spaniard set foot here. A bit east of the Hopi Reservation on Route 264 is Hubbell Trading Post National Historic Site, a working trading post. End your day in **Window Rock,** capital of the Navajo Nation and site of the Navajo Nation Museum. You can overnight here, or make the quick hop over the New Mexico state line via Route 264 and U.S. 666 to Gallup, where tourist facilities are numerous.

To complete your loop tour, drive east on I–40 toward Albuquerque, passing back over the Continental Divide and then stopping in **Grants** to see the famous Inscription Rock at El Morro National Monument. Beginning with Spanish explorer Juan de Oñate in 1605, Old West travelers scratched their names and the dates they passed into the rock face of the bluff. From Grants, it's just 73 mi east on I–40 to Albuquerque.

ARIZONA

I n pages of stone exposed by the geologic forces of uplift on the Colorado Plateau and carved by the relentless flow of the Colorado River, the Grand Canyon, Arizona's most impressive natural wonder, chronicles billions of years of the earth's history. Yet in all of this rocky text, the entirety of human history is absent—not even recorded on a slice of stone the thickness of a piece of paper. But history can be deceptive. Hefty tomes recount the earliest days of the Boston colonies in New England, but those pages often fail to mention that while the Pilgrims were celebrating the first Thanksgiving, the Spanish settlement of Tubac in Arizona had already been around for nearly a quarter of a century.

The first peoples to enter this arid region of the Southwest were roaming bands of Paleo-Indians, who first occupied these lands about 20,000 years ago. But it wasn't until the late 1530s that the Spanish conquistadores entered what is now Arizona. In 1540, the legendary Francisco Vásquez de Coronado led an exploratory expedition across the region in search of the fabled Seven Cities of Cibola. The 30-year-old explorer trekked across the inhospitable Sonoran Desert and up past the Grand Canyon into New Mexico with his party of 336 Spaniards, 1,000 Native Americans, and 1,500 horses and mules. However, instead of finding fame, riches, and cities of gold, all Coronado saw was arid deserts, small Indian villages, and the gaping geological wonder we call the Grand Canyon.

One hundred years later, Father Eusebio Francisco Kino, a Jesuit priest now known to some as the "first Arizonan," explored the area north of Mexico City, creating a chain of missions. His journeys into Arizona's Santa Cruz Valley from 1687 to 1711 resulted in the founding of three missions—Guevavi, Tumacácori, and San Xavier del Bac. To protect the missions from the constant Indian threat, the Spanish government garrisoned the Tubac Presidio in 1752; the garrison remained in Tubac until Apache raids and political unrest forced its relocation to Tucson in 1776.

In 1821, when Mexico seceded from Spain, Arizona flew the Mexican flag. Not until the Texas Revolution of 1835–36 and the Mexican-American War of 1846–48 did most of

Arizona, along with New Mexico, California, Texas, and Utah, come under United States hegemony. The portion of Arizona first acquired by the United States was made part of New Mexico Territory. In 1853 the rest of Arizona was transferred to America via the Gadsden Purchase, still as part of New Mexico.

Soon after the Mexican-American War, the U.S. Army sent troops to set up a series of forts throughout Arizona. In 1860, residents of southern Arizona proclaimed the region a separate territory and announced their affiliation with the Confederacy. Two years later, the westernmost battle of the Civil War was fought at Picacho Pass. After several bills had passed through Congress, President Abraham Lincoln finally announced the creation of the Arizona Territory in 1863. Because of Tucson's Confederate sympathies, the first Territorial Legislature bypassed that city as the capital and set up in Prescott. In 1867, the capital was moved to Tucson and 10 years later back to Prescott. The capital moved for the last time in 1889, to Phoenix, where it remains today.

ARIZONA TIME LINE

1539 Father Marcos de Niza explores Arizona and claims it for New Spain.

1540 Drawn by tales of the Seven Cities of Cibola, Francisco Vásquez de Coronado leads an expedition to Arizona in search of gold.

1692 Father Eusebio Francisco Kino establishes a mission at Guevavi.

1696 San Jose de Tumacácori Mission is founded.

1776 The Tucson Presidio is built.

1821 Mexico discards the mantle of Spanish rule and Arizona becomes a province of Mexico.

1848 At the conclusion of the Mexican-American War most of Arizona becomes the property of the United States.

1853 James Gadsden, ambassador to Mexico, facilitates the Gadsden Purchase of the southern third of Arizona for the United States.

1862 The Battle at Picacho Pass, the westernmost battle of the Civil War, takes place on April 15. Apache chief Cochise attacks U. S. soldiers, igniting a war that lasts 10 years.

1863 President Abraham Lincoln proclaims Arizona a territory on February 24.

1868 The Navajo Indian Reservation, the largest Indian reservation in the country, is established in northeast Arizona, overlapping the four corners into Colorado, Utah, and New Mexico.

1869 John Wesley Powell leads the first river expedition through the Grand Canyon.

1878 John C. Fremont is appointed territorial governor.

1880 The Copper Queen Mine in Bisbee begins large-scale mining that will continue to 1975.

1881 The gunfight between the Earps and the Clantons at the O.K. Corral in Tombstone makes headlines.

1883 The Santa Fe Railroad line spans northern Arizona.

1886 Geronimo surrenders to the U.S. Army, ending the Apache Wars.

1889 The territorial capital moves to its final location, Phoenix.

1899 Joe Boot and Pearl Hart pull the last stagecoach robbery in the West.

1912 Arizona is admitted to the Union as the last of the 48 contiguous states.

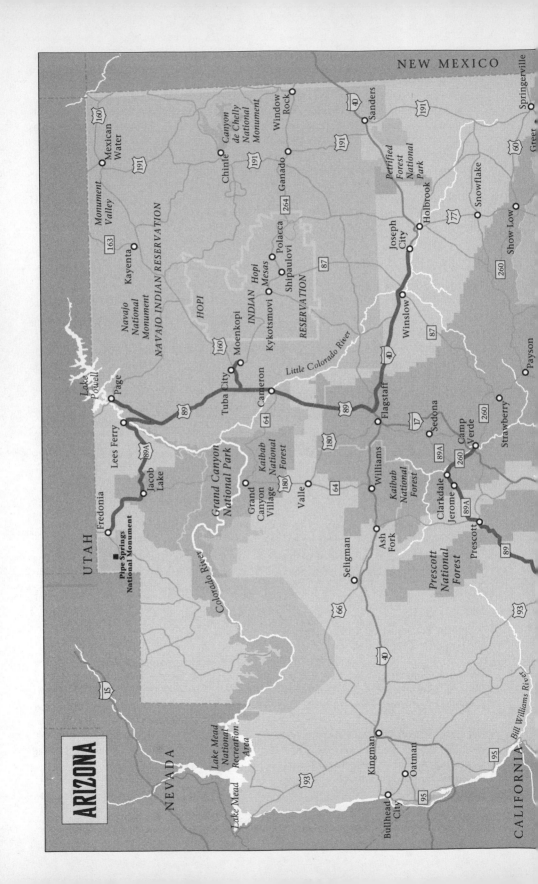

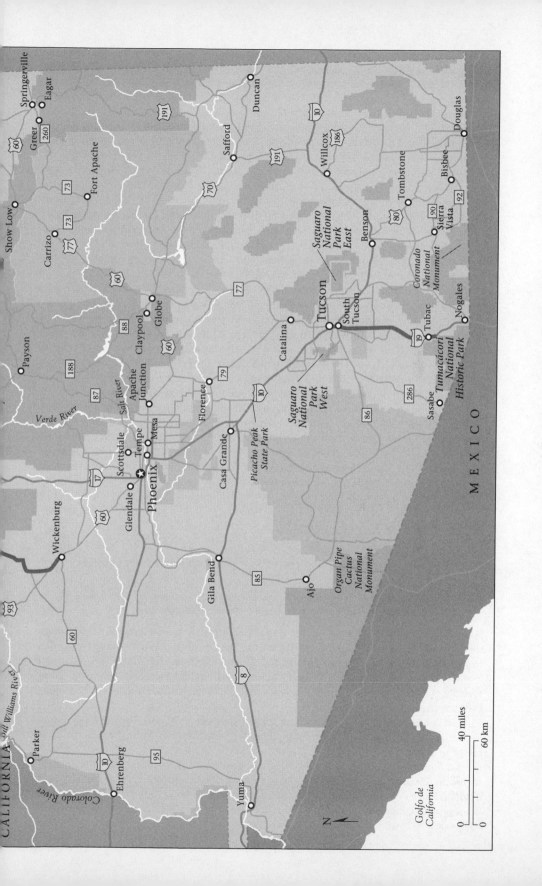

From 1871 to 1886, meanwhile, conflicts between settlers and Apaches culminated in the Apache Wars, a bloody 15-year episode punctuated by numerous massacres on both sides. The last of the 23 independent Apache tribes—the one led by Geronimo—held out in the southeastern Arizona mountains until the bitter end, when the band finally surrendered in the face of General George Crook's persistent campaigns.

Settlers in Arizona concentrated their energies in three arenas: cattle ranching, agriculture, and mining. Cattlemen began raising herds in Arizona in the 1870s; among the ranching empires was the spread of the Aztec Land and Cattle Company, better known as the Hashknife outfit, near Holbrook in northeastern Arizona. The cattle barons allowed the land to be overgrazed, leaving it exposed to erosion in less than 20 years. This proved to be the end of ranching in Arizona. Mormons who arrived from Utah were more adept at sustaining themselves in the arid climate, settling farming communities along the Colorado River, in the White Mountains, and in the southern deserts. Mining in Arizona began in the late 1870s with a brief gold rush, soon followed by a short-lived silver boom. It wasn't until copper was discovered that Arizona found its mineralogical niche. The major mining strikes were at Wickenburg, Tombstone, Bisbee, Oatman, and Jerome.

When most of the United States was living a relatively civilized life, Arizona was a wild frontier that epitomized stereotypes of the Old West. Out in this region of gunfighters, desperados, and prospectors, shootings and robberies were commonplace. The most famous gunfight, the shootout at the O.K. Corral, occurred in Tombstone on October 26, 1881, when the Earp brothers and Doc Holliday confronted the Clanton gang. The last stagecoach robbery in the United States also received its fair share of press. Joe Boot and Pearl Hart unsuccessfully robbed a stagecoach out of Globe in 1899 and were sentenced to terms at the Yuma Territorial Prison, which Hart, the "Lady Bandit," managed to have reduced by faking a pregnancy.

Life in Arizona gradually began to acquire a little polish in the years following the 1880 arrival of the railroad, which allowed entrepreneurs like Sam Hughes, Charles Debrille Poston, and Federico Ronstadt to develop commerce in Tucson and neighboring cities. President William Howard Taft signed the proclamation making Arizona the 48th state on February 14, 1912. The same year, Arizona granted women the right to vote, and seven years later Congress established Grand Canyon National Park.

The Santa Cruz Trail
A DRIVING TOUR FROM TUCSON TO TUMACÁCORI

▼▼▼

Distance: 50 mi   **Time:** 1 day
Breaks: The tiny ranching community of Amado and the artist colony in Tubac offer accommodations in cozy inns and adobe casitas; for meals there you can choose from several cafés and homey eateries.

Following the Gadsden Purchase in 1854, the Mexican army retreated out of Arizona along the Santa Cruz Trail, which follows the Santa Cruz River through the fertile Santa Cruz Valley from Tucson to Mexico. Spanish settlers, militia, and missionaries had followed this route in the opposite direction in the 17th and 18th centuries, establishing along the way the Tubac Presidio, the Tucson Presidio, and the missions at Tumacácori and San Xavier del Bac. Today, I–19 traverses the historic corridor.

Start out in **Tucson,** with a tour of the Tucson Museum of Art and Historic Block, which lies within the original walls of the Tucson Presidio. Several houses dating back to the 1800s create an image of life from the mid-1800s to the early 1900s in the "Old Pueblo." Thirteen miles south on I–19 brings you to one of the most spectacular pieces of Spanish colonial architecture in the United States—the Mission San Xavier del Bac. Another 38 mi south on I–19, a stop in **Tubac** at the Tubac Presidio State Historic Park gives you a look at the military might of the Spanish conquistadores in the 1700s. Drive 3 mi south to the ghostly ruins of the mission of Tumacácori to glimpse the fate of most of Father Kino's forays in the New World.

The Honeymoon Trail

A DRIVING TOUR FROM PIPE SPRING TO JOSEPH CITY

▼▼▼

Distance: 324 mi **Time:** 2 days

Breaks: Basic lodgings and restaurants in this isolated corner of the state can be found in Tuba City and Winslow.

Mormon pioneers headed south out of Utah into Arizona along the Honeymoon Trail, which parallels portions of Route 389, U.S. 89 and 89A, and I–40. The route was known as the Honeymoon Trail because, before the Arizona Temple was dedicated in Mesa in 1927, Arizona Mormon newlyweds had to make the arduous trek back up to St. George, Utah, to have their marriages sealed by the church.

Start your tour at Pipe Spring National Monument, a 72-mi drive north of **Grand Canyon National Park,** near the town of Fredonia. The isolated Pipe Spring settlement was established in 1870 by Mormon leader Brigham Young as a ranch for the Mormon Church's southern cattle operation. Mormon polygamists settled in Fredonia in 1885 in an attempt to evade federal agents. Seventy-six miles east of Fredonia on U.S. 89A, you can pick up the Honeymoon Trail at Lees Ferry, not far from **Page** on the Colorado River. Founded in the 1860s by Mormon leader Jacob Hamblin, the town ran a ferry that facilitated the expansion of Mormon settlement from Utah into Arizona. Another 60 mi south on U.S. 89A and U.S. 89 and an 11-mi jog east on U.S. 160 takes you to **Tuba City,** a good place to spend the night.

Start your second day 2 mi south of Tuba City in the Hopi Indian village of Moenkopi, where Mormon pioneers constructed a woolen mill in 1879. Then head back to U.S. 89 and drive south to I–40, which leads to **Winslow** and the ruins of the Mormon settlement of Brigham City. The Old Trails Museum in Winslow illustrates frontier life and documents the history of the region. Your trek ends a few miles short of **Holbrook,** at Joseph City, the oldest Anglo community in Navajo County, where several spurs of the Honeymoon Trail break off to Heber, Snowflake, Show Low, Safford, St. Johns, and Springerville.

Capitol Riches

A DRIVING TOUR FROM CAMP VERDE TO WICKENBURG

▼▼▼

Distance: 117 mi **Time:** 1 day

Breaks: The many colorful eateries and haunted hotels in Jerome and Prescott offer great places to hang out during an extended exploration of this history-rich region.

Gold strikes in the Mingus and Bradshaw mountains brought miners to the Verde Valley in the 1860s, along with farmers who developed the prime agricultural land here. The displaced Tonto Apache and Yavapai Indians retaliated, forcing the U.S. Army to set up military posts.

Start at one of the army forts, Fort Verde State Historic Park in **Camp Verde.** Twenty miles northwest on Route 260 will take you to the town of **Clarkdale,** where the smelter processed the rich ore from Jerome and shipped it out on the Verde Canyon rail line. Another 5 mi up Cleopatra Hill on Route 260 and you'll enter the funky little hamlet of **Jerome,** once known as the "wickedest town in the West." Sweeping views from town take in the Verde Valley and Sedona, all the way to the towering San Francisco Peaks to the northeast. After you spend some time wandering the steep streets and mining museums, drive the 33 mi to **Prescott.** Founded as the capital of the newly created Arizona Territory (due to its proximity to Fort Whipple), Prescott has more than 500 buildings on the National Register of Historic Places. You can still see the first territorial governor's mansion on the grounds of the Sharlot Hall Museum. For a look at another capital city, travel 59 mi on U.S. 89 to **Wickenburg,** the "Dude Ranch Capital of the World." This frontier town on the Hassayampa River got its start when Henry Wickenburg discovered gold at the Vulture Mine.

APACHE JUNCTION

▼▼

Apache Junction is the western terminus of the Apache Trail, a winding stretch of Route 88 that closely follows a path used by Apache and other Native Americans traveling through the area. In the early 1900s, the road was improved to move construction supplies to build Roosevelt Dam. President Theodore Roosevelt called the scenery along the 150-mi Apache Trail "the most awe-inspiring and most sublimely beautiful panorama nature ever created." Others refer to it as a white-knuckle dirt road because of its sharp switchbacks and steep drop-offs straight down into spectacular Fish Creek Canyon. *Contact Apache Junction Chamber of Commerce | 567 W. Apache Trail, 85220 | 480/982–3141 or 800/252–3141 | www. apachejunctioncoc.com.*

Apache Trail Tours and Superstition Mountain Adventures. Take a narrated jeep ride to the ghost town of Goldfield and learn about the Apache Trail, the Superstition Mountains, and the Lost Dutchman Mine. | 4650 N. Mammoth Mine Rd. | 480/982–7661 | www.apachetrailtours. com | $65–$165.

Goldfield. Located between the Superstition and Goldfield mountains, Goldfield was an instant city of about 4,000 residents after a gold strike in 1892. The town dried up five years later when the gold mine flooded. Today Goldfield Ghost Town is really a tourist trap, but it is nonetheless an interesting place to grab a cool drink at the saloon, pan for gold, or go on a mine tour. Poke around the Superstition Mountain Museum and learn the legend of the Lost Dutchman Mine, named for "Dutchman" Jacob Waltz. The location of the mine (supposedly somewhere in the aptly named Superstition Mountains), not to mention its very existence, has been hotly debated since pioneer days. | 4 mi north of Apache Junction on Rte. 88 | 480/983–0333 | Daily 10–5 | Museum $3.

✦ ON THE CALENDAR: Feb. **Lost Dutchman Days Rodeo.** The ghost of the Lost Dutchman presides over this rodeo, parade, and two-day event at the Apache Junction Rodeo Grounds and Goldfield Ghost Town. | 480/983–0487.

Nov. **Ben Johnson Days.** Named after western actor Ben Johnson, this event at Apache Junction Rodeo Grounds and Goldfield Ghost Town includes equestrian sports such as jackpot team roping and penning, kids' activities, and a memorial ride by the Goldfield Ghost Riders. | 480/983–0487.

HISTORIC DINING

Tortilla Flat Superstition Saloon. Southwestern. Close to the end of the Apache Trail stands a restaurant and country store that once served as a stagecoach stop. Serving travelers since before the turn of the 20th century, this is a fun place to stop for some refreshment while driving the Apache Trail. Sit on a saddle bar stool and enjoy a hearty bowl of killer chili. Save room for prickly-pear-cactus ice cream. | Rte. 88, 18 mi northeast of Apache Junction | $4–$10.

BISBEE

▼▼

The rough, granite Mule Mountains once hoarded hidden riches beyond those found anywhere else in the state. Situated in hostile Apache territory, the region's secrets were well guarded until a civilian scout for the U.S. Army stumbled across a rich outcropping at Mule Pass during a fierce military strike. Through a series of mishaps, the grubstake ended up in the hands of George Warren, a prospector of dubious distinction. In just two years, after claiming a portion of what would become one of the richest mineral sites in the world, Warren

JACOB WALTZ AND THE LOST DUTCHMAN MINE

In the Valley of the Sun, you can almost rest assured that sooner or later the conversation will turn to the famous (or infamous) Lost Dutchman Gold Mine. Did it really ever exist? If so, why hasn't it ever been found? Is the treasure still buried somewhere up there in the Superstition Mountains? There were, in fact, several productive hard-rock gold claims in the Superstitions years before "The Dutchman," appeared on the scene.

Some folks theorize that there was never a Lost Dutchman Mine at all, and that the so-called Dutchman, Jacob Waltz, got his gold elsewhere. Waltz worked up Wickenburg way as a foreman at Arizona's most productive gold mine of the era, the Vulture Mine. The gold came out of the mine in quartzite, which had to be crushed before the precious metal could be retrieved. But to crush the quartzite one needed water, and there was none nearby. The raw ore was transported by wagon down to the Hassayampa River to be crushed for refining.

Workers often placed the very best, richest ore samples on top of the load so they could be easily spotted and stolen. Along the route to the river, some of those samples were "accidentally" dropped by the wayside in a practice known as high-grading—stealing the highest-grade pieces of ore. Later, the samples were recovered and sold privately, cheating the mine owner out of some of his richest ore. Some believe Jacob Waltz acquired his treasure this way, for local lore indicates that he was fired for highgrading at the Vulture Mine.

wagered and lost his claim in a footrace against a horse. Once called the Warren Mining District, Bisbee takes its name from Judge DeWitt Bisbee of San Francisco, a prominent banker who provided financial backing for the Copper Queen Mine. After the earliest mineral strike, in 1877, Bisbee sprawled down Tombstone Canyon—called Main Street—and Brewery Gulch, which was notorious for its shady ladies and wild characters. The Bisbee region yielded more than $6.1 billion in gold, silver, copper, lead, and zinc, all discovered within 6 square mi. The mines closed for good in 1975, but the spirit of this boisterous town lives on. *Contact Bisbee Chamber of Commerce and Visitor Center | 31 Subway St., 85603 | 520/432–5421 or 866/ 2–BISBEE | www.bisbeearizona.com.*

Bisbee Mining and Historical Museum. In the circa-1897 Copper Queen Consolidated Mining Offices, this museum offers a glimpse of the working of Bisbee's early mining community. The first rural museum in the United States to become a member of the Smithsonian Institution Affiliations Program, this facility mounts comprehensive exhibits including the display "Bisbee: Urban Outpost on the Frontier," which offers an in-depth look at this community once known as "The Queen of the Copper Camps." | 5 Copper Queen Plaza | 520/432–7071 | www.bisbeemuseum.org | $4 | Daily 10–4.

Bisbee Trolley Tours. Although this modern trolley doesn't actually ride the rails, it does retrace the original route of the Warren & Bisbee Railway, which transported miners the 7 mi from Warren to the Copper Queen Mine in Bisbee. The trolley opened on March 12, 1908, and ran until the summer of 1928, when a bus system took over. Since that time, Warren has been incorporated into Bisbee. | 81 Main St. | 520/432–7020 | www.bisbeetrolley.com | $10 | Fri.–Mon. 9:30, 11, 1, 2:30, 4.

Copper Queen Mine Underground Tour. This copper mine opened in the 1880s and ran for 60 years, growing to 143 mi of tunnels before closing down for good in 1943. Seventy-five-minute tours into the queen of all copper mines are led by retired miners, who enjoy embellishing their official spiel with tales from the old mining days. Before piling into an ore cart and heading 1,800 ft underground, you get geared up in a yellow slicker, a hard hat, and a battery-operated light. You may want to wear a sweater or light coat under your slicker because the temperature in the mine is a brisk 47°F on average. The mine shaft traveled during the tour reaches ¼ mi back into the Copper Queen Mountain, where there is 900 ft of rock between you and the surface. Those who are a bit claustrophobic might consider taking one of the van tours of the surface mines and historic district that depart from the building at the same times as the mine tours (excluding 9 AM). Reservations for both tours are suggested. | 478 Dart Ave. | 520/432–2071 | $10 | Daily 9, 10:30, noon, 2, and 3:30.

Coronado National Memorial. This memorial dedicated to Francisco Vásquez de Coronado commemorates the conquistador's expedition through the area in 1540 during his search for the mythical Seven Cities of Cibola. It's a little more than 3 mi via a dirt road from the visitor center to Montezuma Pass, and another ½ mi on foot to the top of the nearly 7,000-ft Coronado Peak, where the views are best. An easy hike from the visitor center leads to a shallow cave, a one-time hideout for Apache war parties. The turnoff for the monument is 16 mi south of Sierra Vista on Route 92; the visitor center is 5 mi in. | 4101 E. Montezuma Canyon Rd., Hereford | 520/366–5515 | www.nps.gov/coro | Free | Daily 8–5.

Fort Huachuca Museum. Fort Huachuca, located 32 mi northwest of Bisbee, became the headquarters for the campaign against Geronimo in 1886. Even though the U.S. Army later closed many of its outposts, it kept Fort Huachuca to deal with conflicts on the border and is still in operation today as the longest continuously operating army base in the Southwest. The museum, housed in a late-19th-century bachelor officers' quarters, and the 1880s parade ground across the street provide a fascinating glimpse into military life on the frontier. | U. S. Army Garrison, Sierra Vista | 520/533–5736 | Free | Weekdays 9–4, weekends 1–4.

Muheim Heritage House Museum. Built in stages by Joseph and Carmelita Muheim from 1898 to 1915, this home is a stunning example of late-19th-century architecture. Restored and furnished with period furnishings, this pioneer home offers a look at everyday life during Bisbee's glory years. | 207B Youngblood Hill | 520/432–7698 | $2 | Fri.–Tues. 10–4.

✦ ON THE CALENDAR: July **Annual Fourth of July Celebration.** Bisbee's hard-rock miners battled to prove their skill in the mining technique of double jack in a competition each Independence Day. Two miners named McNichols and Ross set the world record in 1902. Watch the mining competition, a parade, ball games, fireworks, coaster races, and a mucking contest at this annual celebration. | 520/432–6000.

Nov. **Bisbee Historical Home Tour.** See some of Bisbee's late-19th- and early 20th-century architecture on this annual tour. | 520/432–6000.

HISTORIC DINING AND LODGING

St. Elmo's Bar. Bar. Brewery Gulch—a side canyon branching off of Tombstone Canyon or Main Street—was once touted as the hottest spot between El Paso and San Francisco. St. Elmo's Bar, the oldest continuously operated pub in Bisbee, opened its doors in 1902 and has been serving up cold pints ever since. | 36 Brewery Ave. | 520/432–5578 | $3 | No credit cards.

Stock Exchange Bar and the Brewery Steakhouse. American. Known locally as the Brewery, the 1905 Muheim Block Building was built to house the Bisbee Stock Exchange. The original stock tote board still hangs on the wall of the bar upstairs. Downstairs, the dining room serves up everything from burgers to steaks much in the same manner as it has since the beginning. | 15 Brewery Ave. | 520/432–3317 or 520/432–9924 | $7–$32 | MC, V.

Bisbee Grand Hotel. Built in 1906 for mining executives, the Bisbee Grand Hotel reflects the city's turn-of-the-20th-century prosperity in its restored Victorian furnishings. An authentic western-style saloon adds to the hotel's traditional charm. No room phones, no smoking. | 61 Main St., 85603 | 520/432–5900 or 800/421–1909 | fax 520/432–5900 | www.bisbeegrandhotel.com | 5 rooms, 8 suites | $75–$150 | AE, DC, MC, V | BP.

Copper Queen Hotel. The Copper Queen Hotel has been operating since 1902. Built by the Copper Queen Mining Company (which later became the Phelps Dodge Company), this downtown Victorian hotel has rooms named for some of its famous and infamous guests, including "Black Jack" Pershing, John Wayne, and Teddy Roosevelt. Peek into the quaint dining room, but eat elsewhere. Cable TV, meeting rooms. | 11 Howell Ave., 85603 | 520/432–2216 or 800/247–5829 | fax 520/432–4298 | www.copperqueen.com | 47 rooms | $77–$145 | AE, D, DC, MC, V | BP.

High Desert Inn. In the heart of downtown Bisbee, the High Desert Inn is housed in the old (1901) Cochise County Jail building. The structure's classical facade, highlighted by four monumental Doric columns, conceals a very modern, sophisticated establishment. No room phones, no smoking. | 8 Naco Rd., 85603 | 520/432–1442 or 800/281–0510 | www.highdesertinn.com | 5 rooms | $75–$95 | D, MC, V | BP.

CAMP VERDE

▼▼▼

Camp Verde, a military outpost originally known as Fort Verde, was the headquarters of General George Crook's command. Set up to protect the area's white settlers and prospectors against Indian uprisings, the fort gave rise to a town that later boomed with the region's silver- and gold-mining successes. *Contact Chamber of Commerce | 385 S. Main St., 86322 | 520/567–9294 | www.insightable.com/cvcc.*

Crown King. A tiny town with a dirt main street less than the length of a football field, Crown King was named for the Crowned King Gold Mine in the 1870s. More than $2 million worth of ore was extracted from the mine, and in 1895 a new orebody had the mill running 24 hours a day for a year and making $40,000–$50,000 a month. High atop the Bradshaw Mountains, Crown King now houses two saloons, an inn, a general store, a restaurant, cabins for rent, and some of Arizona's best nonprofessional horseshoe throwers. On your way to or from town, make certain to stop at the ghost towns of Bumble Bee and Cleator. Note that after you leave the main highway, parts of the drive to Crown King are unpaved though suitable for passenger cars. | 27 mi south on I–17 from Camp Verde to Exit 259, then Bloody Basin Rd. (NF 259) 10 mi west, then Crown King Rd. 13 mi south | www.crownking.com.

The two-story **Crown King Saloon** (Main St.) once housed a brothel upstairs. Moved to Crown King from the ghost town of Oro Belle in 1916, the saloon recalls the boom years with photos on the walls. You're apt to find a modern-day prospector or two seated at the bar. You can order sandwiches and burgers from a small restaurant attached to the back end of the saloon.

A Day in the West. Take your pick of several different two- to 4½-hour tours, ranging from jeep tours to horseback rides on the 90-acre Bradshaw Ranch, homesteaded in 1902. | 252 N. U.S. 89A, Sedona | 928/282–4320 | fax 928/282–6387 | www.adayinthewest.com | $55–$99.

Fort Verde State Historic Park. The third of three army fortifications in this part of Arizona Territory was built in 1871. To protect the Verde Valley's white farmers and miners from Tonto Apache and Yavapai raids, the fort enforced the removal of nearly 1,500 Native Americans to the San Carlos and Fort Apache reservations. In April 1873, Tonto Apache chief Chalipun and 300 followers surrendered to General George Crook here. At the historic park you can get an idea of what army life was like on this part of the frontier. A museum details the history of the area's military installations, and three furnished officers' quarters show the day-today living conditions of the top brass. | 125 Hollomon St. | 928/567–3275 | www.pr.state.az.us | $2 | Daily 8–5.

✦ ON THE CALENDAR: June–July **Period Reenactments and Encampments.** Occasional encampments and military reenactments of the frontier era take place at Fort Verde State Historic Park. | 928/567–9294.

CASA GRANDE
▼▼▼

Casa Grande, a small town south of Phoenix, was once a stop on the Southern Pacific Railroad. A farming and ranching town, it is infused with Native American history. *Contact Greater Casa Grande Chamber of Commerce | 575 N. Marshall St., 85222 | 520/836–2125 or 800/916–1515 | www.casagrandechamber.org.*

Casa Grande Valley Historical Society and Museum. Artifacts and photographs document local history. One exhibits documents the lives of the Gila Indians, who originally settled the area, including examples of their handcrafted baskets. | 110 W. Florence Blvd., 85222 | 520/836–2223 | $2 | Sept.–May, Tues.–Sun. 10–4.

Picacho Peak State Park. Arizona's only Civil War battle—the westernmost battle of the Civil War—took place at Picacho Pass. A monument commemorates the battle, which lasted 1½ hours and left three Union soldiers dead. Picacho Peak was also a landmark for early explorers. In 1846 the Mormon Battalion constructed a wagon road through here on their way to California to fight in the war with Mexico. The wagon road was subsequently traveled by 49ers on their way to California in search of gold. Five hiking trails in the park have interpretive signage. | 24 mi southeast of Casa Grande off I–10 Exit 219, Picacho | 520/466–3183 | www.pr.state.az.us/parksites.html | $5 per vehicle | Daily sunrise–sunset.

✦ ON THE CALENDAR: Feb. **O'odham Tash–Casa Grande Indian Days.** Held annually in Casa Grande on Presidents' Day weekend, this is the largest Indian event in Arizona. It includes an all-Indian Rodeo, ceremonial dances, a powwow, arts, crafts, food, music, and chicken scratch dances. | 520/836–4723.

DOUGLAS
▼▼▼

This Mexican-border town was founded in 1901 by James Douglas to serve as the copper-smelting center for the Bisbee mines. Before that, this remote region was used primarily as rangeland by cattle barons such as the ex–Texas Ranger John Slaughter. Even back in the early days Douglas had a church on each corner of its single city block: Grace Methodist (built in 1902), St. Stephen's Episcopal (1903), First Baptist (1904), and First Presbyterian (1907). You can see all of them today. *Contact Douglas Chamber of Commerce | 1125 Pan American Ave., 85607 | 520/364–2477 | www.discoverdouglas.com.*

Douglas/Williams House Museum. Now owned by the Arizona Historical Society, Jimmy "Rawhide" Douglas's refurbished Colonial Revival home, built in 1908, is open to the public as a museum. There's not much to see here and hours are limited, but there are some interesting old photographs and mementos. | 1001 D Ave. | 520/364–7370 | Donation requested | Tues.–Thurs. and Sat. 1–4.

Slaughter Ranch. The 73,000-acre San Bernardino Ranch was leased by John Slaughter, the sheriff of Cochise County after Wyatt Earp. Now reduced to a protected 140 acres, the ranch and its outbuildings give a glimpse of the great cattle operations that ran in southeastern Arizona in the late-19th- and early 20th centuries. | 15 mi east of Douglas on 15th St., which turns into Geronimo Trail | 520/558–2474 | www.vtc.net/~sranch | $3 | Wed.–Sun. 10–3.

✦ ON THE CALENDAR: Sept. **Douglas Fiestas.** Weekly events during the month toast the town's history at Veteran's Memorial Park. | 520/364–2477.

HISTORIC LODGING

Gadsden Hotel. Built in 1907, "the best hotel in the West" burned to the ground in 1927. Rebuilt in 1929 as an exact replica of the first, the "last of the grand hotels" has a solid white Italian marble staircase, two authentic Tiffany vaulted skylights, and a 42-ft long stained-glass mural. One thousand ounces of 14-karat gold leaf, costing $20,000 in 1929, were used to decorate the capitals. The bar is lively all day long and still serves as a meeting place for local ranchers. Cable TV, meeting rooms; no a/c in some rooms. | 1046 G Ave., 85607 | 520/364–4481 | fax 520/364–4005 | www.theriver.com/gadsdenhotel | 160 rooms | $40–$85 | AE, DC, MC, V.

FLAGSTAFF
▼▼

Founded in 1876, Flagstaff was named after a pine tree that served as a trail marker for wagon trains making their way to California. Set against a lovely backdrop of ponderosa pine and the snowcapped San Francisco Peaks—the highest mountains in Arizona—the Historic Downtown District still retains its frontier flavor. In 1891, Flagstaff was declared the county seat of Coconino County. *Contact Flagstaff Chamber of Commerce | 101 W. Rte. 66, 86001 | 928/774–4505 | www.flagstaff.az.us. Flagstaff Visitor Center | 1 E. Rte. 66, 86001-5588 | 928/ 774–9541 or 800/842–7293.*

Historic Downtown District. Excellent examples of late Victorian and Tudor Revival architecture in this district resonate with the history of this one-time logging and railroad town. A walking-tour map is available at the **visitor center** (1 E. Rte. 66) in the Tudor Revival–style Santa Fe Depot, an excellent place to begin sightseeing.

The 1888 **Babbitt Brothers Building** (12 E. Aspen Ave.) was constructed as a building-supply store and then turned into a department store by David Babbitt, founding father of one of Flagstaff's wealthiest families. Today, it houses an outdoor camping-hiking-climbing store.

Most of the Flagstaff area's first businesses were saloons catering to railroad construction workers. Such was the case with the 1888 **Vail Building** (1 N. San Francisco St.), a brick structure covered with stucco in 1939. It now houses the Sweet Life ice cream parlor.

Museum of Northern Arizona. Housed in a striking native-stone building shaded by trees, the museum is respected worldwide for its collections centering on the natural and cultural history of the Colorado Plateau; only 1% of its vast holdings on the archaeology, ethnology, geology, biology, and fine arts of the region is on display at any given time. Among the permanent exhibitions are an extensive collection of Navajo rugs and an authentic Hopi kiva (men's ceremonial chamber). The museum's education department sponsors excellent tours of the area and places as far away as New Mexico and Utah. | 3101 N. Fort Valley Rd. | 928/774– 5213 | www.musnaz.org | $5 | Daily 9–5.

Pioneer Museum. Operated by the Arizona Historical Society, the museum occupies a 1908 volcanic-rock building that was Coconino County's first hospital for the poor. Included among the displays are one of the depressingly small nurses' rooms, an old iron lung, and a reconstructed doctor's office. But most of the exhibits touch on more cheerful aspects of Flagstaff history—for example, road signs and children's toys. | 2340 N. Fort Valley Rd. | 928/774– 6272 | $1 suggested donation per individual, $3 per family | Mon.–Sat. 9–5.

Riordan State Historic Park. This must-see artifact of Flagstaff's logging heyday centers on a mansion built in 1904 for lumber-baron brothers Michael and Timothy Riordan. The 40-room log-and-stone structure—designed by Charles Whittlesley, who was also responsible for the El Tovar Hotel at the Grand Canyon—contains furniture by Gustav Stickley, father of the American Arts and Crafts design movement. Fascinating details abound: one room holds "Paul Bunyan's shoes," a 2-ft-long pair of boots made by Timothy in his workshop. Everything on display is original to the house, half of which was occupied by members of the family until 1986. The mansion may be explored by guided tour only. | 1300 Riordan Ranch St. | 928/779–4395 | www.pr.state.az.us | $4 | May–Sept., daily 8–5, with tours on the hr 9–4; Oct.–Apr., daily 11–5, with tours noon–4.

✦ ON THE CALENDAR: July **Folk Crafts Festival.** The Pioneer Museum holds a festival on July 4 with blacksmiths, weavers, spinners, quilters, and candlemakers at work. | 928/774–6272.

HISTORIC LODGING

Inn at 410. This B&B has a quiet but convenient downtown location. All the accommodations in the beautifully restored 1907 residence are suites with private baths. Some have private entrances, fireplaces, or hot tubs; all have coffeemakers. Monet's Garden has a lovely Jacuzzi suite with fireplace. The breakfasts are delicious and healthful; in the afternoon fresh-baked cookies are served. Some in-room hot tubs, refrigerators. | 410 N. Leroux St., 86001 | 928/774–0088 or 800/774–2008 | fax 928/774–6354 | www.inn410.com | 9 suites | MC, V | BP.

FLORENCE
▼▼

Founded in 1866, this territorial town is distinguished by an American Victorian courthouse and more than 150 other sites listed on the National Register of Historic Places. It was a tough town where saloons outnumbered churches by 28 to 1 and even women, such as Pearl Hart, robbed stagecoaches. Walking around the town's historic district is a good way to learn about territorial architecture. *Contact Florence Chamber of Commerce | Box 929, 291 N. Bailey St., 85232 | 520/868–9433 or 800/437–9433 | www.florenceaz.org. Pinal County Visitor's Center | 330 E. Butte St., 85232 | 520/868–4331 or 800/469–0175.*

Clark House. This home was built by mining engineer William Clark in 1884. The house has a ladder and trap door to the upper floor where Clark and his bride could hide in the event of Indian attacks. | Main St. | 520/868–5897.

Conrad Brunenkant City Bakery. Beautifully restored, the bakery was built in 1889 from locally manufactured bricks and granite from the Gila River. The second floor once served as quarters for the local Mexican-American Alliance. | 291 Bailey St., 85232 | 520/868–9433.

McFarland State Park. The 1878 adobe brick building at the heart of the park served as a jail, a courthouse, a hospital, and a World War II POW camp. Exhibits detail the building's history. | Main and Ruggles Sts., 85232 | 520/868–5216 | $2. | Thurs.–Mon. 8–5.

Pinal County Historical Society Museum. Among the displays here are prehistoric Indian artifacts, furnishings from early 20th century houses, and a rather unsettling collection of nooses from actual executions. | 715 S. Main St., 85232 | 520/928–4382 | $2 | Thurs.–Mon. 8–5.

The Silver King Hotel. Stroll down Main St. for a look at the Silver King, which opened for business in 1876. The hotel touted itself as one of the finest in Arizona Territory; historical records show that guests included politicians, film stars, and gunslingers. The hotel has been closed to the public since 1977 and is on the Arizona Preservation Foundation's Most Endangered List. The town continues to raise funds for restoration of the architecturally and contextually irreplaceable building. | Main St.

◆ ON THE CALENDAR: Feb. **Historic Homes Tour.** On this superb tour, residents throughout town open their homes to the public. | 520/868–5797 or 800/437–9433.

May **Cinco de Mayo Celebration.** Florence celebrates its ties to Mexico with homemade Mexican food, a festival, and parade. | 520/868–5797 or 800/437–9433.

GRAND CANYON NATIONAL PARK
▼▼▼

The Grand Canyon is a not-to-be-missed Arizona sight, its grandeur unparalleled in the southwestern United States and few other places in the world. For at least 8,000 to 10,000 years, humans have inhabited the canyon, sometimes building dwellings in the highest, most inaccessible canyon walls. The first Europeans saw the canyon in 1540, when a band of Spanish soldiers under the command of Captain García de Cárdenas came upon the area while searching for the fabled Seven Cities of Cibola. Although Franciscan missionary Francisco Tomás Garcés visited a Havasupai village in the canyon in 1776, the U.S. government didn't begin exploring the area until the army sent Lieutenant Joseph Ives with an expedition in 1857–58. Ives reported that the region was so inhospitable that the Colorado River would "be forever unvisited and undisturbed." After John Wesley Powell explored the canyon floor by boat in 1869, adventurers and mining companies took an interest in the geological wonder. The Grand Canyon was declared a national park in 1919, the year of Theodore Roosevelt's death. *Contact Grand Canyon National Park | Box 129, Grand Canyon 86023 | 928/638–7888 | www.nps.gov/grca | $20 per vehicle; permit good for a wk.*

Bright Angel Trail. On what is perhaps the best known of all the Grand Canyon's trails, you can hike a route followed first by bighorn sheep and later by Havasupai Indians. The trail was widened late in the 19th century for the use of prospectors, and it has since become a well-maintained avenue for mule and foot traffic. If you intend to go very far—the trail descends 8 mi and 5,510 ft to the Colorado River—you should have the proper equipment. | Trailhead adjacent to El Tovar Hotel in Grand Canyon Village.

Canyon View Information Plaza. In Grand Canyon Village at Mather Point, park rangers are on hand to answer questions and help you plan your Grand Canyon excursions. An exhibit examines the area's natural and human history. Nomadic Paleo-Indians, a later Archaic culture, and ancestral Puebloans lived in the canyon before Europeans arrived in the 16th century. The museum traces the arrival of explorers Captain García López de Cárdenas, John Wesley Powell, and others. | Grand Canyon Village, about 1 mi east of El Tovar Hotel | 928/638–7888 | Free | Late May–early Sept., daily 8–6; early Sept.–late May, daily 8–5.

Grandview Point. At an altitude of 7,496 ft, this spot has large stands of ponderosa pine, piñon pine, oak, and juniper. The view is one of the finest in the canyon. Directly below the point and accessible by the Grandview Trail is Horseshoe Mesa, where you can see ruins of the Last Chance Copper Mine. Grandview Point was also the site of the Grandview Hotel, constructed in the late 1890s but closed in 1908; logs salvaged from the hotel were used for the Kiva Room of the Desert View and the Watchtower. | Rte. 64, about 7 mi east of Yaki Point.

Hopi House. Part of an attempt by the Fred Harvey Company to promote Southwest Native American crafts at the turn of the 20th century, Hopi House was one of the first curio stores to open in the Grand Canyon. In the shop's early days, Indians in residence demonstrated their arts and crafts and performed traditional dances. The multi-story structure of rock and mortar was modeled after buildings found in the Hopi village of Oraibi, Arizona, the oldest continuously inhabited community in the United States. | In Grand Canyon Village across from El Tovar Hotel | 928/638–2631 | Daily 8–6.

Kolb Studio. The Grand Canyon's original photographic studio was built in 1904 by the Kolb brothers. From the small corner window that overlooks a trail into the canyon, the brothers photographed tourists as they embarked on mule rides. In the days before a pipeline was installed, Emery Kolb descended 3,300 ft each day to get the water he needed to develop his prints. Kolb was doing something right; he operated the studio until he died in 1976 at age 95. The gallery here presents painting, photography, and crafts exhibits from mid-April through November; there is also a bookstore with an exhibit hall on the lower level. | Canyon Rim Trail, in Grand Canyon Village west of El Tovar Hotel | 928/638–7888 | Free | Dec.–Aug., daily 8–7; Sept.–Oct., daily 8–6; Nov., daily 8–5.

Maricopa Point. On your left as you face the canyon are the Orphan Mine and, below it, a mine shaft and cable lines leading up to the rim. The copper ore in the mine, which started operations in 1893, was of excellent quality, but the cost of removing it finally brought the venture to a halt in 1966. | West Rim Dr. about 1 mi from Trailview Overlook.

Moran Point. This was a favorite spot of American landscape artist Thomas Moran, who painted Grand Canyon scenes from many points on the rim. Moran first visited the canyon with John Wesley Powell in 1873, and his vivid canvases helped persuade Congress to designate the canyon a national park. "Thomas Moran's name, more than any other, with the possible exception of Major Powell's, is to be associated with the Grand Canyon," wrote the canyon photographer Ellsworth Kolb. | East Rim Dr. about 5 mi east of Grandview Point.

Navajo Point. This was probably where the first Spanish descent into the canyon, in 1540, started. Just west of Navajo Point—which at 7,461 ft is the highest elevation on the South Rim—is the head of the unmaintained Tanner Trail (it's also called Horsethief Trail), a rugged route once favored by gold prospectors, rustlers, and bootleggers. | East Rim Dr. about 1 mi east of Lipan Point.

Pipe Spring National Monument. In the vast and desolate Arizona Strip, north of the Grand Canyon and south of Utah, Pipe Spring is named for the natural springs that watered the crops of Pueblo and Kaibab Paiute Indians for nearly 1,000 years. In the late 1800s, Mormon pioneers brought cattle here and the Mormon Church built a fort called Winsor Castle to anchor a large ranching operation and to serve as a waystation for for people traveling across the Arizona Strip. Tours of Winsor Castle are conducted daily on the hour and half-hour. Before making the drive to Pipe Spring, buy plenty of drinking water and top off your gas tank, as services are few and far between in this area. | On Rte. 389, 87 mi northwest of the North Rim, 14 mi southwest of Fredonia | 928/643–7105 | $3 | June–Sept., daily 7–5; Oct.–May, daily 8–5.

Powell Memorial. The large granite monument stands as a tribute to the first white man to ride the wild rapids of the Colorado River through the canyon. In 1869 John Wesley Powell measured, charted, and named many of the canyons and creeks of the river. It was here that the dedication ceremony for Grand Canyon National Park took place on April 3, 1920. | West Rim Dr. about ½ mi beyond Maricopa Point.

HISTORIC DINING AND LODGING

El Tovar Hotel and Dining Room. A National Historic Landmark, El Tovar was built in 1905 of Oregon pine logs and native stone. The hotel has been a focal point of a visit to the South Rim since it opened in 1905 and was quickly recognized as the most elegant hotel west of the Mississippi. The hotel had a coal-fired generator for electricity, a greenhouse to supply fresh vegetables, a henhouse for eggs, and its own diary herd for milk. The rustic elegance of the dining room ($15–$32) makes it popular for breakfast, lunch, and dinner. The restaurant is particularly known for entrées featuring local wild game. Rooms in the hotel are usually booked well in advance, though it's easier to get a reservation here during winter months, and dinner reservations are essential. Restaurant, room service, bar; no a/c. | West Rim Dr.,

Grand Canyon Village (Box 699, Grand Canyon 86023) | 303/297–2757 reservations only; 928/638–2631 ext. 6384 direct to hotel (no reservations) | fax 303/297–3175 reservations only; 928/638–2855 direct to hotel (no reservations) | www.grandcanyonlodges.com | 70 rooms, 8 suites | $118–$289 | AE, D, DC, MC, V.

HOLBROOK

▼▼

In 1884 Edward Kinsley, a stockholder of the Atlantic & Pacific Railroad, inspected the rail line through northern Arizona and saw the lush ranglelands along the Little Colorado River Valley. He returned to New York and persuaded a group of his associates to invest $1.3 million in a cattle ranch. A year later the railroad sold one million acres to the fledgling cattle barons for 50¢ an acre, and the Aztec Land and Cattle Company was born. Better known as the Hashknife outfit, Aztec was the second-largest cattle empire in the country. Like many other communities in Arizona Territory, Holbrook had its share of bloody Wild West shoot-outs, such as the gunfight between Sheriff Commodore Perry Owens and the Cooper-Blevins gang, who were partisans in the Pleasant Valley War. The ranching center became the Navajo County seat in 1895 and the town developed into an important shipping center for the region. *Contact Holbrook Chamber of Commerce | 100 E. Arizona St., 86025 | 520/524–6558 or 800/524–2449 | www.ci.holbrook.az.us.*

Joseph City. In the 1870s, Mormons attempted to establish several colonies along the Little Colorado River, but their irrigation attempts failed repeatedly. After only a few years the settlements were all abandoned, with the exception of Allen's Camp. Known today as Joseph City, this little community is the oldest Anglo settlement in Navajo County. | 11 mi west of Holbrook on I–40.

Navajo County Museum. In the 1898 county courthouse, this museum traces the region's history from the prehistoric Indian era through Arizona's frontier days. | 100 E. Arizona St. | 928/524–6558 or 800/524–2459 | Free | Weekdays 8–5:30.

Petrified Forest National Park. The vast fossilized forest southeast of Holbrook was almost destroyed by the Angell Abrasive Company in the late 1890s. The company set up a mill and began pulverizing the 225-million-year-old petrified trees to make emery for grinding. The federal government quickly put a stop to the millworks and protected the Petrified Forest as a national monument. | 15 mi southeast of Holbrook on U.S. 180 | 928/524–6228 | www.nps.gov/pefo | $10 per vehicle, valid for 1 wk | Mid-Oct.–May, daily 8–5; June–mid-Oct., daily 7–7.

✦ ON THE CALENDAR: June **Old West Day/Bucket of Blood Races.** This event includes Old West reenactments, music, food, and children's activities at the historic Holbrook Old West Courthouse. | 928/524–6558 or 800/524–2449.

HOPI MESAS

▼▼

In northeastern Arizona, the Hopi Reservation is entirely surrounded by the Navajo Nation, an uneasy living arrangement born of ancient rivalries and U.S. government interference. These villages are fascinating to visit, particularly Walpi, the "sky village," which seems to grow right out of the top of a mesa, and Old Oraibi, the oldest continuously inhabited town in the United States. These two villages have changed little since the Hopi's initial contact with the Spanish in 1540, and the same sandstone block houses stand today. The Hopi welcome visitors, but they request that when you come you dress modestly and wear shoes. Photography, sound recording, sketching, or even taking notes is strictly prohibited; do not even attempt to take pictures covertly. | Contact Hopi Office of Public Information, Box 123, Kykotsmovi 86039 | 928/734–3283 | www.hopi.nsn.us.

First Mesa. A narrow gravel road leads up to First Mesa from the more modern town of Polacca. On top, the view of the valley below is sweeping. Some sections of the stone and adobe houses may predate the arrival of Columbus by 300 years. The three interconnected villages include Hano, a settlement formed in 1696 by Tewa Indians who fled Spanish oppression in the Rio Grande valley. The Hopi let them live here on the condition they guard access to the mesa top. Despite centuries of Hopi influence, the Tewa have maintained their own customs and language. Adjacent to Hano is the village of Sichomovi, where the First Mesa Visitor Center stands. Here is where you park and register for a guided walking tour. At the end of the mesa lies tiny Walpi, with ancient houses and old defenses jutting out from the rocky cliffs. | Rte. 264 west of U.S. 191, through the Navajo Reservation and past Keams Canyon | 928/737–2262 | www.hopi.nsn.us | $8 includes tour | Daily 9–6.

Second Mesa. Of the three mesas, this is the most amenable to visitors. The mesa's three villages are Shipaulovi, Mishongnovi, and Shunopavi. At the foot of the mesa's western edge there are a restaurant, a motel, and the Hopi Cultural Center. | Rtes. 264 and 87 | 928/734–2401 | www.hopi.nsn.us | Free | Daily 9–6.

Third Mesa. Just a mile south of Route 264 at the eastern base of Third Mesa stands Kykotsmovi, a town whose name meand "the Mound of Ruined Houses." Two miles west of here is Old Oraibi, which has been inhabited since 1150. In 1906 a dispute erupted between two chiefs, one conservative and one progressive. The leaders staged a "push of war," contest in which opposing groups stood on either side of a line cut into the mesa. The two groups pushed each other until one group pushed across the line. The losing faction, led by Youkeoma, left to establish another village, Hotevilla, a few miles away. | Rte. 264 west of Second Mesa | 928/734–2404 | www.hopi.nsn.us | Free | Daily 9–6; Old Oraibi, daily 9–5.

✦ ON THE CALENDAR: Aug. **Hopi Independence Day Festivities.** A music festival, an arts-and-crafts expo, and a relay race take place at the Hopi Veteran's Memorial Center. | 928/734–6636.

Mid-Aug.–Sept. **Snake, Antelope, Butterfly and Flute Dances.** The katsina dances have significant religious meaning to the Hopi. Request permission before attending. | 928/734–2401.

Oct. **Tuhisma–Hopi Arts and Crafts Market.** A gathering of Hopi artists displays the best of Hopi arts at Hopi Veteran's Memorial Center. There are also entertainment and food. | 928/738–0055.

JEROME
▼▼

Cleopatra Hill was first mined by prehistoric Native Americans, then by the Spanish who were seeking gold and found copper. The first Anglo claims were made in 1876, prompting Eugene Jerome, a frontier financier, to fund a speculative mining venture with the condition that the town be named after him. It wasn't until 1882 that full-scale production ensued. A colorful mining town was soon stacked against the hillside, and Jerome came to be known as the Billion Dollar Copper Camp. In 1903 a New York reporter called Jerome "the wickedest town in America" because of its disproportionate number of saloons and raucous mix of bootleggers, prostitutes, gamblers, and miners. After the last mines closed in 1953, the population shrank to 50. Today Jerome has about 500 residents, who have renovated homes and reopened abandoned shops. *Contact Jerome Chamber of Commerce | 50 Main Ave., 86331 | 520/634–2900 | www.jeromechamber.com.*

Gold King Mine and Ghost Town. One of the most unusual testaments to Jerome's mining days is this mélange of rusting and refurbished antique trucks and mining artifacts, which is patrolled by sheep, goats, and a donkey. Haynes, a gold camp, stood here. Remnants of the mining operation include the old mine shaft, a circa-1901 blacksmith shop, a miner's hut, a boardinghouse, and the world's largest gas engines. You can see demonstrations of antique mining equipment and the operation of a turn-of-the-20th-century sawmill. Take a tour for the full experience. | Perkinsville Rd., 1 mi northeast of Jerome | 928/634–0053 | $3 | Daily 9–5.

Jerome State Historic Park. Of the three mining museums in town, this is the most comprehensive. The museum occupies the 1917 mansion of Jerome's mining king, Dr. James "Rawhide Jimmy" Douglas, Jr., who purchased Little Daisy Mine in 1912. The Douglas mansion is now a museum with exhibits of artifacts, photographs and a 3-D model of the town and its underground mines. The Douglas library is a restored period room. As well, you can see some of the tools and heavy equipment used to grind ore. Drivers note: State Park Road is a short, precipitous road at an elevation of 5,000 ft. | State Park Rd., off U.S. 89A | 928/634–5381 | www.pr.state.az.us | $2 | Daily 8–5.

The Mine Museum. Staffed by the Jerome Historical Society, this museum documents, among other aspects of Jerome's mining past, the role of Chinese, Irish, Italian, and Russian immigrants who came here to find their fortunes. The museum's collection of mining stock certificates alone is worth the (small) price of admission—the amount of money that changed hands in this town around the turn of the 20th century boggles the mind. | 200 Main St. | 928/634–5477 | $2 | Daily 9–5.

Verde Canyon Railroad. On the 22-mi trip through the scenic Verde Valley, knowledgeable announcers regale you with the area's colorful history. They also point out natural attractions along the way—in winter, you're likely to see bald eagles. For an extra $20 you can ride in the living-room-like first-class cars, where hot hors d'oeuvres, coffee, and a cocktail are included in the price. | Arizona Central Railroad Depot, 300 N. Broadway, Clarkdale | 800/293–7245 | www.verdecanyonrr.com | $35.95–$54.95.

HISTORIC DINING
English Kitchen. American/Casual. One of the oldest restaurants in the country, this has operated in one form or another since 1899, when Chinese immigrant Charley Hong arrived in Jerome and set up shop. Nearly a century later, in 1986, Tim and Jayne Toth bought the restaurant, and they now serve salads, burgers, and sandwiches at lunch, as well as the best breakfast in town according to residents, who might prefer to keep this place a secret. | 416 Main St. | 928/634–2733 | $3–$10 | No credit cards | Closed Wed. No dinner.

KAYENTA
▼▼▼

Kayenta, a small town with a small shopping center and some fast-food restaurants, is a good base for exploring Navajo Tribal Park and Navajo National Monument. U.S. 163 runs through Kayenta and has been designated a Scenic Highway by the Arizona Department of Transportation. *Contact Kayenta Visitor's Center | Box 545, 86033 | 520/697–3572.*

Monument Valley. No other western landscape epitomizes America's Old West as do the towering red sandstone monoliths of Monument Valley, situated at the heart of the vast Navajo Nation. Thanks to Hollywood, which over the years has shot scenes for many westerns here, the sight of these geological wonders instantly summons images of John Wayne riding across the desert in search of justice. The sprawling, arid expanse was once populated by ancestral Puebloan people (more popularly known by the Navajo word Anasazi, which means both "ancient ones" and "enemy ancestors") and in the last few centuries has supported generations of Navajo farmers. The soaring red buttes, eroded mesas, deep canyons, and naturally sculpted rock formations of Monument Valley are easy to enjoy on a leisurely drive through Monument Valley Navajo Tribal Park. A 17-mi self-guided driving tour on a rough dirt road (there's only one road, so you can't get lost) passes the memorable Mittens and Totem Pole formations, among others. The Navajo Tribal Park visitor center holds a crafts shop and exhibits devoted to ancient and modern Native American history. | Off U.S. 163, 24 mi north of Kayenta (Box 2520, Window Rock 86515) | 435/727–3353 park visitor center; 928/871–6647 Navajo Parks & Recreation Dept. | www.navajonationparks.org | $3 | Visitor center May–Sept., daily 7–7; Oct.–Apr., daily 8–5.

Navajo Cultural Center of Kayenta. Take a self-guided walking tour through the 2½-acre outdoor cultural park and learn about the history, lifeways, beliefs, and traditions of North America's largest Indian tribe. | U.S. 160, between Hampton Inn and Burger King | 928/697–3170 | Free | Daily 7–sunset.

KINGMAN
▼▼

This mining and ranching area was settled in the late 1800s when the Atlantic & Pacific Railroad made its way here. Today, 62 buildings in the business district are listed on the National Register of Historic Places. Surrounded on three sides by rugged hills, Kingman lies amid the Wild West landscape made famous by Hollywood. *Contact Kingman Area Chamber of Commerce | 120 W. Andy Devine Ave., 86401 | 520/753–6106 | www.kingmanchamber.com.*

Bonelli House. This house is an excellent example of the Anglo-territorial architecture popular in Arizona in the early 1900s. Listed on the National Register of Historic Places, the home is constructed of locally quarried Tufa stone, and every room opens onto sleeping porches for warm summer nights. Inside, you can see how a well-to-do western family lived at the turn of the 20th century. Many of the furnishings on display belonged the Bonnelli family, who lived in the house until it was purchased by the City of Kingman in 1973. | 430 E. Spring St. | 928/753–1413 | Donations accepted | Thurs.–Sun. 1–4.

Chloride. North of Kingman is the ghost town of Chloride. Taking its name from a type of silver ore mined in the area, Chloride is Arizona's oldest silver-mining camp. During its heyday, from 1900 to 1920, there were some 75 mines operating in the area: silver, gold, lead, zinc, molybdenum, and even turquoise were mined here. About 300 folks live here today, some of them artists and craftspeople who run small studios and shops in the historic buildings. Sights include the old jail, Chloride Baptist Church, Silverbelle Playhouse, the 1890 Jim Fritz House, and the Tennessee Saloon, now a general store and dance hall. Don't miss the large murals painted on the rocks by western artist Roy Purcell, who worked the mines here in his youth. | 12 mi north of Kingman, off U.S. 93 | www.oldwesttowns.com.

Colorado River Indian Tribes Museum and Library. This small museum houses a collection of rare photographs that document the Native American presence in the region. There are also baskets and pottery on display. It is in Parker, which is 98 mi south of Kingman via I–40 west and Route 95 south. | 2nd Ave. at Mohave Rd., Parker | 928/669–9211 ext. 1335 | Free | Weekdays 8–5, Sat. 10–3.

Oatman. A worthwhile stop southwest of Kingman is the ghost town of Oatman. Its main street is right out of the Old West; scenes from a number of Hollywood westerns were shot here. Oatman still has a remote, old-time feel: many of the locals carry side arms, and they're not acting. You can wander into one of the three saloons or visit the Oatman Hotel, where Clark Gable and Carole Lombard honeymooned in 1939 after they were secretly married in Kingman. The town's real draw are the burros that often come in from nearby hills and mean-der down the street. A couple of stores sell hay to folks who want to feed these "wild" beasts, which at last count numbered about a dozen and which leave plenty of evidence of their visits in the form of "road apples" (watch your step). The drive here from Kingman is a straight shot across the Mojave Desert valley for a while, but then the road narrows and winds precip-itously for about 15 mi through the Black Mountains. The road is public, but beyond a narrow shoulder the land is privately owned and heavily patrolled, because of the still-active gold mines throughout the hills. | 26 mi southwest of Kingman on Historic Route 66 (now Rte. 68) | 928/768–6222 | www.route66azlastingimpressions.com.

HISTORIC DINING AND LODGING

Brunswick Hotel. The hotel opened its doors in 1909 and was the first three-story building in town. The early 1900s are alive and well here, in guest rooms furnished with antiques. Restaurant, massage, bar; no TV in some rooms, no-smoking rooms. | 315 E. Andy Devine Ave., 86401 | 928/718–1800 | www.hotel-brunswick.com | 18 rooms, 9 with bath; 6 suites | $72–$112 | AE, D, MC, V | CP.

MESA

▼▼

Founded in 1878 by Mormons on their way to Salt Lake City, Utah, Mesa is now a sprawl-ing city east of Phoenix. Its Spanish name for "table" comes from its location on a plateau overlooking the Salt River. *Contact Mesa Convention and Visitors Bureau | 120 N. Center, 85201 | 480/827–4700 or 800/283–6372 | www.mesacvb.com.*

Mesa Southwest Museum. This museum traces local history from prehistoric times to the pres-ent. The interactive exhibits include one in which you can pan for gold, as well as an exhibit of cells from the old Territorial Prison in Yuma. A gallery displays photographs from *Arizona Highways* magazine. | 53 N. MacDonald St. | 480/644–2230 | $6 | Tues.–Sat. 10–5, Sun. 1–5.

♦ ON THE CALENDAR: Feb. **Mesa Territorial Days.** The city of Mesa mounts this Old West celebration of Arizona's statehood. | 480/644–2760.

Oct. **Native American Powwow.** More than 300 Native American dancers from throughout the nation compete in this colorful event in Mesa's Pioneer Park. | 480/827–4700.

HISTORIC DINING

Monte's La Casa Vieja. Steak. In 1871, when Tempe was still known as Hayden's Ferry, this old house was the home of Charles Hayden. Hayden arrived at the east end of the Salt River (then called the Rio Salado) in the 1860s and modeled his adobe hacienda—the town's first building—after Spanish mansions. He built a flour mill and began a ferry service across the river. Although he called the outpost Hayden's Ferry, other settlers thought the butte, river, and fields of green mesquite looked like the Vale of Tempe in Greece. The town's name was changed to Tempe in 1879. Now a steak house, Hayden's former home retains its original dimensions; the lobby and dining rooms contain photographs and historical documents pertaining to the frontier history of Tempe, about 7 mi west of Mesa. | 3 W. 1st St., Tempe | 480/967–7594 | $20–$30 | AE, D, DC, MC, V.

PAGE

▼▼

Though Page itself has no Old West heritage—it was established in 1957 as a construction camp for crews building the Glen Canyon Dam—it is a convenient base for exploring this part of Arizona and the Navajo Nation to the east. *Contact Page/Lake Powell Chamber of Commerce | Box 727, 644 N. Navajo, Tower Plaza, 86040 | 928/645–2741 or 888/261–7243 | www.page-lakepowell.com.*

John Wesley Powell Memorial Museum. This remarkable museum documents John Wesley Powell's explorations of the Grand Canyon. Between 1869 and 1872, Powell led the first known expeditions down the Green River and the rapids-choked Colorado River, through the Grand Canyon. He mapped the rivers and kept detailed records of his trips, naming the Grand Canyon and many other geographical features in northern Arizona. Artifacts from Powell's expeditions are displayed in the museum, which also has a good selection of regional books and maps. The museum doubles as Page's visitor information center. | 6 N. Lake Powell Blvd. at North Navajo Dr. | 928/645–9496 | www.powellmuseum.org | $1 | Early Sept.–late May, weekdays 8:30–5:30; late May–early Sept., Mon.–Sat. 8:30–5:30.

Lees Ferry. A sharp bend in the Colorado River at a break in the Echo Cliffs is considered mile zero of the river, the point from which all distances on the river system are measured. Now known as Lees Ferry, this spot was first visited by Europeans in 1776, when Spanish priests Fray Francisco Atanasio Domínguez and Fray Silvestre Velez de Escalante tried but failed to cross the Colorado here. Explorer John Wesley Powell visited in 1870 on an expedition with Mormon officials. The site is named for John D. Lee, who constructed the first ferry across the Colorado here in 1872, under the direction of Mormon leader Brigham Young. Lees Ferry became a crossing and a supply point for miners and other pioneers. After the ferry was established, it became part of the Honeymoon Trail, on which newlywed Arizona couples traveled to Utah to have their marriages sanctified at the Latter-day Saints temple in St. George. Lees Ferry retains a number of vestiges of the mining era, but it's now primarily known as the starting point for most of the Grand Canyon raft trips. | 43 mi from Page via U.S. 89 south and U.S. 89A north | No phone.

Navajo Village Heritage Tours. These two- to four-hour tours offered by Navajo guides include art demonstrations, native foods tastings, dance performances, and traditional storytelling. | Vermillion Down | 928/660–0304 or 928/645–2741 | $30–$50.

PHOENIX

▼▼

The first inhabitants of the Salt River valley were the Hohokam, who built more than 300 mi of irrigation canals and cultivated cotton, corn, and beans. They constructed a great town and then vanished. Phoenix is built upon the ruins of that town. From the time the Hohokam left until the Civil War, the once fertile valley lay all but forgotten, visited only occasionally by small bands of Pima and Maricopa Indians. Then, in 1865, the U.S. Army established Fort McDowell in the mountains to the east, where the Verde River flows into the Salt River. To feed the soldiers and horses stationed there, Jack Swilling, a former Confederate army officer and part-time prospector, helped reopen the Hohokam canals in 1867. Within a year, fields bright with barley and pumpkins earned the area the name Punkinsville. But by 1870, when the townsite was plotted, the 300 settlers saw their new city rising "like a phoenix" from the ashes of a vanished civilization.

Phoenix would rise indeed. Within 20 years, it had become large enough—its population was about 3,000—to wrest the title of territorial capital from Prescott. By 1912, when Arizona was admitted as the 48th state, the area, irrigated by the brand-new Roosevelt Dam and Salt River Project, had a burgeoning cotton industry. Copper and cattle were mined and raised elsewhere but were banked and traded in Phoenix, and the cattle were slaughtered and packed here in the largest stockyards outside Chicago. *Contact Greater Phoenix Convention and Visitors Bureau Arizona Center, 2nd and Adams Sts., 85004 | 602/254–5521 | www.visitphoenix.com.*

Arizona Hall of Fame Museum. In the former Carnegie Public Library building, this museum documents the lives of the ranchers, Buffalo Soldiers, Mexican miners, early government officials, and others who were instrumental in establishing Arizona. A section called the Arizona Women's Hall of Fame celebrates the women who helped shape Arizona culture and politics. | 1101 W. Washington St. | 602/225–2110 | Free | Weekdays 8–5.

Arizona Military Museum. Artifacts of Arizona's military past are housed here. There's also a photographic collection depicting the Buffalo Soldiers, the African-American army units so named for their "hair like that of the buffalo." | 5636 E. McDowell Rd. | 602/267–2676 | Donations accepted | Tues. and Thurs. 9–2, Sun. 1–4.

Arizona Mining and Mineral Museum. Rocks, minerals, and mining artifacts are on display at this small local museum, which focuses on the copper mining that brought thousands of people to Phoenix and the surrounding areas. An old mining hoist and a mining-car engine are exhibited outside the main building. | 1502 W. Washington St. | 602/255–3791 | Free | Weekdays 8–5, Sat. 11–4.

Arizona State Capitol Museum. This museum has comprehensive displays on Arizona's government and history, state symbols, and governors. The top floor has the original house and senate chambers. Other exhibits focus on territorial life. | 1700 W. Washington St. | 602/542–4581 or 602/542–4675 | Free | Weekdays 8–5.

Arrowhead Desert Tours. Take a four-hour jeep tour out into the Sonoran Desert with cowboy guides and learn how to pan for gold, shoot an authentic six shooter, and throw a tomahawk. | 841 E. Paradise La. | 602/942–3361 | www.arizona-jeeptours.com | $65.

Heard Museum. Pioneer Phoenix settlers Dwight and Maie Heard had a Spanish colonial–revival building erected on their property to house their impressive collection of southwestern art. Today, the site has developed into the nation's premier showcase of Native American art, basketry, pottery, weavings, and beadwork. Events such as the Guild Indian Fair and the Hoop Dancing Competition explore the Native American experience. The museum has a satellite branch in Scottsdale, which displays rotating exhibits on Native American art and history. | 2301 N. Central Ave. | 602/252–8848 or 602/252–8840 | www.heard.org | $7 | Daily 9:30–5 | Heard Museum North: 34505 N. Scottsdale Rd., Scottsdale | 480/488–9817 | $2 | Mon.–Sat. 10–5:30, Sun. noon–5.

Heritage Square. This park-like city-owned area contains the only remaining homes from the original Phoenix townsite. On the south side of the square, along Adams Street, stand several houses built between 1899 and 1901. The Teeter House, the third house in the row, is a Victorian-style tearoom. On the south side of Adams Street is the Thomas House and Baird Machine Shop. | Bounded by 5th and 7th Sts. and Monroe and Adams Sts.

The Stevens House holds the **Arizona Doll and Toy Museum** (602 E. Adams St. | 602/253–9337).

The **Silva House** (5th and Monroe Sts. | 602/236–5451), a bungalow built in 1900, has presentations about the life of turn-of-the-20th-century settlers in Phoenix township.

The grande dame of Heritage Square is the **Rosson House** (6th and Monroe Sts. | 602/495–7000 | $3), an 1895 Victorian in the Queen Anne style. Built by a physician who served a brief term as mayor, it is the sole surviving example of fewer than two dozen Victorians erected in Phoenix. The 30-minute tour is well worth the modest admission price. The house is closed Monday and Tuesday.

Phoenix Art Museum. The museum's American West collection contains the work of painters from Frederic Remington to Georgia O'Keeffe. There's also a clothing-and-costume collection with pieces dating back to 1750. Free tours of the museum collections are given at 2 daily. | 1625 N. Central Ave. | 602/257–1880 | www.phxart.org | $7 | Tues.–Sun. 10–5.

Phoenix Museum of History. This striking glass-and-steel museum documents regional history from the 1860s (when Anglo settlement began) through the 1930s. Interactive exhibits trace the city's multicultural heritage and its growth. | 105 N. 5th St. | 602/253–2734 | www.azcama.com | $5 | Mon.–Sat. 10–5, Sun. noon–5.

Pioneer Arizona Living History Museum. Twenty-eight original and reconstructed buildings from throughout territorial Arizona make up this museum. Costumed guides reenact frontier life and demonstrate pioneer crafts. | Pioneer Rd. (Exit 225) off I–17, 25 mi north of downtown Phoenix | 623/465–1052 | $5.75 | Wed.–Sun. 9–5.

Sahuaro Ranch. Now on the west side of metro Phoenix, Glendale was settled in the late 1880s when W. J. Murphy's dam and canal brought water to this part of the desert, allowing settlers to plant crops in the rich soil. Soon, railroad service and an ice plant made this agricultural center Arizona's largest shipping center as well. Listed on the National Register of Historic Places, Sahuaro Ranch, a turn-of-the-20th-century Glendale homestead, is now an 80-acre historical park. Original buildings include a fruit-packing shed, a bunk house, the main house, and a guest house. There is also a barnyard. Educational exhibits on early pioneer life are shown in the 1899 foreman's house. The rose garden was planted in the 1890s. | 59th Ave. and Mountain View Rd., Glendale | 623/939–5782 | Daily 6 AM–7 PM.

PRESCOTT

▼▼

North of Phoenix, on the gigantic Mogollon Rim behind the dusty Hieroglyphic Mountains (misnamed for Hohokam petroglyphs found there), prospectors found gold in the early 1860s. Soon afterward, in 1864, President Abraham Lincoln designated Prescott the first capitol of Arizona Territory. The town was settled by Yankees, to ensure that gold-rich northern Arizona would remain a Union resource. (Tucson and southern Arizona were strongly pro-Confederacy.) They brought with them a New England architectural style still visible today. Despite a devastating downtown fire in 1900, Prescott remains the Southwest's richest store of New England–style architecture; in fact, it's been called the "West's most eastern town." The city's main drag is Gurley Street, named after John Addison Gurley, who was slated to be the first governor but died days before he was to move to Arizona Territory. Nearby, the town's Victorian neighborhoods contain many restored structures in the Queen Anne style. Street names such as Montezuma, Cortez, and Alarcon reflect early rumors that Aztec Indians once lived in the area. *Contact Prescott Chamber of Commerce | 117 W. Goodwin St., Box 1147, 86302 | 928/445–2000 or 800/266–7534 | www.prescott.org.*

Phippen Museum of Western Art. Included in the permanent collection of the respected museum, about 5 mi north of downtown, is work by many prominent artists of the West, along with the paintings and bronze sculptures of George Phippen. | 4701 U.S. 89 N | 928/778–1385 | www.phippenartmuseum.org | $3 | Mon. and Wed.–Sat. 10–4, Sun. 1–4.

Sharlot Hall Museum. Along with the original ponderosa-pine log cabin—home of the territorial governor—and the museum, named for historian and poet Sharlot Hall, the park-like complex contains three fully restored period homes and a transportation museum. Territorial times are the focus, but natural history and artifacts of the area's prehistoric peoples are also on display. | 415 W. Gurley St., 2 blocks west of Courthouse Plaza | 928/445–3122 | www.

sharlot.org | $5 per family donation requested | Apr.–Oct., Mon.–Sat. 10–5, Sun. 1–5; Nov.–Mar., Mon.–Sat. 10–4, Sun. 1–5.

Smoki Museum. The 1935 stone-and-log building is almost as interesting as the Native American artifacts inside. Priceless baskets and katsinas, as well as pottery, rugs, and beadwork, make up this fine collection, which represents Native American culture from the pre-Columbian period to the present. | 147 N. Arizona St. | 928/445–1230 | $2 | May–Sept., Mon.–Tues. and Thurs.–Sat. 10–4, Sun. 1–4; Oct., Fri.–Sun. 10–4; Nov.–Apr. by appointment only.

Whiskey Row. This strip once held 20 saloons and houses of pleasure. Social activity is more subdued these days, and the historic bars provide an escape from the street's many boutiques. Archaeological digs conducted in 2002 uncovered underground passages housing brothels, opium dens, and gambling facilities. | Montezuma St. between Gurley and Goodwin Sts.

✦ ON THE CALENDAR: May **George Phippen Memorial Western Art Show.** Artists exhibit their work at the annual Memorial Day weekend show in Courthouse Plaza. | 928/445–2000 or 800/266–7534.

June **Territorial Prescott Days.** This festival includes arts and crafts, contests, western reenactors, and tours of the Courthouse Plaza area. | 928/445–2000 or 800/266–7534.

HISTORIC DINING AND LODGING

Murphy's. American. Turn-of-the-20th-century artifacts decorate this former mercantile building, which is on the National Register of Historic Places. The menu stars mesquite-grilled meats and house-brewed beer. Murphy's also has a Sunday brunch. | 201 N. Cortez St. | 520/445–4044 | $8–$25 | AE, D, MC, V.

The Palace. American. Legend has it that the patrons who saved the Palace's ornately carved 1880s Brunswick bar from a Whiskey Row fire in 1900 continued drinking at it while the rest of the row burned across the street. Whatever the case, the bar remains the centerpiece of the beautifully restored turn-of-the-20th-century structure. The tin-embossed ceiling and original woodwork add to the charm. Prime rib is the house speciality; the Tom Mixed Grill (steak, salmon, and shrimp scampi) is a good choice as well. | 120 S. Montezuma St. | 928/541–1996 | $9–$20 | AE, MC, V.

Hotel St. Michael. This hotel sits on the busiest corner of the Courthouse Plaza and offers several rooms with views of the courthouse. The hotel dates from the turn of the 20th century and has furniture dating back to the 1930s. | 205 W. Gurley St., 86301 | 928/776–1999 or 800/678–3757 | fax 928/776–7318 | 71 rooms | $49–$99 | AE, D, DC, MC, V | CP.

SCOTTSDALE
▼▼

Scottsdale began in 1901 as "30-odd tents and a half dozen adobe houses" put up by health-seekers. Touted as "the West's most western town," the chic, sprawling suburb of Phoenix has actually lost most of its old character. The historic Old Town area is trying desperately to hang on to its western flavor, but Scottsdale is better known for its golf courses, shopping, art galleries, and world-class resorts. These days, it's hard to imagine that not too long ago there were still dirt roads and hitching posts here. *Contact Scottsdale Chamber of Commerce | 7343 Scottsdale Mall, 85251 | 480/945–8481 or 800/877–1117 | www.scottsdalecvb.com.*

Arizona Desert Mountain Jeep Tours. These narrated jeep tours will take you past ghost towns and Indian ruins and along the historic Butterfield Overland Trail Route. | 6303 E. Cochise | 480/860–1777 | www.azdesertmountain.com | $75–$100.

Buffalo Museum of America. This quirky little museum pays homage to the American bison and its role in American history. Contents range from a mounted shaggy beast to impressionistic works of art. | 10261 N. Scottsdale Rd. | 480/951–1022 | $3 | Weekdays 9–5.

Old Town Scottsdale. Old Town is a six-block cluster of early 20th-century buildings with rustic storefronts and wooden sidewalks. But the Old West ends at the facades of the shops. Behind the storefronts are boutiques filled with jewelry, crafts items, and Mexican imports, plus the typical souvenir-type establishments. After about three blocks, everything starts looking the same. | Main St.

Scottsdale Historical Museum. This redbrick structure was Scottsdale's first schoolhouse, and it preserves the 1910 schoolroom. Photographs, original furniture owned by the city's founding families, and displays of other treasures from Scottsdale's early days are included in the collection. | 7333 Scottsdale Mall | 480/945–4499 | Free | Sept.–June, Wed.–Sat. 10–5, Sun. noon–4.

✦ ON THE CALENDAR: Jan.–Feb. **Parada del Sol.** This annual event includes a parade down Old Town's main street (billed as the longest nonmechanized parade in the world) and is filled with colorful floats and western reenactors on horseback, including "the wild women of the west." Festivities include a rodeo at the Rawhide Rodeo Arena. | 480/990–3179.

Mar. **Festival of the West.** Held at West World, this festival celebrates the history of the cowboy and the Old West. The four-day event includes a western-music jamboree, cowboy poets, vendor booths, horsemanship and shooting demonstrations, and a rendezvous and mountain-man encampment demonstrating life in the early 1800s. Many western reenactors attend the event, so be on the lookout for Buffalo Bill Cody and Wild Bill Hickock. There's a chuck-wagon cook-off competition; you can buy tickets and dine on traditional pioneer food (beans, biscuits, and beef) prepared by contestants under authentic conditions. | 602/996–4387.

SHOW LOW

▼▼▼

Show Low got its name from a poker game played by two local ranchers in 1876. As local legend has it, Corydon Cooley and his partner, Marion Clark, played a game of seven-up to decide which of them would get the town's original ranch. The game went all night before a weary Cooley finally told Clark: "Show low you win." Clark reputedly pulled a deuce of clubs and said: "Show low it is." *Contact Round Valley Chamber of Commerce | 318 E. Main St., Springerville 85938 | 928/333–2123.*

Fort Apache Museum. South of Show Low in the remote White Mountains, Fort Apache was built as a military post to monitor the Navajo to the north and the Apache to the south. Founded in 1870, the fort now belongs to the White Mountain Apache tribe. Original military buildings are complemented with historical exhibits at the White Mountain Apache Cultural Center. Also at the cultural center, which the Apache call the "House of Our Footprints," you can see demonstrations of Apache basketweaving and storytelling. | 127 Scout Rd. (38 mi south of Show Low on Rte. 73), Fort Apache | 928/338–4625 | www.wmat.nsn.us | $3 | Weekdays 8–5.

Little House Museum. Housed in five buildings dating back to the 1890s, this museum documents the pioneer life of the scenic Show Low region, originally settled by Jacob Noah Butler in 1893. Photos, mementos, vintage fashions, old music boxes, and information on the Old West fill the restored cabins. There is also a private John Wayne collection from the time when the Duke kept a ranch next door. | 541 E. Deuce of Clubs | 928/532–7115 | $5 | May–Aug., Thurs.–Sun. 11–1:30.

Show Low Historical Society Museum. Ten themed rooms with exhibits on Show Low's history and early pioneers preserve the town's ranching heritage. | 541 E. Deuce of Clubs | 928/532–7115 | Donation requested | Mid-Apr.–mid-Oct., Tues.–Sat. 11–3.

Stinson Pioneer Museum. The town of Snowflake, located 19 mi north of Show Low, bears its name not for the local winter weather but for the Mormon official Erastus Snow and the settlement's leader, William Flake. The town is laid out according to the Mormon City of Zion plan and has 45 historic homes built in the late 1800s and early 1900s. The double adobe buildings that house the Stinson Pioneer Museum were built in 1873 as a bunkhouse for cowboys employed by rancher James Stinson. Stinson ended up selling his ranch, which is now the Snowflake townsite, to William Flake, who had been sent south by Mormon leader Brigham Young to set up a settlement in eastern Arizona. Four other historic homes on the museum block, all authentically furnished, are also open to the public: the log Lowcy Rogers Cabin, built in 1878; the Victorian-style James Madison Flake Mansion, built in 1895; the Gothic-style brick John A. Freeman Home, built in 1893; and the Jesse N. Smith Memorial Home, built in 1906. Call for a schedule of daily guided tours. | 102 N. 1st East St., Snowflake | 928/536–4881 | $5 | Tues.–Sat. 10–4.

✦ ON THE CALENDAR: July **Annual Pioneer Days.** St. Johns, the Apache County seat, celebrates its pioneering spirit with a rodeo, a fishing derby, Dutch-oven cooking lessons, storytelling, a parade, and an ice cream social. | 928/337–2000.

Aug. **White Mountain Apache Tribal Fair and Rodeo.** At this Native American event held in Whiteriver, Apache Crown dancers perform as they have for centuries in their trademark black buckskin hoods adorned with colorful crowns of wooden horns. | 928/338–4346.

HISTORIC LODGING

South Fork Guest Ranch. Stay in one of the rustic cabins of this ranch built by Jacob Noah Butler in 1893. Those ready to experience life on the range can join a cattle drive with the ranch's cowboys. Other activities include fly fishing on the Little Colorado River, rock art tours, archaeology programs at the Little Bear archaeological site, and horseback riding. The ranch is in Eagar, 50 mi east of Show Low. Microwaves, cable TV; no a/c, no phones in some rooms, no smoking. | Apache Co. 4124, Eagar 85938 | 928/333–2286 | www.xdiamondranch. com | 7 log cabins | $95–$250 | AE, D, MC, V.

White Mountain Lodge Bed & Breakfast. Mormon settler William Lund began farming this lush region in 1892. His original homestead and rustic lodge now house high-country accommodations. Quilts on the beds, western antiques, and a beaver pond out back make this old farmhouse a fine retreat. The lodge is 45 mi southeast of Show Low, in Greer. No a/c, no room phones, no room TVs, no smoking. | 140 Main St., Greer 85938 | 928/735–7568 or 888/493–7568 | www.wmlodge.com | 7 rooms | $95–$145 | AE, D, DC, MC, V.

TOMBSTONE

▼▼

The legendary headquarters of Wild West rowdies, Tombstone was part of an area called Goose Flats in the late 1800s and was prone to attack by nearby Apache. Ed Schieffelin, an intrepid prospector, wasn't discouraged by those who cautioned that "all you'll find there is your tombstone." In 1877, he struck one of the West's richest veins of silver in the tough old hills and gave the town its name as an ironic "I told you so." Schieffelin sold his interests in the mines and retired to San Francisco. Some said he bailed out too early, but others say he left just in time.

Outlaws like the Clanton gang were drawn to happening Tombstone, while the law—in the form of the Earp brothers—tried to keep order. The Earps dispensed frontier justice to the Clantons on October 26, 1881, in the shoot-out at the O.K. Corral. Fires swept through the streets in June 1881, and May and July 1882, destroying a good portion of the town. After the third fire, residents built their new structures out of brick. Tombstone persevered until 1886, when a fire at the Contention Mine destroyed the water pumps and the mines flooded. The town tried to reclaim the mines from the underground reservoir, but the new pumps broke down and the mines closed for good in 1909. The entire townsite is listed as a National Historic Landmark. *Contact Tombstone Chamber of Commerce | 4th and Allen Sts., 85638 | 520/457–9317 or 888/457–3929 | www.tombstone.org.*

Bird Cage Theater. Described by the *New York Times* in 1882 as "the wildest, wickedest night spot between Basin Street and the Barbary Coast," this music hall staged performances by some of the best in the biz, including Enrico Caruso, Sarah Bernhardt, and Lillian Russell. But the dance hall was even better known for its dancers, who plied their trade in "bird cages" hanging from the ceiling. (One legend attributes the gals as the inspiration for the song "She Was Only a Bird in a Gilded Cage.") In the basement, gamblers played the longest continuous poker game ever recorded. The game started when the Bird Cage opened in 1881 and lasted eight years, five months, and three days. Cards were dealt 'round the clock, and players had to give a 20-minute notice when they were planning to vacate their seats, because there was always a waiting list of at least 10 people ready to shell out $1,000 (the equivalent of about $30,000 today) to get in on the game. In all, some $10 million changed hands. | 517 E. Allen St. | 520/457–3421 | $5 | Daily 8–6.

Boot Hill Graveyard. On the northwestern corner of town lies Tombstone's bone orchard. The more than 350 residents of Tombstone have their final resting place here, including victims from the O.K. Corral gunfight, famous prostitutes, and outlaws with "throat trouble." More than a third of the graves are unmarked, but the ones remaining bear some interesting epitaphs. One of the most famous of these memorializes the luckless Lester Moore: "Here lies Lester Moore. Four Slugs from a .44. No Les. No Moore." | Rte. 80 north of downtown | 520/457–9344 | Free | 7:30–sunset.

O.K. Corral. Details of the infamous gunfight between the Earp brothers and the Clanton gang are still hotly debated, but you can get one version at the corral itself, where life-size figures are posed as the combatants were at the start of the fight. Daily reenactments are held at 2. Photographer C. S. Fly, whose studio was next door to the corral, didn't record the big shoot-out, but he did capture images of Apache chief Geronimo and his pursuers on film. You can take a look at a collection of his fascinating Old West images at the Fly Exhibition Gallery. The 25-minute Historama, a multi-media presentation, gives a dramatic overview of "the town too tough to die." Shows are every 30 minutes, 9–4:30. | 308 E. Allen St. | 520/457–3456 | www.ok-corral.com | Historama $2.50; Historama and Fly Exhibition Gallery $4.50; Historama, Fly Exhibition Gallery, and O.K. Corral reenactment $6.50 | Daily 9–5.

Old Tombstone Tours. A 15-minute stagecoach tour, narrated by a fourth-generation Tombstone resident, takes you past such historic sights as the courthouse, city hall, and the O.K. Corral. | Allen St. between 4th and 5th Sts., Box 545, 85638 | 520/457–3018 | www.oldtombstonetours.com | $5.

Rose Tree Inn Museum. Named for the record-breaking 8,000-square-ft rosebush on its grounds, the museum is in a building that originally served as a boardinghouse for the Vizina Mining Company. Inside are 1880s period rooms and several exhibits detailing Tombstone's boomtown years. The rosebush, planted in 1885, is on record as the world's largest. It still blooms each April. | 116 S. 4th St. | 520/457–3326 | $3 | Daily 9–5.

Tombstone Courthouse State Historic Park. This 1882 redbrick county courthouse doled out frontier justice until the county seat moved to Bisbee in 1929. The venerable building—Arizona's smallest state park—now houses several restored period rooms, including a lawyer's office, a courtroom, and an assay office. Other rooms contains memorabilia and photographs from Tombstone's notorious past. | 219 E. Toughnut St. | 520/457–3311 | www.pr.state.az.us | $4 | Daily 8–5.

Tombstone Epitaph Museum. In 1880, John P. Clum started this newspaper, which earned instant notoriety for its lurid accounts of the gunfight at the O.K. Corral. The *Epitaph* is still being published out of this office. Stop by to see the original printing press and exhibits of old newspaper headlines. | 9 S. 5th St. | 520/457–2211 | Free | Daily 9:30–5.

✦ ON THE CALENDAR: May **Wyatt Earp Days.** Gunfights, chili cook-offs, a fiddling contest, gunfights, and a western fashion show make up this Memorial Day weekend event. | 520/457–3197.

Sept. **Rendezvous of Gunfighters.** Wild West reenactments, games, and food enliven this Labor Day weekend event. | 520/457–3421 or 800/457–3423.

Oct. **Helldorado Days.** Three days of 1880 Tombstone events are reenacted, including the infamous shoot-out at the O.K. Corral. | 520/457–3197.

HISTORIC DINING AND LODGING
Crystal Palace. Bar. If you're looking to wet your whistle, stop by at this 1879 watering hole. Its mirrored mahogany bar, wrought-iron chandeliers, and tinwork ceilings date back to Tombstone's heyday. | Allen and 5th Sts. | 520/457–3611 | $3.

Longhorn Restaurant. American. The site of Big Nose Kate's Saloon, named for Doc Holliday's girlfriend, this was formerly the Owl Cafe and originally the Bucket of Blood Saloon. Old-time saloon keepers may not have had a way with words, but they sure knew what to serve to keep the likes of the Earps, Bat Masterson, and Johnny Ringo coming back for more. | 501 E. Allen St. | 520/457–3405 | $6–$30 | MC, V.

Nellie Cashman's. American. Called an "Irish Rose" and a "Frontier Angel," Nellie Cashman opened this restaurant and boarding house in Tombstone in 1879. Today, the home-style restaurant recalls its past with old photographs and postcards on its walls and old-fashioned meals on the menu. | 117 5th St. | 520/457–2212 | $7–$20 | AE, D, MC, V.

Tombstone Boarding House Bed & Breakfast. This friendly B&B is in two meticulously restored 1880s adobes, complete with period furnishings, that sit side by side in a quiet residential neighborhood: one houses the bedrooms and the other a restaurant. Restaurant, some pets allowed. No room phones, no room TVs, no smoking. | 108 N. 4th St., 85638 | 520/457–3716 or 877/225–1313 | fax 520/457–3038 | 8 rooms | $60–80 | AE, D, MC, V | BP.

TUBA CITY
▼▼▼

An oasis in the western Navajo Nation, Tuba City (it may have been named for Hopi chief Tuve) is the site of many subterranean springs. Native Americans were growing crops here when Father Francisco Garcés passed through in 1776. It was another hundred years, though, before white settlers arrived. Mormons established a settlement, but in 1903 they found out that they had built on Indian land. The federal government bought out the Mormons, made Tuba City the headquarters of the western Navajo Agency, and established an Indian school. Some of the original Mormon structures still stand. *Contact Navajo TourismDepartment | Box 663, Window Rock 86515 | 520/871–6436 or 520/871–7371 | fax 520/871–7381 | www.navajoland. com.*

Cameron Trading Post. Established in 1916 by two brothers, this trading post traded dry goods in exchange for blankets and wool brought in by Navajo and Hopi Indians. The remote outpost came to serve as a post office and dining room as well. Today a gallery displays and sells some examples of old textiles, baskets, and beadwork, along with Old West artifacts and contemporary Indian crafts. After having a look around, order some green chili and Navajo fry bread in the dining room, which has a kiva fireplace. Also on the premises are a gift shop, cafeteria, grocery store, butcher shop, post office, and lodge. | 26 mi southwest of Tuba City via U.S. 160 and U.S. 89 | 928/679–2231 or 800/338–7385 | www.camerontradingpost.com | Free | Daily.

Moenkopi. Chief Tuba of Oribi founded the Hopi Indian village of Moenkopi, "the place of running water," in the 1870s. In 1879 Mormon pioneers constructed a woolen mill here, planning to use the Indians for labor. However, when the Navajo reservation was enlarged, the Mormons were forced to sell their land to the federal government. | Rte. 264, 2 mi southeast of Tuba City.

Tuba City Trading Post. The octagonal trading post founded in the early 1870s sells groceries and authentic Navajo rugs, pottery, baskets, and jewelry. | Main St. | 928/283–5441.

✦ ON THE CALENDAR: Oct. **Western Navajo Fair.** This colorful, weeklong local event includes performances of traditional Navajo songs and dances, a powwow, parades, concerts, arts-and-crafts displays, rodeos, a carnival, and a free barbecue. | 928/283–4716.

TUBAC
▼▼

Since Tubac's inception in 1752, five flags—those of Spain, Mexico, the Confederate States of America, Arizona, and the United States—have flown over this, the oldest European settlement in the country. Regardless of their official nationality, settlers here had repeated troubles with the Apache, abandoning the town eight times over the years. By 1854, when the United States acquired Tubac through the Gadsden Purchase, the presidio lay in ruins. A flurry of mining activity pumped new life into the town and bumped its population to 1,000-plus, but when the troops posted at the presidio were called east to fight in the Civil War, Indian raids routed the residents again. Tubac was—for about three months—part of the Confederate States of America. Following Appomattox, the town revived yet again, but it faced the threat of hostile Apaches until Geronimo's surrender in 1886. *Contact Tubac Chamber of Commerce | Box 1866, 85646 | 520/398–2704 | www.tubacaz.com.*

Tubac Presidio State Historic Park and Museum. The ruins of the 1752 Spanish garrison are protected in an underground museum at this site, which became Arizona's first state park in 1959. Exhibits at the museum include displays of Spanish military might, Arizona's first printing press, and historical diagrams. The Juan Bautista de Anza National Historic Trail, a 4½-mi trail stretching along the Santa Cruz River between the Tubac Presidio and the mission at Tumacácori, is a segment of the 600-mi route traveled by Captain Juan Bautista de Anza and 240 colonists in 1775–76 to create a settlement on San Francisco Bay. | 1 Burrel St. | 520/398–2252 | www.pr.state.az.us | $2 | Daily 8–5.

Tumacácori National Historic Park. Father Eusebio Francisco Kino founded this mission in 1691, but the Jesuits didn't build a church here until 1751. You can still see some ruins of the simple early structure, but the main attraction is the mission of San José de Tumacácori, built by the Franciscans around 1799–1803. A combination of circumstances—Apache attacks, a bad winter, and Mexico's withdrawal of funds and priests—caused the inhabitants to flee in 1848 to San Javier del Bac. Persistent rumors of wealth left behind by both the Franciscans and the Jesuits led treasure seekers to pillage the site unsuccessfully. The ruined mission still bears those scars. It was finally protected in 1908, when it became a national monument. | 1891 E. Frontage Rd. Tumacácori | 520/398–2341 | www.nps.gov/tuma | $3 | Daily 8–5.

✦ ON THE CALENDAR: Oct. **Anza Days.** Revelers in period dress retrace the 1775 trek of Juan Bautista de Anza along the National Historic Trail between Tubac Presidio and Tumacácori. | 520/398–2252.

Oct. **Fall Historic High Mass.** Attendees at this re-creation of an 18th-century mass, held in Tumacácori, must dress in historic costume. The priests giving this authentic mass bless the "soldiers" reenacting the historic Anza expedition of 1775. Reservations are required. | 520/398–2341 Ext. 0.

TUCSON

▼▼

When the Spanish first arrived in the desert valley where Tucson now stands, they came upon *Stjuk-shon,* a Pima Indian village at the base of Sentinel Peak. In 1775, the Spanish adopted the name, which means "spring at the foot of a black mountain," and called their presidio San Agustín del Tucson, a name that has stuck to this day. The settlement, surrounded by adobe walls 12 ft high, became a part of Mexico after the revolution in 1821. Tucson became part of the United States with the Gadsden Purchase of 1854, and soon afterward the Butterfield stage line was extended to this remote town, bringing adventurers, settlers, and more than a few outlaws. Because of Tucson's Confederate sympathies, the Arizona territorial capital was set up in Prescott instead of Tucson. Tucson managed to steal it away for a few years—1867 to 1877—before it was moved back to Prescott. The railroad came to town in 1880, by which time the population had soared to 7,000. Arizona Territorial University, now known as the University of Arizona, opened in 1891 on land donated by a saloon owner and two gamblers. *Contact Metropolitan Tucson Convention and Visitors Bureau | 130 S. Scott Ave., 85701 | 520/624–1817 | www.visittucson.org.*

Arizona Historical Society Museum. Flanking the entrance to the museum are statues of two men: Father Kino, the Jesuit who established a string of missions in Arizona, and John Greenaway, general manager of the Calumet and Arizona Copper Co., which became Phelps Dodge—the copper-mining company that helped Arizona earn statehood in 1912. The museum houses the Southern Arizona Division of the State Historical Society, originally the Society of Arizona Pioneers, and has exhibits tracing the this region's rich history from the prehistoric Indian cultures through Arizona's statehood. | 949 E. 2nd St. | 520/628–5774 | w3.arizona.edu/~azhist | $3 suggested donation | Mon.–Sat. 10–4, Sun. noon–4; library weekdays 10–4, Sat. 10–1.

Arizona State Museum. Founded in 1893, the state's oldest museum houses a world-renowned collection of Native American artifacts. The permanent exhibit "Paths of Life: American Indians of the Southwest" explores the cultural traditions, origins, and contemporary lives of 10 native tribes of Arizona and Sonora, Mexico. | 1013 E. University Blvd., Park Ave. at University Blvd. | 520/621–6302 | www.statemuseum.arizona.edu | Donation requested | Mon.–Sat. 10–5, Sun. noon–5.

Fort Lowell Park and Museum. This onetime site of an ancient Hohokam village became a U.S. Army fort in 1879 to protect Tucson from Apache attacks and to act as a base for the Indian Wars from 1873 to 1891. After the last of the Apache campaigns in 1891, the army abandoned the fort. Some of the original buildings have been restored, while other house exhibits chronicling the fort's military history. | 2900 N. Craycroft Rd. | 520/885–3832 | Free | Wed.–Sat. 10–4.

History of Pharmacy Museum. Curated by former Tucson pharmacist Jesse Hurlbut, this quirky museum at the University of Arizona College of Pharmacy contains a comprehensive collection of Arizona pharmaceutical items dating from 1860 to 1950. Displays in clude memorabilia from Arizona's early days, including apothecary jars, an old steam autoclave, prescription books, mortars and pestles, and homeopathic remedies. | University of Arizona, 1703 E. Mabel St. | 520/626–1427 | www.pharmacy.arizona.edu/museum | Free | Weekdays 8–5.

Mission San Xavier del Bac. Built in the 1700s by Spanish missionaries, this oldest Catholic church in the United States still serves the community for which it was built—the Tohono O'odham Indians. Called the "White Dove of the Desert," the mission was founded in 1692 by Father Eusebio Francisco Kino, who established 22 missions in northern Mexico and southern Arizona. The current structure was constructed out of native materials by Franciscan missionaries between 1777 and 1797 and is one of the finest examples of mission architecture in the United States. Mass is still celebrated at 8:30 AM daily and three times on Sunday morning. | 1950 W. San Xavier Rd., 9 mi southwest of Tucson on I–19 | 520/294–2624 | Church daily 7–5, gift shop daily 8–5.

Old Pueblo Trolley, Inc. Ride historic electric trolleys through the streets of Tucson along University Boulevard and 4th Street past shops and restaurants. The trolley passes restored historic buildings on part of the original 1898 street-car track. The route terminates near the Marriott Hotel, the Arizona Historical Society. | 360 E. 8th St. | 520/792–1802 | www.oldpueblotrolley.org | $1 | Fri. 6 PM–10 PM, Sat. noon–midnight, Sun. noon–6.

Tucson Museum of Art and Historic Block. Situated on the site of Tucson's Spanish Presidio, the Historic Block has five distinctive homes built between 1850 and 1907: La Casa Cordova, an 1848 Sonoran row house; the Stevens Home, the 1856 home of prominent ranch Hiram Sanford Stevens; the J. Knox Corbett House, a two-story, Mission Revival–style residence built in 1906; the Edward Nye Fish House, an 1868 adobe residence; Sosa-Carillo-Fremont House, one of Tucson's oldest adobe residences. | 140 N. Main Ave. | 520/624–2333 | www.tucsonarts.com | $5; Sun. free | Mon.–Sat. 10–4, Sun. noon–4.

✦ ON THE CALENDAR: Oct. **Tucson Heritage Experience Festival.** Native American dancing and other cultural exhibitions round out this citywide annual event. | 520/624–1817.

Dec. **Territorial Christmas.** More than 200 antique toys, cards, and decorated trees herald the holiday season at the Sosa-Carrillo-Fremont House. | 520/622–0956.

HISTORIC LODGING

Rancho de la Osa. This 1889 ranch sits on 250 eucalyptus-shaded acres near the Mexican border and the Buenos Aires nature preserve. The rooms have modern plumbing and fixtures, wood-burning fireplaces, and porches with Adirondack chairs. Bread baked on the premises, salads made with ingredients grown in the garden, and water drawn from the well all contribute to the back-to-basics serenity. The lodge is about an hour from Tucson. No smoking. | Rte. 286, Sasabe | 520/823–4257 or 800/872–6240 | fax 520/823–4238 | www.guestranches.com/ranchodelaosa | 18 rooms | $160–$210 | FAP | 3-night minimum, 5-night minimum during holidays | D, MC, V.

The Royal Elizabeth Bed and Breakfast Inn. Fans of Victoriana will adore this B&B built in 1878. Beautifully furnished with period antiques, the six spacious rooms with high ceilings and casablanca fans have all the modern comforts. All have TVs with VCRs. Two of the larger rooms have separate sitting areas and pull-out sofa beds. Cable TV with videos; no smoking. | 204 S. Scott Ave., 85701 | 520/670–9022 | fax 520/679–9710 | www.royalelizabeth.com | 6 rooms | $130–$160 | AE, MC, V | BP.

WICKENBURG

▼▼▼

Henry Wickenburg owned Vulture Mine, the richest gold mine in Arizona Territory. By the mid-1800s the town bearing his name had become a booming mining center with a seemingly endless supply of gold, copper, and silver in its hills. Wickenburg grew quickly into one of the largest cities in the territory and fell only two votes short of being named the territorial capital in 1866. *Contact Wickenburg Chamber of Commerce | 216 N. Frontier St., 85390 | 928/684–5479 or 928/684–0977 | www.wickenburgchamber.com.*

Desert Caballeros Western Museum. The lore of the American West lives on here, in a wonderful collection of paintings and sculpture by Remington, Bierstadt, Joe Beeler (founder of Cowboy Artists of America), and others. There's a mining and mineral exhibit as well as a re-creation of a late 1800s Main Street. | 21 N. Frontier St. | 928/684–7075 or 928/684–2272 | $5 | Mon.–Sat. 10–5; Sun. noon–4.

Frontier Street. The main drag of Wickenburg is lined with historic buildings, including the Old Santa Fe Train Station (now the chamber of commerce) and the post office, which has a drive-up window once used by people on horseback. | Frontier St. | 928/684–5479 or 928/684–0977 | Free | Daily.

Jail Tree. Check out the tree that once served as Wickenburg's jail: Prisoners were chained to the tree, and the desert heat sometimes finished them off before their sentences were served. | Northeast corner of Wickenburg Way and Tegner St.

Old 761 Santa Fe Steam Locomotive. Behind the town hall you can view this locomotive, which pulled trains across the country in the early 1900s. | Apache Rd. and Tegner St. | 928/684–5479 | Free | Daily 10–4.

Vulture Mine. Legend has it that in 1863 a vulture shot from the sky landed near a gold nugget here. There's still quite a bit to see on a self-guided tour, including the hanging tree used to lynch highgraders (thieves who stole ore) in front of the cottage of mine owner Henry Wickenburg. You can also see an old school house, antique mining equipment, and bunk houses. Many of the tunnels in the mine collapsed, and it's believed that there is plenty of gold ore about 1,200 ft underground. The mine is for sale for approximately $5 million. The exact dates when the mine extends its hours for the spring and summer season vary depending on the weather. | Vulture Mine Rd., 12 mi from Wickenburg (at end of pavement) | 520/859–2743 | $7 | Fall and winter, Thurs.–Mon. 8–4; spring and summer, Fri.–Sun. 8–4.

✦ ON THE CALENDAR: Feb. **Wickenburg Gold Rush Days.** Along with gold-panning and reenactments of the gold-rush days, there is a rodeo and a parade the second week in February. The focal point of activities is Wickenburg Community Center. | 928/684–5479 or 928/684–0977.

Sept. **Septiembre Fiesta.** Wickenburg celebrates its Spanish history and heritage at the Wickenburg Community Center, with mariachi music, folk dancing, salsa contests, and an arts-and-crafts market on the first Saturday in September. | 928/684–5479 or 928/684–0977.

Dec. **Cowboy Christmas.** Cowboy poets gather for evening performances at the Wickenburg Community Center. | 928/684–5479 or 928/684–0977.

WILLCOX

▼▼▼

The small town of Willcox, situated in the heart of the Sulphur Springs Valley, got its start in the late 1870s as a railroad construction camp for the Southern Pacific Railroad line, which arrived in town in 1880. Until spur lines were built to Tombstone and Bisbee, Willcox was the second busiest shipping point in southern Arizona, next to Tucson. The original town-site was called Maley for a rancher whose property stretched across the railroad's right of way. According to legend, residents changed the town's name to honor General Orlando B. Willcox, one of the first passengers to ride the rails into town. Ranchers thrived in the lush valley until overgrazing and a series of droughts transformed the region into a desert. *Contact Willcox Chamber of Commerce, Cochise Information Center | 1500 N. Circle I Rd., 85643 | 520/384–2272 or 800/200–2272 | www.willcoxchamber.com.*

Chiricahua National Monument. The 12,000 acres of wind-sculpted rock formations protected by the monument were the final stronghold of the Chiricahua Apache resistance. On the land here is Far Away Ranch, built in the 1880s by one of the first families in the area. The ranch houses a museum that chronicles the life of the pioneer family that built it. Stones used to construct the fireplace were carted from a nearby monument built by the Buffalo Soldiers in 1885–1886. On one of them you can see the inscription "In memory of Jas. A Garfield"—a radical who proposed equal pay for black soldiers. | 13063 East Bonita Canyon Rd., 36 mi south-east of Willcox on Rte. 181 | 520/824–3560 | www.nps.gov/chir | $5 | Daily 8–5.

Chiricahua Regional Museum and Research Center. Previously known as the Museum of the Southwest, this center documents the region's military history and Native American culture. | 127 E. Maley St. | 520/384–3971 | Free | Mon.–Sat. 10–4.

Fort Bowie National Historic Site. After an 1862 ambush by Cochise's warriors at Apache Pass, the U.S. Army decided a fort was desperately needed in the Dos Cabezas Mountains, and Fort Bowie was built within weeks. The fort protected, among other things, a Butterfield stage stop. There were skirmishes between U.S. Cavalry troops and Apache for the next 10 years, followed by a peaceful decade. Renewed fighting broke out in 1881, and Geronimo, the new leader of the Indian warriors, finally surrendered in 1886. The fort was abandoned eight years later and fell into disrepair. It's a bit of an outing to the site of the last battle between Native Americans and U.S. troops on Arizona soil, but points of historical interest along the way are indicated by markers. After driving down a graded but winding gravel road, you'll come to a parking lot from which a challenging trail leads 1½ mi to the fort. The structure is virtu-ally in ruins, but there's a small ranger-staffed visitor center with historical displays. | 3203 Old Fort Bowie Rd. | 520/847–2500 | www.nps.gov/fobo | Free | Daily 8–5.

Gammons Gulch Ghost Town Movie Set. This 10-acre town contains 1880s buildings collected from around the state by owner Jay Gammons. Restored buildings include a telegraph office, a hotel, a blacksmith shop, an assay office, and a saloon. | 59 E. Rockspring Rd., Pomerene | 520/212–2831 | www.gammonsgulch.com | $5 | Sept.–May, Wed.–Sun. 9–5.

Willcox Commercial Store. Established in 1880, this store is thought to be the oldest retail establishment in Arizona. Locals like to boast that Geronimo used to shop here. Today it's a clothing store with a large selection of western wear. | 180 N. Railroad Ave. | 520/384–2448.

WILLIAMS
▼▼

Named for mountain man "Crazy Bill" Williams, a fur trapper, horse thief, and "preacher of profane sermons" of the 1820s and 1830s, Williams was founded when the railroad passed through in 1882. Once a tough town of saloons, bordellos, and opium dens, modern-day Williams retains a funky frontier charm. Main Street is Historic Route 66 (the town wasn't bypassed by I-40 until 1984). Williams is about an hour from Grand Canyon National Park. *Contact Williams and National Forest Service Visitors Center and Chamber of Commerce | 200 W. Railroad Ave., 86046 | 520/635–4061.*

GHOST TOWNS OF COCHISE COUNTY

Cochise County is dotted with ghost towns, the remnants of mining communities that died when their veins of ore ran out. Their adobe buildings gradually melted back into the desert under the summer monsoons, and some of the towns are only heaps of rubble. Others, such as Gleeson and Fairbank, show strong evidence of better days. The gold camp of Pearce has a post office and one functioning store; the ruins of the mill, the mine, and many old adobes are very much in evidence. Gold was discovered here in 1894, and the town maintained a thriving population of 1,500 until the mine closed in the 1930s. Enough residents remain to keep the post office open in the town of Dos Cabezas, 15 mi southeast of Willcox, where the 1885 Wells Fargo station still stands. A tunnel through a mountain top connects the eastern and western halves of the abandoned town of Hilltop, farther southeast of Willcox. Six miles northwest of Portal in the Chiricahua Mountains, Paradise was active in the 1900s, and a few old-timers still live here. Look for the town jail among the ruined buildings.

Grand Canyon Railway. Restored rail cars chug along a route that was established in 1901 to take early visitors such as Theodore Roosevelt and John Muir to the Grand Canyon. The 65-mi trek from Williams Depot to Grand Canyon Village (2½ hours each way) takes the vintage train through prairie, ranch, and national park land to the 1910 log-cabin Grand Canyon Depot on the South Rim. The ride includes refreshments, commentary, and corny but fun on-board entertainment by Wild West characters. | N. Grand Canyon Blvd. at Fray Marcos Blvd. | 800/843–8724 | www.thetrain.com | Round-trip fare $54.40 plus $6 national park entrance fee | Departs daily from Williams at 9:30 AM, from South Rim at 3:15 PM.

Railroad Museum. Next to the Williams Depot, in the original dining room of the old Harvey House, this small museum holds a collection of old railroad memorabilia and Harvey-girl photographs. | N. Grand Canyon and Fray Marcos Blvds. | 928/635–4253 | Free | Daily 8–5:30.

Williams Depot. Even if you don't take the train, it's worth visiting this depot built in 1908. You can examine a passenger car and the locomotive of a turn-of-the-20th-century steam train and stop at the Williams Visitor Center. | N. Grand Canyon and Fray Marcos Blvds. | 928/635–4253 | Free | Daily 8–5:30.

✦ ON THE CALENDAR: May **Bill Williams Rendezvous Days.** Every Memorial Day weekend the Bill Williams Mountain Men get out their buckskins and reenact the lives of early trappers like "Crazy Bill" Williams. You can see pioneer arts-and-crafts exhibits, a parade, a carnival, a black-powder shooting competition, and a rodeo. | 928/635–4061.

Sept. **Labor Day Rodeo.** A three-day Professional Rodeo Cowboys Association rodeo is the centerpiece of this Old West celebration, which also includes a western parade, dances, and other mountain-town activities. | 928/635–4061.

HISTORIC DINING AND LODGING

Pancho McGillicuddy's. Mexican. Originally the Cabinet Saloon, this restaurant is on the National Register of Historic Places. Gone are the spittoons and pipes—the smoke-free dining area now has a Mexican theme, which sets the scene for such specialties as armadillo eggs, the local name for deep-fried jalapeños stuffed with cheese. | 141 Railroad Ave. | 928/635–4150 | $8–$17 | MC, V.

Red Garter. A restored bordello dating from 1897 now houses a small B&B furnished to retain an old-fashioned feel. Ask for the Best Gal's room, with its own sitting room overlooking the train tracks. Despite the inn's location, all four rooms are very quiet, as the only train traffic is the Grand Canyon Railway, with one daily arrival and departure. | 137 W. Railroad Ave., 86046 | 928/635–1484 or 800/328–1484 | www.redgarter.com | 4 rooms | $72–$134 | AE, D, MC, V | CP | Closed Dec.–mid-Feb.

WINDOW ROCK
▼▼▼

Named for the immense arch-shape "window" in a massive sandstone ridge above the city, Window Rock is the capital of the Navajo Nation and the center of its tribal government. *Contact Navajo Nation Tourism Dept. | Rte. 264 and Loop Rd., Box 663, 86515 | 928/871–6436 or 928/871–7371.*

Hubbell Trading Post National Historic Site. John Lorenzo Hubbell, a merchant and friend of the Navajo, purchased this trading post in 1878. Hubbell taught, translated letters, settled family quarrels, and explained government policy to his customers, and during an 1886 small-pox epidemic he turned his home into a hospital and ministered to the sick and dying. Hubbell died in 1930 and is buried nearby. His family sold the trading post to the National Park Service in 1967, but the business still operates and is famous for the "Ganado red" Navajo rugs sold here (it is just outside the town of Ganado). In addition to the trading post the park site includes the Hubbell family home. At the visitor center, exhibits illustrate the post's history and Navajo weavers frequently demonstrate rug making. The fairly comprehensive book-store specializes in Navajo history, art, and culture. | 28 mi west of Window Rock on Rte. 264 (Box 150, Ganado 86505) | 928/755–3475 | www.nps.gov/hutr | Free | Daily 8–5.

Navajo Nation Museum. This museum is devoted to the art, culture, and history of the Navajo people and has an excellent selection of books on the Navajo Nation. The museum hosts exhibitions of native artists each season; call for a listing of shows. Housed in the same build-ing as the museum is the Navajo Nation Visitor Center, a great resource for information on reservation activities. | Rte. 264, next to Navajo Nation Inn | 928/871–6673 museum; 928/871–7371 visitor center | Free | Weekdays 1–5.

WINSLOW
▼▼▼

Like many towns in the region, Winslow was a child of the railroad, which was built through here in 1881. It's still something of a railroad town and trade center, and it makes a good stopping point for an exploration of the Hopi Nation. *Contact Winslow Chamber of Commerce | 300 W. North Rd., 86047 | 928/289–2434 or 928/289–2435 | www.winslowarizona.org.*

Brigham City. At this old settlement you can see a fort built by Mormon pioneers in 1876. Take a look at the buildings and learn the fort's story. The fort is still undergoing restora-tion, but it is nevertheless worth a visit. | Exit 253 off I-40, then west on North Rd. to La Prade La. | 928/289–5901.

Old Trails Museum. This small museum housed in a 1920 bank building contains exhibits on the Santa Fe Railroad and ranch life, plus displays of vintage clothing and Anasazi arti-facts. You'll find an extensive collection of antique bottles and the best collection of Route 66 memorabilia anywhere in the state. | 212 N. Kinsley Ave. | 928/289–5861 | Donations accepted | Apr.–Oct., Tues.–Sat. 10–4; Nov.–Mar., Tues., Thurs., Sat. 10–4.

YUMA

▼▼

When the Spanish arrived here in the 1500s, looking for a shallow place to cross the Colorado River, Native Americans had already been farming the area for hundreds of years. Several groups attempted to settle at the crossing site, but it wasn't until the U.S. government established Fort Yuma in 1850 that a permanent Anglo settlement was able to thrive despite Indian threats. This spot in the far southwestern corner of Arizona endures blistering heat that can reach 115°F. In 1872, Mark Twain wrote: "Fort Yuma is probably the hottest place on earth. It is a U.S. military post, and its occupants get so used to the terrific heat that they suffer without it. There is a tradition that a very, very wicked soldier died there, once, and of course, went straight to the hottest corner of perdition—and the next day he telegraphed back for his blankets." *Contact Yuma Convention and Visitors Bureau | 377 S. Main St., Suite 102, 85364 | 928/783–0071 or 800/293–0071 | www.visityuma.com.*

Arizona Historical Society Museum. Pioneer merchant E. F. Sanguinetti built the Century House in the 1870s. Today, this historic home, complete with period rooms, houses the Rio Colorado Division of the Arizona Historical Society. Exhibits chronicle Yuma's development from prehistoric times through the early 1900s. | 240 S. Madison Ave. | 928/782–1841 | Free | Tues.–Sat. 10–4.

Colorado King River Cruises. Take a narrated three-hour paddle boat tour up the Lower Colorado River and learn about the steamboat trade that ran the river from 1852 to 1909. | 1636 S. 4th Ave. | 928/782–2412 | www.coloradoking.com | $28–$42.

Fort Yuma Quechan Indian Museum. The 1851 mess hall of the original military camp, which moved four years later and became Fort Yuma, now serves as the tribal headquarters for the Quechan (Yuman) Indians. Exhibits on the Quechan Revolt and displays of military might, native artifacts, and historical photographs fill the small museum. | 350 Picacho Rd. | 760/572–0661 | $1 | Daily 8–5.

Yuma Crossing State Historic Park. This military depot was constructed in 1864 as a supply distribution point for military outposts fighting the Indian Wars. The 1853 home of riverboat captain G. A. Johnson is the earliest building in the depot, which finally closed down for good in 1882. Today the park includes the restored U.S. Quarter Master Depot and the Commanding Officer's Quarters. The park museum has exhibits on early Arizona transportation, including stagecoaches, mule wagons, relics from 1880s steamboats, a 1907 Baldwin steam locomotive, and a 1909 Model T. | 201 N. 4th Ave., between 1st St. and the Colorado River Bridge | 928/329–0471 | www.pr.state.az.us | $4 | Daily 8–5.

Yuma Territorial Prison State Historical Park. Built by the convicts who were incarcerated here, this jail served as the Arizona territorial prison from 1876 until 1909, when it was moved to Florence. When you gaze at the tiny cells that held six inmates each under brutally hot conditions, you are likely to be appalled. The prison was dubbed the "Hell Hole" by the prisoners that spent time behind its bars, but locals called it the Country Club of the Colorado. It was considered a model of enlightenment by turn-of-the-20th-century standards: in an era when inmate beatings were common, the only punishments meted out here were solitary confinement and assignment to a dark cell. The complex housed a hospital as well as Yuma's only public library, where the 25¢ that visitors paid for a prison tour financed the acquisition of new books. The 3,069 prisoners who served time at what was then the territory's only prison included men and women from 21 different countries. They came from all social classes and were sent up for everything from armed robbery and murder to violation of the Mexican Neutrality Act and polygamy. R. L. McDonald, incarcerated for forgery, had been the superintendent of the Phoenix public school system. Chosen as the prison bookkeeper, he absconded with $130 of the inmates' money when he left. Pearl Hart, convicted of stagecoach robbery, gained such notoriety for her crime that she attempted to launch a career in vaudeville after her release. | 1 Prison Hill Rd., near Exit 1 off I-8 | 928/783–4771 | www.pr.state.az.us | $4 | Free interpretive programs at 11, 2, and 3:30 | Daily 8–5.

✦ ON THE CALENDAR: Mar. **Yuma Vigilantes Anniversary.** Gunfight reenactments, live entertainment, and a chili cook-off at the Main Street Plaza commemorate nearly 140 years of vigilante presence in Yuma. | 928/783–2423.

CALIFORNIA

—◆—

Thousands of years before the arrival of Europeans, more than 500 independent groups of indigenous people lived in California. They had little reason to quarrel: the land was prolific, the climate hospitable, and there was plenty of space for all. Far from "primitive" hunter-gatherers, many of these bands—Ohlone, Pomo, Miwok, Maidu, Hupa, and Yurok, among others—lived in permanent settlements governed by complex hierarchies of chiefs and assembly houses. They developed farming techniques to cultivate meadows, control crop pests, and regenerate woodlands to ensure a food supply.

In 1542, European exploration of California started when Juan Rodriguéz Cabrillo sailed up the California coastline from New Spain (Mexico) to map the territory. Cabrillo became—by most accounts—the first European to set foot in present-day California when he came ashore at what is now San Diego Harbor. Seventeen years later, in 1559, Sir Francis Drake, in his attempt to circumnavigate the globe aboard the Golden Hind, weighed anchor somewhere between northernmost California and Vancouver, calling the area Nova Albion. He claimed the land for England's Queen Elizabeth I, but the stake went largely ignored. It was not until 1769, with the discovery of San Francisco Bay to the north and the establishment of Mission San Diego de Alcalá to the south, that permanent European settlement of California began.

In 1770, with the arrival of Don Gaspar de Portola and Father Junípero Serra, Monterey became the military and ecclesiastical capital of Alta California (what the Spanish called the territory north of present-day Baja California). Portola established the first of California's four Spanish presidios; Serra founded the second of 21 Franciscan missions. The mission system decimated Native Americans. Disease and overwork forced by church fathers laid waste the population, and the onslaught of European culture meant the demise of old ways. Spanish settlers radically altered the physical environment, too. As natural as they may appear, California's golden hillsides and woodlands are composed mostly of introduced species. Little of the native prairie survived the influx of great cattle herds from Mexico. This happened after Mexico won its independence from Spain in 1821, claimed California as a territory in 1825, took over the California missions in 1834, and awarded vast amounts of land to ranchers, known as "Californios," who were willing to settle the new territory.

Huge demand for beef and hides made the Californios wealthy—and lazy. They tolerated the occasional European or American arrival who asked to share the wide-open spaces. One such was John Augustus Sutter, a shrewd Swiss man who began building his own fiefdom along the Sacramento River in 1839. In 1846 a group of rowdies, worried by rumors that Mexico might kick American settlers out of California, raided the Sonoma pueblo of General Mariano Vallejo, Mexican *comandante* of northern California. Meeting no resistance, they hoisted a handmade flag embellished with a grizzly bear, declaring the territory part of the Bear Republic. They chose William Ide as their president, but 24 days later they heard of the outbreak of the Mexican-American War. The United States had declared California its own, and the Bear Republic was obsolete. The U.S. flag went up in Monterey, San Francisco, and Los Angeles.

While Mexico and the United States were wrestling over California and the Southwest, James Marshall turned up a gold nugget in the tailrace of a sawmill he was constructing along the American River in Coloma. With Marshall's discovery the United States tightened its grip on the region, and prospectors from all over the world came to seek their fortunes in the mother lode. On January 24, 1848, the Treaty of Guadalupe Hidalgo turned Alta California over from Mexico to the United States.

As gold fever seized the nation, California's population of 15,000 swelled to 265,000 within three years. The mostly young, mostly male adventurers who arrived in search of gold—the '49ers—became part of a culture that discarded many of the conventions of the eastern states. It was also a violent time. Yankee prospectors chased Mexican miners off their claims, and California's leaders initiated a plan to exterminate the local Native American population. Bounties were paid and private militias hired to wipe out the Native Americans or round them up as slaves. California was now to be dominated by the Anglo.

The state's rapid economic growth depended on exploitation of its considerable resources. In 1854, Sacramento became the state capital and the primary center of commerce. The gold rush lasted less than 10 years, but it was followed in the 1860s by a quest for silver in the Comstock Lode, near Lake Tahoe in Virginia City, Nevada. Burgeoning travel and trade made the need for a transcontinental railway obvious by the time businessmen Charles Crocker, Mark Hopkins, Collis Huntington, and Leland Stanford (known as "The Big Four") invested $1,500 each to found the Central Pacific Railroad of California. Built mostly by Chinese labor, the Central Pacific was the western leg of the Transcontinental Railroad joined the East and West coasts at Promontory Point, Utah, in 1869.

With California now accessible to the East by overland routes, San Francisco became an important transfer point between sea and rail. The city became the financial capital of the west coast and by 1870 had grown to become the 10th-largest city in the country. Los Angeles got connected by rail to San Francisco in 1876 and became the end of the line for the Santa Fe Railway in 1888; the railroad and a newly developed way to capture water from the Sierra Nevada ensured the desert city's future growth. San Diego experienced its own boom in the 1880s, based largely on the assumption that the city would become the ultimate terminus of the Santa Fe Railway. The link was completed in 1885, but it proved unsuccessful for a variety of reasons, including the route of the line through Temecula Canyon, where 30 mi of track washed out repeatedly in winter rainstorms. It wasn't until 1908, when Teddy Roosevelt stopped in San Diego on a world tour of the American naval fleet, that the city's destiny as a major U.S. Navy port would be determined.

In 1906, the San Francisco earthquake and fire reduced that city to rubble. Rebuilding took nearly a decade, and in 1915, the city hosted the Panama-Pacific Exposition—the forerunner of today's World's Fairs—which ushered the modern age into California.

CALIFORNIA TIME LINE

1542 Juan Rodriguéz Cabrillo may be first European to sight the California coast; he claims the Monterey Peninsula for Spain.

1559 Sir Francis Drake weighs anchor somewhere around northernmost California.

1769 Father Junípero Serra and followers establish San Diego de Alcalá, the first of a chain of 21 missions along El Camino Real.

1770 Father Junípero Serra and Don Gaspar de Portola establish the mission and presidio in Monterey.

1809 Ivan Kuskov of the Russian-American Co. lands at Bodega Bay.

1821 Mexico gains independence from Spain.

1825 California becomes a territory of the Mexican Republic; Monterey is the territorial capital.

1846 In the Bear Revolt, American settlers defy local Mexican authorities and declare an independent republic. The revolt ends when the United States claims California and the Mexican-American War starts. The Donner Party is snowbound in the Sierra Nevada.

1848 The Mexican-American War ends. California becomes a territory of the United States. Gold is discovered at John Sutter's mill in Coloma.

1850 California gains its statehood.

1854 Sacramento becomes the state capital.

1859 The Silver Bonanza begins with the discovery of silver in the Comstock Lode at Virginia City, Nevada.

1861 The Central Pacific Railroad begins building eastward as part of the Transcontinental Railroad project.

1862 The transcontinental telegraph goes into service between San Francisco and New York.

1869 The Transcontinental Railroad is completed.

1873 Cable-car service begins in San Francisco.

1890 Yosemite National Park is established.

1906 The great earthquake and fire level San Francisco.

1915 San Francisco is rebuilt in time to host the Panama-Pacific Exposition.

The Gold Country
A DRIVING TOUR FROM SONORA TO SACRAMENTO

Distance: 226 mi   **Time:** 5–6 days
Breaks: Murphys, Columbia, Amador City, Placerville, Coloma, Nevada City, and Grass Valley all offer historic lodging in the middle of town.

Most of the towns on this tour sit on or near Route 49, also called the Gold Country Highway—a nearly 300-mi, serpentine two-lane road whose speed limit varies from 25 to 55 mph. Because of the density of sights in the region, choose in advance those that you most want to visit, planning one hour for small museums and historical houses and up to three hours for some of the larger parks. In smaller towns, like Amador City, you may want simply to get out of the car and take a quick stroll, then be on your way. At some of the larger towns, like Columbia, you may want to spend the entire day. This tour is a flexible outline, designed

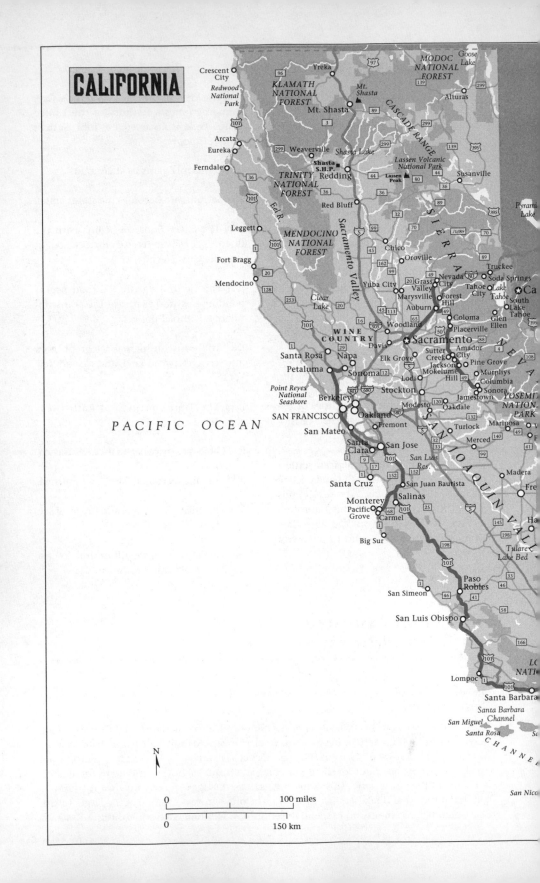

to help you map your own route. If you want to see every single sight in Gold Country, expect to visit one to two towns each day.

Start in **Sonora,** about 2½ hours east of San Francisco, where you can visit the small history museum, then take a quick ride through the old town. From there, drive east on Route 108 to **Columbia.** This is one of the centerpieces of the tour, so plan to spend at least a couple of hours strolling the streets of the restored gold-rush boomtown, poking your head into the candy store, the blacksmith's shop, and the other working businesses around town. From Columbia, return to Route 49 and drive north 18 mi, passing Angels Camp, to Route 4 east to **Murphys.** You can have dinner here, then spend the night.

The next day, drive about an hour via Route 4 west to Route 49 north, to **Jackson.** Visit the Amador County Museum, and if you have time for a break from mining history, see Indian Grinding Rock and the Chaw'se Indian Museum 10 minutes east of town. Return to Route 49 north in Jackson, and drive 20 minutes to **Amador City,** where you can tour the mine. At the end of the day, continue north on Route 49 to **Placerville** and spend the night.

On day three, spend the morning in Placerville and return to Route 49 north, where you'll travel 15 minutes to **Coloma.** This is where California's first gold was discovered; spend a couple of hours in the state historic park, where you can also picnic on the banks of the American River. In the afternoon, drive 30 minutes north on Route 49 to **Auburn.** You can have dinner and spend the night here, or continue another 30 minutes north to **Grass Valley** or **Nevada City**—which are only 4 mi apart—and spend the night in either.

On day four, see Grass Valley and Nevada City. You could easily spend the whole day in either town, but if you're short on time, head to Nevada City just before or after lunch. Because of the number of sights, you may want to spend another night in the area. Otherwise, return south on Route 49 to I–80 west, to **Sacramento.** The drive will take about an hour. Spend the night here.

As California's center of commerce during the late 19th century, Sacramento has a lot to see and do. Devote one or two days to touring the city, making sure to see Old Town, Sutter's Fort, and the California State Capitol. If you can, make it a point to visit the railroad museum, too.

The California Missions

A DRIVING TOUR FROM SAN DIEGO TO SAN FRANCISCO

▼▼

Distance: 600 mi   **Time:** 5 days
Breaks: All of the towns and cities where missions stand are well-established communities, with numerous lodging and dining choices.

Franciscans built 21 missions in California, and the state's original European settlements sprang up around them. The first was constructed in San Diego in 1769 and the last—and northernmost—in Sonoma in 1823. Connected by El Camino Real, the Royal Road, each mission stood approximately one day's journey by horse from the next. Today U.S. 101, I–5, and I–280 trace much of the old route, along with Routes 72, 82, and other roads. In some places El Camino Real is marked with bells, some of cast iron, some of concrete. This tour takes you to 12 of the missions. If you want to see all 21, double the time allotted for this tour.

Starting in **San Diego,** visit Mission San Diego de Alcalá in the morning. Once you've toured the chapel and small museum, drive 30 minutes north via I–805 into I–5 to the town of **Oceanside,** where you'll find Mission San Luis Rey. Leave before rush hour and travel 30 minutes north via I–5 to Ortega Highway west (Rte. 74) into **San Juan Capistrano,** where you'll spend the first night. If you arrive by 4 PM, you'll have an hour to see the Mission San Juan Capistrano, but if you don't want to rush, you can do that in the morning.

On day two, prepare yourself for the always-busy freeways of **Los Angeles.** Travel north on I–5 about 50 mi to I–710 north into I–10 east (San Bernardino Freeway) to Mission San

Gabriel Arcángel at the New Avenue exit. The trip will take about an hour. After seeing where Los Angeles was born, return to I–10 west, which becomes U.S. 101 north (Ventura Freeway). Stay on U.S. 101 to Route 170 north, which will merge with I–5 north. Three miles ahead, exit onto San Fernando Mission Boulevard to reach Mission San Fernando Rey de España. Before rush hour, leave the mission and get back on U.S. 101 north to **Santa Barbara,** where you can spend the night.

In the morning, get an early start and make a quick visit to the reconstructed Mission Santa Barbara before driving north for an hour on U.S. 101 to Route 1 to Lompoc, where it's easy to spend several hours exploring the exquisitely restored La Purisima Mission and State Historic Park. Another 50 mi north brings you to **San Luis Obispo,** site of Mission San Luis Obispo de Tolosa. U.S. 101 will then take you 35 mi north to **Paso Robles,** where you can spend the night. In tiny San Miguel, 8 mi north of Paso Robles at the Mission Avenue exit off of U.S. 101, you'll find Mission San Miguel Arcángel. If you don't arrive in time to see it before closing, stop on your way north the next day.

On day four, continue north on U.S. 101 to Route 156 east to San Juan Bautista State Historic Park. Afterward, travel west on Route 156 all the way to Route 1 south to **Carmel,** where you can tour the Mission San Carlos Borromeo del Rio Carmelo. Stay the night in Carmel or Monterey.

Return to U.S. 101 via Route 156 east on the morning of your fifth day, and travel north to **San Jose.** Turn north at I–280, then north again onto I–880 toward Oakland, and exit the freeway at the Alameda in **Santa Clara,** where you can stop at Mission Santa Clara de Asís. Make it a point to see the rose gardens. Continue via I–280 to **San Francisco,** about an hour north of Santa Clara. Here stands Mission San Francisco de Asís, more commonly called Mission Dolores. End your tour in San Francisco, or if you prefer, continue north to **Sonoma** and Mission San Francisco Solano.

AMADOR CITY
▼▼▼

Tiny Amador City shared the boom-and-bust cycle of many Gold Country towns. With an output of $42 million in gold, its Keystone Mine was one of the most productive in the mother lode. After all the gold was extracted, the miners cleared out and the area suffered. Now it booms again as a tourist town. *Contact Amador County Chamber of Commerce | 125 Peek St., Jackson 95683 | 209/223–0350 | www.amadorcounty.com. Amador City Hall | Box 200, 95601 | 209/267–0682 | www.amador-city.com.*

Sutter Gold Mining Co. At this operating mine you can get a glimpse into the inner workings of a mine and the rough life of a gold miner. There's a one-hour tour that's good for families; no reservations are required. You can take an extended "expedition tour," which takes you deep into the mine; advance reservations are required for this one. Above ground, you can try your luck panning for gold or gemstones. | 13660 Rte. 49, Sutter Creek | 209/736–2708 general information; 888/818–7462 or 866/762–2837 reservations | www.suttergold. com | General tour $14.50; expedition tour $99; gold panning $5 | May–Oct., daily 9–5; Nov.–Apr., daily 10–4.

✦ ON THE CALENDAR: June **Amador Gold Camp Days.** On the second weekend of the month, the town celebrates its gold-rush heritage with bluegrass music, arts and crafts, gold-panning demonstrations, tours of historical buildings, and mock gunfights. | 209/223–0350.

Dec. **Calico Christmas.** On the first weekend of the month, shopkeepers dress in Victorian drag, keep their stores open late, and serve refreshments into the evening. On Saturday at dusk, Christmas carolers proceed down Main Street by candlelight; anyone may join the procession. | 209/223–0350.

HISTORIC DINING AND LODGING

Imperial Hotel. The whimsically decorated mock-Victorian rooms at this 1879 hotel give a modern twist to the excesses of the era. Antique furnishings include iron and brass beds, gingerbread flourishes, and, in one room, art deco appointments. The two front rooms, which can be noisy, have balconies. The hotel's fine dinner-only restaurant (closed Monday), whose menu changes quarterly, serves meals in a bright dining room and on the patio. The cuisine ranges from vegetarian to country hearty to contemporary eclectic. There is a two-night minimum stay on weekends. Restaurant, bar. | Rte. 49, 95601 | 209/267–9172 or 800/242–5594 | fax 209/267–9249 | www.imperialamador.com | 6 rooms | AE, D, DC, MC, V | BP.

ANZA-BORREGO DESERT STATE PARK

▼▼▼

In the western Colorado Desert, east of San Diego, the vast Anza-Borrego Desert State Park holds an accessible portion of one of the most famous pioneer roads in the country, the Southern Emigrant Trail. The park and the surrounding desert are named in honor of Captain Juan Bautista de Anza, who forged the first trail across the southwestern desert from Sonora, Mexico, to San Francisco in 1774. During the gold rush the treacherous route through the Anza-Borrego Desert was the only all-weather trail from the East to the gold fields in northern California. *Contact Visitors Information Center | 200 Palm Canyon Dr., Borrego Springs 92004 | 760/767–5311 | www.anzaborrego.statepark.org.*

Southern Emigrant Trail Historic Route. A trail followed by a number of Native American tribes became the primary route between the San Diego area and points east for Spanish padres and explorers in the 18th century. In 1847, toward the end of the Mexican-American War, Lieutenant Colonel Philip St. George Cooke's Mormon Battalion followed this trail to San Diego. After gold was discovered in the mother lode in 1848, prospectors and adventurers used the trail on their way to the gold fields. In 1858 the Butterfield Overland Stage began using the Southern Emigrant Trail to carry the mail between San Francisco and Missouri. Today you can take a self-guided driving tour of a 26-mi segment of the route. Along the way you will pass through the Blair Valley, the hottest and driest stretch of the entire trail. Passage through this area was often called *La Journada del Muerto* ("the journey of death"). In Box Canyon you can still see the ruts left by wagon wheels. Vallecito Stage Station, built in 1852, was a major stop along the route, especially appreciated by travelers because it meant their journey to San Diego was nearly over. The station is now a county park. | S2 from San Filipe Stage Station to Palm Springs | 760/767–5311 | www.anzaborrego.statepark.org | Free | Daily.

AUBURN

▼▼▼

Auburn's first residents were Nisenan Indians who managed to live a peaceful life apart from Mexican missionaries and European settlers until that moment when California catapulted into the world's consciousness with the discovery of gold. By the end of 1849 the bucolic land was overrun by miners, and the town of Auburn was established as a jumping-off spot to remote gold fields. The Transcontinental Railroad rolled through in 1865. The center of town has many restored 19th-century buildings, including the oldest California post office in continuous operation. *Contact Auburn Area Chamber of Commerce | 601 Lincoln Way, 95603-4803 | 530/885–5616 | www.auburnchamber.net. Placer County Visitor Information Center | 13411 Lincoln Way, 95603 | 530/887–2111 or 866/752–2371 | www.placer.ca.gov.*

Bernhard Museum Complex. Built in 1851, the centerpiece of the complex is the former Traveler's Rest Hotel. A residence and winery buildings reflect family life in the late Victorian era, and the carriage house displays period vehicles. | 291 Auburn-Folsom Rd. | 530/889–6500 | $1 (includes entry to Gold Country Museum) | Tues.–Fri. 10:30–3, weekends noon–4.

Gold Country Museum. Exhibits survey life in the mines and include a walk-through mine tunnel, a gold-panning stream, and a replica saloon. | 1273 High St., off Auburn-Folsom Rd. | 530/889–6500 | $1 (includes entry to Bernhard Museum Complex) | Tues.–Fri. 10–3:30, weekends 11–4.

Placer County Courthouse and Museum. In Auburn's standout gold-dome structure you'll find exhibits on the area's history—Native American, railroad, agricultural, and mining—from the early 1700s to 1900. | 101 Maple St. | 530/889–6500 | Free | Tues.–Sun. 10–4.

✦ ON THE CALENDAR: Sept. **Foresthill Heritage Celebration.** On Forest Hill Road 17 mi east of Auburn, the tiny town of Forest Hill honors Native American heritage, puts on a Wild West shoot-out, offers rides in an original stagecoach, and hosts the California State Gold-panning competition. | 530/367–2474 or 530/367–2110.

HISTORIC DINING AND LODGING
Ore Cart Restaurant. Steak. Enjoy a cut-to-order Black Angus steak inside a 19th-century Wells Fargo bank building with 1½-ft-thick stone walls. In the tiny town of Forest Hill, 17 mi east of Auburn, the building sat empty for many years until the current owners bought it in the 1990s and re-created an Old West saloon and restaurant. They restored the building's original storefront, counters, and floors; numerous 19th-century artifacts from the town's sawmilling and gold-mining days adorn the walls. The kitchen prepares traditional American fare such as chicken, seafood, and salads, but the charbroiled steaks are the real draw. After you eat, you can stroll along Main Street. | 24601 Forest Hill Rd., Forest Hill | 530/367–3644 | $12–$24 | No breakfast Mon.–Sat. | MC, V.

Powers Mansion Inn. This inn hints at the lavish lifestyle enjoyed by the gold-rush gentry. Two light-filled parlors have gleaming oak floors, Asian antiques, and ornate Victorian chairs and settees. A second-floor maze of narrow corridors leads to the guest rooms, which have brass and pencil-post beds. The honeymoon suite has a fireplace and heart-shape hot tub. | 164 Cleveland Ave. 95603 | 530/885–1166 | fax 530/885–1386 | www.vfr.net/~powerinn | 10 rooms, 3 suites | $89–$169 | AE, MC, V | BP.

CARMEL
▼▼▼

Named for the Carmelite friars who accompanied the founding Spanish settlers, Carmel was first visited by Sebastien Vizcaino in 1603. When he arrived the only settled area nearby was Tucutnut, a fertile river valley that now supports wineries and farms. The Spanish chose Monterey as their primary settlement because of its larger port, but Carmel was viewed as preferable for its abundance of elk and other game. *Contact Carmel Business Association | San Carlos St. between 5th and 6th Sts., Box 4444, 93921 | 831/624–2522 | www.carmelcalifornia. org. Carmel Heritage Society | Box 701, Carmel-by-the-Sea 93921 | 831/624–4447 | www. carmelheritage.org. Monterey County Historical Society | Box 3576, Salinas 93912 | 831/757–8085 | users.dedot.com/mchs/index.html.*

Jose Eusebio Boronda Adobe. Built by Mexican homesteaders in the 1840s, this simple adobe 18 mi northeast of Carmel contains furniture and artifacts depicting the lifestyle of early Spanish California. Also on-site is the one-room Old Lagunita School House, built in 1897 and moved here in 1986. The Monterey County Historical Society gives tours of both buildings by appointment. Call for directions. | 333 Boronda Rd., Salinas | 831/757–8085 | Dona-tion | Weekdays 10–2; call for weekend hrs.

Mission San Carlos Borromeo Del Rio Carmelo. One year after it opened in 1770, the Carmel Mission moved from Monterey to Carmel Valley on orders of Father Junípero Serra (who considered the original location too close to the Presidio's corrupt soldiers). Once the head-quarters for the mission system, it now preserves an early kitchen, Serra's spartan sleeping quarters, a tranquil garden, and the oldest college library in California. | 3080 Rio Rd., at Lasuen Dr. | 831/624–3600 | www.carmelmission.org | $2 | Sept.–May, Mon.–Sat. 9:30–4:30, Sun. 10:30–4:30; June–Aug., Mon.–Sat. 9:30–7:30, Sun. 10:30–7:30.

✦ ON THE CALENDAR: June **California Cowboy Show.** Even with hors d'oeuvres and a wine tasting, this show of cowboy poetry and music stays pretty down-home. It's a well-loved local event. | 831/624–9611.

COLOMA
▼▼▼

The great California gold rush started in Coloma. "My eye was caught with the glimpse of something shining in the bottom of the ditch," James Marshall recalled of his 1848 discov-ery. Though crowded with tourists in summer, Coloma hardly resembles the mob scene it was in 1849, when 2,000 prospectors staked out claims along the stream bed. The town's population grew to 4,000, supporting seven hotels, three banks, and many stores and busi-nesses. But when reserves of the precious metal dwindled, prospectors left as quickly as they had come. Ironically, Marshall himself never found any more "color," as gold came to be called. The actual site of his discovery is in the Marshall Gold Discovery State Historic Park. *Contact El Dorado County Chamber of Commerce and Visitors Authority | 542 Main St., Placerville 95667 | 800/457–6279 | www.eldoradocounty.org or www.visit-eldorado.com.*

Marshall Gold Discovery State Historic Park. A working replica of John Sutter's mill stands near the spot where James Marshall first saw gold. A trail leads to a monument marking Marshall's discovery. The museum is not as interesting as the outdoor exhibits. | Rte. 49 | 530/622–3470 | www.parks.ca.gov | $2 per vehicle | Park daily 8 AM–sunset. Museum late May–early Sept., daily 10–5; early Sept.–late May, daily 10–4:30.

Pioneer Cemetery. You can view the graves of more than 600 pioneers in this cemetery. Take a look on your own, or call to arrange a guided tour. | 310 Back St. | 530/622–3470 | Free | Daily.

✦ ON THE CALENDAR: Jan. **Gold Discovery Day.** James Marshall's 1848 discovery of gold at Sutter's Mill is reenacted each year. | 530/295–2170 or 530/622–3470.

Oct. **'49er Family Days.** Over two days, Coloma becomes a gold-rush tent encampment, with period crafts and music, sawmill and trade demonstrations, and a symposium on the area's history. | 530/295–2170 or 530/622–3470.

Dec. **Christmas in Coloma.** The Marshall Gold Discovery Park re-creates an 1850s Christmas, with strolling musicians, carriage rides, and demonstrations of quilting and wreath making. | 530/295–2170 or 530/622–3470.

HISTORIC LODGING

Coloma Country Inn. Gold was discovered a block and a half away from here. Five of the rooms at this B&B on 5 acres in the state historic park are inside a restored 1852 Victorian. The carriage house, built in 1898, has a two-room suite with a kitchenette. Appointments include antique double and queen-size beds, handmade quilts, stenciled friezes, and fresh flowers.

The country breakfast is lavish, and some of the ingredients come from the garden on the property. There are homemade cookies and lemonade in the afternoon; you can swim in a nearby river. Some refrigerators, boccie, horseshoes; no room phones, no room TVs, no smoking. | 345 High St., Box 502, 95613 | 530/622–6919 | fax 530/626–4959 | www.colomacountryinn. com | 5 rooms, 3 with bath; 1 suite | $110–$135 | No credit cards | BP.

COLUMBIA

In 1854 Columbia came within two legislative votes of beating out Sacramento for the title of state capital. Twenty years and $87 million worth of gold later, Columbia's population had nearly vanished. Today the extensively restored buildings and most of the town are within a state historic park that looks like a gold-rush settlement. *Contact Tuolomne County Chamber of Commerce | 222 S. Shepherd St., Sonora 95370 | 209/532–4212 | www.tcchamber.com. Tuolomne County Historical Society | 158 W. Bradford St., Sonora 95370 | 209/532–1317 | www.tchistory. org. Tuolomne County Visitors Bureau | Box 4020, Sonora 95370 | 209/533–4420 or 800/446– 1333 | www.thegreatunfenced.com.*

Columbia State Historic Park. Known as the "Gem of the Southern Mines," Columbia today comes as close to a gold-rush town in its heyday as any site in the Gold Country. You can ride a stagecoach, pan for gold, eat hand-made hard candy, and watch a blacksmith working at an anvil. Street musicians perform in summer. Restored or reconstructed buildings include a Wells Fargo Express office, a Masonic temple, stores, saloons, two hotels, a firehouse, churches, a school, and a newspaper office. All are staffed to simulate a working 1850s town. The park also includes the Historic Fallon House Theater, where a full schedule of entertainment is presented. | Rte. 49, 3 mi north of Sonora | 209/532–0150 | www.parks.ca.gov | Free | Daily 9–5.

✦ ON THE CALENDAR: May **Fireman's Muster.** History springs to life in this commemoration of 19th-century fire companies. You can participate in bucket brigades and pumping contests. | 209/536–1672.

HISTORIC DINING AND LODGING
City Hotel. The rooms in this restored 1856 hostelry are furnished with period antiques. Two have balconies overlooking Main Street, and six rooms open onto a second-floor parlor. All the accommodations have private half-baths with showers nearby; robes and slippers are provided. The What Cheer Saloon is right out of a western movie. The elegant dining room ($16–$24, reservations essential) serves French-inspired Continental and contemporary cuisine; the wine list is exceptional. There is also a very good champagne brunch on Sunday. The hotel offers lodging, dining, and theater packages. Restaurant, bar; no room phones, no smoking, no TVs. | 22768 Main St. Box 1870, 95310 | 209/532–1479 or 800/532–1479 | fax 209/532–7027 | www.cityhotel.com | 10 rooms without bath | $105–$125 | AE, D, MC, V | CP.

Fallon Hotel. The state of California restored this 1857 hotel. All rooms have antiques and a private half-bath; there are separate men's and women's showers. If you occupy one of the five balcony rooms, you can sit outside with your morning coffee and watch the town wake up. Ice cream parlor; no room phones, no smoking, no room TVs. | 11175 Washington St., 95310 | 209/532–1470 | fax 209/532–7027 | www.cityhotel.com | 14 rooms without bath | $70–$125 | AE, D, MC, V | CP.

CORONADO

▼▼

Initially mapped but not visited by Spanish explorer Sebastian Vizcaino in the 1500s, Coronado was a safe harbor for whalers until 1821, when Mexico gained independence from Spain. American developers transformed the nearly vacant land into a resort in the late 1800s, the crowning glory of which is the wedding-cake Victorian Del Coronado hotel, the oldest continuously operating hotel in southern California. The city is packed with high-Victorian treasures. *Contact Coronado Visitor Center | Museum of Art and History Lobby, 1100 Orange Ave., 92118 | 619/435–7242 | www.coronadohistory.org.*

Coronado Museum of History and Art. Home of the Coronado Historical Association, this museum, housed in a 1910 neoclassical building, celebrates Coronado's history with photographs and displays. A permanent exhibit depicts the history of the Tent City, which grew up around the Hotel Del Coronado in the late 1800s. To check out the town's historic houses, pick up a copy of the *Coronado California Centennial History & Tour Guide* in the museum's lobby. | 1100 Orange Ave. | 619/435–7242 | www.coronadohistory.org | Donations | Weekdays 9–5, Sat. 10–5, Sun. 11–4.

Coronado Touring. This 90-minute guided walking tour explores Coronado's old neighborhoods, where streets are lined with high-Victorian mansions. A selection of the 86 designated historic homes may be seen from the outside, including the one occupied by L. Frank Baum while he was writing stories for the *The Wonderful Wizard of Oz*. The tour starts in the enormous Music Room of the Glorietta Bay Inn, which occupies the gleaming white Edwardian residence sugar baron and Coronado developer John D. Spreckles built for himself in 1908. | 1110 Isabella Ave. | 619/435–5993 | $8 | Music Room Tues., Thurs., Sat. at 11 AM.

HISTORIC DINING AND LODGING

Crown Room. American. You can glimpse a bit of the Del's legendary social life by savoring Sunday brunch in the Crown Room, one of the hotel's architectural gems. The room's huge arched ceiling was constructed of unsupported sugar-pine beams without the use of nails. You can tell by looking at this space that the hotel's architect, James Reed, had previously designed railroad stations. *The Wonderful Wizard of Oz* author L. Frank Baum is credited with designing the crown chandeliers that adorn the ceiling. | Hotel Del Coronado, 1500 Orange Ave. | 619/435–6611 | Reservations essential | Sun. brunch only | $46 | AE, D, DC, MC, V.

Glorietta Bay Inn. A grand historic treasure, the original portion of this inn was designed and built by sugar baron and Coronado developer John D. Spreckles. To catch the sense of grandeur that was part of Spreckles' everyday life, pick one of the 11 rooms in the Edwardian-style mansion. Even if you prefer the contemporary rooms of the newer motel-style building, you'll have an opportunity to enjoy breakfast in the Music Room, with its copper-clad doors and gleaming hardwood floors. Ginger snaps and lemonade are served daily from 3 to 5. In-room data ports, some kitchenettes, refrigerators, cable TV with movies, pool, outdoor hot tub, bicycles, library, laundry service, concierge, business services, free parking; no smoking. | 1630 Glorietta Blvd., 92118 | 619/435–3101 or 800/283–9383 | fax 619/435–6182 | www.gloriettabayinn.com | 93 rooms, 7 suites | $150–$345 | AE, MC, V | CP.

Hotel Del Coronado. The Del stands as a social and historical landmark, its whimsical red turrets, white siding, and balconied walkways taking you as far back as 1888, the year it was built. It has hosted the rich and famous, including U.S. presidents dating back to Benjamin Harrison and William H. Taft. The Del is the largest wooden structure west of the Mississippi; its three early 20th-century Otis elevators were among the first installed in any hotel. The original 46-ft hand-crafted mahogany bar in the Babcock & Story Bar came by ship around the Cape Horn from Philadelphia in 1888, and the hotel's first electrically lighted Christmas tree is said to have been illuminated in 1911 by Thomas Edison. All this and more is explained during free tours conducted for guests only, weekdays at 2 and Saturday at 11; the required reservations must be made with the concierge. 2 restaurants, coffee shop, deli, room service, in-room data ports, cable TV with movies, 3 tennis courts, 2 pools, gym, hair salon, outdoor hot tub, massage, sauna, spa, steam room, beach, bicycles, 4 bars, piano bar, shops, children's programs, laundry, concierge, business services, convention center, meeting rooms, parking (fee); no smoking. | 1500 Orange Ave., 92118 | 619/435–6611 or 800/468–3533 | fax 619/522–8262 | www.hoteldel.com | 683 rooms, 4 suites | $250–$460 | AE, D, DC, MC, V.

ESCONDIDO

▼▼

The location of Escondido was first mapped by Juan Bautista de Anza, a Spanish explorer, in 1776. Later, the area became part of the Rancho Rincon del Diablo ("the devil's corner") land grant bestowed to Juan Bautista Alvarado in 1843 by Mexican governor Manuel Micheltorena. During the Mexican-American War, a number of important battles took place in this area. *Contact Escondido Historical Society | 321 N. Broadway, 92025 | 760/743–8207. San Pasqual Battlefield Historic State Park | 15808 San Pasqual Valley Rd., 92025 | 760/737–3301 | www.parks.ca.gov.*

San Pasqual Battlefield State Historic Park. This is the site of one of the most controversial and bloody battles in the war between Mexico and the United States. The battle, which took place on December 6, 1846, pitted 169 U.S. troops led by General Stephen Kearney against a band of 100 "Californios" led by Andres Pico. The Americans suffered heavy casualties, and victory was claimed by both generals. Despite the American defeat, the battle is considered one of the pivotal events in the effort to oust Mexico from California. | 15808 San Pasqual Valley Rd. | 760/737–3301 | www.parks.ca.gov | Donation | Weekends 10–5.

✦ ON THE CALENDAR: Dec. **Battle Day.** This reenactment of the San Pasqual Battle at San Pasqual state park includes a military encampment, period crafts demonstrations, costumed interpretation, and a skirmish between Californios and U.S. dragoons. | 760/737–3301.

EUREKA

▼▼

Eureka started as a mining center and later turned to timbering and fishing. There are nearly 100 Victorian buildings here, many of them well preserved. The splendid Carson Mansion was built in 1885 for timber baron William Carson. Don't miss the Victorian extravaganza popularly known as the Pink Lady. At the Chamber of Commerce you can pick up maps with self-guided driving tours of Eureka's architecture and find out about organized tours. *Contact Eureka/Humboldt County Convention and Visitors Bureau | 1034 2nd St., 95501 | 707/443–5097 or 800/346–3482.*

Clarke Memorial Museum. Extraordinary northwestern California Native American basketry and artifacts of Eureka's Victorian, logging, and maritime eras are on display here. | 240 E St. | 707/443–1947 | Donations | Feb.–Dec., Tues.–Sat. 11–4.

Fort Humboldt State Historic Park. Fort Humboldt once protected white settlers from Native Americans in the area. Ulysses S. Grant was posted here in 1854. The old fort is no longer around, but on its grounds are a museum, some ancient steam engines, and a logger's cabin. | 3431 Fort Ave. | 707/445–6567 or 707/445–6547 | Free | Daily 9–5.

HISTORIC DINING

Samoa Cookhouse. American. Since 1890 this place has been satisfying the mighty appetites of loggers. It's still a loggers' hangout, longer on quantity than quality. The Samoa's cooks serve three substantial set meals family style at long wooden tables. Meat dishes predominate. Save room (if possible) for dessert. | Cookhouse Rd. (from U.S. 101 cross Samoa Bridge, turn left onto Samoa Rd., then left 1 block later onto Cookhouse Rd.) | 707/442–1659 | $12 | AE, D, MC, V.

FERNDALE
▼▼

The residents of the stately town of Ferndale maintain some of the most sumptuous Victorian homes in California, many of them built by 19th-century Scandinavian, Swiss, and Portuguese dairy farmers who were drawn to the mild climate. The queen of them all is the Gingerbread Mansion. A beautiful sloped graveyard sits on Ocean Avenue west of Main Street. Many shops carry a map with self-guided tours of this lovingly preserved town. *Contact Ferndale Chamber of Commerce | Box 325, 95536 | 707/786–4477 | fax 707/786–4477 | www. victorianferndale.org/chamber.*

Ferndale Museum. The main building hosts changing exhibitions of Victoriana and has an old-style barbershop and a display of Wiyot Indian baskets. In the annex are a horse-drawn buggy, a re-created blacksmith shop, and antique farming, fishing, and dairy equipment. | 515 Shaw Ave. | 707/786–4466 | $1 | June–Sept., Tues.–Sat. 11–4, Sun. 1–4; Oct.–Dec. and Feb.–May, Wed.–Sat. 11–4, Sun. 1–4.

HISTORIC LODGING

Gingerbread Mansion. This photogenic Victorian B&B rivals San Francisco's "painted ladies" for dazzle. The mansion's carved friezes set off its gables, and turrets delight the eye. The comfortable parlors and spacious bedrooms are laid out in flowery Victorian splendor. Some rooms have views of the mansion's English garden, and one has side-by-side bathtubs. One spectacular suite is the Veneto, with hand-painted scenes of Venice on the walls and ceiling as well as marble floors. Ask about off-season discounts. | 400 Berding St., 95536 | 707/ 786–4000 or 800/952–4136 | www.gingerbread-mansion.com | 11 rooms, 4 suites | $150–$385 | AE, MC, V | BP.

FREMONT
▼▼

Fremont was named for pioneer John Fremont, who was so enamored of a Spanish-Native Ohlones–built mission that he bought the adjacent land. In the 1840s he mapped a trail for settlers to the southeastern area of San Francisco Bay through what is now called Mission Pass. Established as Washington Township, the area encompassed five small communities, which incorporated into the City of Fremont in 1956. *Contact Fremont Chamber of Commerce | 39488 Stevenson Pl., No. 100, 94539 | 510/795–2244 | www.fremontbusiness.com.*

Ardenwood Historic Farm. This living-history museum on 205 acres portrays life on a late-19th-century California farmstead. Staff members dressed in period costumes demonstrate daily chores. You can view the home of the farm's first owner, tour the grounds in a horse-drawn wagon, and ride in a horse-drawn railcar. Exhibits and events change daily; call in advance to confirm the day's offerings. | Arden Wood Blvd. | 510/796–0663 | www.fremont. gov/recreation/ardenwoodpark | $5 | Tues.–Sun. 10–4.

Mission San Jose Chapel and Museum. A reconstructed 1797 Catholic church with gold-leaf altar, chandeliers, and murals contains a museum documenting the history of the mission, its restoration, and the Ohlone Indians. | 43300 Mission Blvd. | 510/657–1797 | www.thecaliforniamissions.com/sanjos/sanjos.html | Donations | Daily 10–5.

Museum of Local History. In the San Jose Mission district of Fremont, you'll find a small museum and library dedicated to preserving local historical artifacts and records from the period between 1840 and 1940. | 190 Anza St. | 510/623–7907 | www.museumoflocalhistory.org | Donation | Wed.–Fri. 10–4, second Sat. and Sun. of month 10–4.

✦ ON THE CALENDAR: May **Civil War Days.** Held on Memorial Day weekend at Ardenwood Historic Farm are reenactments and exhibits about life on the farm during the Civil War. | 510/796–0663.

GRASS VALLEY

▼▼▼

Grass Valley was incorporated in 1893 as a gold-rush town, but its name predates the period and refers to the pastoral grasslands where the earliest settlers let their cattle graze. After the whirlwind of the gold rush had died down, mining and logging sustained the town. Unlike in many other towns in the region, where the gold was exhausted, a few gold mines still remain here. Look for well-preserved 19th-century buildings in the area where Main and Mill streets meet. *Contact City of Grass Valley | 125 E. Main St., 95945 | 530/274–4310 | fax 530/274–4399 | www.cityof.grass-valley.ca.us. Grass Valley Chamber of Commerce | 248 Mill St., 95945 | 530/273–4667 or 800/655–4667 | www.nccn.net/~gvnc. Nevada County Gold Online Magazine | www.ncgold.com.*

Empire Mine State Historic Park. The hard-rock gold mine here was one of California's richest. An estimated 5.8 million ounces were extracted from its 367 mi of underground passages between 1850 and 1956. On the 50-minute tour you can walk into a mine shaft, peer into the mine's deeper recesses, and view the owner's "cottage," which has exquisite woodwork. The visitor center has mining exhibits. | 10791 E. Empire St. (exit south from Rte. 49) | 530/273–8522 | www.parks.ca.gov | $3 | May–Aug., daily 9–6; Sept.–Apr., daily 10–5. Tours in summer on the hr 11–4; winter weekends only at 1 (cottage only) and 2 (mine yard only), weather permitting.

Grass Valley Museum. Set inside an 1865 structure are artifacts and costumes dating from the founding of the town. Among other exhibits, there is a re-created parlor, music room, doctor's office, and classroom. | 410 S. Church St. | 530/273–5509 | Donation | Tues.–Fri. 12:30–3:30, or by appointment.

Lola Montez House. The notorious dancer Lola Montez, who arrived in Grass Valley in the early 1850s, was wildly popular among the local miners for her suggestive spider dance. She was no great talent, but her loves—who reportedly included composer Franz Liszt—were legendary. According to one account, Lola came to California after having been "permanently retired from her job as Bavarian king Ludwig's mistress," literary muse, and political adviser. She seems to have pushed the king too hard for democracy, which contributed to his overthrow and her banishment as a witch—or so the story goes. A reproduction of her home houses the chamber of commerce. | 248 Mill St. | 530/273–4667 or 800/655–4667 | Weekdays 9:30–5, Sat. 10–3.

North Star Power House and Pelton Wheel Exhibit. The star exhibit here is a 32-ft-high enclosed waterwheel (invented by Lester Allen Pelton), said to be the largest ever built. It was used to power mining operations and was a forerunner of the modern turbines that generate hydroelectricity. Hands-on displays are geared to children. | Empire and McCourtney Sts. (Empire St. exit north from Rte. 49) | 530/273–4255 | Donation | May–mid-Oct., daily 10–5.

✦ ON THE CALENDAR: Sept. **Draft Horse Classic and Harvest Fair.** To honor the horses that used to work the machinery in the mines, this four-day event showcases the "gentle giants" with such events as log pulling and period carriage drives. | 530/273–6217.

Nov.–Dec. **Cornish Christmas.** On four consecutive Fridays after Thanksgiving, Grass Valley celebrates Christmas and the long Cornish heritage of this foothills town. Festivities include hay rides and performances by the Cornish Choir. Have some roasted chestnuts and hot apple cider. | 530/272–8315.

HISTORIC DINING AND LODGING

Holbrooke Hotel. Built in 1851, the hotel is a registered landmark with the state of California. Guests over the years have included Lola Montez, Mark Twain, and Ulysses S. Grant, plus a stream of other U.S. presidents. Accommodations are in brick-walled guest rooms, most with brass canopy beds, and many rooms have private balconies, which you should request when you book. The very good white-tablecloth dining room is one of the longest-operating restaurants west of the Mississippi. It serves steaks and seafood at dinner and sandwiches, soups, and salads at lunch. Restaurant, bar. | 212 W. Main St. 95945 | 530/273–1353 or 800/933–7077 | fax 530/273–0434 | www.holbrookehotel.com | 28 rooms | $85–$125 | AE, D, MC, V | CP.

HANFORD
▼▼

Named for 19th-century Southern Pacific Railroad paymaster James Madison Hanford, this town was defined by the Cantonese immigrants who came to build the railroad. They created one of the largest Chinese communities in California. *Contact Hanford Visitor's Agency | 200 Sante Fe, Suite D, 93230 | 559/582–5024 or 800/722–1114 | www.visithanford.com. Tulare County Historical Society | Box 295, Visalia 93278.*

Hanford Carnegie Museum. This museum is housed in the former Carnegie Library, built in 1905. Inside, displays of fashions, furnishings, toys, and military artifacts tell the personal history of this classic railroad and agricultural town. | 109 E. 8th St. | 559/584–1367 | $1 | Tues.–Fri. noon–3, Sat. noon–4.

Taoist Temple. Built in 1893, the temple has functioned as housing for new immigrants, a school for their children, and a community for Chinese senior citizens. Today the museum displays photos and furnishings from Hanford's once-bustling Chinatown, while the temple upstairs appears much as it has since the turn of the 20th century, with altars, carvings, and ceremonial staves. You can visit as part of a guided walking tour or by calling the temple directly and making an appointment two weeks in advance. | 12 China Alley | 559/582–4508 | Donations welcome.

Tulare County Museum. Twenty miles east of Hanford, this indoor-outdoor museum contains several re-created environments from the pioneer era. On display are Yokuts tribal artifacts (basketry, arrowheads, clamshell-necklace currency) as well as saddles and guns, Victorian-era dolls, and quilts and gowns. | Mooney Grove Park, 27000 S. Mooney Blvd., Visalia | 559/733–6616 | Free | June–Aug., Mon. and Wed.–Fri. 10–4, weekends 10–5; Sept.–Oct., Thurs.–Mon. 10–4; Nov.–Feb., Mon. and Thurs.–Fri. 10–4, weekends 1–4; Mar.–May, Thurs.–Mon. 10–4.

JACKSON

▼▼▼

Jackson wasn't the Gold Country's rowdiest town, but the party lasted longer here than most anywhere else: "Girls' dormitories" (brothels) and nickel slot machines flourished until the mid-1950s. Jackson also had the world's deepest and richest gold mines, the Kennedy and the Argonaut, which together produced $70 million in gold. These were deep-rock mines with tunnels extending as much as a mile underground. Most of the miners who worked the lode were of Serbian or Italian origin, and they gave the town a European character that persists to this day. Jackson has aboveground pioneer cemeteries whose headstones tell the stories of local Serbian and Italian families. A large share of the original 1848 mining settlement burned down in 1862, and most of the structures along Main Street are reproductions of the originals. *Contact Amador County Chamber of Commerce | 125 Peek St., 95683 | 209/223–0350 | www.amadorcountychamber.com. Amador County Archives | 42 Summit St. | 209/223–6389 | www.amadorarchives.org.*

Amador County Museum. Built in the late 1850s as a private home, the museum provides a colorful take on gold-rush life. Displays include a kitchen with a woodstove, the Amador County bicentennial quilt, and a classroom. A time line recounts the county's checkered past. The museum conducts hourly tours of large-scale working models of the nearby Kennedy Mine. | 225 Church St. | 209/223–6386 | www.amadorarchives.org/museum.html | Museum free, mine $1 | Wed.–Sun. 10–4.

National Hotel. In the heart of Jackson's old town, the National Hotel has been in continuous operation since 1863. There's an old-time saloon in the lobby, which gets especially busy on Saturday nights, when people come from miles around for sing-alongs. If you stay for dinner and get too sleepy, you can rent one of the upstairs rooms for the night. | 2 Water St. | 209/223–0500.

St. Sava Serbian Orthodox Church Cemetery. The terraced cemetery is the town's most impressive burial ground, with headstones dating back to 1894, the same year the church was constructed. | 724 N. Main St.

✦ ON THE CALENDAR: Oct. **Lumberjack Days.** Timber was big business in the Sierra Foothills in the late 19th and early 20th centuries. On the first weekend of October, the tiny town of West Point honors the lumberjack with a big kickoff parade, crafts, and axe-throwing and tree-cutting contests. Take Route 88 from Jackson to Route 26 east into the town of West Point. | 209/293–4325.

HISTORIC LODGING

Hotel Leger Bed & Breakfast. The first hotel to stand on this hilltop overlooking a river was built in 1851. That building, the Hotel de France, burned down in 1854, and in its place rose the Hotel Leger (pronounced le-zay). Fire damaged this structure as well, in 1874, but the owners rebuilt, adding a second story. The first building in the town of Mokelumne Hill to install electric lighting, it is still one of the finer lodgings in the area, with balconies off the rooms and complimentary morning newspaper. Mokelumne Hill is about 8 mi south of Jackson on Rte. 49. Restaurant, pool, bar, laundry service, meeting room. | 8304 S. Main St., Mokelumne Hill, 95245 | 209/286–1401 | 13 rooms | $49–$139 | AE, MC, V.

JAMESTOWN

▼▼▼

Not long after James Marshall discovered gold at Sutter's Mill in 1848, Benjamin F. Woods was the first to find gold in Tuolumne County. The incredibly rich diggings around Woods'

Crossing attracted the usual crowds of prospectors, who renamed the town in 1849. They called it Jamestown in honor of one Colonel George James, who treated everyone to champagne when he arrived in town. Before long James left town in a hurry one night, having defrauded many of the prospectors in a mining investment scheme. The townspeople instantly tried to rename the town, but by then Jamestown was an official address in the postal system and its name could not be changed. "Jimtown," as it came to be known, still has several structures from the 1870s. *Contact Tuolomne County Chamber of Commerce | 222 S. Shepherd St., Sonora 95370 | 209/532–4212 | www.tcchamber.com.Tuolumne County Historical Society | 158 W. Bradford St., Sonora 95370 | 209/532–1317 | www.tchistory.org. Tuolumne County Visitors Bureau | Box 4020, Sonora 95370 | 800/446–1333 or 209/533–4420 | www.thegreatunfenced.com.*

Jimtown 1849 Gold Mining Camp. You can pan for gold at this living-history museum, which is set up like an old mining camp, complete with costumed prospectors. | 18170 Main St. | 209/984–4653 or 800/596–0009 | www.goldprospecting.com | Gold panning $15 per hr and up, mining camp free | Daily 9:30–5.

Railtown 1897. The California State Railroad Museum maintains what were the headquarters and general shops of the Sierra Railway from 1897 to 1955. You can view the roundhouse, an air-operated 60-ft turntable, shop rooms, and old locomotives and coaches. Six-mile, 40-minute steam train rides through the countryside operate on weekends in the warmer months. | 5th Ave. and Reservoir Rd., off Rte. 49 | 209/984–3953 | www.csrmf.org | Roundhouse tour $2, train ride $6 | Daily 9:30–4:30 Train rides Apr.–Oct., weekends 11–3; Nov., Sat. 11–3.

HISTORIC DINING AND LODGING
National Hotel. The National has been in business since 1859, and the furnishings here are authentic—brass beds, patchwork quilts, oak-tank pull-chain toilets, and lace curtains—but not overly embellished. The saloon, which still has its original 19th-century redwood bar, is a great place to linger. The popular restaurant serves big lunches: hamburgers and fries, salads, and Italian entrées. More upscale Continental cuisine is prepared for dinner (reservations essential). Restaurant, bar. | 18183 Main St. 95327 | 209/984–3446; 800/894–3446 in California | fax 209/984–5620 | www.national-hotel.com | 9 rooms | $90–$130 | AE, D, DC, MC, V | CP.

JULIAN
▼▼▼

The site of the only significant gold rush in southern California, Julian preserves its historic character with turn-of-the-20th-century false-front buildings. Gold was discovered in 1869, and mining activities lasted for about 30 years, when residents began growing prize-winning apples and pears. Julian was designated a historic site by San Diego County in 1965. *Contact Julian Chamber of Commerce | Town Hall, Box 1866, 92036 | 760/765–1857 | www.julianca.com.*

Eagle Peak Mining Company. Hard hats and flashlights are required to take an hour-long tour of the tunnels of one of Julian's gold mines. Displays include a stamp mill, ore gondolas, picks and shovels, a hoist room where the miners were lowered hundreds of feet into tunnels, and gold-bearing quartz veins. | C St., 5 blocks east of Main St. | 760/765–0036 | $7 | Daily 10–3.

Historic Plaque Tour. You can get a good understanding of how life was lived during Julian's gold-rush era by taking a walking tour of the six-square-block town. The Historic Society has placed informational plaques in front of 29 original houses and shops that remain. Pick up a map from the chamber of commerce in Town Hall. | Town Hall, Washington and Main Sts. | 760/765–1857 | www.julianca.com | Free | Daily 10–4.

Julian Pioneer Museum. In Julian's heyday, mobs of gold miners invaded these valleys and hillsides. When the mines played out, the gold miners left, leaving behind discarded mining tools and empty houses. Today the museum, itself a 19th-century building, displays remnants of that time: mining implements and tools, pioneer clothing, a collection of old lace, and old photographs of the town's historic buildings and mining structures. | 4th and Washington Sts. | 760/765–0027 | $2 | Apr.–Nov., daily 10–4; Dec.–Mar., weekends 10–4.

✦ ON THE CALENDAR: Oct. **Old Time Melodrama.** This annual theatrical battle of good versus evil, Old West style, is performed weekends in Town Hall by the Julian "Floozies" and local actors. A community sing-along follows the show. | 760/765–1857.

HISTORIC DINING AND LODGING

Julian Gold Rush Hotel. As authentic as it can be more than 100 years after it was built, the Julian Hotel was founded as the Hotel Robinson in 1897 by freed slave Albert Robinson. The history of the hotel parallels that of the town: boom, bust, and boom again. Renovation has preserved the styles of the 1890s. Rooms are small, and private bathrooms are about the only modern compromise. You'll find reminders of the hotel's past throughout, including the old guest register, which includes the signatures of Ulysses Grant Jr., members of the Scripps family, and British prime minister David Lloyd George. Rates include full breakfast and afternoon tea. No smoking. | Washington St., Box 1856, 92036 | 760/765–0201 or 800/734–5854 | fax 760/765–0327 | www.julianhotel.com | 14 rooms, 2 cottages | $110–$145 | AE, MC, V | BP.

LAKE TAHOE
▼▼▼

The first white explorer to gaze upon this spectacular region was Captain John C. Fremont, in 1844, guided by the famous scout Kit Carson. Not long afterward, silver was discovered in Nevada's Comstock Lode, at Virginia City. As the mines grew larger and deeper, the Tahoe Basin's forests were leveled to provide lumber for subterranean support. By the early 1900s wealthy Californians were building lakeside estates here, some of which still stand. It was the sight of Lake Tahoe that prompted Mark Twain to write, "I thought it must surely be the fairest picture the whole earth affords." During his 1861 visit he found "not 15 other human beings throughout its wide circumference" and marveled of its beauty that "the eye never tired of gazing, night or day, calm or storm." *Contact Lake Tahoe Visitors Authority | 1156 Ski Run Blvd., South Lake Tahoe 96150 | 530/544–5050 or 800/288–2463 | www.virtualtahoe.com. North Lake Tahoe Historical Society | Box 6141, 96145 | 530/583–1762 | www.tahoecountry. com/nlths. North Lake Tahoe Resort Association Box 5578, Tahoe City 96145 | 530/583–3494 or 800/824–6348 | www.tahoefun.org. Tahoe Heritage Foundation | Box 8586, South Lake Tahoe 96158 | 530/544–7383 | www.tahoeheritage.org.*

Glen Alpine Springs. Built in the 1870s as a private home, this became one of Lake Tahoe's first resorts, known for its "curative" spring water, by 1884. By 1905 the resort had grown to include more than 25 permanent buildings and its own post office. Over the decades, many of the original structures have burned or collapsed, but nine of them remain, including four designed by architect Richard Maybeck in the 1920s. It's hard to get to the Springs—the only roads in are one-lane, narrow, and winding—and you'll have to leave your car in a Forest Service lot and hike the last mile or so. Docents give tours and operate the interpretive center, which shows photographs and historical information about the former resort. | 5 mi west of South Lake Tahoe via Rte. 89 to Fallen Leaf Rd., then south to parking lot at

Lily Lake Box 694, Glen Ellen | 707/996–6354 | fax 707/935–6320 | www.gasprings.org | Donation. | Interpretive center mid-Jun.–mid-Sept., daily 10:30–3:30; grounds dawn–dusk.

Sugar Pine Point State Park. The main attraction at Sugar Pine Point State Park is Ehrman Mansion, a 1903 stone-and-shingle summer home furnished in period style. In its day it was the height of modernity, with a refrigerator, an elevator, and an electric stove. Also in the park are a trapper's log cabin from the mid-19th century. | 10 mi south of Tahoe City on Rte. 89 | 530/525–7232 year-round; 530/525–7982 in season | www.parks.ca.gov | $2 per vehicle | Mansion tours July–early Sept., daily 11–4; park late May–early Sept. daily dawn–dusk.

Watson Cabin Living Museum. Built in 1909 by Robert M. Watson and his son, the log cabin is filled with its original furnishings. Costumed docents act out the daily life of a typical pioneer family. | 560 N. Lake Blvd., Tahoe City | 530/583–8717 or 530/583–1762 | Donation | Mid-June–early Sept., daily noon–4.

LOS ANGELES
▼▼▼

Long before Sunset Boulevard was even a cattle route, Native Americans settled this area, the Chumash along the coast and the Shoshone inland. In 1771, the arrival of Mission San Gabriel Archangel led quickly to the spread of European diseases that would decimate inland communities. Almost a decade later, the Spanish felt increased competition from Russia in the north and Britain overseas and so aimed to build a more agriculturally oriented pueblo to strengthen the mission. For nearly a hundred years the pueblo of Los Angeles was a dusty outpost, isolated from the world by ocean and mountains and generally dismissed by all but the most hopeful (or desperate). In the late 1800s, the fate of this dry town was changed forever by the arrival of a railroad spur line and water piped down from the Sierra Nevada. *Contact Chinese Historical Society of Southern California | Box 862647, 90086-2647 | 323/222–0856 | www.chssc.org. Historical Society of Southern California | 200 E. Ave. 43, 90031 | 323/222–0546 | www.socalhistory.org. Los Angeles City Historical Society | Box 41046, 90071 | 213/891–4600 | www.lacityhistory.com. Los Angeles Convention and Visitors Bureau | 633 W. 5th St., Suite 6000, 90071 | 213/624–7300 or 800/228–2452 | fax 213/624–9746 | www.lacvb.com.*

Autry Museum of Western Heritage. Founded by Gene Autry, this museum in the northeast corner of Griffith Park explores and celebrates local history through its most powerful modern interpretation: the western movie. In addition to the permanent collection, good traveling historical and cultural exhibits often stop here. | Western Heritage Way and Zoo Dr. | 323/667–2000 | www.autry-museum.org | $7.50 | Tues.–Wed. and Fri.–Sun. 10–5, Thurs. 10–8.

El Molino Viejo. Built in 1816 as a gristmill for the San Gabriel Mission, this is one of the last remaining examples in southern California of Spanish Mission architecture. It's a quiet, restful place, with a flower-decked arbor and peaceful garden shaded by sycamores and old oaks. | 1120 Old Mill Rd., San Marino | 626/449–5458 | Free | Tues.–Sun. 1–4.

El Pueblo de Los Angeles Historic Monument. The site of L.A.'s first settlement can offer a full day of strolling, looking, reading, and eating. Self-guided tour brochures are available at the Plaza information desk and at the visitor center within Sepulveda House. The main attraction is **Olvera Street,** center of activity in the early days and still today lined with tile walkways, piñatas, mariachis, vendors, and authentic Mexican food. The street begins at the Plaza, a pleasant Mexican-style park shaded by a huge fig tree. On and around Olvera Street are 27 older buildings that have been restored, among them the 1818 Avila Adobe, considered the oldest building still standing in Los Angeles. Sepulveda House was a Victorian hotel and boardinghouse. The Old Plaza Firehouse, built in 1884, houses antique firefighting equipment, photographs, and an original chemical wagon. The grande dame of monuments here is Nuestra Señora La Reina de Los Angeles, the oldest church in the city. Las Angelitas, El Pueblo's docent organization, provides free tours of the district Tuesday–Saturday at 10 AM, 11 AM, and noon. | Bounded by Alameda, Arcadia, Spring, and Macy Sts. | 213/628–1274 | Free | Hrs vary.

Los Encino State Historic Park. Until the Los Angeles aqueduct was built, the natural spring here made Los Encino the hub of life in dry and dusty Los Angeles, first for Native Americans and then settlers. The 4,500-acre ranch served as a stagecoach stop from 1845 to 1915, and one of the original adobes still stands (though, due to earthquake damage, you can't go inside). | 16756 Moorpark St., Encino | 818/784–4849 | www.parks.ca.gov | Free | Wed.–Sun. 10–5.

Mission San Fernando Rey de España. Built in 1797 and restored beginning in 1923, this mission displays Native American handiwork and artifacts of Spanish craftsmanship from the 18th century. | 15151 San Fernando Mission Blvd., Mission Hills | 818/361–0186 | $4 | Daily 9–4:30.

Mission San Gabriel Archangel. The mission that launched the pueblo of Los Angeles is now tucked between freeways and train tracks. Urban growth has not ruined the 1771 church (though an 1812 earthquake toppled the tower, later rebuilt), and with a little creativity it's not hard to imagine this and the surrounding land as they were once known: the Pride of the Missions. | 428 S. Mission Dr., San Gabriel | 626/457–3035 | www.sangabrielmission.org | $4 | Daily 9–1 and 2–8.

Southwest Museum. Readily spotted from the Pasadena Freeway, this huge Mission Revival building stands halfway up Mt. Washington. Inside is an extensive collection of Native American art and artifacts, including an 18-ft Southern Cheyenne tepee and an outstanding basketry collection that's one of the largest in the country. | 234 Museum Dr. | 323/221–2163 | fax 323/224–8223 | www.southwestmuseum.org | $6 | Tues.–Sun. 10–5.

HISTORIC DINING

La Golondrina. Mexican. Housed in Los Angeles's oldest brick building, the 1855 Pelanconi House, La Golodrina has been serving excellent and imaginative Mexican food since the 1930s. Sitting right on Olvera Street, the shaded, hacienda-style patio is a great place to try your first pickled-cactus margarita. There's breakfast on weekends. | 17 Olvera St. | 213/628–4349 | $9–$16 | AE, MC, V.

MARIPOSA
▼▼▼

Mariposa marks the southern end of the mother lode. Much of the land in this area was part of a 44,000-acre land grant that Colonel John C. Fremont acquired from Mexico before gold was discovered and California became a state. *Contact Mariposa County Chamber of Commerce | 5158 Rte. 140 Box 425, 95338 | 209/966–2456 | www.mariposa.org. Mariposa County Visitors Bureau | Box 967, 95338 | 209/966–7081 | www.homeofyosemite.com.*

California State Mining and Mineral Museum. A glittering 13-pound chunk of crystallized gold on display here makes it clear what the rush was about. You can also see a replica of a typical tunnel dug by hard-rock miners, a miniature stamp mill, and a panning and sluicing exhibit. | Mariposa County Fairgrounds, Rte. 49 | 209/742–7625 | www.parks.ca.gov | $1 | May–Sept., daily 10–6; Oct.–Apr., Wed.–Mon. 10–4.

Mariposa County Courthouse. Much of the legislation that governed the gold rush was drafted here, and the building appears much the same way today as it did then. Built in 1854 and in continuous operation since 1855, the courthouse contains many of the same furnishings it did when it was constructed. | 5088 Bullion St. | 209/966–2005 | Weekdays 8–5. Tours May–Sept., weekends; call for hrs.

Mariposa Museum and History Center. On display here are Native American artifacts, exhibits on the area's Spanish period, and depictions of life during the gold rush, including a one-room miner's cabin. Outside there are large pieces of mining equipment and a small re-creation of an Indian village. | 5119 Jessie St. | 209/966–2924 | Donation | Apr.–Sept., daily 10–4:30; Oct.–Dec. and Feb.–Mar., daily 10–4.

MARYSVILLE

▼▼▼

When Marysville was incorporated in 1851, it called itself the "Gateway to the Gold Fields" of northern California. Indeed, the surrounding mines shipped more than $10 million worth of nuggets back east in 1857 alone. The town took its official name from Mary Murphy, one of the few survivors of the famously unlucky Donner Party. Along with the '49ers came several thousand Chinese immigrants who worked in the mines. Both Marysville and neighboring Yuba City honor their Asian heritage—Marysville's Chinese New Year celebration is among the most elaborate in the nation. *Contact Yuba-Sutter Chamber of Commerce | 429 10th St., Yuba City 95901 | 530/743–6501.*

Bok Kai Temple. The only one of its kind in the United States, this temple was founded by Chinese immigrants in the mid-1800s. The original temple structure burned down and was rebuilt in 1880. | D and 1st Sts. | 530/743–6501 | Free | Tours by appointment only.

Historic D Street. Many of Marysville's original brick and wooden buildings can still be seen south of D Street's 700 block. You can get a self-guided walking tour map at the Mary Aaron museum. | D St. | 530/743–1004 | Free.

Mary Aaron Memorial Museum. Built in 1885 and occupied by the Aaron family until 1935, this Gothic Revival home now houses a museum with old photographs, period clothing, and a display illustrating the experiences of early Chinese immigrants. | 704 D St. | 530/743–1004 | Free | Thurs.–Sat. 1–4 or by appointment.

✦ ON THE CALENDAR: Mar. **Bok Kai Festival and Parade.** Since the turn of the 20th century, this colorful festival has been ringing in the Chinese New Year in downtown Marysville. Festivities, which include food, music, and a 15K run, conclude with a parade down D Street to Chinatown and fireworks. | 530/743–7309.

MENDOCINO

▼▼▼

In 1852, the sole survivor of a shipwreck, German immigrant William Kasten, washed ashore here. He built Mendocino into a logging center, and settlers from New England soon arrived to work here. The craggy, weather-beaten coast must have reminded them of home, for they erected New England–style houses that distinguish it from other California towns. *Contact Fort Bragg–Mendocino Coast Chamber of Commerce | 332 N. Main St., Fort Bragg 95437 | 707/ 961–6300 | www.mendocinocoast.com.*

Ford House. Built in 1854, this is now the visitor center for Mendocino Headlands State Park. The house has a scale model of Mendocino as it looked in 1890, when the town had 34 water towers and a 12-seat public outhouse. History walks leave from Ford House on Saturday afternoon at 1. | Main St. west of Lansing St. | 707/937–5397 | Free ($1 donation suggested) | Daily 11–4, with possible midweek closings in winter.

Kelley House Museum and Library. This is the restored residence of William Henry Kelley, a gold-rush pioneer who arrived in 1852 and bought out the holdings of William Kasten, Mendocino's founder. | 45007 Albion St. | 707/937–5791 | www.homestead.com/kelleyhousemuseum | $2 | Sept.–May, Fri.–Sun. 1–4; June–Aug., daily 1–4.

Temple of Kwan Tai. The oldest Chinese temple on the North Coast, this tiny green-and-red structure dates from 1852. It's open only by appointment, but you can peer in the window and see everything there is to see. | Albion St. west of Kasten St. | 707/937–5123.

HISTORIC LODGING

Noyo River Lodge. Built in 1868 by a lumber baron who was also one of the area's first settlers, this two-story lodge on a redwood bluff above Fort Bragg's harbor overlooks the river, the fishing village, and the Noyo River Bridge. Many of the rooms have antiques and redwood-paneled walls. No room phones. | 500 Casa Del Noyo Dr., Fort Bragg, 95437 | 707/964–8045 or 800/628–1126 | fax 707/964–9366 | www.noyolodge.com | 16 rooms, 8 suites | $115–$155 | AE, MC, V | CP.

Whitegate Inn. With a white-picket fence, a latticework gazebo, and a romantic garden, the Whitegate is a picture-book Victorian B&B. Built in 1883, it has 19th-century French and Victorian antiques, including the owner's collection of Civil War memorabilia. | 499 Howard St., 95460 | 707/937–4892 or 800/531–7282 | www.whitegateinn.com | 7 rooms | $119–$229 | AE, D, DC, MC, V | BP.

MERCED
▼▼

In 1806, the Mexican government in San Francisco sent troops into the San Joaquin Valley to search for marauding bands of Indians. Finding water to be scarce in the dry inner valley, the soldiers named the river here El Rio de Los Mercedes, or the River of Mercy. The name was later shortened to Merced and given also to this town, founded half a century later by American settlers. *Contact Merced Conference and Visitors Bureau | 690 W. 16th St., 95340 | 209/ 384–7092 or 800/446–5353 | www.yosemite-gateway.org. Merced County Historical Society | 21st and N Sts., 95340 | 209/723–2401.*

Merced County Courthouse Museum. The three-story former courthouse, built in 1875, is a striking example of the Victorian Italianate style and is on the National Register of Historic Places. The upper two floors are now a museum of early Merced history. Highlights include an ornate restored courtroom and an 1870 Chinese temple with carved redwood altars. | 21st and N Sts. | 209/723–2401 | www.mercedmuseum.org | Free | Wed.–Sun. 1–4.

Oakdale Cowboy Museum. Housed in the old Southern Pacific Railroad depot 45 mi northwest of Merced, in a town that dubs itself the "Cowboy Capital of the World," this museum is a temple to the rough-riders who tamed this wild country. Displays include saddles, buckles, ranching implements, and artifacts from pioneer ranching families, as well as memorabilia of rodeo stars Ted Nuce, Jerold Camarillo, and Ace Berry. | 355 F St., No. 1, Oakdale | 209/847–7049 | www.oakdalecowboymuseum.org | $1 | Weekdays 11–3.

MONTEREY
▼▼

First claimed for Spain by Juan Rodriguéz Cabrillo in 1542, Monterey was named by Sebastien Vizcaino in 1603 in honor of his patron, the Count of Monte Rey. It was the military and ecclesiastical capital of Alta California through the Spanish period, its deep harbor serving as a strategic hub and the town serving as administrative headquarters of Father Junípero Serra as he oversaw the founding of the California missions. By the mid-1840s Monterey had evolved into a bustling Yankee-dominated fishing port with a whaling industry that flourished until the early 1880s. In that decade, tourism replaced whaling as a major industry in the area when the elegant Del Monte Hotel opened; the golf course added to the resort in 1897 was the first west of the Mississippi. Today, a portion of downtown is protected as Monterey State Historic Park. The 2-mi Path of History, marked by round gold tiles set into the sidewalk, passes by several landmark buildings. *Contact Monterey County Historical Society | Box 3576, Salinas 93912 | 831/757–8085 | users.dedot.com/mchs/index.html. Monterey Peninsula Visitors and Convention Bureau | 380 Alvarado St., 93942 | 408/649–1770 | www.monterey.com.*

Casa Soberanes. This low-ceilinged classic adobe structure, built in 1842, was once a Custom House guard's residence. Exhibits at the house survey life in Monterey from the era of Mexican rule to the present. Don't miss the peaceful garden in back. | 336 Pacific St. | 831/649–7118 | House $5, garden free | Guided tours daily; call for times. Garden daily 8–5.

Colton Hall. A convention of delegates met in 1849 to draft the first state constitution here, at California's equivalent of Independence Hall. The stone building, which has served as a school, a courthouse, and the county seat, is a museum furnished as it was during the constitutional convention. The extensive grounds outside the hall surround the Old Monterey Jail. | 500 block of Pacific St., between Madison and Jefferson Sts. | 831/646–5640 | Free | Mar.–Oct., daily 10–noon and 1–5; Nov.–Feb., daily 10–noon and 1–4.

Cooper-Molera Adobe. This restored 2-acre complex includes a house dating from the 1820s, a visitor center, and a large garden enclosed by a high adobe wall. The mostly Victorian-era antiques and memorabilia that fill the house provide a glimpse into the life of a prosperous pioneer family. | Polk and Munras Sts. | 831/649–7118 | $5 | Guided tours daily; call for times.

Custom House. Built by the Mexican government in 1827 (it is now California's oldest standing public building), this is where, in 1846, Commodore John Sloat raised the American flag and claimed California for the United States during the Mexican-American War. The house's lower floor displays typical cargo from a 19th-century trading ship. | 1 Custom House Plaza, across from Fisherman's Wharf | 831/649–2909 | free | Daily 10–5.

Larkin House. This two-story adobe built in 1835 bears witness to the Mexican and New England influences on the Monterey style. The rooms are furnished with period antiques, many of them brought from New Hampshire by the Larkin family. | 510 Calle Principal, between Jefferson and Pacific Sts. | 831/649–7118 | $5 | Guided tours daily; call for times.

Point Pinos Lighthouse. Built in 1855, this structure 2 mi north of Monterey is the oldest continuously operating lighthouse on the West Coast. In the small museum containing U. S. Coast Guard memorabilia, you can learn about the lighting and foghorn operations. | Lighthouse Ave. off Asilomar Blvd., Pacific Grove | 831/648–3116 | www.pgmuseum.org | Free | Thurs.–Sun. 1–4.

San Juan Bautista State Historic Park. At the heart of the town of San Juan Bautista, which in its entirety is a state historic park, is a wide green plaza ringed by historic buildings: a restored blacksmith shop, a stable, a pioneer cabin, and a jailhouse. The centerpiece, of course, is the Mission San Juan Bautista, a long, low, colonnaded structure founded by Father Fermin Lasuen in 1797. Adjoining it is Mission Cemetery, where more than 4,300 Native Americans who converted to Christianity are buried in unmarked graves. On Living History Day, which takes place on the first Saturday of each month, costumed volunteers engage in quilting bees, tortilla making, butter churning, and other period activities. | 2nd and Franklin Sts., off Rte. 156 | 831/623–4881 | www.cal-parks.ca.gov | $2 | Daily 10–4:30.

✦ **ON THE CALENDAR:** Apr. **Adobe Tour.** Once a year, historic adobe homes open to the public for a tour sponsored by the Monterey History and Art Association. | 831/372–2608.

Apr. **Good Old Days.** This retro-theme small-town festival celebrates bygone times with a Victorian fashion show, parade, arts-and-crafts booths, firefighters' muster, and dancing in the streets. It is held in Pacific Grove. | 831/373–3304.

Oct. **Pacific Grove Historic Home Tour.** Visit—and learn about—Victorian homes, B&Bs, and churches selected each year for this tour. Hostesses decked out in Victorian-era garb narrate high points and architectural details as you tour each locale. | 831/373–3304 | $12.

HISTORIC DINING AND LODGING

Stokes Adobe. Mediterranean. This first-class restaurant is in an adobe, built in 1833 and bought in 1837 by Dr. James Stokes. He enlarged the building throughout the 1840s to accommodate his growing family and lively social life, and after his death the ample kitchen was graced by the first kiln in California and used as a commercial bakery. Continuing its life as a social center in Monterey, the Stokes Adobe now serves imaginative food fused from the cuisines of France, Italy, and Spain. | 500 Hartnell St. | 831/373–1110 | Reservations essential | $12–$25 | AE, MC, V.

Tarpy's Roadhouse. American. This restaurant's namesake is Matt Tarpy, leader of a posse that protected residents against thieves and cattle rustlers in the 1800s. Seems power got the best of Mr. Tarpy, and after a land dispute and subsequent murder, he was lynched here, giving the area the name "Tarpey Flats." Hearty and tasty American food is served in this old stone building, with meat loaf topping the menu. | 2999 Monterey–Salinas Rte. (Rte. 68), at Canyon Del Rey Rd. | 831/647–1444 | Reservations essential | $13–$38 | AE, D, MC, V.

Merritt House Inn. Built around an 1830 adobe house and garden, this inn provides simple yet attractive accommodations. It gains its name and its listing on the National Register of Historic Places from its most famous owner, early Monterey statesman and lawyer Josiah Merritt. All rooms have gas fireplaces and upstairs rooms have vaulted ceilings. Suites are in the adobe. Room service, in-room data ports (some), refrigerators, cable TV, Internet, laundry service; no a/c, no smoking. | 386 Pacific Ave., 93940 | 831/646–9686 | fax 831/646–5392 | www.merritthouseinn.com | 22 rooms, 3 suites | $155–$187 | AE, D, MC, V | CP.

MURPHYS

▼▼

One of the best preserved of the Gold Country towns, Murphys got its start back in 1848, with the opening of a trading post by John and Daniel Murphy. The brothers were settlers with the Stevens-Townsend-Murphy Party, the very first emigrant party to cross the Sierra Nevada successfully with wagons. One of the richest mining areas during the gold rush, the town—also called "Queen of the Sierra Mines"—attracted luminaries and outlaws alike, from Horatio Alger to Black Bart. *Contact Calaveras County Visitors Bureau | 1211 S. Main St., Angels Camp 95222 | 209/736–0049 | visitcalaveras.org. Calaveras County Chamber of Commerce Box 1145 | 1211 S. Main St., 95222 | 209/736–2580 | www.calaveras.org. Murphys On-Line | www. visitmurphys.com.*

Old Timers Museum. Dedicated to preserving the history of Murphys, this museum displays artifacts and old documents. | 470 Main St. | 209/728–1160 | Donation | Fri.–Sun. 11–4.

Saturday Walking Tours. You can take a one-hour guided tour of downtown Murphys every Saturday of the year, provided the weather cooperates and the guide is available. Check the bulletin board at the meeting point in front of the Old Timers Museum, and arrive early: only the first 15 people will be accepted. | 470 Main St. | Free | Sat. 10 AM.

✦ ON THE CALENDAR: Oct. **Calaveras Grape Stomp and Gold Rush Street Fair.** On the first Saturday of October, Main Street in Murphys closes to traffic for a one-day celebration of the town's gold-rush heritage and the area's wine making industry. | 209/754–0127.

HISTORIC LODGING

Dunbar House 1880. The oversize rooms in this elaborate 1880 Italianate-style Victorian home have brass beds, down comforters, gas-burning stoves, and claw-foot tubs. Broad wrap-around verandas encourage lounging, as do the colorful gardens and large elm trees. The Cedar Room's sunporch has a two-person whirlpool tub; in the Sequoia Room you can gaze at the garden while soaking in a bubble bath. In the afternoon you are treated to trays of appetizers and wine in your room. As director of the Calaveras County Visitors Association, the innkeeper, Barbara Costa, is a font of local information. Because of the fragility of some of the antiques, families with children would not be comfortable here. Refrigerators, in-room VCRs, library; no smoking. | 271 Jones St., 95247 | 209/728–2897 or 800/692–6006 | fax 209/728–1451 | www.dunbarhouse.com | 3 rooms, 2 suites | $175–$225 | AE, MC, V | BP.

Murphys Historic Hotel and Lodge. Ulysses S. Grant signed the register here, and the room on the second floor where he slept has been preserved and can be viewed through a Plexiglas wall. Mark Twain, Horatio Alger, and Black Bart also stayed here. Rooms in the original 1855 stone-wall hotel are furnished with antiques, many of them large and hand-carved. However, these rooms are situated above the old-time saloon downstairs (whose walls still bear the bullets of many Wild West shoot-outs), and on a weekend night, raucous crowds and a live band may keep you awake until 2 AM. If you want to sleep in silence, you'll do better to get a room out back in the modern motel-style wing. Restaurant, bar, meeting room; no a/c in some rooms, no phones in some rooms, no TV in some rooms. | 457 Main St., 95247 | 209/728–3444 or 800/532–7684 | fax 209/728–1590 | www.murphyshotel.com | 29 rooms, 20 with bath | $75–$105 | AE, D, DC, MC, V.

NEVADA CITY
▼▼

Nevada City, once known as the "Queen City of the Northern Mines," is the most appealing of the northern mother-lode towns. Set in a gorge along Deer Creek, it's ringed by forested hillsides, where two of the most productive mines yielded half the gold that came out of the gold rush. The well-preserved downtown district is a national historic landmark, with iron-shutter brick buildings lining the narrow downtown streets. At one point in the 1850s Nevada City had a population of nearly 10,000, enough to support lively cultural activity. *Contact Nevada City Chamber of Commerce | 132 Main St., 95959 | 530/265–2692 or 800/655–6569 | www.nevadacitychamber.com. Nevada County Gold Online Magazine | www.ncgold.com.*

Firehouse No. 1. Built in 1851, and featuring a gingerbread-trimmed bell tower, this is one of the most-photographed buildings in the Gold Country. The museum within houses gold-rush artifacts and a Chinese joss house (temple). Also on display are relics of the ill-fated Donner Party. | 214 Main St. | 530/265–5468 | Donation | Apr.–Nov., daily 11–4; Dec.–Mar., Thurs.–Sun. 11:30–4.

Malakoff Diggings State Historic Park. This mine site stands as a symbol of human greed's effect on the landscape. Entire sides of the mountain were washed away by intense hydraulic operations in the last days of the gold rush. The park has reconstructed mining buildings as well as a museum. | 26 mi north of Nevada City, off Rte. 49 | 530/265–2740 or 800/444–7275 | www.parks.ca.gov | $2 per vehicle | Daily dawn–dusk.

Miners Foundry. Erected in 1856, the foundry produced machines for gold mining and logging. The Pelton Water Wheel, a source of power for the mines (the wheel also jump-started the hydroelectric power industry), was invented here. | 325 Spring St. | 530/265–5040 | www.minersfoundry.org | Donation | Tours by appointment; walk-in hours weekdays 9–4, by appointment weekends.

Nevada County Traction Co. Ride a narrow-gauge railway through historic sites just outside of town. As the train makes its 3-mi, 90-minute tour, you'll pass through a reconstructed Maidu Indian village and a mine and disembark at the Chinese Cemetery. | 402 Railroad Ave. | 530/265–0896 or 800/262–3090 | www.northernqueeninn.com | $8 | Mar.–Dec.; call for hrs.

Nevada Theatre. The redbrick theater, constructed in 1865, is California's oldest theater building in continuous use. Mark Twain, Emma Nevada, and many other 19th-century notables appeared on its stage. | 401 Broad St. | 530/265–6161.

✦ ON THE CALENDAR: Sept. **Constitution Day.** This weekend event, usually held early in the month, includes Civil War reenactments in Pioneer Park and a parade. | 530/273–2238.

Dec. **Victorian Christmas.** On the weekends leading up to Christmas, downtown Nevada City is closed to traffic and filled with street vendors in 19th-century costume, selling hot cider and roasted chestnuts. | 530/265–2692.

HISTORIC LODGING
Red Castle Historic Lodgings. A state landmark, this 1857 Gothic Revival mansion stands on a forested hillside overlooking Nevada City. From the brick building trimmed with white-icicle woodwork, a steep private pathway leads down through terraced gardens into town. Handsome antique furnishings and Oriental rugs decorate the rooms, and home-cooked dishes are featured at the opulent afternoon tea and morning breakfast buffet. Families with children would not be comfortable amid the expensive breakables, though there is a large suite that can accommodate older children. Library; no room phones, no room TVs, no smoking. | 109 Prospect St., 95959 | 530/265–5135 or 800/761–4766 | www.historic-lodgings.com | 4 rooms, 3 suites | $110–$165 | MC, V | BP.

OAKLAND
▼▼

On the mainland across the bay from the peninsula city of San Francisco, Oakland is an ideal port. During the gold rush, it became the primary transfer point for people and goods going between the Pacific coast and the Sierra foothills. The town incorporated in 1852, and in 1869 it became the western terminus of the Transcontinental Railroad. After the 1906 earthquake, Oakland's population nearly doubled as San Franciscans fled their ravaged city. Author Jack London was one of Oakland's most famous turn-of-the-20th-century residents. *Contact City of Oakland Official Web Site | www.oaklandnet.com. Oakland Chamber of Commerce | 475 14th St., 94612 | 510/874–4800 | www.oaklandchamber.com. Oakland History Room of the Main Library | 125 14th St., 94612 | 510/238–3222 | www.oaklandlibrary.org.*

Camron-Stanford House. Stately columns, arched windows, and a widow's walk grace the last Victorian left on the shores of Lake Merritt. Built in 1876, it was for many years the Oakland Museum. Now the house stands as an impeccably maintained period piece, filled with 19th-century furnishings, portraits, and documents. | 1418 Lakeside Dr. | 510/444–1876 | $4 | Wed. 11–4, Sun. 1–5.

Dunsmuir House and Gardens. This grand mansion was built in 1899 by Alexander White Dunsmuir (the coal baron who established the town of Dunsmuir) for his wife, Josephine. When they finally married, Alexander fell ill and died during their honeymoon. Josephine died just two years later, and it's said that her unhappy ghost walks the corridors. As there are many events held on the grounds or inside the house, it's a good idea to call before you visit. | 2960 Peralta Oaks Dr. | 510/615–5555 | www.dunsmuir.org | Free | Self-guided tours Feb.–Dec., weekdays 10–4; docent-led tours Apr.–Sept., Wed. at 11 (call to confirm).

Jack London Square. Follow the wolf tracks embedded in walkways around touristy, mall-like Jack London Square to find diamond-shape markers listing historic facts about the area. On the square at the corner of Water and Webster streets you'll find a replica of a Klondike cabin, of the sort London probably occupied as a gold seeker in Alaska (where he got the inspiration for such stories as "White Fang"). You can view the cabin from the outside, but you can't tour the interior. | Embarcadero and Broadway.

Stop in at **Heinold's First and Last Chance Saloon** (56 Jack London Sq. | 510/839–6761), which dates back to 1883, and take a look at the memorabilia on the walls. The story is that the original owner, Johnny Heinold, befriended young Jack London, underwrote his first sailboat, and urged him to continue his education. London referred to the saloon in his novels, several of which are set in Oakland and northern California.

Oakland Museum of California. The premier museum of California culture shows permanent and changing exhibitions celebrating California's art, history, and natural sciences. Permanent exhibits include a collection of artifacts from pre-colonial times to the present in the Cowell Hall of California History; a collection of art dating from the early 19th century in the Gallery of California Art; and a simulated "Walk across California," with dioramas depicting biotic zones from ocean to mountains in the Gallery of Natural Sciences. | 1000 Oak St. | 510/238–3514 or 510/238–2200 | www.museumca.org | $6; free 2nd Sun. of month. | Weds.–Sat. 10–5, Sun. noon–5; 1st Fri. of month noon–9.

Pardee House Museum. Constructed in 1869, this is the house where George Pardee, future governor of California, spent his childhood. Known as the "earthquake governor," Pardee presided over the state in 1906 when San Francisco was devastated by the great earthquake and fire. In addition to the mansion tour, there may also be other exhibits, including intimate period theater pieces presented in the salon. | 672 11th St. | 510/444–2187 | www.pardeehome.org | $5 | Call for hrs; 1-hr tours Fri. and Sat. at noon.

✦ ON THE CALENDAR: Mar. **Tall Ships.** You can step aboard vessels from the 19th century and learn about life on them from docents dressed in period costumes. | 510/814–6000.

June **Juneteenth Celebration.** Celebrating the day when Lincoln's Emancipation Proclamation was read in Galveston, Texas (June 19, 1865), the festival includes plays, music, food, and children's activities at the Oakland Museum. | 510/238–2200 or 888/625–6873.

Dec. **Holidays at Dunsmuir.** Volunteers spend more than 8,000 hours decorating the mansion and grounds of the 1899 estate in turn-of-the-20th-century Christmas style. Highlights include mansion tours, caroling, adult and children's teas, seasonal crafts, and carriage rides. Reservations are essential. | 925/275–9490 | $11–$15; $18 additional for tea service.

OCEANSIDE

One of the oldest communities in San Diego County, Oceanside was founded by the Franciscan friars who built Mission San Luis Rey de Franca. Bisected by El Camino Real, the historic road that connected California's 21 missions, Oceanside holds a handful of reminders of the Spanish and Mexican periods. *Contact California Welcome Center, Oceanside | 928 N. Coast Hwy., 92054 | 760/722–1534 | www.oceansidechamber.com. Oceanside Historical Society | 305 N. Nevada St., 92054 | 760/722–4786.*

Mission San Luis Rey. Known as the "King of the Missions," San Luis Rey was built by Franciscan friars in 1798 under the direction of Father Fermin Lasuen. The 18th and largest of the California missions, it reveals details of mission life within its well-preserved walls. The *sala* (parlor), a friar's bedroom, a weaving room, the kitchen, and a collection of religious art convey much about early mission life. The museum within has the most extensive collection of old Spanish vestments in the United States. Limited, inexpensive dormitory-style accommodations are available in the mission's retreat center. | 4050 Mission Ave. | 760/757–3651 | www.sanluisrey.org | $4 | Daily 10–4:30.

Rancho Guajome Adobe. Helen Hunt Jackson stayed in this 30-room mansion while researching her novel *Ramona* in the late 1800s. Considered the finest example of Anglo-Hispanic architecture in southern California, the beautifully furnished and restored adobe was built in 1853 with profits from the mid-19th-century cattle boom. | 3000 Guajome Lakes Rd., Vista | 760/724–4082 | $3 | Tours weekends 11, 12:30, and 2.

✦ ON THE CALENDAR: June **Intertribal Powwow.** This annual gathering of Native Americans, held on the grounds of Mission San Luis Rey, includes music, dancing, crafts, and art displays. | 760/724–8505.

OROVILLE
▼▼▼

When John Bidwell discovered gold on the Feather River in 1848, it turned out to be a major strike. Thousands flocked to the area, and Oroville was born. The gold played out before too long, and some of the miners planted citrus, nut, and olive orchards and set up cattle ranches. *Contact Oroville Area Chamber of Commerce | 1789 Montgomery St., 95965 | 530/538–2542 or 800/655–4653.*

Butte County Pioneer Museum. Get a glimpse of California's past at this museum, built in 1832 as a replica of a '49ers cabin. Don't miss the extensive arrowhead collection, the Native American baskets, or the preserved invitation card for an 1884 hanging. | 2332 Montgomery St. | 530/538–2529 | $2 | Fri.–Sun. noon–4.

Chinese Temple. This 1863 temple is a testament to the significant presence of Chinese on the California frontier. Decorated with furnishings donated by the emperor of China, there are three structures: one each devoted to Buddhism, Taoism, and Confucianism. | 1500 Broderick St. | 530/538–2496 or 530/538–2497 | $2 | Thurs.–Mon. 11–4:30, Tues.–Wed. 1–4.

✦ ON THE CALENDAR: Mar. **Old Time Fiddlers' Contest.** Music, food, and drink bring people to the old mining town in early spring. | 530/538–2542 or 530/589–4844.

PASO ROBLES
▼▼▼

When Spanish explorers first visited this countryside of tree-dotted hills in 1776, they named it *paso de robles*, or "oak-lined pass." The town was founded on cattle and agriculture by settlers including Jesse James's uncle, Drury James. Today, Paso Robles does a surprisingly good job of maintaining its dual identities: cowboy town and booming winery hub. *Contact Paso Robles Chamber of Commerce | 1225 Park St., 93446 | 805/238–0506 or 800/406–4040 | www.pasorobleschamber.com.*

El Paso de Robles Area Pioneer Museum. In this friendly museum you can see Native American handicrafts, farm and ranching equipment, furniture, clothing, and other artifacts that illustrate life in Paso Robles in the mid-1800s. | 2010 Riverside Ave. | 805/239–4556 | Free | Thurs.–Sun. 1–4.

Mission San Miguel Arcángel. Founded in 1797, this is one of the chain of 21 Spanish missions on the California coast. One of the best-preserved, the structure has been minimally restored—an intentional effort to leave the interior murals and hand-hewn beams in their original state. A self-guided tour with map is available. | 775 Mission St. | 805/467–3256 | Donations | Daily 9:30–4:15.

✦ ON THE CALENDAR: Oct. **Paso Robles Pioneer Day.** A lively parade and historic re-creations celebrate the pioneer past of this small ranching town. | 805/467–3256.

PLACERVILLE
▼▼

Once named Old Dry Diggin's, this boomtown saw so much fast new money and crime that outlaws were hanged in pairs. The settlement was accordingly renamed Hangtown. It's hard to imagine now, but in 1849 about 4,000 miners staked out every gully and hillside in town, turning it into a rip-roaring camp of log cabins, tents, and clapboard houses. It took on the name Placerville in 1854 and became an important supply center for the miners. *Contact El Dorado County Chamber of Commerce and Visitors Authority | 542 Main St., 95667 | 530/621–5885 or 800/457–6279 | www.eldoradocounty.org or www.visit-eldorado.com.*

El Dorado County Historical Museum. The museum has exhibits on local history, mining, logging, and ranching, plus displays devoted to Native American history. You'll also find a stagecoach, country store, and rolling stock from the railroad days. | 104 Placerville Dr. | 530/621–5865 | By donation | Wed.–Sat. 10–4, Sun. noon–4.

Hangtown's Gold Bug Mine. Owned by the City of Placerville, the park centers on a fully lighted mine shaft, open for self-guided touring. You'll also find exhibits and artifacts on display in the interpretive center and books and information in the gift shop. | Bedford Ave., 1 mi north of U.S. 50 | 530/642–5207 | www.goldbugpark.org | $3 | Tours mid-Apr.–Oct., daily 10–4; Nov.–mid-Apr., weekends 10–4. Gift shop Mar.–Nov., daily 10–4.

✦ ON THE CALENDAR: June **Wagon Train Week.** This historical fest celebrates the days when Placerville was called Old Dry Diggin's and was a bustling center of commercial and criminal activity. | 800/457–6279.

HISTORIC LODGING
Cary House Hotel. Constructed in 1915 of the bricks of the destroyed gold rush–era Cary House Hotel, the current Cary House is carefully decorated with period antiques. On Friday and Saturday, the innkeeper hosts a reception for guests, at which the "Hangtown Marshalls," a band of gold rush–era costumed storytellers, appear and recount tales from the town's past. Each room is individually decorated. Some kitchenettes; no smoking. | 300 Main St., 95667 | 530/622–4271 | fax 530/622–0696 | www.caryhouse.com | 26 rooms, 11 suites | $100–$125 | AE, D, MC, V | CP.

Shadowridge Ranch and Lodge. In the wooded hills outside Placerville, you'll find a beautifully restored rustic lodge complex from the 1910s. The immaculate hand-hewn log-and-stone cottages, built on foundations 140 years old, come with wood-burning stoves and are filled with interesting artifacts of ranch and lodge life, including some dramatic taxidermy. Each unit has modern amenities and its own patio. In the afternoon complimentary local wines and a huge appetizer platter are laid out. Minibars, refrigerators, hiking; no-smoking rooms. | 3700 Fort Jim Rd., 95667 | 530/295–1000 or 800/644–3498 | fax 530/626–5613 | www.shadowridgeranch.com | 4 cottages | $130–$185 | Closed Jan.–Mar. | AE, MC, V | BP.

RED BLUFF

▼▼▼

Red Bluff began to flourish as a shipping center in 1850, providing steamer service on the Sacramento River to San Francisco. The town maintains a mix of Old West toughness and late 1800s gentility; restored Victorians line the streets west of Main Street, while the downtown looks like a stage set for a western movie. *Contact Red Bluff Chamber of Commerce | 100 Main St., 96080 | 530/527–6220.*

Kelly-Griggs House Museum. This beautifully restored 1880s home holds an impressive collection of antique furniture, housewares, and clothing arranged as though a refined Victorian-era family were still in residence. A Venetian glass punch bowl sits on the dining-room table. In the upstairs parlor costumed mannequins seem eerily frozen in time (yes, this could be the set of a horror film). The museum's collection includes carved china cabinets and Native American basketry. | 311 Washington St. | 530/527–1129 | Donation | Thurs.–Sun. 1–4.

Shasta State Historic Park. Some 30 mi north of Red Bluff and a few miles west of Redding, this park is on the site of a booming gold-rush town of 2,500. Its 19 acres of half-ruined brick buildings and overgrown graveyards, accessed via trails, are a reminder of the glory days of the California gold rush. The former county courthouse building, jail, and gallows have been restored to their 1860s appearance. The Courthouse Museum (Wednesday–Sunday 10–5) now houses a visitor center, information desk, and interactive exhibits, including a storytelling ghost locked in the jail. Art galleries display paintings created between 1850 and 1950. The Blumb Bakery, which operated in Shasta until 1918, has been revived and now offers free samples and period baking demonstrations. The Litsch General Store, in operation from 1850 to 1950, is now a general merchandise museum, with many of the actual items that were sold in the store. | 15312 Rte. 299 W, Old Shasta | 530/243–8194 | $1 | Daily 10–5.

William B. Ide Adobe State Historic Park. This was the home of the first and only president of the short-lived California Republic of 1846. The park's main attraction is an adobe home built in the 1850s and outfitted with period furnishings. There are also a carriage shed, a blacksmith shop, and a small visitor center. Home tours are available on request. | 21659 Adobe Rd. | 530/529–8599 | www.ideadobe.tehama.k12.ca.us | $2 per vehicle | Daily 8 AM–sunset.

SACRAMENTO

▼▼▼

Founded by John Augustus Sutter, the owner of the mill where gold was discovered in 1848, Sacramento was the scene of a lot of important history and the key center of Gold Country commerce during the mid-19th century. This is where westward-bound emigrants truly arrived in California. In the 1860s Pony Express riders ended their nearly 2,000-mi journeys here. The Transcontinental Railroad, completed in 1869, was conceived here.

Many stately Victorians of various styles still dot the town, standing as reminders of the city's past as a wealthy center of commerce. Be sure to spend some time in Old Sacramento, a national historic landmark that encompasses 28 acres along the Sacramento River waterfront and has more than 100 restored gold rush–era buildings. The *Delta King,* a paddle wheeler that once traveled between San Francisco and Sacramento, is permanently moored here as a hotel and restaurant. *Contact Old Sacramento Events Hotline | 916/558–3912 | www. oldsacramento.com/calendar.htmlx. Old Sacramento Visitor Information Center | 1101 2nd St., at K St., 95814 | 916/442–7644 | www.oldsacramento.com. Sacramento Convention & Visitors Bureau | 1303 J St., Suite 600, 95814 | 916/264–7777 | www.sacramentocvb.org. Sacramento Museum Guide | www.sacmuseums.org. Sacramento Room at the Central Branch of the Public Library | 828 I St., 95814 | 916/264–2920 | www.saclib.org.*

California State Capitol Museum. Built with the wealth dug out of the hills during the gold rush, the Golden State's capitol was built in 1869. The lacy plasterwork of the 120-ft-high rotunda has the complexity and color of a Fabergé egg. Underneath the gilded dome are marble floors, glittering chandeliers, monumental staircases, original artwork, replicas of 19th-century state offices, and legislative chambers decorated in the style of the 1890s. Guides conduct tours of the building and the 40-acre Capitol Park, which contains a rose garden and an impressive display of camellias, Sacramento's city flower. | Capitol Mall and 10th St. | 916/324–0333 | www.parks.ca.gov or www.sacmuseums.org/capitol | Free | Daily 9–5; tours hourly 9–4.

California State Railroad Museum. Near what was once the terminus of the Transcontinental and Sacramento Valley railroads (the actual terminus was at Front and K streets), this big museum has 21 locomotives and railroad cars on display and 46 exhibits. You can walk through a post-office car and peer into cubbyholes and canvas bags of mail and enter a sleeping car that simulates the swaying on the roadbed and the flashing lights of a passing town at night. Allow at least two hours to enjoy the museum. | 125 I St. | 916/445–6645 | www.csrmf.org | $3 | Daily 10–5.

Central Pacific Passenger Depot. At this reconstructed 1876 station there's rolling stock to admire, a typical waiting room, and a small restaurant. Rides on a steam-powered train depart from the freight depot, south of the passenger depot. The train makes a 40-minute loop along the Sacramento riverfront. | 930 Front St. | 916/445–6645 | $3 (free with same-day ticket from California State Railroad Museum); train ride $5 additional | Depot daily 10–5. Train Apr.–Sept., weekends; Oct.–Dec., 1st weekend of month.

Discovery Museum. The building that holds this child-oriented museum is a replica of the 1854 city hall and waterworks. The emphasis is on interactive exhibits that combine history, science, and technology to examine the evolution of everyday life in the Sacramento area. You can sift for gold, examine a Native American thatch hut, or experience the goings-on in the print shop of the old *Sacramento Bee* newspaper. The Gold Gallery displays nuggets and veins. | 101 I St. | 916/264–7057 | www.sacmuseums.org/discovery | $5 | June–Aug., daily 10–5; Sept.–May, Tues.–Sun. 10–5.

Eagle Theater. When the Eagle opened in 1849, audiences paid between $3 and $5 in gold coin or dust to sit on rough boards and watch professional actors. This replica was constructed with the tentlike canvas and ship's-timber walls of olden times, though now there's insulation, and the bench seats are cushioned. The theater hosts programs that range from a 13-minute slide show called *City of the Plains* to puppet shows and juggling acts. | 925 Front St. | 916/323–6343 | www.parks.ca.gov | Varies depending on program | Tues.–Fri. 10–4.

Golden State Museum. Drawing from the vast collections of the California State Archives, this state-of-the-art museum vividly portrays the story of California's land, people, and politics. Exhibits utilize modern technology, but there are also scores of archival drawers that you can pull out to see the real artifacts of history and culture—such as the California State Constitution. Visit a Chinese herb shop inhabited by a holographic proprietor. Admission includes the use of an innovative personal audio guide—choose an adult or children's program and the level of detail you desire for each exhibit. | 1020 O St., at 10th St. | 916/653–7524 | www.goldenstatemuseum.org | $5 | Tues.–Sat. 10–5, Sun. noon–5.

Historic City Cemetery. Many notable figures from California's early history are buried at this cemetery created in 1849, among them John Augustus Sutter (who owned the mill where gold was discovered in 1848, sparking the California gold rush), Edwin and Margaret Crocker (of Crocker Bank fame), and Mark Hopkins (the Nob Hill silver baron). | 1000 Broadway | 916/264–5621 | www.sacmuseums.org/cemetery | Free | Nov.–Apr., daily 7–5; May–Oct., daily 7–7; call for tour times.

Huntington, Hopkins & Co. Store. This museum is a replica of the 1855 hardware store opened by Collis Huntington and Mark Hopkins, two of the Big Four businessmen who established the Central Pacific Railroad. Picks, shovels, gold pans, and other paraphernalia miners used during the gold rush are on display, along with typical household hardware and appliances from the 1880s. Some items, such as blue enamelware, wooden toys, and oil lamps, are for sale. | 113 I St. | 916/323–7234 | Hrs vary.

Old Chinatown. Also known as Sacramento "Yee Fow," this area was populated by Chinese immigrants during the gold rush. | At 3rd and 5th Sts. bounded by I and J Sts.; take I–5, exit J St. | 916/448–6465 | fax 916/448–8969.

State Indian Museum. Among the interesting displays at this well-organized museum is one devoted to Ishi, the last Yahi Indian to emerge from the mountains, in 1911. Ishi provided scientists with insight into the traditions and culture of this group of Native Americans. Arts-and-crafts exhibits, a demonstration village, and an evocative 10-minute video bring to life the multifaceted past and present of California's native peoples. | 2618 K St. | 916/324–0971 | www.parks.ca.gov or www.sacmuseums.org/indian | $1 | Daily 10–5.

Sutter's Fort. Sacramento's earliest Euro-American settlement was formerly an Indian burial ground, chosen because, at that time, it was the highest point in the Sacramento Valley. German-born Swiss immigrant John Augustus Sutter acquired the site as part of a Spanish land grant. In 1839, he built his fort and trading post, which became the destination of westward emigrants to California from the East. Today you can take a self-guided tour. Audio speakers at each stop along the way explain exhibits that include a blacksmith's shop, a bakery, a prison, living quarters, and livestock areas. Costumed docents sometimes reenact fort life, demonstrating crafts, food preparation, and firearms maintenance. | 2701 L St. | 916/445–4422 | www.parks.ca.gov or www.sacmuseums.org/suttersfort | $1 | Daily 10–5.

Wells Fargo History Museum. The histories of Wells Fargo and Sacramento intertwine at this museum, where exhibits include an original, fully restored Concord stagecoach; a functioning telegraph; and treasure boxes. | 400 Capitol Mall | 916/440–4161 | www.wellsfargohistory.com/museums | Free | Weekdays 9–5.

✦ ON THE CALENDAR: Mar. **Ishi Day.** The last surviving member of the Yahi tribe is remembered at this event held the second Saturday of March at the California State Indian Museum. | 2618 K St. | 916/324–0971.

June **Railfair.** This 10-day extravaganza brings steam locomotives, exhibits on railroading, historical reenactments, music, and entertainment to Old Sacramento. | 916/322–8485.

SAN DIEGO

▼▼

The birthplace of California, San Diego was founded in 1769 by Franciscan father Junípero Serra, who established the first of 21 Spanish missions here. Earlier European explorers had visited the San Diego area, but none had paused until Father Serra. San Diego has preserved much of its rich history, starting with the first mission and extending into the 20th century. You'll find museums, historic homes, and designated historic communities to explore here. *Contact Gaslamp Quarter Association | William Heath Davis House, 410 Island Ave., 92101 | 619/233–4692 | www.gaslamp.org. San Diego Convention and Visitors Bureau | 401 B St., Suite 1400, 92101 | 619/236–1212 | www.sandiego.org. San Diego Historical Society | Box 81825, 92138 | 619/232–6203 | www.sandiegohistory.org.*

Cabrillo National Monument. This 144-acre preserve marks the site of the first European visit to San Diego, made by 16th-century explorer Juan Rodriguéz Cabrillo. He came to this spot,

SAN DIEGO CHARACTER

Among the legendary figures who stalked San Diego's Stingaree neighborhood, lawman turned gunslinger Wyatt Earp is one of the most colorful. Later noted for his part in the gunfight at the O.K. Corral in Tombstone, Arizona, Earp arrived in San Diego in 1864 as a teenager with his parents. After hanging around southern California for a few years working as a stagecoach driver, he headed east to Dodge City, Kansas, where he made friends with Doc Holliday and Bat Masterson and established a reputation as a lawman and gambler. Following the incident in Arizona, which involved a dispute with a rival gang over his gambling concession at the Oriental Saloon, he and his wife, Josie, moved on.

The Earps arrived in booming San Diego in the mid-1880s, where Wyatt gambled and speculated heavily in real estate and saloons in the Stingaree district, now the Gaslamp Quarter. Earp frequently stayed in the Brooklyn Hotel during this time; the hotel was later incorporated into the Horton Grand Hotel. While living in San Diego, Earp owned or leased at least four saloons, including the famed Oyster Bar in the Louis Bank Building on 5th Avenue. He and Josie were very fond of horse racing and began to travel the racing circuit. According to legend, Earp enjoyed racing his horse on the beach in front of the Del Coronado hotel. His investments in real estate and mining paid off, and he and Josie were able to retire in Los Angeles, where he died in 1929.

which he called San Miguel, in 1542. The visitor center presents films and lectures about Cabrillo's voyage. Overlooking downtown from a windy promontory, a stone statue of Cabrillo appears rugged and dashing, but he is a creation of an artist's imagination—no portraits of Cabrillo are known to exist. Also within the park is the Old Point Loma Lighthouse, whose oil lamp was first lit in 1855. The light, in a brass-and-iron housing above a white wooden house, shone through a state-of-the-art lens from France and was visible from the sea 25 mi away. | 1800 Cabrillo Memorial Dr. | 619/557–5450 | www.nps.gov/cabr | $5 per vehicle, $3 per person entering on foot or by bicycle | Park daily 9–5:15 (call for later summer hrs, which vary).

Downtown. Downtown San Diego's natural attributes were evident to its original booster, Alonzo Horton (1813–1909), who bought 960 acres along the bay at 27½¢ per acre and gave away the land to those who would develop it or build houses. Within months he had sold or given away 226 city blocks. Once a railroad connection to the East was established (in 1885) the land boom was on, and the population soared from 5,000 to 35,000 in less than a decade. In 1887 the Santa Fe Depot was constructed at the foot of Broadway, two blocks from the water. Freighters chugged in and out of the harbor, and by the early 1900s the U.S. Navy had moved in. Downtown encompasses Balboa Park, the Gaslamp Quarter, and the waterfront. | From the waterfront on the west to 28th St. on the east, and from Upas St. on the north to Imperial on the south.

Gaslamp Quarter. The 16-block National Historic District, between 4th and 5th avenues from Broadway to Market Street, contains most of San Diego's Victorian-style commercial buildings. In the late 1800s, Market Street was the center of downtown, but at the turn of the 20th century downtown's commercial district moved west toward Broadway, and many of San Diego's first buildings fell into disrepair. During the early 1900s the quarter became known as the red-light Stingaree district. Highlights along 5th Avenue include the Mercantile Building (No. 822), the Louis Bank of Commerce (No. 835), and the Watts-Robinson Building (No. 903). The Tudor-style Keating Building at 432 F Street was designed by the same firm that created the famous Hotel Del Coronado. Peer into the Hard Rock Cafe, at the corner of 4th Avenue and F Street, which occupies a restored turn-of-the-20th-century tavern with a

12-ft mahogany bar and a spectacular stained-glass domed ceiling. | 4th and 5th Aves. between Island Ave. and Broadway.

The **William Heath Davis House** (410 Island Ave., at 4th Ave. | 619/233–4692), one of the first residences in town, now serves as the information center for the historic district. Davis, a San Francisco developer, had this prefab saltbox-style house shipped around Cape Horn from the East and assembled in San Diego in 1850. Two-hour tours ($2–$8) of the historic district depart from here Tuesday–Sunday 11–3 and Saturday at 11.

Junípero Serra Museum. The history of Presidio Hill from the time it was occupied by the Kumeyaay Indians until 1929 is exhibited here. Artifacts include Kumeyaay baskets, Spanish riding gear, and a painting that hung in Mission San Diego de Alcalá. The education room has hands-on investigation stations where kids can grind acorns in *metates* (stone mortars), dig for buried artifacts with archaeology tools, or dress up in period costumes. | 2727 Presidio Dr. | 619/297–3258 | www.sandiegohistory.org | $5 | Tues.–Sun. 10–4:30.

Maritime Museum. This collection of three restored ships affords a fascinating glimpse of San Diego during its heyday as a commercial seaport. The *Star of India,* an iron windjammer built in 1863, with high wooden masts and white sails flapping in the wind, has been a harbor landmark since 1927. The *Star of India* made 21 trips around the world in the late 1800s. The oldest active iron sailing ship in the world, it makes rare short excursions. The 1898 steam-driven ferryboat *Berkeley* played its most important role during the great San Francisco earthquake of 1906, when it carried thousands of passengers across San Francisco Bay to Oakland. Its ornate carved-wood paneling, stained-glass windows, and plate-glass mirrors have been restored, and its main deck serves as a floating museum, with permanent exhibits on West Coast maritime history. Anchored next to the *Berkeley* is the small Scottish steam yacht *Medea,* launched in 1904. | 1492 N. Harbor Dr. | 619/234–9153 | www.sdmaritime.com | $6 | Daily 9–8 (until 9 PM in summer).

Mission San Diego de Alcalá. The first of California's 21 missions was established by Father Junípero Serra in 1769 on Presidio Hill and moved to its present location in 1774. The present church is the fifth to be built on the site; it was reconstructed in 1931 following the outlines of the 1813 church. A small museum documents the history of the mission, exhibiting tools and artifacts from the early days. | 10818 San Diego Mission Rd. | 619/281–8449 | www. missionsandiego.com | $3 | Daily 9–4:45.

Old Town San Diego State Historic Park. Old Town, the first European settlement in southern California, had its beginnings during the Mexican period (1821–46), when the Mexican flag flew over the Presidio. Settlers were just then beginning to move down from the Presidio to what is now Old Town. A rectangular plaza along today's San Diego Avenue was the settlement's center. In 1846, during the war between Mexico and the United States, a detachment of U.S. Marines raised the Stars and Stripes over the plaza. The flag was removed once or twice, but by early 1848 Mexico had surrendered California, and the U.S. flag remained. San Diego became an incorporated city in 1850, with Old Town as its center. Some of Old Town's buildings were destroyed in a fire in 1872, but after the site became a state historic park in 1968, efforts were begun to reconstruct or restore the structures that remained. Seven of the original adobes are still intact. The state historic park comprises six square blocks. Most of the 20 historic buildings preserved or re-created by the park cluster around Old Town Plaza. The original commercial hub of Old San Diego, the Robinson-Rose House, held railroad and law offices and the first newspaper press. It now houses the park's visitor center. Living-history events are scheduled at the house each Wednesday 10–1, and walking tours depart from here daily at 1 and 2. | 4002 Wallace St. | 619/220–5422 | www.parks.ca.gov | Free | Daily 10–5.

El Campo Santo (north side of San Diego Ave. S between Arista and Ampudia Sts.), an adobe-walled cemetery established in 1849, was the burial place for many members of Old Town's founding families, as well as for some gamblers and bandits who passed through town until 1880.

Heritage Park (Heritage Park Row | 858/694–3049) contains a number of important Victorian buildings that were moved here and restored, including southern California's first synagogue, a one-room classical revival–style structure built in 1889 for Congregation Beth Israel. The most interesting of the six former residences might be the Sherman Gilbert House, which has a widow's walk and intricate carving on its decorative trim. Bronze plaques detail the history of all the houses.

La Casa de Estudillo (Mason St. between Calhoun St. and San Diego Ave.) was built on Mason Street in 1827 by the commander of the San Diego Presidio, Jose Maria Estudillo. The largest and most elaborate of the original adobe homes, it was purchased and restored in 1910 by John D. Spreckels, who advertised it in bold lettering on the side as "Ramona's Marriage Place." Spreckels' claim that the small chapel in the house was the site of the wedding in Helen Hunt Jackson's novel *Ramona* had no basis in fact.

The **San Diego Union Newspaper Historical Museum** (Twiggs St. and San Diego Ave.) is in a New England–style wood-frame house prefabricated in the eastern United States and shipped around Cape Horn in 1851. The building has been restored to replicate the newspaper's offices of 1868, when the first edition of the *San Diego Union* was printed.

A stage stop in 1867, **Seeley Stable** (Calhoun St. between Mason and Twiggs Sts. | 619/220–5427) was the transportation hub of Old Town until near the turn of the 20th century. The stable houses a collection of horse-drawn vehicles, some so elaborate that you can see where the term "carriage trade" came from. Also inside are western memorabilia, including an exhibit on the California *vaquero,* the original American cowboy, and a collection of Native American artifacts.

Old Town Trolley Tours. Two-hour guided tours visit several historic sites in Old Town and the Gaslamp Quarter, including the Whaley House, Wyatt Earp's home, and the *Star of India*. The 90-minute "Ghosts and Gravestones" tour includes a visit to Villa Montezuma, once the home of spiritualist Jesse Shepard. | Departs Old Town State Park | 619/298–8687 | www.trolleytours.com | $24–$28 | Daily; "Ghosts and Gravestones" Wed.–Sun. at dusk.

✦ ON THE CALENDAR: July **Festival of the Bells.** This is the annual celebration of the founding of the first mission in California, at Mission San Diego de Alcalá. | 619/283–7319.

Aug. **Old Town Fandango.** La Casa de Estudillo hosts an elaborate 1800s-style Mexican fiesta featuring music, food, and dance. | 619/220–5423.

Sept. **Cabrillo Festival.** A festival and reenactment celebrate the exploration of the West Coast by Juan Rodriguéz Cabrillo, at Cabrillo National Monument. | 619/222–8211.

Nov.–Jan. **Historic Holiday Homes Tour.** Historic Villa Montezuma and Marston House are adorned with period holiday decorations. | 619/232–6203.

HISTORIC DINING AND LODGING

Casa de Bandini. Mexican. Built in 1829 by a Peruvian, Juan Bandini, the house in Old Town San Diego State Historic Park reflects the lavish social life enjoyed by the Spanish dons. The building served as Commodore Stockton's headquarters during the Mexican-American War. Albert Seeley, a stagecoach entrepreneur, purchased the home in 1869, built a second story, and turned it into the Cosmopolitan Hotel, a comfortable way station for travelers on the day-long trip south from Los Angeles. Now a popular restaurant with a fountain in the patio and strolling mariachis in the dining rooms serves up giant margaritas and abundant if unremarkable Mexican dishes. Be prepared to wait for a table. | 2754 Calhoun St. | 619/297–8211 | $9–$17 | Reservations not accepted | AE, D, DC, MC, V.

Heritage Park Inn. The beautifully restored mansions in Heritage Park include this romantic 1889 Queen Anne–style bed-and-breakfast with a sweeping covered porch. Rooms range from smallish to ample, and most are bright and cheery. A full breakfast and afternoon tea are included. Some rooms share a bath. Fans, in-room data ports, cable TV, in-room VCRs, library, meeting rooms, airport shuttle; no smoking. | 2470 Heritage Park Row, 92110 | 619/299–6832 or 800/995–2490 | fax 619/299–6832 | www.heritageparkinn.com | 10 rooms, 2 suites | $120–$150 | AE, MC, V.

SAN FRANCISCO
▼▼

In the beginning, San Francisco was little more than a small, well-situated settlement. Founded by Spaniards in 1776, it was prized for its natural harbor, so commodious that "all the navies of the world might fit inside it," as one observer wrote. It was on Montgomery Street, in today's Financial District, that Sam Brannan proclaimed the historic gold discovery that took place at Sutter's Mill on January 24, 1848. The gold rush brought streams of people from across America and Europe, transforming the onetime frontier town into a cosmopolitan city almost overnight. As millions of dollars' worth of gold was panned and blasted out of the hills, a "western Wall Street" sprang up. The population of San Francisco jumped from a mere 800 in 1848 to more than 25,000 in 1850 and to nearly 150,000 in 1870. Frantic crews and passengers caught up in gold fever sometimes abandoned their ships in the harbor; today, under the foundations of many buildings along the former waterfront area (long since filled in, it is now Montgomery Street between California Street and Broadway) lay at least 100 ships abandoned in the gold frenzy.

Along with the prospectors came many other fortune seekers. Saloon keepers, gamblers, and prostitutes all flocked to the so-called Barbary Coast (now Jackson Square and the Financial District). Underground dance halls, casinos, bordellos, and palatial homes sprung up as the city grew into a world-class metropolis. Along with the quick money came a wave of violence. In 1852 the city suffered an average of two murders and one major fire each day. Diarists commented that hardly a day would pass without bloodshed in the city's estimated 500 bars and 1,000 gambling dens.

Just when gold production began to taper off, prospectors turned up a rich vein of silver in Virginia City, Nevada, in 1859. San Francisco, the nearest financial center, saw its population soar to 342,000. But it was the 1869 completion of the Transcontinental Railroad, linking the once-isolated western capital to the rest of the nation, that turned San Francisco into a major city. *Contact Chinese Culture Center | 750 Kearny St., 94108-1809 | 415/986–1822 | www.c-c-c.org. San Francisco Architectural Heritage | 415/441–3000 | www.sfheritage.org. San Francisco Convention and Visitors Bureau | 900 Market St. (lower level of Hallidie Plaza at 5th and Market Sts.) Box 429097, 94142-9097 | 415/391–2000 or 415/974–6900 | www.sfvisitor.org. San Francisco History Association | Box 31907, 94131 | 415/750–9986 | www.sanfranciscohistory.org. San Francisco Public Library | 100 Larkin St., 94102 | 415/557–4400 | sfpl.lib.ca.us.*

Barbary Coast Trail. In the latter half of the 19th century, San Francisco claimed one of the most infamous red-light districts ever to exist—a hotbed for the gold miners who poured into California drunk with quick fortunes (and frequently just as drunk from quick losses). Saloon keepers, gamblers, and prostitutes all flocked to the so-called Barbary Coast, now the Jackson Square Historic District. This area was miraculously spared during the devastation of the 1906 earthquake and remains the oldest section of commercial buildings in San Francisco. The strip of Pacific Avenue between Sansome Street and Columbus Avenue, once called "Terrific Pacific," was the heart of the action: Every building along this street once sheltered a dance hall, saloon, gambling hall, or bordello, although by 1917 the Barbary Coast had been tamed by the Red-Light Abatement Act. In October 1996, the city designated 50 sites as stops along an official, 3.8-mi-long Barbary Coast Trail. Bronze sidewalk plaques have been installed on every street corner. | Starting at the Old Mint, at 5th and Mission Sts., and running north through downtown, Chinatown, Portsmouth Square, Jackson Square, North Beach, and Fisherman's Wharf, ending at Aquatic Park.

SAN FRANCISCO'S CABLE CARS

On a foggy summer day in 1869 the inventor of the cable car, Andrew Hallidie, witnessed a terrible streetcar accident: Five horses had been hauling a heavily weighted car full of passengers up one of San Francisco's steep hills, but the animals lost their footing on the slick cobblestones and slid backward to their deaths. He set to work developing a streetcar that could be drawn mechanically along rail tracks, up and down the city's ubiquitous hills at a set speed, by gripping a constantly moving cable beneath the roadway.

Hallidie's father had invented "wire rope" in Great Britain, and the son, who moved to California in 1852, began manufacturing it in San Francisco, using it in the Gold Country to construct a suspension bridge over the American River and to pull mining cars along their tracks. With that cable, he set about building an experimental line on Clay Street, which he tested with great success at four in the morning on August 2, 1873. One month later, the line went into daily operation, and the city began installing moving cable all over town. At the peak of service 500 cable cars moved along eight lines spanning a network of 110 mi. As the 20th century progressed, cable lines gave way to bus service in many neighborhoods, and in 1947, Mayor Roger Lapham attempted to shut down the last remaining lines. Civic groups forced a measure be placed on the November ballot, and by more than a 3-to-1 margin, the city's residents voted to preserve the last remaining lines. In 1964, San Francisco's cable cars became National Historic Landmarks—the only ones that move. Today, 45 cars move along three remaining lines, covering only 10 mi.

Cable Car Museum. San Francisco's famed cable cars have been trundling up and down its steep hills since August 2, 1873, when young engineer Andrew Hallidie demonstrated his first car on Clay Street. The city once had more than a dozen cable-car barns and powerhouses. The only survivor, this 1907 redbrick structure, is an engaging stopover. Photographs, old cable cars, signposts, ticketing machines, and other memorabilia dating from 1873 document the history of these moving landmarks. The massive powerhouse wheels that move the entire cable-car system steal the show; the design is so simple it seems almost unreal. You can also go downstairs to the sheave room and check out the innards of the system. A 15-minute video describes how it all works—cables must be replaced every three to six months— or you can opt to read the detailed placards. Some of the cable cars in service today date from the 19th century, although the entire network had a complete overhaul in the early 1980s. | 1201 Mason St., at Washington St. | 415/474–1887 | www.cablecarmuseum.com | Free | Oct.–Mar., daily 10–5; Apr.–Sept., daily 10–6.

California Historical Society. The state's official historical society, founded in 1871, has amassed an awesome collection of Californiana: some 500,000 photographs; 150,000 manuscripts; thousands of books, periodicals, prints, and paintings; and gold-rush paraphernalia. The building itself is a former hardware store converted to an airy, skylighted space with a central gallery, two adjacent galleries, the North Baker Research Library, and a storefront bookstore. Exhibitions, all exploring California's history, change every two to three months. Call before visiting, as the galleries close between exhibitions. | 678 Mission St. | 415/357–1848 | www.californiahistoricalsociety.org | $3, free 1st Tues. of month | Tues.–Sat. 11–5 (galleries close between exhibitions).

Chinese Historical Society of America. The fascinating Chinese Historical Society is housed in the historic Chinatown YWCA building. Photos and graphics, accompanied by moving explanations, document the little-publicized history of Chinese immigrants and their descendants from the early 1800s to the present. Among other artifacts, you'll view an altar built in the 1880s and a parade dragon head from 1909. | 965 Clay St. | 415/391–1188 | www.chsa.org | By donation | Tues.–Fri. 11–4, weekends noon–4.

Ferry Building. The beacon of the port area, erected in 1896, has a 230-ft clock tower modeled after the campanile of the cathedral in Seville, Spain. On April 18, 1906, the four great clock faces on the tower, powered by the swinging of a 14-ft pendulum, stopped at 5:17—the moment the great earthquake struck—and stayed still for 12 months. Ferries behind the building sail to Sausalito, Larkspur, Tiburon, and the East Bay. | The Embarcadero at foot of Market St.

Fort Point. Designed to mount 126 cannons with a range of up to 2 mi, Fort Point was constructed between 1853 and 1861 to protect San Francisco from sea attack (which never came) during the Civil War. This National Historic Site is a museum filled with military memorabilia; the building has a gloomy air and is suitably atmospheric. On days when Fort Point is staffed, guided group tours and cannon drills take place. Take care when walking along the front side of the building, as it's slippery and the waves have a dizzying effect. | Marine Dr. off Lincoln Blvd. | 415/556–1693 | www.nps.gov/fopo | Free | Thurs.–Mon. 10–5.

Grant Avenue. Originally called Calle de la Fundación, Grant Avenue is the oldest street in San Francisco. Here you'll find dusty bars that evoke the Wild West flavor of the city's gold-rush years. | Between Columbus Ave. and Filbert St.

Haas-Lilienthal House. San Francisco is filled with splendid Victorian mansions, but this gabled and turreted beauty is the only one open to the public. The 1886 Queen Anne–style house, built for businessman William Haas for $18,500, was considered modest in its day. The original occupants, Alice Lilienthal, daughter of William Haas, and her husband, Samuel Lilienthal, lived here until Alice's death in 1972. One-hour guided tours of the fully furnished interior shed light on turn-of-the-20th-century tastes and lifestyles. | 2007 Franklin St., between Washington and Jackson Sts. | 415/441–3004 | www.sfheritage.org/house.html | $5 | Wed. noon–4 (last tour at 3), Sun. 11–5 (last tour at 4). Pacific Heights tours ($5) leave the house Sun. at 12:30.

Hyde Street Pier. The highlight of the pier is its collection of historic vessels, all of which can be boarded: the *Balclutha,* an 1886 full-rigged three-masted sailing vessel that sailed around Cape Horn 17 times; the *Eureka,* a side-wheel ferry; the *C. A. Thayer,* a three-masted schooner; and the *Hercules,* a steam-powered tugboat. | Hyde and Jefferson Sts. | 415/556–3002 or 415/556–0859 | www.maritime.org | $6 | Mid-May–mid-Sept., daily 9:30–5:30, mid-Sept.–mid-May, daily 9:30–5.

Jackson Square. Here was the heart of the Barbary Coast of the Gay '90s. Though most of the red-light district was destroyed in the 1906 fire, old redbrick buildings and narrow alleys recall the romance and rowdiness of the early days. Some of the city's earliest business buildings, survivors of the 1906 quake, still stand in Jackson Square, between Montgomery and Sansome streets. | Jackson Square district: between Broadway and Washington and Montgomery and Sansome Sts.

Restored 19th-century brick buildings line **Hotaling Place,** which connects Washington and Jackson streets. The lane is named for the head of the A. P. Hotaling Company whiskey distillery, which was the largest liquor repository on the West Coast in its day. A plaque on the side of the Italianate Hotaling building repeats a famous query about the structure's survival of the quake: IF, AS THEY SAY, GOD SPANKED THE TOWN FOR BEING OVER FRISKY, WHY DID HE BURN THE CHURCHES DOWN AND SAVE HOTALING'S WHISKEY?.

Levi Strauss and Co. Factory. The Levi Strauss World Headquarters is downtown, in the Financial District. In the Mission District, however, remains the original Levi Strauss factory, built in 1906 to provide sturdy work clothes to prospectors and pioneers. The factory still turns out thousands of pairs of the world-famous blue jeans annually—making it the oldest jeans-making facility in the west. | 250 Valencia St. | 415/565–9100.

Mission Dolores. Mission Dolores encompasses two churches standing side by side. The humble adobe building known as Mission San Francisco de Asís was constructed between 1782 and 1791 as the sixth of the 21 California missions founded by Father Junípero Serra. The Spanish nicknamed it Dolores after a nearby stream, Arroyo de Nuestra Señora de los Dolores (Stream of Our Lady of the Sorrows), which has long since disappeared. A survivor of three major earthquakes, it is now the oldest building in San Francisco. Architecturally, it's the simplest of all the California missions—it's also one of the most intact. The tiny chapel includes frescoes and a hand-painted wooden altar; some artifacts were brought from Mexico by mule in the late 18th century. The ceiling depicts original Ohlone Indian basket designs hand-painted with vegetable dyes by local Costanoan Indians. The roof consists of timbers lashed with rawhide; the walls are of 4-ft-thick sun-dried adobe mud. Next door to the original mission, the handsome multidomed Mission Dolores Basilica dates from 1913. English- and Spanish-language services are held in both the Mission San Francisco de Asís and in the basilica. There is a small museum, and the pretty little mission cemetery holds the graves of mid-19th-century European immigrants. The remains of an estimated 5,000 Native Americans lie in unmarked graves. | Dolores and 16th Sts. | 415/621–8203 | www.sfmuseum.org/hist5/misdolor.html or | www.missiondolores.citysearch.com | Donation; audio tour $7 | Daily 9–4.

Museum of the City of San Francisco. Historical items, maps, photographs, and other exhibits trace the history of San Francisco, including the earthquake of 1906 and the stories of Chinatown, Golden Gate Park, and the Sutro Baths. The museum is inside City Hall, a 1915 masterpiece of granite and marble modeled after St. Peter's cathedral in Rome. The 700-pound head of the *Goddess of Progress* statue, which crowned the City Hall building that crumbled during the 1906 earthquake, is on display in the museum. | Between Van Ness Ave. and Polk, Grove, and McAllister Sts. | 415/928–0289 | www.sfmuseum.org | Free | Weekdays 8–8, Sat. noon–4.

National Maritime Museum. You'll feel as if you're out to sea when you step inside this sturdy, rounded structure. Part of the San Francisco Maritime National Historical Park, which includes Hyde Street Pier, the museum exhibits ship models, maps, and other artifacts chronicling the development of San Francisco and the West Coast through maritime history. | Aquatic Park at the foot of Polk St. | 415/556–3002 | www.nps.gov/safr | Donation | Daily 10–5.

Nob Hill. Once called the "Hill of Golden Promise," this area was officially dubbed "Nob Hill" during the 1870s when "the Big Four"—Charles Crocker, Leland Stanford, Mark Hopkins, and Collis Huntington, who were involved in the construction of the Transcontinental Railroad—built their hilltop estates. The lingo is thick from this era: those on the hilltop were referred to as "nabobs" (originally meaning a provincial governor from India) and "swells," and the hill itself was called Snob Hill, a term that survives to this day. By 1882 so many estates had sprung up on Nob Hill that Robert Louis Stevenson called it "the hill of palaces." But the 1906 earthquake and fire destroyed all the palatial mansions, except for portions of the Flood brownstone. | The top of the hill is bordered approximately by California, Mason, Jones, and Washington streets.

Now serving as the home of the **Pacific Union Club** (1000 California St.), the former home of silver baron James Flood cost a whopping $1.5 million in 1886, when even a stylish Victorian cost less than $20,000. All that cash did buy some structural stability. The Flood residence (to be precise, its shell) was the only Nob Hill mansion to survive the 1906 earthquake and fire. The Pacific Union Club, a bastion of the wealthy and powerful, purchased the house in 1907 and had it renovated. The ornate fence design dates from the mansion's construction.

Pioneers Monument. The city's largest historical monument stands just north of the San Francisco Main Library. The monument was completed in 1894 and stood firm in the 1906 earthquake and fire, even when City Hall was leveled. Historians believe that a time capsule is buried at the base—but nobody knows for sure. The monument's 30-ft-high granite shaft is topped by a bronze figure whose spear, shield, and bear symbolize California. Figures and bas-reliefs at the base depict scenes from early California and important personalities from that time, such as James Fremont, James Lick, Sir Francis Drake, John Sutter, and Father Junípero Serra. | Fulton St. between Larkin and Hyde Sts.

Portsmouth Square. Captain John B. Montgomery raised the American flag here in 1846, claiming the Bay Area from Mexico. The square—a former potato patch—was the plaza for Yerba Buena, the Mexican settlement that was renamed San Francisco. Robert Louis Stevenson, the author of *Treasure Island,* lived on the edge of Chinatown in the late 19th century and often visited the square, chatting up the sailors who hung out here. Bruce Porter designed the bronze galleon that sits on top of a 9-ft granite shaft in the northwestern corner of the square in honor of the writer. With its pagoda-shape structures, Portsmouth Square is a favorite spot for morning tai chi and afternoon Chinese chess. | Bordered by Walter Lum Pl. and Kearny, Washington, and Clay Sts.

Presidio. Part of the Golden Gate National Recreation Area, the Presidio was a military post for more than 200 years. Don Juan Bautista de Anza and a band of Spanish settlers first claimed the area in 1776. It became a Mexican garrison in 1822 when Mexico gained its independence from Spain; U.S. troops forcibly occupied the Presidio in 1846. The U.S. Sixth Army was stationed here until October 1994, when the coveted space was transferred into civilian hands. Today, after much controversy, the area is being transformed into a self-sustaining national park with a combination of public, commercial, and residential projects. | Between the Marina and Lincoln Park | 415/561–4323 | www.nps.gov/prsf.

National Park Service employees at the **William P. Mott Jr. Visitor Center** (Montgomery St. between Lincoln Blvd. and Sheridan Ave. | 415/561–4323) dispense maps, brochures, and schedules for guided walking and bicycle tours, along with information about the Presidio's past, present, and future.

Just west of the Main Post in the Presidio is the cypress-shaded, 19th-century **San Francisco National Cemetery** (415/561–4323). The final resting place for some 30,000 American servicemen and -women includes some headstones that predate the Civil War. Call for information about free monthly docent-led walking tours of the cemetery.

San Francisco Brewing Company. Built in 1907, this pub looks like a museum piece from the Barbary Coast days. An old upright piano sits in the corner under the original stained-glass windows. Take a seat at the mahogany bar and look down at the white-tile spittoon. In an adjacent room look for the handmade copper brewing kettle used to produce a dozen beers—with names like Pony Express—by means of old-fashioned gravity-flow methods. | 155 Columbus Ave. | 415/434–3344 | www.sfbrewing.com | Daily noon–1 AM.

Seymour Pioneer Museum. The small museum of the Society of California Pioneers, which was founded by pre-gold rush–era Californians and is perpetuated by their descendants, houses permanent exhibits that display clothing, artifacts, paintings, and prints from the years before 1849. The society also holds more than 50,000 archival photographs from the period, and there is a 10,000-volume research library on site, which includes John Sutter's diaries. Call in advance to find out about upcoming exhibits at the museum or to inquire about access to the archives. | 300 4th St. | 415/957–1849 | www.californiapioneers.org | $3 | Wed.–Fri. 10–4, 1st and 3rd Sat. of month 10–4; library Wed. 10–noon and 1–4 by appointment only.

Telegraph Hill. Telegraph Hill got its name from one of its earliest functions—in 1853 it became the location of the first Morse Code signal station. Flower-lined steps flanking the hill make the climb up more than tolerable. The Hill rises from the east end of Lombard Street to a height of 284 ft and is capped by Coit Tower. | Between Lombard, Filbert, Kearny, and Sansome Sts.

Tin How Temple. Day Ju, one of the first three Chinese to arrive in San Francisco, dedicated this temple to the Queen of the Heavens and the Goddess of the Seven Seas in 1852. In the third-floor temple's entryway, elderly ladies can often be seen preparing "money" to be burned as offerings to various Buddhist gods or as funds for ancestors to use in the afterlife. The gold-leaf wood carving suspended from the ceiling depicts the north and east sides of the sea, which Tin How (Tien Hau or Tien Hou in Cantonese) and other gods protect. A statue of Tin How sits in the middle of the back of the temple, flanked by a red lesser god and by a green one. Photography is not permitted, and you are asked not to step onto the balcony. | 125 Waverly Pl. | No phone | Donation | Daily 9–4.

Union Square. The heart of San Francisco's downtown since 1850, the 2½-acre square takes its name from the violent pro-union demonstrations staged here prior to the Civil War. At center stage, the *Victory Monument,* by Robert Ingersoll Aitken, commemorates Commodore George Dewey's victory over the Spanish fleet at Manila in 1898. The 97-ft Corinthian column, topped by a bronze figure symbolizing naval conquest, was dedicated by Theodore Roosevelt in 1903 and withstood the 1906 earthquake. | Between Powell, Stockton, Post, and Geary Sts.

Wells Fargo Bank History Museum. There were no formal banks in San Francisco during the early years of the gold rush, and miners often entrusted their gold dust to saloon keepers. In 1852 Wells Fargo opened its first bank in the city, and the company established banking offices in the mother-lode camps, using stagecoaches and Pony Express riders to service the burgeoning state. The museum displays samples of nuggets and gold dust from mines, a mural-size map of the mother lode, original art by western artists Charles M. Russell and Maynard Dixon, mementos of the poet bandit Black Bart ("Po8," as he signed his poems), and an old telegraph machine on which you can practice sending codes. The showpiece is the red Concord stagecoach, the likes of which carried passengers from St. Joseph, Missouri, to San Francisco in three weeks during the 1850s. | 420 Montgomery St. | 415/396–2619 | www.wellsfargohistory. com | Free | Weekdays 9–5.

HISTORIC DINING AND LODGING

Garden Court. American. This quintessential Old San Francisco restaurant is in the Palace Hotel, the city's oldest lodging. In daytime, light splashes through the Belle Epoque dining room's beautiful 1909 stained-glass ceiling and against the towering Ionic columns and crystal chandeliers. The draw here is not the lunch menu, but rather the truly extravagant Sunday buffet brunch, one of the city's great traditions. Otherwise, if you can't make it to the Palace for breakfast or lunch, try the Saturday-afternoon high tea. | Market and New Montgomery Sts. | 415/546–5011 | Reservations essential | No dinner | $28–$42 | AE, D, DC, MC, V.

Hotel Majestic. Built in Edwardian style as a private home for railroad magnate Milton Schmitt, the 1902 Majestic is today one of San Francisco's most elegant small hotels. Complimentary wine and hors d'oeuvres are served afternoons in the exquisite lobby, replete with glistening granite stairs, antique chandeliers, plush Victorian chairs, and a white-marble fireplace. The hotel's Perlot restaurant has a romantic turn-of-the-20th-century San Francisco feel and an American prix-fixe menu. Glass cases in the bar house a stunning collection of rare butterflies from Africa and New Guinea. Guest rooms and baths are very comfortable and have a combination of French and English antiques and modern amenities. The hotel holds a certificate of recognition for architectural preservation and restoration from the California Heritage Council. Restaurant, room service, in-room data ports, cable TV, bar, dry cleaning, laundry service, parking (fee). | 1500 Sutter St., 94109 | 415/441–1100 or 800/869–8869 | fax 415/ 673–7331 | www.thehotelmajestic.com | 49 rooms, 9 suites | $170 | AE, D, DC, MC, V.

Palace Hotel. This landmark hotel—with a guest list that has included Thomas Edison, Amelia Earhart, and 10 American presidents—was the world's largest and most luxurious hotel when it opened in 1875. Though it survived the tremors of the 1906 earthquake (which sent guest Enrico Caruso into the street wearing nothing but a towel and vowing never to return to San Francisco), the fires that followed gutted the hotel. It reopened in 1909, and today the splendid building includes a stunning entryway. Rooms, with twice-daily maid service and nightly turndown, have high ceilings, antique reproduction furnishings, and marble bathrooms with luxury bath products. 3 restaurants, room service, in-room data ports, minibars, cable TV with movies, indoor lap pool, health club, bar, dry cleaning, laundry service, concierge, business services, meeting rooms, parking (fee); no-smoking rooms. | 2 New Montgomery St., 94105 | 415/512–1111 | fax 415/543–0671 | www.sfpalace.com | 518 rooms, 34 suites | $210–$260 | AE, D, DC, MC, V.

Tadich Grill. Seafood. Owners and locations have changed since Tadich opened in 1849, but the 19th-century atmosphere remains, largely because many of the original fixtures came along when the restaurant moved to its current space. Simple sautés are the best choices, or cioppino during crab season, petrale sole during sole season, and an old-fashioned house-made tartar sauce anytime. The crusty, white-coated waiters are a reminder of good, old-fashioned service. | 240 California St. | 415/391–2373 | Reservations not accepted | Closed Sun. | $11–$24 | MC, V.

SAN JOSE
▼▼

In 1777 San Jose was the place where crops blossomed and cattle fattened before being sent to soldiers stationed at the presidios in San Francisco and Monterey. The farms grew into a thriving town, and, in 1850, San Jose became the state's first capital city. In the Hensley Historic District, a National Historic District, 250 structures built between 1865 and 1930 stand on a street grid laid out in 1848. *Contact Preservation Action Council of San Jose | Box 2287, 95109 | 408/998–8105 | www.preservation.org. San Jose Convention and Visitors Bureau | 125 S. Market St., 3rd floor 95113 | 800/726–5673, 408/295–2265, or 408/295–9600 | www.sanjose.org. San Jose Room of the San Jose Public Library | 180 W. San Carlos St., 95113-2096 | 408/277–4846 | www.sjpl.lib.ca.us. Victorian Preservation Association of Santa Clara Valley | Box 586, 95106-0586 | www.vpa.org.*

Fallon House. San Jose's seventh mayor, Thomas Fallon, built this Victorian mansion in 1855. The house's period-decorated rooms can be viewed on a 90-minute tour that includes the Peralta Adobe and a screening of a video about the two houses. | 175 W. St. John St. | 408/993–8182 | www.historysanjose.org | $6 (includes admission to Peralta Adobe) | Guided tours weekends noon–5.

History San Jose. Southeast of the city center, occupying 25 acres of Kelley Park, this outdoor "museum" highlights the history of San Jose and the Santa Clara Valley. You can see 28 historic and reconstructed buildings, hop a historic trolley, observe letterpress printing, and buy ice cream and candy at O'Brien's. On weekdays the grounds are open but most buildings are closed. | 1650 Senter Rd. | 408/287–2290 | www.historysanjose.org | $6 | Daily noon–5; call for weekend tour times.

Peralta Adobe. California pepper trees shade the last remaining structure (circa 1797) from the pueblo that was once San Jose. The whitewashed two-room home has been furnished to interpret life in the first Spanish civil settlement in California and during the Mexican rancho era. | 184 W. St. John St. | 408/993–8182 | www.historysanjose.org | $6 (includes admission to Fallon House) | Guided tours weekends noon–5.

Winchester Mystery House. This is on the National Register of Historic Places, is 3 mi west of downtown. Convinced that spirits would harm her if construction ever stopped, firearms heiress and house owner Sarah Winchester constantly added to her house. For 38 years, beginning in 1884, she kept hundreds of carpenters working around the clock, creating a bizarre 160-room Victorian labyrinth with stairs going nowhere and doors that open into walls. The brightly painted house is a favorite family attraction, and though the grounds are no longer dark and overgrown, the place retains an air of mystery. Explore the house on the 65-

minute estate tour and the 50-minute behind-the-scenes tour, or come on a Friday the 13th for an evening flashlight tour. Tours usually depart every 20–30 minutes. | 525 S. Winchester Blvd., between Stevens Creek Blvd. and I–280 | 408/247–2101 | www.winchestermysteryhouse.com | Estate tour $16.95, behind-the-scenes tour $13.95, combination ticket $23.95 | Daily 9–5:30 (last admission at 5).

HISTORIC LODGING

Hensley House. This is the only B&B in downtown San Jose, with rooms in neighboring Victorian and Craftsman-style houses. The inn sits in the middle of the Hensley Historic District. The antiques-decorated rooms have thoughtful touches like robes, feather mattresses, and down comforters and pillows. Some rooms have full kitchens. Breakfast frequently includes chorizo and eggs or quiche and homemade bread; dine in the tranquil breakfast room or on the patio. In-room data ports, some in-room hot tubs, some kitchenettes, minibars, refrigerators, cable TV, in-room VCRs, outdoor hot tub, laundry services, concierge, Internet, business services; no smoking. | 456 N. 3rd St., 95112 | 408/298–3537 or 800/498–3537 | fax 408/298–4676 | www.hensleyhouse.com | 11 rooms, 4 suites | $140–$300 | AE, D, DC, MC, V | BP.

SAN JUAN CAPISTRANO
▼▼▼

One of the few noteworthy historical towns in southern California, San Juan Capistrano is best known for its mission. A small historic district, Los Rios, lies along the west side of the railroad tracks and Amtrak station. *Contact San Juan Capistrano Historical Society | 31831 Los Rios St., 92675 | 949/493–8444 | www.sjchistoricalsociety.com.*

Mission San Juan Capistrano. Founded in 1776 by Father Junípero Serra, this was the major Roman Catholic outpost between Los Angeles and San Diego. Though the original Great Stone Church (1806) is permanently supported by scaffolding, many of the mission's adobe buildings have been preserved to illustrate mission life, with exhibits of an olive millstone, tallow ovens, tanning vats, metalworking furnaces, and padres' living quarters. Costumed docents portray early California characters, including founding padres, Native Americans, soldiers, weavers, and miners. The bougainvillea-covered Serra Chapel is believed to be the oldest building standing in California. | Camino Capistrano and Ortega Hwy. | 949/234–1300 | www.missionsjc.com | $6 | Daily 8:30–5.

✦ ON THE CALENDAR: Mar. **Swallow's Day Festival.** Celebration of the annual spring arrival of the swallows at Mission San Juan Capistrano includes traditional bell ringing, music and dance, and living-history characters. | 949/234–1300.

HISTORIC DINING

El Adobe de Capistrano. Mexican. Portions of this building date back to 1797. Consisting of two adobes, the northern portion was the home of Miguel Yorba, and the southern portion was the court and jail. Today the bar occupies the Miquel Yorba Adobe and the dungeon-like jail cells house the wine cellar. You are served what the restaurant calls "early California cuisine"—essentially Cal-Mex standards—in several large dining rooms (the restauraunt does a lot of banquet business). | 31891 Camino Capistrano | 949/830–8620 | AE, D, DC, MC, V.

The Ramos House Cafe. American. One of 20 adobes built in the 1790s on Los Rios Street, the café is the oldest continuously occupied residence in California. The current owner, Steve Rios, is a descendant of Feliciano Rios, who came to San Juan Capistrano in 1776. The focus at this highly regarded spot is on locally grown organic produce; the restaurant grows its own herbs, fruit, and other ingredients. Breakfast is a speciality. | 31752 Los Rios St. | 949/443–1342 | No Dinner. Closed Mon. | $9–$15 | AE, D, MC, V.

SAN LUIS OBISPO

▼▼

While these days it might be hard to imagine, the valley here was once crawling with bears—so much so that on their first trip from San Diego in search of Monterey Bay, Don Gaspar de Portola and his men named it San Luis Obispo, the "Valley of the Bears." One hunting trip by Portola's men is reported to have procured 9,000 pounds of meat, and it was at the site of their prosperous return that the local mission was founded in 1772. *Contact San Luis Obispo County Historical Society | Box 1391, 93406 | 805/543–0638 | www.slochs.org. San Luis Obispo Chamber of Commerce | 1039 Chorro St., 93406 | 805/781–2670 | www.slochamber.org.*

Mission La Purísima Concepción. Founded in 1787, this is the most fully restored mission in the state. Its stark and still-remote setting 60 mi south of San Luis Obispo powerfully evokes the lives of California's Spanish settlers. Docents lead tours twice daily, at 10 and 1, and displays illustrate the secular and religious activities at the mission. From March through October the mission hosts special events including crafts demonstrations by costumed docents. | 2295 Purisima Rd., off Mission Gate Rd., Lompoc | 805/733–3713 | $2 per vehicle | Daily 9–5.

Mission San Luis Obispo de Tolosa. Established in 1772, the mission overlooks San Luis Obispo Creek and holds a museum exhibiting artifacts of the Chumash Indians and early Spanish settlers. | 751 Palm St. | 805/543–6850 | www.thegrid.net/slomission | $2 suggested donation | Late May–Dec., daily 9–5; Jan.–late May, daily 9–4.

San Luis Obispo County Museum and History Center. Across from the mission, this museum presents revolving exhibits on county history—Native American life, California ranchos, railroads, etc. A separate kids' room captivates the younger set with themed activities and the chance to earn prizes. | 696 Monterey St. | 805/543–0638 | $2 | Daily 9–5.

SANTA BARBARA

▼▼

For thousands of years the Chumash Indians lived on this idyllic stretch of coastline, more or less isolated by mountains and sea. The Spanish arrived in 1542 and again in 1602, with Sebastian Vizcaino's party, but the city was not founded until almost 200 years later, when the foundation of the mission was laid. Santa Barbara remained a slow-moving pueblo until wealthy easterners discovered its sublime climate in the 1800s. They quickly developed the town into a health resort and playground for the rich. *Contact Santa Barbara Conference and Visitors Bureau | 12 E. Carrillo St., 93101 | 805/966–9222 or 800/549–5133 | www.santabarbaraca. com. Santa Barbara Historical Society | 136 E. De la Guerra St., 93101 | 805/966–1601.*

Carriage and Western Art Museum. Here is the country's largest collection of old horse-drawn vehicles—everything from polished hearses and police transport buggies to old stagecoaches and circus vehicles. One of the city's hidden gems, this is a wonderful place to help history come alive for children. | 129 Castillo St. | 805/962–2353 | www.carriagemuseum.org | Free | Weekdays 7:30–3:30, Sun. 1–4.

El Presidio State Historic Park. Founded in 1782, El Presidio was one of four military strongholds established by the Spanish along the coast of California. El Cuartel, the adobe guardhouse, is the oldest building in Santa Barbara and the second oldest in California. | 123 E. Cañon Perdido St. | 805/965–0093 | www.sbthp.org | Free | Daily 10:30–4:30.

Mission Santa Barbara. The architecture and layout of this mission, established in 1786, evolved from a few adobe-brick buildings with thatch roofs to more permanent edifices as its population burgeoned. An earthquake in 1812 destroyed the third church built on the site. Its

THE FRUIT OF THE MISSIONS

The grape vines and olive and almond trees that are an integral part of California's land-scape today are fairly recent arrivals in the region. All three came to the New World with the Franciscan friars, whose missions doubled as farms that fed the community and pro-duced surplus for trade.

If Alta California had Mexico's heat or the Northwest's rain, the missionaries would have had to rely on native food sources and farming techniques. But because the climate between San Diego and Sonoma is nearly identical to that of the Franciscans' native Mediter-ranean, they were able to re-create the growing systems they had used in Spain. They built dams and gravity-fed irrigation ditches (*acequias*) to divert mountain streams into the warm and arid lowlands where the missions stood.

To those newly green lands they brought what today are California's top crops: olives, grapes, almonds, and oranges, as well as pears, plums, apricots, peaches, walnuts, figs, and pomegranates. Grapes arrived from Spain on the ship *San Antonio* in 1778. They were first planted at San Juan Capistrano (which came to be known as "Viña Madre," or the "Mother Vineyard") then at San Diego and San Gabriel. Most experts agree that today's mission olives all come from the original planting at San Diego, whose trees were imported from Spain in 1769. Almonds arrived in California around the same time but took longer to flourish. The trees, native to Persia and Egypt, suffered in the coastal fog and struggled until the 19th century, when they were moved into appropriately hot, dry inland valleys.

When the missions were secularized in the mid-1800s, their land went into private hands—and so did their orchards and vineyards. In some cases, as at San Rafael, trees and vines were uprooted and replanted at surrounding *rancherias,* making it extremely difficult for modern horticulturists to trace their provenance. Still, some specimens have withstood the centuries, particularly around Lompoc's Mission La Purísima Concepción, perhaps because it (unlike most other missions) did not spawn a modern metropolis. In its once-extensive orchard, one original pear tree remains. It has since been joined by trees from other missions, transplanted there during the Great Depression by the Civil-ian Conservation Corps. Today, the grounds shelter age-old heritage apples, plums, figs, apricots, pomegranates, and wild cherries. And nearby, on the mission's former rancho in Jalama, a grove of 200-year-old olives trees has been discovered. The grove still bears a crop each year.

While most other original plantings have died, their legacy thrives nearly everywhere you look: in the orchards of Gold Country, the olive groves lining the Central Valley, the lemon trees in backyards from Napa to Palm Springs, and in the single, thick, twisting grapevine that shades the entire courtyard at Mission San Gabriel.

replacement, the present structure, is still a Catholic church, though during the post-mission era it also served as a boys' school and a seminary. | 2201 Laguna St. | 805/682–4713 | www.sbmission.org | $4 | Daily 9–5.

Santa Barbara Historical Museum. The historical society's museum exhibits decorative and fine arts, furniture, costumes, and documents from the town's past. Adjacent is the Gled-hill Library, a collection of books, photographs, maps, and manuscripts. | 136 E. De La Guerra St. | 805/966–1601 | Museum $3 suggested donation; library $2–$5 per hr for research | Museum Tues.–Sat. 10–5, Sun. noon–5; library Tues.–Fri. 10–4, 1st Sat. of month 10–1:30. Free guided tours Wed. and Sat. at 11:30, Sun. at 1:30.

✦ **ON THE CALENDAR:** July–Aug. **Old Spanish Days Fiesta.** This vibrant four-day event celebrates local Spanish, Indian, and Old West history and culture with a rodeo, parade, daily fiestas, and music. | 805/962–8101 | www.oldspanishdays-fiesta.org.

SANTA CLARA
▼▼

Franciscan fathers came to Santa Clara in 1777 to establish the eighth of California's 21 missions. A number of unsuccessful gold miners settled here, and in 1852 Santa Clara incorporated as a city. *Contact Santa Clara Chamber of Commerce and Convention and Visitors Bureau | 1850 Warburton Ave., 95050 | 408/244–8244 | www.santaclara.org.*

De Saisset Art Gallery and Museum. Santa Clara University, founded in 1851 by Jesuits, was California's first college. The campus's gallery has a permanent collection that includes California mission artifacts. There's also a full calendar of temporary exhibits. | 500 El Camino Real | 408/554–4528 | www.scu.edu/desaisset | Free | Tues.–Sun. 11–4.

Harris-Lass Historic Museum. Built in 1864 on Santa Clara's last farmstead, the restored house, summer kitchen, and barn convey a sense of life on the farm from the early 1900s through the 1930s. Guided tours take place every half hour until 3:30. | 500 El Camino Real | 408/554–4023 | www.scu.edu/visitors/mission | Free | Daily 1–sunset for self-guided tours.

Mission Santa Clara de Asís. In the center of Santa Clara University's campus is the eighth of 21 California missions founded under the direction of Father Junípero Serra. The mission's present site was the fifth chosen, after the first four were flooded by the Guadalupe River and destroyed by earthquakes. In 1926 the permanent mission chapel was destroyed by fire. Roof tiles of the current building, a replica of the original, were salvaged from earlier structures, which dated from the 1790s and 1820s. Early adobe walls and a spectacular rose garden with 4,500 roses—many classified as antiques—remain as well. Part of the wooden Memorial Cross, from 1777, is set in front of the church. | 500 El Camino Real | 408/554–4023 | www.scu.edu/visitors/mission | Free | Daily 1–sundown for self-guided tours.

SONOMA
▼▼

The oldest town in the area that is now California's premier wine country had a long history before the first chardonnay grapes were ever planted here. In the early 1800s Franciscan fathers from Mexico established the last of California's 21 missions here. Many Old West adobe and false-front buildings have long since been converted to hotels, restaurants, and shops. *Contact Sonoma Valley Visitors Bureau | 453 1st St. E, 95476 | 707/996–1090 | www.sonomavalley.com.*

Fort Ross State Historic Park. Completed in 1821, this was Russia's major fur-trading outpost in California. The Russians brought Aleut hunters down from Alaska, and by 1841 the area was depleted of seals and otters. The Russians then sold their post to John Sutter, later of gold-rush fame. After the Bear Flag Revolt of 1846 the land fell under U.S. control, becoming part of California in 1850. The state park service has reconstructed Fort Ross, including its Russian Orthodox chapel, a redwood stockade, the officers' barracks, and a blockhouse. The excellent museum here documents the history of the fort and some of the north coast of California. | 9 mi north of Sonoma on U.S. 101, then 35 mi northwest on Rte. 116 to Jenner, then 9 mi north on Rte. 1 | 707/847–3286 | www.parks.ca.gov | $3 per vehicle | Daily 10–4:30.

Mission San Francisco Solano. In Sonoma's central plaza, the mission now houses a museum with a fine collection of 19th-century watercolors. The surrounding Sonoma State Historic Park includes the Sonoma Barracks and the home of Sonoma's founder, General Mariano Guadalupe Vallejo. This is where the Bear Flag Revolt of 1846 took place. Guided tours of the Vallejo house are offered weekdays and some weekends. | 114 Spain St. E | 707/938–1519 | $2 | Daily 10–5.

SONORA

▼▼▼

Miners from Mexico founded Sonora in 1848 and made it the biggest town in the mother lode. Following a period of racial and ethnic strife, the Mexican settlers moved on, and Yankees built the commercial city that is visible today. Sonora's historic downtown section sits atop the Big Bonanza Mine, one of the richest in the state. Another mine, on the site of nearby Sonora High School, yielded 990 pounds of gold in a single week in 1879. Reminders of the gold rush are everywhere in the town's historic heart, in prim Victorian houses, typical Sierra-stone storefronts, and awning-shaded sidewalks. *Contact City of Sonora | 94 N. Washington St., 95370 | 209/532–4541 | www.sonoraca.com. Tuolomne County Chamber of Commerce | 222 S. Shepherd St., 95370 | 209/532–4212 | www.tcchamber.com. Tuolomne County Historical Society | 158 W. Bradford St., 95370 | 209/532–1317 | www.tchistory.org.Tuolomne County Visitors Bureau | 55 W. Stockton Rd., Box 4020, 95370 | 800/446–1333 | www.thegreatunfenced.com.*

Angels Camp. This gold-rush town is famed chiefly for its jumping-frog contest (third weekend in May), inspired by Mark Twain's story "The Jumping Frog of Calaveras County," written in 1865. The writer reputedly heard the story of the jumping frog from Ross Coon, proprietor of Angels Hotel, which has been in operation since 1856. Today, the town retains much of its 19th-century appearance, with restored gold rush–era buildings and wood plank sidewalks. | 18 mi north of Sonora on Rte. 49.

At the **Angels Camp Museum** (753 S. Main St. | 209/736–2963 | $2) you'll find lots of gold rush–era relics, including photos, rocks, petrified wood, mineral specimens, and old mining equipment. The carriage house out back holds 25 horse-drawn carriages, most notable among them a hearse. Open daily Mar.–Nov., the museum is closed in December and open only on weekends in January and February.

Tuolumne County Museum and History Center. Constructed in 1857 and reconstructed after a fire 1865, the building that houses the museum served as a jail until 1951. It contains a jail museum; vintage firearms, household items, and clothing; a case with gold nuggets; exhibits on logging, mining, and irrigation; and the libraries of a historical society and a genealogical society. | 158 W. Bradford St. | 209/532–1317 | Free | Sun.–Mon. 9–4, Tues.–Fri. 10–4, Sat. 10–3:30.

✦ ON THE CALENDAR: May **Mother Lode Roundup Parade and Rodeo.** On Mother's Day weekend the town of Sonora celebrates its gold-mining, agricultural, and lumbering history with a parade, rodeo, entertainment, and food. | Motherlode Fairgrounds, 220 Southgate Dr. | 209/532–7428 or 800/446–1333.

TRUCKEE

▼▼▼

The Truckee River Basin has been the overland crossing route for westward immigration into California since the Stevens Party successfully crossed the Sierra Crest here in 1844. In the fall of 1846, the Donner Party got trapped by early snows just west of what is now Truckee, and causing a sharp drop-off in westward migration until the gold rush of 1849. In the 1860s, the Truckee River attracted gold miners and prospectors, but when the ore proved to be poor, many followed the river to present-day Tahoe City. Around 1863, the town of Truckee was

TO CALIFORNIA, WITH LOVE

For almost 30 years in the early 19th century, more than a century before the cold war, Russia had a colony in what would become the state of California. Russia had been pushing its influence eastward for hundreds of years, since the time of Ivan the Terrible. By the time Ivan Kuskov of the Russian-American Company first landed at Bodega Bay around the turn of the 19th century, the Russians had crossed Siberia, established settlements on the Aleutian Islands and in Alaska, and intended to press on down the North American continent.

Twenty-five Russians and 80 Alaskans arrived in March 1812 at what would become Fort Ross and started building a stockade. Comany officers lived within the stockade, while the native Alaskan laborers lived outside in a separate village. As intermarriage between Russians and Alaskans increased, a village of more than 60 buildings appeared near the stockade. The settlement came to be known as Fort Ross, for "Rossiya," another name for Russia. Hunting the waters from the Baja peninsula to the present-day Oregon border, the Alaskans used traditional kayaks and atlatls. The sea-otter population was seriously depleted by 1820, and the colony had to rely more heavily on farming, ranching, and shipbuilding to support itself. Losing thousands of rubles every year, they finally sold out to John Sutter in 1841 for some $30,000 in wheat installments, paid over three years. Today, the Russian foray into California is commemorated at Fort Ross State Historic Park, north of Jenner.

officially established, and by 1868, it went from a stage-coach resting stop to a station for trains bound for the Pacific via the new Transcontinental Railroad. Old West facades line the main street of Truckee, and freight and passenger trains still stop every day at the depot right in the middle of town. *Contact Town of Truckee | 10183 Truckee Airport Rd., 96161 | 530/ 582–7700 | www.townoftruckee.com. Truckee Chamber of Commerce | 10065 Donner Pass Rd., 96161 | 530/587–2757 | www.truckee.com. Truckee-Donner Historical Society | Box 893, 96160 | 530/582– 0893 | truckeehistory.tripod.com.*

Big Bend Visitor Center. The center occupies a state historic landmark 10 mi west of Donner Summit. This area has been on major cross-country routes for centuries; Native Americans crossed through, trading acorns and salt for pelts, obsidian, and other materials. Between 1844 and 1860, more than 200,000 emigrants traveled to California along the Emigrant Trail, which passed nearby; you can see ruts left by wagon wheels scraping the famously hard granite. Later, the nation's first Transcontinental Railroad ran through here (and still does), as did the old national road (now I–80). Exhibits in the visitor center explore the area's transportation history. There are also occasional exhibits focusing on natural history. Take the Rainbow–Big Bend exit off I–80. | Old U.S. 40, Soda Springs | 530/426–3609 or 530/587–3558 | www.r5.fs.fed.us/tahoe/big_bend/ | Free | Thurs.–Mon. 8:30–5.

Donner Memorial State Park and Emigrant Trail Museum. The park commemorates the sojourn of the Donner Party, a group of 89 westward-bound pioneers who were trapped in the Sierra in the winter of 1846–47. In snow 22 ft deep, only half survived—⅔ of the women and ⅓ of the men—some by resorting to cannibalism and others by eating animal hides. The museum's hourly slide show details the Donner Party's plight; other displays relate the stories of other settlers and of railroad development through the Sierra. | Off I–80, 2 mi west of Truckee | 530/582–7892 | ceres.ca.gov/sierradsp/donner.html | Museum $2 | Daily 9–4.

Old Truckee Jail Museum. First opened in 1875, this was the longest-operating jail in California until 1964. Today, you can tour the cells and see exhibits mounted by the town's histor-

TRAGEDY ON THE OREGON TRAIL

The Oregon Trail, the first viable route for wagon trains crossing the continent, brought thousands of families westward. In the spring of 1846, the year after the first books that mapped the trail had been published, about 2,700 people set out from Independence, Missouri, 1,500 of them bound for California, the rest for Oregon. Entire families packed their possessions into Conestoga wagons and hitched them to teams of oxen. Young and old, they essentially walked across the continent, covering an average of 15 mi per day across 2,000 mi of terrain over the course of five months.

Among the throngs were 14 families and 21 teamsters who later become known as the Donner Party. They sought to save time by taking a route known as Hastings' Cut-off, named for Lansford Hastings, a lawyer who had designs of becoming California's first governor. After traveling to Oregon and California by horseback in 1842 and 1843, Hastings published "The Emigrant's Guide to Oregon and California" and wrote with certainty of a faster, nearer route that would save several hundred miles. In actuality, Hastings had never traveled the length of the trail he proposed, and he had certainly never navigated it with wagons.

Led by George Donner, the group of 89 emigrants who decided to follow Hastings' Cutoff saved no time. Instead they added two precious weeks to their journey. Peril after peril befell them, and in late October they arrived at the base of the Sierra Crest, a fortnight after other emigrants had already safely arrived at Sutter's Fort in Sacramento. Severely shaken, exhausted, and very near starvation, the group rested their oxen for several days before the final push over the mountain range. During the night of October 30, it began to snow, and in the morning, the party frantically scrambled to make it across the pass, but the trail disappeared, the wind blew at gale force, and the summit became impassible. They had traveled five months and more than 2,000 mi, only to miss by one day the season's last chance to cross the Sierra Crest.

Forced to set up makeshift camps for the remainder of what proved to be one of the worst Sierra winters ever recorded, the families survived on the remaining scraps of their provisions and the hides of their slaughtered oxen until there was nothing left to eat. Frozen and starving, people began to die. In January of 1847, a group of several emigrants, calling themselves the "Forlorn Hope," pushed over the summit on makeshift snowshoes. Some died, some turned back, but those who survived the crossing summoned help. The first of three rescue parties arrived in late February, though it was not until mid-April that the last of the survivors was carried out of the mountains. Many—but not all—of those who lived through the ordeal did so only by consuming the emaciated remains of the dead. Of the 89 emigrants, only half survived. As the gruesome details of the party's fate spread across the nation, westward migration slowed to a trickle, and it was not until the discovery of gold at Sutter's Mill in 1849 that emigrants would again risk the journey west.

ical society and displays of Native American artifacts. | 10142 Jibboom St. | 530/582–0893 | truckeehistory.tripod.com | Free | May–early Sept., weekends 11–4.

✦ ON THE CALENDAR: Sept. **Truckee Railroad Days.** At this celebration of town's railroad heritage, you're invited to tour railroad cars, visit a model train exhibit, and take in other goings-on around town. | 530/546–1221.

Oct. **Donner Party Hike.** Guides from the Truckee Chamber of Commerce lead hikes through the surrounding mountains to commemorate the Donner Party's ill-fated trip west. | 530/587–2757.

HISTORIC LODGING

Richardson House. On a hill overlooking downtown, Warren Richardson, who developed a steam engine capable of carrying lumbered logs to the town's mill, built this 1880s green-and-gold gingerbread Victorian. Today it is filled with antiques, vintage fixtures, and plenty of period lace. It has views of the surrounding Sierra. Some rooms have four-poster canopy beds and claw-foot tubs. Two adjoining rooms share a bath and can be rented together as a family-style suite. Dining room; no smoking, no room TVs. | 10154 High St., 96161 | 530/587–5388 or 888/229–0365 | fax 530/587–0927 | www.richardsonhouse.com | 8 rooms, 2 with shared bath | $100–$175 | AE, D, MC, V | BP.

Truckee Hotel. Constructed in 1873, the four-story hotel has housed passengers on the stage coaches, laborers on the Transcontinental Railroad, and early workers at the lumber mills. Antiques fill the Victorian-style rooms; several have private bathrooms with claw-foot tubs. Restaurant, bar; no a/c, no smoking, no TV in some rooms. | 10007 Bridge St., 96161 | 916/587–4444 or 800/659–6921 | fax 916/587–1599 | www.truckeehotel.com | 37 rooms, 29 with shared bath | $55–$88 | AE, MC, V | CP.

WEAVERVILLE
▼▼

Set in a mountain valley, Weaverville was settled in 1850 during the first wave of the gold rush. Named after John Weaver, who was one of three men who built the first cabin here, the town has an impressive downtown historic district. *Contact Trinity County Chamber of Commerce | 211 Lakes Blvd., 96093 | 530/623–6101 | www.trinitycounty.com.*

J. J. Jackson Museum and Historical Park. Artifacts of Trinity County's pioneer and prospector past fill this museum, among them a functioning steam-powered stamp mill used to extract gold from ore. | 508 Main St. | 530/623–5211 | www.trinitycounty.com/museum | Donation | May–Oct., daily 10–5; Apr. and Nov., daily noon–4; Dec.–Mar., Tues. and Sat. noon–4.

Joss House State Historical Park. This colorful, ornate Taoist temple was built and decorated in 1875 by Chinese gold miners, who called it Won Lim Miao (The Temple of the Forest Beneath the Clouds). The oldest continuously used Chinese temple in California, it attracts worshipers from around the world. With its golden altar, carved wooden canopies, and intriguing artifacts, the Joss House is a remarkable piece of California history. The original temple building and many of its furnishings—some of which had come from China—were burned in 1873, but members of the local Chinese community soon rebuilt it. It contains a museum, and you can take a 40-minute tour. | 404 Main St. | 530/623–5284 | www.cal-parks.ca.gov/districts/nobuttes/wjhshp/wjhshp127.htm | $1 | Call for hrs.

YOSEMITE NATIONAL PARK
▼▼

Native Americans—the Southern Sierra Miwok people—lived in the Yosemite region as long as 8,000 years ago, hunting, fishing, and harvesting acorns. The members of the Joseph Walker Party of 1833 were probably the first non-natives to see Yosemite, but white settlers did not arrive until 1849. Throughout the Sierra Nevada foothills prospectors searched for gold, while the Miwoks fought to protect their homeland. The conflict known as the Mariposa Indian War brought a battalion of soldiers to Yosemite in 1851, and the Miwoks were forced out. Reports of the valley's beauty spread, and in 1864 President Abraham Lincoln granted Yosemite Valley and the Mariposa Grove of Giant Sequoias to the State of California as land to be preserved for the enjoyment of the people. This was first such act ever taken by a federal government. As more and more people came to Yosemite conservationist John Muir worked to protect the subalpine meadows from damage. His efforts resulted in the creation of Yosemite National Park on October 1, 1890.

Ahwahneechee Village. Tucked behind the Valley visitor center, a short loop trail of about 100 yards circles through a re-creation of an Ahwahneechee Native American village as it might have appeared in 1872, 23 years after non-natives arrived in the area. Markers explain the lifestyle of Yosemite's first residents. Allow 30 minutes to see it all. | Yosemite Village | Daily sunrise–sunset | Free.

Bodie Ghost Town. Old shacks and shops, abandoned mine shafts, a Methodist church, the mining village of Rattlesnake Gulch, and the remains of a small Chinatown are among the sights at this fascinating ghost town. Bodie boomed from about 1878 to 1881, but by the late 1940s, all its residents had departed. A state park was established in 1962, with a mandate to preserve but not restore the town. Evidence of Bodie's wild past survives at an excellent museum, and you can tour an old stamp mill and a ridge that contains many mine sites. Bodie is well worth the 71-mi drive from Yosemite Village, via Route 120 east and I–395 north to Route 270. Portions of Route 270 may be closed by weather, and the last 3 mi to the ghost town is unpaved. | Rte. 270 (Bodie Rd.), 13 mi off I–395, Bodie | 760/647–6445 | $1 | Late May–early Sept., daily 8–7; last 3 weeks in Sept.–first 3 weeks in May, daily 8–4.

Indian Cultural Museum. With demonstrations in beadwork, basket-weaving, and other traditional activities, the museum presents the cultural history of Yosemite's Miwok and Paiute people. | Yosemite Village | 209/372–0299 | Daily 9–4:30 | Free.

Pioneer Yosemite History Center. Yosemite's first log buildings, relocated here from around the park, make up this historic collection near the Wawona Hotel. Enter on the covered bridge that welcomed the park's first tourists. There's also a homesteader's cabin, a blacksmith's shop, a bakery, and a U.S. Cavalry headquarters, all from the late-19th or early 20th centuries. In summer, costumed docents play the roles of the pioneers. Ranger-led walks leave from the covered bridge, Saturday at 10 in summer. | Rte. 41, Wawona | 209/379–2646 | Buildings are open mid-June–early Sept., Wed.–Sun. 9–1, Mon. and Tues. 2–5 | Free.

Yosemite Mountain–Sugar Pine Railroad. Take a 4-mi narrow-guage railroad excursion near Yosemite's south gate. The railroad is a restoration of the Madera Sugar Pine Lumber Company Railroad, which operated from 1899 to 1931. During that time, five wood-burning Shay locomotives hauled massive log trains through the mountains to the mills. You can ride a train powered by a vintage Shay steam locomotive, or climb aboard trolley-like Jenny cars for a trip behind an antique Model "A" Ford gas engine. | 56001 Rte. 41, about 8 mi south of Yosemite, Fish Camp | 559/683–7273 | www.ymsprr.com | Jenny railcar $9; steam train $12.50 | Mid-Mar.–Oct., daily.

Yosemite Theater. Theatrical and musical presentations are offered at various times throughout the year. One of the best-loved is Lee Stetson's portrayal of John Muir in *Conversation with a Tramp, John Muir's Stickeen and Other Fellow Mortals,* and *The Spirit of John Muir.* Buy your tickets in advance at the Valley visitor center. Unsold seats are available at the door at performance time, 8 PM. | Valley visitor center auditorium; Yosemite Lodge Theater | 209/372–0299 | $7–$10.

HISTORIC DINING AND LODGING

Tioga Lodge. A creek flows through the meadows and woods of this property on the shores of Mono Lake, just 2½ mi north of Yosemite's eastern gateway. By turns a store, a bordello, a saloon, a tollbooth, and a boarding house, the white wood-frame buildings that house the current lodge office, saloon, and restaurant date from the late 1800s. Some of the buildings were moved 15 mi to the site from the mining town of Bodie, starting around 1897. Guest rooms, some in modern buildings, are uniquely furnished with period artifacts meant to recall the 1890s. Restaurant, bar, shop. No room phones, no TV. | U.S. 395, about 40 mi east of Yosemite Village via Rte. 120, Lee Vining | 760/647–6423 or 888/647–6423 | fax 760/647–6074 | www.tiogalodge.com | 13 rooms | $95–$105 | AE, D, MC, V.

Wawona Hotel. An old-fashioned Victorian estate of whitewashed buildings with wrap-around verandas, this circa-1879 National Historic Landmark is in the southern end of the national park. The hotel annexes are also turn-of-the-20th-century, the last built in 1918. Most rooms are small, and only half have a private bath, but almost all open onto a verandah. The cozy Victorian parlor in the main hotel is pleasant and romantic, with a fireplace, board games, and a pianist who plays ragtime tunes most evenings. Restaurant, pool, golf course, putting green, tennis, bar. No a/c, no room phones, no pets, no smoking. | Rte. 41, Wawona | 209/375–1425 | 104 rooms (54 with shared bath) | $96–$148.

COLORADO

—◆—

owboys and Indians. Prospectors and pioneers. Mountain men and mining-town madams. No state conjures up quite so many colorful images of the wide-open Wild West as Colorado. Bisected by the towering peaks of the Continental Divide, the country's highest state is steeped in legends, lore, and legitimate history.

When Spanish explorers became the first Europeans to explore what is now Colorado, they encountered multiple tribes of Native Americans. Cheyenne, Arapaho, Comanche, and Kiowa were prominent among the tribes roaming the central and eastern plains. The formidable Ute tribe held dominion in the mountains. Spain first claimed title to Colorado based on the 1540 expedition of Francisco Vásquez de Coronado, though most authorities assert that his expedition never passed through the state's current boundaries. But subsequent Spanish explorations, based out of the Spanish settlement of Santa Fe (now in New Mexico), did venture into Colorado's interior, exploring much of the Rio Grande drainage and considerable territory in the state's southwest.

While the Spanish were making inroads through the south, the French were encroaching from the east. Famed Mississippi River explorer René Robert Cavelier (more widely known by his title, La Salle) claimed the northeastern part of Colorado for France in 1682 but never actually set foot in the area. The first known French exploration of Colorado was led by brothers Paul and Pierre Mallet, who, in 1739, made the first documented crossing of the Great Plains from the Missouri River to Santa Fe. Their eight-man party followed the Arkansas and Purgatoire rivers as they cut diagonally across the southeastern portion of Colorado, passing through what is now Trinidad.

Although claims to the northeastern part of the state were disputed by Spain and France throughout the 1700s, the matter would be put to rest in 1803. That year, Thomas Jefferson brokered the Louisiana Purchase with Napoléon and the northeastern section of Colorado became U.S. territory. The remainder of Colorado—first controlled by Spain, then Mexico after the latter won its independence in 1821—wouldn't come under U.S. rule until the end of the Mexican-American War in 1848.

By the time the United States held all of the land that would become Colorado, exploration of the territory by the U.S. Army was well under way. Lieutenant Zebulon Pike had explored the headwaters of the Arkansas River, west of what is now Pueblo, in 1806. That expedition had not gone exactly as planned: Once Pike made his way into the mountains he became lost and confused, wandering from South Park (west of the peak that would later bear his name) deep into Spanish land in the San Luis Valley. He was ultimately arrested by Spanish soldiers and hauled off to Mexico, though he was later released (Spain was loathe to set off a war with the United States). Muddled as it was, Pike's adventure did yield the first detailed report and maps of eastern Colorado.

Anglo adventurers eager to explore and exploit the natural riches of the Rockies didn't wait for published reports or accurate maps. When the market for beaver pelts took off in the early 19th century, rugged trappers—some working for syndicates, others trading for themselves—infiltrated Colorado's myriad river valleys in search of the "hairy bank notes." The beaver trade, which was pretty profitable from 1815 to the 1830s, was just the first of Colorado's booms.

In mid-century, with the Mexican-American War finished and the vast stretch of the West under federal control, American industrialists were itching for a railway connection between eastern cities and the Pacific Coast. In 1853, Captain John W. Gunnison surveyed a central route through the Rocky Mountains, following the Gunnison River from central Colorado (near what is now the town of Gunnison) to the Colorado River, and the Colorado into Utah. In Utah, Paiute killed Gunnison and most of his command, but his artist and cartographer survived to produce reports, illustrations, and the first good maps of west-central Colorado.

Nothing, however, brought people to Colorado like the mining bonanza of the late 1850s. For millennia, gold dust had washed out of the rugged mountains and accumulated at the mouths of stream beds along the front range. In May 1858, William Russell, a prospector from Georgia, discovered a deposit of such "placer" gold in Cherry Creek (in present-day Denver), and the rush was on. "Pike's Peak or Bust" became the slogan of the throngs of gold seekers who converged on the area. Historians estimate that approximately 50,000 people came to Colorado in 1858–1859. Most left disappointed, but a lucky few struck it rich. Russell's discovery was followed in quick succession by others around the newly founded village of Denver City and in the foothills and mountains to the west.

The placer gold found in streams was easy pickings and was snatched up quickly. The real riches—the gold ore and pure gold in veins—were harder to unlock, but prospectors dug and blasted their way into the mountainsides. Mining claims and camps quickly dotted the Rocky Mountains. When a strike was made, a town appeared virtually overnight. These were lawless, rowdy outposts filled with hard-drinking men and industrious women. Central City, Black Hawk, Cripple Creek, Victor, Idaho Springs, Gold Hill, Tarryall, Georgetown, Nevadaville . . . in all, about 300 mining settlements sprang up throughout Colorado, all fueled by dreams of wealth and grandeur. For almost 20 years enormous amounts of gold were extracted from Colorado's mountains, making many people wealthy.

Politicians in Washington, D.C., quickly agreed that the vast, gold-bearing region should become part of the Union. In February 1861 Congress bestowed territorial status on Colorado and immediately began to study ways to capitalize on the area's wealth. Conveniently, Colorado Territory was born two months before the Civil War erupted in South Carolina, and its gold would provide badly needed funds to finance the Union's efforts in the conflict. No combat between Confederate and Union forces ever took place on Colorado soil, but territorial militia companies kept a wary eye out for a feared invasion by Southerners. None came, and for the duration of the war the only fighting in Colorado Territory were skirmishes between various Indian groups and white settlers. The bloodiest of these occurred in late November 1864, when the Third Colorado Cavalry, a volunteer regiment under the dubious command of Colonel John Chivington, massacred the inhabitants of a peaceful Cheyenne Indian camp at Sand Creek.

As the Civil War drew to a close, a boom of a different kind hit Colorado Territory. Folks had ranched in the area for years to provide beef to the local miners, but in 1866, trail drivers started herding longhorns along the new Goodnight-Loving Trail, which crossed Colorado on its way from Texas to Montana. In 1870, when the railroad arrived in Colorado and linked Denver to the eastern cities, an enormous market for western beef opened up. Close to 5 million head traveled to or through Colorado on the Goodnight-Loving Trail between 1866 and 1884.

As Colorado's economy developed, settlers streamed steadily into the territory. By 1876 Colorado met the minimum population requirement for statehood and was officially admitted to the Union as the 38th state. The young state soon found itself in the national limelight when prospectors discovered another precious metal—silver—in its mountains in the mid-1870s. As they had 20 years earlier, fortune hunters flocked to the Rocky Mountains by the thousands, hoping to become the nation's newest millionaires.

Between 1880 and 1890 Colorado's population more than doubled, approaching half a million. Prosperous citizens put down roots and built the imposing Victorian structures for which the state came to be known. They founded the University of Colorado and the University of Denver, as well as the renowned Colorado School of Mines. The silver boom went bust in 1893, when the Sherman Act took the nation's currency off the silver standard, but by then the state was well established. As it entered the 20th century Colorado built its farming and ranching economy, and by 1909 it was the most widely irrigated state in the nation. In 1906, the inaugural National Western Stock Show, a livestock and horse show and a celebration of the state's ranching heritage, was held in Denver.

The Golden Era

A DRIVING TOUR FROM DENVER TO CRIPPLE CREEK

▼▼

Distance: 327 mi   **Time:** 3 Days
Breaks: Georgetown, Leadville, and Cripple Creek have plenty of lodgings and restaurants, historic and otherwise, to keep you well fed and rested on this trip.

No single event influenced the course of Colorado's history more than the 1858 discovery of gold in what is now Denver. Camps, settlements, and full-fledged towns sprang up overnight. Most are ghost towns now, but some of these boomtowns have survived remarkably intact. This tour will take you to some of the most legendary mining camps and provide a glimpse of Colorado's golden era.

Start your tour where it all began, in **Denver**'s Larimer Square. Near the confluence of Cherry Creek and the South Platte River, the oldest street in Denver lies close to the spot where prospector William Russell first hit pay dirt. From downtown Denver, drive west via U.S. 40/I–70 west, Route 93 north, and U.S. 6 west to the twin towns of **Central City** and Black Hawk. Look past the monster casinos at Black Hawk to see the real history—silver rush buildings line Main and Gregory streets. The 1878 Opera House is the centerpiece of Central City's impressive historic district. From Central City, drive the appropriately nicknamed, unpaved but well-maintained "Oh My God" road (CR-279/281) to Idaho Springs. Here you can have lunch and tour the still operating Phoenix Gold Mine. Get back on I–70 and head west about 12 mi to the turnoff for **Georgetown**—a town happily obsessed with the preservation of its many historic structures. Take the 6-mi round-trip ride on the Georgetown Loop Railroad, a marvel of engineering built in 1877. Spend the night in Georgetown.

On your second day, drive about 75 mi southwest via I–70 and Route 9 to **Leadville,** which got its start as a gold-mining town but achieved its real glory during the silver years. From Leadville, head south on U.S. 24, part of the Top of the Rockies Scenic Byway. For a glimpse

COLORADO TIMELINE

1541 Spanish explorer Francisco Vásquez de Coronado passes near or through Colorado while hunting for the Seven Cities of Cibola. He claims the territory for Spain.

1682 Robert Cavelier, sieur de La Salle, claims for France all of Colorado east of the Rocky Mountains.

1763 France cedes all claims in eastern Colorado to Spain.

1800 French First Consul Napoléon Bonaparte reclaims title to the vast Louisiana territory (including eastern Colorado) from a weakened Spain.

1803 President Thomas Jefferson makes the Louisiana Purchase for $15 million. The territory gains for the United States most of eastern Colorado.

1832 Brothers Charles and William Bent and veteran trapper-trader Ceran St. Vrain open Bent's Fort on the Mountain Branch of the Santa Fe Trail.

1848 The Treaty of Guadalupe Hidalgo ends the Mexican War, granting most of Colorado west of the Rockies to the United States.

1851 The first permanent non-Indian settlement in Colorado is founded at San Luis.

1858 William Russell discovers placer gold near the confluence of Cherry Creek and the South Platte River, precipitating Colorado's first gold rush.

1864 Colonel John Chivington leads the Third Colorado Volunteers in the massacre of Chief Black Kettle's peaceful Cheyenne village, at Sand Creek in southeastern Colorado.

1865–1869 Retaliatory attacks from Indians (predominantly the Cheyenne Dog Soldiers) wreak havoc on overland trails and white settlements.

1868 Represented by Chief Ouray, the Ute give up the Central Rockies and San Luis Valley.

1870 Nathan Meeker and Horace Greeley found a utopian community called Union Colony, in the town of Greeley. The railroad era begins in Colorado when the Denver Pacific Railroad connects Denver with Cheyenne, Wyoming. The Kansas Pacific Railroad enters from the east. General William Palmer begins building the Denver Rio Grande Railroad south from Denver. The competing railroads begin the race to western gold fields.

1871 Palmer establishes Colorado Springs as a resort community.

1875 Prospectors find lead carbonate ores, rich in silver, near present-day Leadville.

1876 Colorado is admitted to the Union as the 38th state.

1881 The Ute are sent to two reservations in southwestern Colorado.

1886 The Denver Union Stockyards are established, later becoming the nation's largest receiving market for sheep.

1893 Repeal of the Sherman Act demonetizes silver. Many silver boom towns go bust overnight.

1900 Gold production at Cripple Creek reaches its peak of more than $20 million annually.

1906 Congress creates Mesa Verde National Park to protect the ancient Indian sites there.

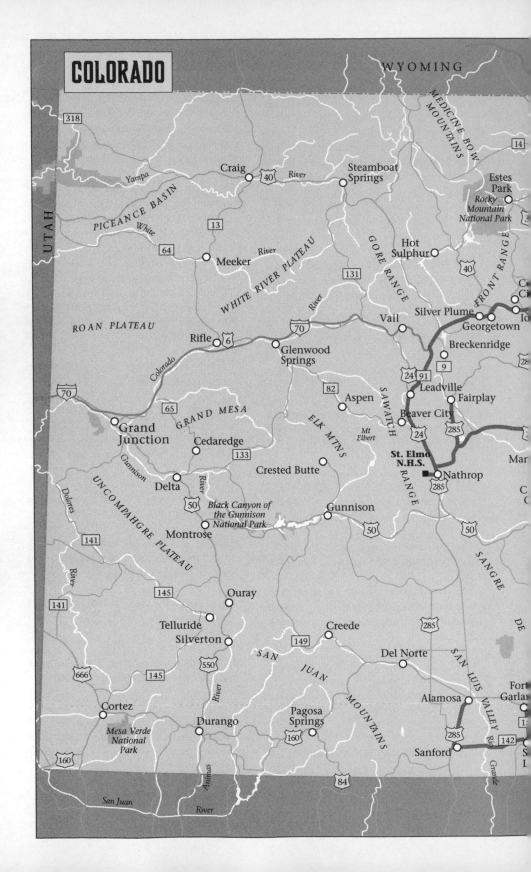

COLORADO

WYOMING

UTAH

318

14

Craig

40 River

Steamboat
Springs

Estes
Park

Rocky
Mountain
National Park

MEDICINE BOW MOUNTAINS

Yampa

PICEANCE BASIN

White

13

64

Meeker

River

131

Hot
Sulphur

40

C

C

ROAN PLATEAU

WHITE RIVER PLATEAU

River

70

Vail

Silver Plume

Georgetown

Io

Colorado

Rifle

6

Glenwood
Springs

Breckenridge

9

28

GORE RANGE

FRONT RANGE

70

65

GRAND MESA

82

Aspen

24 91

Leadville

Fairplay

Grand
Junction

Cedaredge

Beaver City

Mt
Elbert

Gunnison

133

Crested Butte

ELK MTNS

SAWATCH

St. Elmo
N.H.S.

Nathrop

Mar

Delta

River

285

24

285

UNCOMPAHGRE PLATEAU

Dolores

50

Black Canyon of
the Gunnison
National Park

Gunnison

50

50

50

C

Montrose

141

RANGE

SANGRE

141

145

Ouray

149

Creede

285

River

Telluride

Silverton

550

San Juan

San Juan

MOUNTAINS

Del Norte

285

SAN LUIS VALLEY

DE

666

145

Cortez

Pagosa
Springs

160

Alamosa

Fort
Garla

1

160

Mesa Verde
National
Park

Durango

Animas

142

River

Sanford

285

Río

S
I

San Juan

River

84

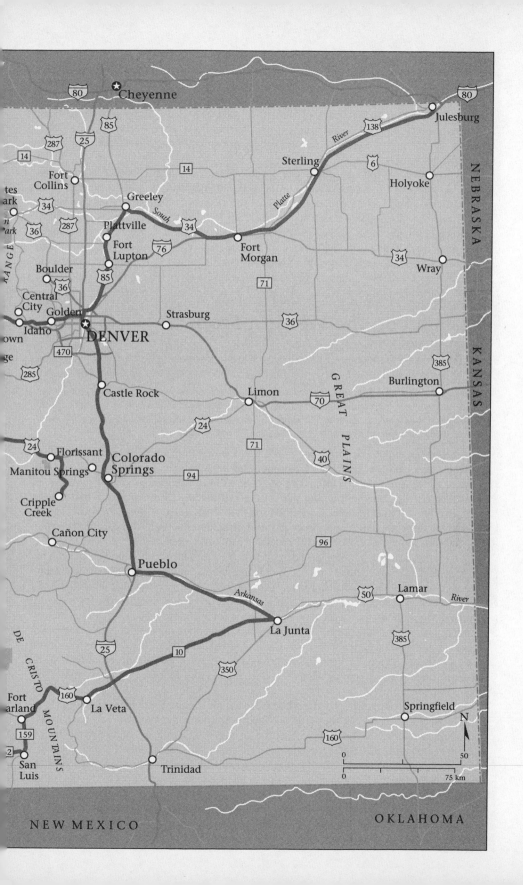

at some mining ghost towns in advanced stages of disintegration, turn west off U.S. 24 just south of Granite, onto CR 390, a good gravel road that's fine for two-wheel-drive cars. About 14 mi along this road you'll hit what's left of Beaver City. Travel a few miles farther to see the remains of Vicksburg, Rockdale, and Winfield, which were once bustling mining towns. Backtrack on CR 390 and head south 26 mi via U.S. 24 and U.S. 285 to Nathrop. Here, turn right (west) on CR 162 and follow the road 16 mi to St. Elmo National Historic Site, one of the best-preserved (but unrestored) ghost towns in the state. Backtrack to Leadville and spend the night there.

On day three, drive 40 mi north on U.S. 285 to **Fairplay.** There, South Park City is an impressive assemblage of mining-era cabins, commercial buildings, and equipment. Now drive 18 mi south on Route 9 and 32 mi east on U.S. 24 to the town of Florissant. Turn south onto the Cripple Creek/Florissant Road, part of the Gold Belt Scenic Byway. It's about 20 mi to the town of **Cripple Creek,** known as "the World's Greatest Gold Camp." The Molly Kathleen mine offers tours. Cripple Creek's ghostly sister city, Victor, is just a few miles down the road; between them is a mammoth ongoing mining project that is steadily displacing a mountain of rock. You can overnight in one of several historic lodgings in Cripple Creek.

Disquiet on the Western Front

A DRIVING TOUR FROM ALAMOSA TO JULESBURG

▼▼

Distance: 567 mi   **Time:** 3 days
Breaks: Stop for lunch in San Luis (Colorado's oldest town) or Fort Garland; in La Junta; and in Greeley, whose old downtown offers several options. La Veta is a sleepy little town that the masses have yet to discover, and the best reason to stay there is that the surrounding Cuchara Valley is flat-out gorgeous. Colorado Springs, by contrast, has lots of lodgings, including some Victorian-era B&Bs.

To protect trappers, pioneers, railroad workers, and miners from attack by Indians and other hostile forces, the U.S. military (and sometimes private citizens) built many forts and armored installations in Colorado. The peak period for fort building was the tumultuous mid-19th century, but by the later part of the century the threat of attack had largely subsided. Most of the forts were abandoned and have disappeared. A few old forts still stand, some have been re-created, and plenty of historic sites dot the rugged landscape. This tour takes you to some of Colorado's most noteworthy military sites.

Your tour starts where Colorado's first documented fort, Pike's Stockade, was built. A re-created stockade now stands 17 mi south of **Alamosa** near Sanford, on the site where Zebulon Pike was captured by Spanish forces. From Sanford, make your way 45 mi northeast via Routes 142 and 159 (passing through San Luis, Colorado's oldest town) to the town of Fort Garland. The fort itself, now a museum, was constructed in 1858 to replace Fort Massachusetts (built in 1852, 6 mi to the north). Both forts were intended to protect settlers and their roads from Ute and Apache raiders. From Fort Garland, take U.S. 160 east for 37 mi to the turnoff for **La Veta** (Rte. 12). In La Veta, follow the signs to Francisco Fort. Built in 1862 by local citizens, the fort also served as the town's central plaza and commercial center. Spend the night in La Veta.

Day two of your tour starts with an 88-mi drive from La Veta northeast to **La Junta,** via U.S. 160 east and Route 10. On Route 194 northeast of town is Bent's Old Fort National Historic Site. Built in 1833 on the banks of the Arkansas River, Bent's Fort was an important safe haven along the Santa Fe Trail. The current structure is a reproduction built in the 1970s to the exact specifications of the original. After leaving Bent's Old Fort, head west on U.S. 50 for 54 mi to the city of **Pueblo,** the location of the first permanent American settlement in the Colorado. No traces remain of the trading post–fort built at this location in 1842, but the El Pueblo Museum has displays about and a reconstruction of the fort. Spend the night in **Colorado Springs**—at the Broadmoor, if you feel like splurging—40 mi north of Pueblo on I–25.

TAKING THE HIGH ROAD: THE MOUNTAIN BRANCH OF THE SANTA FE TRAIL

Spanning 900 mi of America's Great Plains, from Independence, Missouri, to Santa Fe, New Mexico, the Santa Fe Trail was, for about 60 years, an unrivaled route of commercial and cultural exchange. The original route of the trail, known as the Cimarron Cutoff, barely nicked the southeastern-most corner of present-day Colorado, but the Mountain Branch cut an arched swath deeper into the area. Although portions of the Mountain Branch had been used for centuries by Native Americans and Spanish explorers, traffic picked up in earnest after Mexico won independence from Spain in 1821. Many American merchant-traders brought goods from the East along the trail to exchange them for furs and other western products. At the same time, caravans of Mexican traders started traveling the trail from Santa Fe to the east. When the Treaty of Guadalupe Hidalgo ended the Mexican-American War in 1848, granting much of Mexico's northern territory to the United States, the Santa Fe Trail became a national road connecting the eastern states to the new southwestern territories. From this point forward, southeastern Colorado became an important landmark in the opening of the West to white settlement.

After traveling west through Kansas, traders and emigrants following the Santa Fe Trail had two options: they could take the original southern route, which was shorter but included a long stretch with no reliable water sources, or they could follow the Mountain Branch, which crossed more difficult terrain but had more water. The Mountain Branch crossed the Kansas-Colorado border where the Arkansas River did and followed the river about 70 mi west to Bent's Fort. Brothers William and Charles Bent of St. Louis and veteran trapper and trader Ceran St. Vrain of Taos built the fort in 1833. For 17 years, it served as the most important center of trade on the entire the trail from Independence, Missouri, to Santa Fe, New Mexico. An oasis in the "Great American Desert" between Eastern Kansas and the Rocky Mountains, the fort was a rare haven where travelers could rest and re-supply. (William died in 1847, and a few years later Charles abandoned the fort to build a new trading post about 40 mi downriver.) Past Bent's Fort the trail curved southwest, leaving the river behind and heading south into New Mexico.

As crucial to western travel as the Santa Fe Trail was in the middle of the 19th century, it became obsolete as railroads pushed ever farther west. When the tracks of the Santa Fe Railroad reached its namesake city in 1880, the venerable trail faded into history. Today, U.S. 50 roughly follows the route of the Mountain Branch from the Kansas border through the pioneer towns of Lamar and Las Animas to La Junta, where U.S. 350 picks up the trail, traveling southwest to Trinidad. If you detour off the highway onto the quiet country roads, you can still discern the Mountain Branch's faint outline over the gentle hump of swales and dip of arroyos. Wagon ruts are still visible at Iron Springs (27 mi southwest of La Junta on U.S. 350), an important water stop along the route. At the Sierra Vista overlook (13 mi southwest of La Junta on U.S. 350, then 1 mi north on Rte. 71) you can hike a 3-mi section of the Santa Fe National Historic Trail. Here, amid the magpies and prairie dogs, it takes little imagination to conjure visions of pioneers in oxcarts, struggling westward 10 mi a day on the Santa Fe Trail.

On your third day, take I–25 north approximately 80 mi to the junction of I–76 at Denver. Drive east on I–76 for 13 mi and north on U.S. 85 for 16 mi to the town of Fort Lupton. The Fort Lupton Museum has a model of the town's namesake fort, the southernmost of four competing trading forts built along the banks of the South Platte River during the 1830s. Another of the four forts, Fort Vasquez stood 9 mi north of Fort Lupton. On its site near the town of Platteville on U.S. 85, Fort Vasquez Museum is a living-history museum in a reconstruction of the fort. Another 18 mi north is **Greeley,** the major town along this stretch of U.S. 85. From here, take U.S. 34 east to I–76 east, and drive 12 mi to the town of Fort Morgan, where the Fort Morgan Museum preserves that fort's history. Continue east on I–76 and U.S. 6, about 45 mi to **Sterling.** At the Overland Trail Museum, take in the displays about the trail and the forts and stage stops along its route. Finally, move on to the town of Julesburg, 48 mi east of Sterling via U.S. 138. Julesburg's Fort Sedgwick Museum tells the story of the old military fort that once served this area.

ALAMOSA
▼▼▼

Early Spanish explorers and Native Americans are known to have passed through the lovely valley of the San Luis River, but it was the Spanish who left their indelible imprint in the town names and local architecture. Hispanic emigrants from nearby New Mexico first settled Alamosa in 1851. Almost three decades later, a trainload of Anglo settlers traveled west from Fort Garland to stake their claim to the area. They dubbed the cottonwood-shaded hamlet Alamosa, a Spanish word for "cottonwood." The citizens of Alamosa raised wheat, oats, barley, and other crops and built large supply houses along the tracks when the railroad arrived. As a major shipping point supplying ranchers and miners, the town became a hub of the San Luis Valley. *Contact Alamosa County Chamber of Commerce/Visitor's Center | Cole Park, 81101 | 719/589–3681 or 800/258–7597 | www.alamosa.org.*

Cumbres & Toltec Scenic Railroad. Constructed in 1880 as part of the Rio Grande Railroad's San Juan Extension, the Cumbres & Toltec served the silver-mining district of the San Juan Mountains. Today, the steam-era railroad is a registered state and national historic site. You can choose from among several types of rides, including a round-trip between Chama and Osier or between Antonito and Osier, or you can travel the entire 64-mi line and return by motorcoach. Comfortable rail coaches with windows that open, a paneled and carpeted parlor car with open seating, complimentary snacks, and attendant service as well as the open-air gondola on top are your seating options. The trains stop for lunch at the remote stagecoach town of Osier. The depot is in Antonito, 28 mi south of Alamosa. | U.S. 285 at Rte. 17 | 719/376–5483 or 888/286–2737 | www.cumbresandtoltec.com | $45–$60 | Late-May–mid-Oct.; call for schedule.

Fort Garland Museum. Colorado's first military post, established in 1856 to protect settlers from Indians, was commanded by the legendary Kit Carson. The museum, which depicts army life in the 1860s–70s, is housed in six of the fort's original adobe structures. You will also find a re-creation of the commandant's quarters, various period military displays, and a rotating local folk-art exhibit. Fort Garland is 24 mi east of Alamosa. | 29477 Hwy. 159 | 719/379–3512 | www.museumtrail.org/fortgarlandmuseum.asp | $3 | Apr.–Oct., daily 9–5; Nov.–Mar., Thurs.–Mon. 8–4.

Pike's Stockade State Historic Monument. Pike's Stockade, located east of Sanford, is a replica of a log stockade that explorer Zebulon Pike built near the Conejos River in 1807. Pike and his men, who didn't realize they were in Spanish territory, were captured while they camped here during the harsh winter. The replica stockade was built in the 1950s from notes in Pike's journal. It stands north of Sanford, which is 14 mi south of Alamosa on U.S. 285, then about 3 mi east on Route 136. | From Sanford, CR 20 north 2 mi to CR Y. East on CR Y 4 mi to Pikes Stockade entrance. Turn right over cattle guard onto CR 24, then 1 mi to stockade | 719/379–3512 | Free | Late May–early Sept., daily.

San Luis. Founded in 1851, San Luis is the oldest incorporated town in Colorado. Murals depicting famous stories and legends of the area adorn the buildings along the gracious tree-lined streets. Stop by the Town of San Luis Visitors Center (408½ Main St. | 719/379–3002) for information. The town's Hispanic heritage is celebrated in the San Luis Museum and Cultural Center (401 Church Pl. | 719/672–3611 | $2), which displays an extensive collection of *santos* (decorated figures of saints used for household devotions), *retablos* (paintings on wood), and *bultos* (carved religious figures). | 24 mi east of Alamosa on U.S. 160 to Fort Gartland, then 16 mi south on Rte. 159 | www.slvguide.com.

✦ ON THE CALENDAR: Apr. **Train Day.** The community celebrates its railroad heritage in skits on local history and tours of old Engine 169, which is parked next to the Chamber of Commerce office. | 719/589–3681.

ASPEN
▼▼

Originally called Ute City, Aspen was founded in the late 1870s during a silver rush. The most prominent early citizen was Jerome Wheeler, who in 1889 at the height of Aspen's prosperity opened two of the town's enduring landmarks: the Hotel Jerome and the Wheeler Opera House. After the silver market crashed in 1893, Aspen's population dwindled from 15,000 to 250—even though one of the largest (almost 2,200 lbs) nuggets of native silver ever found was mined in 1894. Aspen survived as a rural county seat and ranching center. The town received a new lease on life in the 1940s when it was developed into a recreational destination with an emphasis on skiing. HeritageAspen, Aspen's historical society, is dedicated to preserving the city's past through educational programs, research, publishing, and the collecting and exhibiting of historical artifacts. *Contact Aspen Chamber Resort Association | 425 Rio Grande Pl., 81611 | 970/925–1940 or 800/262–7736 | www. aspenchamber.org. HeritageAspen | 620 W. Bleeker, 81611 | 970/925–3721 | fax 970/925–5347 | www.aspenhistory.org.*

Walking Tours. Discover Aspen's fascinating history on a walking tour. You can pick up a self-guided tour brochure at HeritageAspen or the Wheeler Opera House visitor center. Or you can take one of the two-hour walks on Monday or Friday morning with a Victorian-costumed guide. Tours start at the Wheeler-Stallard Museum and finish at the Hotel Jerome. Private tours are also available. | 620 W. Bleeker St. | 970/925–3721 | www.aspenhistory.org | $10 | June–Aug., Mon. and Fri. 9:30.

Wheeler Opera House. Built in 1889, the Wheeler Opera House debuted with a gala event that included a tantalizing performance by a group of Viennese lady fencers. Jerome B. Wheeler, a wealthy entrepreneur from New York, had spared no expense in building the plush opera house. It was loaded with crimson velvet drapes, gold plush seats with Moroccan leather cushioned arms, an azure ceiling studded with silver stars, and a chandelier with 36 electric light bulbs. Today, the opera house has been fully restored to its original appearance and continues to be the center of Aspen's art scene, hosting more than 300 events annually. Public one-hour tours are available, though the tour schedule varies greatly. | 320 E. Hyman Ave. | 970/920–7148 | www.wheeleroperahouse.com | Tours $3 | Box office daily 10–6; call for tour and performance schedules.

Wheeler-Stallard Museum. You can obtain great insight into Victorian high life at this restored Queen Anne home, which displays period memorabilia collected by HeritageAspen. Some exhibits depict Aspen's early history. Jerome B. Wheeler built the home in 1888, but his wife, Harriet Macy Valentine Wheeler, refused to leave their mansion in Manitou Springs and the family never lived here. The Stallard family moved into the home in 1905. | 620 W. Bleeker St. | 970/925–3721 | www.aspenhistory.org | $6 | June–early Sept., Tues.–Sat. 10–4.

✦ ON THE CALENDAR: June–Aug. **Snowmass Village Rodeo.** This authentic western rodeo, held a few miles northwest of Aspen in the tiny town of Snowmass, features bull riding, barrel racing, and rope tricks. You can also pan for silver, eat some barbecue, listen to country-and-western music, and do some dancing. | 970/923–4433.

HISTORIC DINING AND LODGING

Century Room. Continental. Nineteenth-century western antiques fill the the Hotel Jerome's restaurant, which has been in operation since Old West days. Step back in time and play the mining tycoon amid rich burgundy velvet, Italian tapestries, and overstuffed Victorian furniture and a warm fire. The Wheeler Room, a private dining room, is even more elegant, with French crystal chandeliers and gold-leaf accents. The kitchen does a good job with trout and prime beef. Signature items include lobster and crab cakes with spicy fried angel-hair pasta and native rack of lamb with toasted barley cassoulet and lamb jus. | 330 E. Main St. | 970/920–1000 | Reservations essential | $24–$34 | AE, DC, MC, V.

Hotel Jerome. This gold rush–era grande dame is Victorian to the core, with lavishly patterned wallpaper and ornate guest rooms. One of the state's truly grand hotels since 1889, the solid redbrick property has vintage furnishings, crystal chandeliers, intricate woodwork, and gold-laced tile flooring throughout. Rooms are large, with high ceilings, oversize beds with down comforters, antique armoires and chests, and huge bathtubs. Book six months in advance for big savings. 3 restaurants, room service, in-room data ports, refrigerators, cable TV, in-room VCRs with movies, pool, gym, hot tub, massage, ski shop, 2 bars, business services, airport shuttle, pets allowed (fee). | 330 E. Main St., 81611 | 970/920–1000 or 800/331–7213 | fax 970/925–2784 | www.hoteljerome.com | 76 rooms, 15 suites | $560–$1,125 suites | AE, DC, MC, V.

BOULDER

▼▼

Unabashedly new-age and forward thinking, many Boulderites seem oblivious to the rich history they jog, pedal, and stroll through daily. Settled in the gold rush years of the 1860s and '70s, the town was an important service and supply center for the booming mining areas tucked into the adjacent Flatiron mountains and points west. Pearl Street pedestrian mall is the most frequently visited portion of the town's nationally listed Downtown Historic District. *Contact Convention and Visitors Bureau | 2440 Pearl St., 80302 | 303/442–2911 or 800/444–0447 | www.bouldercoloradousa.com. Historic Boulder Inc. | 646 Pearl St., 80302 | 303/444–5192 | www. historicboulder.org.*

Boulder Museum of History. Housed in the 1889 Harbeck-Bergheim mansion, the museum's exhibits document the history of Boulder and the surrounding region from 1858 to the present. If you're interested in the sartorial styles of the 19th century (whether rugged cowboy and miner duds or high-society finery), this museum will delight. It is home to one of Colorado's largest clothing collections, with items dating as far back as 1820. | 1206 Euclid Ave. | 303/449–3464 | www.bcn.boulder.co.us/arts/bmh | $3 | Tues.–Fri. 10–4, weekends noon–4.

Downtown Boulder Historic District. The late-19th- and early 20th-century commercial structures that once housed mercantile stores and saloons more likely peddle designer lattes and Tibetan prayer flags now. Nevertheless, the period architecture—including Queen Anne, Italianate, and Romanesque styles in stone or brick—has been preserved. Historic Boulder (646 Pearl St. | 303/444–5192) sponsors both guided and self-guided tours of this district and Boulder's other designated historic areas. You can buy a 22-page guidebook for $4, or take a guided walk in summer and the Christmas season. | South side of Spruce St. from 10th to 16th St.; Pearl St. from 9th to 16th St.; north side of Walnut St. from Broadway to 9th St.

Mapleton Hill Historic District. Three blocks north of Pearl Street and west of Broadway, this neighborhood of turn-of-the-20th-century homes is shaded by old maple and cottonwood trees. Historic Boulder (646 Pearl St. | 303/444–5192) sponsors both guided and self-guided tours of this district and Boulder's other designated historic areas. You can buy a 22-page guidebook for $4, or take a guided walk in summer and the Christmas season. | Roughly bounded by Broadway, the alley between Pearl and Spruce Sts., 4th St., and the alley between Dewey St. and Concord Ave.

✦ ON THE CALENDAR: Sept. **Walker Ranch: A Glimpse of the Past.** Homesteaded in the 1880s and retaining many of its original buildings, Walker Ranch is listed on the National Historic Register as a "Historic Cultural Landscape." This event, usually held the last two weekends in September, is the only time you can visit the ranch. You'll see costumed men, women, and children demonstrating the daily chores of a turn-of-the-20th-century working ranch. You are invited to participate in a wide range of activities. | 303/441–4594.

HISTORIC LODGING

Hotel Boulderado. Boulder's first luxury hotel opened to admiring crowds on New Year's Day 1909. Listed on the National Register of Historic Places, this Victorian gem has been meticulously restored to its original appearance. Architectural highlights include the lobby's elegant stained-glass ceiling and a cantilevered cherry staircase. Antique and reproduction furnishings lend historical charm to the rooms. 3 restaurants, in-room data ports, 2 bars, business services, meeting rooms. | 2115 13th St., 80302 | 303/442–4344 | fax 303/442–4378 | www.boulderado.com | 160 rooms | $185–$215 | AE, D, DC, MC, V.

BRECKENRIDGE

▼▼▼

Breckenridge owes its existence to the discovery of gold here during the Pikes Peak gold rush of 1859. After the precious metal played out, prospectors moved on to greener pastures, leaving the once prosperous and bustling community almost deserted. The town came back to life when the skiing industry arrived. It's a resort town, but Breckenridge has managed to preserve much of its Old West heritage in a 12-square-block downtown historic district. The district contains a whopping 254 buildings listed on the National Register of Historic Places, making it one of the largest such districts in Colorado. *Contact Breckenridge Resort Chamber | 311 S. Ridge St., 80424 | 970/453–2913 | www.gobreck.com.*

Gold Rush Tours. Grab a hardhat and walk along ore-car tracks into the Washington Mine, where old-time miners drilled and blasted gold from the rock. The hands-on tour lets you peer down into a manway and shaft and see tools and equipment the miners used in the 19th century—things like candles, carbide lights, rock drills, and dynamite. You will also learn why the prospectors dug where they did. On the Lomax Placer Gulch Tour, you can visit a miner's cabin and pan for gold. The tours last approximately 1½ hours; tickets are available at the Information Cabin (309 N. Main St.), at the Activity Center in Blue River Plaza (137 S. Main St.), or at the mine site. | Washington Mine: 465 Illinois Gulch Rd. off Boreas Pass Rd.; Lomax Mine: 301 Ski Hill Rd. | 970/453–9022 | www.summithistorical.org | $6 | June–early Sept., Tues.–Sat. at 1 (Washington); at 3 (Lomax).

Walking Tours. The Summit Historical Society has laid out walking tours of the historical homes and businesses of Breckenridge, which you can take on your own or guided by a docent. On a guided tour of the 1880 Alice G. Milne House, the Edwin Carter Museum, and the 1896 W. H. Briggle House you can hear about the town's colorful past. In one incident, infamous gangster Pug Ryan is said to have interrupted a poker game at the now defunct Denver Hotel and made off with the loot. You can see the centerpiece of the hotel, a mahogany-and-oak Brunswick bar, at the Horseshoe II Restaurant next door to where the hotel once stood. Tickets for the tour can be purchased at the Information Cabin (309 N. Main St.) or at the Activity Center in Blue River Plaza (137 S. Main St.). The tours start from the plaza. | 970/453–9022 | www.summithistorical.org | $6 | June–early Sept., Tues.–Sat. 10 AM.

BURLINGTON
▼▼

Founded as a railroad town along the Rock Island Railroad, Burlington was incorporated in 1888 and became the county seat of newly formed Kit Carson County shortly thereafter. Twelve miles from the Kansas border, it was a fairly isolated agricultural outpost. *Contact Burlington Chamber of Commerce | 415 15th St., 80807 | 719/346–8070.*

Beecher Island Battlefield. In 1868, one of the last battles between the U.S. Army and Native American tribes was fought on a small island in the Arikaree River about 17 mi south of what is now the town of Wray. Among the nearly 100 who died here (75 of whom were Native Americans) were the legendary Cheyenne warrior Roman Nose and the Army troop's second in command, Lieutenant Fred H. Beecher, for whom the island and battle were named. A monument is surrounded by memorial markers commemorating the army soldiers who died in the battle. | CR KK, 44 mi north of Burlington off U.S. 385 | 970/332–5063 | Free | Daily dawn–dusk.

Old Town. Folks in Burlington take their history seriously, and Exhibit A proving this point is an authentic re-creation of an Old West village. More than 20 restored turn-of-the-20th-century buildings are complete with antique frontier memorabilia. Daily cancans take place throughout the summer in the Longhorn Saloon, a happily cheesy reproduction of an Old West watering hole. It's a hoot and a half. | I–70, Exit 437 | 719/346–7382 | $6 | Late May–early Sept., daily 9–6; early Sept.–late May, daily 9–5.

Wray Museum. In 1992, the Smithsonian Institution opened a permanent exhibit in this unlikely location, highlighting thousands of artifacts uncovered from a huge Ice Age bison kill site discovered near here in the mid-1970s. But more interesting to fans of more recent western history will be the permanent exhibit on the Battle of Beecher Island, which occurred about 15 mi to the south. A diorama depicts the Battle of Beecher Island, and a cannon from the battle is on display. The museum is also the tourist information office for Wray, 54 mi north of Burlington. | 203 E. 3rd St., at U.S. 34, Wray | 970/332–5063 | $1 | Tues.–Sat. 10–noon and 1–5.

CAÑON CITY
▼▼

When the West got wild, the wild got sent to Cañon City. This no-nonsense town has been the undisputed bad-guy capital of Colorado since pre-statehood days. The austere limestone enclosure at the west end of town is the original territorial prison of Colorado, which began welcoming ne'er-do-wells and no-good varmints way back in 1871. Famous residents of the joint have included "Colorado Cannibal" Alferd Packer and 11-year-old murderer Anton Woode. U.S. 50 is the garish main drag through town, but you can jump back a century by going one block west to the town's turn-of-the-20th-century Main Street. The restored 1883 St. Cloud Hotel at the corner of 7th and Main is one of the town's architectural jewels. *Contact Cañon City Chamber of Commerce | 403 Royal Gorge Blvd., 81212 | 719/275–2331 or 800/876–7922 | www.canoncitychamber.com.*

Cañon City Municipal Museum. While the territorial prison may have put Cañon City on the map, early ranching, farming, and ore processing all played a part in making it a thriving community. This museum complex includes a 1860 log cabin built by the first warden of the territorial prison and located at its original site, a pioneer cabin moved from another location, and a small three-story stone house built in 1881. Artifacts include old firearms, blacksmith's tools, and a collection of 19th-century furnishings. The museum's Amick Gallery highlights the work of noted (and locally born and raised) western artist and illustrator Robert Wesley Amick. | 612 Royal Gorge Blvd. | 719/269–9018 | $2 | Early May–early Sept., Tues.–Sun. 10–4; early Sept.–early May, Tues.–Sat. 10–4.

CENTRAL CITY
▼▼

In 1859, John Gregory struck gold in Clear Creek canyon west of Denver. A manic few years followed, and the area became known as the richest square mile on earth. The first town was called Mountain City, and others—with colorful names like Dog Town, Eureka, Black Hawk Point, and Enterprise City—soon dotted the surrounding gulches and hillsides. Central City quickly emerged as the most important town in the district and was named the county seat when Gilpin County was organized in 1861, a full 15 years before Colorado statehood. By the turn of the 20th century, the area's mining glory days were over and the towns began a gradual slide into decline. In 1990, the legalization of limited-stakes gambling reawakened the historically significant but barely surviving towns of Central City and Black Hawk, and many of the grand hotels and commercial buildings found new life as casinos. *Contact Gilpin County Chamber of Commerce | Box 343, Black Hawk 80422 | 303/582–5077 or 800/331–5825 | www.peaknet.org/webpages/gilchamber.*

Argo Gold Mine, Mill and Museum. The huge, rust-red "Mighty Argo" gold mill has stood on the hillside above the town of Idaho Springs for more than 100 years. Restored and listed on the National Register of Historic Places, the mill now houses a mining museum within a complex that also includes a reproduction of a western mining town. You can pan for gold, see the old mill at work grinding ore, and visit the mines. The museum displays mining artifacts, old payrolls, and photographs of the miners who worked here. | 2350 Riverside Dr., Idaho Springs | 303/567–2421 | $9.50 | May–Sept., daily 9–6; Oct.–Apr. by appointment only.

Black Hawk. Though the casinos have come to town and erected massive structures completely out-of-scale with the original Victorian architecture, there's no denying Black Hawk's historic significance. The entire town is part of the Central City-Black Hawk Historic District, and many 19th-century buildings have been preserved along Gregory and Main streets. But the true heart of historic Black Hawk is the filligreed Lace House, a gingerbread confection that has stood in the center of town since 1863 and at the center of controversy for a number of years. The adjacent casino wants to move it to make room for more parking. Historic preservations are fighting to keep the house on its own foundation at its original address (161 Main St.). In the end, Lace House may (or may not) be moved into a historic village being cobbled together up the road a bit in Mountain City (between Black Hawk and Central City). Either way, you'll have to be satisfied with a look at the exterior of the little house, which is considered Colorado's finest example of Carpenter Gothic architecture. | Rte. 279, 1 mi east of Central City.

Central City Opera House. The centerpiece of Central City's Historic District, the Opera House has played host to scores of legendary performers since first opening in 1878. It was built at a time when Central City rivaled Denver in glamour and importance, and the interior is lavish. If you have the chance to attend a performance (that's the only way you can get in), check out the elaborately frescoed ceiling and the excellent acoustics. Because there's no central heating, performances are held in summer only. | 200 Eureka St. | 303/292–6700 box office | www.centralcityopera.org.

Gilpin County Historical Society Museum. Housed in the town's old schoolhouse, a handsome two-story stone structure built by Cornish masons in 1870, the museum focuses on 19th-century life in Central City and the surrounding gold camps and boomtowns. Highlights include a replica of the town's Main Street, circa 1900; displays of a doctor's office and a barbershop of the Victorian era; home furnishings, toys, and clothing; and remnants from the original Black Hawk and Central City post offices. | 228 E. High St. | 303/582–5283 | $3; $5 combined admission to Thomas House Museum | June–Sept., daily 11–4; Oct.–May by appointment only.

Phoenix Gold Mine. The notable difference that sets the Phoenix Mine tour apart from many other mine tours is that this is a working gold mine, where you can see all aspects of hard-rock gold mining and processing being done by actual miners. Co-owner and lead tour-guide Al Mosch is a born storyteller and engaging host. | Box 3236, Idaho Springs | 303/567–0422 | $9 | Daily 10–6 | www.phoenixmine.com.

Thomas House Museum. This 1874 house is an example of Colorado's Victorian mountain elegance. Family photos and heirlooms, such as period quilts and feather hats, document the life of the Billings-Thomas family, who owned the house from 1894 until 1987. | 209 Eureka St. | 303/582–5283 | $3; $5 combined admission to Gilpin County Historical Society Museum | June–Sept., Fri.–Mon. 11–4; Oct.–May by appointment only.

✦ ON THE CALENDAR: June **Lou Bunch Day.** In honor of the town's last madam, Central City throws bed races, a formal costume ball, and other festivities. | 303/582–5251.

COLORADO SPRINGS

▼▼

Colorado Springs' place in history is inextricably tied to its geography and geology. Centuries before white explorers arrived, Cheyenne, Ute, Arapaho, and other Native American tribes hunted in the high plains to the east and frequented the abundant mineral springs in the foothills to the west. Towering above those foothills is the great white peak named for Zebulon Pike, who was a 27-year-old army lieutenant when he first saw the mountain in 1806. In 1859 prospectors established a village called Colorado City as a supply depot and jumping-off point for the goldfields lying on the backside of the front range. It was still a rough-around-the-edges frontier outpost when railroad tycoon General William Jackson Palmer passed through the area in 1870. A Quaker, strict teetotaler, and gentleman accustomed to the finer things in life, he judged this the perfect place to build a genteel resort like those back East. Palmer staked out the first streets of Colorado Springs a year after he arrived. For many decades, the well-mannered and well-moneyed spa town, which came to be known as "the Saratoga of the West," stood in stark contrast to the wide-open, Wild West mining settlement on its western fringes.

The seminal moment in the Springs' evolution occurred in 1891, when gold was discovered in nearby Cripple Creek. Within 10 years, the Colorado Springs' population had tripled to 35,000. Sprinkled among its residents were a fair number of newly minted millionaires, many of whom built magnificent mansions in the North End of the city. When the gold played out sometime after 1915, Colorado Springs returned to its original incarnation as quiet resort town, but it has kept growing ever since. *Contact Colorado Springs Convention and Visitor Bureau | 104 S. Cascade Ave., Suite 104, 80903 | 719/635–7506 or 800/368–4748 | www.coloradosprings-travel.com. Old Colorado City Historical Society | One South 24th St. | 719/636–1225 | http://history.oldcolo.com.*

Colorado Springs Pioneers Museum. Colorado pioneers get their due at the municipal museum of Colorado Springs, which is housed in the elegant former El Paso County courthouse. Built in 1903, it is listed on the National Register of Historic Places. The museum's holdings include artifacts of the colorful history of the region's Native Americans, Spanish, and 19th-century immigrants from Europe. Especially worthwhile is the in-depth exhibit on the great western surveys and explorations of Hayden, Pike, Long, and Fremont. | 215 S. Tejon St. | 719/385–5990 | www.colorado-springs.com/fmp/cspm | Free | May–Oct., Tues.–Sat. 10–5, Sun. 1–5; Nov.–Apr., Tues.–Sat. 10–5.

Ghost Town Museum. Like the other Old West ghost-town attractions around Colorado, this one is built around authentic turn-of-the-20th-century buildings relocated from their original sites. The blacksmith shop, general store, saloon, and other edifices come mostly from played-out mining towns, and the entire "town" of 20-odd structures is housed in a vintage 1899 Colorado Midlands Railroad building. Low-tech moving mannequins liven up (kind of) several of the displays. | 400 S. 21st St. | 719/634–0696 | $5 | May–early Sept., Mon.–Sat. 9–6, Sun. noon–6; early Sept.–Apr., Mon.–Sat. 10–5, Sun. noon–5.

Old Colorado City. Once a separate, rowdier town where miners caroused, Old Colorado City is today a National Historic Landmark District in Colorado Springs. Colorado City served as Colorado's original territorial capital, hosting the first legislative caucus in 1862. The small log building where the legislature met still stands in Bancroft Park near the center of the old town. | Colorado Ave. from 24th to 27th St. | 719/636–1225 | www.history.oldcolo.com.

Rock Ledge Ranch Historic Site. This living-history farm and outdoor museum preserves three periods in Pikes Peak regional history from 1860 to 1910. Guides in period clothing serve as living historians, leading tours of homesteads typical to the three eras. You can see the 1860s Galloway homestead, the 1880s Chambers farm and blacksmith shop, and the lavish "Orchard House" built by General William Jackson Palmer in 1907. The American Indian Interpretive Area, also a living-history installation, depicts Ute life along the central front range as it was between 1775 and 1835. | 3202 Chambers Way | 719/578–6777 | $5 | June–early Sept., Wed.–Sun. 10–5; mid-late Sept., Sat. 10–4, Sun. noon–4.

Western Museum of Mining and Industry. Rivaled only by the National Mining Museum in Leadville as a repository of the West's rich mining heritage, the museum exhibits everything from a simple gold pan to a massive (and still working) 1895 Corliss Steam Engine. A guided tour is the best way to experience this unusual museum, for the knowledgeable and enthusiastic guides discuss the equipment and demonstrate techniques from mining's early days. | Exit 156A off I-25 N | 719/488–0880 | www.wmmi.org | $6 | June–Oct., Mon.–Sat. 9–4, Sun. noon–4; Nov.–May, Mon.–Sat. 9–4.

HISTORIC LODGING

Holden House. Luxurious amenities like turn-down service and complimentary refreshments bring modern comfort to two Victorian houses and a carriage house. Five guest suites are outfitted with fireplaces, sitting areas, and two-person tubs, and decorated with antiques. On a residential street near Old Colorado City, the inn offers mountain views from the porch swings and fountains in the garden. No children, no pets, no smoking. | 1102 W. Pikes Peak Ave., 80904 | 719/471–3980 or 888/565–3980 | fax 719/471-4740 | www.bbonline.com/co/holden | 5 suites | $130–$145 | AE, D, DC, MC, V | BP.

CORTEZ

▼▼

The Navajos called Cortez "Tsaya-toh," meaning "rock water," for Mitchell Springs, a spring that once watered Navajo sheep. The water supply also attracted ranchers to the area in the early 1880s, and cattle became the town's economic mainstay. Founded in 1886, Cortez still sees plenty of modern-day cattle drives and action-packed rodeos. Much as they did in the late 1800s, Navajo and Ute still frequent the area to sell traditional artwork at trading posts. *Contact Colorado Welcome Center | 928 E. Main St., 81321 | 970/565–3414 or 800/253–1616 | www.swcolo.org.*

Cortez Cultural Center. Painted to resemble the cliff dwellings of Mesa Verde, the circa-1909 home of the Cortez Cultural Center also has a mural on its back wall depicting a traditional pueblo. Also outside, in the Cultural Park, are an authentic Navajo hogan and Ute tepee. When you finally make it inside, you'll see exhibits such as the Southwest Pioneers display, which features clothing from the frontier era. The Ute Collection, on loan from the tribe, showcases artifacts ranging from beaded vests and moccasins to ceremonial pipes and baskets. | 25 N. Market St. | 970/565–1151 | www.cortezculturalcenter.org | Free | Late May–early Sept., Mon.–Sat. 10–10; early Sept.–late May, Mon.–Sat. 10–5.

✦ ON THE CALENDAR: May–Sept. **Native American Dances.** The Cortez Cultural Center invites performers from the Ute, Navajo, and Hopi tribes to perform traditional dances from their respective cultures. | 970/565–1151.

June **Ute Mountain Round Up Rodeo.** A parade and rodeo competition are the centerpieces of this Old West celebration at the Legion Arena. | 970/565–4485.

CRAIG
▼▼

Mention Moffat County, and images of Butch Cassidy and the Sundance Kid, the Wild Bunch, the Hole-in-the-Wall Gang, Harry Tracy, and David Lant immediately come to mind. But though this area is most famous for its outlaw past, it has a respectable history as well. The first settler arrived in 1881, and eight years later an entrepreneur by the name of W. H. Tucker traveled here from Glenwood Springs to set up a townsite in anticipation of the arrival of the railroad. He named the town after his chief financial backer. Tucker built himself a house and started a general mercantile business, and Craig was on its way. *Contact Moffat County Visitor's Center | 360 E. Victory Way, Craig 81625 | 800/864–4405 | www.craig-chamber.com.*

Museum of Northwest Colorado. Everything from arrowheads to old photos and from railroad memorabilia to a fire truck shows up in this museum in a restored county courthouse and former state armory. On the second floor is the Cowboy and Gunfighter Museum, the world's largest private collection of cowboy artifacts—guns, bits, saddles, bootjacks, holsters, and spurs of all descriptions. The museum also houses the largest stretched-canvas oil painting on the Western Slope of Colorado. The painting by local artist F. Williams-Reust, titled *Craig, Colorado 1895,* shows the town on an early September morning. A life-size bronze statue of James Robinson, a turn-of-the-20th-century cowboy, stands in Estey Memorial Park on the north side of the museum. | 590 Yampa Ave. | 970/824–6360 | www.museumnwco.org | Free | Mon.–Sat. 9–5.

✦ ON THE CALENDAR: May **Grand Olde West Days.** On Memorial Day weekend, people converge on the Moffat County Fairgrounds for live music, rides, arts and crafts, western history displays, quickdraw shooting exhibitions, bull riding, a rodeo, and a parade. | 970/824–5689 or 800/864–4405.

CREEDE
▼▼

Creede's reputation as one of Colorado's rowdiest mining camps was immortalized in a poem by the local newspaper editor, Cy Warman: "It's day all day in daytime, and there is no night in Creede." The last silver boomtown in Colorado, Creede was populated by the usual cast of characters: Along with the prospectors and miners came gamblers, saloonkeepers, and ladies of the evening. The boom peaked in 1892, when every other building was either a saloon or a bordello. Bob Ford, who killed Jesse James, was himself gunned down here; other notorious residents included Calamity Jane, Bat Masterson, and the cigar-smoking, gun-toting Poker Alice Tubbs. *Contact Creede-Mineral County Chamber of Commerce | 1207 N. Main St., 81130 | 719/658–2374 or 800/327–2102 | www.creede.com.*

Bachelor Historic Tour. Take a 17-mi driving tour through Creede's old silver mining district and nearby ghost towns. The driving loop starts north of Creede and ends south of town. You can buy a guidebook with a map at area businesses, the chamber of commerce, or the visitor center. | FS Rd. 503 north, then FS Rd. 504 south | Free | Daily.

Creede Museum. Housed in the town's original Denver & Rio Grande Railroad Depot, the museum paints a vivid portrait of Creede's rough-and-tumble Old West days. You can see the first local hand-drawn fire wagon, a horse-drawn hearse, early pioneer utensils, a photo collection, early newspapers, and troves of memorabilia gathered from homesteaders, prospectors, miners, and notorious characters who helped make Creede what it is today. | 6th and San Luis Sts. | 719/658–2004 | www.creede.com/attract.htm#museum | $1 | Late May–early Sept, Mon.–Sat. 10–4.

Underground Mining Museum and Mining Tour. Learn about early mining techniques while gaining insight into an important part of western history. Demonstrations and exhibits give you a first-hand look at what it was like to be a miner. The museum, one of Creede's most popular attractions, is housed in a series of rooms and tunnels blasted into the cliff face of Willow Creek Canyon, at the north edge of town. The gift shop sells minerals and gemstones as well as reproductions of mining and historic artifacts. | 13 Forest Service Rd. | 719/658–0811 | www.creede.com/attract.htm | Audio tour $6, guided tour $10 | June–Aug., daily 10–4; Sept.–May, weekdays 10–3.

✦ ON THE CALENDAR: May **Mountain Man Rendezvous.** The mountain man era of the 1830s is celebrated at this festival, where participants wear period clothing and test their skills in events like the black-powder shoot and storytelling contests. | 719/658–0420 or 800/327–2102.

July **Knife and Tomahawk Throwing Contest.** Wearing period clothing, participants throw knives and tomahawks at targets in a typical Old West contest. Competitors are required to use authentic equipment, meaning handles must be made out of bone, antler, or wood. | 719/658–0420 or 800/327–2102.

HISTORIC DINING AND LODGING

The Creede Hotel and Restaurant. A relic of the silver bonanza days, this two-story 1890s structure has hosted many famous borders, including Poker Alice Tubbs, Calamity Jane, and Bob Ford, the baby-face killer of Jessie James. Back in its heyday, it was known as Zang's Hotel (it was named for its owner) and was considered one of the finest in town. The four guest rooms have been restored, and two of the upstairs bedrooms share a balcony overlooking Main Street. In the restaurant ($12–$25), which draws patrons from as far away as Taos and San Francisco, an Old West atmosphere prevails. The menu includes everything from hamburgers and steaks to fresh trout to pheasant and venison. Dining reservations are essential; in slower months (October–December) the restaurant is open only for Friday and Saturday dinner and Sunday brunch. Restaurant; no a/c, no room phones, no cable TV, no smoking. | 120 N. Main St., 81130 | 719/658–2608 | fax 719/658–0725 | www.creedehotel. com | 4 rooms | $80–$95 | Closed Jan. | AE, D, DC, MC, V | BP.

CRESTED BUTTE

▼▼

Before the first gold and silver prospectors arrived in the Crested Butte area in the 1870s, Ute Indians used the area as summer hunting grounds. The former mining center has been declared a National Historic District, and a stroll down Elk Avenue will show you why. Crested Butte still looks like a bustling 19th-century boomtown, even though the trading posts are now occupied by art dealers, restaurants, and pottery studios. In the residential neighborhoods, exquisite Victorian gingerbread-trim houses—albeit painted in whimsical shades of hot pink, magenta, and chartreuse—remain from the old days. *Contact Crested Butte Chamber of Commerce | Box 1288, 81224 | 970/349–6438 or 800/545–4505 | www.crestedbuttechamber.com.*

Crested Butte Mountain Heritage Museum. A former blacksmith shop, hardware store, and the site of the town's first gas station, this 1883 building now serves as the town museum. Some evidence of the building's past is retained in the potbelly stove that has warmed the building since the early 1900s. The stove, which sits in the center of the building, is still in use today. Exhibits cover the history of the town, particularly its origins as a mining camp (catch the life-size coal-mine diorama) and ranching in the region. Attention is also given to the ethnic heritage of the area's settlers: Welsh and English arrived in the early 1880s, followed by Slovenians and Croats in the late 1890s to mid-1900s. | 331 Elk Ave. | 970/349–1880 | www.discovercolorado.com/crestedbuttemuseum | $2 | Late Nov.–mid-Apr., Tues.–Sun. 2–7; early June–late Sept., Tues.–Sun 1–6.

Historic District Walking Tour. Pick up a map at the chamber of commerce office (601 Elk Ave. | 970/349–6438) and wander the streets at your own pace to learn about the city's landmarks. Some of the more interesting buildings include the Railroad Depot, the Princess Theatre, the Wooden Nickel Saloon, and the Old Town Hall. | Bounded by 7th St. to the east and 1st St. to the west, and by Gothic Ave. to the north and Whiterock Ave. to the south | 970/349–6438 or 800/545–4505 | www.crestedbuttechamber.com | Free | Daily.

CRIPPLE CREEK

▼▼

Three decades after prospectors hit pay dirt in the gold camps west of Denver, Cripple Creek overshadowed them all. In 1890, a cowhand and part-time prospector named Bob Womack was the first to strike gold here, in the weirdly misnamed Poverty Gulch. Womack sold it, but his claim eventually yielded $5 million in gold. The strike was just the beginning for this town, which earned the moniker "the World's Greatest Gold Camp." At the height of its glory, the town was home to more than 25,000, and there were 10 post-office towns in the Cripple Creek district. Frenzied prospectors operated more than 500 mines, producing more gold than the Alaska and California gold rushes combined. Two infernos destroyed much of the old settlement in 1896, but the town rebuilt in stone and brick, and those structures still stand as a testament to the town's gung-ho spirit. Today, Cripple Creek has a population of 584. *Contact Cripple Creek Chamber of Commerce | Box 650, 80813 | 719/689–2169 or 800/526–8777 | www.cripple-creek.co.us. Cripple Creek Historic District | Box 430, 80813 | 719/689–3315 or 877/858–4653.*

Cripple Creek District Museum. Providing a glimpse into mining life at the turn of the 20th century, the museum's holdings are spread among three buildings: the 1895 Midland Terminal Railway Depot, the 1893 Colorado Trading and Transfer Building, and a turn-of-the-20th-century assay office. Among the displays are mining machinery and memorabilia, Victorian clothing and furniture, American Indian artifacts, photographs, maps, letters, and a broad array of items salvaged from the mining district's many towns and camps. | East end of Bennett Ave. | 719/689–2634 | $2.50 | Late May–mid-Oct., daily 10–5; mid-Oct.–late May, weekends noon–4.

Cripple Creek & Victor Narrow Gauge Railroad. In bygone days, more than 50 ore-laden trains a day made the run between Cripple Creek and its rival, Victor, 6 mi to the south. You can climb aboard for the meandering ride past abandoned mines and stroll the streets of Victor, which is almost a ghost town. Walking among the abandoned and partially restored buildings is an eerie experience that does far more to evoke the mining (and post-mining) days than its tarted-up neighbor. | Depot at Cripple Creek District Museum, east end of Bennett Ave. | 719/689–2640 | $9 | Late May–Oct., daily 10–5; departs every 45 mins.

Golden Loop Historic Parkway. This self-guided driving tour to the abandoned mining districts of Cripple Creek and Victor focuses on gold rush–era history and includes some of the ghost towns and abandoned mines in the area. You can pick up a map at the Cripple Creek Welcome Center. Allow at least two to three hours for the tour, which involves a minimum of 60 mi of driving. | Loop follows U.S. 67 and Teller County Rd. 81 | 719/689–3315 or 800/858–4653 | www.cripple-creek.co.us/attr.html | Map 50¢.

Molly Kathleen Mine Tour. In 1891 Molly Kathleen Gortner became the first woman ever to strike a gold claim in her own name in the gold fields west of Pikes Peak. The eponymous gold mine ceased mining operations in 1961, but this popular mine tour keeps her name alive. On the nation's only vertical shaft gold-mine tour, you ride the Man Skip elevator to a depth of 1,000 ft to tour the mine's 10th level. | 1 mi north of Cripple Creek on U.S. 67 | 719/689–2466 or 888/291–5689 | $11 | Apr.–Oct., daily 8–6 | www.goldminetours.com.

Old Homestead Museum. Built in 1896, the Homestead was, during the boom years, one of Cripple Creek's most notable brothels. See if you can avoid blushing while the gracious gray-haired tour guides describe the operations and activities of the old parlor house. | 353 Myers Ave. | 719/689–3090 | $3 | May and Oct., weekends 11–4; June, daily 11–4; July–Sept., daily 10–5.

HISTORIC LODGING
Imperial Hotel and Casino. Dating from 1896, this hotel has been restored to its turn-of-the-20th-century appearance and is furnished with period antiques. Some rooms have bathrooms with claw-foot tubs; others share bathrooms down the hall. The hotel operates a three-level gaming parlor in an adjacent building. 2 restaurants, lounge, business services. | 123 N. 3rd St., 80813 | 719/689–7777 or 800/235–2922 | fax 719/689–1008 | www.imperialcasinohotel.com | 29 rooms | $65–$95 | AE, D, DC, MC, V.

DELTA
▼▼

Delta lies along the banks of the Gunnison River in the midst of Colorado's fruit-growing region. Originally inhabited by a band of Ute Indians and a few white fur traders, Delta got its start in 1826 as a fur-trading post called Fort Uncompahgre. However, the name "Uncompahgre" was so difficult to pronounce that the settlement's name was changed to Delta, for the wedge of land where the Uncompahgre and Gunnison rivers meet. The fort remained in operation until 1844, when the Ute became tired of intrusion into their lands and torched the post. Relations between whites and Indians continued to deteriorate. After gold was discovered in the Rocky Mountains, the Ute were forced off their land and taken to a reservation in Utah, allowing for white settlement of much of western Colorado. By 1882, Delta had grown to include two stores, two saloons, and a dozen other buildings, including a church and post office. The town's economic base was ranching, which continues today. *Contact Delta Area Chamber of Commerce | 301 Main St., 81416 | 970/874–8616 | www.deltacolorado.org.*

Confluence Park. The primary feature of this park is its replica of Fort Uncompahgre, staffed by guides in period dress. A visit to the fort sends you back to when trapping beaver was the only occupation around. Take a guided tour into the trade room, where Indians and trappers exchanged furs for guns, knives, beads, and other prized goods. | 205 Gunnison River Dr. | 970/874–8349 | $5 | June–Aug., Tues.–Sat. 10–5; Mar.–May and Sept.–mid-Dec., weekdays 10–4.

Delta County Museum. Among this museum's idiosyncratic collection, one of the more interesting exhibits is of guns used in a failed bank-robbery attempt in Delta on September 7, 1893. That day, the notorious McCarty Gang rode into town to rob the Farmers & Merchants Bank. The robbery went bad almost from the start, when one of the robbers shot and killed the cashier. The gunfire alerted a hardware-store clerk, who grabbed his Sharps rifle and killed two of the robbers during their getaway. | 251 Meeker St. | 970/874–8721 | $2 | May–Sept., Tues.–Sat. 10–4; Oct.–Apr., Wed. and Sat. 10–4.

Escalante Canyon. Named after Spanish missionary explorer Francisco Silvestre Velez de Escalante, who with father Francisco Atanasio Dominguez led an expedition through the area in 1776, Escalante Canyon shelters homesteader cabins (including the 1911 Walker Cabin), Indian rock art, and hiking trails. One of the pioneer homes was built by Captain H. A. Smith. His stone cabin, built into the side of a boulder, has a hollowed-out slab for a bed and a smaller niche carved out of the stone wall to hold a bedside pistol. Signs are visible from the main highway, and the sites are well marked. You can hike the several miles on the dirt road off the main highway or drive right up to the site. | 10 mi north of Delta on U.S. 50 | 970/874–8616 | Free | Daily.

Pioneer Town. Take a step back in time and discover how the early settlers of Colorado once lived. Main Street in Pioneer Town is made up of wooden sidewalks and a cluster of 23 authentic buildings furnished and outfitted with artifacts of the period. You will find a country chapel, the Lizard Head Saloon, a working blacksmith shop, and the famous wooden silos from the Bar-I Ranch, the last surviving original ranch structures. | 315 S.W. 3rd Ave., Cedaredge | 970/856–7554 | www.cedaredgecolorado.com | $5 | Late May–Sept., Mon.–Sat. 9–4, Sun. 1–4.

✦ ON THE CALENDAR: Sept. **Council Tree Pow Wow and Cultural Festival.** American Indians groups gather to share their heritage and culture through dance, music, and song in Confluence Park. | 970/874–1718 or 800/874–1741.

DENVER
▼▼

If you could go back in time to a summer's day in 1857 and stand at the confluence of Cherry Creek and the South Platte River, you would likely have seen a large encampment of Arapaho Indians and perhaps a few French trappers trading beaver pelts for buffalo robes. If you could go back to the same spot a few years later, you would scarcely believe your eyes. In May of 1858, William Russell discovered gold in Cherry Creek, and no single event had a greater impact on the settlement and development of Colorado than the gold rush that followed. By 1860, an estimated 100,000 fortune seekers had flocked to the site of the old Arapaho camp.

The manic rush for riches forever changed the central Rockies from a frontier wilderness of trading forts and Indian encampments to a hub of commerce and a land of irresistible opportunity. The land where Denver sits today was, at the time of the gold strike, legally owned by the Arapaho by virtue of the 1851 Fort Laramie Treaty. But when the richness of the land was revealed, the treaty—and the Arapaho—didn't stand a chance. Spurred on by early movers like town founder William Larimer, Colorado territorial governor John Evans, and founding editor of the *Rocky Mountain News* William N. Byers, Denver rode out early booms and busts to become the great metropolis of the Rockies.

Denver's emergence as the most important city of the mountain west could scarcely have been less likely. Six hundred miles from the closest industrial towns along the Missouri River, far from any navigable waters, and cut off from the West by the formidable barrier of the Continental Divide, Denver might well have remained an isolated outpost. But its ambitious early leaders anticipated the importance of railroads and, putting the state's mineral wealth to good use, struck deals with the major lines to use their city as a hub. Between 1870, when the first railroads arrived, and 1890 Denver's population grew from 4,759 to 106,713. In a single generation, it became the second most populous city in the West, behind only to San Francisco. *Contact Denver Metro Convention and Visitors Bureau | 1555 California St., Suite 300, 80202 | 303/892–1112 or 800/645–3446 | www.denver.org. Historic Denver | 1536 Wynkoop, Suite 400A, 80202 | 303/534–5288 | www.historicdenver.org.*

Black American West Museum and Heritage Center. This grass-roots museum, housed in the former home of Denver's first black female physician (a good story in itself), looks at western heritage from a perspective unfamiliar to most Americans. The photographs, documents, and artifacts here depict the vast contributions that African-Americans made to settling the West. One section of the museum is devoted to black cowboys, another to military troops such as the Buffalo Soldiers. Changing exhibits focus on topics such as the history of black churches in the West. | 3091 California St. | 303/292–2566 | $4 | May–Sept., daily 10–5; Oct.–Apr., Wed.–Fri. 10–2, weekends 10–5.

Colorado History Museum. The state's frontier past is vibrantly depicted in changing exhibits on different eras. Permanent displays include detailed dioramas of pioneer settlements, Indian encampments, and mining camps, Conestoga wagons, the requisite mining paraphernalia, and a powerful exhibit relating the stories of the Cheyenne Dog Soldiers, the Sand Creek Massacre and the battle at Summit Springs. The entire museum is excellent, but the jewel is the extraordinary time line called "The Colorado Chronicle 1800–1950," which depicts the state's history in amazing detail. The mixed-media display stretches 112 ft, 6 inches and dedicates 9 inches to each year. It's crammed with artifacts from rifles to land-grant surveys and old daguerreotypes. | 1300 Broadway | 303/866–3682 | www.coloradohistory.org | $5 | Mon.–Sat. 10–4:30, Sun. noon–4:30.

Comanche Crossing Museum. This collection of historic buildings 30 mi east of Denver on I–70 includes two schoolhouses (one dating from 1891), a depot, and a barn. Exhibits detail the history of the area as well as of the Transcontinental Railroad. It was at this location, in 1870, that the Kansas Pacific Railroad laid the final tracks that first connected the Atlantic to the Pacific. (The tracks that were joined 15 months earlier at Promontory Point—of "golden spike" fame—in Utah only connected Omaha and Sacramento.) | 56060 E. Colfax Ave., Strasburg | 303/622–4322 | Free | June–Aug., daily 1–4.

LoDo. The historic lower downtown area was once the city's thriving retail center; then it fell into disuse and slid into slums. Since the early 1990s, LoDo has metamorphosed into the city's cultural center, thanks to its resident avant-garde artists, retailers, and loft dwellers who have taken over the old warehouses and redbricks. Walking tours of historic LoDo are conducted every Saturday from late May through early October. | From Larimer St. to the South Platte River, between 14th and 22nd Sts. | 303/628–5428 | www.lodo.org.

HISTORIC LODGING

Brown Palace. Built in 1892, Denver's hotel empress is still considered the city's most prestigious address. Reputedly, this was the first atrium hotel in the United States: Its ornate, nine-story-high lobby is crowned by a Tiffany stained-glass window. The Victorian-style rooms will give you a taste of the past even as they provide you with all the modern comforts. Free guided tours are offered at 2 each Wednesday and Saturday. 4 restaurants, in-room data ports, in-room fax, gym, 2 bars, laundry service, concierge, business services, parking (fee). | 321 17th St., 80202 | 303/297–3111 or 800/321–2599 | fax 303/297–2954 | www.brownpalace.com | 230 rooms, 25 suites | $225–$255 | AE, D, DC, MC, V.

DURANGO
▼▼

Unlike so many other Colorado towns, Durango wasn't founded by prospectors looking for gold. It was established as a railroad town in 1879 by General William Palmer, president of the all-powerful Denver & Rio Grande Railroad. When nearby Animas City refused to donate land for a railroad depot, Palmer decided to set up shop on his own. By 1881, Durango was a full-fledged town with its own government. The following year, the railroad tracks to nearby Silverton were complete and the train began hauling both passengers and freight. It's estimated that more than $300 million in precious metals was hauled over this route. Shortly before the turn of the 20th century, Durango had electric power, a streetcar, several newspapers, and more than 2,700 inhabitants. *Contact Durango Area Chamber Resort Association | 111 S. Camino Del Rio, 81301 | 970/247–0312 or 800/GO–DURANGO | www.durango.org.*

Durango & Silverton Narrow Gauge Railroad. The most entertaining way to relive the Old West days of Durango is to take a ride on the train. You'll travel in comfort in restored 1882 parlor cars as the train's shrill whistle accompanies the chugging of the locomotive. The route wends its way through the fertile Animas River valley and at times clings precariously to the hillside. You will want to set aside the better part of a day for the eight-hour round-trip journey along the 45-mi railway. | 479 Main Ave. | 970/247–2733 | www.durangotrain.com | $55–$60 | May–Oct., 8:15 and 9 AM; June–Aug., 7:30 and 9:45 AM.

Durango National Historic District. In the city's historic district, old-fashioned gas lamps grace streets lined with superlative Victorian-era buildings. A hodgepodge of architectural styles shows up in the restored structures: Greek Revival, Gothic Revival, Queen Anne, Spanish colonial mission. The heart of the district is the intersection of 13th Avenue and Main Avenue (also known as Main Street), where chic shops and restaurants now occupy the old buildings. Mustsees include the 1882 train depot, the 1887 Strater Hotel, and the three-story sandstone Newman Building. For an authentic saloon experience, stop in at the Diamond Belle in the Strater Hotel. Piano music fills a room awash in velour and lace, and waitresses clad in scanty Gay '90s outfits deliver drinks from a gilt-and-mahogany bar. You may also want to check out the district's Victorian residences, which range from the imposing mansions of railroad and smelting executives to the more modest homes of well-to-do merchants. One-hour trolley tours ($10) on the Queen City Trolley depart three times a day from either the Strater Hotel or the Doubletree Hotel. Maps for self-guided tours are available at the visitor center (111 S. Camino Del Rio). | Bounded by 15th St. to the north and 5th St. to the south, and by 3rd Ave. to the east and Main St. to the west | 970/247–0312 or 800/GO–DURANGO | Free | Daily.

✦ ON THE CALENDAR: Oct. **Durango Cowboy Gathering.** The first weekend in October, working cowboys and their imitators gather for a rodeo, western art exhibition, cowboy poetry slam, storytelling sessions, and a dance. The event is held at the Diamond Circle Theater. | 970/385–8904.

HISTORIC DINING AND LODGING
Strater Hotel. Opened in 1887, this fabulously elegant Victorian beauty has been lovingly restored. The hotel owns the largest collection of Victorian walnut antiques in the country

and even has its own on-site wood shop to create accurate period reproductions. So it is no wonder that your room, which might have accommodated Butch Cassidy or Louis L'Amour (he wrote *The Sacketts* here), is swooningly exquisite. Each chamber is individually decorated with Victorian furniture. There are wood carvings on the ceiling, rich wool carpeting, velvet draperies, exquisite crystal lamps and chandeliers, and luxurious linens on beds topped with Victorian-stitch bedspreads. The hotel's restaurant, Henry's ($12–$26), looks like a set from an Old West movie, with flocked wallpaper, plush velour curtains, beveled windows, crystal chandeliers, and original oak beams. When it comes to the food, though, forget about beans and biscuits. Try the grilled buffalo steak or the famous pepper steak Herbert. You'll need reservations to eat here. Restaurant, bar, in-room data ports, room service, cable TV, hot tub, business services. | 699 Main Ave., 81301 | 970/247–4431 or 800/247–4431 | fax 970/259–2208 | www.strater.com | 93 rooms | $129–$235 | AE, D, DC, MC, V.

ESTES PARK
▼▼▼

Rancher Joel Estes, the first white settler in this area, built two log cabins here in 1860. Great hunting, abundant grazing land, and spectacular scenery soon began to draw many visitors and some other homesteaders. But Estes sold out to a Welshman who converted Estes's small ranch cabins into guest houses, launching Estes Park's now well-established career as a resort destination. Tourism and ranching kept population growth steady throughout the 1880s and '90s, but it wasn't until the turn of the 20th century that the town itself began to take shape. In 1905, local businessman Freelan O. Stanley (who made his fortune as the inventor of the Stanley Steamer automobile) platted a downtown. Often called "The Grand Old Man of Estes Park," Stanley also donated land for the growing town, built an electric plant, and donated considerable sums for road improvement. But Stanley's most obvious legacy is the stately Stanley Hotel, which has stood sentry over the town since 1909. *Contact Information Center at the Chamber of Commerce | 500 Big Thompson Ave., 80517 | 970/586–4431 or 800/443–7837 | www.estesparkresort.com.*

Enos Mills Original Cabin. Enos Mills, sometimes called the father of Rocky Mountain National Park, once lived in this cabin 8 mi south of Estes Park. Built in 1885, it stands on 200 undeveloped acres in the shadow of Long's Peak. A nature guide and self-guided nature trails are also available. | 6760 Rte. 7, 8 mi south of Estes Park | 970/586–4706 | Free | Late May–early Sept., Tues.–Sun. 11–4; early Sept.–late May by appointment only.

Estes Park Area Historical Museum. The museum presents four (or so) rotating exhibits each year, along with its permanent exhibit, "Tracks in Time," which presents the history of the Estes Park area from the Ice Age to today. The archaeological evidence displayed makes an eloquent case that Native Americans used the area as a summer resort. | 200 4th St. | 970/586–6256 | $2.50 | May–Oct., Mon.–Sat. 10–5, Sun. 1–5; Nov.–Apr., Fri.–Sat. 10–5, Sun. 1–5.

MacGregor Ranch Museum. This 1,200-acre ranch, one of the first in the area to be homesteaded, is now operated as a pioneer living history museum in the summer. You can tour the 1896 ranch house to see furniture and possessions of three generations of the MacGregor family, which owned the property until 1970. Outside, early ranching and farming equipment is not only on display, but still in service. On the National Register of Historic Places, the ranch also conducts free educational programs covering aspects of life on a homestead-era cattle ranch. | MacGregor Ave., off U.S. 34 | 970/586–3749 | Free | June–Aug., Tues.–Fri. 10–4.

HISTORIC DINING AND LODGING
Stanley Hotel. Estes Park had a growing reputation as a resort town in 1909, when entrepreneur F. O. Stanley constructed this regal hotel on a promontory overlooking town. The

white-pillared Georgian hotel soon became one of the most glamorous resorts in the Rockies, a position it holds to this day. As is often the case with these grand dames, the sunny rooms, decorated with antiques and period reproductions, are not as sumptuous as they once were. Still, there is an incomparable air of history to the hotel, along with all the modern conveniences. The McGregor Room is the nicest restaurant in town. Restaurant, some refrigerators, cable TV, tennis court, pool, croquet, bar, playground, laundry service, meeting room. | 333 Wonder View Ave., 80517 | 970/586–3371 or 800/976–1377 | fax 970/586–4964 | 138 rooms | $189–$229 | AE, D, DC, MC, V.

FAIRPLAY

▼▼▼

In the center of Colorado, at an elevation of 8,500 ft, lies the 900-square-mi alpine valley of South Park. The lush valley, watered by three forks of the Platte River, was long a favorite hunting ground of the Ute people and, later, of French and Spanish trappers and traders. The first gold discovered in the area was found in Tarryall Creek in 1859. As usual, prospectors rushed in, and when some found themselves shut out of the Tarryall diggings, they set up camp along the South Platte. Vowing to offer a fair share of the wealth to all comers, they christened their settlement Fairplay. Many other mining camps once dotted the hillsides of South Park, but today only Fairplay, Alma, and a few other vestiges of the boom days remain. *Contact Fairplay Town Clerk | 400 Front St., Box 267, 80440 | 719/836–2622.*

Monument to Prunes, a Burro. This monument honors a faithful burro who hauled supplies to area mines for more than 60 years. | Between 16th and 17th Sts. | 719/836–2622 | Free | Daily.

St. Elmo. In the late 1800s, there were several old towns along the Denver, South Park & Pacific Railroad line west of Nathrop, but St. Elmo is now literally the last one standing. In its heyday, the town at the end of the line was home to about 1,000 residents. There are still a few solitude seekers living in the town, but it is chiefly known as one of the most visited and best-preserved ghost towns in the state. | 40 mi south of Fairplay via U.S. 285 and U.S. 24 to Nathrop, then about 15 mi west on Chalk Creek Canyon Rd. (CR 162).

South Park City. Restored or re-created pioneer villages are not hard to come by in Colorado, but nowhere in the state is there a better one. The cobbled-together 19th-century mining town offers a fascinating glimpse of gold rush–era mountain life. The buildings—which have been restored but not overly prettied—include the requisite log cabins and livery but also more unusual structures like a two-story sandstone brewery and a dual-purpose morgue and carpentry shop. Seven of the buildings sit on their original sites, and the remaining 27 have been relocated from other areas in the South Park region. | 100 4th St. | 719/836–2387 | $5 | Late May–early Sept., daily 9–7; early Sept.–late May, daily 9–5.

✦ ON THE CALENDAR: July **Burro Days.** Surely no town in America professes more devotion to the jackass than tiny Fairplay. This annual celebration of the shaggy little workhorse includes a mountain-man rendezvous and what is billed as the World-Champion Pack Burro Race. | 719/836–2659.

FORT COLLINS

▼▼▼

Fort Collins was established as a U.S. Cavalry camp in 1864 to protect traders traveling the treacherous Overland Trail from local Indians. When the military pulled out of the camp just two years later, squatters moved into the abandoned site on the Cache la Poudre River.

Congress opened the old camp to legal homesteading in 1872, and the town was officially incorporated a year later. *Contact Fort Collins Convention and Visitors Bureau | 420 S. Howes St., Suite 101, 80521 | 970/482–5821 or 800/274–3678 | fax 970/493–8061 | www.ftcollins.com.*

Avery House Historic District. The distinctive wide streets and avenues of Fort Collins are the legacy of Franklin Avery, the surveyor who platted the town in 1873. He later founded the town's First National Bank and was instrumental in developing water projects that enabled agriculture (and the town itself) to flourish in northern Colorado. The Avery House, the stately sandstone home he built in 1879, is the centerpiece of the Avery House Historic District— but it is by no means the only highlight. More than 20 notable buildings surviving from Fort Collins's early days are included on a walking tour of the district mapped out by the Fort Collins Convention and Visitors Bureau. You can tour Avery House Wednesday and Sunday between 1 and 3. | 328 W. Mountain Ave. | 970/221–0533 | Free.

Fort Collins Museum. The permanent exhibits are the best reason to visit this museum. The three historic buildings in the Pioneer Courtyard paint a vivid picture of a settler's life on the northern Colorado plains. An 1844 homesteader's cabin is one of the oldest buildings in the state, the Auntie Stone cabin is the only surviving structure from the cavalry fort era, and the 1884 schoolhouse remained in use until 1951. Inside each building are period artifacts and furnishings. The museum itself is housed in the city's 1904 Carnegie Library building and contains interpretive exhibits on the history of Fort Collins and northern Colorado as well as rotating exhibits of regional interest. | 200 Matthews St. | 970/221–6738 | www.fcgov.com/museum | Free | Tues.–Sat. 10–5, Sun. noon–5.

Old Town Square. In this National Historic District you'll find restored buildings bustling with commerce and culture. The majority of the ornate brick and stone commercial structures were built between the early 1880s and 1910. Highlights among the 22 historic structures include the Opera House Block (built in 1880), the firehouse (1882), and the Linden, Antlers, and Northern hotels. A free self-guided walking-tour brochure is available at the Fort Collins Museum and at many downtown businesses. | Mountain and College Aves. | 970/482–5821 or 800/274–3678.

✦ ON THE CALENDAR: July **Skookum Day.** "Skookum" is a Chinook Indian word meaning "full of pep," and this celebration of early pioneer life lives up to its name with a mountain-man rendezvous; demonstrations of homestead-era activities including blacksmithing, quilting, and beading; and a parade. | 970/482–5821 or 800/274–3678.

GEORGETOWN

▼▼▼

Georgetown rode the crest of the silver boom during the second half of the 19th century. Most of its elegant, impeccably maintained brick buildings, which make up a five-square-block National Historic District, date from that period. Fortunately, Georgetown hasn't been tarted up at all, so it provides a fairly accurate sense of what gracious living meant in those rough-and-tumble times. *Contact Georgetown Visitor Center | Box 426, 80444 | 800/472–8230 | www.georgetowncolorado.com.*

Georgetown Loop Railroad and Historic Mine. Hop on the 1920s narrow-gauge steam train that connects the town with the equally historic community of Silver Plume (site of the Lebanon Silver Mine). Along the way it winds through huge stands of pine and fir before crossing the 95-ft-high Devil's Gate Bridge, where the track loops back over itself as it gains elevation. The 6-mi round-trip excursion takes about 70 minutes. | 100 Loop Dr. | 303/569–2403 or 800/691–4386 | georgetownloop.com | $14.50 | Train May–Oct., daily 9:20–4.

Georgetown National Historic District. Pick up a map at the visitor center (613 Argentine St.) and stroll the streets of the five-square-block district to learn about the city's landmarks. Some of the more interesting buildings include the Hamill House Museum, once the home of silver magnate William Arthur Hamill; the elaborate Hotel de Paris, built almost single-handedly by Frenchman Louis Dupuy in 1878; and the narrow-gauge train depot. The district's 200-plus Victorian buildings include businesses and residences. | Bounded by 2nd St. to the south and 15th St. to the north, and by Argentine St. to the west and Main St. to the east | 800/472–8230 | www.georgetowncolorado.com | Free.

Lebanon Silver Mine Tour. Ever wonder what it was like to be a hard-rock miner back in the old days? Here, Colorado Historical Society guides lead you through the mine and show you the mine manager's office, the change room (also called a "dry"), and the blacksmith shop and tool shed. The walking tour lasts about one hour and 20 minutes, so wear comfortable walking shoes, and the temperature inside the mine is a chilly 44°F, so a sweater or jacket is a must. The mine, in the community of Silver Plume, is only accessible by the Georgetown Loop Railroad train (except the last trip of the day). | 100 Loop Dr., Silver Plume | 303/569–2403 or 800/691–4386 | georgetownloop.com/minetour | $6 | May–Sept., daily 10–4.

✦ ON THE CALENDAR: July **Historic Homes Tour.** On this annual tour of Georgetown's 19th-century buildings you can peek into approximately a dozen Victorian homes, churches, and the Hamill House Museum. The homes are mostly scattered throughout the historic district. Shuttle bus service is provided. | 303/569–2840.

GLENWOOD SPRINGS
▼▼

The Ute Indians first discovered the healing powers of the hot springs here and treated their animals as well as their sick with the waters. In the summer of 1860, U.S. Army captain Richard Sopris stumbled upon Yamapah Hot Springs ("Yampah" is Ute for "big medicine"), apparently the first Anglo to do so. The man credited with turning the springs into a health spa was Walter Devereux, a coal tycoon. In 1887, Devereux bought the hot springs and vapor caves for $125,000 and began planning a pool and spa resort. Some colorful characters, including gunfighter Doc Holliday and President Theodore Roosevelt, have taken the waters in Glenwood Springs. In addition to the famous hot springs, the town was also known for coal mining and ranching. *Contact Glenwood Springs Chamber Resort Association | 1102 Grand Ave., 81601 | 970/945–6589 or 888/445–3696 | www.glenscape.com.*

Frontier Historical Museum. Built in 1905 by a doctor, a former residence now houses exhibits on the Ute Indians and pioneer life in Glenwood Springs and Garfield County. The parlor, which houses a display on Doc Holliday, still retains the home's original carpets and coal-burning fireplace. Note the charcoal portrait done for Holliday in 1885 by Dutch-American artist A. Van Martin. | 1001 Colorado Ave. | 970/945–4448 | www.glenwoodguide.com/museum | $3 | May–Sept., Mon.–Sat. 11–4; Oct.–Apr., Mon. and Thurs.–Sat. 1–4.

Hot Springs. Since 1888 tourists have come to Glenwood Springs seeking the restorative effects of its water. At the Hot Springs Lodge and Pool, you can soak in 104°F water in a 100-ft-long pool or in 90°F water in a pool that is more than two city blocks (405 ft) long and contains in excess of a million gallons of water. The red sandstone bathhouse and lodge, completed in 1890, now houses a snack bar and fitness center. | 401 N. River St. | 970/945–7131 | www.hotspringspool.com | $10.25 | Late May–early Sept., daily 7:30 AM–10 PM; early Sept.–late May, daily 9 AM–10 PM.

DOC HOLLIDAY

John Henry "Doc" Holliday was a gunslinger with an attitude. Part scholar, part rebel, he was often only one step ahead of the law. Born on August 14, 1851, in Griffin, Georgia, Holliday went to dental school. Shortly after opening his practice, he was diagnosed with tuberculosis. On the advice of his doctor, Holliday moved west in 1873 in search of a drier climate.

While living in Texas, Holliday took up gambling, which became his sole means of support. His violent temper turned him into a killer: After shooting a prominent citizen and leaving him for dead, Holliday had to flee Texas. Carrying one gun in a shoulder holster, another on his hip, and a long-bladed knife (just in case), he blazed a trail of death across the Southwest. It's not known just how many men died at his hands, but some have estimated the number to be as high as 25 or more. However, historians generally believe the true number is considerably less. Holliday's reasons for killing run the gamut from fights over cards to self-defense—or so he claimed. He will forever be known for his role in one of the most famous gunfights in the history of the Wild West: a 30-second gunfight at the O.K. Corral, in Tombstone, Arizona.

In May of 1887 Holliday moved to Glenwood Springs, hoping that the sulfur vapors of the hot springs there would help his failing lungs. He lived out his dying days at the Hotel Glenwood. On the last day of his life, Holliday knocked back a glass of whiskey and remarked, "This is funny." A few minutes later he was dead. Holliday was 36 years old.

✦ **ON THE CALENDAR:** June **Strawberry Days Festival.** At the first Strawberry Days Celebration, held in 1898, fresh berries and homemade pies were the highlights. Today's festival has a rodeo competition, parade, music, arts-and-crafts booths, and free strawberries and ice cream. | 970/945–6589 or 888/445–3696.

HISTORIC LODGING

Hotel Colorado. Soon after it opened its doors in 1893, this hotel at the Glenwood hot springs became a fashionable retreat. Teddy Roosevelt even made it his unofficial "Little White House" in 1905, and the building is now listed on the National Historic Register. Modeled after the Villa de Medici in Italy, the structure is adorned with graceful sandstone colonnades and Italianate campaniles. The luxury continues in the imposing yet gracious marble lobby and public rooms. The sunny, individually decorated rooms and suites have high ceilings, fireplaces, gorgeous period wainscoting, and balconies affording superlative vistas. Restaurant, café, cable TV, hair salon, gym, bar, meeting room, pets allowed (fee). | 526 Pine St., 81601 | 970/945–6511 or 800/544–3998 | fax 970/945–7030 | www.hotelcolorado.com | 129 rooms, 32 suites | $129–$149 | AE, D, DC, MC, V.

GOLDEN
▼▼

In 1859, during the earliest days of the Colorado gold rush, Golden was born as Golden City. Proximity to mining camps like Black Hawk, Central City, Idaho Springs, and Sliver Plume made this an ideal location for a supply town, and Golden grew with gusto throughout the 1860s. Once a fierce rival of neighboring Denver, Golden served as the Colorado territorial capital from 1862 to 1867—when the Mile High City snatched that honor away. Golden is famous for the Coors Brewing Company, the Colorado School of Mines, and the gravesite of William F. "Buffalo Bill" Cody. *Contact Greater Golden Chamber of Commerce | Box 1035, 80402 | 303/279–3113 or 800/590–3113 | www.goldenchamber.org.*

12th Street Historic Residential District. This row of handsome 1860s brick buildings includes the Astor House, a former hotel dating from 1867, which is now a museum with period furnishings. The restored and replica structures—a tepee, a prospector's camp, a schoolhouse, and cabins—within Clear Creek History Park preserve the history of Golden circa 1843–1900. Tours of the park start on the hour in season. | 11th and 12th Sts. between Maple St. and Washington Ave. | 303/278–3557 | Astor House Museum early Jan.–late Dec., Tues.–Sat. 11–4; Clear Creek History Park tours daily mid-May–mid-Oct. | Astor House or Clear Creek $3, combined $4.

Buffalo Bill Grave and Museum. Contrary to popular belief, Bill Cody—Pony Express rider, cavalry scout, and tireless promoter of the myth of the West—never expressed a burning desire to be buried here. The story of how he arrived at his final resting place is more macabre: the *Denver Post* bought the corpse from Bill's sister and bribed her to concoct a teary story about his dying wish. Adjacent to the grave is a small but satisfying museum with art and artifacts detailing Cody's life and times as well as exhibits highlighting the colorful careers of other western legends like Annie Oakley, Wyatt Earp, Wild Bill Hickok, and Sitting Bull. You can also hike up Lariat Look, a winding trail that leads to Buffalo Bill's Grave, starting at 19th Avenue in west Golden. | Rte. 5 off I–70 Exit 256, or 19th Ave. out of Golden | 303/526–0747 | www.buffalobill.org | $3 | May–Oct., daily 9–5; Nov.–Apr., Tues.–Sun. 9–4.

Colorado Railroad Museum. Just outside Golden is this must-visit for any choo-choo lover. More than 50 vintage locomotives and cars are displayed outside. Inside the replica-1880 masonry depot are historical photos and steam-train memorabilia, along with an astounding model train set that chugs through a scale model of Golden. In the roundhouse you can witness a train's restoration in progress. | 17155 W. 44th Ave. | 303/279–4591 | www.crrm.org | $6 | Daily 9–5.

Golden Pioneer Museum. The collection on display at this museum includes mining artifacts, period clothing and furniture, Golden's first galvanized bathtub, and a turn-of-the-20th-century piano covered in orange velvet (really!). | 923 10th St. | 303/278–7151 | www.henge1.henge.com/~goldenpm | Free | Mon.–Sat. 10–4:30.

✦ ON THE CALENDAR: July **Buffalo Bill Days.** A celebration of Golden's most famous permanent resident features Old West–style entertainment, a parade, and turn-of-the-20th-century crafts demonstrations. | 303/279–3113 or 800/590–3113.

GRAND JUNCTION
▼▼▼

Grand Junction gets its name naturally, situated as it is at the junction of the Colorado and Gunnison rivers. This is also where the railroad that connected Salt Lake City and Denver was joined, in 1882. The city became the seat for Mesa County in 1883, drawing settlers who built dams and irrigation canals, established ranches and farms, and planted orchards, laying the foundation of the fruit industry that thrives in the area today. *Contact Grand Junction Visitor and Convention Bureau | 740 Horizon Dr., 81506 | 970/244–1480 or 800/962–2547 | www.grand-junction.net.*

Cross Orchards Living History Farm. A re-creation of an early 20th-century agricultural community, this farm is listed on the National Register of Historic Places. Take the 1½- to 2-hour tour to see the workers' bunkhouse, blacksmith shop, country store, and an extensive collection of vintage farming and road-building equipment. | 3073 F Rd. | 970/434–9814 | www.wcmuseum.org | $4 | May–Oct., Tues. and Fri.–Sat. 9–3. Tours mid-May–Oct.

Little Bookcliffs Wild Horse Range. The true spirit of the Wild West is literally kept alive at this preserve, just one of three that the United States has set aside specifically for wild horses. Rugged canyons, windswept plateaus, and sagebrush-covered hills shelter 80 to 120 wild horses, most of whom are believed to be descendants of horses that escaped from their owners in the late 1800s or early 1900s. The best season for riding, hiking, or biking the trails here is May to September. In spring and early summer most years, you can spot new foals with their mothers on the hillsides just off the main trails. In summer, you might glimpse some wild horses in Indian Park or North Soda, but it's a matter of luck. The locals' favorite trails include Coal Canyon Trail and Main Canyon Trail, which leads through an area that the herd frequents in winter. | About 8 mi north of Grand Junction on 2815 H Rd. | 970/244–3000 | www.co.blm.gov/gjra/lbc | Free | Daily dawn–dusk.

Museum of Western Colorado. Here you can learn about the history of the Grand Junction area since the 1880s. The Thrailkill firearms collection contains Winchesters, carbines, and pistols carried by lawmen and outlaws. Another display documents the life and times of "Colorado Cannibal" AlferdPacker (1842–1907). | 462 Ute Ave. | 970/242–0971 | www.wcmuseum.org | $5.50 | Mon.–Sat. 9–5, Sun. noon–4.

GREELEY

▼▼

Named in honor of Horace Greeley, the *New York Tribune* publisher who urged America's youth to "Go West, young man, go West," Greeley was founded in 1870 by his agricultural editor, Nathan Meeker. Meeker and Greeley shared a fascination with the notion of utopian societies, and the town of Greeley was their grand experiment for building one. Of the 3,000 prospects who answered Horace Greeley's call to go West, 59 individuals that Greeley deemed of adequate means and moral character were selected. They formed a joint stock company called Union Colony and made the journey west. Within a year the venture was a success. By 1871 the town had a population of 1,500, plus 36 mi of irrigation canals and many businesses, including Meeker's newspaper, the *Greeley Tribune*. Meeker was a tireless promoter of the town but in 1878 he accepted an appointment as a federal Indian Agent in northwestern Colorado. There, he was killed in an Indian attack known as the Meeker Massacre, and the town that later grew up was named for him. *Contact Greeley Convention and Visitors Bureau | 902 7th Ave., 80631 | 970/352–3566 or 800/449–3866 | www.greeleycvb.com.*

Centennial Village. This meticulously maintained reconstructed village preserves Greeley and Weld County history from 1860 to 1920. The dwellings here run the gamut of northern plains architecture, from Southern Cheyenne and Arapaho teepees to humble homes of German, Russian, and Swedish settlers to a magnificent Victorian mansion. Most of the structures have been relocated from their original sites nearby. The village is a favorite site for festivals, many focusing on pioneer life in what (before irrigation) was known as the "Great American Desert." | 1475 A St., at N. 14th Ave. | 970/350–9220 or 970/350–9224 | www.greeleycvb.com/centennial.html | $3.50 | Late May–early Sept., Tues.–Sat. 9–4; mid-Apr.–late May and early Sept.–mid-Oct., Tues.–Sat. 10–3.

Fort Lupton Museum. This one-room municipal museum features Weld County artifacts, with special emphasis on the fur-trading era, the Indian uprisings of the 1860s, and the original Fort Lupton, which once stood nearby on the banks of the South Platte River. Other exhibits include vintage clothing, medical equipment, and household items as well as arrowheads and other Native American artifacts. | 453 1st St. | 303/857–1634 | Free | Weekends by appointment.

Fort Vasquez Museum. A reconstruction of a fur-trading post built in the 1830s, this museum is 18 mi south of Greeley near Platteville. Fort Vasquez served as an important center for trade between Native Americans and Euro-American settlers along the busy South Platte River corridor. The museum, which is operated by the Colorado Historical Society, is on the fort's original site and was built to approximate the original fort as closely as possible. Exhibits illuminate the fur-trading era with hundreds of artifacts from both the Native American and Euro-American sides of the trading equation. | U.S. 85 | 970/785–2832 | Free | Late May–early Sept., Mon.–Sat. 9:30–4:30, Sun. 1–4:30; early Sept.–late May, Wed.–Sat. 9:30–4:30, Sun. 1–4:30.

Meeker Home. This 1870 adobe house was the home of Greeley's founder, Nathan Meeker. Meeker's personal belongings and other historical artifacts from the region are on display. | 1324 9th Ave. | 970/350–9220 | Free | Late May–early Sept., Tues.–Fri. 10–5; early Sept.–mid-Oct. and mid-Apr.–late May, Tues.–Sat. 10–3.

LA JUNTA
▼▼

Although La Junta lies on the route of the Mountain Branch of the Santa Fe Trail, the town was not established until around 1875, some years after the trail's heyday. La Junta (which roughly translated from Spanish means "the meeting place") came to life as a railroad town, serving as a stop for the Santa Fe and Kansas Pacific railroads. The town stands near Sand Creek Massacre National Historic Site, which has been authorized but is not yet open to the public. The opening date will depend on how soon the National Park Service can acquire the land it needs within the authorized boundary. *Contact Chamber of Commerce | 110 Santa Fe Ave., La Junta 81050 | 719/384–7411 | www.lajunta.net.*

Bent's Old Fort National Historic Site. A living museum resides in this painstaking re-creation of the original adobe fort. The fort anchored the commercially vital Santa Fe Trail, providing both protection and a meeting place for the military, trappers, and traders of the era. Inside is a smithy and soldiers' and trappers' barracks. The guided tour is most informative. | 35110 Rte. 194 E | 719/383–5010 | www.nps.gov/beol | $2 | Daily 9–4.

Koshare Indian Museum. Extensive holdings of Native American artifacts and crafts (Navajo silver, Zuni pottery, Shoshone buckskin clothing) fill this museum. Pieces by Anglo artists, such as Frederic Remington, known for their depictions of Native Americans are also included in the collection. The Koshare Indian Dancers (actually a local Boy Scout troop) perform regularly. | 115 W. 18th St. | 719/384–4411 | www.koshare.org | $2 | Daily 10–5.

Otero Museum. This museum complex includes seven buildings, among them an 1890 home and a grocery store listed on the National Register of Historic Places, an 1873 boarding house, and a replica of La Junta's 1876 schoolhouse. The Santa Fe Railroad (which gave the town a major boost when it laid tracks through in 1875) and the region's agricultural history get much attention in the museum's exhibits. | 3rd and Anderson Sts. | 719/384–7500 | Free | June–Sept., Mon.–Sat. 1–5.

✦ ON THE CALENDAR: Sept. **Early Settlers Day.** Arts and crafts, a parade, and a fiddlers' contest bring pioneer history alive on the Saturday after Labor Day. | 719/384–7411.

LA VETA
▼▼

Las Cumbres Españolas, the Spanish Peaks of south-central Colorado, have served as landmarks for hundreds of years. Even before Spanish conquistadors named them, the twin peaks were held sacred by the Apache, Comanche, and Ute tribes of the region, the last of which

SAVAGERY ON THE PLAINS: THE SAND CREEK MASSACRE

Under the 1861 Treaty of Fort, the Southern Cheyenne were moved to a desolate reservation along Sand Creek in southeastern Colorado. Their chief was Black Kettle, widely known as a "peace" chief who advocated cooperation with the ever more abundant white man. But as his band struggled to survive on the arid plains, many young Cheyenne warriors defied the chief, launching raids against white settlements, running off livestock, and attacking freight shipments along the Smoky Hill Trail. These fighters were known as Dog Soldiers. By 1864, after three years of escalating violence on the eastern plains, territorial governor John Evans was eager to put the "Indian problem" to rest. He received permission from Washington to raise a regiment of soldiers to protect white settlers from Indian attack. Commanding the troop was Colonel John M. Chivington, a former Methodist preacher with political ambitions of his own. There was little mystery in Chivington's goal. In a Denver speech in August 1864, he articulated his strategy to an applauding crowd " . . . kill and scalp all, little and big . . . nits make lice."

Evans called a meeting among Indian tribal leaders at Fort Lyon, an army garrison 40 mi from Black Kettle's camp on Sand Creek. At the meeting, Black Kettle again pledged peace and was presented a white flag by Major Scott J. Anthony, who instructed him to fly it over his camp as a sign of his cooperation. The flag—along with a huge U.S. flag given Black Kettle by the Commissioner of Indian Affairs—was flying on the morning of November 29, 1864, but Chivington and his regiment paid no heed. They opened fire on the camp from two sides and over the course of several hours killed more than 100 women and children and at least 28 men. It is estimated that about 500 Indians managed to escape across the prairie, among them Black Kettle and his wife. After the slaughter, Chivington's men sexually mutilated and scalped many of the dead. The colonel received a hero's welcome back in Denver, proudly exhibiting his trophy scalps to cheering crowds. An editorial in the *Rocky Mountain News* effused, "Colorado soldiers have again covered themselves with glory."

In the years following the Sand Creek Massacre, the Dog Soldiers led raids on white settlements on the eastern Colorado plains and on stage stations along the Overland Trail. These fierce final hold-outs in the Plains Indian battles of the 1860s were finally defeated at the Battle of Summit Springs (about 30 mi southeast of Sterling) in 1869. After this last battle, the Cheyenne were moved to reservations in Oklahoma and Wyoming.

And what of Chivington? Witnesses—including several soldiers who had been under Chivington's command—eventually leaked the horrendous details of the Sand Creek Massacre. Three years after the slaughter, a Congressional inquest renounced Chivington, and the Joint Committee on the Conduct of War called the episode a massacre that " . . . scarcely had its parallel in the records of Indian barbarity." The colonel was brought up on court-martial charges for his involvement in the massacre, but since he had already quit the U.S. Army he could not be punished. No criminal charges were ever filed against him.

---

knew them as Huajatolla, or "breasts of the world." In addition to serving as landmarks for explorers from Spain's Diego de Vergas (who passed nearby in 1694) to Lieutenant Zebulon Pike, Colonel John C. Fremont, and Captain John Gunnison, the peaks have long inspired legends of Spanish gold supposedly buried among their crags and canyons. Nestled at the foot of the peaks is a gem that's easier to find. The small town of La Veta (Spanish for "the vein") grew up around a fortified adobe central plaza built by Colonel John M. Francisco, a Virginian who came west in 1839 and became sutler for nearby Fort Garland in the 1850s. Today, Francisco Plaza is listed on the National Register of Historic Places. *Contact La*

Veta/Cuchara Chamber of Commerce | 124 N. Main St., Box 32, 81055 | 719/742–3676 | www. lavetacucharachamber.com.

Fort Francisco Museum. Built in 1862 as protection from Indian threat, this adobe structure surrounds a plaza, opening only to the north. In addition to the original structure, the museum here includes three buildings moved from other sites: the Ritter School House (built in 1876), the Saloon (built in the 1880s), and a log structure that was used as a blacksmith shop. Within the museum are many fine artifacts donated by county residents. | 308 N. Main St. | 719/742–5501 | $4 | Late May–early Sept., daily 9–5.

LEADVILLE

▼▼▼

Born in the early days of the Colorado gold rush and raised in the silver-boom years, Leadville was once home to many self-made millionaires. Prospecting came to this area as early as the 1867 gold rush, but when the boom went bust the town became a ghost village. The real action started when the silver boom of 1879 revitalized the area. Then mines like the Tasmania, the Fortune, the Banker, and the Swiss Boy erupted everywhere in the canyon. The wealth was a magnet for all sorts, famous and infamous, who arrived by foot, mule, and train. The crowd in Leadville's streets was a colorful mix of conmen, prostitutes, miners, and merchants, all looking to make a fast buck. Although Leadville at times rivaled Denver as the most important city in Colorado, the 1893 repeal of the Sherman Silver Purchase Act effectively wiped out much of the town's wealth. Today Leadville has been restored to its bonanza-years appearance. *Contact Greater Leadville Area Chamber of Commerce | 809 Harrison Ave., 80461 | 719/486–3900 or 888/264–5344 | www.leadvilleusa.com.*

Ghost Towns. At one time, bustling mining towns such as Beaver City, Vicksburg, Rockdale, and Winfield surrounded Leadville. Some of the original buildings in Beaver City and Rockdale stand today, but only Vicksburg and Winfield have been restored and preserved. Once the site of more than 75 buildings, Vicksburg is maintained by the Clear Creek Canyon Historical Society of Chaffee County. Two buildings and a small park serve as museums where interesting artifacts from the area are on display. Winfield was once home to 1,500 residents, but three years after its peak the town was nearly deserted. Today, Winfield has preserved several buildings and restored them to their original condition, although they can usually only be viewed from the outside or by peeking in through the windows. Many buildings remain private; observe the "no trespassing" signs where posted. | U.S. 24 south of Leadville for about 20 mi, then CR 390 west for about 14 mi | www.coloradoghosttowns.com.

Leadville, Colorado & Southern Railroad Train Tour. As the train chugs across the Arksansas River valley, guides regale you with humorous narratives about Leadville's colorful past. The 23-mi round trip snakes along the headwaters of the Arkansas River, revealing breathtaking panoramas. The tour takes approximately 2½ hours. | 326 E. 7th St. | 719/486–3936 | www. leadville-train.com | $24 | Late May–mid-June, daily 1 PM; mid-June–early Sept., daily 10 AM and 2 PM; early Sept.–early Oct., daily 1 PM.

Tabor Opera House. The beautifully restored opera house was built in 1879 by Colorado's "silver king," Horace Tabor. Like the boomtown it was in, the theater went up quickly—it was built in 100 days with materials brought in by wagon. Most of the original 880 seats are still in the auditorium. The Metropolitan Opera and the Chicago Symphony, as well as notable names like Houdini, John Philip Sousa, Oscar Wilde, and Anna Held, played here during Leadville's heyday. You can see the opera house on a guided tour. | 308 Harrison Ave. | 303/471–0984 | www.taboroperahouse.net | $4 | Late May–Sept., daily 8–5:30.

✦ ON THE CALENDAR: Aug. **Boom Days Celebration.** A parade, a burro race (to the summit of Mosquito Pass and back to the town center), and mining demonstrations are highlights of this downtown celebration of Leadville's heritage. | 719/486–3900.

HISTORIC LODGING

Delaware Hotel. This redbrick Victorian with a grand lobby was built in 1886 as a state-of-the-art hotel, with steam heat, gas light, and six bathrooms to serve the 50 guest rooms. (All of the rooms now have private baths.) Located in the center of the National Historic District in Leadville, the hotel transports you back in time in high-ceilinged rooms maintained in authentic Victorian style. Come for a murder mystery weekend to solve a case based on actual Leadville events—with plenty of fantasy mixed in. A costumer will dress you in the clothing of the 1880s and 1890s for the occasion. Restaurant, library, meeting rooms, business services. No pets, no smoking. | 700 Harrison Ave. | 719/486–1418 or 800/748–2004 | www.delawarehotel.com | 36 rooms | $65–$139 | AE, MC, V | CP.

MEEKER

▼▼

This remote area in the northwest corner of Colorado was once inhabited by the White River Ute and their prized racing ponies. Soon after whites arrived, it became the site of the infamous Meeker Massacre of September, 1879. Angered by Indian agent Nathan Meeker's strong-arm efforts to Christianize them and force them to become farmers, the local Ute attacked the white settlement, killed 11 people, and took 5 people hostage. The army arrived quickly and established the Camp on the White River, banishing the Indians to a reservation in eastern Utah. When the army moved out in 1883, it sold all of its buildings to settlers eager to take the land and build a town named after the slain Indian agent. Four of these buildings still stand on their original locations. Meeker became the regional hub of business and banking for pioneers who moved to the area. *Contact Meeker Chamber of Commerce | Box 869, 81641 | 970/878–5510 | www.meekerchamber.com.*

White River Museum. The log building that houses the museum was built in 1880 as a barracks for U.S. Army officers. Inside are exhibits such as a collection of guns dating back to the Civil War and the plow used by Nathan Meeker to dig up the Ute's pony racetrack. Other items include Chief Colorow's peace pipe, a pair of moccasins made by a Ute woman for a pioneer boy, a bear-hide coat that belonged to a stagecoach driver, and a large Victorian mourning wreath made of human hair. | 565 Park St. | 970/878–9982 | www.meekercolorado.com/museum.htm | Free | May–Oct., weekdays 9–5; Nov.–Apr., weekdays 11–3.

✦ ON THE CALENDAR: July **Range Call Celebration.** Held since 1885, this western festival includes reenactments of the Meeker Massacre and the Last Ute Indian Uprising (otherwise known as the Ute War of 1887, it was the last major conflict between whites and Ute Indians), as well as a parade and rodeo. It all happens at the Rio Blanco County Fairgrounds. | 970/878–5510.

HISTORIC DINING AND LODGING

Meeker Cafe. American/Casual. At this Old West–style restaurant in a building dating back to the early 20th century, you can peruse vintage photographs and lively stories of Meeker's past in the menu. Try the homemade soup, chicken-fried steak, and mashed potatoes with cream gravy. The inside of the café has been remodeled numerous times and unfortunately does not retain much in the way of the original architecture. | 560 Main St. | 970/878–5062 | Reservations not accepted | $4–$23 | MC, V.

THE MEEKER MASSACRE

It started over a clash of cultures, with Nathan C. Meeker, an Indian agent for the U.S. government, on one side and the White River Band of the Ute Indians on the other. With the mining boom in full swing, tension was rising between the Indians and the white prospectors and settlers. As soon as he arrived in the White River valley in 1878, Meeker, a former agricultural editor for the *New York Tribune,* set out to "civilize" the Ute and turn them into farmers. The Ute weren't about to adopt white customs; they considered farming to be woman's work. The horse was their most prized possession, and Ute men preferred to spend their time perfecting their horsemanship.

Meeker became increasingly frustrated with the Ute's defiance and threatened to take their land if they did not cooperate with him. In a test of wills, he ordered one of his men to plow up a pasture where the Ute kept their treasured horses, in order to turn it into farmland. On September 29, 1879, the Ute attacked the Indian agency, killing all 11 of the agency employees, including Meeker. They took five white women and children captive and looted and torched the agency. Those held captive were released 23 days later after negotiations between Ute chief Ouray and his wife, Chipeta, and former Indian agent General Charles Adams.

Meanwhile, the U.S. Army arrived at the site and set up a military camp on the White River to keep peace after the massacre. Negotiations began immediately for a new Ute agreement that would open the Ute reservation to settlers. In 1881, the Ute Indians of western Colorado were forced onto a reservation in northeastern Utah.

Meeker Hotel. The original false wood front of this rustic hotel, an adobe structure built in 1886, was replaced 10 years later with bricks. The hotel is listed on the National Register of Historic Places. The walls of the lobby are lined with framed broadsheet biographies of famous figures—such as Teddy Roosevelt—who stayed here, along with a painting of the Meeker Massacre. A blend of modern and antique furnishings fills the rooms, which are more eclectic than western. One room, dubbed the Woman's Room, features frilly pink furnishings, including an old-fashioned western love seat. Another is decorated in shades of blue and features a canopy bed. The economy, or bunk, wing has rooms with shared baths. Restaurant, café, cable TV, bar; no-smoking rooms, no room phones. | 560 Main St., 81641 | 970/878–5255 | fax 970/878–3412 | www.meekerhotel.com | 24 rooms, 17 with bath | $65–$80 | AE, D, MC, V.

MONTROSE

Before the rough-and-rowdy frontier cattle town appeared on the map, this area was home to the legendary Ute Indian chief Ouray and his wife, Chipeta. Founded in 1882, Montrose was a supply station for nearby mining camps. The 7-mi Gunnison Tunnel opened in 1909, bringing water from the Gunnison River into the Uncompahgre Valley and enabling Montrose to become the agricultural hub that it is today. *Contact Montrose Chamber of Commerce | 1519 E. Main St., 81401 | 970/249–5000 or 800/923–5515 | www.montrosechamber.com.*

Montrose County Historical Museum. The exhibits at this museum in the Depot Building include antique farm machinery, a railroad caboose, and a toy collection. A pioneer cabin and a country store dating back to the mid-1800s were moved here for display. The Depot Building was

CHIEF OURAY

Crawling with prospectors and settlers in search of their fortunes, Colorado was undergoing great social and political change in the mid-1800s. The Ute Indians, who until then occupied all of Colorado except for the eastern slope, wanted nothing to do with the newcomers.

Chief Ouray (whose Ute name means arrow) found himself caught in the middle. On the one hand, if he didn't learn the white man's politics, what chance did he stand of striking a deal with the United States government to save the best part of his people's land? On the other hand, would his people think he was a traitor if he negotiated with the white man and adopted his ways?

One of Ouray's major accomplishments was the negotiation of the Great Ute Treaty of 1868, which granted some 6 million acres of land to the Ute. The treaty was considered to be the most favorable ever negotiated with the U.S. government by an Indian tribe. But it wouldn't last. By 1874, discontent among the Ute was rising after the discovery of gold in the San Juan Mountains attracted fortune seekers by the dozens to Ute land. While most of the Ute favored violent retaliation, Ouray insisted on peaceful negotiation. The United States drew up another treaty, proposing that the Ute give up almost 4 million acres of their land in return for some $60,000 in annuities and allotments. Ouray, who was still convinced that cooperation with the U.S. government was best for his people, reluctantly signed the agreement, known as the Brunot Treaty. The tribe never received any money from the United States.

The Brunot Treaty recognized Ouray as head chief of the entire Ute nation and granted him an annual salary of $1,000. Even though he preferred the traditional ways, Ouray knew his people could not stop the march of history, something he believed his fellow Ute would never understand. He took up residence with his wife, Chipeta, on a small government-owned farm south of Montrose to show his people that it was possible for them to adjust to white ways. The couple adopted Euro-American customs, furnishing their home with curtains, china, and teapots. Ouray even wore the white man's broadcloth and boots for a time, but he refused to cut his long hair, which he wore in braids that hung down on his chest in typical Ute fashion. Most Ute felt Ouray had sold out to the whites. He was even accused of treason and several attempts were made on his life.

Ouray, who was instrumental in negotiating the release of white hostages kidnapped during the Meeker Massacre in 1879, continued to act as a negotiator between his people and the government until his death in 1880. One top-ranking Washington official said that "Ouray was by far the brightest Indian I have ever met." A great negotiator, Ouray is remembered as a man who believed in peace more than war.

erected in 1912 and retains many of its original features, including freight scales that still work. | 21 N. Rio Grande | 970/249–2085 | www.montrose-colo.com/virtual/museum.htm | $2.50 | May–Sept., Mon.–Sat. 9–5.

Ute Indian Museum and Chief Ouray Memorial Park. Commemorating the life of Chief Ouray and his wife, Chipeta, the museum occupies the couple's 8-acre homestead site. You can see dioramas depicting a Ute hunting party and a traditional Ute village, plus Colorado's most comprehensive collection of Ute artifacts. Be sure to check out Chipeta's Crypt and the native plants garden. There are also a gallery and museum store on the grounds. | 17253 Chipeta Rd. | 970/249–3098 | www.coloradohistory.org/hist_sites/UteIndian/Ute_indian.htm | $3 | May–Sept., Mon.–Sat. 9–4:30, Sun. 11–4:30; Oct.–Apr., Mon.–Sat. 9–4:30.

OURAY

▼▼▼

Named in honor of Ute Indian chief Ouray, this town was founded in 1876 when gold and silver were still being mined in the area. The former mining camp sits at an elevation of nearly 8,000 ft, surrounded by mountain peaks that reach 12,000 to 14,000 ft. Ouray was mostly built between 1880 and 1900, and virtually all of its original buildings are still standing. The entire town is on the National Register of Historic Places. *Contact Ouray Chamber Resort Association | Box 145, 81427 | 970/325–4746 or 800/228–1876 | www.ouraycolorado.com.*

Bachelor-Syracuse Mine. This mine 1 mi north of Ouray via U.S. 550 has been in continuous operation since the 1880s. You can ride a mine train deep into the mountain to see mining equipment, work areas, and explosives demonstrations. | 1222 CR 14 | 970/325–0220 | $15.95 | Mid-May–mid-Sept., daily 9–5.

Historic District Walking Tour. Visit more than 25 classic edifices on a walking tour of Ouray's historic district. Among the points of interest are the grandiose Wright Opera House, the Beaumont, Western, and St. Elmo hotels, and the Elks Lodge. You can pick up a brochure at the chamber of commerce office (1222 Main St.). | Bounded by 2nd St. to the south and 10th Ave. to the north, and by 6th St. to the east and Oak St. to the west | 970/325–4746 | Free | Daily.

Sheridan Opera House. Built in 1913, this former vaudeville house in Telluride is now home to the Sheridan Arts Foundation. As of this writing its 240-seat auditorium was being restored to its original appearance. The theater is a popular venue for visiting musicians and for theater productions, including those of the Telluride Repertory Theatre Company. No organized tours are available, but you can sneak a peek at the inside when performances are not scheduled. Check out the 1914 roll curtain painted with a Venetian scene. | 110 N. Oak St., Telluride | 970/728–6363 | www.sheridanoperahouse.com | Free; performance costs vary | Daily 9–5; call for performance schedules.

HISTORIC DINING AND LODGING

Bon Ton Restaurant. Continental. This casual spot is in the St. Elmo Hotel, an 1898 hostelry that was a haven for miners down on their luck. According to the story, original owner Kitty Heit couldn't resist a sob story, so she let broke miners eat for free and pay dirt-cheap room rates. Her son's ghost reputedly hovers protectively about the property. The restaurant's rock-lined walls and Victorian furnishings create an intimate setting in which you can dine on beef Wellington, veal piccata, and other dishes off the frequently changing menu. The St. Elmo Hotel currently operates as a bed-and-breakfast. | 426 Main St. | 970/325–4951 | No lunch | $11–$24 | AE, D, DC, MC, V.

Beaumont Hotel. Built in 1886 during the mining boom, these swanky digs were modeled after the Brown Palace Hotel in Denver. Check in at the original registration desk in the lobby, where a massive oak staircase leads to an open rotunda ringed with ornate railings. Perhaps the most striking feature is the cathedral glass skylight above. During the hotel's renovation, designers painstakingly matched the wood, wallpaper, and trim as closely as possible to the originals. At this writing the public areas had been restored but the rooms were awaiting improvement. The hotel has 12 minisuites, each individually decorated and furnished with antique furniture. The Tower Room is named for its spiral staircase to a 32-ft-high loft. 2 restaurants, coffee bar, in-room data ports, some kitchens, some microwaves, some refrigerators, cable TV, hot tub, massage, spa, wine bar, business services; no smoking. | 505 Main St., 81427 | 970/325–0152 | fax 970/325–0460 | 12 rooms | $165–$300 | AE, MC, V.

PUEBLO

▼▼▼

Fur trappers worked the Arkansas River and its tributaries around here as early as the 1820s, but it wasn't until 1842 that the first non-native people settled in the area. That year, Fort Independence, a trading post–fort that later became known as Fort El Pueblo, was built. At the time, the Arkansas served as the international border between the United States and Mexico, and the settlement, called El Pueblo, that grew up around the fort was an important cultural crossroads where Anglo, French, and African-American trappers, Mexican settlers, and various Indian tribes lived in relative harmony. It didn't last. On Christmas Day in 1854, Ute and Jicarilla Apache unsatisfied with U.S. treaties attacked the post, killing or capturing all of its inhabitants. Within a few years, though, a new town began growing on the same site. The Denver & Rio Grande Railroad laid tracks into the town of Pueblo in 1872, establishing the city as a transportation hub. By the turn of the century, Pueblo had become the home of enormous smelting operations and had the largest steel plant west of the Mississippi. No traces of the fort remain. *Contact Pueblo Chamber of Commerce | Box 697, 81002 | 719/542–1704 | www.pueblochamber.org.*

Pueblo History Museum. Pueblo's history as a cultural and geographical crossroads is documented here, in displays such as a reconstruction of Fort Independence/El Pueblo. The museum also extends its scope to chronicle life on the Great Plains from the prehistoric era onward. The museum is located in temporary quarters while a new museum building is under construction, slated to be completed in August, 2003. | 119 Central Plaza | 719/583–0453 | www.coloradohistory.org | $2.50 | Mon.–Sat. 10–3, Sun. noon–3.

Rosemount Victorian Museum. Unquestionably the glory of Pueblo, this is one of Colorado's finest historical institutions. The splendid 37-room mansion, built in 1893 by merchant and banker John A. Thatcher, features exquisite maple, oak, and mahogany woodwork throughout, with ivory glaze and gold-leaf trim. Italian marble fireplaces, Tiffany-glass fixtures, and frescoed ceilings are the height of opulence. The top floor—originally the servants' quarters—houses a collection of objects of curiosity (including an Egyptian mummy) acquired by eccentric Pueblo businessman and philanthropist Andrew McClelland on a worldwide tour he took in 1904. | 419 W. 14th St. | 719/545–5290 | www.rosemount.org | $5 | Tues.–Sat. 10–4; tours every ½ hr.

Union Avenue and Pitkin Avenue Historic Districts. During the 1880s, Union Avenue linked the then-separate towns of South and Central Pueblo. After consolidation, the street became the hub of business and entertainment. A repository of turn-of-the-20th-century stores and warehouses, including the glorious 1889 sandstone-and-brick Union Avenue Depot, this is now a fashionable commercial district. Among the landmarks are Mesa Junction, which celebrates Pueblo as a crossroads, at the point where two trolleys met. Pitkin Avenue, which intersects Union Avenue, is lined with fabulous gabled and turreted mansions; the Pitkin Avenue Historic District is comprised of seven elegant Victorian homes along the south side of the 300 block. Walking-tour brochures of each district are available at many shops and at the Chamber of Commerce office. | Union Ave. Historic District: bounded by Grand and Victoria Aves. and Main and B Sts. | Historic Pueblo Business Center Assn.: 719/543–5804 | www.puebloonline.com | Free | Daily.

STERLING

▼▼▼

Settlers in the northeastern section of Colorado, especially on the Overland Trail along the South Platte River, were the primary targets of retaliatory strikes by Plains Indians in the years following the Sand Creek Massacre of 1864. Of the many stage stations along the trail, only Godfrey's Ranch Station, nicknamed Fort Wicked, avoided capture by Indians during the 1865 raids. Fort Wicked was on the banks of the South Platte where the town of Sterling stands today. Sterling was founded by settlers who moved east from Greeley in search of better farmland. In the early 1870s, they built sod huts and dugouts along the banks of the South Platte River about 4 mi north of the present townsite. When the Union Pacific Railroad laid tracks from Julesburg to La Salle in 1881, town leaders offered the railroad 80 acres of land for a right-of-way and a roundhouse. The railroad agreed, but under the agreement, tracks would be laid a few miles to the south, so the town was reestablished at its current location. Sterling's decision to accommodate the railroad paid off. When the trains started arriving, the town began growing in earnest. By 1884, the town had incorporated. *Contact City of Sterling | 421 N. 4th St., 80751 | 970/522–9700 | www.sterlingcolo.com.*

Fort Morgan Museum. This three-room museum traces the history of the frontier fort that stood near here in 1864–68, and of the town (44 mi southwest of Sterling) that grew up around it. Exhibits focus on the fort itself, the Arapaho and Cheyenne tribes that once hunted in the area, the influence of early railroads in northeastern Colorado, and early ranching and farming implements. | 414 Main St., Fort Morgan | 970/867–6331 | www.ftmorganmus.org | Free | Mon., Wed., and Fri. 10–5; Tues. and Thurs. 6 PM–8 PM; Sat. 11–5.

Fort Sedgwick Depot Museum. Housed in a 1930s Union Pacific Railroad depot, this museum, along with the Fort Sedgwick Museum a few blocks away, is operated by the Fort Sedgwick Historical Society. The Depot Museum focuses on early pioneer life in the region and houses a collection of Native American artifacts, household tools and utensils, railroad equipment, firearms, and period clothing. Julesburg (55 mi northeast of Sterling) was home to Colorado's only Pony Express station, and the museum also has some Pony Express memorabilia. | 201 W. 1st. St., Julesburg | 970/474–2264 | www.kci.net/~history | $1 | Late May–early Sept., Mon.–Sat. 9–5, Sun. 11–5.

Fort Sedgwick Museum. The old fort itself is the primary focus at this interpretive center and museum (55 mi northeast of Sterling). Although nothing remains of the fort that once protected settlers and travelers along the South Platte River, the museum houses a vast collection of archived documents, drawings, and photographs. Offices for the Fort Sedgwick Historical Society are also here. | 114 E. 1st. St., Julesburg | 970/474–2061 | www.kci.net/~history | $1 | By appointment.

Overland Trail Museum. When goldfields drew thousands upon thousands of fortune seekers westward in the mid-19th century, many traveled a path along the South Platte River corridor that became known as the Overland Trail. But they were far from the first to do so. Fur traders and explorers used the route as early as the 1820s, and Native Americans had traveled this way for generations before them. Located near the historic trail, the Overland Trail Museum highlights pioneer life along this route. Built to replicate an early fur-trading fort, the museum's original building is a small stone structure erected in 1936 as a Works Progress Administration project. The museum has expanded twice to make room for exhibits of pioneer tools, household furnishings, clothing, early firearms, and a huge collection of branding irons, along with Native American artifacts. | 21053 CR 26.5 | 970/522–3895 | Free | Apr.–Oct., Mon.–Sat. 9–5, Sun. 10–5; Nov.–May, Tues.–Sat. 10–4.

TRINIDAD
▼▼

You'll never forget where you are in Trinidad. Virtually every street in the town's core is paved with bricks stamped TRINIDAD—the product of the now-defunct Trinidad Brick & Tile Company, which began making the distinctive pavers in 1910. In fact, much of Trinidad's rich and fascinating history can be gleaned from its streets. The city's slightly canted Main Street follows the original path of the Santa Fe Trail, the historic trade route that literally put Trinidad on the map. As the last rest-and-water stop before the trail's strenuous climb over Raton Pass to the south, Trinidad was an important supply town in the 1860s and incorporated as a city in 1876. The city has known its share of western legends. Bat Masterson served as town marshal in the 1880s, and Wyatt Earp was once driver of the stage between Trinidad and Box Springs, New Mexico. Scout and Indian Agent Kit Carson made his home here in the later years of his life in the mid-1860s. With discovery of coal nearby and the arrival of the railroad, Trinidad enjoyed boom years from the 1880s through 1910, and the town's wealth of surviving architecture from this period is one of its real charms. *Contact Trinidad–Las Animas County Chamber of Commerce | 309 Nevada Ave., 81082 | 719/846–9285 | www.trinidadco.com.*

A. R. Mitchell Memorial Museum and Gallery. Come here to see the work of the famous western illustrator, whose distinctive oils, charcoal drawings, and watercolors graced the pages of pulp magazines and ranch romances. Not only did Mitchell preserve the Old West in pictures, he was responsible for saving Trinidad's Baca and Bloom houses from demolition, and he spearheaded numerous campaigns to restore the historic downtown. The museum also houses his collection of other western masters, such as Larry Heller and Harvey Dunn. For a glimpse into Trinidad history, take in the museum's Aultman Collection of Photography, which includes Aultman family photos of Trinidad dating back to 1889. | 150 E. Main St. | 719/846–4224 | Free | Mid-Apr.–Sept., Mon.–Sat. 10–4.

Cokedale. Nestled in Reilly Canyon, this derelict turn-of-the-20th-century coal-coke camp is a National Historic Landmark District. As you drive through the area, note the leftover slag heaps and the spooky abandoned mining buildings that dot the hillsides. Telltale streaks of black in the sandstone and granite bluffs fronting the Purgatoire River and its tributaries bear testimony to the area's mineral riches. | 6 mi west of Trinidad via Rte. 12.

Corazon de Trinidad. Downtown Trinidad, a National Historic Landmark District, is filled with splendid Victorian mansions, churches, and the glorious, bright red domes and turrets of Temple Aaron, Colorado's oldest operating synagogue. The Trinidad/Las Animas Chamber of Commerce publishes a brochure detailing an excellent walking tour of the neighborhood. | Bordered by Brown, Chestnut, Elm, Walnut, 3rd, Animas, 1st, and Nevada Sts.

Trinidad History Museum. Four museums in one, this complex takes you back in time to Trinidad's early years. The Santa Fe Trail Museum, housed in an old adobe, displays relics of trade along the trail, such as commercial goods and a fringed buckskin coat supposedly worn by Kit Carson. Photographs depict Trinidad at the turn of the 20th century, when the town was at its peak. The Historic Gardens replicate the southwestern vegetable and herb gardens kept by Trinidad's pioneers. One of those pioneers was Felipe Baca, who was a prominent trader. His 1870 residence—the Baca House—shows off its original furnishings in the parlor, sitting room, kitchen, dining room, and bedrooms. Displays of the Baca family's personal possessions—from clothing to rosaries—reveal the mix of Anglo and Hispanic influences on Trinidad's history. Next door, the 1880s Bloom House shows another side of life in the town. Owner Frank Bloom made his fortune in ranching, banking, and railroading, and although he was no wealthier than Baca, his mansion reveals a very different lifestyle. He filled his ornate Second Empire–style Victorian (with mansard roof and elaborate wrought ironwork) with fine furnishings and fabrics brought from New York and Europe. | 300 E. Main St. | 719/846–7217 | www.coloradohistory.org | $5 | May–Sept., daily 10–4.

✦ ON THE CALENDAR: June **Santa Fe Trail Festival.** This celebration honors the history of the Santa Fe Trail, which once ran through the town of Trinidad. Crafts, period costume contests, live music, and a melodrama are part of the event. | 719/846–9285.

IDAHO

American Indians have lived for generations in the area that is now Idaho: the Shoshone and Bannock tribes to the south and east and the Nez Perce and Coeur d'Alene tribes in the north. The region's recorded history begins with the arrival of the Lewis and Clark expedition, which in 1804–06 sought a route to the Pacific Ocean through the vast territory acquired by the United States in the Louisiana Purchase. In 1805 Meriwether Lewis, William Clark, and their Corps of Discovery followed the Missouri River to the Lemhi Pass area in the Bitterroot Mountains. Finding the way too rugged there, they crossed Lolo Pass instead and made their way from the Clearwater and Lochsa River valleys to the Snake River at Idaho's western border.

Like much of the Northwest, Idaho was opened to further exploration and exploitation by fur trappers. In 1809 David Thompson built Kullyspell House near Lake Pend Oreille, the first non-native establishment in the Northwest. It served British and Canadian trappers who cut trails through the region as they sought beaver and other furs. Fort Henry was established near St. Anthony in 1810 and became the first American fur-trading post west of the Rocky Mountains.

In 1818, the United States and Great Britain signed a joint occupation treaty for Oregon Territory, which included what is today Idaho. Idaho's southern boundary was determined in 1819 under the Adams-Onis Treaty between Spain and the United States. During the next two decades, Fort Boise and Fort Hall were established to serve the fur trade in Idaho. Missionaries began arriving in the West in the 1830s, and the Reverend Henry Spalding organized a mission in Idaho's present panhandle region near Lapwai. It had the first school, the first irrigation system, and the first crop of Idaho potatoes.

Narcissa Whitman and Eliza Spalding traveled across the country in 1835 with their missionary husbands, demonstrating that not only men but women, and therefore families, could make a cross-country trip. American families began to look west. The first wagon train of emigrants to travel the Oregon Trail was the party led by John Bidwell and John Bartleson

IDAHO TIME LINE

1805 Meriwether Lewis and William Clark cross into northern Idaho over the Lolo Trail, then meet with Nez Perce Indians at Weippe Prairie.

1806 Canadian David Thompson establishes a fur-trading post near Bonners Ferry.

1810 The Missouri Fur Company establishes Fort Henry near St. Anthony, the first American fur-trading post.

1811 Wilson Price Hunt's Astorians head east from Fort Astoria, crossing through Idaho on a route that later becomes the Oregon Trail.

1818 Great Britain and the United States agree that the Oregon region, including Idaho, is open to settlement by citizens of both nations.

1832 Captain Benjamin L. E. Bonneville leads the first covered wagons across the Rocky Mountains.

1832–42 Fort Hall becomes a hub for trails and roads to the western United States, while several Jesuit missions are established in north-central Idaho and the Panhandle.

1841 The first overland emigrants travel the route blazed by the Astorians.

1843 Full-scale migration over the Oregon Trail begins, with emigrants traveling across Idaho along the Snake River.

1848 Oregon Territory, which includes Idaho, is established.

1852 French Canadians discover gold on the Pend Oreille River.

1857–1859 Oregon's eastern boundary is established and Oregon becomes a state, leaving all of Idaho in Washington Territory. Gold is discovered on Orofino Creek.

1863–1865 Idaho Territory is organized, with the capital at Lewiston. The territory includes a portion of present-day western Montana. The town of Boise is laid out and replaces Lewiston as the capital.

1877 Nez Perce Indians cross Idaho as they seek refuge in Canada. Along their route they engage in several skirmishes with the U.S. Army, including battles at White Bird.

1890 Idaho becomes the nation's 43rd state.

1902 The Carey Act provides for an irrigation project that opens the Snake River valley to agriculture.

in 1841, but the major migration started two years later, in 1843, with a wagon train involving around 1,000 people. In 1849 gold seekers headed toward California also made their way across southern Idaho.

The discovery of gold along the Pend Oreille River by French Canadians in 1852 marked the beginning of Idaho's mining era. A year later Congress created Washington Territory, which included most of Idaho. In 1863, Idaho became a territory in its own right following gold strikes in the north and central region, particularly around Idaho City and near Boise. The next 20 years saw several battles with Indian tribes, including the 1877 Nez Perce War, the Bannock War in 1878, and the 1879 Sheepeater campaign. Railroads pushed their way across Idaho from the 1880s onward, allowing mining camps to grow into communities.

Another mining boom began near Coeur d'Alene in 1884 with the discovery of silver; the boom continued through 1890, when Idaho became a state. The earth held further promise for the State of Idaho. Completion of Milner Dam, under the Carey Act of 1902, spawned irrigation projects across the Snake River Plain and turned the region into a fertile cropland. Still, much of Idaho remains wild and looks the way it did before Euro-Americans ever stepped foot here.

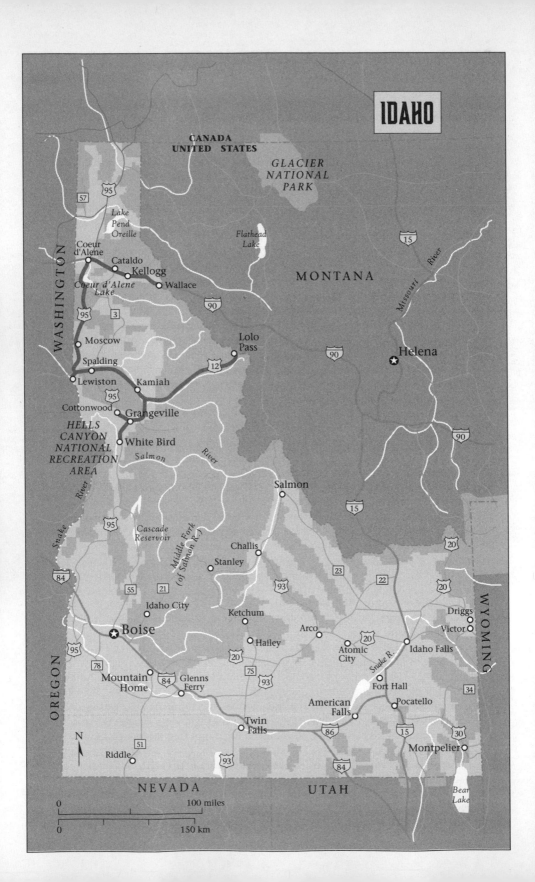

Northern Trails

A DRIVING TOUR FROM LOLO PASS TO WALLACE

▼▼

Distance: 341 mi   **Time:** 4 days

Breaks: Plan to spend one night each in Grangeville, Coeur d'Alene, and Wallace so you have plenty of time to see sites all along this route.

This tour begins where Lewis and Clark entered present-day Idaho: at Lolo Pass, where U.S. 12 crosses from Montana into Idaho. Traveling west on U.S. 12 from Missoula, Montana, you'll follow the route of the explorers along the Lolo Trail, to where they were assisted by Nez Perce Indians; several interpretive signs mark the way the explorers took. The highway itself passes along the Lochsa Wild and Scenic River corridor. After 100 mi on U.S. 12, drive 26 mi south on Route 13 to **Grangeville,** just south of the present Nez Perce Indian Reservation in the southwestern portion of Idaho's panhandle. Visit the Bicentennial Historical Museum, and then stop at the chamber of commerce to pick up some driving-tour brochures. From Grangeville you can take an auto tour south on U.S. 95 to the White Bird battle site, scene of the first battle in the Nez Perce War, or visit White Bird Summit. Another option is to take U.S. 95 north from Grangeville through the western portion of the Nez Perce Indian Reservation, stopping at the historical museum at St. Gertrude in Cottonwood. Overnight in the Grangeville area.

Departing Grangeville on your second day, head back up Route 13 to U.S. 12 (this is the Northwest Passage Scenic Byway) along the east side of the Nez Perce reservation. Thirteen miles out of Grangeville is Harpster, where, if you have the time and a high-clearance vehicle, you can explore the Elk City Wagon Road, a freight road used to supply mining camps. Farther north on U.S. 12, around present-day Kamiah, is the area where the Nez Perce spent their winters, fishing for steelhead (some of which they shared with Lewis and Clark in 1806) and making ropes. Continue on U.S. 12 to Spalding and the headquarters of the Nez Perce National Historic Park. When you leave the historical park headquarters turn your vehicle northwest on U.S. 12 and north on U.S. 95, 124 mi to **Coeur d'Alene.** Stop at the Museum of Northern Idaho for information on the Mullan Road, including a look at the Mullan Tree. East of town, I–90 follows much of the Mullan Road, which brought soldiers, miners, and settlers to the area. About 8 mi out of town is the Mullan Road Historical Site in 4th of July Canyon. There you can actually hike on a bit of the original road. Return to Coeur d'Alene for a night's rest.

On day three, drive 27 mi east on I–90 to Old Mission State Park in Cataldo, which contains the oldest building in Idaho, the Mission of the Sacred Heart, built in the 1850s. Another 11 mi east brings you to **Kellogg,** a silver-mining town surrounded by ghost towns. Poke around the mining museum there and continue on to **Wallace,** 11 mi east on I–90. Here's your chance to step back into mining-camp life by visiting a mine and stopping in at the Oasis Bordello Museum and the Wallace District Mining Museum.

AMERICAN FALLS

▼▼

The waterfalls where the Snake River cascaded 50 ft over basalt boulders gave this town its name, long before dams and a huge reservoir were built here. Emigrants following the Oregon Trail across the Snake River Plain often wrote of the music of the falls in their diaries. One traveler recalled, "The sound of the falls was heard some time before reaching them. The scene was truly magnificent. Here was an entire change in the face of the country as well as the river." The look of the town and the river changed again beginning in 1901, as power plants and later a dam were built on the Snake, eventually slowing the falls to a trickle.

By 1925 the town of 4,000 had packed up and moved south to make way for what would become a 36-mi-long reservoir. Today the town sits at the southern tip of the lake. When the water level is low you can still see the original town's skeletal remains—streets, sidewalks, and the foundations of buildings—in the northwestern section of the lake. Some buildings, such as the brick church at Fort Hall Avenue and Polk Street, were taken apart, moved, and reconstructed in the new town. *Contact American Falls Chamber of Commerce | 239 Idaho St., 83211 | 208/226–7214 | fax 208/226–7214 | www.governet.net/id/ci/amf/area.cfm.*

Fort Hall Indian Reservation. The Shoshone-Bannock Indian tribe is headquartered at the Fort Hall Indian Reservation, a 544,000-acre tract that is only a small portion of the area that the Shoshone and Bannock once inhabited. The two tribes hunted, gathered, and fished for salmon in what is now Wyoming, Utah, Nevada, and Idaho. They obtained horses in the early 1700s, allowing them to hunt buffalo in Montana and Wyoming. To open land to white exploitation, a Presidential Executive Order established a 1.8-million-acre reservation for the tribes in 1867, confirmed by the Fort Bridger Treaty of 1868. Over the years the reservation was whittled down to its present size. You can still see wagon-wheel ruts on the Oregon Trail near the monument marking the former location of Fort Hall. Along with remnants of the trail are remains of buildings from the old Fort Hall Indian Agency. In the "bottoms area" along the Snake River, a protected herd of tribal buffalo roams. At the Clothes Horse store you can purchase the tribe's colorful bead and quill work. | About 35 mi northeast of American Falls via I–86 east and I–15 north Shoshone-Bannock Tribal Enterprises, Fort Hall 83221 | 208/237–9791 or 800/806–9229 | www.sho-ban.com.

The **Fort Hall Replica** (3002 Alvord Loop, Exit 67 off I–15, Pocatello | 208/234–1795 | $2.25) is a re-creation of the fort that Nathaniel Wyeth built for the Hudson Bay Company in 1834. Trappers in the region came to the post to exchange beaver and other hides for supplies. After 1841, Fort Hall also became a major supply point for travelers on the Oregon and California trails. Nothing remains of Wyeth's fort, which stood on the Portneuf River. The Fort Hall Replica has massive wooden gates, trading rooms, and a blacksmith shop. Living-history re-enactors are usually on hand to speak with you about the fur-trade era or the trail days. The fort is closed October–March and on weekends in April and May.

The exhibits at the **Shoshone-Bannock Tribal Museum** (Simplot Rd., Exit 80 off I–15 | 208/237–9791 | $2.50) include beaded ceremonial clothing, headdresses, weapons, and historical photographs commemorating tribal heritage.

Massacre Rocks State Park. You can see where the wheels of pioneer wagons carved ruts into the land on this section of the Oregon Trail. The spot is named for an 1862 attack by Indians on pioneer travelers. A ¼-mi walk along the trail itself leads to huge Register Rock, where pioneers inscribed their names. At the visitor center you'll find information about the Oregon Trail, Shoshone Indians, the geology of the area, and fur trapping. From Memorial Day through Labor Day, costumed performers depict pioneer days in Living History Campfire Programs. | 3592 N. Park La., 10 mi west of American Falls off I–86, Exit 28 | 208/548–2672 | www.idahoparks.org/parks/massacre.html | $3 per vehicle | Daily.

✦ ON THE CALENDAR: June **Portneuf Muzzleloader Blackpowder Rendezvous.** The fur trapper and trader way of life is reenacted by modern-day mountain men with a tepee village and a traders' row where you can purchase items such as beaver pelts, fur hats, beads, and leather clothing. Black-powder shoots and a knife-throwing contest are among the events in Massacre Rocks State Park. | 208/548–2672.

Aug. **Sho-Ban Indian Festival.** The Shoshone-Bannock tribe sponsors this four-day Indian festival on the reservation the second weekend in August. It has powwow dancing by members of many tribes in one of the largest traditional dancing competitions in the country. You can watch an Indian stick game, pony relay races, or an all-Indian rodeo, or shop for authentic Indian clothing, beadwork, and art. | 208/237–9791.

HISTORIC DINING

Oregon Trail Restaurant. Native American. Traditional American Indian foods are served at this restaurant on the Fort Hall Indian Reservation. Try buffalo steaks, buffalo burgers, buffalo stew, Indian tacos, and Indian fry bread. | 110 E. Idaho Ave. | 208/237–2704 | $5–$11 | MC, V.

BOISE

▼▼

From a distance, Boise looks like a dreamy desert oasis rising above the seemingly endless sagebrush flats of the Boise Basin. The welcoming patch of green attracted Captain B.L.E. Bonneville and his party of trappers as they trudged across the barren Snake River Plain in 1832, causing them to exclaim, *"Les bois! Les bois!"* ("Trees!"). The French name stuck, though it is now pronounced *boy*–see. A year after Bonneville's group discovered the riverside oasis, the Hudson Bay Company, a British fur-trading enterprise, constructed a fort near the mouth of the Boise River. By the 1840s, pioneers were driving wagons along the Oregon Trail across southern Idaho and through what is now downtown Boise. Gold-rush trails leading to the Boise Basin and Owyhee mines also brought settlement to the area. But it was not until 1863 that Boise actually became a town. The U.S. Army decided to build a fort to protect the seemingly endless stream of pioneers passing along the Oregon Trail. Boise was incorporated and named the capital of Idaho Territory in 1865. Although gold fever had swelled the town's population to 1,658 in 1864, by 1869 it had shrunk to just under 1,000. The town resumed its growth in the 1870s, and by 1887, three years before Idaho became a state, it had a functioning streetcar system.

As it was in most other western frontier towns, growth was spurred by the arrival of the railroad. A branch of the Oregon Short Line reached Boise in 1887, and the Boise Basin became a booming rail center. Among the settlers attracted to the area were Basque immigrants from the western Pyrenees. They were not sheepherders when they arrived, but they found employment with sheep companies owned by Scottish and English concerns. Today the Snake River Plain has the largest concentration of Basques in the United States, many of them carrying on the sheepherding traditions of their forebears. Other Basques found employment in the mining and logging industries. Agriculture thrived after irrigation turned stretches of the once barren valley into lush farmland. By 1910, with the construction of a dam and a canal, Ada County had 1,500 irrigated farms. *Contact Boise Convention and Visitors Bureau | Box 2106, 83701 | 208/344–6236 | www.boise.org.*

Basque Block. The culture of Boise's Basque pioneers lives on in a group of buildings on Grove Street. The 1864 Cyrus Jacobs-Uberuaga house at No. 607 served as a boarding house for Basques and is the city's oldest building. The Fronton Building, No. 619, was built as a boarding house by the Anduiza family in 1912 and is unique for the fronton, or Basque handball court, inside. At the Basque Center at No. 601, the Oinkari Basque Dancers and the Boise'ko Gasteak Dancers hold practices, and older Basques meet on many afternoons for coffee, conversation, and maybe a round of Mus, a Basque card game. | Grove St. between 6th St. and Capitol Blvd. | 208/343–2671 | www.boisebasques.com.

Basque Museum and Cultural Center. This museum and cultural center is in a former rooming house that served young Basque sheepherders and other immigrants from 1910 onward. The exhibits cover Basque culture and traditions and the story of the Basques in Idaho. Basque language classes are offered two times a week. | 611 Grove St. | 208/343–2671 | www. boisebasques.com | Donation | Tues.–Fri. 10–4, Sat. 11–3.

Idaho Museum of Mining and Geology. Mining tools and old photographs tell the story of the state's colorful history of gold, silver, and gemstone mining. You can also take field trips to nearby geological sites. | 2445 Old Penitentiary Rd. | 208/368–9876 | Donation | Apr.–Oct., weekdays 9–5, weekends noon–5; Nov.–Mar., Wed.–Sun. 11–5.

Idaho State Historical Museum. Very detailed reconstructions of building interiors make you feel as if you've actually stepped back to pioneer days. Two log cabins built in 1863 have been relocated to the park grounds. Isaac Coston, a pioneer farmer east of the city, used his cabin for more than 50 years. Originally located near 5th and Main streets, the Pearce Cabin was a blacksmith shop and then the home of a Chinese family. Other original buildings moved to the museum grounds include the adobe house of four-term Boise mayor Thomas E. Logan, built in 1865. The house is restored and furnished in the style of the 1870s. The Richard C. Adelmann House is a reconstruction typical of Boise dwellings during the period 1870–1890, while the Colson Homestead Shack is a modest board-and-batten house built in 1909 and typical of homestead houses in southern Idaho. The museum also has exhibits related to Idaho's Indian, Chinese, and Basque peoples. A working wood shop is open Saturday 11–3. | Julia Davis Park, 610 N. Julia Davis Dr., off Capitol Blvd. | 208/334–2120 | idahohistory. net/museum.html | $2 | Tues.–Sat. 9–5.

Old Idaho Territorial Penitentiary. Built in 1870, the Idaho Penitentiary was used for just over a century and is one of only three territorial prisons still standing. You can take a 90-minute self-guided tour to see the cell blocks, some of which were damaged during riots just before the prison closed in 1974. | 2445 Old Penitentiary Rd., off Warm Springs Ave. | 208/368–6080 | $4 | Late May–early Sept., daily 10–5; early Sept.–late May, daily noon–5.

✦ ON THE CALENDAR: July **Basque Feast Day of Saint Ignatius of Loyola.** Basque music, dancing, cultural activities, and sports fill this annual celebration of St. Ignatius of Loyola, patron saint of the Basques and founder of the Jesuit religious order. It takes place the last weekend in July. | 208/343–2671.

Sept. **Museum Comes to Life.** The last weekend in September, costumed interpreters at the Idaho State Historical Museum show you what it was like to live in a homesteader's house and demonstrate 19th-century crafts and activities. | 208/334–2120.

HISTORIC DINING AND LODGING

Gernika Basque Pub and Eatery. Basque. Although it was opened in 1991, this bar and café is a window on Idaho's long history of Basque culture. The menu includes Basque cuisine with spicy meat and tomato sauces and Basque wines. | 202 S. Capitol Blvd. | 208/344–2175 | Closed Sun. | $6–$8 | MC, V.

Idaho Heritage Inn Bed & Breakfast. In the Warm Springs District near downtown, this imposing turn-of-the-20th-century former governor's mansion has a seemingly endless supply of natural geothermal spring water that you can use to fill deep tiled tubs. The Governor's Suite's dark walls and shiny white woodwork are accented by an heirloom quilt on the oak sleigh bed, while the Judge's Chambers has a private entrance to the covered veranda and Eastlake walnut furnishings. The separate Carriage House is a private retreat complete with a microwave, refrigerator, and deck overlooking the courtyard. Dining room, in-room data ports, bicycles, business services; no smoking, no TV in some rooms. | 109 W. Idaho St., 83702 | 208/342–8066 or 800/342–8445 | fax 208/343–2325 | www.idheritageinn.com | 3 rooms, 2 suites, 1 carriage house | $75–$110 | AE, MC, V.

CHALLIS

▼▼

The gateway to central Idaho's rugged river and mountain wilderness, this town of 1,200 is surrounded by the 2.3-million-acre Frank Church–River of No Return Wilderness, the largest such area in the lower 48 states. Trappers first lived and worked the Challis area in 1822, and some 50 years later gold brought a mining boom to the town that lasted almost three decades. The town was laid out by Alvah P. Challis in 1876 and became an important trading and shipping center, serving mining camps and ranches. The Challis mineral belt is still mined for gold, silver, molybdenum, and 40 other minerals. You can take a self-guided driving tour along the Salmon River valley that traces Yankee Fork mining history. A walking tour of the Old Challis Historic District takes you past a number of buildings on the National Register of Historic Places. *Contact Challis Area Chamber of Commerce | 700 N. Main St., 83220 | 208/879–2771 | fax 208/879–5836 | www.salmonbyway.com.*

Custer Motorway Adventure Road. The 35-mi route had its start when miners rushed to the Yankee Fork gold mines in the 1870s. By 1879, Alex Toponce, an enterprising freighter, had built a toll road from Challis to Bonanza. Townsites, mines, and several stations served those venturing along the rugged back road. (Back then, the trip from the Yankee Fork mines to Challis took nine hours and cost $8.) The driving tour takes about three hours and passes through the ghost towns of Bonanza and Custer. Along the way you can see the remains of stations that provided services to early travelers. The narrow dirt road is suitable for high-clearance and four-wheel-drive vehicles. | Forest Service Rd. 070 between Challis and Sunbeam.

A brochure with a map of the motorway is available from the **Idaho Department of Parks and Recreation, Challis Ranger District** (HC 63, Box 1669, 83227 | 208/879–4321 | www.fs. fed.us/r4/sc).

Land of the Yankee Fork Historic Area. This 6,000-acre historic area showcases Idaho's frontier mining history. The Land of the Yankee Fork attracted gold seekers from 1870 onward, and within six years the communities of Custer and Bonanza were working mines like the Lucky Boy, General Custer, and Montana. Custer reached a population of 600, but by 1911 both it and Bonanza had become ghost towns. | Along Custer Motorway Adventure Rd., from Challis 45 mi southwest to Sunbeam Dam | 208/879–5244 | www.idahoparks. org/parks/yankeefork.html | Free | Daily dawn–dusk.

The **Custer Museum** displays nine buildings, including a school, the former Empire Saloon, and five homes of people from various income levels. The miner's cabin has little more than a rough bed, while the homes of more prosperous residents had better furnishings and even, sometimes, a piano. The museum also has exhibits of miners' lanterns, drills, and mining tools, as well as photographs. | Custer Motorway Adventure Rd., about 35 mi southwest of Challis | No phone | Free | Late May–early Sept., daily 10–5.

An **interpretive center** styled like an old mining mill has displays with photographs and written descriptions of Yankee Fork mining activity. Items on hand include a collection of Chinese opium pipes, a doctor's buggy, poker tables, and blacksmith tools. | U.S. 93 at Rte. 75, about 2 mi southeast of Challis | 208/879–5244 | Free | Late May–early Sept., daily 8–6; early Sept.–late May, daily 9–5.

✦ ON THE CALENDAR: Aug. **Sacajawea/Heritage Days.** Born in the Lemhi Valley, Sacajawea was a Shoshone woman who was part of Lewis and Clark's Corps of Discovery. This festival celebrates the expedition and the woman with three days of programs, Indian dances, and hot-air balloon flights. | 800/727–2540.

COEUR D'ALENE
▼▼

About 4 million acres around Coeur d'Alene and in the southern portion of Idaho's Panhandle were once held by the Coeur d'Alene Indian tribe, which gave Jesuit missionary Father Pierre De Smet a warm reception in the 1840s. The origin of the name Coeur d'Alene is subject to debate; its literal translation from French is "heart of awl." In the late 1850s army captain John Mullan and his crew started hacking the Mullan Road out of the wooded wilderness.

In 1877 the Mullan Road carried General William Tecumseh Sherman to the area, where he surveyed the lakefront for potential sites for a military fort. A tent city was followed in 1878 by a military stockade, Fort Coeur d'Alene, on the north shore of Coeur d'Alene Lake near the Spokane River inlet. Pioneers soon began settling in the area, which was incorporated as a town in 1887 with a population of 1,000. The discovery of gold, silver, and lead brought a rush of miners from 1883 to 1885. Today, part of the city's Sherman Avenue follows a segment of the Mullan Road. *Contact Coeur d'Alene Chamber of Commerce | 1621 N. 3rd St., Suite 100, 83816 | 208/664–3194 or 877/782–9232 | fax 208/667–9338 | www.coeurdalene.org.*

Fort Sherman Museum. The city of Coeur d'Alene didn't exist when the fort was built as Fort Coeur d'Alene in 1878, but a small community called Slabtown sprang up nearby. The fort was later renamed for General William Tecumseh Sherman and the new town became Coeur d'Alene. The museum is on the grounds of Northern Idaho College, which in turn sits on the original Fort Sherman grounds. The Fort Sherman Powder House contains weapons and information on Fort Sherman. | 1000 W. Garden Ave. | 208/664–3448 | Free | May–Sept., Tues.– Sat. 1–4:45.

Mullan Road Historic Site. Captain John Mullan and the men who helped him built the Mullan Road between Fort Walla Walla, Washington, and Fort Benton, Montana, spent July 4, 1861, about 8 mi east of Coeur d'Alene at a place called Fourth of July Pass. They celebrated the holiday by firing their rifles and carving "MR July 4, 1861" and their names into a large redwood tree, now known as the Mullan Tree. The tree was struck by lighting many years later, and the part with the inscription was relocated to the Museum of Northern Idaho, where lightning struck it again. There is an interpretive area at Fourth of July Canyon. | 8 mi east of Coeur d'Alene on I–90 to Fourth of July Canyon Rd. | 208/769–3000 | Free | Daily dawn–dusk.

Museum of Northern Idaho. The museum's major exhibits focus on Native American culture, steamboats, the logging industry, and nearby communities. Each year the museum has a new theme and rotating exhibits, such as one showcasing handmade quilts. | 115 Northwest Blvd. | 208/664–3448 | $1.50 | Apr.–Oct., Tues.–Sat. 11–5.

✦ ON THE CALENDAR: July **Julyamsh Powwow.** The Coeur d'Alene Tribal Encampment Powwow is held at Greyhound Park and Events Center in Post Falls. | 800/523–2464.

GLENNS FERRY
▼▼

Here was one of the most dangerous river crossings on the 2,000-mi Oregon Trail. Those who made it this far had to decide whether to risk their lives crossing the fast-flowing Snake River, which would give them a shorter, easier route on the north side, or to plod through the barren, rocky desert south of the river where there was little water and feed for livestock. The first emigrants to attempt the crossing were two missionaries, Marcus Whitman and Henry Spalding. Their wagon broke up in mid-crossing, but they salvaged the pieces, constructed a cart, and continued on their way. Some 300,000 people are believed to have crossed the river here in a 30-year period beginning in the early 1840s. The town is named for Gus Glenn, who in 1869 began offering pioneers a safe crossing 2 mi upriver. *Contact Glenns Ferry Chamber of Commerce | 108 E. 1st Ave. | 208/366–7345 or 208/366–2433 | fax 208/366–2238 | www.mountain-home.org/chamber/gfchamber.htm.*

Glenns Ferry Historical Museum. Housed in a native stone schoolhouse built in 1909, this small museum has artifacts from the Oregon Trail as well as ranch and railroad memorabilia. Check out the photographs of the horse teams dragging 1,000-lb. sturgeon out of the Snake River. | 200 W. Cleveland St. | No phone | Donation | June–Sept., Fri.–Sat. noon–5.

Three Island Crossing State Park. The three islands in this state park mark the spot where many pioneers attempted to cross the Snake River on their way along the Oregon Trail. Here you can see ruts left by their wagon wheels. At the Oregon Trail History and Education Center at the park's entrance, life-size dioramas showing trail life, wagon replicas, diary entries, and interactive displays tell the pioneers' stories, and an eight-minute film shows wagons crossing the river. From time to time, buffalo and longhorn cattle are pastured in the enclosure at the southeast corner of the park. | Off Commercial St. ½ mi from town, then 1 mi down paved road | Park 208/366–2394; history center 208/366–7121 | www.idahoparks. org/parks/threeisland.html | Park: $3 per vehicle; history center $3 | Park daily dawn–dusk; history center hours vary seasonally.

✦ ON THE CALENDAR: Aug. **A Crossing in Time Festival and Three Island Crossing Re-enactment.** This annual event commemorates the hundreds of pioneers who lost their lives crossing the river. In a reenactment, wagons cross the Snake River where they did in the 1840s and 1850s. The festival includes a horse parade, cowboy poetry, a pioneer breakfast and barbecue, a mountain-man rendezvous, and arts and crafts. | 208/366–7375.

GRANGEVILLE
▼▼

At the foot of the Bitterroot Mountains on the Camas Prairie, a 200,000-acre stretch of foothills bordered by the Clearwater and Snake rivers, the Nez Perce Indians each summer gathered camas roots, a mainstay of their diet. This was a supply town for mines in the Gospel Mountains and Buffalo Hump region. It got its first building in 1874, when a grange hall was built. The structure housed what is thought to have been the first Northwestern chapter of the National Grange of the Patrons of Husbandry, a secret fraternal organization for farmers. From this, the town got its name. *Contact Grangeville Chamber of Commerce | U.S. 95 at Pine St., Box 212, 83530 | 208/983–0460 | fax 208/983–1429 | www.grangevilleidaho.com.*

Bicentennial Historical Museum. In this museum you will find an extensive collection of Nez Perce items, including a beaded buckskin jacket worn by Eagle Boy, a scout for General Howard during the Nez Perce War of 1877. Several buckskin ceremonial dresses decorated with trade beads and shells are on display. One ceremonial dress is made of red Hudson Bay trade cloth and decorated with shells, ribbons, and coins. Other Nez Perce items are corn-husk bags, beaded bags, saddlebags, pipes, beads, moccasins, gloves, dolls, leggings, a strike-a-lite bag, a beaded awl holder, and a pack saddle. | 305 N. College | 208/983–2104 | www.grangevilleidaho.com/historical_museum.htm | Donation | June–Sept., Wed. and Fri. 1–5.

Elk City Wagon Road. You'll need a high-clearance vehicle and most of a day to drive this 53-mi unpaved route. For centuries it was used by Native Americans traveling through the Clearwater Mountains to the Bitterroot Valley and points eastward. After 1861 thousands of miners used the same route to reach the goldfields of Newsome, Elk City, Buffalo Hump, and Thunder Mountain. So heavy was the traffic that a new road had to be built along the route; construction began in 1894. The road to Elk City, funded mostly by public subscription, was completed July 15, 1895. To help you follow the road there are "Elk City Wagon Road" posts and 22 interpretive signs, and you can get a tour guide book from Nez Perce National Forest Headquarters in Grangeville or any other ranger district in the forest. In Elk City there is a ranger station where you can get additional information. | Starts in Harpster, 10 mi east of Grangeville on Rte. 13 and 3 mi north on U.S. 12 | 208/842–2245 or 208/983–1950 | www.fs.fed.us/r1/nezperce/ | Summer and fall, weather permitting.

Historical Driving Tours. Starting from Grangeville, you can take three driving tours that focus on the history of the region. The Camas Prairie Driving Tour takes you from Grangeville to

LEWIS AND CLARK IN IDAHO

When Lewis and Clark made their way into Idaho at Lemhi Pass they believed they had reached the headwaters of the Missouri. They figured they only needed to cross the pass and travel down the west slope of the Rockies to the Columbia River. But when they reached the top of Lemhi Pass the view stunned the explorers. Before them lay what looked like hundreds of miles of mountains. With the help of a Lemhi Shoshone guide they called Old Toby, the Corps of Discovery headed west (to present-day Tendoy) and then north (along present-day U.S. 93) to the North Fork of the Salmon River. Captain Clark set out with 11 men from the party to make an exploratory trip along that branch of the Salmon and found the region too rough for travel. The explorers continued north to cross Lost Trail Pass, into the Bitterroot Valley of what is now Montana.

Lewis and Clark reentered Idaho at Lolo Pass and followed the northern Nez Perce Trail along the Lochsa River corridor (now traversed by U.S. 12), but they found themselves struggling through snow and cold weather. Nearly out of food by September 14, 1805, they killed one of their colts at a place since known as Killed Colt Creek. Clark and an advance party of six companions met three Nez Perce (Ni Mii Pu) boys on September 22 near present-day Weippe. The Indians allowed the Corps of Discovery to spend time in the Nez Perce camp, where they were provided with food and a map, plus guides who would travel west with them. The guides took the explorers along the Clearwater River, and they exited present Idaho near Lewiston.

After spending the winter at Fort Clatsop on the west coast, the Corps of Discovery began its return trip in March 1806. On this journey they followed a similar route in reverse, though three of the party along with some Nez Perce guides made a southerly detour along the Snake River. Near the mouth of the Salmon River they purchased salmon before turning north and east, passing north of present-day Cottonwood and Grangeville and rejoining the other travelers in the Kamiah Valley. They thought it would take them two days to make their salmon-buying expedition; it actually took seven. The Nez Perce warned Lewis and Clark not to continue traveling until more snow melted. Some Corps members had been ill, and the party was low on food. But on June 10, 1806, Lewis and Clark made the decision to move on. Before they were able to cross Lolo Pass on June 29, they endured excruciatingly difficult travel through snow "from 8 to 12 feet deep."

Many interpretive areas have been developed across Idaho along the various routes the Corps of Discovery took. You can follow their trail on the Lolo Motorway or the Lewis and Clark Back Country Byway. Portions of these are rough, steep dirt roads suitable only for high clearance or four-wheel-drive vehicles. Information is available from the Bureau of Land Management in Salmon (208/756–5400), the National Forest Service Salmon-Challis Forest (208/756–5100), or Lolo National Forest in Missoula, Montana (406/329–3814), or check out www.lewisandclarkidaho.org.

Cottonwood. Mining history and the Chinese influence in the region are the focus of the Elk City Driving Tour. On the Salmon River Driving Tour you travel along the Salmon River to the town of White Bird and various Nez Perce sites. The Chamber of Commerce has developed brochures to show you the way.

Historical Museum at St. Gertrude. The museum houses an extensive collection of military artifacts, including many from the Nez Perce War of 1877; uniforms from the Spanish-American War; and a collection of 19th-century firearms. Gold scales from 1880 and a miner's rocker cradle are among the items in exhibits on mining in the region. Objects from everyday pioneer life include a complete cobbler's bench with sewing machine, shoe lasts, and leather tools; a Hoosier cabinet with old bowls and serving pieces; a kitchen work table (circa 1900); handmade tools dating back to 1834; and clocks, dolls, butter churns, kitchen tools, and lanterns dating to 1865. | 121 Keuterville Rd., Cottonwood | 208/962–7123 | www. historicalmuseumstgertrude.com | $4 | May–Sept., Tues.–Sat. 9:30–4:30, Sun. 1:30–4:30; Oct.–Apr., Tues.–Sat. 9:30–4:30.

Nez Perce National Historical Park. The park itself is made up of 38 sites in several states—most in Idaho—strung along the route the Nez Perce took in 1877 as they left their native lands after conflicts with settlers. The park headquarters that manages all of them is in Spalding (61 mi northwest of Grangeville), where a visitor center provides background on the Nez Perce Indians, or Ne-Mee-Poo, as they called themselves, and their history. A 30-minute film details the tribe's contacts with Lewis and Clark and their lives today. A small museum exhibits artifacts from Chiefs Joseph and White Bird, including textiles, pipes, and, poignantly, a ribbon and a coin given to the tribe by Meriwether Lewis as thanks for help. | 39063 U.S. 95, Spalding | 208/843–2261 | www.nps.gov/nepe | Free | Late May–early Sept., daily 8–5:30; early Sept.–late May, daily 8–4:30.

White Bird Hill Battlefield Auto Tour. The first battle of the Nez Perce War was fought here on June 17, 1877. Thirty-four U.S. Army soldiers were killed, while the Nez Perce lost none. After the initial confrontations, the Nez Perce made their way across Idaho as they sought refuge in Montana and ultimately attempted to reach Canada. The White Bird Interpretive Shelter has exhibits that explain the sequence of the battle. | 12 mi south of Grangeville on U. S. 95 | 208/843–2261 | Free | Daily dawn–dusk.

✦ ON THE CALENDAR: May **Victorian Tea.** The refectory (dining room) of the Monastery of St. Gertrude is transformed into a Victorian garden for a formal tea. The Victorian lifestyle is re-created with emphasis on the food, fashions, and live music of the period. It's not required, but you are urged to dress in Victorian attire. Reservations are required, and admission is $15 per person. | 208/962–7123.

May **Nez Perce Indian Powwow and Root Festival.** This powwow celebrates the ancient Nez Perce tradition of gathering camas roots, an important staple of their diet, each summer on the Camas Prairie. | 208/935–2290.

July **Grangeville Border Days.** This is the oldest running rodeo in Idaho, with wild horse races, bronc and bull riding, calf roping, and three parades. | 208/983–0460.

IDAHO CITY
▼▼

As you stroll along the wooden sidewalks of Idaho City, you will be immersed in the gold-mining history of the community. Prospectors found gold here in 1862, and the rush to the Boise Basin was the biggest since California's gold rush. In 1863, during the mining boom, Idaho City was Idaho's largest town, with a population of 6,275. At one time more than 200 buildings stood along the town's dusty streets. By 1898, the mining area surrounding the frontier town of Idaho City was ravaged by dredging operations; the scars from the giant machines that raked the earth can be seen for miles today. Idaho City is now part historic mining ghost town and part thriving community at the confluence of More's and Elk creeks. You can see weathered buildings from the town's heyday, including the oldest operating Masonic hall west of the Mississippi, the former county courthouse, the Independent Order of Odd Fellows (IOOF) hall, and a Catholic church. The town publishes a walking-tour map and brochure that points out these and other sights. *Contact Idaho City Visitors Center | 511 Main St., 83631 | 208/392–6040 | www.idahocitychamber.com.*

Boise Basin Museum. Originally a post office, the brick building that houses the museum was built in 1867 and later became a stagecoach station. It also served at times as a private residence before it was turned into a museum. Mining-boom days are illustrated with exhibits, and there is also a short movie on the gold rush. | 501 Montgomery St. | 208/392–4550 | www.idahocitychamber.com | $2 | Late May–early Sept., daily 11–4.

✦ ON THE CALENDAR: Sept. **Gold Rush Days.** Relive the excitement of the rush by riding a stagecoach, eating a meal prepared in a dutch oven, and attending a melodrama. | 208/392–4550.

KELLOGG

▼▼

Smack in the middle of Silver Valley—an area 23 mi long and 9 mi wide, extending from the Montana border to Coeur d'Alene—Kellogg was born a mining town. In the 1880s, thick veins of lead, zinc, silver, and gold ore were discovered. A century later, the district led the nation in silver production, ringing up more than $3 billion in sales. The town is named after miner Noah Kellogg, whose mule Jimmy supposedly kicked over a rock and uncovered the largest vein of silver ever seen in Idaho. Local legend holds that this was the event that kicked off a rush that has been likened to the one in California. Miners swarmed the community, and by the 1890s the town of Kellogg had been established. Today mining museums recall the district's past. *Contact Historic Silver Valley Chamber of Commerce | 10 Station Ave., 83837 | 208/784–0821 | fax 208/783–4343 | www.historicsilvervalleychamberofcommerce.com.*

Kellogg Mining District Ghost Towns. Retrace the colorful mining era by visiting the historic towns of Murray, Pritchard, and Enaville. Some still thrive, while others are deserted clusters of decaying wood. Maps and information are available at the Kellogg Chamber of Commerce.

Old Mission State Park. This 18-acre park contains the oldest surviving building in Idaho, the Mission of the Sacred Heart. It was built in the early 1850s from plans developed by Father Anthony Ravalli, who came to the area from St. Mary's Mission in Montana. The foot-thick mission walls were built without nails, using straw, mud, and wooden pegs in the "wattle and daub" method. More than 300 members of the Coeur d'Alene tribe labored on the building's construction. Inside, there are no pews because the Indians preferred to worship in an open room. The recently restored parish house is next door, and a cemetery is nearby. A short trail links the mission to the visitor center, where you can see interpretive exhibits on the Coeur d'Alene Indians, with samples of Indian beadwork, clothing, and saddles, and on the Jesuit missionaries, known as the Black Robes. | 15 mi east of Kellogg via I–90, Exit 39, Cataldo | 208/682–3814 | www.idahoparks.org/oldmission.html | $3 per vehicle | June–Aug., daily 8–6; Sept.–May, daily 9–5.

Staff House Mining and Smelting Museum. Exhibits trace the history of the Bunker Hill Mining and Smelting Company, one of the oldest and largest mining companies in the Coeur d'Alene district. On display in the historic home are mineral and metallurgical exhibits, a scale model of the Bunker Hill mine, and mining and smelting equipment. | 820 McKinley Ave. | 208/786–4141 | $3 | Late May–Sept., daily 10–5.

✦ ON THE CALENDAR: July **Historic Skills Fair.** Living-history reenactors demonstrate frontier skills such as weaving, spinning, blacksmithing, and fiddle playing. The fair takes place at Old Mission State Park in Cataldo. | 208/682–3814.

Aug. **Mountain Man Rendezvous.** Old Mission State Park in Cataldo is the site of this gathering of buckskinners, who demonstrate the art of black-powder shooting and show trade goods such as buckskin clothing. | 208/682–3814.

KETCHUM

Ketchum held a place of distinction in the Wood River valley as the smelting center for the Warm Springs mining district. The town was first known as Leadville; then because the postal service objected to overuse of the name, it was named Ketchum after David Ketchum, who had staked a claim there in the late 1880s. From 1895 to 1930, the town was a major sheep-shipping center. Today the trailing of the sheep is still an annual event, when herds move through town en route to the high pastures in the Big Wood River valley to the north. *Contact Sun Valley/Ketchum Chamber of Commerce | Box 2420, Sun Valley 83353 | 800/634–3347 | fax 208/726–4533 | www.visitketchum.com.*

Blaine County Historical Museum. Housed in an adobe structure built in 1883, the museum commemorates pioneer life in the Wood River Valley. Mining was how the area got its start, with casinos and brothels popping up before farms, churchs, and schools appeared. Exhibits focus on Chinese railroad and mine workers, Basque sheepherders, mining, and the Oregon Short Line the railroad that came to the Valley in 1883. The museum is in the historic town of Hailey, 12 mi south of Ketchum on Rte. 75. | 218 N. Main St., Hailey | 208/788–1801 | www.bchistoricalmuseum.org.

Ore Wagon Museum. The centerpiece of this museum is the collection of huge ore wagons that are taken out once a year for Ketchum's Wagon Days. In the 1880s, the wagons hauled as much as 24,000 pounds of ore per trip, with a team of up to 20 mules. Related exhibits on the town's mining past are also on display. | East Ave. at 5th | No phone | Free | Daily 10–5.

✦ ON THE CALENDAR: Oct. **Trailing of Sheep.** In keeping with a century-old tradition, sheepherders move their flocks from summer pastures in the mountains north of Ketchum and Sun Valley, south through the Wood River valley to winter grazing areas. For one after-noon the sheep trail down Main Street Ketchum past restaurants, boutique shops, coffee-houses, and hotels as all other traffic halts. Other events include programs relating to the history of sheep ranching in the Wood River valley. There are wool-carding demonstrations, spinning and weaving, shearing, herding sheep with stock dogs, storytelling, sheepherder-bread making, a traditional Basque lamb dinner, music, sheep wagons on display, and Basque and Scottish dancing. | 208/725–2101.

Aug.–Sept. **Wagon Days.** A popular four-day event is held in both Sun Valley and Ketchum. The Big Hitch parade, showcasing dozens of horse-drawn vehicles, is one of the largest non-motorized parades in the West and highlights the Lewis String ore wagons that were donated to the city by the Lewis family. These massive wagons are awesome examples of how mate-rials were transported during the mining boom of the late 1800s. There are also pancake breakfasts, evening western dances, antiques shows, live entertainment, and a rodeo. A multi-day wagon-train trip often takes place in the area, ending during Wagon Days. | 208/726–3423 or 800/634–3347.

MONTPELIER

Montpelier has long been a rest stop for travelers, first used by those trudging the Califor-nia and Oregon trails, which passed nearby. Settled in 1864, the community was named by Mormon Church leader Brigham Young, who was born in Montpelier, Vermont. The noto-rious outlaw Butch Cassidy once robbed the local bank. *Contact Greater Bear Lake Valley Cham-ber of Commerce | 322 N. 4th St., 83254 | 208/847–0067 | www.bearlakechamber.org.*

IDAHO'S HISTORIC ROADS

The first roads and trails across Idaho were those charted by Indians, who were most likely following game trails. Then Lewis and Clark made their way across the north-central portion of what is now Idaho, followed by fur trappers and traders. But the first major thoroughfare across Idaho came with the development of the Oregon Trail. Though fur trappers crossed portions of it and missionaries also traveled the route, the first emigrants to make their way with covered wagons headed west in 1841. Two years later the great wave of emigration to Oregon began.

The main route of the Oregon Trail entered Idaho in the Bear River valley, near Montpelier. It struck to the northwest and Fort Hall, where emigrants rested (they called it recruiting) before they followed the Snake River to the western side of Idaho. Pioneer Tim Goodale eventually forged a "cutoff" on the Oregon Trail that took travelers farther north. A new wave of travelers arrived in 1849, when emigrants seeking their fortune crossed southeast Idaho on their way to the goldfields in California. Their route took them southwest from the Oregon Trail at the Raft River (about 35 mi southwest of present-day American Falls), to the Humboldt River in northern Nevada and then over the Sierra Nevada to California. As for the Oregon Trail, there were various branches and cutoffs for the California Trail. In northern Idaho, a military road constructed by Captain John Mullan between 1859 and 1861 linked Fort Walla Walla in Washington with Fort Benton in Montana. Not only did the road serve the U.S. Army, it provided access to Jesuit missions such as the one at Cataldo.

In all, around 500,000 travelers made their way across Idaho as they sought land in Oregon or gold in California. U.S. 30 and I–84 roughly parallel the main branch of the Oregon Trail across Idaho. You can follow parts of the California trail on Route 77 (about 15 mi south of I–84 via Rte. 81) and the City of Rocks Back Country Byway. I–90 follows parts of the Mullan Road across northern Idaho.

Border Summit Oregon Trail Ruts. At an elevation of 6,335 ft, Border Summit offers a good view of an undisturbed portion of the Oregon Trail. | 12 mi south of Montpelier off U.S. 30.

The National Oregon-California Trail Center. Visit with living-history reenactors and learn what it was like to travel the Oregon and California trails, which brought emigrants through the Montpelier area from 1843 to 1870. The center is built on the site of the Clover Creek campsite used by pioneer travelers; one exhibit places you amid real wagons and around a campfire with reenactors who share actual stories from the trail. The center also has a Rails and Trails Museum, with examples of tools and photos from early settlers. Among the items on display are Native American stone tools, a spinning wheel, and several butter churns. | 320 N. 4th St. | 208/847–3800 or 800/448–2327 | www.oregontrailcenter.org | $6 | Late May–Sept., daily 10–5; Oct.–late May, weekdays 10–2.

Paris Tabernacle. Mormon pioneers built this redbrick tabernacle in 1889 when they settled in the Bear Lake area. In summer you can tour the building, where there are periodic organ recitals. | 10 mi south of Montpelier in Paris, on U.S. 89 | 208/945–3333 | Free | Late May–early Sept., daily 9:30–5.

✦ ON THE CALENDAR: Aug. **Butch Cassidy Bank Robbery Reenactment.** Held during a non-historical celebration called Butch Cassidy Days, this bank-robbery reenactment memorializes the August 13, 1896, robbery of the Montpelier bank carried off by outlaw Butch Cassidy and some of his cohorts. | 208/847–0067.

WALLACE

▼▼

The mining town of Wallace is one of the few towns to be included in their entirety on the National Register of Historic Places. It was first settled in the 1880s mining rush, and today much of the town center looks exactly as it did in the early 1900s. A fire in 1910 reduced a third of the town to ashes, but much of the gracious turn-of-the-20th-century architecture created during Wallace's heyday as the capital of the Silver Valley mining area remains intact. Known for its turreted and decorative storefronts—which today house eateries and hotels— it has a dozen museums that recall its mining and railroad years. *Contact Wallace Chamber of Commerce | 10 River St., Box 1167, 83873 | 208/753–7151 | www.wallace-id.com.*

Historic Wallace Walking Tour. This self-guided tour of Wallace is outlined in a brochure that has a map and descriptions of the town's historic buildings. The complete tour takes about one hour. The brochure is available at the chamber of commerce.

Northern Pacific Depot Railroad Museum. Exhibits trace the history of railroading in the Coeur d'Alene mining district. On display is a rare 13-ft glass map of the Northern Pacific Railroad route. | 219 6th St. | 208/752–0111 | $2 | Apr.–mid-Oct., daily 10–5.

Oasis Bordello Museum. The museum depicts the days of the Oasis Rooms, one of the town's five bordellos. An accurate and tasteful tour is presented by proprietor Michelle Mayfield, who shares a 20-minute glimpse into the past, with details that range from poignant to hilarious. In addition to visiting the second-floor brothel, the tour stops by an old wine press in the basement and traces the history of the Bi-Metallic Building, which began as a hotel and saloon in 1895 and later became the bordello. Of particular interest are the mosaic floor tiles imported from China. | 605 Cedar St. | 208/753–0801 | www.silver-country.com | Donation; $5 for tour | May–Oct., Mon.–Sat. 9:30–6:30, Sun. 10–5.

Sierra Silver Mine Tour. An open-air trolley transports you to the mine, where you are fitted with a hard hat. Tours include a brief overview of the mine's history and early mineral discoveries in Wallace. Underground displays explain how minerals were extracted in the 19th century using hard-rock mining methods. Kids over 4 only. | 420 5th St. | 208/752–5151 | $9 | May– June and Sept., daily 9–4; July–Aug., daily 9–6.

Wallace District Mining Museum. Housed in the old Rice's Bakery building, the museum mounts exhibits on the history of local mining methods and operations from the 1880s to modern times. Among the displays you can see lighting devices from old stearic candles and oil lamps to today's rechargeable electric cap lamps. In addition, the museum has the only complete steam-driven diamond drill known to have been preserved. The video "Northern Idaho's Silver Legacy" relates the history of the area from the 1850s to the present. | 509 Bank St. | 208/556–1592 | $1.50 | May, daily 9–5; June, daily 8–6; July–Aug., daily 8–7; Sept., daily 9– 5; Oct.–Apr., weekdays 9–4, Sat. 10–3.

✦ ON THE CALENDAR: Aug. **Huckleberry and Heritage Festival.** Local residents dress up as turn-of-the-20th-century characters during this festival, which also has a parade, pancake breakfast, and peddlers. | 208/753–7151.

HISTORIC LODGING

The Beale House B&B. This 1904 home has original parquet floors and antique furnishings. The five second-floor guest rooms are distinctive, with a fireplace in one, a balcony for another, and still another with two full walls of windows. A massive Palladian window in the library area provides a view of the grounds and mountains. There is a two-night minimum. Dining room, outdoor hot tub; no kids, no room phones, no room TVs. | 107 Cedar St., 83873 | 208/ 752–7151 or 888/752–7151 | $115 | No credit cards.

Historic Jameson Hotel. In 1890 the local newspaper reported: "The bar and billiard hall of Jameson & Horton, corner of Sixth and Pine streets, is without exception the handsomest in northern Idaho." The three-story redbrick building was opened as saloon and billiard hall in 1889 and was later converted to a hostelry and saloon. Though it was damaged by fire in the 1940s, it has been restored; ceiling fans, bentwood chairs, polished brass, chandeliers, and Oriental carpets evoke the Old West at the turn of the 20th century. The six rooms are small, and none have a private bath, but each has hardwood floors, period wall coverings and vintage photographs and prints on the walls, and antique furnishings including ornate headboards and mirrored armoires. Restaurant, bar; no room phones, no room TVs. | 314 6th St., 83873 | 208/556–1554 | fax 208/753–0981 | wallace-id.com/jameson/index.html | 6 rooms | Closed Nov.–Apr. | $70–$90 | MC, V.

KANSAS

————◆————

From its eastern border to the western horizon, Kansas unfolds across the miles of rolling Flint Hills, through the Gypsum and Smoky Hills, and onto the High Plains. On these wide-open grasslands abundant buffalo herds once supplied the needs of resident Plains Apache, Kaw, Osage, Pawnee, and Wichita. European exploration began in 1541 when Francisco Vásquez de Coronado journeyed from Mexico northeast to present-day Lyons. Other French and Spanish explorers followed in the 1700s, claiming the land for their countries before the United States ultimately acquired it in 1803 as part of the Louisiana Purchase. Thomas Jefferson promptly sent Meriwether Lewis and William Clark to map the new acquisition.

Traders and trappers crisscrossed the territory, and beginning in the 1820s the first of hundreds of thousands of merchants and settlers surged westward along the Santa Fe and Oregon trails, leaving wagon ruts still visible today in the prairie grasses. Religious missionaries also ventured westward and established schools to Christianize Kaw, Osage, Shawnee, Potawatomie, and others and to educate them in "civilized ways." Culture clashes resulted in bitterness, broken treaties, and ultimately the compression of Native American lands to a few small reservations.

In 1854, as tensions mounted between the northern and southern states over the slavery issue, the Kansas-Nebraska Act officially established Kansas Territory boundaries, opening the area for settlement and decreeing that the territory's residents would decide for themselves whether Kansas would enter the Union as a slave or free state. People on both sides of the debate, including such renowned figures as John Brown, converged on the territory in an attempt to influence the politics of the future state. In the ensuing conflict dozens of towns were burned to the ground and many others were threatened. The territory was soon called "bleeding Kansas." The free-state faction eventually triumphed, and Kansas became the 34th state on January 29, 1861, but the struggle over the state's position on slavery continued throughout the Civil War. Many eastern Kansas towns suffered William Quantrill's guerrilla raids, the most famous of which was his attack on Lawrence in August 1863, when more than 200 buildings were burned and 150 people were killed. Kansas freestaters, or "jayhawkers" (a mythical Irish bird that worries its prey to death before devouring it), and Union troops took revenge on Missouri towns and factions.

Meanwhile, settlers continued to stake their claims. The U.S. Army established military posts across the frontier to guard supply trains and to subdue native tribes who resisted the seizing of open land. Forts Leavenworth and Riley supplied the western forts of Harker, Larned, Hays, Dodge, and Wallace. Soldiers at these posts endured long and lonely service; those who survived the extreme temperatures, poor food, and epidemics of influenza or cholera often deserted. Colonel George Custer served on this frontier, as did the African-American Buffalo Soldiers.

Technology also had an impact on the new state. In the early 1860s the arrival of telegraph lines and steel rails made the short-lived Pony Express mail route obsolete. Six years later, entrepreneur Joseph McCoy convinced Texas cowboys to drive their herds up the Chisholm Trail to the Abilene railhead, where cattle merchants set their prices and loaded the steers onto freight cars headed for eastern markets. Other cattle towns appeared: Newton, Ellsworth, and Wichita, and later Caldwell and Dodge City. These wild and wicked places deprived many a young drover of a season's wages in return for fancy clothes, strong liquor, and the services of "soiled doves." Wyatt Earp, Doc Holliday, Bat Masterson, and "Wild Bill" Hickok all called these towns home.

On the Early Frontier

A DRIVING TOUR FROM REPUBLIC TO FORT SCOTT

▼▼

Distance: 350 mi   **Time:** 4 days
Breaks: Don't miss Leavenworth's historic High Noon Saloon or Fort Scott's Victorian inns.

Before establishing Kansas Territory in 1854, the U.S. government did not allow pioneer settlement in the Louisiana Purchase, which had long been inhabited by Native Americans. Trappers, traders, and missionaries, however, accessed the territory on the Santa Fe and Oregon trails. Fights between Indians and whites were sometimes resolved by troops from Forts Leavenworth and Scott. This tour highlights Native American and early settlements and follows the historic Military Byway from Fort Leavenworth to Fort Scott.

Start your journey near **Belleville,** at Pawnee Indian Village State Historic Site, where displays of artifacts and the excavated floor of an 1820s earth lodge tell the story of the mighty Pawnee Nation. Drive 8 mi south on Route 266 to U.S. 36 east, then 55 mi to Route 148 in the vicinity of **Marysville.** On Route 148, drive 4 mi north to Hollenberg Station State Historic Site, a trails way station on the Pony Express mail route. Then return to U.S. 36 and continue east 44 mi to Seneca, where the only original Pony Express barn still stands. Overnight in this area.

On your second day, continue east 42 mi on U.S. 36 to Route 120 north. Arrive in Highland in mid-morning and visit the Native American Heritage Museum, a former site of Iowa and Sac and Fox encampments. Returning to U.S. 36, continue 10 mi to Troy; then go south 20 mi on Route 7 for a drive-through of **Atchison.** Drive south 25 mi on U.S. 73 to the Missouri River bluff city of **Leavenworth,** site of the frontier's first fort, commemorated in the Frontier Army Museum. The short esplanade in town affords a breathtaking view across the river. Overnight here.

Depart Leavenworth before mid-morning on day three, heading south on the Frontier Scenic Military Byway (Route 5), a former Army trail. Don't let the sudden appearance of **Kansas City**'s sprawl fool you: here early settlement history surrounds you. Take I–435 south to I–70 east, then I–635 south to I–35 south. U.S. 56 will then take you east to Shawnee Indian Mission State Historic Site. This 1839 manual training school for Native Americans also provided supplies for overland travelers. Back on I–35, drive south to Santa Fe Road west, turn right on Ridgeview Road, and then go left at Kansas City Road. Here the 1858 Mahaffie Farmstead

KANSAS TIME LINE

1541 The Wichita Tribe meets Francisco Vásquez de Coronado as he explores central Kansas.

1650 Taos Indians build El Quartelejo, the only known Indian pueblo in Kansas.

1803 Future Kansas land is bought by the United States as a part of the Louisiana Purchase.

1821 The Santa Fe Trail opens.

1825 Congress passes the first legislation forcing Native American tribes into eastern Kansas.

1827 Fort Leavenworth is built.

1838–1844 The Frontier Military Road is constructed from Fort Leavenworth to Fort Scott and Fort Gibson in present-day Oklahoma.

1842 Overland immigration begins on the Oregon Trail; Fort Scott is established.

1844 John C. Fremont explores the Smoky Hill Trail.

1854 Congress passes the Kansas-Nebraska Bill, creating Kansas Territory and opening it for settlement.

1854–1861 During the "Bleeding Kansas" years, violence erupts over the future of Kansas as a free or slave state.

1855 Lecompton is named the capital of Kansas Territory; abolitionist John Brown moves to Osawatomie, 30 mi south of Kansas City, and begins his campaigns against pro-slavery advocates. Brown helps escaped slaves to freedom.

1857 The pro-slavery Lecompton Constitution is drafted but rejected.

1860 The Pony Express begins its 18-month service; Cyrus K. Holliday founds the Atchison, Topeka & Santa Fe Railroad Company in Atchison.

1861 Kansas becomes the 34th state in the Union, with its capital in Topeka.

1863 Quantrill and his Confederate guerrillas sack towns in eastern Kansas.

1864 The Battle of Mine Creek takes place.

1867 The Great Plains Peace Treaty is signed at Medicine Lodge; Abilene becomes the trailhead of the Chisholm Trail.

1874 The Western Cattle Trail opens; Mennonites, bringing hardy Turkey Red wheat, begin immigration to central Kansas.

1877 African-American pioneers establish the settlement of Nicodemus.

1878 The last Indian attempt to return to their homelands in northern Kansas turns violent.

1882 Russian Jews establish Beersheba, the first Jewish agricultural colony in Kansas.

1890 Temperance leader Carry Nation arrives in Kansas.

1892 The Dalton Gang's attempt to rob both of Coffeyville's banks ends in the death of four of its members. The first oil well of the Mid-Continent field, the nation's largest, is drilled in Wilson County.

1893 Arkansas City becomes the rendezvous point for the great Cherokee Strip Land Rush.

1900 Kansas population reaches 1,470,495.

1901 Carrie Nation, who launched her saloon smashing campaign in Medicine Lodge and Kiowa, brings her show to Topeka.

1912 Kansas woman suffrage amendment ratified.

and Stagecoach Stop demonstrates how meals and livery service were provided for westbound stagecoaches. Now follow I–35 southwest about 18 mi to Exit 215, and take U.S. 169 south to Route 68 east. U.S. 69 south puts you on a 54-mi stretch of the Frontier Scenic Military Byway, which cuts through the Osage Cuestas near **Pleasanton.** Slaves on the Underground Railroad hid in these hills. Also along this roadway is Mine Creek Battlefield State Historic Site, a Civil War site. Overnight in **Fort Scott.**

Make day four a leisurely one to round out your tour. Stroll the parade grounds of Fort Scott and view the barracks and block house. Daily trolley rides take you through the 1850s downtown and past 1880s Victorian homes.

Prairie Pioneer Trails
A DRIVING TOUR FROM DODGE CITY TO WICHITA

▼▼▼

Distance: 420 mi   **Time:** 4 days
Breaks: Hays, Ellsworth, and Abilene all have bed-and-breakfasts in historic buildings. Downtown Council Grove offers historic lodgings in walking distance of the renowned Hays House Restaurant.

Immigrant trails crisscrossed the plains of Kansas from the time trappers and traders first realized the economic potential of the Louisiana Purchase. Entrepreneurs and settlers headed west on the Santa Fe, Oregon, and Smoky Hill trails to claim land in and beyond Kansas. The Chisholm and Western Cattle trails snaked north from Texas as drovers herded cattle to market. Along these dusty, rutted routes the Old West gained its wild and dangerous reputation.

Begin in **Dodge City,** where Santa Fe Trail wagon trains camped. The former Fort Dodge grew from a few sod and adobe buildings in 1865 to a full military outpost. Between 1874 and 1890 the Western Cattle Trail brought cowboys to the booming town to indulge in a few vices and gunfights. Drive U.S. 56 northeast to **Larned,** the location of Fort Larned National Historic Site and the Santa Fe Trail Center. Next, head west 7 mi on Route 156, and then take U.S. 183 north to **Hays,** on the Oregon Trail. Travelers, mail carriers, and railmen depended on the fort here for protection. Overnight here.

Driving I–70 east on your second day, watch for fences. You're in post rock country, where early settlers had no trees and instead quarried fence posts of soft Greenhorn Limestone. **Ellsworth,** a one-time military supply post, protected stage lines and travelers on the Smoky Hill Trail and had a reputation as a wild cowtown. Farther east on I–70, the history of notorious **Abilene** is preserved at the Dickinson County Heritage Center. Overnight in either of the cities.

On day three, head to history-rich **Council Grove,** dropping south from I–70 on Route 57/177. Here, museums and historic sites preserve the heritage of the Kaw Nation, the story of the Santa Fe Trail, trail town culture, and Osage Tribe history. You can stay in one of the town's historic hotels and have dinner where Jesse James and George Custer ate.

Your last day begins with a drive along Route 57/177, a beautiful scenic byway. When you reach the Kansas Turnpike (I–35), turn south to **Wichita.** Here, you can spend a day reliving the city's 1865–80 heyday at an open-air living history museum and a chuck wagon dinner. Don't miss Wichita/Sedgwick County Historical Museum's Chisholm Trail exhibit.

ABILENE
▼▼▼

Abilene, a simple plains town founded in 1857, changed drastically when the Atchison, Topeka & Santa Fe Railroad arrived in 1867 and entrepreneur Joseph McCoy proposed bringing together eastern cattle merchants and Texas cattle drovers. Almost overnight Abilene became a booming cattle town. Cowboys, gambling establishments, and at least a dozen saloons made this

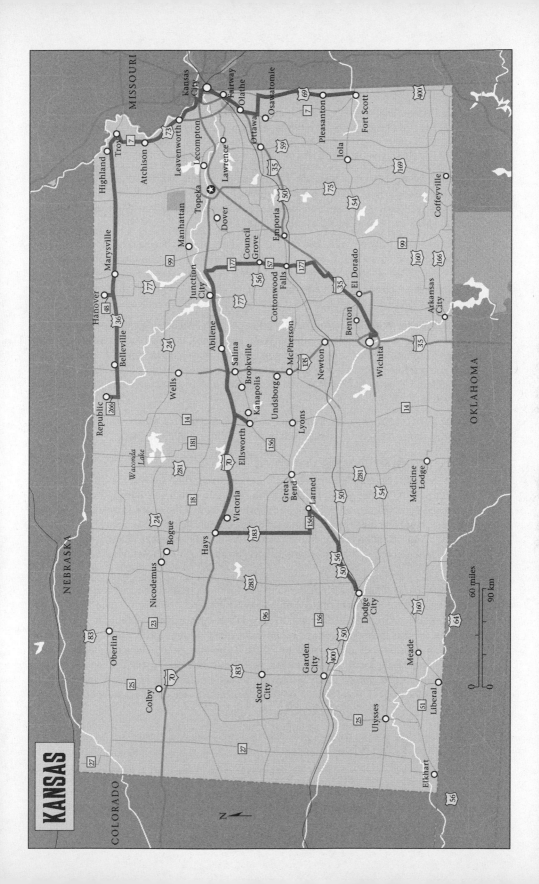

KANSAS

railhead a wild and wicked place, and their attempts to maintain law and order here made Tom Smith and Wild Bill Hickok famous. *Contact Abilene Convention and Visitors Bureau | 201 N.W. 2nd St., Box 146, 67410 | 800/569–5915 | www.abileneks.com.*

Abilene Historic Van Tours. On a one-hour guided tour, you'll hear about the history of the town at the end of the Chisholm trail while touring the sites. Tours start in the Abilene Visitor Center in the restored Union Pacific Depot. | 201 NW 2 St. | 785/263–2231 | fax 785/263–4125 | June–Aug., Mon.–Sat. 9:30–7 | $3.

Dickinson County Historical Museum. The museum presents exhibits on Indians, pioneers, railroads, agriculture, cowboys on the Chisholm Trail, and cow towns. | 412 S. Campbell St. | 785/263–2681 | www.heritagecenterdk.com | $3 | Early Sept.–late May, Mon.–Sat. 10–4, Sun. 1–5; late May–early Sept., Mon.–Sat. 10–8, Sun. 1–8.

Lebold Mansion. Abilene mayor, banker, and real estate mogul Conrad Lebold commissioned this house to be "the finest home west of Topeka." The site he chose was where Abilene's first home (1858) stood; in the mansion's basement is the original stone dugout. The Italianate mansion, complete with a 4-story tower, was built in 1880 for $18,000. | 106 N. Vine | 785/263–4356 | www.abilenecityhall.com/lebold.htm | $10 | Tours Tues.–Sun., 11, 1, and 3.

Patent Medicine Museum. Starting in 1890, the A.B. Seelye Medical Company produced such cure-alls as Wasa-Tusa, Fro-zona, and Ner-vena. Take a look at the artifacts here for a glimpse of health care in the Old West. The museum is in the 1905 Georgian Seelye Mansion, whose 25 rooms are filled with the original furniture. You can take a tour of the house and stroll the gardens. | 1104 N. Buckeye | 785/263–1084 | www.seelyemansion.com | $10 | Mon.–Sat. 9–6, Sun. 1–6.

✦ ON THE CALENDAR: Oct. **Chisholm Trail Day.** An antique tractor show and pioneer-skills demonstrations take center stage at the Heritage Center. | 785/263–2681.

HISTORIC DINING AND LODGING

Brookville Hotel. American. Formerly in Brookville, this restaurant was relocated to Abilene in spring 2000. The building replicates the original, which the Kansas Pacific Railway constructed in 1870. Since 1896 the same family has owned the establishment, serving only one thing: complete fried chicken dinners with real cream cole slaw and creamed corn, mashed potatoes, and biscuits—the best anywhere. | 105 E. Lafayette St. | 785/263–2244 | www.brookvillehotel.com | Reservations essential. | Closed Mon. No lunch weekdays. | $12 | D, MC, V.

Ehrsam Place B&B Inn. Danish miller John J. Thompson built this three-story, 1879 Greek Revival mansion 5 mi east of Abilene on more than 18 acres of Flint Hills land where Native Americans once camped and drovers later rested their cattle before shipping them to market. The hosts of this lavishly decorated home know much about local history. All rooms have queen-size canopy beds and guest bathrobes, and you may arrange for a candlelight dinner. Dining room, grill, picnic area, cable TV, in-room data ports, fishing, bicycles, croquet, hiking, horseshoes, shop, laundry facilities, Internet, no smoking. | 103 S. Grant, Enterprise 67441 | 785/263–8747 | fax 785/263–8548 | www.ehrsamplace.com | 4 suites | $65–$105 | BP | AE, D, MC, V.

ATCHISON

▼▼▼

Kansa, and later Kickapoo, Indians once occupied the Independence Creek valley of present-day Atchison, where Lewis and Clark also briefly camped in 1804. Pro-slavery Missourians settled the town in 1854, and as steamboats arrived with settlers headed west, Atchison became a crucial jumping-off and supply point. The Pony Express and the Overland State & Mail Company headquartered here; in 1860 Cyrus K. Holliday founded the Atchison, Topeka & Santa Fe Railroad on North 2nd Street. *Contact Atchison Area Chamber of Commerce | 200 S. 10th St., 66002 | 913/367–2427 or 800/234–1854 | www.atchisonkansas.net.*

Atchison Trolley. The Santa Fe Depot conducts a fascinating 45-minute tour of historic Atchison. Four designated points allow passengers to jump off and rejoin the tour later as the trolley comes back around. | 200 S. 10th St. | 800/234–1854 | www.atchisonkansas.net | $4 | May and Aug.–Oct., Fri.–Sat. 10–4, Sun. noon–4; June–July, Wed.–Sat. 10–4, Sun. noon–4.

Native American Heritage Museum State Historic Site. About 30 mi north of town, near Highland, this cultural center uses ancient artifacts and modern-day art to share the moving stories of tribes of present-day Kansas: the Iowa, Kickapoo, Potawatomi, and Sac and Fox. | 1727 Elgin Rd., 3 mi east of Highland | 785/442–3304 | www.kshs.org/places/sites.htm | $3 | Wed.–Sat. 10–5, Sun. 1–5.

HISTORIC DINING AND LODGING

River House Restaurant. Contemporary. This plain white structure has perched on the Missouri River's edge since the riverboat era, and the staff enjoys telling of the building's colorful past. The restaurant serves creatively presented and flavorful meals. Start with the hot artichoke and garlic dip, and then try a cut of Kansas City beef or chef Michael's always tasty salmon of the day. | 101 Commercial St. | 913/367–1010 | Closed Sun. | $11.95–$24.95 | AE, D, MC, V.

The Majestic House. In 1890 the brothers of Saint Benedict's Abbey built this three-story native stone farmhouse on their 600-acre dairy farm. The abbey abandoned the property in the mid-1900s and it stood unused for years, but hard work brought back the high ceilings and rich pine woodwork. Cable TV, outdoor hot tub, fishing, hiking, Internet; no kids, no smoking. | 18936 262nd Rd., 66002 | 913/367–3696 | www.themajestichouse.com | 5 rooms | $90–$130 | BP | D, MC, V.

BELLEVILLE
▼▼

Generations of Pawnee Indians made their homes here near the Republican River before settlers built the area's first log cabin, in 1861. Belleville, the seat of Republic County, was founded in 1869 and named after Arabelle Tutton, the wife of one of the town's founders. A tourist information center is on U.S. 81 just north of town. *Contact Belleville Chamber of Commerce | 1819 L St., 66935 | 785/527–2310 | skyways.lib.ks.us/towns/Belleville.*

Crossroads of Yesteryear Museum. Tour the museum's restored school, church, and log cabin, similar to the first one built in the county, and see tools used by early settlers. | 2726 U.S. 36 | 785/527–5971 | $2 suggested donation | Weekdays 1–5, Sun. 1:30–4:30, Sat. by appointment.

Pawnee Indian Village State Historic Site. The story of the powerful Pawnee Nation is preserved at this 6-acre site northwest of Belleville. Learn why the Pawnee were known as the "astronomers of the Plains" and explore the archaeological remains of the 19th-century earth-lodge village, including items left behind by the Pawnee, such as a rare Pawnee sacred bundle hanging above the altar. Some artifacts date back thousands of years. The museum encloses the excavated floor of one of the largest earth lodges. Take U.S. 36 west out of Belleville for approximately 10 mi, then Route 266 north for another 8 mi. | Rte. 266, Republic | 785/361–2255 | www.kshs.org | $3 | Wed.–Sat. 10–5, Sun. 1–5.

COFFEYVILLE

▼▼

When the U.S. completed the Louisiana Purchase, the Black Dog band of Osage Indians occupied the land around present-day Coffeyville. As settlers displaced Native Americans in the area, Colonel James A. Coffey set up his trading post here. By 1869 the town had been settled around his store and named Coffeyville in his honor. Cowboys arrived in the 1880s, herding their cattle northward. The Dalton Gang made the town famous in 1892 for its failed and fatal attempt to rob two Coffeyville banks on the same morning. *Contact Coffeyville Area Chamber of Commerce | 807 Walnut, Box 457, 67337-0457 | 620/251–2550 or 800/626–3357 | fax 620/251–5448 | www.coffeyville.com.*

Dalton Defenders Museum. Guns, saddles, photos, and the original First National Bank doors tell the tale of the ill-fated Dalton Raid. | 113 E. 8th St. | 316/251–5944 | www.terraworld. net/lbarndollar/dalton/dalton.htm | $3 | Daily 9–5.

To take the **Walking Tour of the Dalton Raid,** begin at the Dalton Defenders Museum and, following the map painted on the side of the building in their parking lot, retrace the Dalton Gang's short path through town. The tour takes you to the Old Condon Bank where the 1892 raid took place, and through Dalton Defenders Plaza; markers show where four citizens died defending their town. Bullet holes are still visible in Death Alley, site of the gun battle that claimed three Dalton Gang members, and the Jail is still in its original location.

Little House on the Prairie. This authentic reconstruction of a log cabin and other early frontier structures sit near the original homestead site where children's author Laura Ingalls Wilder lived briefly in the 1870s. 13 mi southwest of Independence off U.S. 75. | 620/289–4238 in season, 620/289–4737 off season | www.littlehouseonprairie.com | Donations accepted | May–Oct. Wed.–Sat. 10–5, Sun. 1–5.

✦ ON THE CALENDAR: Oct. **Dalton Defenders Days.** Raid reenactments, stage-coach rides, and other entertainment help preserve the memory of the famous robbery. | 316/251–2550.

COUNCIL GROVE

▼▼

Kit Carson supposedly carved the name Council Grove on a buffalo hide in 1820 and nailed it to an oak tree, thus creating this little city. The name came from a huge gathering (or council) of Indian chiefs and government leaders that agreed to the sale of much of this area to the United States. The Council Oak tree stump commemorates the 1825 treaty between the Osage Tribe and U.S. government, which promised travelers safe passage through Osage territory. Nestled in the Flint Hills, Council Grove watched thousands of settlers head west on the trails and hosted George Armstrong Custer with his 7th Cavalry. The Conn Store, a trading post, and the Last Chance, a trail supplier, both still stand on Main Street. *Contact Council Grove Convention and Visitors Bureau. | 212 W. Main St., 66846 | 620/767–5882 | www.councilgrove.com.*

Chase County Historical Society and Museum. Twenty-two miles south of town in Cottonwood Falls, the Chase County National Bank originally owned this two-story building, constructed in 1882 of native stone. A National Register of Historic Places structure, it now houses an old chuck wagon, a stone burr mill, and cowboy memorabilia. | 301 Broadway, Cottonwood Falls | 620/273–8500 | skyways.lib.ks.us/genweb/society/cottonwd | $1 | Tues.–Sat. 1–5.

Flint Hills Overland Wagon Train Trips. Relive the experiences of mid-19th century pioneers for a weekend, on a covered wagon trip through a pristine area of the American tallgrass prairie. Trips start and end in the town of Bazaar | Box 1076, El Dorado, 67042 | 316/321–6300 | www.wagontrainkansas.com | Certain weekends in June, July, and Sept. | $150.

Kaw Mission State Historic Site. Methodist Episcopal missionaries built this school for Kaw Indian children in 1851; today this state historic site uses photographs, video, and artifacts such as letter, books, and household items to explain the heritage of the Kaw Indians, the Santa Fe Trail, and early Council Grove. | 500 N. Mission St. | 620/767–5410 | www.kshs.org/places/sites.htm | $3 | Tues.–Sat. 10–5, Sun. 1–5.

Post Office Oak and Museum. Travelers along the Santa Fe Trail left messages in a hole of this tree, which served as the area's official post office. In an 1864 brewery building, the museum presents agricultural and household artifacts collected from the area during its long history. | E. Main St. | 620/767–5882 | www.councilgrove.com | $1 | Sun. 1–4 or by appointment.

Santa Fe Trail Ruts. Thousands of wagon wheels cut deep ruts in the prairie earth on their way westward on the Santa Fe Trail. You can still see the marks of the wheels on this private property. | 5 mi west of Council Grove on U.S. 56, then ½ mi south on 1400 Rd. | www.councilgrove.com/san_fe.htm | Free | Daily.

Self-Guided Tour. Kaw Mission provides maps for the outstanding 21-point driving or walking tour of this historic town. | www.councilgrove.com | Free | Daily.

✦ ON THE CALENDAR: June **Flint Hills Folklife Festival.** Come to the Chase County Courthouse to see how pioneers made baskets, soap, and rope in frontier times. A Civil War encampment, blacksmith shop, and reenactors in period dress set the scene for the mid-1800s. | 620/273–8686 or 620/273–6020.

June **Wah-Shun-Gah Days.** A powwow, parade, and carnival highlight this festival of Native American heritage at the Kaw Mission. | 620/767–5413.

HISTORIC DINING AND LODGING

Hays House 1857 Restaurant & Tavern. American. Kaw Indian trader Seth Hays built this establishment in 1857 for Santa Fe Trail travelers. This National Register of Historic Places landmark has continuously served townfolk and visitors, including Jesse James and General George Custer, since it opened. Try the steak and quail, skillet fried chicken, prime rib (on Friday or Saturday), and the Godiva chocolate pie. Kids' menu. | 112 W. Main St. | 620/767–5911 | Closed Mon. | $8–$13 | D, MC, V.

Cottage House Hotel. The original 1867 three-room cottage and blacksmith shop at this site grew in stages to become a Victorian hotel. Each guest room is individually decorated with period antiques. In-room data ports, some microwaves, some refrigerators, some in-room hot tubs, sauna, cable TV, business services, meeting rooms, some pets allowed (fee). | 25 N. Neosho St., 66846 | 620/767–6828 or 800/727–7903 | fax 620/767–6414 | www.councilgrove.com/cot_hou.htm | 40 rooms | $50–$155 | CP | AE, D, DC, MC, V.

Grand Central Hotel. Here's a Victorian hotel, opened in 1884, that still serves the purpose for which it was built. The original brick walls and stockyard brick flooring are still visible. Each luxurious room, decorated in a western motif, bears the brand of a Chase County ranch. The hotel is about 22 mi south of Council Grove in Cottonwood Falls. Dining room, in-room hot tubs, cable TV, massage, bar, concierge, business services, meeting rooms, some pets allowed. | 215 Broadway, Cottonwood Falls 66845 | 800/951–6763 | www.grandcentralhotel.com | 10 suites | $139–$179 | AE, D, MC, V | CP.

DODGE CITY

One of the wildest towns in the Old West traces its roots to 1865 when a military fort was established to protect wagon trains on the Santa Fe Trail. Thousands of wagon trains traveled the Mountain Branch of the Santa Fe Trail west from Dodge City into Colorado from the opening of the trail in 1821 until 1880. Originally called Buffalo City, Dodge City was founded in 1872, 5 mi west of Fort Dodge, and quickly became a trade center for buffalo hunters because of the new railroad access. Cowboys from the Texas cattle drives helped establish Dodge City's reputation as the wildest town on the western frontier. Bat Masterson and Wyatt Earp became legends in their attempts to bring law and order to Front Street. Scenic overlook signs can mean views of massive feedlots, as cattle are still the area's primary income source. *Contact Dodge City Convention and Visitors Bureau | 400 W. Wyatt Earp Blvd., 67801 | 620/225–8186 or 800/OLD–WEST | www.dodgecity.org.*

Boot Hill Museum and Front Street. After an orientation video, climb up to Boot Hill to see the famous cemetery, so named because cowboys were buried immediately—with their boots on. The replica of Front Street as it was in 1876 houses exhibits such as "The Guns That Won the West." Summer entertainment includes stagecoach rides, Long Branch saloon shows, and gunfights at high noon. The site also includes an original 1865 jail, 1890 cook shack, and 1879 house. | Front St. | 620/227–8188 | www.boothill.org | $7 | June–Aug., daily 8–8; Sept.–May, Mon.–Sat. 9–5, Sun. 1–5.

Dodge City Trolley. Take a trip back in time with a narrated tour that tells the history of Front Street, Fort Dodge, the Santa Fe Trail, and historic homes and churches. | 400 W. Wyatt Earp Blvd. | 620/225–8186 | $5 | Late May–early Sept., daily.

Fort Dodge. Established in 1865 on the Santa Fe Trail midway between two major Indian crossings on the Arkansas River, the site is now the Kansas Soldiers' Home. Several original buildings remain of the fort, which defended the area from 1865 to 1882 and served as a supply depot. The fort is 5 mi east of Dodge City on U.S. 400. | 101 Pershing Ave. | 620/227–2121 | Free | Museum and library daily 1–4.

Home of Stone. The three-story 1881 Mueller-Schmidt House was built of native limestone and remains the lone stone house in Dodge City. It is also the oldest building still on its original site. The house was built by German immigrant John Mueller, who came to Dodge from St. Louis in 1875 and started building the house in 1879. The house is listed on the National Register of Historic Places. | 112 E. Vine St. | 620/227–6791 or 620/225–4926 | Free | June–Aug., Mon.–Sat. 9–5, Sun. 2–4; Sept.–May, by appointment.

Santa Fe Trail Tracks. The wide-open prairie reveals the vastness of the pioneers' undertaking as miles of wagon ruts, found 9 mi west of Dodge City, stretch to the horizon. | On U.S. 50/400 | 620/227–8188 | Free | Daily.

✦ ON THE CALENDAR: June **Cowboy Heritage Festival.** Listen to the tales of cowboy poets and storytellers, witness gunfights, sample chuck-wagon food, and attend an 1880s Cowboy Ball at Boot Hill Museum. | 800/653–9378.

July–Aug. **Dodge City Days.** In addition to one of the largest Professional Rodeo Cowboys Association rodeos in the country, the 10-day event includes western arts and crafts, a chuck-wagon breakfast, parade, and barbecue. | 800/653–9378.

ELLSWORTH
▼▼

This former cow town once had a reputation as wild and wooly as that of Dodge City. Its ties to the cattle trade attracted gunmen, thieves, saloons, and brothels. The histories of Ellsworth and Kanopolis mingle at Fort Ellsworth, which was established in 1864 to protect the route of the Butterfield Overland Despatch and the Smoky Hill shortcut to Denver. In

A TALE OF TWO FRONT STREETS

It was mostly the worst of times in 1870s Dodge City. Helpless to maintain law and order, city founders decided that they would maintain the law on one side of the railroad tracks and disregard it on the other side. Thus emerged two Front Streets, one on each side of Dodge City's "deadline."

In 1876, 19 Dodge City businesses had licenses to sell liquor, even though the town had only 1,200 residents. Its streets, however, often swelled with transient cowboys, gamblers, buffalo hunters, railroad workers, soldiers, and drifters, who were inclined to settle their disputes with shoot-outs. With names like the Alamo and the Lone Star, the Front Street saloons catered to Texans who had money to spend after driving their longhorns north and selling them. In 1878, the year Bat Masterson was elected sheriff and Wyatt Earp was hired as law enforcement, a New York City newspaper observed: "There is more concentrated hell in Dodge City than any other place of equal size . . . ."

Prostitutes saw ample opportunity to do business here, and by 1879 the town had 47 prostitutes, such as "Squirrel Tooth" Alice Chamber, Big Emma, and Sadie Ratzell. The term "red light district" supposedly originated in Dodge City to describe the railroaders' habit of leaving their lanterns in front of the brothels they patronized.

Alcohol was banned in Dodge City 1880, but the law was largely ignored until 1885, when state law enforcement visited the city. Saloon owners had a simple solution: They crossed out the word "Saloon" on their signs and replaced it with "Drugstore," since it was legal to sell alcohol as medicine. Their patrons now ordered tonics such as a Methodist cocktail or a Baptist lemonade. Churches, which had begun to sprout up on the hill above Front Street on what became known as Gospel Ridge, literally looked down in disapproval.

It wasn't Bat Masterson and Wyatt Earp who finally tamed Dodge City—it took a devastating cattle quarantine, downtown fires, and a blizzard to quiet the city, sometime after 1886.

1866 Fort Ellsworth was moved to its current site in Kanopolis on the western edge of an Indian reservation and renamed Fort Harker. The post suffered a devastating cholera epidemic the following year, and the operation disbanded in 1873. By this time, cowboys had made city of Ellsworth (established 1867) into a rowdy cattle town where they sold their steers and celebrated the end of another long drive from Texas. Today, ranchers still swap stories in the Drovers Mercantile. A downtown walking tour has 17 stops, designated by black silhouettes of 1880s townsfolk, each with written material explaining such historic sites as the Plaza, bank, hotel, jail, general store, and saloon. *Contact Ellsworth/Kanopolis Area Chamber of Commerce | 114½ N. Douglas Ave., 67439 | 785/472–4071 | www.cityofellsworth.com.*

Drover's Mercantile/Johnny Bingo's Hats. You'll find everything you need to dress and cook like a real cowboy. Historically accurate Stetson hats, women's dresses, pants, and boots are for sale, as are chuck-wagon utensils, dutch ovens, bridles, and Old West books and music. Co-owner Jim Gray, known locally as "The Cowboy," is a wealth of information on the area. | 119–121 N. Douglas Ave. | 785/472–4703 or 877/376–8377 | www.droversmercantile.com | Mon.–Sat. 10–5.

Fort Harker Guardhouse Museum Complex. The Guardhouse Museum commemorates the days of the Seventh Cavalry and the military of the late 1860s when the fort was one of the earliest protecting travelers along the Smoky Hill and Santa Fe trails. In 1866 young Bill Cody took his first scouting job at the fort and the next year earned the nickname Buffalo Bill because of his success hunting buffalo for the railroads. Within the complex are the original guardhouse, junior officers' quarters, and exhibits. | 308 W. Ohio St., Kanopolis | 785/472–3059 | $2 includes Hodgden House Museum | May–Sept., Tues.–Sat. 9–noon and 1–5, Sun. 1–5; Oct.–Apr., Sat. 9–noon and 1–5, Sun. 1–5.

Hodgden House Museum Complex. The Hodgden House Historical Complex stands along South Main Street, once known as "Snake Row." A collection of 1880s buildings, including the home of one of Ellsworth's early residents, provides a look at the town as it was during its cattle days. Structures in the complex include the 1878 Hodgden House, 1880s livery stable, 1912 one-room school, 1900 train depot, 1880s church, 1911 caboose, and small log cabin. | 104 W. South Main | 785/472–3059 | $2 includes Fort Harker | May–Sept., Tues.–Sat. 9–noon and 1–5, Sun. 1–5; Oct.–Apr., Tues.–Fri. 1–5, Sat. 9–noon and 1–5, Sun. 1–5.

◆ ON THE CALENDAR: Apr. **C.O.W.B.O.Y.S. Spring Gathering, Trade Show and Rodeo.** Old West events are planned throughout Ellsworth to celebrate the cowboy tradition. | 785/472–4071.

FORT SCOTT
▼▼▼

The military established this post in 1846 to help maintain peaceful relations between traders and native tribes along the Indian frontier. The fort closed in 1853, but homesteaders bought the buildings in 1855 and proceeded to build one of the largest towns in Kansas Territory. Fort Scott witnessed social unrest and violence in the Bleeding Kansas period. During the Civil War the fort served as the U.S. Army District Headquarters, recruitment station and training center, and quartermaster supply depot. Downtown Fort Scott contains a number of Victorian-era buildings. *Contact Fort Scott Convention and Visitors Bureau | 231 E. Wall St., 66701 | 620/223–3566 or 800/245–3678 | www.fortscott.com.*

Fort Scott National Historic Site. Experience the lives of dragoons and infantry during westward expansion in each of the fort's 20 historic structures. Weekday tours are available June–Aug. | Old Fort Blvd. off Wall St. | 620/223–0310 | www.nps.gov/fosc | $3 | Apr.–Oct., daily 8–5; Nov.–Mar., daily 9–5.

HISTORIC LODGING
Courtland Hotel. The Courtland, in the heart of the Victorian downtown, has accommodated travelers and railroad executives since 1906. Lace curtains and a tin ceiling adorn the common East Parlor, and a broad stairway leads you to the guest rooms on the second floor. The owners keep the gift shop well stocked with collectibles. You may arrange for in-house catering in the private dining rooms. Restaurant, snack bar, cable TV, snack bar, shop, no smoking. | 121 E. 1st St. 66701 | 316/223–6800 | fax 620/223–1708 | www.courtlandhotel.com | 15 rooms | $50–$70 | CP | AE, D, MC, V.

Lyons' Victorian Mansion B&B. One of two identical homes built in the 1870s for a wealthy banker's daughters, this four-story Victorian is completely restored in rich velvets, tapestries, and detailed walnut carvings. Grounds include a koi pond and a butterfly garden. Innkeeper Pat Lyons, who dresses in period clothes, will help coordinate biking, hiking, or other excursions across the state. Dining room, grill, picnic area, in-room data ports, some in-room hot tubs, minibars, refrigerators, cable TV, in-room VCRs, outdoor hot tub, massage, badminton, croquet, dry cleaning, laundry facilities, laundry service, Internet, business services, meeting rooms; no smoking. | 742 S. National St. 66701 | 316/223–3644 or 800/784–8378 | fax 316/223–0062 | www.lyonsmansion.com | 6 rooms, 1 suite | $90–$150 | BP | AE, D, DC, MC, V.

GARDEN CITY

▼▼

Many who first traveled this area along the Santa Fe Trail claimed nothing could possibly live in this "Great American Desert," except Native Americans and buffalo. Two of the town's founders, brothers William and James Fulton, ranged the region for several years hunting buffalo and wild horses before they helped establish the town in 1878. Settlers found flowers and vegetables could grow here, and the town's name was chosen because of the Fulton's garden. *Contact Finney County Convention and Tourism Bureau | 1511 E. Fulton Terr., 67846 | 620/276–3264 or 800/879–9803 | www.garden-city.org.*

Finney County Historical Museum. At the entrance to Finnup Park, this museum is dedicated to preserving and honoring the heritage of the southwest Kansas plains and the history of the county. | 403 S. 4th St. | 620/272–3664 | Free | Late May–early Sept., Mon.–Sat. 10–5, Sun. 1–5; early Sept.–late May, daily 1–5.

Finney Game Refuge. This 3,670-acre reserve looks as it did centuries ago when herds of bison roamed the plains. It now protects Kansas's largest publicly owned herd of buffalo, which was started in 1924. Guided driving tours are available for viewing buffalo and other prairie animals by reservation; you can also drive through on your own. | 785 S. U.S. 83, south of river bridge | 620/276–3264 or 620/276–9400 | www.gardencity.net/chamber/ctb/buffalo.html | Free (donations accepted) | Daily.

El Quartelejo Museum. This museum on the edge of Scott City (30 mi north of Garden City) chronicles the life of the local Pueblo Indians through displays of artifacts. | 902 W. Rte. 96, Scott City | 620/872–5912 or 620/872–3523 | Free | Weekdays 1–5 or by appointment.

El Quartelejo Pueblo Ruins. For thousands of years early Nomadic Indians camped in the area that is now Scott County State Park. An important archaeological relic of early life in Scott County is the ruins of an old pueblo, El Quartelejo, established around 1702 by Picurís Pueblo Indians who were fleeing Spanish oppression in New Mexico. Unearthed by professors from the University of Kansas in 1898, the pueblo originally was divided into seven rooms and constructed of stone. It is thought to be the first walled house in Kansas. The Apache also lived in the area in the 17th and 18th centuries. | 520 W. Scott Lake Dr., Scott City | 620/872–2061 | www.scottcity.com/history.html | $5 per vehicle | Daily.

✦ ON THE CALENDAR: June **Beef Empire Days.** The 12-day salute to the cattle industry and its heritage in southwestern Kansas includes a Professional Rodeo Cowboys Association rodeo, chuck-wagon meals, cowboy poets, a cattle show, and a parade. | 620/276–3264 or 800/879–9803.

HAYS

▼▼

First known as Fort Fletcher, Fort Hays was built as a military post along the Smoky Hill stagecoach line from Kansas City to Denver in 1865. Wild Bill Hickok served as sheriff of the nearby town, which was filled with saloons, dance halls, and illegal activities; Calamity Jane and Buffalo Bill Cody found their way here. The fort was abandoned in 1889, and soon after the state designated land for an agriculture college. Early settlers, such as the Volga-Germans from Russia, brought some stability to the rowdy town. *Contact Hays Convention and Visitors Bureau | 1301 Pine St., Suite B, 67601 | 800/569–4505 | www.haysusa.com.*

Ellis County Historical Society and Museum. More than 25,000 artifacts tell the story of the buffalo hunters, soldiers, cowboys, and scouts who settled Ellis County. Original buildings from the 19th century, including a harness shop and a limestone church, evoke the untamed spirit of these times. Children can experience a one-room school and see toys, clothes, and books. | 100 W. 7th St. | 785/628–2624 | $2 | June–Sept., Tues.–Fri. 10–5, Sat. 1–5; Oct.–May, Tues.–Fri. 10–5.

Fort Hays State Historic Site. See the original block house, guardhouse, and two officers' quarters at the 65-acre fort, which was built in 1867 to protect travelers and railroad workers. Buffalo Bill Cody, Wild Bill Hickok, and U.S. Army generals George Custer, Nelson Miles, and Philip Sheridan all visited the post. At its peak 560 soldiers were stationed here; the fort was closed in 1889. It is 4 mi south of Exit 157 on I–70. A gift shop stocks Old West books. | 1472 U.S. 183A | 785/625–6812 | www.kshs.org | $3 | Tues.–Sat. 9–5, Sun.–Mon. 1–5.

✦ ON THE CALENDAR: July **Wild West Festival.** Enjoy country-western music, crafts, and activities in Frontier Park. | 800/569–4505.

Sept. **Old Fort Hays Days.** Educational programs, demonstrations, and military living history bring Fort Hays to life as it was in the 1800s. | 785/625–6812.

HISTORIC LODGING
Tea Rose Inn Bed and Breakfast. Built in 1909, this gracious home stands in the heart of downtown Hays. Relax on the front porch or stroll to restaurants and art galleries. Modern amenities complement period furnishings in each room. The inn's gardens supply flowers and herbs for breakfast and tea. No smoking. | 117 W. 13th St., 67601 | 785/623–4060 or 888/623–1125 | www.tearose.net | 4 rooms | $60–$100 | AE, DC, MC, V | BP.

KANSAS CITY
▼▼▼

In 1869, Kansas City sprang to life in the bottom lands along the Kansas-Missouri state line. It developed alongside the Missouri city of the same name, and little more than the Kansas River separates the history and activities of the people who live in each state. Stockyards and other agricultural enterprises took advantage of the railroads on the Kansas side of the river, which has witnessed immigration on overland trails, steamship commerce, and bitter struggles surrounding the Civil War. *Contact Kansas City Convention and Visitor's Bureau | 727 Minnesota Ave., Box 171337, 66117 | 913/321–5800 or 800/264–1563 | www.kckcvb.org.*

Grinter Place State Historic Site. Moses Grinter built this brick farmhouse in 1862 at a site near his trading post, where he did business with the Delaware Indians. Original furnishings and displays about the Grinter family history help explain the area's settlement. | 1420 S. 78th St., Kansas City | 913/299–0373 | www.kshs.org/places/grinter.htm | $3 | Wed.–Sat. 10–5, Sun. 1–5.

Mahaffie Farmstead and Stagecoach Stop. This stagecoach stop operated from 1863 to 1869 on the Westport Cut-off of the Santa Fe and Oregon trails. Join a half-hour guided tour of the stone house, then wander through the three farmstead buildings listed on the National Register of Historic Places. | 1100 Kansas City Rd., Olathe | 913/782–6972 | www.mahaffie.com | $3 | Feb.–Mar., weekdays 10–4; Apr.–Dec., Mon.–Sat. 10–4, Sun. noon–4.

Old Shawnee Town. More than 20 historic buildings and replicas dot the grounds here, including the original 1843 Shawnee jail, an undertaker's shop, and a smoke house. Guided tours are available. | 11501 W. 57th St., Shawnee | 913/248–2360 | www.cityofshawnee.org | $1 | Jan.–mid-Dec., Tues.–Sat. 10–5.

Shawnee Indian Mission State Historic Site. Missionaries built this school in 1839 to teach English and trade skills to Native Americans. Later it became a supply point on the Santa Fe and Oregon trails and a camp for Union soldiers during the Civil War. It is now a National Historic Landmark. Original furnishings and photographs assist curators in describing the building's place in eastern Kansas history. | 3403 W. 53rd St., Fairway | 913/262–0867 | www.kshs.org/places/shawnmis.htm | $3 | Tues.–Sat 10–5, Sun. 1–5.

✦ ON THE CALENDAR: July **Forgotten Skills Remembered Day.** Reenactors on the grounds of Shawnee Indian Mission perform such daily activities as spinning, weaving, and candle-dipping that settlers performed during frontier times. | 913/262–0867.

Sept. **Grinter Place AppleFest.** Reenactors demonstrate historic arts and crafts such as spinning, weaving, and wood carving and explain how they hone their skills. | 913/299–0373.

Sept. **Mahaffie's Old Glory Blowout and 1800s Wild West Weekend.** Indians, cowboys, mountain men, cavalry soldiers, and dance-hall gals all converge at the Mahaffie Farm for an Old West good time. | 913/782–6972.

Oct. **Fall Festival.** The Shawnee Indian Mission presents pioneer skills, reenactors, and a large collection of arts and crafts. | 913/262–0867.

LARNED
▼▼

Fort Larned was established in 1859 as a base of military operations against hostile Indians of the Central Plains, to protect traffic along the Santa Fe Trail, and as an agency for the administration of the Central Plains Indians by the Bureau of Indian Affairs under the terms of the Fort Wise Treaty of 1861. The town of Larned became the seat of Pawnee County, which was established in 1872 and named after the Pawnee Indians, who made this area their hunting grounds. Pawnee Rock, one of the most prominent landmarks on the Santa Fe Trail, still stands tall ½ mi north on U.S. 56. *Contact Larned Area Chamber of Commerce | 502 Broadway, 67550 | 620/285–6916 or 800/747–6919 | www.larned.org.*

Fort Larned National Historic Site. Established in 1859 to protect the mail coaches and travelers on the Santa Fe Trail, the site survives as one of the best examples of Indian Wars period forts. Nine restored 1860 sandstone buildings remain, many with restored and furnished rooms surrounding the parade ground. Exhibits, and tour guides relate the story of the Indian Wars. | 6 mi west of Larned on Rte. 156 | 620/285–6911 | $3 | Daily 8:30–5.

Santa Fe Trail Center. Set near the midpoint of the trail, the center operates two museums, which detail the history of the trail and displays artifacts such as tools and items carried along the trade route between the United States and Mexico that opened up in 1821. Exhibits take you back to the days when millions of buffalo roamed the prairie and Wichita Indians lived in grass hunting lodges. On site are sod and dugout houses that show early life on the prairie. | 2 mi west of Larned on Rte. 156 | 620/285–2054 | $4 | Late May–early Sept., daily 9–5; early Sept.–late May, Tues.–Sun. 9–5.

✦ ON THE CALENDAR: May **Santa Fe Trail Days.** At Fort Larned there are living history reenactments, and around town there is cowboy music, food, and humor, as well as a Buffalo Bill Cody Show. | 800/747–6919.

LAWRENCE
▼▼

Settlers in the Wakarusa and Kansas River valleys asked the U.S. government to push Native Americans off this area's fertile lands. In 1854 the abolitionist New England Emigrant Aid

Company founded the town in honor of Amos A. Lawrence, the society's leading supporter. Discord over the slavery issue during the Bleeding Kansas period prompted pro-slavery advocates to burn the town to the ground in May 1856, an act repeated by William Quantrill and his Confederate guerrillas in August 1863. Citizens determinedly rebuilt, often saying Lawrence rose from its own ashes. *Contact Lawrence Visitor Information Center | Old Union Pacific depot, N. 2nd and Locust Sts., 66044 | 888/529–5267 | www.visitlawrence.com.*

Constitution Hall State Historic Site. In 1858 pro-slavery delegates to the Constitutional Convention gathered here to debate the slavery issue, but abolitionist settlers came by the thousands to the ground-floor land office and filed the homestead claims that ultimately made Kansas a free state. Visit this National Historic Landmark to see exhibits of early documents and tour the rooms where history was made. | 319 Elmore, Lecompton | 785/887–6520 | www.kshs.org/places/constit.htm | $3 | Wed.–Sat. 10–5, Sun. 1–5.

Self-Guided Tour. At the Lawrence Visitor Information Center, you can find out about tours that focus on Quantrill's Raid, John Brown, or the Oregon and Santa Fe trails. | Old Union Pacific Depot, N. 2nd and Locust Sts. | 785/832–7955 | www.visitlawrence.com | Free | Daily.

✦ **ON THE CALENDAR:** June **Territorial Capital Festival.** Reenactments, demonstrations, and general festivities in Lecompton mark the significance of this town in the state's history. | 785/887–6691.

Aug. Civil War on the Frontier Commemoration. This weeklong series of events, including encampments, black-powder shoots, and walking tours, commemorates Quantrill's Raid and the Civil War in Kansas. | 785/841–4109.

HISTORIC LODGING

Eldridge Hotel. Distinctly Victorian, this downtown Lawrence establishment was built in 1855 and is now on the National Register of Historic Places. Spacious rooms provide most of the necessities, and 24-hour room service is available. Restaurant, in-room data ports, minibars, cable TV, hair salon, hot tub, lounge shop, baby-sitting, dry cleaning, laundry service, concierge, Internet, business services, meeting rooms, some pets allowed (fee); no-smoking floors. | 701 Massachusetts St., 66044 | 785/749–5011 or 800/527–0909 | fax 785/749–4512 | www.eldridgehotel.com | 48 suites | $89–$295 | AE, D, DC, MC, V | BP.

LEAVENWORTH

▼▼▼

On the Missouri River bluffs where Kansa, Delaware, and Osage tribes once lived, the U.S. government established a fort in 1827 to regulate relations between traders and Native Americans. This locale boomed after Kansas Territory opened, and the new city become a major jumping-off point for travelers on the Santa Fe and Oregon trails. The Kansas State Penitentiary was opened in 1868 on a site that is now in neighboring Lansing. In 1881 General William T. Sherman established the U.S. Army Command and General Staff College, which still matriculates some of the army's finest leaders. An esplanade in town offers stunning river views. *Contact Leavenworth/Lansing Convention and Visitors Bureau | 518 Shawnee St., Box 44, 66048 | 913/682–4113 or 800/844–4114 | www.lvarea.com/chamber/lv_cvb.htm.*

Frontier Army Museum. Learn the story of Fort Leavenworth in exquisite detail from its founding in 1827, and the history of the U.S. Regular Army on the frontier from the time of the Lewis and Clark expedition in 1804. Uniforms, weapons, and military equipment abound, and you'll see the carriage Abraham Lincoln used during his 1859 visit. Photo IDs are mandatory on the post. | Reynolds Ave. | 913/684–3191 | leav-www.army.mil/museum | Donations accepted | Weekdays 9–4, Sat. 10–4, Sun. noon–4.

✦ ON THE CALENDAR: Apr. **Frontier Army Encampment.** This encampment lets you witness 1800s army men cooking at their tents and firing their arms. | 913/684–3767.

HISTORIC DINING
High Noon Saloon and Brewery. Steak. Rustic wooden floors and an authentic saloon bar constructed in 1894 set the mood for a hearty western meal in the historic Great Western Manufacturing Building. The High Noon serves up juicy burgers, sizzling cuts of Kansas beef, smoked barbecue, home cooking, and lighter fare: you won't go wrong on anything you order. Ask about the seasonal fresh-brewed beers, and don't forget the made-from-scratch Chocolate Stout Cake. | 206 Choctaw | 913/682–4876 | $6–$15 | MC, V.

LIBERAL
▼▼

Coronado crossed near here in 1541 when the short-grass country was the home of the Plains Apache, and later the Kiowa, Cheyenne, Comanche, and Arapaho. Captain John R. Bell reported in 1820 that the area was not suitable for civilized men because of the lack of rain. Congress designated this territory as Indian Territory in 1830, and until 1872 western Kansas was practically uninhabited. Settlement came to the area only after the railroads came through. Seward County was established in 1873, and a post office was set up at the town of Liberal in 1886. A vote in 1892 made Liberal the county seat. The town got its name from parched settlers who passed through this dry area in the 1880s. Whenever they received free water from a homesteader, they were said to reply, "That's mighty liberal of you." *Contact Liberal Convention and Tourism Bureau | 1 Yellowbrick Rd., 67901 | 800/542–3725 | www.liberal.net.*

Cimarron National Grassland. Take a self-guided tour of the grasslands, which cover key Santa Fe Trail sites in Morton County. Although you can take the tour anytime, you can only pick up a map at the office weekdays from 8 to 5. The office is in Elkhart, a 65-mi drive west from Liberal. | 242 E. U.S. 56, Elkhart | 620/697–4621 | Free | Daily.

Coronado Museum. A search for the Seven Golden Cities of Cibola brought Spanish explorers here in the 1500s. Items such as an extensive weapons display, household furnishings, and photographs tell the story of the pioneers who arrived and settled Seward County. | 567 E. Cedar St. | 620/624–7624 | Free | Late May–early Sept., Mon.–Sat. 10–5, Sun. 1–5; early Sept.–late May, Tues.–Sat. 10–5, Sun. 1–5.

Dalton Gang Hideout. After Eva Dalton moved out of this house in 1892, the new owners didn't realize it had an underground tunnel—until a man popped up through the floor boards in the kitchen one day. The tunnel was created from her house to the barn by the Dalton Gang to use as an escape route. Eva, one of 15 Dalton siblings, moved there with her husband in 1887. Walk through the tunnel from the house to the barn and view exhibits about the notorious Dalton brothers, who were wiped out in 1892 during an overly ambitious attempt to rob two banks at once in Coffeyville. | 502 S. Pearlette, Meade (39 mi northeast of Liberal) | 620/873–2731 or 800/354–2743 | $2 | Mon.–Sat. 10–5, Sun. 1–5.

Historic Adobe Museum. Constructed of adobe blocks in the 1930s, this institution in Ulysses, 65 mi northwest of Liberal, underwent a renovation that turned it into one of the premier small museums in the state. Life on the High Plains is told through scenes, murals, and exhibits such as a freight wagon loaded with trade goods. The sod house on the wind-swept prairie depicts what the first home was like for many pioneers. The 1887 Hotel Edwards has been moved to the museum complex and furnished. | 300 E. Oklahoma, Ulysses | 620/356–3009 | Donation requested | Weekdays 10–5, weekends 1–5.

MANHATTAN

In 1855, Isaac Goodnow and five members of a New England company reached this spot in the Flint Hills by the Big Blue and Kansas rivers. The town, originally named Boston, soon welcomed another group of anti-slavery settlers from Cincinnati, which brought along prefabricated buildings. Officials changed the name to Manhattan, which was incorporated in 1857. Later that year the Methodist Episcopal Church chartered Blue Mont College, which later became the land-grant Kansas State Agricultural College, today Kansas State University. *Contact Fort Riley Public Affairs Office | Building 405, Fort Riley, 66442 | 785/239–6727 or 785/239–3911 | www.riley.army.mil. Manhattan Chamber of Commerce | 501 Poyntz Ave., 66502 | 785/776–8829 or 800/528–4748 | www.manhattan.org.*

Fort Riley. Established in 1852 to protect settlers and commerce along the Santa Fe and Oregon trails, this complex still retains a link to its past in the form of the Commanding General's Mounted Color Guard. You need a photo ID to enter the post. | Public Affairs Office, Building 405 | 785/239–6727 | www.riley.army.mil | Free | By appointment.

At the native limestone **First Territorial Capital State Historic Site** (Building 693, Huebner Rd. | 785/784–5535 | $3), in 1855, pro-slavery forces convened the first territorial legislature in an attempt to bring slavery to the area that would become Kansas. The building is open Wed.–Sat. 10–5, Sun. 1–5.

The **U.S. Cavalry Museum** (Building 205 | 785/239–2743 | Donation accepted), in the 1855 Post Hospital building that in 1887 became the Cavalry School, displays the colorful history of the American mounted horse soldier since the American Revolution. The museum is open Mon.–Sat. 9–4:30, Sun. noon–4:30.

Geary County Historical Museum. Rotating exhibits depicting early Native American through present day history are on display in this three-story native limestone building, which once served as the town's first high school. | 6th and Adams Sts. | 785/238–1666 | www.junctioncity. org/cvb/attract.html | Donations accepted | Tues.–Sun. 1–4.

Goodnow House State Historic Site. Free-state leader Isaac Goodnow built this stone house in the 1860s. His interest in education led him to establish Kansas State University, one of the first land-grant colleges. See the inside of the home with its original furnishings, interpretive exhibits, and knowledgeable staff, who will provide tours. | 2309 Claflin Rd. | 785/565–6490 | www.kshs.org/places/goodnow.htm | $3 | Tues.–Fri. 8:30–5, weekends 2–5.

✦ ON THE CALENDAR: July **Geary County Historical Gala.** Celebrate the area's rich history at an old-time hometown festival with music, dancing, and food at the Geary County Historical Museum. | 785/238–1666.

MARYSVILLE

Frank Marshall, a trading post operator and later pro-slavery candidate for governor, paid tribute to his wife by naming the town after her when he set up the first civilian post office in Kansas Territory, in 1854. Marshall ran a rope ferry across the steep-banked Big Blue River. Eight historic trails crossed through or near Marysville, including the Oregon and California trails and the Pony Express route. Cattlemen drove their herds to this town, for shipment out on the Union Pacific rail lines. *Contact Marysville Chamber of Commerce | 101 N. 10th St., 66508 | 785/562–3101 or 800/752–3965 | skyways.lib.ks.us/kansas/towns/ Marysville/index.html.*

THE SPRINGS OF THE NEW FRONTIER

The glaciers that once covered northeastern Kansas worked the rocky earth like a master artisan chiseling rare marble. Native Americans who lived as one with the land revered and respected what Nature had left them, and they looked upon one particular feature as a special gift. Tucked in among the trees along a creek by the Big Blue River, they discovered a waterfall flowing near a rock shelf, and beneath the falls, even in the driest of seasons, a natural spring provided a constant supply of fresh water to the ground around it.

This small miracle in the vastness of the prairie became known as Alcove Spring. Immigrants learned of it in the 1840s as they crossed this territory, headed west on the Oregon and California trails. The trails took advantage of natural pathways that wagons could fairly easily traverse—pathways that traders had cut into the land after the Louisiana Purchase secured U.S. rights to the region. Before tackling the steep crossing of the Big Blue, the wagon trains paused for a few days to rest at Alcove Spring, where they watered their oxen and restocked their stores of fish and game before heading on into the unknown. The spring became a necessary rest stop, and today wagon tracks to this peaceful haven are still visible in a nearby pasture. Here, too, you'll find a memorial to traveler Sarah Keyes, who passed away here in 1846.

When the Kansas-Nebraska Act opened Kansas Territory for settlement in 1854, greatly increasing the numbers of travelers crossing on the trails, one shrewd entrepreneur, Frank Marshall, recognized the potential of the Alcove Spring site. He set up his trading post along the Big Blue that same year and then organized the first civilian post office in Kansas Territory, naming it Marysville, after his wife. Recognizing that the steep sides of the river made crossing with wagons and livestock difficult, he set up a rope ferry across the water, pressing his advantage by charging as much as $5 per wagon and 25¢ a head for cattle to cross—an exorbitant amount of money in those days.

Ultimately, eight frontier trails passed through or near Marysville: the Oregon, California, Missouriana, and Mormon trails, the St. Joe Road, the Overland Stage route, the Leavenworth–Fort Kearney Military Road, and the Pony Express route.

Alcove Spring. Native Americans relied on this natural spring for their water source years before the thousands of Oregon Trail travelers, who rested here before crossing the Big Blue. Wagon ruts still mark the adjacent field. | U.S. 77, 6½ mi north of Blue Rapids | 785/363–7736 | Free | Daily.

Historic Trail Park/Marshall Ferry. You can cross the steep-banked Big Blue River on this replica of the ferry the pioneers used and read historic markers that explain the many historic trails that crossed at this location. | U.S. 36 (west side of town) | 785/562–3101 | Free | Daily.

Hollenberg Station State Historic Site. Gerat and Sofia Hollenberg established a way station in 1858 for trail travelers, turning it into a Pony Express station in 1860. The museum inside this National Historic Landmark 28 mi northwest of Marysville preserves saddles, tack, and stables from the days when horses galloped up to its door. | 2889 23rd St., Hanover | 785/337–2635 | www.kshs.org/places/sites.htm | $4 | Wed.–Sat. 10–5, Sun. 1–5.

Pony Express Barn Museum. Although it existed for only 18 months, the Pony Express captured the imagination of the world, its daring riders and thundering, sweating steeds racing to deliver urgent messages to military outposts and civilians alike. Thirty-one miles east of Marysville, the only original Pony Express barn that remains in its original location invites you to step into 1860, to see artifacts of the service. | 106 S. 8th St., Seneca | www.lasr.net/leisure/kansas/marshall/marysville/attractions.html | 785/562–3825 | $2 | Apr. or May–early Nov., Wed.–Sat. 10–4, Sun. noon–4.

✦ ON THE CALENDAR: Aug. **Pony Express Festival.** Reenactors at the Hollenberg Station State Historic Site make candles, grind wheat and corn, and demonstrate blacksmithing; a black-powder shoot rounds out this weekend festival. | 785/337–2635.

MCPHERSON
▼▼

The county seat of McPherson was founded in 1872 and named after a Union general in the Civil War. One of the earliest settlements in the county was Lindsborg, where immigrants from Sweden began building dugout homes in the late 1860s and where the shops and homes still radiate this Swedish heritage. *Contact McPherson Convention and Visitors Bureau | 306 N. Main St., 67460 | 620/241–3340 or 800/324–8022 | www.mcphersonks.org. Lindsborg Chamber of Commerce | 104 E. Lincoln, 67456 | 785/227–3706 or 888/227–2227 | www.lindsborg.org.*

Coronado Quivira Museum. Exhibits upstairs at this museum 30 mi west of McPherson chronicle Coronado's explorations through the area and the blazing of the Santa Fe Trail. See a rare piece of Spanish chain mail (circa 1500) uncovered in the county during a Smithsonian Institution dig in 1940. A Quivera Indian exhibit shows a life-size replica of a grass lodge as it would have been in 1500. Also on display are Spanish weapons, bridle ornaments, 1864 moccasins, and a peace pipe used in the 1860s by Chief White Horse in the Dakotas. The downstairs area captures a slice of life in Rice County in 1902. | 105 N. Lyon, Lyons | 620/257–3941 | $2 | Mon.–Sat. 9–5, Sun. 1–5.

McPherson County Old Mill Museum and Park. Inside a historic mill on the bank of the Smoky River, this museum houses exhibits that demonstrate the process of early flour milling as well as life in the settlement years of 1870 to 1910. Two buildings on the National Register of Historic Places and the 1904 Swedish Pavilion from the World's Fair preserve the cultural history of the county. | 120 Mill St. | 785/227–3595 | www.oldmillmuseum.org | $2 | Mon.–Sat. 9–5, Sun. 1–5.

✦ ON THE CALENDAR: Dec. **Lucia Fest and Heritage Christmas.** The Swedish tradition of opening the holiday season with the crowning of St. Lucia is maintained here. Festivities take place throughout Lindsborg and at the Old Mill complex, where evening historical reenactments include the telling of tales by a *tomte,* the Swedish version of a gnome. | 785/227–3706 or 888/227–2227.

HISTORIC LODGING
Swedish Country Inn. Built at the turn of the 20th century, this building is now a cozy inn with pine furnishings, colorful quilts, and hand-painted cupboards reminiscent of Sweden. It's a little taste of McPherson county's immigrant past. A family suite sleeps six. Price includes full Swedish buffet breakfast. Cable TV, sauna. | 112 W. Lincoln, Lindsborg 67456 | 785/227–2985 or 800/231–0266 | www.swedishcountryinn.com | 17 rooms, 2 suites | $55–$95 | AE, DC, MC, V | BP.

MEDICINE LODGE
▼▼

Named for the Indian council house that sat alongside the legendary healing waters of the Medicine River, the town was the site of the signing of the historic Medicine Lodge Peace

Treaty between the U.S. government and the five tribes of Plains Indians in 1867. Founded in 1873, this was the home of temperance legend Carry Nation. *Contact Medicine Lodge Area Chamber of Commerce | 108 W. 1st St., 67104 | 620/886–3417 | www.cyberlodge.com/mlchamber.*

Carry A. Nation Home. The home of this international crusader against tobacco and alcohol is filled with items such as her pump organ, writing desk, and a hatchet pin she sold to pay her fines. She moved into the house in 1890 and lived there for 13 years. The site is a National Historic Landmark. | 211 W. Fowler Ave. | 620/886–3553 | $4 includes admission to Medicine Lodge Stockade | Daily 10:30–5.

Medicine Lodge Stockade. The museum is housed in a replica of the stockade built in 1874 to protect settlers. Within the stockade walls are the Old Courthouse Jail and Uncle Bob Smith's 1877 two-story furnished log cabin. | 209 W. Fowler Ave. | 620/886–3553 | $4 includes admission to Carry A. Nation Home | Daily 10:30–5.

✦ ON THE CALENDAR: Sept. **Peace Treaty Pageant and Intertribal Powwow** Every three years a cast of more than 1,000 people and animals reenacts the signing of the 1867 peace treaty between the United States and the Arapaho, Apache, Cheyenne, Comanche, and Kiowa tribes. Staged in a natural prairie amphitheater near the site of the actual council, the pageant, which was first presented in 1927, covers 300 years of history, starting with Coronado's trip through the region. A reenactment is scheduled for 2003. | 620/886–9815.

NEWTON
▼▼

Both the Chisholm Trail and the railroad—which brought gunslingers, gamblers, "soiled doves," and cowboys to the area—helped Newton become one of the wickedest towns in the West. The Atchison, Topeka & Santa Fe Railroad established a western terminal and railhead for Texas cattle here in 1872, the year the town was founded. In 1874 a group of German Mennonites left Russia to avoid military service for the czar and settled here, bringing with them the hardy Turkey Red winter wheat, which saved the economic fortunes of the region. *Contact Newton Area Chamber of Commerce | 500 N. Main St., Suite 101, 67114 | 620/283–2560 or 800/ 899–0455 | www.infonewtonks.org.*

Country Boys Carriage and Prairie Adventure. If you are fascinated by pioneer life but don't want to relive its hardships, you might enjoy these full-day or overnight covered wagon trips in the Flint Hills. Ride beneath the wide blue sky during the day and settle down at night in a secluded but easily accessible campsite on the Homestead Ranch. Entertainers and reenactors take you back to earlier days as you grind wheat into flour, maybe shell come corn, and observe other skills that pioneers needed in the Old West. Your supper is a campfire-cooked "prairie meal." | 1504 S. Rock Rd. | 620/283–2636 | www.kscoveredwagon.com/flinthills. htm | Overnight trip $140.00; $80.00 for trail riders who bring their own horses and feed | June–Sept. weekends; privately scheduled trips Apr.–Oct.

Harvey County Historical Society & Museum. Housed in the 1914 Carnegie Library, this museum not only displays railroad and Harvey Girl memorabilia but also enables you to see how a turn-of-the-20th-century station agent and telegraph office looked. | 203 N. Main St. | 316/283–2221 | $2 | Wed.–Sun. 1–4.

Kauffman Museum. Exhibits explore the relationship of the area's first inhabitants—primarily the Cheyenne—with their prairie home. See examples of wildlife as well as quilts, organs, clothing, and other items brought by early immigrants, especially the German-Russian Mennonites. | 2701 N. Main St. | 316/283–1612 | $3 | Tues.–Fri. 9:30–4:30, weekends 1:30–4:30.

Warkentin House. Walk through the 16-room furnished home of Bernhard Warkentin, a Mennonite who immigrated from the Ukraine in 1874. Bringing with him Turkey Red winter wheat, Warkentin helped Kansas become a major grain producer. The house was built in 1886–1887 and contains many of the original furnishings. The four fireplaces and woodwork are beautifully preserved. | 211 E. 1st St. | 316/283–7555 | $3 | June–Aug., Tues.–Sun. 1–4:30; Apr.–May and Sept.–Dec., weekends 1–4:30; Jan.–Mar., by appointment.

NICODEMUS

This is the only remaining all-black town west of the Mississippi River founded after the Civil War. Promised by promoters that they would find a temperate climate, lush trees, wild horses, and rich soil in the free state of Kansas, 300 freed slaves from Kentucky came here in 1877. What they found was not the paradise they'd been promised but instead stubborn soil, no trees, drought, frigid winters, sweltering summers, and lots of wind. They survived the first winter by selling buffalo bones or working for the railroad. Many returned home, but those who stayed established churches, schools, banks, and two newspapers. The town thrived in the 1890s, when it grew to 700 residents, but it declined after it was bypassed by the railroad. Today there are 21 residents. *Contact Graham County Economic Development | 521 W. Main St., Hill City 67642 | 785/421–2211.*

Nicodemus Livery Company. Take a Black West history tour, eat barbeque while learning about the town's history, or go on a horse-drawn wagon tour around Nicodemus National Historic Site. Contact the company for a schedule of events. | U.S. 24, Box 29, Bogue, 67625 | 785/ 421–3311 | $15–$60.

Nicodemus National Historic Landmark District. Five historic buildings still stand, including the Old First Baptist Church, which started as a dugout and was replaced in 1907. Start your visit of the last remaining black township west of the Mississippi River at the visitor center in Nicodemus Township Hall. Exhibits tell the story of Nicodemus's first settlers as well as of its black cowboys and Buffalo Soldiers. | U.S. 24 | 785/839–4233 | Free | Daily 8:30–5.

✦ ON THE CALENDAR: July **Emancipation Proclamation Celebration.** Since the late 19th century, Nicodemus has welcomed former residents and relatives in an annual homecoming celebration with traditional food and music, church services, and Buffalo Soldier reenactments. | 785/839–4233.

OBERLIN

First called Sappa after the creek here, the town was renamed Oberlin to honor the Ohio hometown of one of the men who donated the land for the town. Founded in 1873, Oberlin is remembered as the site of the last Indian raid on Kansas soil, when settlers were killed in 1878 by Cheyenne avenging a similar massacre years earlier. A Last Indian Raid monument is in the Oberlin Cemetery. *Contact Decatur Area Chamber of Commerce | 132 S. Penn Ave., 67749 | 785/475–3441.*

Last Indian Raid/Decatur County Museum. A video and exhibits tell the story of the last Indian raid on Kansas soil, which happened after 100 armed warriors and their families broke loose in September 1878 from a camp in Oklahoma where they had not been treated well. Artifacts in 13 buildings—including an 1885 depot and jail, sod-house replica, and 1906 Bohemian dance hall—relay the area's heritage. | 258 S. Penn Ave. | 785/475–2712 | $3 | Apr.–Nov., Tues.–Sat. 10–noon and 1–5.

HISTORIC LODGING

LandMark Inn. An oasis of Victorian gentility on the plains of western Kansas, this 1886 bank was where many homesteaders claimed their 160 acres. The building is now on the National Register of Historic Places. Rooms are filled with antiques and such Old West reminders as an oversize portrait of Buffalo Bill Cody and a stuffed bobcat. Breakfast, which might include stuffed french toast with homemade butter-pecan syrup drizzled on top, is served downstairs in the Teller Room Restaurant. Restaurant, exercise equipment. | 189 S. Penn Ave., 67749 | 888/639–0003 | www.landmarkinn.com | 7 suites | $79–$109 | AE, D, MC, V | BP.

PLEASANTON
▼▼

Within the sloping hills where Osage, Potawatomie, and Miami once lived, a chapter of Kansas's rich Civil War history played out. Slaves on the Underground Railroad hid in the wooded hills, and blood was spilled over the slavery issue. Here, too, Kansas's only Civil War battle took place, along the old Military Road between Kansas City and Fort Scott. The town itself, founded in 1869, bears the name of the Union general who commanded that battle. *Contact Mine Creek Battlefield State Historic Site. | R.R. 1, Box 97A, Pleasanton 66075 | 913/352–8890 | www.kshs.org/places/sites.htm.*

John Brown Museum State Historic Site. This wooden cabin preserves the original belongings of Samuel and Florella Adair, pioneers who embraced abolitionist beliefs. John Brown, Florella's half-brother, stayed here as well. | 10th and Main St., Osawatomie | 913/755–4384 | www.kshs.org/places/sites.htm | $3 | Wed.–Sat. 11–5, Sun. 1–5.

Marais des Cygnes Massacre State Historic Site. Printed outdoor signs and markers detail the May 1858 shooting of free-state men by pro-slavery advocates in a ravine that is now a National Historic Landmark. The massacre was a major event in the Bleeding Kansas era. Tours are available. | 6 mi north of Pleasanton on U.S. 69, east 3 mi on Rte. 52 | 913/352–8890 | www.kshs.org/places/marais.htm | $3 | Apr.–Sept., Wed.–Sat. 10–5, Sun. 1–5.

Mine Creek Battlefield State Historic Site. In October 1864 Union forces began an attack on the Confederates outside Kansas City and ran the Southern troops south along the Military Road until they reached this site. The skirmishes erupted into one of the largest cavalry engagements of the Civil War. Bullet casings and military gear are on display, and written exhibits guide you through the battle. You can also walk the actual battlefield. | 2 mi south on U.S 69, west ½ mi on Rte. 52 | 913/352–8890 | www.kshs.org/places/minecrek.htm | $3 | Wed.–Mon. 9–5.

✦ ON THE CALENDAR: May **Border War Days.** Reenactors dressed in period clothing commemorate the Marais des Cygnes Massacre at the state historic site; there are also talks by historians. | 913/352–8890.

SALINA
▼▼

Before the railroad arrived in 1867, this settlement along the banks of the Smoky Hill and Saline rivers consisted of only a few families, who made their living by hunting and trapping. *Contact Salina Area Chamber of Commerce | 120 W. Ash, 67402 | 785/827–9301 | www. salinakansas.org.*

Central Kansas Flywheels Historical Museum. Several buildings house an 1880s print shop, a Kansas general store, and machinery used in the region in years gone by. The collection focuses on regional heritage. | 1100 W. Diamond Dr., off I–70 at Exit 252 | 785/825–8473 | $2 | May–Sept., Tues.–Sun. 1–7.

Smoky Hill Museum. A sod dugout replicates a 1858 dwelling originally on the banks of the Smoky Hill River near Iron Street. The one-room dugout has log walls set into the river embankment and a sod roof. Inside are a rope bed with buffalo-skin blanket, hand-hewn table and log seats, small stove, and a sewing machine. The site also has a 1900 mercantile. | 211 W. Iron Ave. | 785/309–5776 | www.smokyhillmuseum.org | Free | Tues.–Fri. noon–5, Sat. 10–5, Sun. 1–5.

HISTORIC LODGING

Trader's Lodge. Step back in time to the life of the Rocky Mountain fur trader of the 1820s in this lodge of fir and native stone. The lodge was built in the late 20th century, and is filled with antiques, furs, and Indian artifacts. Each room has its own theme. There are beaver pelts and a muzzle-loading rifle in the Trapper's Room and a medicine bag and Sioux war clubs in the Plains Indian room. Historian-in-residence Neal Kindall can arrange for a private guide and nature hikes through the northern Smoky Hills. By special arrangement you can sleep under the stars in an 18-ft Sioux teepee, learn Indian beadwork, or tan a deer skin. Generous breakfasts include homemade cinnamon rolls. No room phones. | 1392 210th Rd., Wells 67467 | 785/488–3930 or 866/360–1813 | www.come.to/traderslodge | 4 rooms | $65–$85 | AE, DC | BP.

TOPEKA

▼▼▼

Kansa Indians recognized the convenience of the fords across this stretch of the Kansas River, and they made their homes on the rich river bottomland. The earliest white settlers in the area that would become Topeka established a ferry across the river for travelers on the Oregon Trail. The city quickly grew, and Topeka's first mayor, Atchison, Topeka & Santa Fe Railroad tycoon Cyrus K. Holliday, oversaw Topeka's incorporation on February 14, 1857. When Kansas gained its statehood in 1861, Topeka became the state capital. *Contact Kansas State Historical Society | 6425 S.W. 6th St., 66615 | 785/272–8681 | www.kshs.org. Topeka Convention and Visitors Bureau | 1275 S.W. Topeka Blvd., 66612 | 785/234–1030 or 800/235–1030 | www. topekacvb.org.*

Kansas History Center. The center serves as the state-run repository for Kansas's rich heritage. The Kansas Museum of History traces the state's past from the Native American era through the times of frontier settlers and on to the present. The Potawatomi Mission, a Baptist manual-labor school for Potawatomi children, still stands in its original location on the site. | 6425 S.W. 6th St. | 785/272–8681 | www.kshs.org | $4 | Mon.–Sat. 9–4:30, Sun. 12:30–4:30.

✦ ON THE CALENDAR: Aug. **Lake Shawnee Inter-Tribal Pow Wow.** Against the scenic Lake Shawnee backdrop witness traditional Native American dancing, crafts, and culture. | 785/272–5489.

HISTORIC LODGING

1878 Sage Inn & Stage Coach Station. Since 1878, this three-story limestone stone inn has provided hospitality on the frontier. Listed on the National Register of Historic Places, the building still retains its underground stone chamber, which may have been used as a raid hideout or Underground Railroad station. A deposit is required for kids under 16. Dining room, massage, library, business services; no smoking, no room phones, no TVs in some rooms. | 13553 S.W. K-4, Dover, 66420 | 785/256–6050 or 866/INN–OPEN | fax 785/256–6291 | www. historicsageinn.com | 4 rooms | $70–$85 | MC, V | BP.

WICHITA

▼▼▼

Jesse Chisholm established a trading post at the confluence of the Big and Little Arkansas rivers in what is now the state's largest city. His trading trail south into Indian Territory, known as Chisholm's Trail, was used by Texans to bring wild longhorns to the Kansas railheads. Named after the Indian tribe, the town of Wichita was founded in 1868 along the trail near Chisholm's trading post. The city grew quickly after it was incorporated, thanks to the cattle trade along the trail and the rail lines, which reached Wichita in 1873. *Contact Wichita Area Convention and Visitors Bureau | 350 W. Douglas Ave., 67202 | 316/265–2800 or 800/288–9424 | www.wichitakansas.org.*

Indian Center Museum. Exhibits such as ceremonial dress, photos, tools, and beadwork trace the history of the Wichita and Plains Indians. An outdoor village (open spring to fall, weather permitting) includes a reconstructed Wichita grass house, 1850 tepee, and garden. Indian tacos available for lunch on Tuesday and Thursday. | 650 N. Seneca St. | 316/262–5221 | www.theindiancenter.com | $3, museum and village $6 | Tues.–Sat. 10–5, Sun. 1–5.

Old Cowtown Museum. See what it was like to live in an Old West cattletown by strolling the boardwalks at this 17-acre living-history village dedicated to preserving and presenting life on the frontier from 1865 to 1880. The site comprises 40 buildings of historic significance, including the area's first homes and jail as well as a marshal's office, undertaker parlor, saloon, general store, church, school, livery stable, dentist, train depot, and farm. During the summer, living-history interpreters, saloon shows, and gunfight reenactments add to the experience. | 1871 Sim Park Dr. | 316/264–0671 | www.old-cowtown.org | $7 | Apr.–Oct., Mon.–Sat. 10–5, Sun. noon–5.

Prairie Rose Chuckwagon Supper. After taking a ride in a horse-drawn wagon, belly up to all-you-can-eat barbecue served next to a large stone fireplace. A heaping helping of cowboy music is provided by the nationally known Prairie Rose Wranglers, who have played Las Vegas and Carnegie Hall. Family entertainment includes a kids' corral during the main show. The venue is 15 mi northeast of Wichita off Route 254. No alcohol is served, and reservations are required. | 15231 S.W. Parallel Rd., Benton | 316/778–2121 | www.prairierosechuckwagon.com | $25 | Dinner shows Thurs.–Sat., with additional shows in Dec.

Wichita-Sedgwick County Historical Museum. Trading trinkets, a Plains Indian headdress, and an 1860s beaded Kiowa cradle board are among the artifacts from the area's earliest days. The museum is housed in an impressive four-story Richardsonian Romanesque structure built of Kansas limestone in 1890–92. Turrets and a 170-ft clock tower highlight the architecture. | 204 S. Main St. | 316/265–9314 | $2 | Tues.–Fri. 11–4, weekends 1–5.

✦ ON THE CALENDAR: July **Annual Powwow.** A weekend of drumming and dance competitions takes place at the Indian Center. Native American vendors and food keep you busy between events. | 316/262–5221.

Oct. **Old Sedgwick County Fair.** Experience an 1870s county fair with music, games, gunfights, saloon shows, and demonstrations at Old Cowtown Museum. | 316/264–6398.

HISTORIC LODGING

Castle Inn Riverside. In 1886–88 a wealthy cattle baron built this mansion on the banks of the Arkansas River to resemble a Scottish castle. Listed on the National Register of Historic Places, the edifice has stone walls, stained-glass from Germany, and carved-oak lattice work. Twelve rooms have fireplaces, and one is in the castle's turret. Complimentary hors d'oeuvres, wine, fresh desserts, premium coffee, and a choice of liqueurs are served every evening in the library. Cable TV, in-room data ports, meeting rooms; no kids under 10. | 1155 N. River Blvd., 67203 | 800/580–1131 | www.castleinnriverside.com | 14 rooms | $125–$275 | AE, D, MC, V | BP.

MONTANA

───❖───

The name Montana, a Spanish word for "mountain," conjures up majestic scenes of snowcapped mountain peaks, raging rivers, and weathered cowboys herding cattle over vast prairies that have felt few footsteps over the course of time. Indeed, with an area of 147,138 square mi (it's the fourth largest state), and a population of only 904,000, Montana is still rugged frontier land, with gorgeous, untrammeled public lands and historic sites unchanged in 200 years.

As in much of the western United States, humans are believed to have arrived in Montana 10,000 to 30,000 years ago. Historians believe that these Paleo-Indians were direct ancestors of today's Native American tribes—including the Assiniboine, Blackfeet, Chippewa-Cree, Crow, Gros Ventre, Kootenai, Northern Cheyenne, Pend d'Oreille, Salish, and Sioux. These itinerant peoples flourished on the Great Plains and in Montana's western valleys. Aside from a few French trappers, who may have made their way to Montana as early as the 1740s, European-Americans did not venture to the area until the 19th century.

The Corps of Discovery, led by Meriwether Lewis and William Clark, traveled through Montana in 1805–06, following the traditional hunting and trading passages of the Plains people by canoe, horse, and on foot. Lewis and Clark documented a land thickly populated with beaver, otter, bison, and grizzly bears. The explorers' journals unlocked the West for enterprising traders and trappers eager to cash in on the state's abundant natural resources. Between 1806 and about 1880, trappers hunted for valuable furs throughout Montana's waterways. During this time, many fur-trading forts were built, including Manuel Lisa's trading post, established by the Missouri Fur Company at the confluence of the Bighorn and Yellowstone rivers, and Fort Union Trading Post, established by John Jacob Astor's American Fur Company at the mouth of the Yellowstone River. The fur market crashed when the beaver population was depleted around the same time beaver-pelt hats went out of fashion.

Miners arrived in Montana not long after the trappers. Montana's first major gold strike occurred near the present-day town of Dillon in 1862. Gold deposits were discovered near

Virginia City and Nevada City in 1863, drawing thousands of fortune seekers to Montana. Rough-and-tumble towns sprouted in the gold-dust gulches, and became the scene of robberies, lynchings, and general lawlessness. But the wealth of the mines drew the attention of the U.S. government, and in 1864 Montana Territory was created. The territory's crowning stroke of good luck came in 1882, when a thick vein of copper was found beneath the played-out gold-mining camp of Butte. At the time, it was the richest cache of copper ore in the world. For the next 73 years, Butte, Helena, Anaconda and much of west-central Montana continued to attract miners.

Cattle and sheep ranchers made their way to Montana's wide-open spaces in the 1850s, and open-range cattle ranching appeared on the prairies in 1870. By 1880 the bison were almost completely wiped out, killed by white entrepreneurs for their hides and for the prairies that were their habitat. As the number of bison declined, so did the population of the Plains tribes, who depended wholly on bison for meat and hides with which to make shelter and clothing. The tribes began to trade and sell land for food, horses, weapons, shelter, blankets, and whisky, a European import that became a huge commodity on reservations. Sometimes the blankets they acquired were infected with smallpox, to which the Indians had no immunity. Smallpox epidemics ravaged the native Montanan population, killing thousands. The few Native Americans who survived starvation and smallpox were pushed onto reservations, no longer free to roam the land.

In 1880 the first railroad reached Montana; the Northern Pacific crossed the territory by 1883. Loggers, stockmen, and sodbusters arrived from the east using the same routes of travel along the Missouri and Yellowstone rivers that Lewis and Clark had followed. Montana became the nation's 41st state in 1889, sparking a tumultuous battle between copper barons Marcus Daly in Anaconda and William Clark in Helena. Each of the would-be politicians spent hundreds of thousands of dollars from his own fortune to promote his home town as the state capital. Both were accused of bribery, and though Daly outspent Clark, Helena was finally selected as the state capital in a run-off election against Anaconda. Meanwhile, agriculture had been gaining on mining as the state's leading industry, and by the early 20th century wheat and cattle surpassed gold and copper as the state's top commodities. Miners turned to farming and ranching on land previously controlled by Native Americans. In 1909, the Homestead Act was amended to provide for ownership of larger tracts of land, further encouraging settlers to set up homesteads in Montana. The Montana frontier faded into history, but on the high plains and in small towns and ghost towns, the spirit of the Wild West still reigns today.

Along the Missouri River
A DRIVING TOUR FROM FORT BENTON TO THREE FORKS

▼▼

Distance: 200 mi   **Time:** 3 days
Breaks: Overnight in Great Falls, Helena, and Three Forks, ranching and mining communities with historic hotels and museums.

The stops in this tour sit along the traditional migration routes Native Americans used for 10,000 years. In 1805 and 1806, when the Corps of Discovery paddled, hiked, and rode horses across then-unmapped Montana, they camped at many of these same spots. In the next century, fur trappers, gold miners, and homesteaders retraced the route, settling and developing communities along the Missouri River and among the foothills of the Rocky Mountains.

Begin at **Fort Benton** with visits to the Museum of the Upper Missouri and Old Fort Benton, where the significance of Montana's first steamboat landing is revealed. The Wild and Scenic Missouri River, visible as it roils through town, flows past ancient teepee rings and the dramatic White Cliffs. Drive 45 mi southwest of Fort Benton on U.S. 87 to **Great Falls,** where the Great

MONTANA TIME LINE

1803 The United States purchases Louisiana Territory from France, including Montana east of the Rocky Mountains, for 3¢ an acre.

1805–06 Explorers Meriwether Lewis and William Clark travel through Montana on their transcontinental expedition.

1807 American fur trade begins with Manuel Lisa's construction of the Missouri Fur Company's trading post at the confluence of the Bighorn and Yellowstone rivers.

1828 John Jacob Astor's American Fur Co. builds Fort Union Trading Post at the mouth of the Yellowstone River.

1859 The first steamboat from St. Louis arrives in Fort Benton, the farthest-inland port in the world.

1862 Montana's first major gold strike occurs near the present-day town of Dillon. John Bozeman blazes the Bozeman Trail. Congress passes the Homestead Act, opening thousands of acres to pioneer settlers.

1863 Gold is discovered near Virginia City and Nevada City (east of Dillon).

1864 Montana Territory is created on May 26, with the first capital at Bannack. John M. Bozeman leads the first wagon train over Bozeman Trail.

1872 Congress establishes Yellowstone National Park, overlapping Montana's southern border. It is the world's first national park.

1876 Lieutentant Colonel George Armstrong Custer and his 7th Cavalry fall to Sioux and Cheyenne warriors at the Battle of the Little Bighorn, southeast of Billings.

1877 The Nez Perce, led by Chief Joseph, surrender to the U.S. Army near present-day Chinook after a six-month, 1,170-mi trek that includes nearly a dozen battles.

1880 Hide hunters shoot buffalo to near extinction.

1882 A thick vein of copper is discovered beneath the played-out gold-mining camp of Butte. It is the richest cache of copper ore in the world.

1888 The Sweetgrass Hills Treaty establishes boundaries for Fort Peck, Fort Belknap, and the Blackfeet reservations.

1889 Montana is admitted to the Union on November 8 as the 41st state.

1894 In a runoff against Anaconda, Helena is selected as Montana's state capital.

1910 Glacier National Park is established by act of Congress.

Falls of the Missouri once roared and are now tamed by four dams. Don't miss the preeminent Lewis and Clark National Historic Trail Interpretive Center and the C. M. Russell Museum. End the day with a stroll along the River's Edge Trail, where you can see what remains of the Great Falls.

On your second morning, drive south on I–15 to **Helena,** 88 mi south. Last Chance Gulch and the Montana Historical Society Museum reveal Helena's colorful past.

On your third morning, drive south on U.S. 287 for 70 mi, past ranches, public lands, and Canyon Ferry Reservoir, to **Three Forks,** where the Jefferson, Madison, and Gallatin rivers meet. Visit Missouri Headwaters State Park to see where Lewis and Clark explored the best route to the Pacific, or the misnamed Lewis and Clark Caverns, which in fact were discovered by two hunters more than 80 years after Lewis and Clark passed through the area.

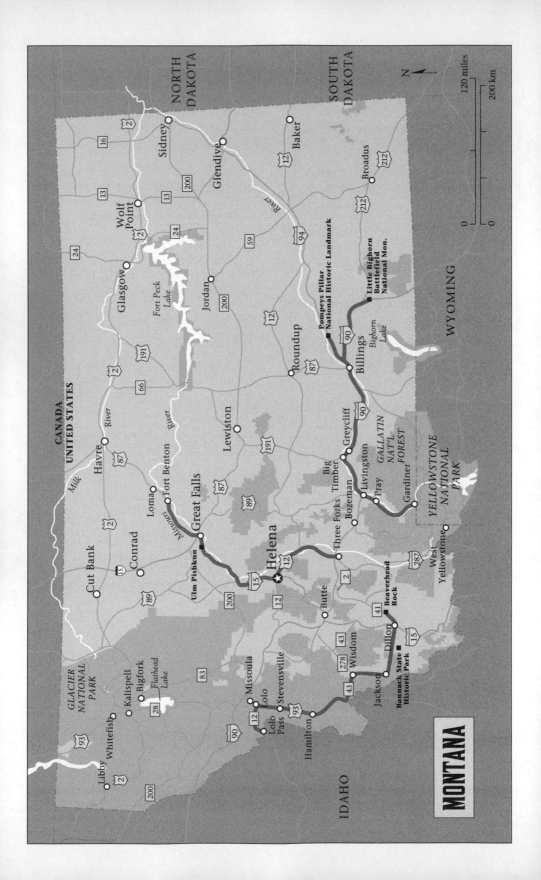

MONTANA

Along the Yellowstone River

A DRIVING TOUR FROM YELLOWSTONE NATIONAL PARK TO POMPEYS PILLAR

▼▼▼

Distance: 200 mi   **Time:** 3 days
Breaks: Overnight in Livingston, Big Timber, and Billings, which sprouted along the Yellowstone River as mining, ranching, and the railroad brought settlers westward.

For more than 10,000 years, the Yellowstone River has been a major commercial route. The Plains Indians hunted along its game-thick banks, followed by European fur trappers, mountain men, and settlers. Today the Yellowstone is the last undammed major river in the lower 48 states. The Yellowstone churns a frothy white where it exits Yellowstone National Park at Gardiner, your starting point for this tour.

From the north entrance of **Yellowstone National Park,** the world's first national park, drive north on U.S. 89, where you might see some of the estimated 16,000 to 18,000 elk that live in the Northern Range Elk Herd in lush Paradise Valley. You also may see mule deer and bighorn sheep. About 30 mi north of Gardinert, at Emigrant's flashing light, turn east and drive 2 mi to the Chico Hot Springs Resort for a soak, lunch, and a look at the historic photos in the turn-of-the-20th-century lobby. Return to U.S. 89, following the Yellowstone River toward Livingston. You're likely to see fly fishermen, deer, and even eagles along the way. Where the river turns eastward at Livingston, you'll meet the 1863 gold-rush Bozeman Trail and the Lewis and Clark Trail.

Spend the afternoon in **Livingston** visiting the Yellowstone Gateway Museum of Park County, where you can see evidence of the region's earliest residents, and Livingston Depot Center in the Northern Pacific Depot, which was the departure point of the Northern Pacific Railway's "Gateway to Yellowstone National Park" during the golden age of America's railroads.

On your second morning, drive east 27 mi on I–90 to **Big Timber** and visit Crazy Mountain Museum, where exhibits show what it was like to be a cowboy or settle on a homestead in Montana in the 1800s. In the afternoon, join an outfitter on a history-tracking float trip on the Yellowstone River from the area William Clark called "Rivers Across." The river wends its way down to Greycliff Prairie Dog Town State Park, where the expedition noted the "barking squirrels." Overnight in Big Timber's historic downtown district. If you don't stay in the Grand Hotel, be sure to take a peek at the 1890s saloon inside.

On your third morning, continue eastward on I–90 for 80 mi, following the Yellowstone River to **Billings,** where you will find several museums and historical sites, including the Western Heritage Center and Moss Mansion. Each sight illustrates a different era in the state's varied history. The final leg of your journey follows the Yellowstone River east on I–90 for 5 mi, then east on I–94 for 23 mi to Pompeys Pillar National Historic Landmark, where William Clark carved his name into sandstone. As an extension to your tour or an alternative to Pompeys Pillar, head back west to the junction of I–90 and I–94, and go south on I–90 for about 60 mi to Little Bighorn Battlefield National Monument.

The Bitterroot Valley Corridor

A DRIVING TOUR FROM DILLON TO LOLO PASS

▼▼▼

Distance: 232 mi   **Time:** 3 days
Breaks: Overnight in Jackson and Lolo.

Begin in **Dillon,** just west of the Beaverhead River, which Lewis and Clark followed down from Three Forks. Drive north on Route 41 for 14 mi to see Beaverhead Rock, which Sacagawea recognized as a landmark not far from her Shoshone tribe's summer home. Head back to Dillon and go south on I–15 for 2 mi to Exit 58, then west on Route 278 for 20 mi, then south on Route 5 for 4 mi, to the state's first territorial capitol, at Bannack State Park, a remarkably preserved ghost town. Back to Route 278, drive west and north into the Big Hole Valley. Near Dillon, overnight in Jackson, where members of the Corps of Discovery cooked their food in the hot springs.

On your second morning, continue northwest on Route 278 until you reach the town of Wisdom. At the intersection of Route 43, turn west and drive 10 mi on the Nez Perce National Historic Trail to Big Hole National Battlefield, where the Nez Perce and a U.S. regiment fought a bloody battle. Next, continue west 16 mi to U.S. 93 and turn north to drive 80 mi to **Lolo.** Notice the wetter, greener landscape on the western side of the Rockies. Spend the night in Lolo, and on your third day take U.S. 12 west to Travelers Rest National Historic Landmark and State Park, Lolo Hot Springs, and finally Lolo Pass.

BIG TIMBER

▼▼

This ranching community on the banks of the Yellowstone River is the only city in Sweet Grass County. Two streams empty into the Yellowstone at a point north of town, noted in William Clark's journals as "Rivers Across." Big Timber, named for the large cottonwoods that dominate the river's shore, attracted sheepherding operations in the early 20th century, and at one time the surrounding ranches were among the West's largest wool producers. The rough-and-tumble town is framed by the Crazy Mountains, whose name conjured several etymological theories, from Native American lore to a certain pioneer woman's behavior. *Contact Sweet Grass Chamber of Commerce | Box 1012, 59011 | 406/932–5131 | www.bigtimber.com.*

Big Timber Guides and Rollin' Boulder Outfitters. Float the Yellowstone River starting from "Rivers Across," the point where William Clark stopped during his return trip on July 17, 1806. Knowledgeable guides point out some of the wildlife that Clark saw here, including white pelicans, bald eagles, white-tailed deer, and cutthroat trout. | 406/932–4080 or 406/932–5836 | www.rboutfitters.com | Late May–late Oct.

Crazy Mountain Museum. This beautiful building is filled with exhibits that represent Big Timber's history, its people, the sheepherding business, the famous Cramer Rodeo, and the Crazy Mountains. There's a room dedicated to pioneers with artifacts dating to the late 1890s; a detailed miniature of Big Timber in 1907; the restored Sour Dough School House; and the "stabbur"—a reconstruction of an early Norwegian grain storehouse. | Cemetery Rd., I–90 at Exit 367 | 406/932–5126 | Donations accepted | Late May–early Sept., Tues.–Sun. 1–4:30, or by appointment.

Greycliff Prairie Dog Town State Park. Ranchers don't like prairie dogs, but the animals are undeniably fascinating to observe, as noted in the Lewis and Clark journals. At this large prairie-dog town, a preserved habitat, you can wander trails created for easy viewing. Watch out for rattlesnakes. | Off I–90 at Exit 377, Greycliff, 10 mi southeast of Big Timber | 406/247–2940 | www.fwp.state.mt.us | $1 | May–Sept., daily dawn–dusk.

✦ ON THE CALENDAR: July **Yellowstone Boat Float.** This annual float trip begins at Livingston, with overnight stops in Big Timber and Reed Point, and ends at Laurel. | 406/248–7182.

Sept. **Running of the Sheep.** Hundreds of sturdy Montana-bred sheep join this drive in celebration of the state's agricultural history. There's the ugliest-sheep and prettiest-ewe contest, and a precision draft-horse cultivation event, all just downriver in Reed Point. | 406/326–2288.

HISTORIC LODGING
The Grand Hotel B&B. The Grand has hosted travelers and sheepherders since 1890. The owners will regale you with histories of Big Timber's rowdier days, when a room could be had for

$2. The hotel is fully restored, but rooms are still simple with comfortable furnishings, and some baths in the hall. The views of the Crazy Mountains are unsurpassed. Restaurant, fishing, bar, free parking, some pets allowed; no room TVs, no smoking. | 139 McLeod St., 59011 | 406/932–4459 | fax 406/932–4248 | www.thegrand-hotel.com | 10 rooms, 4 with bath | $59–$145 | D, MC, V | CP.

BILLINGS

▼▼▼

This high-plains city helped forge Montana Territory. As a major stop on the Yellowstone River, the area saw passage of native warriors, the Lewis and Clark expedition, railroad barons, cattle punchers, sod busters, and pioneers heading west. Named for railroad developer Frederick Billings, it was nicknamed "the Magic City" for its rapid growth beginning in 1882. It's surrounded by six mountain ranges and flanked in the east by sandstone cliffs called the rimrocks. The area around Billings was the scene of several important historic events featuring such headliners as George Armstrong Custer and Sitting Bull, who battled at Little Bighorn in 1876, and skilled frontierswoman Calamity Jane, who lived in Billings at one time. *Contact Billings Area Visitor Center and Cattle Drive Monument. | 815 S. 27th St., 59107 | 406/252–4016 or 800/735–2635 | www.billingscvb.visitmt.com.*

Billings Trolley. Take a tour of Billings in a 1930 trolley. The 1½-hour tour takes you through the rimrock area for an overview of the Yellowstone Valley, with stops at local museums. Guides tell stories about General Custer, Calamity Jane, Lewis and Clark, and other characters of the Old West. Reservations are essential. | Depart from Broadway at 1st Ave. | 888/618–4386 | www.montanafunadventures.com | $20 | Tues.–Sat.

Boothill Cemetery. H. M. Muggins Taylor, the army scout who carried word of Custer's defeat through 180 mi of hostile territory to Fort Ellis, is one of the many citizens and outlaws of early Billings buried here. | Airport Rd. and Main St. | 406/252–4016 | Free | Daily.

Chief Black Otter Trail. Drive along this scenic, 2-mi dirt road atop the rimrocks to look for the burial site of Chief Black Otter, a Crow Indian who was killed by a Sioux war party. Also along the trail is the gravesite of famous frontier scout Yellowstone Kelly. Go north on 27th Street to Airport Road and follow the signs. | Off Airport Rd. | 406/252–4016 | Free | Daily dawn–dusk.

Lewis and Clark Expedition Tours. Join Montana Fun Adventures' knowledgeable guides for a visit to Pompeys Pillar, a canoe trip on the Yellowstone River, or a horseback ride along the route taken by Sergeant Pryor, a member of the Corps of Discovery and responsible for herding the expedition's horses. | 888/618–4386 | www.montanafunadventures.com | Apr.–Oct.

Little Bighorn Battlefield National Monument. When the smoke cleared on June 25, 1876, neither Lieutenant Colonel George Armstrong Custer nor his 200 or so blue-shirted troopers were alive to tell the story of their battle against several thousand Northern Plains natives on this windswept prairie along the Little Bighorn River. It was a Pyrrhic victory for the tribes; the loss would force the U.S. government to redouble its efforts to clear them off the plains. Now a national monument, and formerly called Custer's Last Stand, the site, on the Crow Indian Reservation, has a new interpretive display that includes material from recent archaeological excavations. The display explains what led to the momentous clash of two cultures and speculates on what might have happened during the battle. A new Indian Memorial dedicated to the Plains Indians who took part in the battle opened in 2002. Beware of rattlesnakes. | U.S. 212, 1½ mi from I–90 at Exit 510, 3 mi south of Crow Agency and 60 mi southeast of Billings | 406/638–2621 | www.nps.gov/libi | $10 per vehicle | Late May–early Sept., daily 8 AM–9 PM; Sept., Apr., and 1st 3 weeks in May, daily 8–6; Oct.–Mar., daily 8–4:30.

Peter Yegen Jr.–Yellowstone County Museum. In an 1893 log cabin, this eclectic collection of Northern Plains tribes artifacts and ranching, mining, and trapping tools includes antique saddles, Native American clothing, an authentic chuckwagon, and a barbed-wire collection. Teddy Roosevelt attended meetings in this building. | 1950 Terminal Cir., south of Billings Logan International Airport's parking lot | 406/256–6811 | www.pyjrycm.org | Donations accepted | Weekdays 10:30–5, Sat. 10:30–3.

Pompeys Pillar National Historic Landmark. Captain William Clark carved his name on this immense sandstone butte in 1806, leaving the only remaining evidence of the Lewis and Clark expedition on the trail. Stop at the visitor center or take an interpretive tour. | Off I–94 at Exit 23 | 406/896–5013 | www.mt.blm.gov | $4 | Visitor center late May–Sept., daily 8–8.

Western Heritage Center. Permanent exhibits at this downtown museum include artifacts and kid-friendly interactive displays that trace the lives of Native Americans, ranchers, homesteaders, immigrants, and railroad workers who lived in the Yellowstone River region between 1880 and 1940. Interpretive programs and courses for all ages are available. | 2822 Montana Ave. | 406/256–6809 | www.ywhc.org | Donations accepted | Tues.–Sat. 10–5.

Yellowstone Art Museum. Come to the original Yellowstone County jail to see western artworks from a 4,000-piece permanent collection, plus changing exhibits of regional artists' works. Artists represented include Joseph Henry Sharp (1859–1953), Charles M. Russell (1864–1926), and Will James (1892–1942). | 401 N. 27th St. | 406/256–6804 | www.yellowstone. artmuseum.org | $5 | Tues.–Sat. 10–5, Sun. noon–5.

✦ ON THE CALENDAR: July **Clark Day.** Celebrate William Clark's visit to Pompeys Pillar in 1806 with your own visit to the landmark. There's free admission during the festival, plus a buffalo burger cookout and live music. | 406/896–5235 or 406/875–2233.

DILLON

▼▼▼

Beaverhead Rock, a massive sandstone outcrop resembling a swimming beaver, has long been an important landmark. Native American hunting parties traveling the Jefferson and Beaverhead rivers passed it on their way to the bison territory in the east. Likewise, when the Lewis and Clark expedition paddled up river, Sacajawea recognized the rock. Her Shoshone tribe's summer camp was near here, and beyond lay their route to the Bitterroot Mountains. Today the Big Hole Valley region is still pristine and largely unsettled. You can see parts of the Nez Perce National Historic Trail and several mining ghost towns, including Bannack, once the territorial capital and now a state park. *Contact Beaverhead Chamber of Commerce | Box 425, Dillon 59725 | 406/683–5511 | www.beaverheadchamber.com.*

Bannack State Park. Bannack was Montana's first territorial capital and the site of the state's first major gold strike, in 1862. The frontier boomtown is now a state park; 19th-century wood and brick structures, including a Methodist church, a saloon, a jail, the Meade Hotel and Beaverhead County courthouse, and a Masonic temple and schoolhouse line the main street. Renegade sheriff Henry Plummer and his gang of outlaws terrorized Bannack residents until the legendary Montana Vigilantes, also acting outside the law, hunted down and hanged Plummer and his associates. Rumors persist that Plummer's stash of stolen gold was hidden somewhere in the mountains near Bannack and never found. Gallows stand in town as a reminder of the Wild West. Take Route 278 and watch for a sign indicating a left turn (south) just before Badger Pass. A well-maintained gravel road leads for 3 mi to the park. | Rte. 278, 25 mi west of Dillon | 406/834–3413 | www.bannack.org | $2 | Park daily dawn– dusk. Visitor center late May–early Sept., daily 8 AM–9 PM; early Sept.–late May, daily 8–5.

BANNACK, THE GOLD RUSH CAPITAL

As gold fever gripped the nation, Montana stepped into the nation's headlines with reports of the area's first gold strike, in 1862. Soon after, prospectors arrived in south-central Montana near today's community of Dillon in search of the glistening ore.

Not far from where Lewis and Clark mapped the Beaverhead River, a gold seeker named Jack White panned for gold among the gravel of Grasshopper Creek and struck it rich. Fortune seekers poured into to the mining camp that developed and called it Bannack, the name of a tribe of local Native Americans. Two years later, in 1864, Montana achieved territorial status, and Bannack, with a population of 3,000, became the territorial capital.

Riches brought more and more people to the remote region, including some unsavory characters who robbed the miners and stagecoaches and terrorized the citizenry. A group of men looking for speedy justice formed the Vigilantes to hunt down the band of robbers, who turned out to include Bannack Sheriff Henry Plummer. The Vigilantes hanged Plummer and two of his gang and continued to deal with outlaws according to their own understanding of the law.

When the gold played out, so did interest in Bannack. In 1865 the territorial capital was moved east to Virginia City, and Bannack was on its way to becoming a ghost town. It is now preserved as a state park.

Beaverhead County Museum. Here you can see Native American artifacts; ranching, farming, and mining memorabilia; a homesteader's cabin; and a boardwalk imprinted with the area's ranch brands. | 15 S. Montana St. | 406/683–5027 | Donations accepted | Late May–early Sept., weekdays 8–8, Sat. noon–4; early Sept.–late May, weekdays 8–5.

Beaverhead Rock State Park. The park is named for the massive rock, shaped like the head of a beaver, that anchors it. Beaverhead Rock was recognized by Lewis and Clark's Shoshone guide, Sacajawea, in 1805, giving the expedition renewed hope of finding the friendly tribe and a route to the Bitterroot Mountains. The best place to view the rock is from an overlook on Route 41. Watch out for rattlesnakes. | Rte. 41, 14 mi north of Dillon | 406/834–3413 | Free | Daily dawn–dusk.

Big Hole National Battlefield. One of the West's most tragic stories played out on this battlefield. In 1877, the U.S. Army was charged with forcing resistant Nez Perce Indians onto a reservation in Idaho. In the same year, a few Nez Perce warriors killed several white settlers as retribution for Nez Perce deaths and mistreatment at the hands of white people. The bloodshed provoked a massive manhunt and the beginning of a 1,500-mi odyssey. The Nez Perce fled north from their homeland in central Idaho, pursued by the U.S. Army. The tribe engaged 10 separate U.S. commands in 13 battles and skirmishes. One of the fiercest of these took place at Big Hole Battlefield, where both sides suffered serious losses. A visitor center overlooks the meadows of Big Hole, which remain as they were at the time of the battle. Teepees erected by the park service mark the site of the Nez Perce village that was attacked, serving as haunting reminders of what transpired here. Call in advance to arrange for a ranger-led talk or tour. | About 65 mi northwest of Dillon on Rte. 278, then 10 mi west on Rte. 43 | 406/689–3155 | www.nps.gov/biho | $5 per vehicle late May–early Sept., free rest of yr | May–early Sept., daily 8:30–6; early Sept.–Apr., daily 9–5.

HISTORIC DINING AND LODGING

Jackson Hot Springs Lodge. The spacious lodge here isn't an historic structure—it was built in 1950—but it rests on land where Lewis and Clark camped and beside which they cooked their dinner in natural hot springs. Now in a large, man-made pool, the artesian well water still averages 104°F (138°F at its source) year-round. The log lodge is decorated with elk antlers, stuffed mountain lions, and other critters. There are simple rooms in separate cabins, four RV sites with electrical hook-ups, and a field where campers can set up tents. The dining room specializes in wild game like pheasant, bison, and elk. Restaurant, pool, fishing, bar, piano, meeting rooms, some pets allowed (fee); no room phones, no room TVs. | Main St. (Box 808, Jackson 59736), 48 mi northwest of Dillon | 406/834–3151 or 888/438–6938 | fax 406/834–3157 | www.jacksonhotsprings.com | 20 cabins, 4 RV sites | $34–$78, camping $15–$30 | AE, MC, V.

✦ ON THE CALENDAR: June **Dale Tash Montana History Day.** You can take a guided tour of the 19th-century buildings, sit through a mock school day in the old schoolhouse, or learn to make a log cabin during this event at Bannack State Park. | 406/843–3548.

July **Bannack Days.** Take in stagecoach rides, candle making, a Main Street gunfight, old-time dancing, and music during this celebration of life in Montana's first territorial capital in Bannack State Park. | 406/834–3413.

Aug. **Commemoration of the Battle of the Big Hole.** Ceremonies, demonstrations, traditional music, and park rangers help you understand this battle fought on August 9 and 10, 1877, between the U.S. military and the Nez Perce. The events are held at Big Hole National Battlefield on Route 43. | 406/689–3155.

FORT BENTON

▼▼

Fort Benton became a major landing point for fur traders, gold miners, and homesteaders arriving from St. Louis on steamships via the Missouri River. The original 1846 fort is known as the "Birthplace of Montana," around which the state's oldest town developed. Teepee rings from Plains tribes such as the Blackfeet are still visible on the bench lands along the river, and Lewis and Clark passed the site en route to the Pacific and back. *Contact Fort Benton Chamber of Commerce | Box 12, 59442 | 406/622–3864 | www.fortbenton.com.*

Museum of the Upper Missouri. Find out what Fort Benton was like from 1800 to 1900 and about the role it played as a trading post, military fort, and the head of steamboat navigation. Next door is Old Fort Benton, considered the birthplace of Montana. Its 1846 blockhouse is the oldest standing structure in Montana. | Old Fort Park, Main and 21st Sts. | 406/622–5316 | www.fortbenton.com/museums | $4 | May, daily 11:30–4:30; June–Sept., daily 10–5; Oct.–Apr., by appointment only.

Upper Missouri National Wild and Scenic River. In 1805–06 Lewis and Clark explored the Missouri River and camped on its banks. Today the designated National Wild and Scenic stretch of the river runs 149 mi down from Fort Benton. Highlights include the scenic White Cliffs area, Citadel Rock, Hole in the Wall, the Lewis and Clark camp at Slaughter River, abandoned homesteads, and abundant wildlife. Commercial boat tours, shuttle service, and rentals of rowboats, power boats, and canoes are offered at Fort Benton and Virgelle. | Visitor center: 1718 Front St. | 406/622–5185 or 406/538–7461 | www.mt.blm.gov/ldo/umnwsr.html | Free | Visitor center May–Oct., daily 9–5.

Virgelle Merc and Missouri River Canoe Co. This canoe outfitter is 75 mi northeast of Great Falls on the Missouri River. The Virgelle Merc itself is a restored homestead-era settlement offering accommodations. The river outfitter offers guided eco-tours in canoes or kayaks following Lewis and Clark's river trail and lasting 1–10 days. You'll float sections of the river from almost-a-ghost-town Virgelle, where one of the state's last river-crossing cable ferries oper-

GLACIER NATIONAL PARK

The "Crown of the Continent," Glacier National Park encompasses 1.2 million acres of wilderness straddling the Continental Divide. Although they never lived in Glacier's mountains, area Native Americans, including the Blackfeet, Kootenai, and Salish Indians, regularly traversed the valleys for centuries before white immigrants arrived. For the most part, these migratory people crossed the mountains in search of sustenance in the form of roots, grasses, berries, and game. Many tribes felt that the mountains, with their unusual glacier-carved horns, cirques, and arêtes, were spiritually charged.

The first white trappers arrived in the area as early as the 1780s. Then, in 1805, Lewis and Clark passed south of what is now Glacier National Park. Attracted by the expedition's quickly disseminated reports of abundant beaver, many more trappers, primarily British, French, and Spanish, began migrating to the region from the north, south, and east. For most of the early to mid-1800s, human activity in the area was limited to lone trappers and migrating Native Americans.

On their journey west, Lewis and Clark sought but did not find the elusive pass over the Rockies, now known as Marias Pass on the southern edge of Glacier National Park. Whether their scouts were unaware of the relatively low elevation—5,200 ft—in the pass, or whether they feared the Blackfeet that controlled the region, is unknown. The pass was not discovered, in fact, until 1889, when surveyors for the Great Northern Railway finally found it in the dead of winter. By 1891 the Great Northern Railway's tracks had crossed Marias Pass, and by 1895 the railroad had completed its westward expansion, thus ensuring continued settlement of the West.

As homesteaders, miners, and trappers poured into the Glacier area in the late 1800s, the Native American population seriously declined. The Blackfeet were devastated by smallpox epidemics—a disease previously unknown in North America—from the mid-1800s until the early 1900s. The disease, and a reduced food supply due the overhunting of buffalo, stripped the Blackfeet of their power and, eventually, their land. In 1895, the tribe sold the area now within the national park to the U.S. government, who opened it to miners. Returns on the mines were never very substantial, and most were abandoned by the 1905.

Between the late 1880s and 1900, *Forest and Stream* magazine editor George Grinnel made several trips to the mountains of northwestern Montana. He was awed by the beauty of the area, and he urged the U.S. government to give it park status, thereby protecting it from mining interests and homesteaders. At the same time, the Great Northern Railway company, eager to bring customers out from the east, also was spreading the word about the area's recreational opportunities. The company built seven backcountry chalets to house guests, and promised tourists from the East a back-to-nature experience with day-long hikes and horseback rides between the strategically placed chalets. Visitors arrived by train at West Glacier, took a stagecoach to Lake McDonald, a boat to the lakeside Snyder Hotel, and began their nature adventures from there. Between Grinnel's political influence and the Great Northern's financial interests, Congress found reason enough to establish Glacier National Park; the bill was signed by President William Howard Taft in 1910. **Information:** | Box 128, West Glacier, 59936 | 406/888–7800 | www.nps.gov/glac.

ates. | 7485 Virgelle Ferry Rd. N, Loma 59460 | 800/426–2926 | www.canoemontana.com | AE, DC, MC, V.

✦ ON THE CALENDAR: June **Fort Benton Summer Celebration.** Fort Benton celebrates its role as Montana's first community with a parade, arts, crafts, antiques, a street dance, fireworks, Missouri River boat rides, and historical tours of Old Fort Benton. | 406/622–3351.

HISTORIC DINING AND LODGING

Grand Union Hotel. This completely restored steamboat-era hotel on the shaded banks of the Missouri River is the centerpiece of town. Opened in 1882, it's the state's oldest hotel and listed on the National Register of Historic Places. Large rooms, elegantly appointed and trimmed with massive windows, overlook either the downtown area or the Missouri's lush riverside grasses, willows, and cottonwood trees. The restaurant walls are lined with photographs of the town and hotel in the 1800s. Restaurant, in-room data ports, cable TV, boating, fishing, bar; no smoking. | 1 Grand Union Sq. 59442 | 404/622–1882 or 888/838–1882 | fax 404/622–5985 | www.grandunionhotel.com | 26 rooms | $99–$159 | AE, D, MC, V | CP.

GREAT FALLS

▼▼

Named for the famous Great Falls of the Missouri River, which cost the Lewis and Clark expedition a monthlong, 18-mi portage, this city was founded in the 1880s by flour and wood merchant Paris Gibson. Great Falls soon became one of the state's industrial centers, populated with shipping, railway-merchandizing, and copper-mining companies. This is the site of the first power dam on the Missouri River, built in 1890. Four dams now control the Missouri River and stem the falls, although during spring runoff snowmelt returns the falls to formidable size. Great Falls was the home of one of the West's most famous artists, painter and sculptor Charlie Russell. *Contact Great Falls Chamber of Commerce | 710 1st Ave. N, 59403 | 406/761–4434 | www.greatfallsonline.net.*

C. M. Russell Museum. Charlie Russell's former home and log studio, replete with the artist's tools and work, is open to the public. A separate 46,000-square-ft facility next door to the home displays watercolors, sculptures, oil paintings, and illustrated notes and letters from the prolific and often humorous artist. Russell completed 4,000 works of art, primarily portraying the vanishing era of the Old West. You can also see works by O. C. Seltzer, Joseph Henry Sharp, and Edward Curtis. | 400 13th St. N | 406/727–8787 | www.cmrussell.org | $6 | May–Sept., Mon.–Sat. 9–6, Sun. noon–5; Oct.–Apr., Tues.–Sat. 10–5, Sun. 1–5.

Great Falls Historic Trolley. Tour the greater Great Falls area aboard a 21-seat trolley. The ride takes you through historic neighborhoods and past sites where Lewis and Clark stopped, including the spot where a grizzly bear chased Captain Lewis into the river. The tour's one stop is at Rainbow Falls. Tours start at the visitor center at Broadwater Overlook Park, off 10th Avenue South on the west end of town, or at the High Plains Heritage Center, off 2nd Street South. | 315 5th St. S | 406/771–1100 or 888/707–1100 | www.greatfallshistorictrolley.com | $20 | June–Sept., daily; Oct.–May, by appointment only.

High Plains Heritage Center. In the old warehouse district of Machinery Row (where farm machinery businesses were located from the early 1900s until the 1980s), this county museum displays an eclectic collection of homesteading and ranching items. Look for a barbedwire collection, leather horse collars, hand plows, and other exhibits that explain why the region became known as the Golden Triangle of farming. | 422 2nd St. S | 406/452–3462 | www.highplainsheritage.org | $2 | Early Sept.–late May, Tues.–Fri. 10–5, weekends noon–5; late May–early Sept., weekdays 10–5, weekends noon–5.

Lewis and Clark National Historic Trail Interpretive Center. Trace the trail that the Lewis and Clark expedition traveled at the dawn of the 19th century in search of an overland route to the Pacific Ocean, and find out about their struggles and successes. This premier Lewis and Clark Trail information center, overlooking the Missouri River, exhibits tools, canoes, furs, leather clothing, and other materials used by travelers and Native Americans of the era. Films, tours, and costumed interpreters tell the stories of the expedition's members and their adventures. | 4201 Giant Springs Rd. | 406/727–8733 | www.fs.fed.us/r1/lewisclark/lcic.htm | $5 | Late May–Sept., daily 9–6; Oct.–late May, Tues.–Sat. 9–5, Sun. noon–5.

River's Edge Trail. This 25-mi path, about half of which is paved, skirts the Missouri River's banks and passes the waterfalls that intimidated the Corps of Discovery. Five dams control the river here, diminishing or obscuring some the famous falls, but you can still see Black Eagle and Rainbow falls. Free maps are available at the four parking areas and trailheads along River Drive. | River Dr. | 406/771–1265 | Donations accepted | Daily dawn–dusk.

✦ ON THE CALENDAR: June **Lewis and Clark Festival.** During the "week of rediscovery," Great Falls celebrates the Corps of Discovery's adventures here with presentations, ceremonies, and tours. Reenactors are in period dress, and food booths have samplings of what the expedition ate. | 406/452–5661.

June **Touch the Trail of Lewis and Clark.** Spend a day in buckskins and linen, with muskets and knives, and learn early survival skills like hide-tanning. The event, conducted with the Missouri River Canoe Company, takes place on the Missouri River at the Virgelle Mercantile. | 406/378–3110 or 800/426–2926.

HISTORIC LODGING
Collins Mansion B&B. With an ornate Victorian interior, spacious rooms, and private baths, the Collins Mansion, which is listed on the National Register of Historic Places, is a premier local lodging. The house was built in 1891 by banker T. C. Collins, who founded the local bank and waterworks and also became a state senator. The luxurious master suite has a fireplace. In-room data ports, laundry facilities; no smoking, no room TVs. | 1003 2nd Ave. NW, Great Falls 59401 | 406/452–6798 or 877/452–6798 | fax 406/452–6787 | www.collinsmansion. com | 4 rooms, 1 suite | $85–$100 | AE, MC, V | BP.

HELENA
▼▼▼

Helena is a city of Victorian mansions and abandoned gold mines, tucked into the foothills of the Rockies and surrounded by wilderness. Last Chance Gulch, the town's main street, was named for the gulch that eventually yielded more than $15 million in gold between 1864 and 1893. Helena was one of the seats of the territorial government and, ultimately, after a bribe-induced election in 1894, became the state's permanent capital. *Contact Helena Chamber of Commerce | 225 Cruse Ave., Suite A, 59601 | 406/442–4120 or 800/743–5362 | www. helenachamber.com. Downtown Helena | 121 N. Last Chance Gulch | 406/442–9869 | www. downtownhelena.com.*

Gates of the Mountains Boat Tours. On July 19, 1805, Lewis and Clark were paddling upstream in between towering rocks that really seemed "ready to tumble," as Lewis wrote. "I shall call them Gates of the Mountains," he continued. Today, you can take a 105-minute boat cruise to see these 1,200-ft limestone cliffs, plus ancient Native American pictographs. | Off I–15 at Exit 209, 17 mi north of Helena | 406/458–5241 | www.gatesofthemountains.com | $9.50 | June–Sept., weekends at 10, noon, 2, and 4; weekdays at 11 and 2. Additional cruises July–Aug.

Last Chance Train Tour. Hour-long tours begin in front of the Historical Society Museum and thread through Helena's historic neighborhood, filled with miners' mansions, on the west side to the site where four miners made the first gold discovery in Helena on Last Chance Gulch. | Roberts St. | 406/442–1023 or 888/432–1023 | www.lctours.com | $6.50 | May–June and Sept., daily 10–3; July–Aug., daily 10–6. Tours on the hr.

THE CORPS OF DISCOVERY IN MONTANA

On April 27, 1805, Lewis and Clark, with a party of 45 seasoned soldiers, scouts, and interpreters, paddled canoes and poled a keelboat up the Missouri River into what is now Montana. They followed the Missouri to its Montana headwaters—the confluence of the Jefferson, Madison and Gallatin rivers. After they reached the Continental Divide, Shoshone Indians helped them cross the Rockies into the present-day state of Idaho. On their return trip from the West Coast, Lewis and Clark split the expedition into two groups in Montana and explored several rivers, including the Yellowstone. All told, Lewis and Clark spent more than a quarter of their great expedition in Montana, where much of the land the intrepid explorers observed, mapped, and pondered in their timeless journals remains unchanged today.

Today you can retrace Lewis and Clark's footsteps; LEWIS AND CLARK TRAIL signs mark the expedition's route along portions of many state, U.S., and interstate highways in Montana. The best place to start is the Lewis and Clark National Historic Trail Interpretive Center in Great Falls, where the adventure unfolds before you. Missouri Headwaters State Park near Three Forks preserves the spot where the explorers traced the river to its birthplace. The Lolo Pass Visitor Center, on U.S. 12 at the Montana-Idaho border, has exhibits on the Lewis and Clark expedition and the Nez Perce Indians in this part of the state.

Another memorable way to relive Lewis and Clark's voyage of discovery is to take a boat tour on the "Mighty Mo." Several commercial operators offer tours at Gates of the Mountains, north of Helena off I–15, and also at the White Cliffs area of the Upper Missouri National Wild and Scenic River below Fort Benton. For those who prefer to go it alone, a canoe rental and shuttle service operates on the Missouri near Loma.

Montana Historical Society Museum. One of the most important collections of western artist Charlie Russell's work is on display here in the MacKay Gallery, and you can also see some beautiful black-and-white photographs of Yellowstone National Park taken by Frank Jay Haynes in the 1880s. Additionally, nearly 2,000 artifacts, documents, and more photographs tell the story of Montana history from the time of the first settlers to the present. Special family-friendly events in summer include programs on folk music, Native American culture, and cowboys. | 225 N. Roberts St. | 406/444–2694 or 800/243–9900 | www.montanahistoricalsociety. org | Donations accepted | Late May–early Sept., weekdays 8–6, weekends 9–5; early Sept.– late May, weekdays 8–5, Sat. 9–5.

Montana State Capitol. With a bright copper dome, the Greek Renaissance–style state capitol (built 1899–1902 and expanded in 1912) is hard to miss. Step inside to see the beautifully restored interior, filled with detailed woodwork and original paintings and murals. Charlie Russell's largest painting, a 12-by-25-ft mural of Lewis and Clark. Guided tours are offered on the hour in summer from 9 to 4. | 6th and Montana Sts. | 406/444–2511 or 800/243–9900 | www.montanacapitol.com | Free | Daily 8–5.

Reeder's Alley. Carefully restored, this part of old Helena has some distinctive shops, restaurants, a pioneer cabin, and a visitor center. Miners' quarters from the late 1800s line the narrow, winding street where brick mortar reveals fingerprints from the gold rush. | Near the south end of Last Chance Gulch and S. Park Ave. | Free | Daily.

Wells Fargo Bank. Step into the bank's lobby to see a collection of gold nuggets, including one worth $600,000, taken from area diggings in the late 1800s. | 350 N. Last Chance Gulch, at Lawrence St. | 406/447–2000 | Free | Weekdays 9–4.

HISTORIC LODGING

Sanders-Helena B&B. This three-story Victorian mansion was built in 1875 by Colonel Wilbur Sanders, the prosecuting attorney at some of the summary trials hosted by the Montana Vigilantes. The colonel's rock collection and some original furnishings are still in the home. Most rooms overlook the mountain-ringed downtown area. Breakfasts are a work of art: Grand Marnier French toast, orange soufflé, and gingerbread waffles. Refrigerator, cable TV, in-room VCRs; no smoking. | 328 N. Ewing St., Helena 59601 | 406/442–3309 | fax 406/443–2361 | www.sandersbb.com.com | 7 rooms | $100–$130 | AE, D, DC, MC, V | BP.

LIVINGSTON

▼▼▼

Evidence of ice-age natives from the Anzick Site near town dates back 13,000 years. Much later, William Clark reached the Yellowstone River here on July 16, 1806, and, with his party, killed a bull bison, made "mockersons," and caught fish, probably cutthroat trout. An 1870s trading post and ferry brought the first round of settlers, and the laying of Northern Pacific railroad tracks in 1882 secured Livingston's future. *Contact Livingston Area Chamber of Commerce | 303 E. Park St., 59047 | 406/222–0850 | www.yellowstone-chamber.com.*

Livingston Depot Center in the Northern Pacific Depot. The 1902 brick Northern Pacific depot is an Italian villa–style structure with mosaic trim, a terrazzo floor, and wrought-iron ticket windows. It now holds a museum with displays on western and railroad history. | 200 W. Park St. | 406/222–2300 | www.livingstonmuseums.org | $3 | Mid-May–Oct., Mon.–Sat. 9–5, Sun. 1–5.

Yellowstone Gateway Museum of Park County. Occupying a turn-of-the-20th-century schoolhouse, this museum has a remarkable display on the Anzick Site, the oldest known Native American burial site in North America. Other exhibits include early mining, farm, and railroad tools; Native American arrowheads; antique furniture; and early photographs and documents. | 118 W. Chinook St. | 406/222–4184 | www.livingstonmuseums.org | $3 | June–early Sept., daily 10–5:30; early Sept.–May, by appointment only.

✦ ON THE CALENDAR: July **Western Days and Roundup Parade.** The city-wide western celebration includes one of the state's largest parades, a PRCA rodeo, fireworks, arts and crafts, music, and dance, all at the fairgrounds. | 406/222–0850.

HISTORIC LODGING

Chico Hot Springs Resort. During the gold rush of the 1860s, a miner noted, "I washed my dirty duds" in the hot springs near the Yellowstone River. Soon a series of bath houses was established, attracting people to the so-called medicinal waters, and, in 1900, the Chico Warm Springs Hotel opened. Famous folk like painter Charlie Russell came to soak in the 104°F–107°F pools and dine and dance in the chic hotel. Today the resort is surrounded by the large, modernized outdoor pools. Luxury cottages open out to 10,920-ft Emigrant Peak and the Absoroka-Beartooth Wilderness beyond. Pray is 23 mi south of Livingston. Restaurant, pizzeria, snack bar, room service, in-room data ports, some in-room hot tubs, some kitchens, some refrigerators, pools, massage, spa, fishing, hiking, horseback riding, cross-country skiing, bars, piano, shop, business services, convention center, airstrip, some pets allowed; no-smoking rooms, no room TVs. | 1 Old Chico Rd., Pray 59065 | 406/333–4933 or 800/468–9232 | fax 406/333–4694 | www.chicohotsprings.com | 82 rooms, 4 suites, 16 cottages | $45–$315 | AE, D, MC, V.

The Murray Hotel. This turn-of-the-20th-century town institution is known for attracting silver-tipped cowboy boots, fly-fishing waders, and the sparkling heels of Hollywood players.

Historic photos and taxidermied game animals decorate the lobby and surround the antique elevator, which is still in use. In-room data ports, cable TV, outdoor hot tub, fishing, bar; no-smoking floors. | 201 W. Park St., 59047 | 406/222–1350 | fax 406/222–2752 | www. murrayhotel.com | 30 rooms | $69–$108 | AE, D, MC, V.

LOLO
▼▼

Native Americans frequented the natural hot springs in the area and created pools with stones, as noted by Lewis and Clark. It's here that Meriwether Lewis wrote, "The weather appearing settled and fair I determined to halt the next day, rest our horses and take some celestial observations. We called the creek Travellers Rest." The Nez Perce assisted the expedition, but in 1877 they were pursued by General Oliver Howard's army on what's now called the Nez Perce National Historic Trail, past Fort Fizzle in Lolo Canyon. *Contact Bitterroot Valley Chamber of Commerce | 105 E. Main St., Hamilton 59840 | 406/363–2400 | www.bvchamber.com.*

Lolo Pass Visitor Center. At 5,260 ft elevation in the formidable Bitterroot Mountains, Lolo Pass crosses the Continental Divide. Lewis and Clark followed a Nez Perce trail through this snow-clogged pass in September 1805 during their westward trip, and again in June 1806 on their homeward journey. The visitor center has intrepretive exhibits, such as maps and dioramas, on the Lewis and Clark expedition, the Nez Perce National Historic Trail, and other local history. | U.S. 12 at the Idaho–Montana border, 28 mi west of Lolo | Powell Ranger Station, 208/942–3113 | www.fs.fed.us/r1/clearwater | $5 per vehicle | June–Sept., daily 8–5; Dec.–Mar., Fri.–Sun. 10–6; Apr.–May and Oct.–Nov., hours vary.

Travelers Rest National Historic Landmark and State Park. This is the site of Lewis and Clark's 1805 camp after they found the Bitterroot Range beyond Lemhi Pass impenetrable. They camped here again in 1806 when returning from the Pacific. | 6550 Mormon Creek Rd., ¼ mi west of U.S. 93 | 406/273–4253 | www.travelersrest.org | Free | Weekdays 11–4, weekends 8–5.

STEVENSVILLE
▼▼

Originally inhabited by the Salish tribe, Stevensville was settled by Jesuit missionaries in 1840 and today is known as the first permanent white community in Montana. Similarly, St. Mary's Mission was the first permanent building raised by white immigrants. In 1850, the missionaries sold the building to Major John Owen, who converted it to a trading post. Trappers and traders trickled into the area, and records show that by 1872 there were close to 500 residents in what would become Ravalli County. Jesuit Father Anthony Ravalli came to Stevensville in 1866 to reopen St. Mary's Mission at a different site not far from Fort Owen. Ravalli County and Stevensville continued to be settled by traders, homesteaders, and miners eager to reap the benefits of the fertile Bitterroot Valley. *Contact Bitterroot Valley Chamber of Commerce | 105 E. Main St., Hamilton 59840 | 406/363–2400 | www.bvchamber.com.*

Fort Owen State Park. Fort Owen was built in 1850 by Major John Owen as a trading post for grain and livestock. A store on the property provided supplies to nearby gold-mining camps and settlers. You can take a self-guided tour of the barracks and a few other preserved buildings. A small museum displays period furnishings and artifacts.| Rte. 269, ½ mi east of Stevensville Junction off U.S. 93 | 406/542–5531 | www.fwp.state.mt.us | Donations accepted | Daily 8 AM–10 PM.

St. Mary's Mission. St. Mary's Mission was established in 1841 by the Jesuit Father Pierre DeSmet as the first in the Northwest. It was closed in 1850, and the building you can visit today was built in 1866 by the Italian Jesuit Father Anthony Ravalli. The landmark memorializes the relationship between the Jesuits, then called "blackrobes," and the Flathead tribe. There is a small museum and a cemetery. | West end of 4th St. | 406/777–5734 | www.saintmarysmission.org | $3 | Daily 10–4.

✦ ON THE CALENDAR: July **Clark's Days.** Commemorating William Clark's passage through the Bitterroot Valley, the three-day event is filled with reenactments, an art show, live music, and an auction. | 406/777–3773.

THREE FORKS
▼▼

Centuries of travelers used the Missouri River and its tributaries, the Gallatin, Madison, and Jefferson rivers, which merge 3 mi north of town. Lewis and Clark explored the forks July 25–30, 1805, looking for the one that could take them through the Continental Divide. Sacagawea showed the explorers where her people's camp had been when Hidatsa braves captured her five years earlier. It was also here, in 1808, that Corps of Discovery veteran John Colter met 800 Blackfeet who killed his partner John Potts, then stripped Colter naked and ordered him to run for his life. He ran 200 mi east to Manuel Lisa's trapping post. The town is the surviving one of four that sprouted up at the headwaters of the Missouri River around 1862. *Contact Three Forks Chamber of Commerce | Box 1103, 59752 | 406/285–4753 | www. threeforksmontana.com.*

Headwaters Heritage Museum. A gem off the well-traveled highway, the museum contains thousands of local historical artifacts. The largest brown trout caught in Montana is displayed, as well as a small anvil, all that is left of a trading post, Fort Three Forks, established in 1810. | Main and Cedar Sts. | 406/285–4778 | www.threeforksmontana.com/history | Free | June–mid-Sept., Mon.–Sat. 9–5, Sun. 1–5, or by appointment.

Lewis and Clark Caverns. Opened to the public in 1901, this is one of Montana's first tourist attractions, and its oldest state park (established 1937). Native tribes in the region had known of the cave for many years, but despite the name Lewis and Clark never came across it. The first white person to stumble upon the caverns was a hunter named Tom Williams. Williams brought it to the attention of Dan Morrison, a local miner, who built wooden stairs inside the cave and opened it up for visitors. It's no wonder intrepid turn-of-the-20th-century travelers made their way here: the caverns offer some of the most beautiful underground landscape in the nation. Two-hour tours lead through narrow passages and vaulted chambers past colorful, intriguingly varied limestone formations. The temperature in the cave stays in the 50s year-round; jackets and rubber-sole shoes are recommended. The hike to the cavern entrance is mildly strenuous. The cave trip involves lots of bending, stooping, and some crawling. Bring a flashlight, even though each cave area is lit during the tour. | Rte. 2, 19 mi west of Three Forks | 406/287–3541 | www.fwp.state.mt.us | $8 | June–early Sept., daily 9–6:30; May and early Sept.–end of Sept., daily 9–4:30.

Missouri Headwaters State Park. The Madison, Jefferson, and Gallatin rivers merge to become the mighty Missouri River at a National Historic Landmark in this park. The Missouri is the country's second-longest river, at 2,565 mi. Lewis and Clark named the three forks after Secretary of the Treasury Albert Gallatin, Secretary of State James Madison, and President Thomas Jefferson. The park has historical exhibits, interpretive signs, picnic sites, hiking trails (watch out for rattlesnakes), and camping. | Trident Rd., 3 mi northeast of Three Forks on I–90, exit at the Three Forks off-ramp, then go east on Rte. 205 and 3 mi north on Rte. 286, Three

Forks | 406/994–4042 | www.fwp.state.mt.us | $4 per vehicle (includes admission to Madison Buffalo Jump) | Daily dawn–dusk.

✦ ON THE CALENDAR: July **Lewis and Clark Encampment.** Break out the buckskins for this late-July reenactment of the Corps of Discovery's adventures at the Three Forks of the Missouri River. A Children's Festival of Discovery includes teepees and demonstrations. | 406/285–4753.

Sept. **John Colter Run.** This race commemorates John Colter's famous naked 1809 escape from the Blackfeet Indians. Today's runners are required to wear clothes. | 406/994–6934.

HISTORIC DINING AND LODGING

Historic Headwaters Restaurant. Contemporary. Now restored to its original appearance, the 1908 brick restaurant originally served railroad tourists on their way to see Yellowstone National Park. The smoke-free dining area now includes a summertime dining patio surrounded by native plants, flowers, and a stream where you can eat better than Lewis and Clark: try buffalo chorizo enchiladas with black-bean sauce and smoked corn salsa, from the owner-chef, a graduate of the Culinary Institute of America. | 105 S. Main St. | 406/285–4511 | Closed Mon.–Tues. | $8–$22 | MC, V.

Sacajawea Hotel. Built in 1910 by the Old Milwaukee Railroad, the original portion of the hotel was rolled on logs to higher ground where it became a railroad hotel for travelers heading to Yellowstone National Park. The lofty lobby and cozy rooms retain the 19th-century style, and the front porch has rockers where you can relax with a book or watch the sunset. Restaurant, in-room data ports, cable TV, fishing, bar, piano, meeting rooms, free parking, some pets allowed (fee); no smoking. | 5 N. Main St. 59752 | 406/285–6515 or 888/722–2529 | fax 406/285–4210 | www.sacajaweahotel.com | 30 rooms, 1 suite | $58–$90 | AE, D, DC, MC, V | CP.

NEBRASKA

———◆———

The first citizens of Nebraska were the Pawnee, Omaha, Osage, Ponca, Otoe, Missouria, Arapaho, Cheyenne, Comanche, and Lakota (also called Nebraska) Indians. The Spanish made the earliest documented explorations by Europeans, in 1714 and 1720, but it was French explorers and fur traders who made the earliest white claims to the region. The United States acquired Nebraska as part of the 1803 Louisiana Purchase. In 1804, Meriwether Lewis and William Clark's Corps of Discovery made their journey up the Missouri River and had their first council with Native Americans in the vicinity of today's Omaha.

For many pioneers dreaming of prosperity and freedom in the Great American West, the journey began in Nebraska. Three great trails—the Oregon, the California, and the Mormon— all crossed this state, passing famous natural trail markers: Scotts Bluff, Chimney Rock, and Courthouse Rocks. Much of Nebraska's terrain was lush and welcoming, but other parts were harsh and unforgiving (though not as difficult as the land the pioneers would cross in Wyoming, Utah, and beyond). By following the Platte River much of the way through Nebraska, pioneers had a constant source of water and relatively easy ground to cover. However, the farther west they traveled, the scarcer water and trees became, and the rockier and more diffi- cult to traverse became the land. Nebraska was a land to be endured on the route to pros- perity, a stretch of the "Great American Desert," as explorer Stephen Long so ungallantly named the Great Plains. Nebraska was a testing ground, preparing the pioneers for what lay ahead, and it did many pioneers in. A cemetery filled with more than 700 Mormons lies on the banks of the Missouri River near Omaha, and hundreds of trail markers identify the remains of others who could not withstand the perils Nebraska presented.

The Homestead Act of 1862 changed the way some pioneers saw Nebraska. Recogniz- ing that the region was not a great desert but in fact possessed some of the richest, most productive soil in the world, white settlers began claiming their dream, 160 acres at a time. In the midst of all of this movement, another migration was taking place. Nebraska entered the Union as a "free" state in 1867, and fugitive slaves from the south began to find their way here. Several spots in eastern Nebraska became important stops along the Underground Railroad.

Nebraska still has a strong Native American presence, and there are other communities rich in Irish, Danish, German, and Czech heritage. Great Nebraskans such as authors Willa Cather and Mari Sandoz, oil painter Gene Ronca, and legendary showman Buffalo Bill helped to create the image of the Old West. Folklore and legends about such people as Calamity Jane, Wild Bill Hickock, Crazy Horse, and Dull Knife add some spice to the roster of famous characters. Nebraska is still a land of cowboys and Indians. Cowboys on horseback ride the range in much of the panhandle and northern Nebraska, and rodeos dominate the summer culture of many communities. Native Americans, including Lakota, Pawnee, and Ponca, live on and off reservations throughout the state, keeping their heritage alive in small but vibrant pockets. Nebraskans continue to struggle with the natural elements of weather, land, and wildlife, to maintain their way of life as they have for hundreds of years.

Lewis and Clark's Nebraska Journey

A DRIVING TOUR FROM BROWNVILLE TO CROFTON

▼▼▼

Distance: 404 mi   **Time:** 3 days
Breaks: Nebraska City and Omaha are good choices for a night's stay.

This tour takes you along the Missouri River, following much of the same route taken by the Corps of Discovery in 1804. You will visit small river towns, agriculture communities, and Omaha, the state's largest metropolitan area.

Begin in **Brownville,** one of the first towns established in Nebraska Territory. Spend the morning walking through the historic district to see the many homes dating to the 1860s and '70s and visiting local businesses like Brownville Mills and the Whiskey Run Creek Vineyard & Winery, which will give you a sense of what Brownville was like in wilder times. Leave Brownville around noon, heading west on U.S. 136 to Auburn. Along the way, you will pass the Half-Breed Tract Historical Marker, which identifies land set aside for the children of white trappers and Native American women. At Auburn, turn north on U.S. 75 toward **Nebraska City,** home of Arbor Day founder J. Sterling Morton. Spend the afternoon at the Arbor Lodge State Historical Park, where you can tour Morton's home and original tree farm, saving an hour to visit the Mayhew Cabin and Historical Village. This cabin was a vital link on the Underground Railroad, whose history is told in a tour of the cabin, root cellar, and property.

On your second day, drive north on U.S. 75 to **Bellevue,** the site of a fur-trading post established in the early 1800s. A walking tour of downtown is well worth the 90 minutes. Stop in to see cowboy hats made the old-fashioned way at the Great Plains Hat Company. Leaving Bellevue, head north on U.S. 75 to **Omaha.** This is where more than 4,000 Mormons camped and 700 died, during the winter of 1846–47 en route to Utah. The visitor center at Winter Quarters doucuments the plight of the Mormons on that journey. A visit to old Fort Omaha and the General Crook House will give you an inside look at military life in the 1870s. You can also learn about the trial of Standing Bear, which resulted in the granting of the first legal rights for Native Americans. Take a minute for an old-fashioned phosphate soda at the Durham Western Heritage Museum, which has hours worth of displays on overland travel in the 1800s.

On day three, drive north from Omaha on U.S. 75 for a visit to Fort Calhoun in Fort Atkinson State Historical Park. After 2½ months on the trail, this is where Lewis and Clark held their first council with Native Americans on August 2, 1804. As you exit the park, continue north on U.S. 75 to **Blair,** then turn east on U.S. 30 and continue for 3 mi to the Desoto

NEBRASKA TIME LINE

1675 French traders first visit Pawnee villages along the Republican River.

1720 French traders and Pawnee allies attack the Spanish explorer Pedro de Villasur and his troops near Columbus.

1730 The Kiowa migrate into northwestern Nebraska, eventually becoming the Kiowa Apaches.

1795 James Mackay opens the first fur-trading post in Nebraska, near Bellevue.

1803 The Sioux move into northwestern Nebraska, forcing the Kiowa Apaches, the Crow, and the Cheyenne out of the region.

1803 On April 30, the United States acquires Nebraska through the Louisiana Purchase.

1804 Meriwether Lewis and William Clark explore the Louisiana Territory, including part of Nebraska.

1806 Zebulon Pike crosses southeast Nebraska en route to Santa Fe, New Mexico, meeting with the Pawnee near Guide Rock.

1812 Manuel Lisa opens a fur-trading post at Bellevue, later known as Fort Lisa.

1815 Omaha Indians negotiate their first treaty with the U.S. government at Portage des Sioux.

1819 The U.S. Army establishes Cantonment Missouri (later Fort Atkinson) as its first western outpost.

1819–20 Major Stephen Long launches his exploration of the western country and reaches Nebraska in the steamboat *Western Engineer.* He calls the area "The Great American Desert."

1828 Hiram Scott dies near the bluff that now bears his name.

1833 The Pawnee enter their first treaty with the U.S. government.

1837 Alfred Jacob Miller sketches Chimney Rock, probably the first artist to do so.

1841 The Bidwell–Bartleson wagon train crosses the plains, carrying the first emigrants on the Oregon Trail.

1843 The Oregon migration begins; during the next 30 years more than 400,000 emigrants cross Nebraska en route to Oregon and California.

1846 Brigham Young and the first of the Mormon emigrants cross the Missouri River and establish winter quarters at Florence.

1847 Mormon migration from winter quarters to Utah begins.

1849 Thousands of gold seekers follow the California Trail, crossing Nebraska.

1854 On March 15–16, in exchange for two reservations, the Otoe, Missouria, and Omaha cede lands west of the Missouri River, opening most of eastern Nebraska to white settlement. On May 30, Congress approves the Kansas-Nebraska Act, establishing Nebraska Territory.

1857 On September 24, Pawnees sign away the last of their land in Nebraska in the Table Rock Treaty in Nebraska City; they move to a reservation at Genoa.

1860–61 William Russell, Alexander Majors, and William Waddell of Nebraska City start the Pony Express.

1862 President Abraham Lincoln signs the Pacific Railway Act, leading to construction of the Union Pacific Railroad across Nebraska.

1862 Congress approves the Homestead Act to encourage pioneers to settle the West. The first homestead claimed under the act is that of Daniel Freeman, near Beatrice.

1867 On March 1, Nebraska becomes a state; Lincoln becomes its permanent capital.

1869 The first Texas cattle ship to market on the Union Pacific Railroad from Schuyler, Nebraska.

1869 The University of Nebraska gets its charter. It opens in Lincoln in 1871.

1872 The Nebraska State Department of Agriculture approves Arbor Day as a holiday.

1877 On September 5, a sentry at Fort Robinson stabs and kills Lakota Chief Crazy Horse.

1878 On November 27, homesteaders Ami Ketchum and Luther Mitchell shoot and kill cattleman Bob Olive. Olive's brother Print leads a vigilante group that hangs Mitchell and Ketchum. The homesteaders' bodies are burned, and Nebraska becomes known as the "Man Burner State."

1880S Omaha becomes a center of livestock shipping and processing.

1891 William F. Cody organizes his first Wild West Show in Columbus, Nebraska.

1896 William Jennings Bryan of Lincoln, "The Great Commoner," is the Democratic candidate for U.S. President.

1902 President Theodore Roosevelt creates the Nebraska National Forest, a completely man-made preserve.

National Wildlife Refuge. The cargo from a steamboat that sank here in 1865 is on display at the visitor center. Return to U.S. 75 and head north until you reach U.S. 20. Go west 5 mi, and then turn north on Route 12. As you drive, you'll be able to see the Missouri River; this area is considered to be the least disturbed and most genuine in appearance to what Lewis and Clark experienced. Route 12 turns west toward **Crofton,** where Lewis and Clark eventually crossed the Missouri River into South Dakota. A historical marker 3 mi west of Newcastle marks the location. At the Lewis and Clark Lake Visitor Center exhibits illustrate the progress of the expedition through this region. Five miles farther, the Corps of Discovery Welcome Center has additional information and hosts numerous reenactments of the period.

Across the Panhandle

A DRIVING TOUR FROM OGALLALA TO SCOTTSBLUFF AND CHADRON

▼▼

Distance: 350 mi   **Time:** 3 days
Breaks: Overnight in the Scottsbluff area and the Chadron-Crawford area.

This drive explores the Nebraska Panhandle, a region Native American conflict, fur-trading posts, and the Oregon, California, and Mormon trails. The land is rugged with outcrops that mark the beginning of Pine Ridge country.

Start in **Ogallala,** a community still known as the cowboy capital of Nebraska. Visit Boot Hill Cemetery to see where some of the cowboys that took part in the Texas cattle drives of the late 1800s ended up. As you leave Ogallala, take U.S. 26 west about 30 mi to Ash Hollow State Historical Park. Here you can see the ruts where travelers on their way west locked the wheels on their wagons, skidding to the bottom of Windlass Hill. Animal bones and fossils dating back 6,000 years are also on display. When you've finished exploring Ash Hollow, drive west on U.S. 26 about 75 mi to Courthouse and Jail Rocks, near Bridgeport. As the wagon trains headed west, they guided themselves by natural landmarks, including these rocks. More

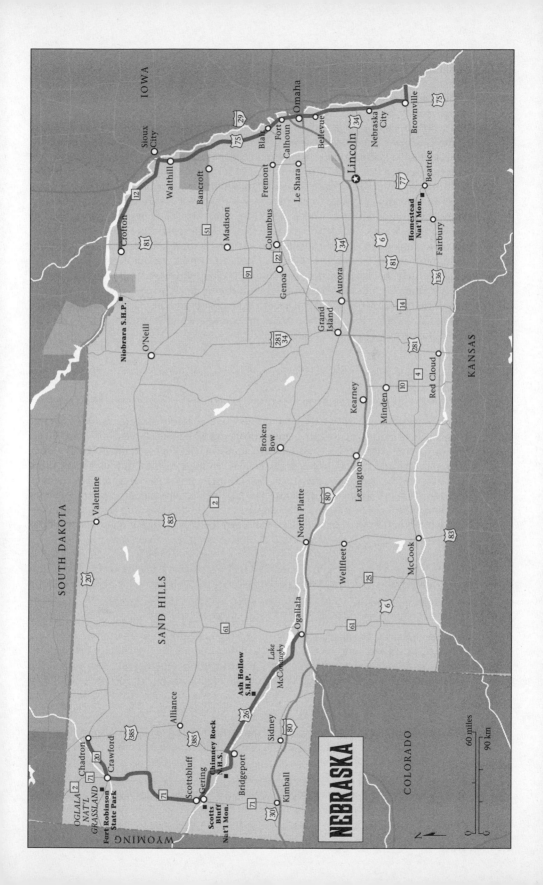

IOWA

SIOUX CITY

29

75

Walthill

Bancroft

12

Crofton

81

51

Madison

Blair
Fort
Calhoun

Omaha

Bellevue

75

Nebraska
City

34

Lincoln

77

Beatrice

Brownville

75

Fremont

Le Shara

Columbus

22

Genoa

91

Homestead
Nat'l Mon.

Fairbury

6

34

81

136

Niobrara S.H.P.

O'Neill

281
34

Grand
Island

Aurora

14

281

Red Cloud

KANSAS

4

Kearney

Minden

10

Valentine

Broken
Bow

2

Lexington

80

North Platte

Wellfleet

McCook

83

83

SAND HILLS

61

Ogallala

61

6

25

SOUTH DAKOTA

20

Lake
McConaughy

Ash Hollow
S.H.P.

26

Sidney

80

Alliance

385

385

Chimney Rock
N.H.S.

Bridgeport

Kimball

Chadron

20

Crawford

Scottsbluff

Gering

71

71

30

OGLALA
NAT'L
GRASSLAND

2

71

Fort Robinson
State Park

Scotts
Bluff
Nat'l Mon.

COLORADO

WYOMING

NEBRASKA

60 miles

90 km

0

noted are the rocks 20 mi farther west, near **Scotsbluff,** at what is now Chimney Rock National Historic Site. The visitor center there has several interactive exhibits on the Oregon Trail and the geology of the area, and you can get up close to Chimney Rock on a three-hour Oregon Trail Wagon Train tour. See the North Platte Valley Museum and Western History Archives, with the world's largest collection of Oregon Trail artifacts. Two other natural Oregon Trail markers in the Scottsbluff area are Robidoux Pass and the promontory at Scotts Bluff National Monument. Enter the 3,000-acre preserve of the monument at the intersection of Routes 71 and 92, and drive to the top of what pioneers called "the lighthouse of the plains."

On your second day, travel north on Route 71 until it joins Route 2 heading into **Crawford.** This small community is the center of an area inhabited by Native Americans as far back as 10,000 years ago. More recent history is documented at Fort Robinson State Park, 3 mi west of Crawford. This was where Chief Crazy Horse was killed in captivity, the Buffalo Soldiers prepared for action at Wounded Knee, and 64 Cheyenne were killed attempting to flee in the winter of 1869, during what is now known as the Cheyenne Outbreak. Barracks remain much as they were in the 1870s, and you can spend the night if you like.

On day three, head east from Crawford on U.S. 20 to **Chadron** and the Museum of the Fur Trade, on the site of a former fur-trading post. There's much to see and learn on a historic walking tour of the town or a visit to Chadron State College and the Mari Sandoz High Plains Heritage Center. You can spend the night at the barracks at Fort Robinson or at the historic Olde Main Street Inn.

BEATRICE

▼▼

More than 300,000 settlers following the Oregon Trail crossed the Missouri River here and continued west along various routes. One of those paths, originally an Otoe-Omaha Indian Trail, was known as the DeRoin Trail. It passed along what is now Court Street, a major thoroughfare in Beatrice, and across the Big Blue River, on the rock-bottom ford known as the Scott Street ford. Most pioneers passed through Beatrice without stopping, until the passage of the 1862 Homestead Act. On January 1, 1863, Daniel Freeman obtained the title to land just west of Beatrice. His homestead is believed to be the first recorded claim in the West and is now part of Homestead National Monument. *Contact Beatrice Visitors Bureau | 226 S. 6th St., 68310 | 402/223–2338 or 800/755–7745 | www.beatricene.com/visitor.*

Filley Stone Barn. When a plague of grasshoppers threatened the livelihood of area farmers in 1874, Elijah Filley persuaded the farmers not to leave the area by hiring them to build this three-story barn, the largest limestone barn in Nebraska. | 13282 E. Scott Rd., 10 mi east of Beatrice on U.S. 136 | 402/228–1679 | Free | During special events.

Homestead National Monument. By granting 160 acres of land to any household head who would live, work, and build on them, the Homestead Act of 1862 encouraged pioneers to travel and settle in the western United States. This monument and museum, located on what was believed to be the first homestead, includes an original cabin, school, and undisturbed prairie. | 8523 W. Rte. 4 | 402/223–3514 | www.nps.gov/home | Free | Late May–early Sept., daily 8:30–5; early Sept.–late May, weekdays 8:30–5, weekends 9–5.

✦ ON THE CALENDAR: May **Heartland Storytelling Festival.** Regionally and nationally known artists gather at the Homestead National Monument to tell tales of the Midwest and its pioneers. | 402/223–3514 or 402/223–2338.

June **Annual Homestead Days.** Learn to make lye soap, sheer a sheep, tan a hide, or track down family history. The festival also includes musicals, horseshoes, and an old-time baseball game. | 402/223–3514.

HISTORIC DINING

The Black Crow. American. This popular restaurant, in a building that dates to 1888, is downstairs from what once was a brothel. Today the menu includes pheasant, quail, duck, and other types of game hunted in Gage County for years. | 405 Court St. | 402/228–7200 | Closed Mon.–Tues. | $15–$20 | D, MC, V.

BELLEVUE
▼▼▼

Early on, Bellevue's strategic position near the juncture of the Platte and Missouri rivers made it an important site for early traders and explorers. In 1795, James Mackay, working for Spain, established a fur trading post in the area. When Meriwether Lewis and William Clark hoisted an American flag in the vicinity on July 23, 1804, it was likely the first time the United States banner had ever flown over Nebraska. Bellevue has some of the state's oldest buildings, which you can see on a guided or self-guided tour. *Contact Bellevue Tourism Office | 204 W. Mission Ave., 68005 | 402/291–8565 | www.bellevue.net. Sarpy County Tourism. | 1210 Golden Gate Dr., No. 1129, Papillion 68046 | 402/593–4354 | www.gosarpy.com. Sarpy County Historical Society | 2402 Clay St., 68005 | 402/292–1880.*

Great Plains Hat Company. More than 100 years ago cowboys came here to get fitted for their hats, and you can do the same today. Cowboy hats and fedoras, among other styles, are made on original equipment from the 19th century. A visit with owner Herb Gindulis, who is also a history professor, is like talking with the cowboys who wore these hats 150 years ago. | 2245 Franklin St. | 402/292–6018 | Weekdays 5 PM–7 PM.

Olde Towne Bellevue. Bellevue's small historic district is comprised of some of Nebraska's oldest buildings, including a bank, a log cabin, and an 1850 Presbyterian church. Sign up for a 90-minute guided tour through the buildings, cemetery, and the state's oldest train depot. You also can pick up a map of the historic sites at the tourism office, but you can't see the interiors of the buildings unless you're on the tour. | Between Main and Madison Sts., south of 19th St. and north of 25th St. | 402/293–3080 | Free | Daily.

Sarpy County Historical Museum. The large collection of pioneer dolls here draws the most people, but you can also see old traps, knives, buffalo-hide clothing, and other artifacts that reflect the early history of Sarpy County, home to some of the state's first settlements. | 2402 Clay St. | 402/292–1880 | $2 | Tues.–Sun. 9–4.

✦ ON THE CALENDAR: May **Native American Festival.** Native American performers and musicians stage concerts at the Fontenelle Forest Learning Center the first or second weekend of the month. | 402/731–3140.

BLAIR
▼▼▼

History in Blair is tied to Dana College, started in 1884 as a seminary by the Danish Evangelical Lutheran Church. Oglala Sioux holy man Black Elk, immortalized by the poet John Neihardt, was an important figure in the area. Not far away is Fort Atkinson, a stopover for Lewis and Clark that later became the first American military fort in present-day Nebraska. *Contact Blair Area Chamber of Commerce | 1526 Washington St., 68008 | 402/533–4455 | www. blairchamber.org.*

DeSoto National Wildlife Refuge. The visitor center, 3 mi east of Blair, has more than 200,000 well-preserved items recovered from the steamboat *Bertrand,* which sank in the region in 1865. The almost 8,000 acres of protected land in Nebraska and Iowa are home to thousands of species of wildlife, including migrating waterfowl, and especially snow geese. | Off U.S. 30, 3 mi east of Blair | 712/642–4121 | www.midest.fws.gov | $3 per vehicle | Daily.

Fort Atkinson State Historical Park. Fort Atkinson was built in 1820 close to the site, 10 mi south of Blair, where Lewis and Clark met with Otoe and Missouria chiefs in 1804. A re-created fort with barracks and log walls illustrates what life was like for the 1,000 men billeted there. | 7th and Madison, Fort Calhoun | 402/468–5611 | www.ngpc.state.ne.us/parks | $2.50 | Grounds daily 8–7; visitor center late May–early Sept., daily 9–5.

✦ ON THE CALENDAR: May–Oct. **Living History Days.** The first weekend of each month, Fort Atkinson re-creates life at the fort during the 1820s with costumed infantrymen, trades- men, laundresses, and cooks. | 402/468–5611.

BROWNVILLE
▼▼

In 1854, Richard Brown crossed the Missouri River and built a cabin in the newly formed Nebraska Territory. Two years later, Brownville was incorporated and soon became an impor- tant river town and a jumping-off point for travelers headed west. Thirty-two of the origi- nal buildings remain and are a part of a National Historic District. *Contact Brownville Historical Society | Box 1, 68321 | 402/825–4131 or 800/305–7990 | www.ci.brownville.ne.us.*

Brownville Historic District. The buildings and homes in the district might best be described as antebellum with a midwestern sensibility. Many of the structures are red brick, with a spare, squared-off shape, yet some ornately carved details and the size of the lots around them bear testimony to the prosperity of their owners and the riverside community in the mid-1800s. | Along Main St. | 402/825–6001 | Free; $1–$3 at some homes | June–early Sept., daily 10–5; early Sept.–May, weekends 10–5.

Brownville Mills. In the 1860s, this building was the Lone Tree Saloon, a popular stop for Jesse James and his gang as they avoided pursuit across the Missouri River. Over the years, the property has operated as a grocery store, gambling hall, opera house, and, since the 1950s, a mill where you can purchase organically grown wheat, rye, and buckskin flour made the old-fashioned way. Stop by to see the store and talk to owner Harold Davis, an active member of the historical society who will do his best to answer questions about the area. | 116 Main St. | 402/825–4131 | www.brownvillemills.com | Free | Mon.–Sat. 9–5, Sun. 1–5.

Half-Breed Tract Historical Marker. This politically incorrect marker identifies the boundaries of a tract of land put aside in 1836 by the federal government for children born of white men and Native American women (primarily Otoe, Iowa, Omaha, and Santee Sioux tribes) of the region. | 9 mi west of Brownville on U.S. 136.

Whiskey Run Creek Vineyard & Winery. More than 3,000 barrels of beer a year were produced by a brewery here in the 1860s. The brewery closed in the 1920s, probably due to prohibi- tion laws, but reopened as a winery in 2002. Weekends, when the winery often holds special events, are the best time to visit the grounds. Ask for a tour of the original 1866 brewery caves and the turn-of-the-20th-century barn. | 702 Main St. | 402/825–4601 | www. whiskeyruncreek.com | Free | Daily 10–5.

✦ ON THE CALENDAR: Oct. **Old Time Autumn.** Broom makers, blacksmiths, and fiddlers fill the downtown streets demonstrating life in Brownville in its heyday. | 402/825–4131 or 800/305–7990.

CHADRON

▼▼

Chadron was named for Louis Chartran, a fur trapper who ran a trading post on Bordeaux Creek. The area was traditionally used by the Lakota, Cheyenne, and Kiowa tribes. When a railroad station was built a few miles to the south, many of the buildings were moved from their original location on the banks of Bordeaux Creek to the town's current site. *Contact Chadron Chamber of Commerce | 706 W. 3rd St., 69337 | 308/432–4401 or 800/603–2937 | www.chadron. com. Dawes County Travel Board | Box 746, Chadron 69337 | 308/432–4401 or 800/603–2937.*

Chadron State College/Mari Sandoz High Plains Heritage Center. This former campus library honors area native Mari Sandoz, who wrote *Cheyenne Autumn, Old Jules, Crazy Horse,* and other books about the history and people of western Nebraska. Many original manuscripts and artifacts from the Sandoz home are part of the exhibits. | 1000 Main St. | 308/432–6066 | www.csc.edu | Free | Weekdays 9–4.

Chadron Historic Walking Tour. See Victorian homes, municipal buildings, theaters, and the 1892 Blaine Hotel on this self-guided 2½-mi tour of downtown. Pick up maps at the chamber office. | 706 W. 3rd St. | 308/432–4401 or 800/603–2937 | Free.

Dawes County Historical Museum. Memorabilia from the 1,000 Mile Horse Race, from Chadron to Chicago, are among the fun exhibits here. You'll also see a log house and barn, a 1890s schoolhouse, a pioneer church, and a train caboose. | 341 Country Club Rd., 3 mi south of Chadron | 308/432–4999 | www.chadron.com/dchm | Free | Mon.–Sat. 10–4, Sun. 1–5.

Museum of the Fur Trade. On the land where James Bordeaux ran his trading post, this museum and reconstructed outpost display trade goods, weapons, furs, and other items relating to the history of fur trading in North America. Furs trapped along the White River are for sale. | 6321 E. U.S. 20 | 308/432–3843 | www.furtrade.org | $2.50 | Late May–Sept., daily 8–5; Oct.– late May, by appointment only.

✦ ON THE CALENDAR: July **Buckskinners Camp.** Held at a campground in the Pine Ridge National Forest, this event brings together competitors for muzzle-loader contests and for tomahawk- and knife-throwing. Participants dress in period costume and demonstrate crafts and skills from the late 1800s. | 800/603–2937.

HISTORIC LODGING

Olde Main Street Inn. Built in 1890, the hotel served as headquarters for General Nelson Miles during the Wounded Knee Massacre in late December 1890. Four generations of the Goetzinger family have operated the inn, which has a fireplace and a working 1890s well pump in the lobby. Dining room, cable TV, lounge. | 115 Main St., 69337 | 308/432–3380 | www. chadron.com/oldemain | 6 rooms, 3 suites | $50–$72 | AE, D, MC, V | BP.

COLUMBUS

▼▼

In 1720, Spanish general Don Pedro de Villasur led an army of Spanish soldiers, Pueblo allies, and Apache scouts from Santa Fe, New Mexico, to Nebraska to discover the extent of French forces near the Missouri River. When the army reached the area near the confluence of the Loup and Platte rivers on August 14, Pawnee warriors attacked them at dawn, killing almost all of the soldiers, including Villasur. The conflict was the biggest defeat for Europeans in Nebraska to that time, and the reverberations were felt all the way back to Santa Fe.

A century and a half later Frank and Luther North recruited Pawnees to be scouts for the American Frontier Army. These Pawnees were likely the first Native Americans to ally themselves with frontier troops against other tribes. The North brothers also became acquainted with scout William F. "Buffalo Bill" Cody and helped him to develop his Buffalo Bill Wild West Show. The troupe presented its first performance in Columbus in 1881. *Contact Platte County Convention & Visitors Bureau | 764 33rd Ave., 68601 | 402/564–2769 | www.ci.columbus.ne.us.*

Genoa Indian School. Young Pawnees were housed and schooled here in an attempt to assimilate them into European-based cultures. Built in 1874, the school operated for nearly 50 years with a peak enrollment of about 600 students. The Genoa Museum, also on site, has exhibits on the Pawnees and on the Mormon Trail. Genoa is 20 mi west of Columbus off Route 22. | 209 E. Webster Ave., Genoa | 402/993–2349 or 402/993–6636 | www.ci.genoa.ne.us | Free | Fri.–Sun. 1–5, or by appointment.

Madison County Historical Society Museum. This is the official site of the Nebraska Archives for Orphan Train Riders, a program implemented from the 1850s to the 1930s to send orphaned children from New York to work on western farms. Exhibits include an 1880s fire pumper, a telegraph system, and a working railroad model depicting a rural Nebraska town. Madison is 15 mi north of Columbus on U.S. 81. | 210 W. 3rd St., Madison | 402/454–2827 or 402/454–3733 | www.madisoncountyhistory.org | Weekdays 2–5, weekends by appointment.

✦ ON THE CALENDAR: Aug. **Buffalo Bill Tours.** During a weeklong town carnival, Tom Martin, a leading authority on Buffalo Bill, hosts bus tours around Columbus pointing out various sites frequented by Buffalo Bill. | 402/564–2769.

Sept. **Nebraska State Hand Cornhusking Contest.** This three-day event includes square dancing, tractor pulls, and corn husking the old-fashioned way by hundreds of people in the city park and a corn field east of town. | 402/564–2769.

HISTORIC DINING

Glur's Tavern. American/Casual. Built in 1876, Glur's is the oldest operating tavern west of the Missouri River. Showman Buffalo Bill once visited this tavern while in town and paid for a round for the house with a $1,000 bill. That bill, no longer legal tender, is framed at the bar. Glur's is a great place for burgers and chicken sandwiches. | 2301 11th St. | 402/564–8615 | Closed Sun. | $2–$5 | No credit cards.

CRAWFORD

▼▼

This land of rolling prairie interrupted by stark sandstone buttes, ponderosa pines, and cottonwood trees was home to the Lakota for centuries before Fort Robinson was established on the White River in 1874. White settlers followed, and hostilities between the native peoples and the frontier army became a pattern. Crazy Horse, one of the greatest of all Lakota warriors, died when he was stabbed while troops were trying to arrest him at Fort Robinson. *Contact Crawford Area Chamber of Commerce | Rte. 271 and U.S. 20, 69339 | 308/665–1817 or 800/647–3213 | www.crawfordnebraska.com.*

Fort Robinson State Park. If ever there were a place to walk in the footsteps of great military and Native American leaders, Fort Robinson is it. An active military post for more than 70 years, Fort Robinson was the scene of the Cheyenne Outbreak, recounted in Mari Sandoz's book *Cheyenne Autumn*. It also was where Chief Crazy Horse was killed while in captivity and where the Buffalo Soldiers prepared for the battle at Wounded Knee. It is now considered Nebraska's premier state park, where you can ride horses, take a stagecoach ride, and stay in a lodge created from former officers' quarters and cavalry barracks. | 308/665–2900 | www.ngpc.state.ne.us/parks | $2.50 | Late May–early Sept., daily 9–6.

Warbonnet Battlefield. On a hill in the Oglala National Grassland is a monument honoring troops who held off a war party of 800 Cheyenne attempting to join the victors of the Battle of Little Big Horn. | 3 mi east of Harrison on U.S. 20 | 308/668–2428.

✦ ON THE CALENDAR: July **Fiddle Contest.** Instrumental and vocal music performed by contestants from around the world accompanies a quilt show at Crawford City Park. | 800/647–3213.

HISTORIC DINING AND LODGING

The Ranch House. Steak. Army general Walter Reed (stationed at Fort Robinson) was one of the original investors in this building, which operated first as a hardware store and mortuary. The tin ceiling and walnut bar date to the 1880s. Nebraska-raised Hereford beef is the most popular item on the menu. | 448 2nd St. | 308/665–1231 | Closed Sun. No lunch | $5–$15 | MC, V.

Fort Robinson Lodge. The cabins here are simple and stark, just as they were when military officers occupied them (1874–1909). Portraits of the officers hang above the beds. Enlisted men's rooms, with no kitchen facilities, are also available. Dining room, kitchens, indoor pool, children's program (ages 2–12); no room phones, no room TVs. | 3200 U.S. 20 | 308/665–2900 | fax 308/665–2906 | www.ngpc.state.ne.us/parks | 22 rooms, 9 cabins | Rooms $35–$40, cabins $80–$160 | Closed Dec.–Apr. | MC, V.

CROFTON

▼▼

Although Lewis and Clark spent a week in 1804 crossing the Missouri just north of where Crofton now sits, the area remained unsettled until railroad workers pitched their tents here in 1892 while they constructed a route linking Norfolk, Nebraska, and Yankton, South Dakota. Railroad promoter J. T. M. Pearce liked the spot and started a town, named for Crofton Courts, his home in England. *Contact Crofton Chamber of Commerce | Box 81, 68730 | 402/388–4385 | www.crofton-ne.com.*

Corps of Discovery Welcome Center. At the intersection of the Lewis and Clark Trail and the Pan American Highway, this center hosts weekly historical programs and has abundant tourist information about the area. | 89705 U.S. 81, 3 mi east of Crofton | 402/667–6557 | www.crofton-ne.com/discover.htm | Free | Late May–early Sept., daily 9–6; early Sept.–late May, daily 9–4.

Lewis and Clark Lake Visitor Center. The center, maintained by the U.S. Army Corps of Engineers, sits on a bluff overlooking the Missouri River and Lewis and Clark Lake. Interior and exterior exhibits, a 30-minute film, and a bookstore provide detailed information about the Corps of Discovery's trek through this region and councils with the Yankton Sioux. | 402/667–2546 | www.nwo.usace.army.mil | Free | Late May–early Sept., Sun.–Thurs. 8–6, Fri.–Sat. 8 AM–9 PM; early Sept.–late May, weekdays 8–4:30, weekends 10–6.

Niobrara State Park. Take a three-hour float trip along the Upper Missouri River with park rangers who provide a history of the river, the Lewis and Clark expedition, and the Ponca nation who once lived in this area. The park protects the least disturbed stretch of the Missouri River. Offered from late May through early fall, the trip ($12) is aboard a 20-ft, 11-person rubber raft. | 28 mi west of Crofton on Rte. 12, Niobrara | 402/857–3373 | fax 402/857–3420 | Free | Daily.

✦ ON THE CALENDAR: Aug. **Lewis and Clark Festival.** The Lewis and Clark Lake Visitor Center hosts this annual festival commemorating the famous expedition with reenactments, speakers, and demonstrations. | 402/667–2546.

Sept.–Oct. **Lewis and Clark Motor Coach Tours.** A daylong motor coach tour departing from Crofton includes lunch and stops at several locations where Lewis and Clark traveled. | 402/582–4866.

FAIRBURY

▼▼▼

James Butler "Wild Bill" Hickok launched his career as an Old West gunfighter when he shot and killed David McCanles on July 12, 1861, at Rock Creek Station near Fairbury. In the early 1900s, Fairbury was the home of the Campbell Brothers Circus, the second largest circus in the world at that time. *Contact Fairbury Chamber of Commerce | 518 East St., 68352 | 402/729–3000 | www.visitoregontrail.org. Jefferson County Historical Society | 910 2nd St., 68352 | 402/729–5131 | www.jeffersoncountyhistory.com.*

District 10 School Museum. The school house was built in 1898, but long before school children came to learn here, the Pony Express, and the Oregon and Mormon trails crossed the land. Historical markers for each are nearby, as well as the graves of some who died on the trails. | 5 mi north of Fairbury on Rte. 15, then 9 mi west on 717th Rd. | 402/729–5131 | Free | Late May–early Sept., Sun. 2–4:30.

Rock Creek Station State Historical Park. Although the station's buildings and covered wagons are re-creations, the ruts are real, cut into the soil by the thousands who traveled the Oregon Trail. The visitor center covers the history of the trail and the station's connection with Wild Bill Hickok, who was a young ranch hand when he killed three men in a dispute over rent money and began his path to becoming part of the lore of the West. | 6 mi southeast of Fairbury via Rte. 8 | 402/729–5777 | www.ngpc.state.ne.us/parks | $2.50 | Late May–early Sept., daily 9–5; mid-Sept.–May, weekends 9–5.

✦ ON THE CALENDAR: Apr. **Windmill Days.** Celebrating the history of the windmills once made in Fairbury to bring power to the plains, this event at the city park combines kite-flying contests, Frisbee contests, and more, to demonstrate how windmills work. | 402/729–3000.

June **Rock Creek Trail Days.** Try some buffalo stew during the cookout at this annual festival, when Fairbury residents gather to re-create Pony Express runs and enjoy entertainment on part of the Oregon Trail. | 402/729–5777.

FREMONT

▼▼▼

Fremont was named for John C. Fremont, the controversial explorer, soldier, and one-time Republican candidate for president whose writings did much to inspire many Americans to head west to seek a new life. A cottonwood tree near Fremont was one of the many places where travelers on the Mormon Trail left mesages for each other by attaching to the tree a white flag and a note. *Contact Fremont Area Chamber of Commerce | 605 N. Broad St., 68025 | 402/721–2641 or 800/727–8323 | www.visitdodgecountyne.org.*

Fremont-Elkhorn Valley Railroad and Museum. The first tracks for this rail line, which eventually extended into Lander, Wyoming, were laid in 1869. By 1899, the line carried more passengers north into the Black Hills than the Union-Pacific took passengers west. Costumed characters provide narration on the 16-mi, 3½-hour round-trip. The depot museum, open only when trains are preparing for departure, includes a history of the routes, as well as a telegraph office, and other memorabilia. | 1835 N. Somers Ave. | 402/727–0615 | $8–$12 | Apr.–Nov., weekends at 1:30.

Louis E. May Historical Museum. Living-history programs bring the past to life in this large, brick mansion, where the Dodge County Historical Society is headquartered. You can also see an 1868 log home and a Victorian garden. | 1643 N. Nye Ave. | 402/721–4515 | www.connectfremont.org | $3 | Apr.–Dec., Wed.–Sun. 1:30–4:30.

The Old Poor Farm. This is where the homeless and needy of Dodge County came to live and work, from 1872 until 1945. A two-hour walking tour of the remaining 4 acres includes outbuildings, animals, and a vivid oral history of this former social-service agency. | 1777 County Rd. 23, 4 mi north of Fremont | 402/721–8087 | $3.50 | By appointment only.

✦ ON THE CALENDAR: July **John C. Fremont Days.** You can mix history with pure fun during this weekend tribute to the man known as "the Pathfinder." There are living-history encampments, arts-and-crafts shows, and antiques displays. | 402/727–9428.

Oct. **Homesteaders Fair.** Admission to the May Museum is free while it hosts this event, which includes demonstrations in blacksmithing, quilting, and butter churning. | 402/721–4515.

HISTORIC DINING
Long Branch Saloon. Steak. Built in 1900, this restaurant and bar 12 mi south of Fremont has shotgun blasts in its tin ceiling that date back to the days when saloon keepers had forceful ways of quieting rowdy crowds. Today, customers are a little more sedate while they enjoy prime rib, steaks, and barbecue. | 212 Main St., LeShara | 402/721–8882 | Closed Mon.–Tues. No lunch | $8–$12 | No credit cards.

GRAND ISLAND
▼▼

This large island flanked by the middle and south channels of the Platte River was a landmark for early travelers to the area. It was first named Grand Island City, then Grand Island Station when the railroad came through in 1866, then simply Grand Island when it was finally incorporated in 1872. *Contact Grand Island/Hall County Convention and Visitors Bureau | 309 W. 2nd, 68801 | 308/382–4400 or 800/658–3178 | www.visitgrandisland.com or www.gionline.com. Hall County Historical Society | Box 1663, 68802 | 308/385–1545 | www.hallchs.org.*

Murdock Mormon Trail Site. Travelers on the Mormon and Oregon trails were funneled onto a narrow ridge here between Wood River and the Platte wetlands. A marker identifies and explains the significance of these undisturbed wagon ruts from more than 150 years ago. | 7½ mi southwest of Grand Island on U.S. 30, Alda.

Plainsman Museum. Among the 19th-century buildings moved to this site 22 mi southeast of Grand Island are the General Deleven Bates home, a homestead house, a barn with farm equipment, a blacksmith shop, and a one-room school where classes met from 1848 to 1950. | 210 16th St., off Rte. 14, Aurora | 402/694–6531 | www.plainsmanmuseum.org | $6 | Apr.–Oct., Mon.–Sat. 9–5, Sun. 1–5; Nov.–Mar., daily 1–5.

The Stuhr Museum of the Prairie Pioneer. Buildings and artifacts on more than 200 acres tell the stories of Native Americans and settlers who lived on the plains in the 19th century. Start your tour, which could take all day, with a multimedia presentation in the main building followed by a visit to an 1880s railroad town where costumed merchants and a marshal stroll the grounds, relating their stories of life on the plains. The museum is the site of numerous special programs and exhibits throughout the year. | U.S. 34 at U.S. 281 | 308/385–5316

| www.stuhrmuseum.org | $7.25 May–Oct., $4.25 Nov.–Apr. | May–Oct., daily 9–5; Nov.–Apr., Mon.–Sat. 9–5, Sun. 1–5.

KEARNEY

▼▼

Fort Kearny, named for Colonel Stephen Watts Kearny, was originally established near Nebraska City. It was transferred to this area on the Platte River in 1848 to provide protection for travelers along the various trails. According to an official War Department report, more than 30,000 people bound for California, Oregon, and Utah passed through Fort Kearny in an 18-month period during the gold rush of 1849. The first homestead claim was filed in 1871, and at one point residents attempted to have the nation's capital moved to Kearney. The spelling of Kearney gained an extra "e" sometime in the mid-1800s because of an error by the post office. *Contact Kearney Chamber of Commerce and Visitors Bureau | 1007 2nd Ave., 68848 | 308/237–3101 or 800/652–9435 | www.ci.kearney.ne.us or www.kearneycoc.org.*

Fort Kearny State Historical Park. In its 23 years as a military post, Fort Kearny was the headquarters of military and civil government, a home station of the Pony Express, an outfitting depot for numerous Indian campaigns, and the home of the famed Pawnee Scouts, who were the first Native Americans to join a military regiment under the leadership of Frank and Luther North. Today, excavated earthenworks and exhibits in the interpretive center document the development of the fort. | Rte. 44, 2 mi south of I–80 at Exit 272 | 308/865–5305 | www.ngpc.state.ne.us/parks | $2.50 | Mar.–May, weekends 9–5; June–Sept., daily 9–5.

Great Platte River Road Archway. This eight-story-high archway, the length of a football field, spans I–80 between Grand Island and Kearney and is the only historical monument granted air rights over an interstate highway. Inside the big red structure you'll find 12 exhibits that immerse you in the history of the Oregon Trail and other aspects of 19th-century life in the Platte River valley. | I–80 at Exit 272 | 877/511–2724 | www.archway.org | $8.50 | May–Sept., daily 9–6; Oct.–Apr., weekdays 10–4.

Trails and Rails Museum. In a former Union Pacific depot, you can see everything from old tickets and schedules to luggage and conductor uniforms. Outside are a steam engine and caboose, an 1880s hotel, and an 1871 school. | 710 W. 11th St. | 308/234–3041 | Free | Late May–early Sept., Mon. 1–8, Tues.–Sat. 11–5, Sun. 1–5.

✦ ON THE CALENDAR: Aug. **Living History Days.** This three-day celebration at Fort Kearny State Historical Park includes an 1800s-style dance, vintage baseball games, a lantern tour of the park, and a nighttime firing of the cannon. | 308/865–5305.

June **Pony Express Reride.** Because Fort Kearny was a Pony Express stop, the annual ride retracing the route of the mail service comes through the park and is met by food, music, and spectators. | 308/865–5305.

LEXINGTON

▼▼

Lexington started as a frontier trading post named Plum Creek for the nearby creek that pours into the Platte River. The Oregon and Mormon trails crossed here and the county has four markers detailing the journeys. On August 8, 1964, a party of Cheyenne attacked the Plum Creek Station and a train of freight wagons, leaving 11 men dead and taking a woman and child hostage. *Contact Lexington Area Chamber of Commerce | 709 E. Pacific St., 68850 | 308/ 324–5504 or 888/966–0564 | www.lexingtonnebraskavisitorbureau.com.*

Dawson County Historical Museum. The diary of Nancy Jane Morton, who was taken hostage by Cheyenne after the Plum Creek massacre, is among the artifacts here. Pick up a copy of Morton's book and a map that identifies 25 historic sites in the county, including Oregon Trail marker sites, wagon ruts, and cemeteries. A school house, train depot, and steam locomotive are also part of the museum. | 805 N. Taft St. | 308/324–5340 | Free | Mon.–Sat. 9–5.

Pony Express Station. Originally a fur-trading post and ranch house, this log structure later was a stop for Pony Express riders delivering mail. Later, it was moved intact to Gothenburg's Ehmen Park (29 mi southeast of Lexington via I–80). You may drop your mail in an old mailbag for an official Pony Express delivery mark; the bag is delivered to a post office. | Rte. 47 about 1 mi north of Exit 211 on I–80, Gothenburg | 308/537–2143 | Free | May–Oct., daily 8–8.

Sod House Museum. Homesteaders in the prairie regions often started their new lives in sod houses built from the dirt they'd claimed, like this example now resting near a typical windmill and a barn in Gothenburg. Sod houses were very durable and long-lasting, and you can see many of them still out on the prairies today. | Exit 211 off I–80, north ½ mi on Rte. 47, Gothenburg | 308/537–2076 2680 | $1 | May and Sept., daily 9–6; June–Aug., daily 8–8.

Turkey Leg Raid Site. On August 7, 1867, the Cheyenne, under the command of Chief Turkey Leg, used material from a nearby telegraph line to build a barricade that derailed a Union Pacific train, killing most of its passengers. A stone monument marks the site. | U.S. 30, 3 mi west of Lexington | 308/324–5340.

✦ ON THE CALENDAR: June **The Olive Tea.** Held at the former home of an outlaw turned respectable businessman, this Victorian teatime includes stories about the Olive family and highlights the Victorian era. | 308/324–5504 or 888/966–0564.

LINCOLN
▼▼

Salt, so important in preserving food, was the primary reason early travelers, both Native Americans and European immigrants, came to the area that is now Lincoln. Salt deposits once filled Capital Beach Lake, and early residents simply scraped the salt off the ground. In the 1850s, salt companies from the east sent representatives to Lincoln in an attempt to begin salt production plants, but the process was too costly. One of those salt company scouts, W. T. Donovan of Lancaster, Pennsylvania, named the developing community after his hometown. When Nebraska became a state in 1867, a fierce battle broke out between Omaha, a much bigger and more established town, and Lancaster over which would become the state capital. Lancaster eventually won, but an angry Omaha representative introduced a bill to change the name of the town to Lincoln, in honor of the late president. The move passed, perturbing many of the Southern sympathizers in the Lancaster area. *Contact Lincoln Chamber of Commerce | Box 83006, 1135 M St., 68501 | 402/436–2350 | www.lcoc.com. Lincoln Convention and Visitors Bureau | Box 83737, 1135 M St., 3rd floor, 68501 | 402/434–5335 or 800/423–8212 | www.lincoln.org.*

Museum of Nebraska History. One of the nation's best archives of western history is kept by the Nebraska State Historical Society at this museum. You can see the first good maps of the Oregon Trail, by Charles Preuss; an inflatable india-rubber seat cushion used by a Pony Express rider to ease saddle sores; a buckskin coat worn by an overland migrant in 1849; and materials related to the Mormon Trail and California and Pikes Peak gold rushes. An exhibit on 10,000 years of Native American history allows you to touch bison fur, among other items. The gift shop sells authentic Native American beadwork, basketry, and pottery made in

Nebraska. | 131 Centennial Mall N | 402/471–4754 | www.nebraskahistory.org | Free | Weekdays 9–4:30, weekends 1–4:30.

Pioneers Park. Forty acres of this 900-acre city park are virgin prairie, meaning they were never plowed or otherwise disturbed by man. Another 80 acres of the park are restored prairie. Protected buffalo and elk roam the park as they used to do before the area was developed. You can hike, picnic, or visit the park's nature center. | 3201 S. Coddington St. | 402/441–7895 | June–Aug., Mon.–Sat. 8:30–8:30, Sun. noon–8:30; Sept.–May, Mon.–Sat. 8:30–5, Sun. noon–5.

✦ ON THE CALENDAR: July **Camp Creek Threshers Show.** The antique threshers displayed here were once the backbone of Nebraska farm and village life. Along with demonstrations of threshers and steam-powered engines, the grounds in Waverly, 15 mi east of Lincoln, have a train, an 1873 schoolhouse, a broom maker, and a blacksmith shop. | 402/786–3003.

Aug. **Picnic on the Prairie.** Hosted by Pioneers Park staff, you'll be invited to walk alongside a covered wagon—because the pioneers didn't ride either—as you head out on the prairie for a picnic and oral history of the Great Plains. | 402/441–7895.

MCCOOK
▼▼

The fertile Republican River valley, once home to the Pawnee, was first explored by French fur traders as early as 1675. A small farming community eventually emerged, its growth spurred by the coming of the the the Burlington-Quincy Railroad in 1882. Named for General Alexander McCook, a decorated officer of the Indian wars, the town of McCook has been home to three Nebraska governors. *Contact Southwest Nebraska Convention and Visitors Bureau/McCook Chamber of Commerce | 107 Norris Ave., 69001 | 308/345–3200 or 800/657–2179 | www.ci.mccook. ne.us or www.aboutmccook.com.*

Massacre Canyon. It was here in August 1873 that 1,400 Sioux warriors and 700 Pawnee staged a bloody battle, considered the last battle between the Indian nations and an influential factor in the Pawnees' decision to leave Nebraska. | U.S. 34, 20 mi west of McCook | 308/285–3833 or 800/657–2179.

Museum of the High Plains. An eclectic mix of exhibits explores different facets of early life in Red Willow County and southwest Nebraska. Among them are Native American artifacts and the farm implements used by Germans who emigrated to Russia before immigrating to the United States. You'll see a room full of railroad mementos and rooms furnished in period style, including an old drugstore. | 421 Norris Ave. | 308/345–3661 | Free | Tues.–Sat. 1–5, Sun. 2–4.

✦ ON THE CALENDAR: May **Buffalo Commons Storytelling Festival.** Watch storytellers perform songs, cowboy poetry, and ghost tales at Norris Park, the Fox Theater, and the High Plains Museum. | 308/345–6223.

MINDEN
▼▼

Prior to the arrival of European settlers around 1813, the Pawnees made their home on the primarily treeless prairies of southern Nebraska. Fur trappers with the Astor Fur Company were probably the first white people in the area. Stephen Long's Yellowstone Expedition came through in 1819–20, and the first wagons of the Oregon Trail crossed through here in 1832. *Contact Minden Chamber of Commerce | 325 N. Colorado Ave., 68959 | 308/832–1811 | www. mindenne.com.*

Harold Warp's Pioneer Village. Among the early white settlers of Minden were the ancestors of Harold Warp, who built this village dedicated to the pioneers. The town within a town is made up of such buildings as Warp's original barn, a schoolhouse, a church, and a blacksmith shop. The buildings house more than 50,000 artifacts, from vehicles to furniture to fountain pens and salt shakers, representing in Warp's view every era of "Man's Progress since 1838." This is considered one of the country's most extensive collections of pioneer memorabilia. You can take a horse-drawn, covered-wagon ride and view crafts demonstrations. | U.S. 6/34 at Rte. 10 | 308/832–1181 or 800/445–4447 | www.pioneer-village.org | $8.50 | Daily 8–5.

Willa Cather Pioneer Memorial Historical Center. This museum and research center in Red Cloud, 42 mi southeast of Minden, is dedicated to the writer who loved the plains and wrote such classics as *My Àntonia, O Pioneers!,* and *A Lost Lady.* Organized tours of five buildings include Cather's childhood home, Grace Episcopal Church, the Depot, the museum, and St. Juliana Catholic Church, all of significance to Cather's writings. | 413 N. Webster St., Red Cloud | 402/746–2653 | www.willacather.org | $1 | Apr.–Oct., Mon.–Sat. 8–5, Sun. 1–5; Nov.–Mar., weekdays 8–5.

✦ ON THE CALENDAR: June **Pioneer Village Days.** From fiddling to dancing to more strenuous tasks, such as blacksmithing and barn building, this festival at the Pioneer Village features activities that occupied folks on the frontier. | 800/445–4447.

NEBRASKA CITY
▼▼

Nebraska City started as a trading post, ferry crossing, and riverboat stop where boatloads of goods were unloaded to be shipped west by ox teams. Among the first freight companies to set up in Nebraska City was the firm of William Russell, Alexander Majors, and William Waddell, which gained a national reputation when it launched the Pony Express in 1861. Nebraska City was also an important stop on the Underground Railroad. *Contact Nebraska City Tourism | 806 1st Ave., 68410 | 402/873–3000 or 800/514–9113 | www.nebraskacity.com. Nebraska City Historical Society | Box 175, 68410 | 402/873–4240.*

John Brown's Cave and Historical Village. The Mayhew Cabin, located 20 ft from its original site, and its root cellar were an integral part of the Underground Railroad of Nebraska. Other buildings transferred to the property include a school, blacksmith shop, and African-American church. | 2012 4th Corso | 402/873–3115 | www.johnbrownscave.com | $6 | Apr.–Nov., daily 10–4.

Old Freighter's Museum. The former headquarters of the company that ran the Pony Express, this museum commemorates the freight companies that delivered supplies to the Army on the Oxbow and Cutoff trails from 1858 to 1866. | 407 N. 14th St. | 402/873–9360 or 402/873–4868 | $2 | Tours by appointment.

✦ ON THE CALENDAR: Sept. **Applejack Festival.** Recognizing the place of apple-growing in the city's history and economy, this citywide festival has a parade, air show, crafts and quilt show, and living-history demonstrations, as well as an apple bowl game, scarecrow contest, and apple jam fest. | 402/873–3000.

NORTH PLATTE
▼▼

The rich and fertile river valley here was superb hunting grounds for Native Americans for centuries and attracted sportsmen from around the world, including Grand Duke Alexis of

Russia, who came to hunt buffalo in the 1870s. The Mormon Trail passed just north of town, the Oregon Trail passed to the south, and the Pony Express came right through the middle. At one point, an estimated 1,000 covered wagons came through North Platte each day. Buffalo Bill Cody had two homes in the area. *Contact North Platte/Lincoln County Convention & Visitors Bureau | 219 S. Dewey St., 69103 | 308/532–4729 or 800/955–4528 | www.northplatte-tourism.com.*

Buffalo Bill Ranch State Historical Park. A self-guided tour takes you through the 16-room mansion Buffalo Bill had built in 1886 and lived in until 1913. The 625-acre park also includes the original barn, outbuildings, and a small herd of buffalo. | 2921 Scout's Rest Ranch Rd., 6 mi northwest of I–80 at Exit 177 | 308/535–8035 | www.ngpc.state.ne.us/parks | $2.50 | Apr.– late May and early Sept.–Oct., weekdays 9–5; late May–early Sept., daily 9–5.

Dancing Leaf Earth Lodge Cultural Learning Center. Owners Jan and Les Hofik have spent their entire lives in the Medicine Creek area learning and teaching about Native Americans and the history of the region. Inside their museum and re-created earthen lodge, 25 mi south of North Platte, are Native American artifacts from 25 years' worth of archaeological digs. | 6100 E. Opal Springs Rd., Wellfleet | 308/963–4233 | $7 | Late May–early Sept., daily tours at 9 AM and 2 PM or by appointment.

Fort McPherson National Cemetery. Nebraska's only national cemetery was established in 1873 on the grounds of a fort that was used to guard the Oregon Trail. Seventy African-American cavalry troopers, known as Buffalo Soldiers, are buried here. | 2 mi south of I–80 off Exit 190, 13 mi east of North Platte | 308/582–4433 | Free | Daily.

✦ ON THE CALENDAR: June **Nebraskaland Days.** This four-day event includes the state rodeo, the governor's western and wildlife art show, a quilt show, parades, and readings by cowboy poets. | 308/532–7939 | www.nebraskalanddays.com.

HISTORIC DINING AND LODGING

Dancing Leaf Earth Lodge. A night spent at this museum and cultural center means sleeping in an earthen lodge under the cover of a deer hide as the first people of this region did 1,300 years ago. Cabins are also available. Dinner ($7) is usually buffalo stew with Pawnee flint corn and corn-meal muffins; nonguests are welcome to join the meal. | 6100 E. Opal Springs Rd., Wellfleet | 308/963–4233 | 3 cabins, 1 earthen lodge | Cabins $50–$75, lodge $30 per person | Reservations essential | No credit cards | BP.

OGALLALA
▼▼

Ogallala, named for the Native American tribe (whose name is spelled with only one "L"), was the end of the line for hundreds of Texas cattle drives from 1875 to 1885. The city became known as the Gomorrah of the Plains for the saloons, gaming halls, and brothels frequented by the weary cowboys. There were more than 50 such businesses in Ogallala during that decade, but not one church. More than 125,000 head a year were shipped from Ogallala to eastern markets, and today's livestock auctions continue to be a major event. *Contact Ogallala/Keith County Chamber of Commerce | 204 E. A St., 69153 | 308/284–4066 or 800/658–4390 | www.visitogallala.com.*

Ash Hollow State Historical Park. You can follow a walkway along Windlass Hill to look down at the deep ruts made when immigrants on the Oregon Trail locked the wheels on their wagons and skidded down to the spring below. | U.S. 26, about 3½ south of Lewellen | 308/778–5651 | www.ngpc.state.ne.us/parks | $2.50 | Grounds daily, visitor center Tues.–Sun. 8–4.

Boot Hill Cemetery. Cowboys were typically buried with their boots on, thus the name of this graveyard with more than 100 markers. One marker is for Rattlesnake Morely, who was killed over a $9 gambling debt. | W. 10th St. and Parkhill Dr. | 308/284–4066 or 800/658–4390.

Mansion on the Hill. This home was built in 1887 for a prominent businessman. It now houses a museum with exhibits about 19th-century cattle drives of the area. | W. 10th St. and Spruce | 308/284–4066 | $2 | Late May–mid-Sept., Tues.–Sun. 9–4.

✦ ON THE CALENDAR: June **Ash Hollow Pageant.** Listen to readings from the journals of travelers on the Oregon Trail and join a chuck-wagon supper during this outdoor festival. | 308/778–5548.

OMAHA

▼▼

The Omaha area was originally the homeland of the Omaha and Otoe Native Americans. The first fur traders established posts on the western bank of the Missouri River in the early 1800s. In 1846, the Mormons built a city called Winter Quarters, which housed 4,000. Omaha grew quickly after Nebraska Territory was created in 1854. It expanded further in 1863 when it became the terminus of the Union Pacific Railroad. Omaha was also the site of the trial of Standing Bear, at which a Native American was given the legal rights of a U.S. citizen for the first time. *Contact Greater Omaha Convention and Visitors Bureau | 6800 Mercy Rd., Suite 202, 68106-2627 | 402/444–4660 or 800/332–1819 | www.visitomaha.com. Douglas County Historical Society | 30th and Fort Sts., Building 11A, 68111 | 402/455–9990 or 402/451–1013 | www. omahahistory.org.*

Durham Western Heritage Museum. Formerly Omaha's Union Station, the museum highlights the history of Omaha and the role it played in westward expansion. Lifelike sculptures of soldiers, salesmen, and other rail travelers sit in restored train cars and "talk" about the politics, music, and the society of the time. | 801 S. 10th St. | 402/444–5071 | www.dwhm.org | $5 | Tues.–Sat. 10–5, Sun. 1–5.

Fort Omaha. Established as a supply fort in 1868, Fort Omaha is best known as the site of the landmark trial of Standing Bear in 1879. The military abandoned it in 1913, and now the fort is part of Metropolitan Community College. | 30th and Fort Sts. | 402/455–9990.

General Crook House. The house, now a museum, was originally owned by General George Crook. Crook testified on behalf of Standing Bear in the 1879 trial. The two-story Victorian was the first brick house inside old Fort Omaha. | 30th and Fort Sts., Building 11B | 402/455–9990 | www.omahahistory.org | $5 | Weekdays 10–4, weekends 1–4.

Mormon Trail Visitors Center at Winter Quarters. Explore a pioneer cabin, pull a handcart, and see what life was like for thousands of Mormons who spent the winter of 1846 here. | 3215 State St. | 402/453–9372 | www.placestovisit.lds.org | Free | Daily 9–9.

Omaha History Tours. These 2-hour tours aboard a trolley car highlight residential areas of the city, but may be customized to meet your interests. A guide from the Douglas County Historical Society provides narration. | Douglas County Historical Society, Historic Fort Omaha, 30th and Fort Sts. | 402/455–9990 | www.omahahistory.org | $12.

✦ ON THE CALENDAR: Sept. **River City Round-up.** This agriculture and western-heritage festival held at the convention center includes a rodeo, a barbecue, trail rides, and a western-theme parade. | 402/554–9610 or 800/840–3057.

THE TRIAL OF STANDING BEAR

The 1879 trial of Standing Bear, the great Ponca chief, was a pivotal point in Native American history. The Ponca had been forced from their land to a reservation in Oklahoma, and during that forced march, known as the Ponca Trail of Tears, Chief Standing Bear's young son, Bear Shield, became ill and died. The chief refused to bury his son along the trail and, according to tribal custom, was attempting to return to his homeland with the body when he was arrested for violating a government order.

With the help of Thomas Tibbles, a reporter for the *Omaha World Herald,* Chief Standing Bear filed suit against the government, asserting that he had the right to return home. The trial took place at Fort Omaha, and General George Crook, then the Commander of the Department of the Platte, quietly lobbied for the chief's cause, garnering newspaper and public support. Eventually, the general testified in court on behalf of Standing Bear. The court found in favor of Standing Bear in a decision that marked the first time the U. S. Government recognized that "an Indian is a person within the meaning of the law" and has the right of citizenship.

SCOTTSBLUFF
▼▼▼

The North Platte Valley was prime hunting territory for the Sioux, Cheyenne, Pawnee, and Lakota for centuries and remains a fertile agricultural and hunting area. In the 1830s, white religious leaders came to the region hoping to convert the Native Americans to Christianity. Then the Oregon, California, and Mormon trails brought as many as 1 million pioneers through the valley, past several large sandstone outcroppings that served as trail markers. Wagon ruts are visible in several locations, particularly at the Robidoux Pass. This was also the path Pony Express riders took in 1860–61. *Contact Gering and Scottsbluff Chamber of Commerce | 1517 Broadway, Suite 104, Scottsbluff 69361 | 308/632–2133 or 800/788–9475 | www.scottsbluff. net/chamber.*

Chimney Rock National Historic Site. One pioneer described this impressive outcrop as "towering to the heavens." Rising 325 ft from base to top, with a spire of 120 ft, the rock became the most famous landmark passed by nearly half a million travelers on the Oregon, California, and Mormon trails. The visitor center has a hands-on exhibit that lets kids pack a wagon. | 22 mi southeast of Scottsbluf, 1 mi south of junction of U.S. 26 and Rte. 92 | 308/586–2581 | www.nebraskahistory.org/sites/rock | $3 | Apr.–Sept., daily 9–6; Oct.–Mar., daily 9–5.

Courthouse and Jail Rocks. These two large, rocky outcroppings were some of the first natural Oregon Trail markers pioneers saw after they had crossed the long, dusty miles of the plains. Today, you may hike around the rocks. | 22 mi southeast of Scottsbluff on Rte. 88 | 308/262–9925 | Free | Daily.

North Platte Valley Museum and Western History Archives. A fur trapper's boat, 19th-century tools and weapons, a log cabin, and an 1880 homestead dwelling illustrate pioneer life in the North Platte Valley. In Gering, the museum has the world's largest collection of Oregon Trail artifacts. | Overland Trails Rd. at J St., Gering | 308/436–5411 | www.npvm.org | $3 | May–Sept., weekdays 9–4, Sun. 1–4; Oct.–Apr., weekdays 9–4.

Oregon Trail Wagon Train. You can travel part of the route of the Oregon Trail and Pony Express in an old-fashioned wagon-train excursion that circles Chimney Rock. The trips leave from

WHO WAS THE SCOTT IN SCOTTS BLUFF?

His name was Hiram Scott, a clerk for the American Fur Company. In 1827–28, he and a party of company employees were returning east from a fur-trading rendezvous when Scott fell ill. Some say he was injured during an attack by the Blackfeet tribe; others say he may have had pneumonia. Either way, Scott's condition was slowing down the group and he was left behind near the bluffs that now bear his name. The next spring, trappers found his remains and personal effects nearly 100 mi east of the bluffs on the banks of the North Platte River. Today, Hiram Scott's final resting place is not known, but a plaque dedicated to his memory is located on the North Overlook Trail of the bluff that bears his name.

Bayard, 25 mi southeast of Scottsbluff on U.S. 26, and last 24 hours or four days. They include chuck-wagon cookouts with homemade ice cream and sourdough bread. | Oregon Trail Rd., Bayard | 308/586–1850 | www.oregontrailwagontrain.com | $200 for 24 hrs or $575 for 4 days | May–Aug.

Join one of the guided **Historic Old West Tours** ($15) to the base of Chimney Rock via a covered wagon. You'll have an opportunity to climb on the rocks during this three-hour trip.

Robidoux Pass. As you drive through Carter Canyon on U.S. 71, the ruts you'll see intersecting the gravel road were made by the thousands of wagons that came this way as they headed west. The route looks much the same as it did 150 years ago. Late in the Oregon Trail migration, the route shifted north of Robidoux Pass to the more forgiving landscape by present-day Scotts Bluff National Monument. | 11 mi south of Scottsbluff on Rte. 71 | 800/788–9475 | Free | Daily.

Scotts Bluff National Monument. Once described as the "Lighthouse of the Plains," this towering sandstone rock was a prominent trail marker for those on the Oregon, California, and Mormon trails. Three thousand acres around the outcropping have been preserved, and a museum and visitor center invite you to learn the social and natural history of the area. You may drive to the top of the bluff or hike around its base. | 6 mi south of Scottsbluff on Rte. 92 | 308/436–4340 | www.nps.gov/scbl | $5 per vehicle | Late May–early Sept., daily 8–7; early Sept.–late May, daily 8–5.

✦ ON THE CALENDAR: June–Aug. **Tuesday Evening at the Monument.** This educational program series sponsored by the National Park Service focuses on themes of westward migration and is held at the outdoor amphitheater behind the Scotts Bluff National Monument visitor center. | 308/436–4340.

July **Oregon Trail Days.** You can revisit the past at a historically themed play, see a quilt show and western-art show, take part in music and dance events, and eat your fill at the state-championship chili cook-off during this four-day festival. | 308/436–4457.

Sept. **Chimney Rock Pioneer Days.** You could get kidnaped by outlaws during this lively festival in Bayard's Library Park. You'll also find street dances, a saloon, crafts fairs, and a horseshoe competition. | 308/586–2830.

HISTORIC DINING

Chuck Wagon Cookout. Steak. Watch your 16-ounce rib eye cook over an open fire while you hear stories from days on the Oregon Trail. Homemade bread and ice cream top off a great meal and entertainment. | Oregon Trail Rd., Bayard | 308/586–1850 | Reservations essential. | Closed Sept.–Apr. | $18.95 | MC, V.

SIDNEY

▼▼

Travelers on the Union Pacific Railroad, which came through Sidney 1867, were warned not to get off the train here because they were likely to be robbed before they got back on. More than 100 saloons, brothels, and gaming halls lined the tracks, and the area became a favorite hangout of Calamity Jane and her gang. Sidney also was a major jumping-off point for gold seekers taking the Sidney-Deadwood Trail to South Dakota during the Black Hills gold rush of the 1870s. Of course, long before the trains and gold seekers, thousands of settlers came through on the Oregon, California, and Mormon trails. *Contact Cheyenne County Chamber of Commerce | 740 Illinois St., 69162 | 308/254–5851 or 800/421–4769 | www.sidney-nebraska.com.*

Fort Sidney Museum and Post Commander's Home. The residence of the army post commander, and the first hospital General Walter Reed was assigned to, is among the few remaining buildings of the army garrison built here in the 1880s to protect railroad crews. The museum displays period military uniforms and Native American dress. | 1153 6th Ave. | 308/254–2150 | Free | Late May–early Sept., daily 9–11 and 1–3.

Historic Walking Tours. The self-guided tour takes you past 43 buildings on the National Register of Historic Places, including one that houses the Sidney Telegraph, a continuously operating newspaper since 1873. Brochures are available at the Chamber of Commerce office. | 740 Illinois St. | 308/254–5851 or 800/421–4769.

Sidney-Deadwood Trail Marker. Wagon and stagecoach ruts are visible as far as the eye can see on this route used by gold seekers heading to the Black Hills. | 3 mi west of Sidney on U.S. 30 | 308/254–5851 or 800/421–4769.

NEVADA

Nevada was one of the last sections of the Old West to be explored—and with good reason. Remote, desolate, and dry, the region was unforgiving to newcomers unfamiliar with its ways. Many early trappers and traders nearly died of thirst and hunger exploring its vast, inhospitable terrain, and emigrants remembered the Nevada stretch of their trail west with bitterness. Even rugged prospectors were challenged by the harsh face that this place presented. Native Americans in northern Nevada eked out a subsistence lifestyle, but early white explorers considered aboriginal southern Nevadans the lowest form of humanity they had even seen. Only when gold and silver were discovered in unimaginable quantities did Euro-American settlers begin to tame Nevada. But to this day, the state remains slightly uncivilized.

The first Europeans—two Spanish friars surveying a traders' trail from Santa Fe, New Mexico, to the southern California coast—passed through Nevada in 1776. Exactly 50 years passed before another white man stepped foot in the area. In the fall of 1826 Jedediah Smith led a party of fur trappers along the trail blazed by the Franciscans through what's now southern Nevada. On his way back the following spring, Smith crossed central Nevada, getting a look at the Great Basin Desert, which occupies the northern half of the state. In 1829, fur trapper and trader Peter Skene Ogden traipsed through northern Nevada in search of beaver pelts. A year later Rafael Rivera, a scout for a Mexican trading party traveling along the Spanish Trail, discovered a shortcut that led through a large valley with a fresh-water spring and abundant vegetation. He named the valley Las Vegas, meaning "The Meadows."

Exploration of Nevada commenced in earnest in 1832, when John C. Fremont, a lieutenant in the U.S. Army's Topographical Corps, set out to explore and map much of what would become Nevada. The famous Kit Carson—who'd earlier explored southern Nevada and had become renowned for his Far West exploits—was his guide. Fremont named many features of the landscape, including Pyramid Lake, the Carson River, and the Great Basin

Desert. (Much later, the main drag that runs through downtown Las Vegas, Fremont Street, was named in honor of this great namer of places.) Fremont was followed in 1833 by explorer Joseph Walker, who blazed a trail along the Humboldt and Carson rivers from eastern Nevada to California.

As Nevada's vast expanse was charted, Euro-American settlers began to arrive. In 1841 the Bidwell-Bartleson party came in on Walker's route, bringing the first wagons, cattle, and white woman and child (one of each) to the area. The trail blazed by Joseph Walker, by then known as the Emigrant Trail, crossed from Utah into Nevada at Pilot's Peak (near present-day Wendover), then followed the Humboldt and Carson rivers to the Sierra Nevada range and into central California. In the late 1840s and early 1850s, after gold was discovered at Sutter's Mill in California, more than 100,000 fortune-seekers passed through Nevada on the Emigrant Trail, most without a second glance. But some decided to stay, settling the verdant valleys at the eastern base of the Sierra Nevada. Latter-day Saints from Utah established trading posts to supply the settlers and emigrants; they founded Mormon Station (today Genoa), the first town in Nevada, in 1851. Other Mormons built a mission at Las Vegas's Big Spring in 1855, founding the first settlement in what would become southern Nevada.

A handful of hardy prospectors drifted back from California to look for gold in the creeks of the Sierra Nevada's eastern slope. They didn't find a lot, just enough to keep them interested. For nearly 10 years these desert rats swished pans at Gold Flats (now Dayton) and up Gold Creek to its source on Sun Mountain (now Mt. Davidson). There, a couple of intuitive prospectors sunk their shovels into the mountain itself, and struck the richest body of ore ever discovered in the Lower 48.

With a bang, the Comstock Lode put Nevada on the map in 1859. Virginia City, directly atop the Comstock mines on Sun Mountain, was the Las Vegas of its day—a fast-paced, no-holds-barred kind of place. For a time, Virginia City rivaled San Francisco in size and splendor. Indeed, wealth from the Comstock Lode inaugurated the golden age of San Francisco, when mansions were built atop the hills, the mint and the stock market were established, and every other west-coast settlement looked to the sparkling city on the bay with awe and envy. The United States was quick to claim glittering Nevada as its own: in 1861 this former chunk of Utah Territory became a U.S. territory in its own right, and in 1864 it became the 36th state in the Union. Carson City was designated the capital of Nevada.

Virginia City's boom lasted a full 20 years—an eternity when compared to the flash-in-the-pan booms of most other mining towns. Prospectors fanned out from the Comstock to find new lodes and stake their claims in new Virginia Cities. Towns such as Austin, Eureka, Tuscorora, Ely, Belmont, and Pioche sprouted where miners found orebodies of gold and silver. The Central Pacific Railroad laid the tracks of the Transcontinental Railroad across northern Nevada in 1868–69, spawning the towns of Reno, Winnemucca, Battle Mountain, Carlin, Elko, and Wells in the process.

Borrasca ("bust" in Spanish) overtook Nevada's lesser mining towns in the 1860s and 1870s, and even the great Virginia City busted for good around 1879. Reno emerged from Virginia City's shadow and soon made a name for itself as the economic center of the state: it was the Central Pacific Railroad's transshipment center for northern and western Nevada. The mining recession lasted a good two decades, up through the turn of the 20th century. Then, in 1900, a prospector from Belmont struck silver at Tonopah, and a huge copper deposit was unearthed at Ely. A new boom was on. In 1902, gold was discovered 25 mi south of Tonopah in Goldfield, which in its heyday grew nearly to the size of boom-time Virginia City. From there, prospectors kept moving and founded the mining towns of Manhattan, Round Mountain, and Rhyolite.

Meanwhile, farmers and ranchers had been putting down roots for several decades. Farms in the Carson, Smith, and Mason valleys in western Nevada, watered by the Carson and Walker rivers, grew alfalfa for ranches throughout the state. The largest ranches were in northeastern Nevada, in the basins at the foot of the mountain ranges around Elko, Wells,

NEVADA TIME LINE

1776 Two Spanish missionaries travel through southern Nevada.

1826 Jedediah Smith leads a party of fur trappers along the Spanish Trail.

1830 Rafael Rivera blazes a shortcut on the Spanish Trail via Big Spring; he names it Las Vegas, "the Meadows."

1833 Joseph Walker establishes a trail through northern and western Nevada.

1841 The Bidwell-Bartleson party is the first to emigrate from Missouri to California following Walker's route through Nevada.

1843 John C. Fremont explores, maps, and names large sections of Nevada.

1848 In the Treaty of Guadalupe Hidalgo, Mexico cedes the Southwest, including Nevada, to the U.S.

1851 Latter-day Saints from Salt Lake City build a trading post at Mormon Station (now Genoa).

1855 Nevada is officially designated Carson County of the Utah Territory; Mormons build a mission at Las Vegas's Big Springs.

1859 Two Irish immigrants dig a hole near a spring high up on Sun Mountain (now Mt. Davidson) and discover the Comstock Lode.

1860 A rush of prospectors back across the Sierra Nevada from California establishes Virginia City.

1861 Nevada becomes a U.S. territory; Samuel Clemens, age 20, travels to Carson City with his brother Orion, personal secretary to territorial governor James Nye.

1864 Nevada becomes the nation's 36th state.

1869 The Transcontinental Railroad is laid across northern Nevada.

1872 The Big Bonanza, the Comstock's richest orebody, is discovered.

1876 Fire rages through Virginia City, destroying nearly the whole town.

1880 The 20-year bust, during which white emigrants desert most of Nevada, begins.

1900 Jim Butler discovers silver at Tonopah, launching a 20-year boom.

1905 The city of Las Vegas is founded as a watering stop on the San Pedro, Los Angeles & Salt Lake Railroad.

and Ely. Basque shepherds coexisted (sometimes uneasily) with these cattle barons. Many Basque adventurers migrated west during and after the gold rush; when the mining dried up, they turned to sheep-ranching. To run their large herds of sheep, they imported family, friends, and neighbors from the Old Country. Their legacy endures throughout northern Nevada.

In 1905, the San Pedro, Los Angeles & Salt Lake Railroad pushed through southern Nevada, giving rise to the town of Las Vegas, a sleepy little outpost that would soon experience the biggest Nevada boom of them all. Like Reno before it, Las Vegas would flourish thanks to Nevada's liberal divorce laws, wide-open gambling, legal prostitution, and other libertine policies. These same policies, as well as the state's miles and miles of open space and the undying hopes of prospectors, allowed Nevada's Old West spirit—whether you call it bold or reckless, independent or lawless—to live on.

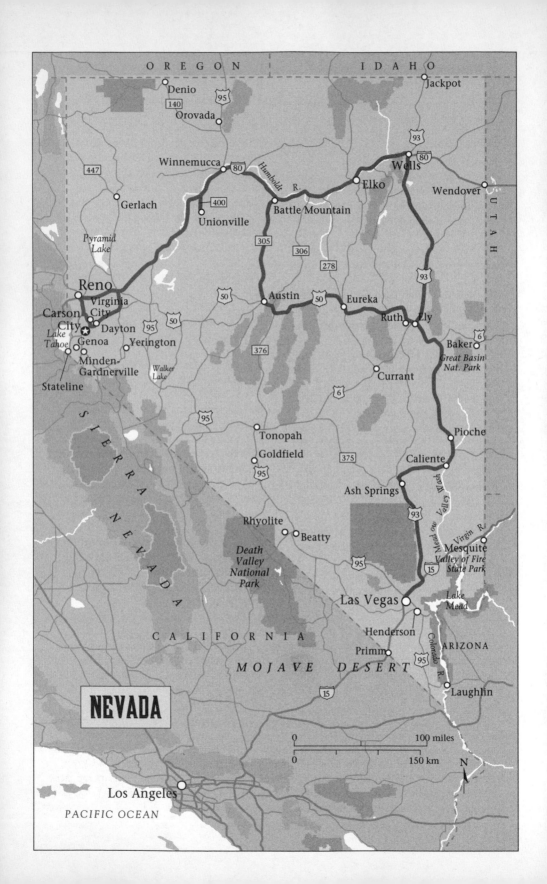

O R E G O N · I D A H O

Denio
[140] [95]
Orovada
Jackpot
[93]

Winnemucca [80] Humboldt R.
[447]
Wells [80]
Gerlach
Elko
Wendover
[400]
Unionville
Battle Mountain
U T A H

Pyramid Lake
[305] [306]
[278]
[93]

Reno
Virginia City
[50] Austin [50] Eureka
Ruth Ely
Carson City
Dayton
[50]
Baker
Lake Tahoe
Genoa [95]
Great Basin Nat. Park
Minden-
Gardnerville Yerington
[376]
Currant
[6]
Stateline
Walker Lake
[95]
Pioche

Tonopah
[375]
Caliente
Goldfield
[95]
Ash Springs
Rhyolite
[93]
Beatty

S I E R R A   N E V A D A
Death Valley National Park
[95]
Meadow Valley Wash
Mesquite
Valley of Fire State Park
[15]

Las Vegas
Lake Mead

Henderson
Colorado R.
A R I Z O N A
Primm
[95]
C A L I F O R N I A
[15]
Laughlin

M O J A V E   D E S E R T

NEVADA

0 ___ 100 miles
0 ___ 150 km
N

Los Angeles
PACIFIC OCEAN

Boomtowns

A DRIVING TOUR FROM VIRGINIA CITY TO RHYOLITE

▼▼

Distance: 1,000 miles   **Time:** 4 days
Breaks: Overnight in Unionville at the Old Pioneer Garden B&B, and in Eureka, at the beautifully restored Jackson House Hotel. Spend the third night at any of a half-dozen motels in Tonopah, and your final night at one of the casino resorts in Vegas.

The late-19th and early 20th century history of Nevada is all about mining boomtowns. Hundreds of hastily built settlements erupted from the desert, only to be abandoned after a few years when the mines gave out. Most returned to the sand and sagebrush, but a handful have survived. All are treasure troves of artifacts, photographs, and architecture from mining days.

Start your tour where Nevada's mining bonanza started: **Virginia City.** Though it's been overtaken by gift shops, many of the old buildings still stand, and D Street, the main drag, still has wooden sidewalks. Take half a day to look around; then head south through Gold Hill and Silver City and east on U.S. 50 to Dayton, site of Gold Creek. Make your way via U.S. 50 and U.S. Alt. 50/95 to I–80 (about 45 mi) and drive east on the interstate toward **Winnemucca.** At the Mill City exit, follow Route 400 south to the gorgeous and tiny settlement of Unionville (20 mi), where you can spend the night at an atmospheric B&B.

In the morning, head back to I–80 east past Winnemucca and stop at Battle Mountain (100 mi) to visit the Trail of the '49ers Interpretive Center. From here, drive south on Route 305 to **Austin** (80 mi) and have lunch. Look around the town; then head move on to lovely **Eureka** (70 mi east on U.S. 50). There you can tour the shops, stroll the streets, and spend the night at the Jackson House.

On day three, continue east on U.S. 50 to Ruth (70 mi), with its vast open-pit copper mine, and **Ely,** with its fine museums and crossroads-town bustle. Next, drive south on U. S. 93 to **Pioche** (106 mi); here the ore buckets still hang on the overhead tramway where they stopped in 1923. It's a long 200 mi west on U.S. 93, Route 375, and U.S. 6, past Rachel (home of Area 51 of UFO fame), to **Tonopah.** Visit the Central Nevada Museum; then have dinner and spend the night in the busy town.

Goldfield, 25 mi south south of Tonopah on U.S. 95, is your first stop on the fourth and final day of the tour. Visit the Esmeralda County Courthouse; then drive another 60 mi south to the ghost town of Rhyolite, near Beatty. Another 110 mi south on U.S. 95 brings you to **Las Vegas,** where you can get a taste of Nevada's latest gold rush.

Railroad Towns

A DRIVING TOUR FROM RENO TO LAS VEGAS

▼▼

Distance: 700 miles   **Time:** 3 days
Breaks: Winnemucca is prime for a Basque dinner at the Winnemucca Hotel and a night at a motel. Ely has the historic Nevada Hotel. In Las Vegas you can choose from 130,000 hotel and motel rooms, and 1,000 eateries of all descriptions.

Start off in **Reno,** where freight and passenger trains clog up downtown traffic several times each day and you can take in exhibits on railroad history at the Nevada Historical Society Museum. A 30-mi round-trip side trip to **Virginia City** gives you the chance to ride the restored Virginia & Truckee short line to Gold Hill and back. From Reno, catch I–80 east for 160 mi to **Winnemucca,** where you can take in the Humboldt Historical Museum, with its exhibit on the railroading heritage of the town. Spend the night in Winnemucca.

On your second morning pick up where you left off, heading east on I–80 along the Humboldt River, the route of the Transcontinental Railroad. It's 120 mi east to **Elko,** the only town in Nevada that diverted its railroad tracks away from downtown; the original right-of-way is plainly evident in the wide and seemingly out-of-place parking lots on Railroad Street. Head east on I–80 to Wells (60 mi). The storefronts on 7th Street, the original downtown area across from the Central Pacific tracks, have been completely abandoned; though boarded up, the buildings are still intact. From Wells, it's a fast jaunt south on U.S. 93 to **Ely** (130 mi), where you can spend the night in any of a dozen motels or in the historic Hotel Nevada.

You can spend an entire day in Ely touring the Nevada Northern Railway Museum and taking rides on the railroad if it's running. But leave some daylight to drive south past **Pioche** to Caliente (130 mi south on U.S. 93), where the last leg of the southern Transcontinental Railroad (from Salt Lake City to Los Angeles) enters Nevada. Many original railroad-company town bungalows still stand in Caliente, and there's a spectacular drive through Rainbow Canyon along the railroad tracks. From Caliente it's a fast 150 mi to Las Vegas, passing Ash Springs (where there's a public hot spring) and the verdant Pahranagat Valley. Spend your last night in **Las Vegas,** which was a railroad-company town until it became a casino company town. When the pig train passes through on a hot and still night, it suffuses half the city with an aromatic reminder of its railroad origins.

AUSTIN
▼▼

A town of 300 souls, Austin lies 12 mi from the exact center of Nevada. When silver was discovered here in 1863, it became the first offspring boomtown of Virginia City. Austin's residents were a civic-minded bunch. In one case, a man named Gridley pulled a stunt to raise money for the Sanitary Fund (the 1870s version of the Red Cross). The sack of flour that he bought at auction wound up being re-auctioned around the West, raising $250,000. Locals were also imbued with a frontier sense of humor: One Fred Ward, editor of the local daily newspaper, invented the Sazerac Lying Club, for the tall-tale-telling habitués of the Sazerac Saloon (the whole hilarious story is immortalized in Oscar Lewis's *The Town That Died Laughing*). Today, Austin still has numerous original buildings, including a hotel, the county courthouse, and three churches. *Contact Austin Chamber of Commerce / Lander County Courthouse, 100 Main St., 89310 / 775/964–2200 / www.austinnevada.com.*

Lander County Courthouse. This wood-and-brick building was constructed in the mid-1860s, when Austin was the seat of Lander County (Battle Mountain wrested the county administration from Austin in 1980). One of the oldest courthouses in the state, it's bedecked with 150-year-old woodwork, lamp shades, and other fixtures. Pick up some informational brochures from the rack in the foyer. The chamber of commerce, upstairs, is open most weekdays. | 12 Main St. | 775/964–2447 | Free | Weekdays 9–noon and 1–4.

✦ ON THE CALENDAR: June **Gridley Days.** Local, state, and regional competitions include the Gridley Sack of Flour foot race, the Nevada State Fiddler's Championship, mining competitions, and a Civil War encampment. | 775/964–2200.

HISTORIC DINING
The International. American. One of the oldest buildings in Nevada, the International Hotel was originally built in Virginia City, then dismantled and moved by wagon 100 mi to Austin in the 1860s. You can't sleep here, but three meals are served daily in the dining room. Bacon and eggs, burgers, and twice-baked potatoes are the attractions. | Main St. | 775/964–1297 | $5–$13 | MC, V.

CARSON CITY

▼▼▼

Named for famed western explorer Kit Carson, Carson City has been the seat of Nevada's government since 1861, when Nevada became a territory of the United States. Mark Twain describes the struggles of the newborn territorial government in his classic of the Old West, *Roughing It.* A prizefight in 1897 between Bob Fitzsimmons and Gentleman Jim Corbett attracted so many spectators to Carson City that the city and state fathers launched a tourism campaign that has continued to this day. A number of government buildings (made of sandstone quarried locally), houses, and trees date from the late 19th century; walk or drive through the neighborhood just west of downtown to see them. Today Carson City is a bustling burg, but it remains one of the nation's smallest state capitals. *Contact Carson City Area Chamber of Commerce | 1900 S. Carson St., Suite 100, 89701 | 775/882–1565 | www.carsonvalleynv.org. Carson City Convention and Visitors Bureau | 1900 S. Carson St., Suite 200, 89701 | 775/687–7410 | www.virtualtahoe.com.*

Bowers Mansion. This 16-room house, 10 mi north of town in Washoe Valley, was built in 1867 by Sandy and Eilley Bowers, who made a fortune in the early days of the Comstock Lode. It was restored, stocked with donated period pieces, and opened as a museum in 1968. To see this example of how two of the Comstock's earliest mining barons lived, you must take a tour (conducted every half hour in summer). The small exhibit in the original root cellar has excellent displays of the V flume that transported logs from the Lake Tahoe basin to the Comstock and of the pipes and siphons that supplied water for Virginia City. | U.S. 395 | 775/849–0201 | $3 | Late May–early Sept., daily 11–4:30; first 3 weeks of May and Sept.–Oct., weekends 11–4:30.

Nevada State Museum. A U.S. mint from 1870 to 1893, the museum building is packed with exhibits on early mining days, Carson City–minted silver and gold coins, and willow baskets woven by Washoe artisans around the turn of the 20th century. | 600 N. Carson St. | 775/687–4811 | $3 | Daily 8–4:30.

Nevada State Railroad Museum. Here you can see an extensive collection of passenger and freight cars from railroads from around the Old West. There are two meticulously restored Virginia & Truckee trains that transported Comstock ore from the mines of Virginia City to the mills of Carson City from 1869 to 1888. Be sure to take the tour of the restoration shop. | 2180 S. Carson St. | 775/687–6953 | $2 | Daily 8–4:30.

State Capitol. Completed in 1871, the building now houses a small museum on its second floor. The collection of Nevada memorabilia includes a map of Nevada Territory circa 1862; the front page of the November 2, 1864, *New York Herald* announcing statehood for Nevada; and an exhibit of all the state symbols. Portraits of Nevada's governors hang from the walls. | N. Carson and Musser Sts. | 775/687–5000 | www.carsoncity.nv.us | Free | Daily 8–5.

Warren Engine Company No. 1 Fire Museum. Carson City claims the oldest volunteer fire department in the West—it has operated continuously since 1863. In the course of time most early Nevada settlements succumbed to raging fires—some, like Virginia City, more than once—which often made the volunteer fire departments the only thing standing between a boomtown and a potential ghost town. The museum displays 140 years' worth of gear used by the squad, including a 1913 Seagrave, Nevada's first motorized fire engine. | 777 S. Stewart St. | 775/887–2210 | Donations accepted | Daily by appointment.

✦ ON THE CALENDAR: June **Kit Carson Rendezvous.** This big mountain-man fair in Mills Park includes musket loading and shooting demonstrations, battle reenactments, Native American storytelling and teepee decorating, and western music. | 775/687–7410 or 800/638–2321.

ABE CURRY, CITY FATHER

Something about the desert inspires strange and wondrous visions in the eyes of select men and women. One such visionary was Abraham Curry. An entrepreneur from upstate New York, Curry had been a longshoreman in Cleveland, a contractor in San Francisco, and a prospector around the Motherlode. His vision came to him in early fall of 1858, when at the age of 43, he acquired 900 acres of strange and wondrous sand and sagebrush—a tract otherwise known as Eagle Ranch. It was a patch of the Eagle Valley, on the eastern slope of the Sierra Nevada a bit north of the seven-year-old Mormon settlement of Genoa. Curry bought it from one John Mankin for the princely sum of $1,000.

Curry was immediately full of lofty ambitions for his new "ranch." Looking over his desolate spread, he envisioned a town with wide downtown streets, small lots for hundreds of homes, and a government plaza—in short, a glorious state capital, where there wasn't yet a state, not even a territory. The closest people, in fact, were more than 10 mi away.

Everyone who heard of Curry's plan considered him a lunatic, and Eagle Ranch was soon known as "Curry's Folly." Old Abe, however, was not to be discouraged or denied. He discovered a source of clay, a limestone outcrop, and warm springs on his land. The clay he used for bricks to construct a trading post in "town," the limestone he began to quarry for the permanent government buildings, and the warm springs he dammed. At the springs he built a bathhouse, which attracted dusty ranchers, prospectors, and travelers.

Less than a year after Curry bought Eagle Ranch, in July 1859, the Comstock Lode was discovered and the rush was on. Thousands of frenzied fortune seekers passed through Curry's Folly on the way to Virginia City and some of them stayed, or returned after catching a glimpse of the lawlessness and harsh conditions on the Comstock. Curry, the self-proclaimed "mayor" of the newly named Carson City, obliged them by deeding them free lots. By spring 1860, Carson City had a population of more than 500.

When the United States Congress declared Nevada a territory in 1861, booming Carson City was designated territorial capital, beating out rough-and-tumble Virginia City and declining Genoa for the honor. On October 31, 1864, when Nevada was declared the nation's 36th state, Carson City ascended to the rank of state capital. Abe Curry's vision had come to fruition in a mere six years.

For the next decade, Uncle Abe, as he came to be known, built the first Nevada state house, courthouse, and prison; the roundhouse and maintenance shops for the Virginia & Truckee Railroad; and even a U.S. mint, among other buildings (many of which still stand today). He also served as the first warden of the prison and the first superintendent of the mint.

Abraham Curry died of a stroke in 1873, at age 58. He's remembered to this day as one of Nevada's most civic-spirited, honest, generous, and prophetic pioneers.

HISTORIC LODGING

Bliss Mansion B&B. Built in 1879, this magnificent home is a State Historical Landmark that was restored in 1994. It is furnished with museum-quality Victorian furniture and artwork. The four guest rooms are upstairs; each has a private bath. The view across the street is of the Governor's Mansion. Refrigerators. | 710 W. Robinson St., 89570 | 775/887–8988 or 800/320–0627 | www.blissmansion.com | 4 rooms | $175 | AE, D, MC, V | CP.

ELKO

▼▼

Elko started life in 1869 the same way that Reno, Winnemucca, Battle Mountain, and Carlin did: as a railroad town. No one seems to know how the town got its name, but Elko quickly became the major supply center for all the mines and ranches within 200 mi. The town and its people were rugged, self-sufficient, and industrious, making Elko the largest settlement in an area the size of New England. The Commercial Hotel opened downtown in 1869; it's still there today. Some of the town's homes date back before the turn of the 20th century. The Basque influence is strong here: Basque shepherds arrived in the area around the turn of the 20th century, and they congregated in Elko's Basque hotels, which still exist today. *Contact Elko Chamber of Commerce | 1405 Idaho St., 89801 | 775/738–7135 or 800/428–7143 | www.cattle-log.com/elkocc.htm. Elko Convention and Visitors Authority | 700 Moren Way, 89801 | 775/738–4091 or 800/428–7143 | www.cattle-log.com/ecva.htm.*

Northeastern Nevada Museum. Your first stop in northeastern Nevada should be this fine museum dedicated to the history, industry, and cultural tapestry of this vast, underpopulated corner of the state. Here you'll see a life-size pioneer kitchen, school room, and type shop, along with exhibits from the short-lived Elko Chinatown and a slide show on the local gold-mining business (Elko is the center of one of the largest gold-producing regions on earth). | 1515 Idaho St. | 775/738–3418 | www.nenv-museum.org | Free | Mon.–Sat. 9–5, Sun. 1–5.

Wells. An hour east of Elko via I–80 is Wells, founded by the Central Pacific Railroad in the 1860s. The original downtown directly across from the tracks, 7th Street, is completely derelict; the block of buildings stands, but they're all abandoned and boarded up. It's a graphic illustration of the evolution of railroad towns across the West: the business district migrated from the tracks on 7th to the old U.S. 40 highway on 6th to the I–80 superhighway exit ramps on either side of town.

✦ ON THE CALENDAR: Jan. **Cowboy Poetry Gathering.** One of the largest cowboy poetry and music festivals in the country, this one is sponsored by the Western Folklife Center, which is responsible for the resurgence in popularity of this 19th-century folk art. Five days of poetry readings, yodeling, concerts, art exhibits, and serious partying fill the Elko Convention Center. | 775/738–7508 or 888/880–5885.

HISTORIC DINING
Star Basque Restaurant. Basque. Built in 1910, this restaurant–rooming house has been in continuous operation ever since. A good example of the type of inn Basque shepherds frequented throughout Nevada around the turn of the 20th century, it's a typical Basque set-up: family-style seating and serving. The soup, salad, bread, beans, and fries are all-you-can-eat, while entrées include your choice of pork, beef, chicken, lamb, trout, and salted cod. Try the Basque cocktail, Picon Punch (Amer liqueur, brandy, and grenadine) and say *"Oso garria!"* to toast the house. | 246 Silver St. | 775/753–8696 | $11–$16 | MC, V.

ELY

▼▼

Ely rose on the wave of the second Nevada mining boom, right at the optimistic turn of the 20th century. But it wasn't the usual gold, silver, lead, barite, or mercury that fed the mining frenzy here. It was copper—billions of tons of ore to produce hundreds of millions of tons of metal at a few bucks per ton. Ely became the headquarters for the area's open-pit mines (5 mi west in Ruth), the giant mill (5 mi north in McGill), and the railroad (1 mi east in East Ely). Copper was Ely's number one industry as late as the early 1980s. *Contact Ely Bristlecone*

Convention Center | 150 6th St., 89301 | 775/289–3720 or 800/496–9350. White Pine Chamber of Commerce | 636 Aultman St., 89301 | 775/289–8877 | www.elynevada.com.

Nevada Northern Railway Museum. Though the Nevada Northern Railway was built in the waning years of the Old West (1904), a tour of this museum—actually, a collection of 30 buildings that supported the railroad operations—is not to be missed when you're in Ely. You can visit the depot, offices, warehouses, yard, roundhouses, and repair shops, and you'll see train cars and machinery that date back to the early 1900s. You can also catch a ride on one of the trains in the summer. | 1100 Ave. A | 775/289–2085 | www.pages.prodigy.com/nevadanorthern/index. htm | $4, train rides $16–$18 | Late May–early Sept., daily 9:30–4.

Ward Charcoal Ovens Historic State Monument. You can see this row of ovens, the biggest group in a single spot in Nevada, in the desert south of Ely. They were used between 1876 and 1887 to turn piñon and juniper into charcoal, which in turn was used for refining silver and copper from the local ore. It's worth the 12-mi drive from Ely to take in this well-preserved piece of Nevada mining history. | U.S. 6/50 | www.state.nv.us/stparks | Free | Daily.

White Pine County Museum. At this small-town museum packed with an eclectic accumulation of local memorabilia, you can see an 1876 cannon, an 1891 bicycle, a model of late-19th-century mine timbering, more than 300 types of minerals mined locally, and some Nevada Northern rolling stock outside. | 2000 Aultman St. | 775/289–4710 | www.webpanda. com/white_pine_county/museum | Donations accepted | Daily 9–3.

HISTORIC LODGING
Hotel Nevada. Among the oldest hotels in Nevada, this six-story specimen was once the tallest building in the state. Artifacts from the Old West, such as guns, cattle brands, prospecting tools, and wagon wheels, pack nearly every inch of wall space throughout the casino. The rooms are small but have been renovated and upgraded several times. Coffee shop, casino. | 501 Aultman St., 89301 | 888/406–3055 | www.hotelnevada.com | 60 rooms | $28–$48 | AE, D, MC, V | CP.

EUREKA
▼▼

Eureka boomed to life in 1864, with the discovery of silver here. The ore contained a high percentage of lead, however, and the smelting process produced highly toxic fumes. The town suffered an inordinately high mortality rate, especially among infants. This pall hung over Eureka for 15 years until the boom went bust. It remained a semi-ghost town through the rest of the Old West period. But hardy residents maintained the town's status as the Eureka County seat and a supply center for surrounding ranches. Today Eureka is an attractive town of stately brick buildings and well-kept houses and yards. *Contact Eureka Chamber of Commerce | Monroe and Bateman Sts. (Box 14, 89316) | 775/237–5544 | www.ecc.com.*

Eureka Opera House. Built in 1880, this structure remained the focal point of entertainment in Eureka for 100 years. Its first public event was a masquerade ball on New Year's Eve in 1881. Completely renovated, it reopened in 1994 and is once again the pride of downtown Eureka. You can stroll in and take a look during business hours; call for an appointment at other times. | 100 Main St. | 775/237–6006 | Free | Weekdays 8–noon and 1–5.

Eureka Sentinel Museum. This 1879 building served for 90 years as the offices of the town's newspaper. Exhibits on mining history, railroad history, and newspaper history are displayed as newspaper stories. Read all about the short-lived Eureka-Palisade Railroad, the challenges of refining silver from lead, and the disastrous fires that consumed the town. You can also view the newspaper office, which displays 1880s posters on the walls. | Ruby Hill and Monroe | 775/237–5010 | Free | Apr.–Oct., weekdays 9–5; Nov.–Mar., Tues.–Sat. 9–5.

HISTORIC LODGING
Jackson House Hotel. Built in 1877, burned in 1880, rebuilt, abandoned, renamed—the Jackson House saw it all before being restored and reopened in the 1990s. Downstairs is a veranda; the rooms, all upstairs, are outfitted with wood floors and walls, quilts, antique furniture, and private baths. Restaurant, bar. | Main St., 89316 | 775/237–5518 | www.elywave. com/jackson | 9 rooms | $79–$119 | AE, D, MC, V | CP.

GENOA
▼▼▼

Only two years after gold was discovered in California, Mormon settlers from Salt Lake City established a trading post in a lush valley at the eastern foot of the Sierra Nevada. The trading post did a brisk business with prospectors and emigrants passing through and homesteaders settling down. Genoa (pronounced juh-*noa*) is the oldest town in Nevada, and so it has bragging rights to many state firsts: first house, first town meeting, and first newspaper. Genoa claims the oldest bar in Nevada: it was built in 1863, so you won't be the first to hoist a brew here. Genoa was quickly eclipsed in the news by Virginia City, Carson City, and Reno, but its large homesteads sustained the town. Its scenic beauty and historic significance endure. *Contact Carson Valley Chamber of Commerce | 1512 U.S. 395, Suite 1, 89410 | 775/782–8144 or 800/727–7677 | www.carsonvalleynv.org. Greater Genoa Business Association | c/o Genoa Country Store, Box 571, 89411 | 775/782–5974.*

Carson Valley Museum and Cultural Center. The old Douglas County High School, built in 1915, has been restored and now serves as the area historical museum. Exhibits spotlight the Washoe Tribe, early Carson Valley pioneers, agriculture in the area, and the local Basque influence with exhibits such as a telephone time line (starting in 1876), 19th-century printshop and wooden-tool displays, and a life-size diorama of a Basque sheep camp. The museum is in Gardnerville, 8mi southeast of Genoa. | 721 Main St., Gardnerville | 775/782–2555 | Donations accepted | Daily 10–4.

Genoa Courthouse Museum. This building was a courthouse from 1865 to 1916. Now a museum, it contains exhibits of Washoe basketry, a model stamp mill, 19th-century furniture, and a life-size courtroom diorama; see if you can figure out what's going on in the scene. | 100 Foothill Rd. | 775/782–4325 | Donations accepted | May–Oct., daily 10–5.

Mormon Station State Historic Park. Though the local Washoe Indians were peaceful and kept to themselves, the Mormons built a stockade along with their trading post. At this small, historic park you can explore re-creations of the original structures, an early log cabin, and exhibits on pioneer life. | Foothill Rd. and Genoa La. | 775/687–4379 | www.state.nv.us/stparks | Free | May–Oct., daily 8–5.

GOLDFIELD
▼▼▼

Shortly after Tonopah became a silver boomtown in 1900, a couple of prospectors located metal of a more precious variety nearby, and Goldfield quickly became the largest city in Nevada. Large stone buildings rose out of the desert and bank vaults bulged with gold and cash. Goldfield attracted a national prizefight in 1906, and labor strife attracted the International Workers of the World (known as Wobblies) a year later; in 1910, the population peaked at 20,000. It's been downhill ever since, and today only 400 people live in Goldfield. Take a leisurely drive around town to see the buildings left over from the boom, such as the high school, the telegraph office, and the Goldfield Hotel. If it's open, you can wander around the Esmeralda County Courthouse. *Contact Goldfield Chamber of Commerce | Box 219, 89013 | 775/485–3560.*

Esmeralda County Courthouse. Built in 1907, this is one of the best preserved turn-of-the-20th-century courthouses in the state. You can wander around on your own, but if the courtroom's locked, ask someone to unlock it for you. You'll see the original Tiffany lamps on the judge's bench, 100-year-old chairs and fixtures, the judge's chambers, and a huge bighorn sheep trophy. | U.S. 95 | 775/485–3560 | Free | Weekdays 9–5.

Rhyolite. In 1904, a couple of prospectors were examining rocks in the desolate hills just south of the Beatty Ranch, on the trickling Amargosa River, when they found free-gold-bearing quartz. Within two months, 2,000 claims covered every square inch of ground within 30 miles, and the boomtown of Rhyolite was born. At the pinnacle of its success, in 1907, the city had a three-story bank, hotels, a large schoolhouse, an ice plant, and even electricity. But by 1910 the place was essentially deserted. Today, you can explore ruins such as the walls of the bank, part of the old jail, and the train depot. Stop by Tom Kelly's Bottle House (yes, it's made of bottles) for a free information brochure. | 4 mi west of Beatty off Rte. 374; 71 mi south of Goldfield via U.S. 95 | www.rhyolitesite.com | Free | Daily.

Santa Fe Saloon. This turn-of-the-20th-century bar hasn't been upgraded since it was built, so you can drink your fill of gold-rush ambience. Check out the framed newspapers, photos of Goldfield during its Old West period, antique Jolly Joker poker-pinball machine, and rickety floor. | 5th Ave. | 775/485–3431 | Free.

LAS VEGAS
▼▼

It's possible that no other city in the world is less devoted to its past than Las Vegas. The city was founded in 1905 by the San Pedro, Los Angeles & Salt Lake Railroad, and it didn't really get rolling until the 1930s. The one remaining 19th-century site is perhaps the least-visited attraction in the city, and other than two hard-to-find historic museums and the old fort, there are no other notable reminders of the railroad era. *Contact Las Vegas Chamber of Commerce | 3720 Howard Hughes Pkwy., 89109 | 702/735–1616 | fax 702/735–2011 | www.lvchamber.com. Las Vegas Convention and Visitors Authority | 3150 Paradise Rd., 89109 | 702/ 892–0711 or 800/332–5333 | www.lasvegas24hours.com.*

Marjorie Barrick Museum of Natural History. On the campus of University of Nevada at Las Vegas, this museum jam-packed with Gila monsters and dinosaur skeletons also has a comprehensive exhibit on southern Nevada history. Check out the displays of Native American baskets, masks, and jewelry; the painting of Fremont at Big Springs in 1844; and a "before-and-after" (1900 and 1978) look at Las Vegas Creek. | 4505 Maryland Pkwy. | 702/895–3381 | www.hrcweb.lv-hrc.nevada.edu/mbm/mbmmain.htm | Free | Weekdays 8–4:45, Sat. 10–2.

Nevada State Museum and Historical Society. Everything you wanted to know about the history and ecology of southern Nevada is covered in this extensive and fine collection in Lorenzi Park. There's a huge tribal map of Nevada, an exhibit on mining in southern Nevada, a ranching exhibit, and more. | 700 Twin Lakes Dr. | 702/486–52205 | www.state.nv.us | $2 | Daily 9–5.

Old Las Vegas Mormon Fort. Southern Nevada's oldest extant historical site is this agricultural mission, built by Mormons in 1855 to supply emigrants and traders traveling along the Old Mormon Trail. Abandoned for a decade (1858–68), the fort was resettled and later turned into a resort in the 1880s, with Las Vegas's first swimming hole. Today, a tiny remnant of the fort remains; inside you can see displays on the early history of Las Vegas, and antiques. | 500 E. Washington Ave. | 702/486–3511 | www.state.nv.us | $2 | Daily 8:30–4:30.

HISTORIC LODGING

Golden Gate Hotel and Casino. The closest you'll come to genuine Old West accommodations in Las Vegas is this hotel, which stands downtown at the corner of Fremont and Main. Built in 1905, the hotel has been restored; its exterior is in its original condition. The rooms are small but comfortable and affordable, and many are furnished with early 20th century antiques. coffee shop, deli, bar, casino. | 1 Fremont St., 89101 | 702/382–6300 or 800/426–1906. | www.goldengatehotel.com | 202 rooms | $32–$75 | AE, D, MC, V | CP.

PIOCHE
▼▼▼♦

Gold was discovered in the hills around Pioche (pronounced pee-*oach*) in 1869, and a notorious boomtown sprang up. Like Bodie, California, and Tombstone, Arizona, Pioche gained a reputation as one of the most rough-and-tumble Old West mining communities. Local legend has it that upward of 50 men died here violently before anyone succumbed to natural causes. During a boisterous block party in 1871, someone accidentally exploded 300 kegs of gunpowder, burning nearly the whole town to the ground. *Contact Pioche Chamber of Commerce | Main St. (Box 127, 89043) | 775/962–5544 | www.piochenevada.com. Regional Development Authority of Lincoln County | 100 Depot Ave., Suite 6, Caliente 89008 | 775/726–3209 | www.tradecon.com/lincoln/lincoln.html.*

Caliente. The San Pedro, Los Angeles & Salt Lake Railroad founded the town of Caliente in 1905 as a watering stop for its steam engines and named the town for its hot springs. Caliente was the site of the only railroad "war" in Nevada, when E. H. Harriman's Union Pacific claimed the same right of way as William Clark's San Pedro, Los Angeles & Salt Lake; in a race to lay track through narrow Rainbow Canyon south of the townsite, each line deployed thugs armed with axe handles and shovels. Eventually, the courts sided with Clark, who convinced Harriman to partner up on the one line. Railroad-company town bungalows, schools, a post office, even apartment buildings all date back to the earliest years. Rainbow Canyon, just outside town, is one of the most spectacular scenic drives in Nevada. | 22 mi south of Pioche on Rte. 93

In an old boxcar, the **Caliente Railroad Depot and Boxcar Museum** (100 Depot St. | 775/726–3199) documents the history of Lincoln County, including the railroad years. The old depot, open weekdays 10–2, now houses the chamber of commerce, city hall, and library, and most of its walls are covered with artwork by local artists. To see the museum ($1), you need to make an appointment.

Lincoln County Historical Museum. This two-room museum is chock-full of mining displays and pioneer dioramas and memorabilia. You'll find guns, medicines, clocks, and all the back issues of the local newspapers in one room. The other contains displays such as black-and-white photos of Pioche in its heyday and a large map of town from the 1870s. | Main St. | 775/962–5207 | Donations accepted | Tues.–Sun. 9–4.

Million-Dollar Courthouse. Docents will take you on a tour of this two-story building completed in 1876. Visit a historical photo room, the offices of the sheriff, district attorney, and assessor, the courtroom and the judge's chambers (the judge's bench and nearby chairs are original), and a jailhouse out back (the middle cell has the original bunk and leg chain). | Delmar St. | 775/962–5182 | Donations accepted | Apr.–Oct., daily 10–5.

PIOCHE'S MILLION-DOLLAR COURTHOUSE

In the beginning, Nevada was slightly more than half its current size. Carved out of the vast Utah Territory, Nevada Territory was originally assigned an eastern border that passed through what would become Elko and Eureka—roughly 100 mi west of Utah today. Its southern border with Arizona Territory was drawn through what is now Beatty on the west and Mesquite on the east, cutting off the whole southern tip of the state, including present-day Nevada's 150 mi of the Colorado River.

It wasn't until three years after statehood, in 1867, that the addition of three tracts of land—two from Utah and one from Arizona—perfected Nevada's distinctive shape. The vast southeastern tract, 18,500 square mi (roughly half the size of Virginia), became Lincoln County, and Pioche, a lawless mining boomtown where silver and gold had been discovered in 1869, was eventually named the county seat.

County administrative duties began to tame the town, and women arrived on the scene. Some miners married and settled down, but others, according to one historian, grew reluctant to walk down the street "for fear of coming home with a wife." The Single Men's Protective Association was formed in 1876 to help bachelors "withstand the wiles of the fair sex."

Street violence subsided, but behind the scenes corruption reigned supreme. Lincoln County politicians developed a fondness for running up expenses that far exceeded the government's revenues. Residents and local mining companies disdained taxes of any kind, and what little taxes the sheriff's department managed to collect rarely made it into the county coffers. To make up for shortfalls in the county's official and unofficial budgets, politicians floated bonds, printed local scrip, and quickly doomed the county to decades of debt.

Though it had a tenuous grasp on law and order, Pioche required a courthouse. The Lincoln County Courthouse proved to be the enduring symbol of those early free-wheeling days. When it was designed in 1871, it was projected to cost $16,000, but construction overruns nearly doubled the budget. The price tag came to $26,000 when the building was completed in 1876. The county struggled to make scheduled payments on the high-interest bonds that it had issued to finance the courthouse. By 1890, officials had yet to pay down the principal, while accrued interest totaled $400,000—nearly 70% of the assessed value of the entire county.

The politicians tried to default on the bonds, but the state would not allow it, so the county's commissioners refinanced the debt. This only made things worse, and the debt increased another quarter million dollars by 1907. When the bonds were finally paid off in 1938, almost seven decades after the construction project was planned, the courthouse had cost a cool mil. Four years earlier, the million-dollar courthouse had been condemned as uninhabitable, though it still stands and has been refurbished into a museum. The same year the debt was retired, a new courthouse was completed.

RENO

▼▼

Reno was founded in the late 1860s as a depot on the Central Pacific Railroad, part of the transcontinental line. The closest main-line station to Virginia City and the Comstock Lode, Reno prospered when the Virginia & Truckee short line connected it in 1872 to the mines and mills to its south. After the Comstock played out in the late 1870s, Reno's fortunes continued to rise, even as the rest of the state descended into the Big Bust. Brick buildings were built downtown, the railroad kept commerce steady, saloons and gambling parlors lined Virginia Street, banks and hotels flourished, and even a fire in 1879 barely slowed the city's steady growth. As the largest city in Nevada, Reno attracted prosperity, culture, and people; only in the 1950s was it finally eclipsed by Las Vegas. The city gained a measure of notoriety in the early 1900s, when a New York lawyer discovered Nevada's liberal divorce laws and publicized Reno as a divorce haven. Soon afterward the town named itself "the Biggest Little City in the World." *Contact Greater Reno-Sparks Chamber of Commerce | 405 Marsh Ave., 89505 | 775/686–3030 | www.reno-sparkschamber.org. Reno/Sparks Convention and Visitor Authority | 4950 S. Virginia St., 89502 | 775/827–7366 or 800/367–7366 | www.playreno.com.*

Nevada Historical Society Museum. One of the best museums in the state, the Nevada Historical Society has numerous exhibits on Native Nevada cultures, mining, the Pony Express, the railroad, and recent state history. The time line alone is good for an hour's perusal. | 1650 N. Virginia Ave. | 775/688–1190 | Donations accepted | Mon.–Sat. 10–5.

TONOPAH

▼▼▼

In the fall of 1900, Jim Butler staked several claims on Mizpah Hill in central Nevada and dug out some ore containing a large percentage of high-grade gold and silver. Immediately, Tonopah burst onto the scene, launching Nevada's second 20-year mining boom. The town rode high for 15 years, and many young mine superintendents, bankers, and politicians, such as Tasker Oddie (later governor), Key Pittman and Patrick McCarran (later U.S. senators), and George Nixon and George Wingfield (later big bankers) rose to prominence during that time. In the Castle House, built in 1906, the wife of a prominent banker held seances in the tower room. A ghost is said to have haunted the house since then. *Contact Tonopah Chamber of Commerce | 301 Brougher Ave., 89049 | 775/482–3859 | www.tonopahnevada.com. Tonopah Convention Center | 301 Brougher Ave., 89049 | 775/482–3558 | www.tonopahminingpark.org.*

Central Nevada Museum. This museum houses an excellent and extensive collection of later Old West items from all over central Nevada. The outdoor exhibit contains big mining machinery and a replica of the town site as it was at the turn of the 20th century. Inside are Shoshone baskets, a 1900s assay office, Tonopah's first organ, an old barber chair from the Goldfield Hotel, and photos of the early mines and miners. | Logan Field Rd. | 775/482–9676 | Donations accepted | Apr.–Sept., daily 9–5; Oct.–Mar., daily 11–5.

Mizpah Hotel. The tallest building in town—in fact, the tallest building between Carson City and Las Vegas—the Mizpah (built in 1906) stands at the center of Tonopah. The hotel has been shut down and re-opened a number of times since the 1990s, so you may only be able to see it from the outside. | 100 Main St.

Tonopah Mining Park. At this 70-acre park you can see silver mines just as they were left when they shut down. A one-hour guided tour, which leaves from the Central Nevada Museum, takes you through the Top and Mizpah mines, where hoistworks, warehouses, and a 100-ft-deep glory hole (mining pit) are preserved. There's an excellent view of downtown Tonopah from the park. | At the top of Mizpah Ave. | 775/482–9676 | fax 775/482–5423 | www.tonopahnevada.com/tonopahhistoricminingpark.htm | $3 | May–Sept., daily 10–5; Oct.–Apr., Tues.–Sat. 11–4.

✦ ON THE CALENDAR: July **Jim Butler Days.** One of Nevada's most popular pioneer festivals draws people from all over the state. Three days of events include a parade, a barbecue and chili cook-off, an arts-and-crafts fair, a dance, and the state's biggest pancake breakfast. | 775/482–3878.

VIRGINIA CITY

▼▼

Prospectors had been working the creeks at the bottom of Sun Mountain for nearly a decade before a couple of them climbed up the steep eastern slope in 1859, stuck a shovel into the ground, and discovered the richest lode of silver and gold in the history of the continental United States. Another prospector, Henry Comstock, claimed that the land on the mountain was part of his ranch. The lode was named for him, but he sold out several months after the first strike for a few hundred dollars. A few months later, the Comstock Lode had attracted more than 10,000 fortune seekers and the town of Virginia City mushroomed on the hillside.

The Comstock boom raged for 20 years, and Virginia City reigned as one of the largest cities in the United States. At its peak, Virginia City's population hovered around 25,000. Mark Twain, then in his early 20s was one of those who came to town; here he got his start as a frontier journalist and teller of tall tales. He hired on as a correspondent for the local newspaper, the *Territorial Enterprise*. Below the city streets miners dug and blasted silver and gold from the underground hard-rock mines, earning $4 a day, a princely sum for laborers in a boomtown where a fancy steak dinner cost $1 and rent for a month in a rooming house ran $10.

The mines kept getting deeper and more dangerous, and the largest orebody on the Comstock, the Big Bonanza, was struck in 1872 at 1,200 ft. It was so rich that the mine owner, John Mackay, was able to build a mansion and open a bank in San Francisco, endow the University of Nevada, and send the better part of a ton of silver to Tiffany & Co. in New York City, which fabricated a 1,600-piece silver dining service and shipped it back to Nevada. When the Great Fire of 1875 burned 33 blocks of Virginia City, including all of downtown, the Big Bonanza funded the rebuilding. Most of the town's major structures date from that year. In all, the Comstock yielded precious metal valued at roughly $750 million in 1880 dollars—that's about $10 billion today. But the boom eventually went bust around 1879, and the gold-hungry hordes moved on.

Today Virginia City is a caricature of its Old West self, with dozens of themed tourist traps dispensing souvenirs, gifts, candy, jewelry, crafts, leather goods, candles, glassware, cigars, mineral samples, and books. Nevertheless the town is photogenic, with Old West storefronts and wooden sidewalks along D Street, the main drag. Add the museums, mansions, mine tours, churches, cemeteries, saloons, back streets, and a railroad ride, and Virginia City can entertain you for two or three days. *Contact Virginia City Chamber of Commerce | Box 464, 89440 | 775/847–0311 | www.virginiacity-nv.org. Virginia City Convention and Tourism Authority | Box 920, 89440 | 775/847–7500 | www.virginiacity-nv.org.*

The Castle. Perhaps the most authentic historical attraction in the state, the Castle has never been restored. It was built in 1868 by a mine superintendent and sold only twice, with all of its furnishings included. The museum portion of the house is outfitted with an excellent collection of the original European accoutrements, such as French wallpaper, Italian marble fireplaces, Dutch vases, Czech crystal chandeliers, Belgian lace, and German furniture. Your guide will tell you all about the Italian hanging staircase. | 70 B St. | 775/847–0275 | $4 | Daily 10–5.

Dayton. It claims to be older than Genoa, but Dayton is probably the second-oldest town in Nevada. Here, in Gold Creek, prospectors found the first gold in Nevada in 1849. The strike was just enough to keep a handful of gold panners in nuggets for nearly a decade. In the small downtown historic district are restored 19th-century buildings such as the Dayton Grammar School (1865) and Odeon Hall (1870). In the Dayton Cemetery (founded 1861) up the hill from downtown is the grave of James "Old Virginny" Finney, who gave Virginia City its name. | 11 mi southeast of Virginia City via Rte. 341 and U.S. 50 | 775/246–7909 | www. daytonnvchamber.org.

Fourth Ward School. Built in 1876, this is one of the few schools of this size and type still standing in the United States. The four-story structure, which accommodated 1,000 students, served as a school through 1936. Several classrooms have been restored to their original appearance. The museum contains a good retrospective of the Comstock, with models of the mines and mills, exhibits on mining technology, a look at the entertainment of the time, background on Mark Twain, and more. | C St. | 775/847–0975 | Donations accepted. | Mid-May–Oct., daily 10–5.

Mackay Mansion. The lavish interior of the 1870s home of one of the Bonanza Kings is open for self-guided tours. The layout remains the same as when the house was built, and the rooms are decorated with period furniture. | 129 D St. | 775/847–0173 | $4 | Daily 10–6.

Mark Twain Museum. Virginia City's most famous resident was Mark Twain, who lived here from 1861 to 1864 while working as a reporter for the *Territorial Enterprise*. The exhibit room occupies the newspaper's pressroom and displays 19th-century printing equipment. Oddly, though, there's nothing on Twain himself in the museum. | 47 S. C St. | 775/847–0525 | $1 | Daily 10–5.

Silver City. Along with Gold Hill and Virginia City, this was one of the Comstock's original tri-towns. Among the sights to see here are the Keystone mine's headframe, built in the 1850s. Devil's Gate, a natural rock outcropping that's split in two (the road runs through it) formed a natural boundary between the residential district and the blasting, drilling, and digging of the mining district. | 4 mi south of Virginia City on Rte. 342.

Virginia & Truckee Railroad. One of the most profitable and celebrated short-line railroads in American history, the V&T was completed in 1869 and hauled millions of dollars of gold and silver ore from the Comstock mines to the mills in Carson City. Today, the steam-powered train makes 35-minute round trips nine times daily between Virginia City and the town of Gold Hill, passing through Tunnel No. 4. You can ride in open or covered cars. | Washington and F Sts. | 775/847–0380 | $5.50 | Late Apr.–Sept., daily 10:30–5:45

The Way It Was Museum. For insight into local history, spend some time at this museum. Watch a 16-minute video on Comstock Lode history and check out mining displays such as a working model of an early water-powered stamp mill. Costumed mannequins, pioneer tools, and a blacksmith shop are also among the exhibits. | C St. and Sutton Dr. | 775/847–0766 | $2.50 | Daily 10–6.

HISTORIC DINING AND LODGING

The Gold Hill Hotel. Probably the finest historic accommodations in Nevada, this is also the state's oldest operating inn, opened in 1860. There are four guest rooms in the original two-story structure; they're small, but each has a private bath and the two front rooms have private balconies overlooking the road. Another eight rooms are in the new wing, built in 1987; four have working fireplaces and balconies. The Great Room on the main floor is original and looks it; the cozy stone bar looks it too, though it was added in 1960. The Crown Point Restaurant serves lunch and dinner daily. Restaurant, bar. | Main St., Gold Hill 89440 | 775/847–0111 | www.goldhillhotel.net | 12 rooms | $45–$125 | AE, D, MC, V.

WINNEMUCCA
▼▼

In the 1860s, the great Paiute chief Winnemucca made a lasting peace between the Northern Paiute and white settlers in northern Nevada, which was only broken by a handful of minor skirmishes. This town named after him supported a ferry service for emigrants crossing the Humboldt River to turn north into Oregon. The establishment here of a station on the Transcontinental Railroad ensured the town's survival. *Contact Winnemucca Chamber of Commerce | 30 Winnemucca Blvd., 89445 | 775/623–2225 or 800/962–2638 | www.winnemucca-nv.org. Winnemucca Convention and Visitors Bureau | 50 W. Winnemucca Blvd., 89445 | 775/623–5071 or 800/962–2638 | www.winnemucca-nv.org.*

Humboldt Museum. A church built in 1907 now houses local Native American objects and artifacts of early Winnemucca life, including the town's first piano, brought here in 1868. A newer building adjacent contains a wall-length mural depicting the town at the turn of the 20th century. | Jungo Rd. and Maple Ave. | 775/623–2912 | www.humboldt-county-nv.net | Donations accepted | Weekdays 10–noon and 1–4, Sat. 1–4.

Trail of the '49ers Interpretive Center. This small museum, 54 mi southeast of Winnemucca, packs a big historical punch, with displays of artifacts from the Humboldt Trail, which the gold-rushers followed through northern Nevada. You can see exhibits of antique firearms, stock animals, and covered wagons (ask the docent to describe the mechanics of the Conestoga wagon centerpiece). | 453 N. 2nd St., Battle Mountain | 775/635–5720 | Donations accepted | Weekdays 10–5, Sat. noon–4.

HISTORIC DINING AND LODGING

Old Pioneer Garden B&B. Scattered among Unionville's well-kept houses and gardens and the huge old trees lining the main street are a number of gold-rush ruins. The place to stay hereabouts (46 mi southwest of Winnemucca) is a complex of three rustic buildings. Six rooms are in the Hadley House, a stone structure that dates from 1861. The Tack Room is in a stone-floor barn where your horses can stay, too (in separate quarters). The Field House contains four more rooms. Your full breakfast is prepared with the inn's own eggs, fruit, and dairy products; dinner is available by advance arrangement for a small fee. Dining room, fishing, piano; no room phones, no room TVs. | 2805 Unionville Rd., Unionville 89418 | 775/538–7585 or 800/538–7556 | www.virtualcities.com/ons/nv/c/nvc4101.htm | 11 rooms, 6 with bath | $75–$95 | No credit cards.

Winnemucca Hotel. Basque. The oldest building (1863) in town, the Winnemucca Hotel is actually a boarding house offering long-term rentals to Basques. But you can get a taste of the area's Basque heritage in the dining room, which serves an ample lunch and dinner family-style. The ornately carved and mirrored bar is one of the most spectacular in Nevada, with a collection of international currency displayed above; the cash register is ancient. | 95 Bridge St. | 775/623–2908 | $6–$16 | MC, V.

YERINGTON
▾▾▾

Since the 1860s, Yerington has been a small supply town for the Smith and Mason valleys, which shelter some of the richest agricultural land in Nevada, watered by the Walker River. When the Carson & Colorado Railroad laid tracks nearby in 1890, it ensured the farm town's future by giving it access to larger markets. Today, the pace here is probably no faster than it was in 1876. *Contact Mason Valley Chamber of Commerce | 227 S. Main St., 89447 | 775/463–2245 | www.tele-net.net/mvcc.*

Fort Churchill State Historic Park. The first and largest army outpost in Nevada, Fort Churchill was built in 1860 to protect white travelers and miners from marauding Paiutes. A 700-acre park 32 mi north of Yerington contains the extensive ruins of the fort buildings, which you can wander through and around. Exhibits in the visitor center tell the fort's story, from its service as a Pony Express stop, through the Civil War, to the arrival of the telegraph. The park's campground lies under towering cottonwoods near the Carson River. | U.S. 95A | 775/577–2345 | www.state.nv.us/stparks | Free | Daily 10–4.

Lyon County Museum. This museum overflows with local history: Paiute baskets, cradle boards, and the like are on display along with a large copper-mining exhibit. You can also see re-creations of an Old West sheriff's office, a pioneer kitchen, and a barber shop. | 215 S. Main St. | 775/463–6576 | Donations accepted | Fri. noon–4, Sat. 10–4, Sun. 1–4, or by appointment.

✦ ON THE CALENDAR: Aug. **Wovoka Days.** A small spiritual powwow honors Wovoka, who started the Ghost Dance movement that culminated in the massacre at Wounded Knee. Wovoka was from the Yerington area, and the powwow is held on the Yerington Paiute Reservation. | 775/463–2350.

NEW MEXICO

———>◆<———

New Mexico's long and intriguing history is a saga of three cultures. From the time Spanish conquistadores first set foot here to the day New Mexico became the 47th of the United States—and beyond—the conflicts between and intermingling of three distinctly different peoples has given rise to a unique hybrid culture, language, architecture, and cuisine. Pueblo Indian and Spanish ways melded in many respects in the nearly 250 years New Mexico was ruled by New Spain. The Anglos (any non-indigenous, non-Hispanic person in New Mexico is considered an Anglo—even those who don't normally identify with the Anglo-Saxon tradition) were the last to arrive, bringing with them railroads, prospecting, and the ways of the Wild West.

Ancestral Puebloan civilizations waxed and waned in New Mexico for centuries before Europeans arrived. The first significant exploration of New Mexico by Europeans was made in 1540, when conquistador Francisco Vázquez de Coronado came looking for legendary cities of gold. Forty-odd years later the rulers of Nueva España (New Spain) laid claim to the northern province they called Nuevo Mexico (New Mexico). In 1598 Juan de Oñate established the first Spanish settlement in New Mexico, near present-day Espanola. Don Pedro de Peralta founded La Villa Real de la Santa Fe de San Francisco de Asís (the Royal City of the Holy Faith of St. Francis of Assisi), known simply as Santa Fe, in the first decade of the 17th century, at least 10 years before the first European pilgrims landed at Plymouth Rock in Massachusetts. At the time, English colonists were making a go of it in Jamestown, Virginia.

At first the Spanish brutally enslaved and mistreated the Indians, largely through a system of exploitative Franciscan missions. In 1680 the Pueblo people rose in revolt, burning Spanish homes and churches and killing hundreds of Spaniards. After an extended siege in Santa Fe, the colonists were driven out of New Mexico. The tide turned 12 years later, when General Don Diego de Vargas returned with a new army from El Paso and recaptured

Santa Fe. The then-grand El Camino Real (Royal Road), stretching from Mexico City to Santa Fe, brought an army of conquistadores, clergymen, and settlers to New Mexico. It seems the Spanish took a lesson from the Pueblo revolt, practicing from here on in a certain degree of tolerance for Pueblo culture and religion.

Perhaps that was because they needed the Indians. The colonists of this remote outpost of New Spain struggled to eke out a living with little help from the empire. The two peoples faced a common enemy in the warlike Plains Indians, including Comanche and Apache, who roamed farther and farther from their eastward homes on horses newly acquired from Spanish explorers and traders. Then there were the elements. To survive in New Mexico, Spanish farmers and merchants eventually aligned themselves with the agrarian Pueblo tribes. The Indians passed on their uses for chile, beans, and corn, and the Spanish shared their skill at metalwork, influencing the Indian jewelry that has become typical of the region. The Spanish also shared their architecture, which itself had been influenced by 700 years of Arab domination of Spain, and the *acequia* method of irrigation still in use in the villages of northern New Mexico. Colonial authorities even extended some land grants to various Pueblos, enabling residents to keep their ancestral homes.

The relationship between Indian and Spaniard was not, however, one of equals. Armed with Bibles instead of swords, Spanish Catholic missionaries infiltrated the native cultures. They forced the Indians to build adobe missions—some that still exist—and filled them with crosses and candle-lit shrines. Pueblo people were often converted (sometimes against their will) to Catholicism, and intermarriage between Native Americans and the isolated Spanish colonists was common. For nearly 150 years after their reconquest of New Mexico the Spanish ruled the region, establishing outposts throughout the area. Santa Cruz was founded in 1695 and Albuquerque in 1706; Franciscan priests built churches in Pecos (1717), Las Trampas (1776), and elsewhere; and land grants were given to people (many of them mestizos, of mixed blood) willing to establish settlements beyond the relatively populous Rio Grande valley. Throughout the 18th century, the Spanish defended the colony from nearly constant incursions by Plains Indians.

New Mexicans under Spanish rule lived on the fringes of civilization, forbidden to trade with Anglo-Americans. But the westward expansion of the United States could not be halted, and in 1820 the Santa Fe Trail was inaugurated. The trail started in Missouri and crossed much of Kansas before splitting into northern (Mountain Route) and southern (Cimarron Cut-Off) branches, which came together at Fort Union, New Mexico and terminated at Santa Fe's central Plaza. After Mexico achieved independence from Spain in 1821, its subsequent rule of New Mexico officially opened the door to Anglo-American traders. A booming commerce with the United States was born, and a flood of covered wagons spilled along the Santa Fe Trail. As the economy developed, the region became more desirable. Mexico suppressed a revolt against its rule of New Mexico in 1837 and rebuffed an invasion from Texas in 1841.

But like Spain before it, Mexico could not withstand the relentless advance of American interest in New Mexico. In 1846 the U.S. claimed the territory (which at the time also included Arizona) as its own. The Mexican-American War raged across the Southwest before the United States emerged victorious in 1848. After centuries of almost exclusive occupation by people of Spanish and Native American descent, New Mexico fell under U.S. rule. The Territory of New Mexico (which included parts of Colorado as well as Arizona) was organized in 1850 and was quickly drawn into the maelstrom of America's westward expansion. During the Civil War, Confederates troops from Texas invaded in hopes of gaining control of access routes to California ports and Colorado gold and silver mines. The Confederates retreated within a year, unable to live off the hostile land long enough to defeat Union forces. In 1863, Arizona became a territory separate from New Mexico, and the boundary between New Mexico and Colorado was finalized.

As soon as New Mexico became a U.S. territory, the U.S. Army started building forts to subdue local and invading Indian tribes, so white settlement could increase. Violence became a way of life in New Mexico. Anglos were less inclined than Spaniards to blend with people of other cultures, and they began to persecute the Indian and Hispanic populations. Campaigns against the Navajo (1849–61), the Comanche (1867–75), and the Apache (1873, 1885–86) forced the Indians onto ever-smaller and more remote reservations. Fierce Chiricahua Apache leaders such as Cochise, Geronimo, and Victorio fought back, hiding out in the rugged back country, raiding settlements, and ambushing soldiers and posses. By 1886, when Geronimo surrendered for the last time (in Arizona), any Indians who had not fled or been deported from New Mexico were confined to reservations within the territory.

New Mexico's reputation for lawlessness grew, and the territory was often regarded as a haven for outlaws. Though the territory was open for settlement, most civilized folk went elsewhere, choosing to sidestep the "badlands." The forbidding landscape and Indian wars of New Mexico didn't put off ranchers like John Chisum, who first drove longhorns up the Chisum Trail (not to be confused with the Chisholm Trail from Fort Worth, Texas, to Kansas) from Paris, Texas, to Roswell in 1872. He and his compatriots, Englishman John Tunstall and attorney Alexander McSween, soon found themselves in a battle against powerful merchant Lawrence Murphy for political and economic control of Lincoln County. As the conflict intensified, gunfighters like Billy the Kid signed on to one side or the other, and violence was inevitable. The infamous Lincoln County War broke out in 1878 and raged in a series of gunfights and murders until 1881, when Sheriff Pat Garrett became a national hero for gunning down Billy the Kid in Fort Sumner.

Episodes like the Lincoln County War made the rest of the nation leery of New Mexico, and Congress hesitated to grant the territory statehood. But the same year the Lincoln County War started, the Atchison, Topeka & Santa Fe Railway laid the first tracks into New Mexico. The line reached Santa Fe in 1880. Other railroads soon followed, and with them came rapid growth. Part of the white demand for New Mexican lands had to do with the area's mineral riches. Indians had mined sacred turquoise for hundreds of years and copper had been mined as early as 1804, near Santa Rita, and gold as early as 1828, in the Ortiz Mountains, but it was not until after the Civil War and the suppression of the Indian threat that mining in New Mexico started in earnest. As they did throughout the Old West, boomtowns sprang up and then died, their fortunes tied to discoveries of gold, silver, and copper. Today, more than 1,000 ghost towns are scattered across New Mexico.

Its mineral wealth and increasing stability began to earn New Mexico some respect in the United States. The territory gained further respect in 1898, when Theodore Roosevelt recruited his regiment of Rough Riders in New Mexico and took them to Cuba to fight in the Spanish-American War. The Rough Riders were instrumental to the American victory in Cuba. New Mexico began to look toward statehood, though some miners feared the regulation and taxation that would come with it. Finally, in 1912 New Mexico became the 47th of the United States.

The past is present in New Mexico today. In isolated villages of northern New Mexico, ancient Spanish linguistic styles and native Pueblo languages are still sometimes intermingled, and throughout the state the English spoken today is peppered with words and phrases from Spanish and the many Indian tongues indigenous to the region. Native Americans still dwell in pueblos near Albuquerque, Taos, and Santa Fe, within the same multistory adobe habitats occupied by their ancestors centuries ago. Some cities retain their old-town Spanish adobe neighborhoods built around cobbled plazas. Foods usually thought of as Mexican appear on almost every restaurant menu and in almost every market. Cowboy boots and hats, frontier-era storefronts, and vast ranches reflect the Anglo influence. And everywhere, you can see the Old West in the faces of New Mexico's people.

NEW MEXICO TIME LINE

1540 Francisco Vázquez de Coronado conducts the first significant exploration of New Mexico in a search for rumored cities of gold.

1583 New Spain declares Nuevo Mexico (New Mexico) a province.

1598 Juan de Oñate, the first governor of New Mexico, claims the Rio Grande drainage for Spain and establishes the first Spanish capital near what is now Espanola.

1610 Santa Fe is named the capital of Spanish New Mexico.

1680 Northern New Mexico Pueblo Indians, outraged by atrocities committed by Spanish explorers and colonists, revolt. Many settlers are killed and the rest are driven south.

1692 Don Diego de Vargas leads new colonists into New Mexico, with promises to the Indians of better treatment. The Pueblo revolt ends.

1706 Villa de Albuquerque is founded.

1820 The first American traders arrive in Santa Fe's Plaza via the Santa Fe Trail.

1821 Mexico wins its independence from Spain.

1824 Mexico claims New Mexico as a territory.

1846 The Mexican-American war begins after the United States declares ownership of New Mexico.

1848 The war between Mexico and the United States ends with the Treaty of Guadalupe Hidalgo, which makes New Mexico part of the U.S.

1850 The United States establishes New Mexico Territory.

1854 Purchase from Mexico adds the Mesilla Valley to New Mexico.

1861 During the Civil War, Confederate forces from Texas invade New Mexico. A year later they retreat.

1872 Texas cattle king John Chisum drives his first herd of longhorns up the Chisum Trail and sets up a huge ranch near present-day Roswell.

1878 The Lincoln County War begins. It ends three years later.

1879 New Mexico's first railroad, the Atchison, Topeka & Santa Fe, reaches Las Vegas.

1886 The Apache Wars end with the surrender of Geronimo.

1912 New Mexico is admitted to the Union as the 47th state.

Along El Camino Real

A DRIVING TOUR FROM SANTA FE TO MESILLA

Distance: 285 mi   **Time:** 3 days
Breaks: Take refuge in Santa Fe in the rooftop garden of the city's oldest hotel, La Fonda. In Albuquerque, sample traditional Indian fry bread at the Indian Pueblo Cultural Center's restaurant. Dine on Mexican food at the old stage stop of La Posta in Mesilla.

In the late 1500s, long before the arrival of the pilgrims in New England, Spanish colonists established an inland trade route between Mexico City in the heart of Mexico and Santa

NEW MEXICO

OKLAHOMA   TEXAS

UTAH

COLORADO

ARIZONA

Clayton
Springer
Raton
Cimarron
Tres Piedras
Taos
Taos Pueblo
Rancho de Taos
Chimayó
Española
Abiquiú
Chama
Aztec
Shiprock
Farmington
Gallup
Grants
Santa Fe
Las Vegas
Pecos
Cerillos
Madrid
Golden
San Felipe Pueblo
Sandia Pueblo
Bernalillo
Coronado State Mon.
Albuquerque
Isleta Pueblo
Belén
Tijeras
Acoma Pueblo
Encino
Mountainair
Salinas Pueblo Missions Nat'l Mon.
Tucumcari
Clovis
Fort Sumner
Fort Sumner State Mon.
Watrous
Ft. Union Nat'l Mon.
Ute Cr.
Mosquero
Conchas Lake
Conchas R.
Canadian R.
Canadian
Vermejo R.
Mora R.
Catalinas R.
Pecos R.
Rio Grande
Rio Grande
Rio Puerco
Rio
Chaco R.
Chaco R.
Chaco R.
San Juan R.

KIOWA NAT'L GRASSLANDS
CARSON NAT'L FOR.
CIBOLA NAT'L FOR.
CIBOLA NAT'L FOR.
ZUNI INDIAN RES.
Chaco Culture Nat'l Historic Park

456
406
370
402
551
325
562
102
420
420
54
40
209
467
64 87
56
412
120
39
420
39
40
285
40
54
252
60 84
20
203
156
104
84
285
60
58
21
161
518
161
518
434
64
522
196
285
285
84
64
84
502
501
4
550
550
537
539
511
550
573
574
666
371
57
57
9
400
602
264
40
53
117
117
603
36
601
53
117
47
6
337
55
41
42
55
60
3
3
68
518
25
25
25
25

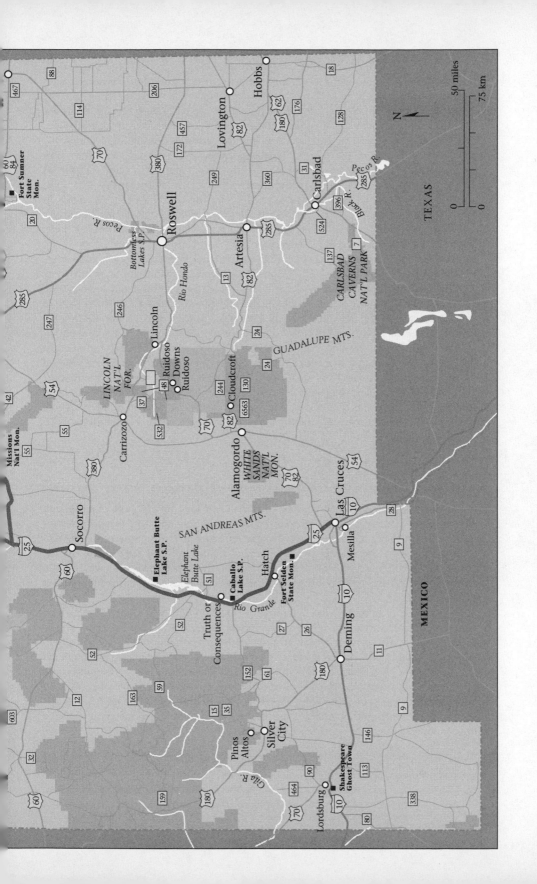

Fe in New Mexico. Known as the royal road—El Camino Real—the road brought Spanish goods, settlers, and influence into New Mexico. Interstate 25 follows the north–south route of El Camino Real along the Rio Grande between Santa Fe and the Texas border south of Mesilla.

Begin your trip in what once was Spain's provincial capital in New Mexico, **Santa Fe.** Plan to spend at least a day and an evening visiting 17th- and 18th-century Spanish sites, such as the Plaza, the Palace of the Governors, and the centuries-old San Miguel mission.

On day two, drive 62 mi south on I–25 to **Albuquerque,** where you can spend the morning in the city's Old Town district, noted for its 18th-century architecture and for galleries full of paintings and icons from early Spanish New Mexico. In the afternoon, take I–25 south 36 mi to Belén and pick up Route 47 southeast for 19 mi and U.S. 60 east for 22 mi to Salinas Pueblo Missions National Monument. Three sites, each with the ruins of a 17th-century Spanish-colonial Franciscan missionary church and an associated pueblo, await you there. Backtrack and spend the night in Albuquerque.

Get an early start on your third day for a 227-mi drive south on I–25. Traders and settlers from New Spain made their way north through these sparse grasslands and stark hills in ox carts, 400 years ago. Indian attacks were frequent, disease was common and some hapless travelers died of thirst in the desert. When you reach Elephant Butte Lake north of Truth or Consequences, you'll be at the northern tip of a notorious portion of El Camino Real known as *Jornada del Muerto,* or Journey of Death. Some of this stretch of the old road is now underwater and some is on private land, but your drive will give you a taste of what the trail must have been like. Legend has it that the city of Las Cruces (the crosses), about 75 mi south of Truth of Consequences, takes its name for the crosses used to mark the place where some travelers on El Camino Real were ambushed and killed by Indians. The end of your trail is in **Mesilla,** whose 19th century Mexican-style plaza is lined with old adobe buildings. Those on their way to Mexico City would have had another 900 mi to go on El Camino Real.

ALBUQUERQUE
▼▼

Albuquerque's rich colonial history begins with the city's founding in 1796 as an agricultural settlement. The city is named for Spain's duke of Alburquerque (the first "r" was later dropped), who at the time was viceroy of New Spain. The name was chosen by Don Francisco Cuervo y Valdés, a provincial governor of New Mexico, who hoped flattery would induce the duke to waive the requirement that a town have 30 families before a charter was issued— there were only 15 families here at the time. The duke acquiesced. (Albuquerque is to this day nicknamed the "Duke City.")

The settlement prospered thanks to its strategic location on the El Camino Real, which wound from Mexico City to Santa Fe and was for centuries New Mexico's primary link to the outside world. Also helping to spur economic growth was Albuquerque's proximity to several Indian pueblos, which were a source of commerce and provided protection from raiding nomadic tribes. As in other Spanish settlements, Albuquerque's homes were built around a central plaza for protection. The fortresslike community could be entered from the four corners only, making it easier to defend. This four-block area is now called Old Town. In the 19th century Albuquerque became the starting point of the Turquoise Trail, along which a string of mining communities prospered. *Contact Albuquerque Convention and Visitors Bureau | 20 1st Plaza NW, Suite 601, 87125 | 505/842–9918 or 800/284–2282 | www.abqcvb.org.*

Albuquerque Museum of Art and History. Housed in a modern structure, this expansive facility in Old Town contains the largest collection of Spanish colonial artifacts in the nation, along with relics of the city's birth and development. The centerpiece of the colonial exhibit is a pair of life-size models of Spanish conquistadores in original chain mail and armor. | 2000 Mountain Rd. NW | 505/243–7255 or 505/242–4600 | $2 | Tues.–Sun. 9–5.

El Camino Real Visitors Center. A small, workaday town 35 mi south of Albuquerque via I–25, Belén grew up as an important stop on the El Camino Real. Here, exhibits at the El Camino Real Visitors Center tell the story of the Spanish *entrada* along this ageless highway to empire. | 201 Rio Communities Blvd., Belén | 505/864–8091 | Free | Daily 10–2.

Indian Pueblo Cultural Center. Here you can find out what you need to know about each of the state's 19 pueblos; the center is an excellent general resource for learning about the state's indigenous tribes and how they adapted to the period of Spanish colonization beginning in the mid-1500s. On the upper level exhibits represent the arts and crafts of each of the 19 pueblos, while on the lower level you'll find exhibits that trace the history of each pueblo. Learn how the pueblos have preserved many traditions and ideals that date back many hundreds of years and how they both adopted and rejected aspects of Spanish culture and Catholic religion during the colonial period. | 2401 12th St. NW | 505/843–7270 or 800/766–4405 | www.indianpueblo.org | $4 | Daily 9–5:30.

Isleta Pueblo. Isleta was one of the few pueblos that didn't participate in the Pueblo Revolt of 1680, during which Isleta was abandoned. Facing the quiet plaza is Isleta's church, St. Augustine, built in 1629. One of the oldest churches in New Mexico, it has thick adobe walls, a viga-crossed ceiling, and simple interior decor. The pueblo is 13 mi south of Albuquerque via I–25 to Route 47; follow signs. | Tribal Rd. 40 | 505/869–3111 | Free | Camera use restricted; only church may be photographed.

Old Town Plaza. Don Francisco Cuervo y Valdés, a provincial governor of New Mexico, laid out this small plaza in 1706. Today the plaza is an oasis of tranquillity filled with shade trees, wrought-iron benches, a graceful white gazebo, and strips of grass. Mock gunfights are staged on Romero Street on Sunday afternoons, and during fiestas, Old Town comes alive with mariachi bands and dancing señoritas. | Bounded by Mountain Rd., San Felipe, Old Town Rd., and Tiguex Park | 505/243–3215.

Built in 1793, **San Felipe de Neri Church** (2005 Plaza NW | 505/243–4628) is still active. The building, which replaced Albuquerque's first Catholic church, has been enlarged and expanded several times, but its adobe walls and other original features remain. Next to it is a small museum that displays relics—vestments, paintings, carvings—dating from the 17th century.

Salinas Pueblo Missions National Monument. When Francisco Vásquez de Coronado arrived in what is now New Mexico in 1540, he found a dozen or so villages along the Rio Grande in the province of Tiguex, between what is now Bernalillo to the north of Albuquerque and Isleta to the south. Salinas Pueblo Missions National Monument, about 65 mi southeast of Albuquerque, comprises three sites—Quarai, Abó, and Gran Quivira—each with the ruins of a 17th-century Spanish-colonial Franciscan missionary church and an associated pueblo. Quarai was abandoned about 50 years after its mission church, San Purísima Concepción de Cuarac, was built in 1630. At Abó are the remains of the three-story church of San Gregorio and a large unexcavated pueblo. A video about Salinas Pueblo can be viewed at Gran Quivira, which contains two churches and some excavated Native American structures. | 15 mi east on I–40 to Rte. 337, then 30 mi south on Rte. 337 and 24 mi south on Rte. 55 | 505/847–2585 | Free | Late May–early Sept., daily 9–7; early Sept.–late May, daily 9–5.

♦ ON THE CALENDAR: Apr. **Founders' Day.** This annual event celebrates Albuquerque's 1706 founding by Spanish conquistadores. It's held at Tiguex Park in Old Town, and festivities include a parade, arts festival, and two-day carnival. | 505/768–3555.

HISTORIC DINING AND LODGING

La Placita. Southwestern. It's touristy, but this restaurant housed in a historic hacienda on Old Town Plaza serves tasty chiles rellenos, enchiladas, tacos, sopaipillas, and other traditional New Mexican fare. The building dates from 1706—the adobe walls are 3 ft thick in places. For years it housed Ambrosio Armijo's mercantile store. The six dining rooms are also art galleries—patrons dine surrounded by outstanding examples of Native American and southwestern painting. | 208 San Felipe St. NW | 505/247–2204 | $14–$28 | AE, D, MC, V.

Pueblo Harvest Cafe. Native American. This restaurant at the Indian Pueblo Cultural Center, open only for breakfast and lunch, serves foods that are authentic to New Mexico's Pueblo Indian traditions. You might sample blue-corn enchiladas, *posole* (a thick soup with pork, hominy, chile, garlic, and cilantro), Indian bread pudding, and, of course, fry bread—that addictive popover-like creation that is served plain or topped with honey, beans, chile, or powdered sugar. | 2401 12th St. NW | 505/843–7270 | No dinner | $4–$8 | MC, V.

Brittania & W. E. Mauger Estate B&B. Popular with businesspeople because of its downtown location, this fine B&B is in an 1897 Queen Anne Victorian, the first home in Albuquerque to have electricity. Oval windows with beveled and "feather-pattern" glass, hardwood floors, a bright redbrick exterior, and an Old West front veranda are among the noteworthy design elements. In-room data ports, free parking. | 701 Roma Ave. NW, 87102 | 505/242–8755 or 800/719–9189 | fax 505/842–8855 | www.maugerbb.com | 8 rooms | $79–$179 | AE, D, DC, MC, V | BP.

CERRILLOS

▼▼

As early as 1680 Spanish dons enslaved Indians to mine the rocky outcrops along the Turquoise Trail (Route 14) for the prized stone. In the 19th century, coal, silver, zinc, and gold were discovered in the region, and numerous boomtowns, among them Cerrillos, sprang up almost overnight. Once the home of four hotels and 21 saloons, Cerrillos has reverted to a sleepy little village—almost a ghost town. Other villages, such as Golden and Madrid, along the 52-mi Turquoise Trail offer a glimpse into the area's mining past. *Contact Turquoise Trail Box 303, Sandia Park, 87047 | 505/471–1054 or 505/281–5233.*

Casa Grande. This funky 21-room adobe (several rooms of which are part of a shop) contains a small museum with a display of early mining exhibits. The shop sells all kinds of mining-related curiosities and gems. | 17 Waldo St. | 505/438–3008 | $1 | Daily 8–8.

Golden. The site of the first gold rush (in 1825) west of the Mississippi, tiny Golden now contains a small number of homes, a rock shop, and a mercantile store. The rustic adobe church and graveyard are popular with photographers. Be aware that locals are very protective of this area and aren't known to warm up to strangers. La Casita, a gift shop at the north end of the village, serves as the unofficial chamber of commerce. | 20 mi south of Cerrillos on Rte. 14, Golden.

Old Coal Mine Museum and Engine House Theater. This museum in Madrid, 5 mi south of Cerrillos, is a remnant of the once-flourishing local mining industry. Explore the old tunnel, climb aboard a 1900 steam train, and poke through antique buildings full of marvelous relics. On weekends between Memorial Day and Labor Day you can cheer the heroes and hiss the villains of the old-fashioned melodramas performed at the Engine House Theater. The theater, inside a converted roundhouse machine shop, has a full-size steam train that comes chugging onto the stage. | 2846 Rte. 14, Madrid | 505/438–3780 | Museum $3, melodrama $9 | Daily 9:30–dusk.

CIMARRON

▼▼

As you approach Cimarron from the south or east, you can't help but notice a huge rock looming over the town. Known as the Tooth of Time, it indicated to Santa Fe Trail travelers that their journey was nearing an end, for Santa Fe was only seven days away by wagon. In a land that was once home to Jicarilla Apache and Ute, Cimarron became a refuge for gamblers and outlaws and a stopping point for soldiers, gold seekers, and mountain men. (Its name means "untamed" in Spanish.) Founded in the early 1840s, it was the home of land baron Lucien Maxwell. These days, sleepy Cimarron (population 900) is a trove of Old West artifacts and lore. *Contact Cimarron Chamber of Commerce | 104 N. Lincoln Ave., 87714 | 505/376–2417 or 800/700–4298 | www.cimarronnm.com.*

Kit Carson Museum. A short drive south of town, this complex of adobe buildings presents costumed reenactments of life in 19th-century New Mexico and period crafts demonstrations. You'll see working horno oven, a blacksmith shop, and a trading post stocked as it might have been during Santa Fe Trail days. | Rte. 21, 11 mi south of Cimarron | 505/376–2281 | Free | Mid-June–Aug., daily 8–5.

Old Mill Museum. The workers who toiled inside this sturdy stone building once processed 300 barrels of flour a day for the Maxwell Ranch and the Jicarilla Apache reservation. Now the mill houses four floors of vintage photos, clothing, tools, and memorabilia depicting life in Colfax County from the 1860s into the 20th century. | 220 W. 17th St. | 505/376–2417 | $2 | Late May–early Sept., Mon.–Wed. and Fri.–Sat. 9–5, Sun. 1–5; early May–late May and early Sept.–end of Sept., Sat. 9–5, Sun. 1–5.

✦ ON THE CALENDAR: Sept. **Cimarron Days.** This Labor Day weekend festival in Cimarron's Village Park celebrates the arts-and-crafts heritage of the Santa Fe Trail. | 505/376–2417.

HISTORIC DINING AND LODGING
St. James Hotel. With 27 bullet holes in the tin dining-room ceiling, resident ghosts, and a guest book signed by someone using a known alias of Jesse James, this creaky old hotel is nothing if not atmospheric. Every notable outlaw of the late 19th century is said to have visited this place. It opened first as a saloon in 1872 and then eight years later developed into a hotel. The lobby is filled with western Victoriana: overstuffed sofas, fringed lamp shades, and mounted hunting trophies. Even if you don't stay here you can take a tour for $2. Lace curtains and Victorian-era antiques adorn the 12 rooms (there are also 10 modern but less distinctive motel rooms). There's a bit of a chill in the air, and the rooms aren't well sound-proofed or especially luxurious, but it's just what you'd expect in an allegedly haunted hotel. The dining room, Lambert's, serves steaks and pastas. Restaurant, café, lounge. | Rte. 21 at 17th St., 87714 | 505/376–2664 or 800/748–2694 | fax 505/376–2623 | 21 rooms, 1 suite | $60–$120 | AE, MC, V.

FORT SUMNER

▼▼

One of the area's earliest military outposts, Fort Sumner is where Sheriff Pat Garrett gunned down escaped outlaw Billy the Kid in 1881. The fort is even more infamous for its earlier role as the holding area for hundreds of Navajo and Apache who were forced to farm the inhospitable land. The Kid is buried here. *Contact DeBaca County Chamber of Commerce Box 28, 88119 | 505/355–7705.*

Billy the Kid Museum. Most everyone already knows that Sheriff Pat Garrett shot and killed Billy the Kid at Pete Maxwell's house in Fort Sumner. Here you'll find exhibits about the young scofflaw, as well as antique wagon trains, guns, household goods, and other artifacts of the frontier era. | 1601 Sumner Ave. (U.S. 60/84) | 505/355–2380 | $4 | Mid-May–Sept., daily 8:30–5; Oct.–Dec. and mid-Jan.–mid-May, Mon.–Sat. 8:30–5, Sun. 11–5.

Fort Sumner State Monument. Artifacts and photographs illustrate the history of the fort, which was established in 1862 on the east bank of the Pecos River. From 1863 to 1868 it was the site of a disastrous attempt to force the Navajo people and some Apache bands— after their defeat on various battlefields in the Southwest—into farming. Natural disasters destroyed crops, wood was scarce, and even the water from the Pecos proved unhealthful. Those who survived the harsh treatment and wretched conditions (3,000 out of 12,000 didn't) were allowed to return to reservations elsewhere in 1868. The post was then sold and converted into a large ranch, where in 1881 Sheriff Pat Garrett gunned down Billy the Kid. | East of town on U.S. 60/84, then south on Billy the Kid Rd. (parts of which are marked Rte. 212) | 505/355–2573 | $3 | Daily 8:30–5.

Old Fort Museum. Next to Fort Sumner State Monument, this small museum has written displays about Billy the Kid and is adjacent to the outlaw's grave. The Kid's headstone was secured in a barred cage after it was stolen and recovered. | East of town on U.S. 60/84, then south on Billy the Kid Rd. (parts of which are marked Rte. 212) | 505/355–2942 | $3 | Call for hrs.

✦ ON THE CALENDAR: June **Old Fort Days.** Living-history re-enactments, a staged bank robbery, and mock shoot-outs recreate the Wild West days of Fort Sumner. Food booths, a rodeo, a parade, and a barbecue are featured during the weeklong celebration at the De Baca County Fairgrounds. | 505/355–7705.

GRANTS
▼▼

Cibola County, of which Grants is the county seat, didn't exist until 1981, but by then people had been living in the town for more than 100 years. It started as a railroad town, established in the 1870s by three brothers by the name of Grant. Farming was the mainstay of the economy until well into the 20th century, when uranium was discovered in the vicinity. *Contact Grants/Cibola County Chamber of Commerce | 100 N. Iron Ave., 87020 | 800/748–2142 | www.grants.org.*

Acoma Pueblo. Atop a 367-ft mesa that rises abruptly from the valley floor, Acoma Pueblo's terraced, multistory Sky City is like no other pueblo. It's one of the oldest continually inhabited spots in North America, with portions believed to be more than 1,500 years old. Captain Hernando de Alvarado, a member of Francisco Vásquez de Coronado's expedition of 1540, was the first European to see Acoma. He reported that he had "found a rock with a village on top, the strongest position ever seen in the world." The Spanish eventually conquered the Acomas and brutally compelled them to build San Estéban del Rey, the immense adobe church that stands to this day. Visitation is by an hour-long guided tour. | On Rte. 22, 30 mi southeast of Grants via I-40 and Rte. 38 | 505/552–6604 or 800/747–0181 | www.puebloofacoma. org | $9 | Apr.–Oct., daily 8–7, tours daily 8–6; Nov.–Mar., daily 8–4, tours daily 8–3 | Closed certain periods; call first | Video cameras prohibited, still-camera permit $10.

El Morro National Monument. When you see the imposing 200-ft-high sandstone bluff that served as a rest stop for explorers, soldiers, and pioneers, you'll understand how El Morro ("the Headlands") got its name. The bluff is the famous Inscription Rock, where wayfarers, beginning with Juan de Oñate in 1605, stopped to carve their names and leave messages.

Petroglyphs mark the passage of travelers of earlier times. The Inscription Trail makes a quick ½-mi round-trip from the visitor center. The monument's museum chronicles 700 years of human history in this region. | 37 mi southwest of Grants via I–40 to Rte. 53 | 505/783–4226 | $2 per passenger, maximum of $4 per vehicle | Late May–early Sept., daily 9–7; early Sept.–late May, daily 9–5 | Trails close 1 hr before monument.

✦ ON THE CALENDAR: July **Wild West Days.** Along with a parade down Santa Fe Avenue, there is an art show, crafts, and old-fashioned games like a pie-eating contest, watermelon-seed-spitting contest, and tug of war. | 505/287–4802 or 800/748–2142.

LAS VEGAS

▼▼▼

In August 1846, before several hundred Mexican residents, General Stephen Watts Kearny stood on a rooftop in the small village of Las Vegas and declared that from that time forward all of New Mexico belonged to the United States. The town had its beginnings as a settlement along the Santa Fe Trail, but by the 1880s, when most commerce had shifted to the railroad, it had blossomed into a sizable community. With an improvement in the economy came an increase in lawlessness, and during the latter part of the 19th century Las Vegas was known as a wild and woolly town. Las Vegas lists more than 900 buildings in the National Register of Historic Places. You can pick up walking-tour maps at the Chamber of Commerce office. *Contact Las Vegas Chamber of Commerce | 727 Grand Ave., Box 128, 87701 | 505/425–8631 or 800/832–5947 | www.lasvegasnewmexico.com.*

Fort Union National Monument. The ruins of New Mexico's largest frontier-era fort sit on an empty, windswept plain that still echoes with the isolation surely felt by the soldiers stationed here between 1851 and 1890. The fort was established to protect travelers and settlers along the Santa Fe Trail. It became a military supply depot for the Southwest, but with the "taming" of the West it was abandoned. The visitor center provides historical background about the fort and the Santa Fe Trail. Talks on the Santa Fe Trail and Fort Union are given daily, and guided tours are available by reservation. The fort is 26 mi north of Las Vegas via I–25. | Off Rte. 161, Watrous | 505/425–8025 | www.fortunion.areaparks.com | $3 | Early Sept.–late may, daily 8–5; late May–early Sept., daily 8–6.

La Cueva Historic District. On Route 518, 20 mi north of Las Vegas, be sure to stop in this curious village. It had its origins in the 1850s, when pioneer Vicente Romero established a ranch and stone-wall mill here to supply the soldiers of Fort Union. La Cueva means "the cave," and it's said Romero slept in caves while he built the ranch. The town's San Rafael Church, dating from the 1870s, is also worth a look. | Rte. 518 at Rte. 442 | 505/387–2900 | Free.

Las Vegas City Museum and Rough Riders Collection. This small museum houses historical photos, medals, uniforms, and memorabilia from the Spanish-American War; documents pertaining to the city's history; and Native American artifacts. Theodore Roosevelt recruited many of his Rough Riders—the men the future president led into battle in Cuba in 1898—from northeastern New Mexico, and their first reunion was held here. | 725 Grand Ave. | 505/454–1401 Ext. 283 | Free | Weekdays 9–noon and 1–4, Sat. 10–3.

✦ ON THE CALENDAR: May **Santa Fe Trail Heritage Days.** This yearly celebration of life on the Santa Fe Trail includes demonstrations of frontier cooking, weaving, soap making, and sheep shearing, along with other entertainment and a crafts fair, all in Plaza Park. | 505/425–8631 or 800/832–5947.

THE SANTA FE TRAIL

The 900-mi Santa Fe Trail played a pivotal role in the history of the American South-west and remains today a source of intrigue and inspiration. The trail traversed treach-erous terrain that lacked adequate water supplies and was vulnerable to Indian attacks. But mostly, the challenges encountered by travelers on the eight-week journey from Franklin, Missouri, to Santa Fe, New Mexico, came in the form of tedium, dust, and pes-tering insects.

The heyday of the trail started in 1821, when Americans living on the Great Plains saw the promise of trade with the wealthy Spanish colony of New Mexico. Spanish author-ities had long forbidden New Mexican colonists from engaging in foreign commerce, but Americans saw hope in the prospect of revolution in New Spain. Sure enough, just as the Americans finished charting their route to New Mexico the Spanish colonists revolted and gained Mexico's independence, taking New Mexico with them. For the next 25 years, the Santa Fe Trail proved to be an incredibly profitable route, a conduit for trade between interior Mexico—which was linked to Santa Fe via El Camino Real— and the United States.

During the Mexican-American War of 1846–48, U.S. soldiers used the trail to invade New Mexico. When the two countries reached an agreement through the 1848 Treaty of Guadalupe Hidalgo, New Mexico became part of the United States, and the Santa Fe Trail became a national highway, still of great value. It was not until the 1880 con-struction of the railroad between Atchison, Kansas, and Santa Fe that the trail was ren-dered obsolete.

Today the Santa Fe National Historic Trail is administered by the National Park Ser-vice, which maintains a string of historic sites that trace the trail's two routes—the orig-inal Cimarron Cut-Off and the Mountain Route. At Lakin, Kansas travelers could choose either to continue across Kansas into Colorado and down through Raton, New Mexico, over the Mountain Route, or they could cut south through the Oklahoma panhandle and across northeastern New Mexico via the Cimarron Route. The latter cut-off shaved about 60 mi off the trip but also lacked sources of water, so quite a few wagon trains took the long but well-watered mountain route.

The Santa Fe Trail Museum in Springer, Fort Union National Monument in Watrous, and Pecos National Historic Park in Pecos preserve the history of the trail. You can also drive near parts of the original trail on modern highways like I–25 from Trinidad, Col-orado, to Santa Fe and U.S. 56 from Dodge City, Kansas, to Springer. For information on the trail, contact **Santa Fe National Historic Trail** (Box 728, Santa Fe, 87504 | 505/988–6888 | www.nps.gov/safe).

HISTORIC LODGING

Plaza Hotel. Opened in 1882, this hotel on the National Register of Historic Places overlooks the town plaza. Political and business leaders stayed here, as well as outlaws like Doc Holl-iday and Big Nose Kate. Rooms balance the old and the new—they are not fancy, but very nice. In addition to plenty of space, rooms have painted trim and borders, high stamped-tin ceilings, a sprinkling of antiques, and coffeemakers. Continental breakfast is included in your rate. Restaurant, room service, cable TV, bar, Internet, meeting rooms, some pets allowed (fee). | 230 Old Town Plaza, 87701 | 505/425–3591 or 800/328–1882 | fax 505/425–9659 | www.plazahotel-nm.com | 32 rooms, 4 suites | $59–$72 | AE, D, DC, MC, V.

LINCOLN

▼▼

Lincoln is best known as the nexus of the Lincoln County War, in which Billy the Kid figured prominently. The war was a struggle for economic and political control of the county. In the fight, John Chisum, cattle king in this area from 1872 onward, was allied with Englishman John Tunstall and attorney Alexander McSween. Their financial interests clashed with those of others in Lincoln County, especially merchant Lawrence Murphy, who had made the town of Lincoln his personal fiefdom, and John Riley and J. J. Dolan, who bought Murphy's business. Small ranchers in the area, resentful of Chisum's strong-arm control of grazing lands, sided with Murphy et al. But Tunstall and McSween could not be intimidated, and they opened a store in Lincoln to compete with Murphy's. When lucrative government contracts to provide food for the U.S. Army at Fort Stanton and area Indian reservations came up for grabs, the conflict between the two rival factions deepened.

Tunstall recruited gunfighters like Billy the Kid, while Sheriff William Brady sided with the merchants against the ranchers. Gunfights erupted on a regular basis, and Tunstall was killed in early 1878, igniting the Lincoln County War. Billy the Kid shot down Sheriff Brady on April Fool's Day that year, and three months later McSween's house was torched. The five-day shoot-out that followed left 17 dead, including McSween. The Lincoln County War finally ended in 1881, and Sheriff Pat Garrett became a national hero for gunning down Billy the Kid in Fort Sumner. Mellowing with age, the notorious one-street town has become a National Historic Landmark and a New Mexico state monument, preserved and reconstructed to look much as it was in the days of the Lincoln County War. A single ticket ($6) grants entry to the seven historic buildings that make up the monument. *Contact Lincoln State Monument Box 36, Lincoln 88338 | 505/653–4372 | www.museumofnewmexico.org.*

Billy the Kid Trail National Scenic Byway Visitor Center. This headquarters for information about Lincoln County and Billy the Kid is adjacent to the Hubbard Museum of the American West in Ruidoso Downs. | U.S. 70 E, Ruidoso Downs | 505/378–5318 | www.byways.org | Free | Late May–early Sept., daily 9–5:30; early Sept.–late May, daily 10–5.

Dr. Woods House. This residence was once occupied by a country doctor specializing in tuberculosis treatments. | Main St. (U.S. 380) | no phone | $6 pass grants access to all historic buildings | Daily 9–5.

Historic Lincoln Center. On the eastern end of town, the information center has a 12-minute video about Lincoln and exhibits devoted to Billy the Kid, the Lincoln County War, cowboys, Apache Indians, and the Buffalo Soldiers. The center's guides and attendants dress in period costumes and lead a walking tour through town on the hour, vividly describing each building's role as a setting in the Lincoln County War. | Main St. (U.S. 380) | 505/653–4025 | $6 pass grants access to all historic buildings | Daily 8:30–5.

Hubbard Museum of the American West. This museum in Ruidoso Downs displays saddles from the Pony Express, carriages and wagons, a horse-drawn grain thresher, and clothing worn by Native Americans and cowboys. The museum also oversees many of the exhibits in Lincoln. | U.S. 70 E, Ruidoso Downs | 505/378–4142 or 800/263–5929 | www.zianet.com/museum | $6 | Daily 10–5.

Lincoln County Courthouse Museum. Billy the Kid made his famous escape from this building, where you can view the room where the outlaw was imprisoned. Check out the hole in the wall, which was probably made by gunfire during his escape. Display cases contain historical documents. You can read one of Billy's eloquent handwritten letters to Governor Lew Wallace, in which he defends his reputation. | Main St. (U.S. 380) | 505/653–4372 | $6 pass grants access to all historic buildings | Daily 8:30–5.

Montaño Store. José Montaño ran a saloon and boardinghouse at this site for more than 30 years following the Civil War. Governor Lew Wallace stayed here when trying to arrange a meeting with Billy the Kid. On view today are written displays about adobe making and Lincoln's Hispanic community. | Main St. (U.S. 380) | No phone | $6 pass grants access to all historic buildings | Daily 8:30–5.

Torreon. When Spanish settlers first arrived in Lincoln in the 1840s, this short, round fortress served as protection from Apache raids. | Main St. (U.S. 380) | No phone | $6 pass grants access to all historic buildings | Daily 8:30–5.

Tunstall Store Museum. One of the flashpoints of the Lincoln County War, this is the store that John Tunstall and Alexander McSween opened to compete with L. G. Murphy & Co. (that building now houses the Lincoln County Courthouse Museum). When the state of New Mexico purchased the store in 1957, boxes of unused stock (such as clothing and butter churns) dating from the late-19th and early 20th centuries were discovered on the premises. Those goods are on display. | Main St. (U.S. 380) | 505/653–4049 | $6 pass grants access to all historic buildings | Daily 9–5.

✦ ON THE CALENDAR: Aug. **Old Lincoln Days.** Historic reenactments, arts and crafts, and the "Billy the Kid Pageant," a dramatization of the original shoot-out, fill this weekend in Lincoln. | 505/653–4025.

HISTORIC DINING AND LODGING

Casa de Patrón Bed-and-Breakfast. This adobe was once the home of Juan Patrón, an early Lincoln settler who was gunned down at age 29 in the violence that swept Lincoln County. Billy the Kid really did sleep here, more than once: as a guest of Patrón and again while being held by the sheriff under protective custody. If you stay in the main house you'll get a full country breakfast; in the casitas you are served a Continental breakfast. Some kitchens, some microwaves, some refrigerators, meeting rooms; no smoking. | U.S. 380 (Box 27, 88338) | 505/653–4676 or 800/524–5202 | fax 505/653–4671 | www.casapatron.com | 5 rooms, 2 casitas | $87–$117 | MC, V | BP, CP.

Ellis Store Country Inn. This B&B has a rich history dating from 1850. Settlers and Mescalero Indians clashed in the area, and Billy the Kid was known to frequent the place during the Lincoln County War. Restaurant; no smoking. | U.S. 380, Mile Marker 98 (Box 15, 88338) | 505/653–4609 or 800/653–6460 | fax 505/653–4610 | www.ellisstore.com | 10 rooms, 6 with bath; 2 suites | $79–$139 | AE, D, MC, V | BP.

Wortley Pat Garrett Hotel. At this ranch-style inn, rooms are named after characters in the Lincoln County War. Antiques and old newspaper accounts are displayed throughout the inn, where historical field trips and classes are part of the experience. Rebuilt after a fire in 1935, the inn is on the site where Deputy U.S. Marshal Bob Olinger ate his last meal at noon on April 28, 1881. As the lawman consumed roast beef and mashed potatoes, he heard gunfire from the courthouse down the street. He ran outside and met up with a bullet fired by Billy the Kid during his famous escape. The hotel's restaurant does not accept credit cards. Restaurant. | U.S. 380, 88338 | 505/653–4300 or 877/967–8539 | fax 505/653–4686 | www.patgarretthotel.com | 7 rooms | Closed Nov.–Apr. | $65 | AE, MC, V.

MESILLA

▼▼▼

Some say Mesilla occupies the spot that Spanish explorer Don Juan de Oñate declared to be "the first pueblo of this kingdom" in 1598. Mesilla was the largest station between El Paso and Los Angeles along the Butterfield Stage Line in the mid-1800s. *Contact Mesilla Visitor's Center | 2340 Ave. de Mesilla, 88046 | 505/647–9698 | www.oldmesilla.org.*

Gadsden Museum. This museum three blocks from the Mesilla Plaza includes a painting that commemorates the Gadsden Purchase, when the U.S. officially acquired the area from Mexico. | W. Boutz Rd. at Rte. 28 | 505/526–6293 | $2 | Mon.–Sat. 9–11 and 1–5.

San Albino Church. Built in 1855, this still-active adobe and stained-glass Catholic church was reconstructed in 1906. | Mesilla Plaza | 505/526–9349 | Free | Mon.–Sat. 1–3.

HISTORIC DINING

La Posta. Mexican. Once a way station for the Butterfield Overland Mail and Wells Fargo stages, the adobe restaurant has hosted celebrities such as Mexican revolutionary Pancho Villa. Some of the Mexican entrées are made according to recipes dating back before the turn of the 20th century. | 2410 C. de San Albino | 505/524–3524 | Closed Mon. | $4–$15 | AE, D, MC, V.

RATON

▼▼

Originally a Santa Fe Trail forage station called Willow Springs, Raton was born in 1880 when the Atchison, Topeka & Santa Fe Railway established a repair shop at the bottom of Raton Pass. The town grew up around 1st Street, which paralleled the railroad tracks. Much of the Raton Downtown Historic District, which has 70-odd buildings on the National Register of Historic Places, lies along several restored blocks of Historic 1st Street. As it has since the late 19th century, Raton runs on ranching, railroading, and the industry for which it's most famous, mining. In the early 1900s there were about 35 coal camps around Raton, most of them occupied by immigrants from Italy, Greece, and Eastern Europe. It was hard living in these camps and a tough road out, but a familial, close-knit interdependence grew out of mining life—a spirit that still prevails in Raton today. *Contact Raton Chamber of Commerce Box 1211, Raton, 87740 | 505/445–3689 or 800/638–6161 | www.raton.com.*

Clayton. This remote town had its beginnings as a watering hole on the Santa Fe Trail. In time a settlement took hold, and by 1888, when the railroad came through, it counted several hundred residents. In 1901 the notorious rain robber Thomas E. "Blackjack" Ketchum was hanged there. His last words were: "I had breakfast in Clayton, but I'll have dinner in hell!" Legend has it that when the trapdoor of the gallows was sprung open and Blackjack dropped through, the weight of his body snapped his neck and his head rolled away into the mob of curious onlookers. Clayton lies close to what was known as the Cimarron Cut-Off of the Santa Fe Trail. Nearby is a natural stone formation called the Rabbit Ears, which was used by early travelers as a landmark. | 73 mi southeast of Raton on U.S. 64/87 | 505/374–9253 or 800/390–7858 | www.claytonnewmexico.org.

Raton Museum. This tiny trove of history inside the 1906 Coors Building (the beer manufacturer used it as a warehouse) brims with artifacts of the coal camps, railroading, ranch life, and the Santa Fe Trail. The museum, which has a large and interesting photo collection, is a good first stop on a visit to the area. | 218 S. 1st St. | 505/445–8979 | Free | May–Sept., Tues.–Sat. 9–5; Oct.–Apr., Wed.–Sat. 10–4.

Springer. A stroll under the shady oaks of Springer's main street is a journey into the past. Long a shipping center for cattle, sheep, and mining machinery, the town was founded in 1870 when land baron Lucien Maxwell deeded 320 acres to his lawyer, Frank Springer, for handling the sale of the Maxwell Land Grant to the Dutch East India Company. More than a few locals here still seem a bit rankled about losing the title of county seat to Raton—way back in 1897. | 37 mi south of Raton via I–25 | 505/483–2998.

In the middle of nowhere (about 37 mi northeast of Springer) stands the **Dorsey Mansion** (505/375–2222 | www.dorseymansion.com | $3), a curious 36-room log-and-masonry castle built in 1886 by Stephen Dorsey, a U.S. senator from Arkansas. Its grand furnishings include a cherrywood staircase from Chicago, gargoyles depicting Dorsey family members, a dining room that seats 60, and a swank billiard room. The career of the ambitious senator, who owned the mansion for 15 years, dissolved in a mail-fraud scandal. He was acquitted after two trials but went bankrupt defending himself. You must make reservations by phone to visit the mansion. To get here, drive 25 mi east of Springer on U.S. 56/412; then turn north (left) at the rest stop at Mile Marker 24 and take the dirt road 12 mi.

When Springer was the Colfax County seat, the 1883 structure that houses the **Santa Fe Trail Museum** served as a courthouse. The museum has a curious jumble of documents, maps, memorabilia, and other artifacts. | 606 Maxwell St. | 505/483–2998 | $2 | Late May–early Sept., Mon.–Sat. 9–4, with limited hrs in early fall and late spring (call ahead).

HISTORIC DINING

Eklund Hotel Dining Room & Saloon. Eclectic. The guest rooms here have been closed since the 1970s, but the splendid Victorian dining room still welcomes guests with its crystal chandeliers, apricot tufted-velvet booths, gilt-flocked wallpaper, and marble fireplaces. The atmosphere in the saloon is quite different but no less authentic. Here you'll find a large raw-rock fireplace, wooden booths, and mounted heads of elk and buffalo, plus historic photos and clippings documenting Clayton's past. American standards and Mexican and New Mexican fare (good sopaipillas) are served in both the dining room and saloon. Hand-cut steaks are the house specialty, and you can order hamburgers, beef stew, chicken-fried steak, and a decent club sandwich. | 15 Main St., Clayton | 505/374–2551 | No lunch in dining room Mon.–Sat. | $10–$25 | MC, V.

SANTA FE

▼▼

La Villa Real de la Santa Fe de San Francisco de Asís (the Royal City of the Holy Faith of St. Francis of Assisi) was founded in the first decade of the 17th century and became capital of Spanish colonial New Mexico in 1610. This was the center of Spanish political and religious power in the region and became the target of Pueblo Indian discontent in 1680, when the Indians rose up against Spanish oppression and forced the colonists out of Santa Fe. The Spanish returned 12 years later and retook the city. The terminus of El Camino Real, the road that connected the territorial outpost with Mexico City, Santa Fe also became the end of the Santa Fe Trail, a prime artery of U.S. westward expansion. The city was thus a major center of trade, first with New Spain and later with the United States. The heyday of the Santa Fe Trail ended with the arrival of the Atchison, Topeka & Santa Fe Railway in 1880. The trains brought greater numbers of Anglo settlers to New Mexico, and Santa Fe continued to grow, though most of its citizens were not particularly prosperous. Later, a new type of pioneer arrived in Santa Fe—artists who fell in love with its cultural diversity, history, and magical color and light. Their presence attracted some of America's earliest tourists, who came to Santa Fe to experience the Old West before it disappeared. *Contact Santa Fe Convention and Visitors Bureau | 201 W. Marcy St., Box 909, 87501 | 505/955–6200 or 800/777–2489 | www. santafe.org.*

Barrio de Analco. Along the south bank of the Santa Fe River, the barrio—its name means "district on the other side of the water"—is one of America's oldest neighborhoods, settled in the early 1600s by the Tlaxcalan Indians (who were forbidden to live with the Spanish near the Plaza) and in the 1690s by soldiers who had helped recapture New Mexico after the Pueblo Revolt. Plaques on houses on East De Vargas Street identify important structures. | Old Santa Fe Trail between the Santa Fe River and E. De Vargas.

El Rancho de Las Golondrinas. The "Williamsburg of the Southwest," El Rancho de las Golondrinas ("the ranch of the swallows") is a reconstruction of a small agricultural village. Originally a *paraje*, or stopping place, on El Camino Real, it was where travelers could rest and regroup before making the final leg of their journey north to Santa Fe, a half-day ride in horse-and-wagon days. The living-history village has buildings dating from the 17th to 19th century and maintains an authentic character. Guided tours (April–October) survey Spanish-colonial and U.S. territorial lifestyles in New Mexico from 1660 to 1890: you can view a molasses mill, threshing grounds, and wheelwright and blacksmith shops, as well as a mountain village. | 334 Los Pinos Rd., 15 mi south of downtown Santa Fe via I–25 | 505/471–2261 | www.golondrinas.org | $5 | Wed.–Sun. 10–4.

Museum of Indian Arts and Culture. An interactive multimedia exhibition tells the story of Native American history in the Southwest, merging contemporary Native American experience with historical accounts and artifacts. The collection has some of New Mexico's oldest works of art: pottery vessels, fine stone and silver jewelry, intricate textiles, and other arts and crafts created by Pueblo, Navajo, and Apache artisans. | 710 Camino Lejo | 505/476–1250 | www.miaclab.org | $7, 4-day pass $15 (good at all 5 state museums in Santa Fe) | Tues.–Sun. 10–5.

Museum of International Folk Art. Although this first-rate museum focuses chiefly on contemporary art, the facility contains an excellent Hispanic Heritage Wing, with art and artifacts dating from the Spanish-colonial period. The 5,000-piece exhibit includes religious works such as *bultos* (carved wooden statues of saints) and *retablos* (holy images painted on wood or tin). | 706 Camino Lejo | 505/476–1200 | www.moifa.org | $7, 4-day pass $15 (good at all 5 state museums in Santa Fe) | Tues.–Sun. 10–5.

Museum of Spanish Colonial Art. The museum, which stands next to the Museum of New Mexico complex, displays the fruits of the Spanish Colonial Art Society's efforts to preserve traditional Spanish-colonial art and culture. This is one of the most comprehensive collections of Spanish-colonial art in the world. Objects here, dating from the 16th century to the present, include retablos, elaborate santos, tinwork, straw appliqué, furniture, ceramics, and ironwork. | 750 Camino Lejo | 505/982–2226 | www.spanishcolonial.org/museum.shtml | $6, 4-day pass $15 (good at all 5 state museums in Santa Fe) | Daily 10–5.

Palace of the Governors. A humble-looking one-story adobe on the north side of the Plaza, the palace is the oldest public building in the United States. Built at the same time as the Plaza, around 1610 (scholars debate the exact year), it was abandoned in 1680 following the Pueblo Revolt but resumed its role as Spanish government headquarters when Don Diego de Vargas returned to Santa Fe in 1692. The seat of four regional governments—those of Spain, Mexico, the Confederacy, and New Mexico Territory—the building served as the residence for 100 Spanish, Mexican, and American governors. The palace has been the central headquarters of the Museum of New Mexico since 1913 and houses the main section of the State History Museum. Permanent exhibits chronicle 450 years of New Mexico history, using maps, furniture, clothing, housewares, weaponry, and village models. | Palace Ave., north side of the Plaza | 505/476–5100 | www.palaceofthegovernors.org | $7, 4-day pass $15 (good at all 5 state museums in Santa Fe), free Fri. 5–8 | Tues.–Thurs. and weekends 10–5, Fri. 10–8.

Pecos National Historic Park. Pecos was the last major encampment that travelers on the Santa Fe Trail reached before they got to Santa Fe. Today the little village is mostly a starting point for exploring Pecos National Historic Park, the centerpiece of which is the ruins of Pecos, once a major Pueblo with more than 1,100 rooms. The Spanish built two missions here, and the Pueblo was abandoned in 1838. Anglo travelers on the Santa Fe Trail observed

HOODWINKED

Promoters sometimes employed colorful exaggerations—a more polite term for lies—in the late 1800s to lure hapless settlers to southeastern New Mexico's rugged Pecos Valley. Drawn by advertisements touting the valley as a paradise similar to California, one group of Swiss immigrants journeyed to a spot near what is now Carlsbad, only to find they had been hoodwinked. The terrain around their settlement—which they called Vaud but which is now named Loving—was arid and inhospitable. To save face, they wrote their own lies back home, describing in their letters lush, fertile surroundings that simply did not exist. For a while the folks back home were themselves hoodwinked, until a visitor to the area discovered the awful truth: many of the Swiss pioneers were sick, dying, and financially ruined. The scandal filled newspapers in French-speaking sectors of Switzerland for weeks, and in some areas of that country the term "Pecos" was used to describe things that are too good to be true. Markers in a graveyard at Loving are filled with the names of the unlucky settlers.

the mission ruins with a great sense of fascination (and relief—for they knew it meant their journey was nearly over). A couple of miles from the ruins, Andrew Kozlowski's Ranch served as a stage depot, where a fresh spring quenched the thirsts of weary horses and passengers. You can view the mission ruins and the excavated pueblo on a ¼-mi self-guided tour in about two hours. In late March 1862, the pivotal Civil War battle of Glorieta Pass took place on what is now an outlying parcel of park land; a victory over Confederate forces firmly established the Union army's control over New Mexico Territory. | 31 mi east of Santa Fe via I–25 to Exit 307, then 4 mi north on Rte. 63, Pecos | 505/757–6414 | www.nps.gov/peco | $3 | Late May–early Sept., daily 8–6; early Sept.–late May, daily 8–5.

St. Francis Cathedral. This magnificent Romanesque-style cathedral, a block east of the Plaza, was built in 1869 by Jean Baptiste Lamy, Santa Fe's first archbishop, working with French architects and Italian stonemasons. The circuit-riding archbishop was sent by the Catholic Church to the Southwest to change the religious practices of its native population (to "civilize" them, as one period document puts it) and is buried in the crypt beneath the church's high altar. A small adobe chapel on the northeast side of the cathedral, the remnant of an earlier church, embodies the Hispanic architectural influence so conspicuously absent from the cathedral itself. The chapel's *Nuestra Señora de la Paz* (Our Lady of Peace), popularly known as *La Conquistadora,* the oldest Madonna statue in the United States, accompanied Don Diego de Vargas on his reconquest of Santa Fe in 1692. | 231 Cathedral Pl. | 505/982–5619 | Daily 8–5:45, except during mass. Mass Mon.–Sat. at 7 and 8:15 AM, 12:10 and 5:15 PM; Sun. at 6, 8, and 10 AM, noon, and 7 PM. Museum weekdays 9–noon and 1–4.

San Miguel Mission. The oldest church still in use in the United States, this simple earth-hue adobe structure was built in the early 17th century by the Tlaxcalan Indians of Mexico, who came to New Mexico as servants of the Spanish. Badly damaged in the 1680 Pueblo Revolt, the structure was restored and enlarged in 1710. On display in the chapel are priceless statues and paintings and the San José Bell, weighing nearly 800 pounds, which is believed to have been cast in Spain in 1356. | 401 Old Santa Fe Trail | 505/983–3974 | $1 | Mon.–Sat. 10–4, Sun. 3–4:30.

Santa Fe Plaza. The city's placid central Plaza, which dates from Santa Fe's earliest days, has been the site of bullfights, public floggings, gunfights, battles, political rallies, promenades, and public markets. Much of the history of Santa Fe, New Mexico, the Southwest, and even the Old West as a whole has some association with this central Plaza, which was laid out in 1607. Freight wagons unloaded here after completing their arduous journey along the Santa Fe Trail. The American flag was first raised over the Plaza in 1846, during the Mexican-American War. | Bounded by Lincoln, Palace, and Washington Aves. and San Francisco St.

Santuario de Chimayó. This small frontier adobe church is in tiny Chimayó, the first town you hit heading north along the "High Road to Taos" (Rte. 76). The Santuario has a fantastically carved and painted Spanish-colonial wood altar and is built on the site where, believers say, a mysterious light came from the ground on Good Friday in 1810 and where a large wooden crucifix was found beneath the earth. The Santuario draws a steady stream of worshipers all year long—Chimayó is considered the Lourdes of the Southwest. | 28 mi north of Santa Fe on Rte. 76 to CR 98; look for sign | 505/351–4889 | Free | Daily 9–5:30.

✦ ON THE CALENDAR: Sept. **Las Fiestas de Santa Fe.** To commemorate the reconquest of New Mexico after the Pueblo Revolt of 1680, Las Fiestas de Santa Fe have been held every year since 1712. The nation's oldest community celebration takes place on the Plaza the weekend after Labor Day, with parades, mariachi bands, pageants, and the burning in effigy of Zozóbra, Old Man Gloom. | 505/984–6760 or 800/777–2489.

HISTORIC DINING AND LODGING

El Farol. Spanish. Touted as the oldest continuously operated restaurant in Santa Fe, El Farol (built in 1835) has a relaxed ambience, a unique blend of the western frontier and contemporary Santa Fe. Order a classic entrée like paella or make a meal from the nearly 30 different tapas—from tiny fried squid to wild mushrooms. Dining is indoors and out. There's usually a festive flamenco performance weekly. | 808 Canyon Rd. | 505/983–9912 | $22–$29 | D, DC, MC, V.

Rancho de Chimayó. Southwestern. In a turn-of-the-20th-century adobe hacienda tucked into the mountains, with whitewashed walls, hand-stripped vigas, and cozy dining rooms, Rancho de Chimayó is still owned and operated by the family that first occupied the house. There's a roaring fire in the fireplace in winter and, in summer, a terraced patio shaded by catalpa trees. Traditional, if predictable, New Mexican fare is served, but the ambience is the real draw here. You can take an after-dinner stroll on the grounds. | CR 98, Chimayó, 28 mi north of Santa Fe | 505/351–4444 | Closed Mon. Nov.–mid-May | $10–$14 | AE, D, DC, MC, V.

SILVER CITY

▼▼

Silver City sprouted as a tough and lawless mining camp in 1870, struggling to become a more respectable—and permanent—settlement. Henry McCarty spent part of his boyhood here, perhaps learning some of the ruthlessness that led to his later infamy under his nickname—Billy the Kid. Thanks to the efforts of preservationists, Silver City's origins are evident in the many distinctive houses and storefronts that have been salvaged. *Contact Silver City/Grant County Chamber of Commerce | 201 N. Hudson St., 88061 | 505/538–3785 or 800/ 548–9378 | www.silvercity.org.*

Lake Valley National Back Country Byway. The 48-mi Lake Valley National Back Country Byway— a stretch of Route 152 between Silver City and Hillsboro—provides an exhilarating link to the Wild West. This remote drive (there are no gas stations) follows part of the route taken by the Kingston Lake Valley Stage Line, which operated in a region terrorized by Apache leaders like Geronimo and outlaw bands led by Butch Cassidy and other notorious figures. The old silver-mining town of Lake Valley was once home to 4,000 people. Its mine produced 2.5 million ounces of pure silver and gave up one nugget weighing several hundred pounds.

You can visit the schoolhouse (which later served as a saloon) and walk around the chapel, the railroad depot, and some old homes. At the junction of Route 152 and Route 27 is another mining-era boomtown, Hillsboro, where gold was discovered as well as silver (about $6 million worth of the two ores was extracted). The town has a small museum and some shops, restaurants, and galleries. | East of Silver City 8 mi via U.S. 180/Rte. 152, then Rte. 152 east to Hillsboro | 800/548–9378 or 505/538–3785.

Shakespeare Ghost Town. This abandoned gold- and silver-mining town (it now stands on a working ranch) 2½ mi southwest of Lordsburg is complete with a saloon, blacksmith shop, and stables. Billy the Kid was its most famous inhabitant and allegedly washed dishes in the Stratford Hotel here to earn his keep as a boy. Historical reenactments take place several times a year. | 44 mi southwest of Silver City via Rte. 90 to Lordsburg, then I–10 to Exit 22; turn south to follow signs to Shakespeare (Box 253, Lordsburg 88045) | 505/542–9034 | www.shakespeareghostown.com | $3, special events $4 | Mar.–Dec., 2nd weekend of month 10–2, or by appointment.

Silver City Museum. The Ailman House, built in 1881, is now a museum that presents a good overview of the area's colorful history. Displays include pottery and other relics from the area's Mimbres and Mogollon Native American cultures. From the museum's upper level you can catch a glimpse of Silver City's three historic districts. | 312 W. Broadway | 505/538–5921 | www.silvercitymuseum.org | Free | Tues.–Fri. 9–4:30, weekends 10–4.

✦ ON THE CALENDAR: Oct. **Special Night Tour.** Several times a year, particularly in October just before Halloween, Shakespeare is eerily lit with candles and lanterns while performers tell ghost stories. | 505/542–9034.

HISTORIC DINING AND LODGING

Buckhorn Saloon and Opera House. Steak. Seven miles north of Silver City on Route 15, mosey up to the wooden bar at this genuine 1800s saloon and slug down a taste of the Old West. The complex also includes the Opera House, where melodramas are performed (on Friday and Saturday at 8), and Pinos Altos Mercantile, a business founded in the 1860s that's now an ice cream parlor and soda shop. Restaurant reservations are recommended. | 32 Main St., Pinos Altos | 505/538–9911, 505/388–3848 for opera house | Closed Sun. No lunch | $10–$30 | MC, V.

Palace Hotel. Owners Nancy and Cal Thompson have replicated the intimacy of a small European hotel at the Palace, a grand structure that was a first-class lodging when it opened in 1900. It saw less fabulous times as an apartment building before the Thompsons took over and renovated it in the late 1980s. Some rooms have western furnishings, others a distinctly Victorian decor. The upstairs garden room provides solitude for playing games or reading. Cable TV; no pets. | 106 W. Broadway, 88061 | 505/388–1811 | www.zianet.com/palacehotel | 11 rooms, 7 suites | $59–$109 | AE, D, DC, MC, V | CP.

TAOS
▼▼▼

The first European explorers of the Taos Valley came here with Captain Hernando de Alvarado, a member of Francisco Vásquez de Coronado's expedition of 1540. Don Juan de Oñate arrived in Taos in July 1598 and established a mission and trading arrangements with residents of Taos Pueblo. On a mesa at the base of the Sangre de Cristo Mountains, Taos today is actually three towns in one, all of them of considerable historical note. One is the low-key business district of art galleries, restaurants, and shops that recalls the Santa Fe of a few decades ago. Another, 4 mi south of downtown, is Ranchos de Taos, a farming and ranching community settled by the Spanish. And 3 mi north of downtown is Taos Pueblo, home to Tiwa-speaking Native Americans. Unlike many nomadic Native American tribes that were forced to relocate to government-designated reservations, the residents of Taos Pueblo have inhabited their land for centuries, since long before the arrival of the Spanish in the 1500s. Taos became famous at the end of the 19th century as one of America's earliest and most prominent artists colonies. *Contact Taos County Chamber of Commerce | 1139 Paseo del Pueblo Sur, Drawer I, Taos 87571 | 505/758–3873 or 800/732–8267 | www.taosguide.com.*

Chama. About 95 mi west of Taos, Chama has endured a series of booms and busts that have largely coincided with the popularity of train transportation. The town's earliest boom, which precipitated its founding, occurred in the 1880s when workers piled into town to construct the Denver & Rio Grande Railroad. In those days, narrow-gauge trains chugged over the high ranges carrying gold and silver from the mines of the San Juan Mountains. Gambling halls, moonshine stills, speakeasies, and brothels were a fixture along the main drag, Terrace Avenue. The lumber industry also thrived during the early years, and the town still has quite a few houses and buildings fashioned out of spare hand-hewn railroad ties. | 95 mi west of Taos on U.S. 64 | 505/756–2306 or 800/477–0149 | www.chama.org.

You can get a sense of Chama's Victorian railroading days with a tour on the **Cumbres & Toltec Scenic Railroad** (15 S. Terrace Ave., Chama | 505/756–2151 or 888/286–2737), a narrow-gauge railroad pulled by a coal-driven steam engine. As it runs through the San Juan Mountains and over the Cumbres Pass, the train chugs over elderly trestles, around breath-taking bends, and high above the Los Pinos River. Trains depart at 8 AM and 10:30 AM daily, late May–mid-October, and fares run $45–$60.

El Rincón. This small private museum exhibits Native American and Spanish-colonial arti-facts as well as a pair of Kit Carson's leather pants. Some of the other items on display include a holy water cup from the San Miguel mission dating to 1610, Plains Indians buckskin items, and various Native American church artifacts. | 114 Kit Carson Rd. | 505/758–9188 | Free | Daily.

Governor Bent Museum. In 1846, when the United States claimed New Mexico, a trader, trap-per, and mountain man by the name of Charles Bent was appointed governor. Less than a year later he was killed in his house by an angry mob protesting New Mexico's annexation by the United States. A collection of Native American artifacts, western Americana, and family possessions is squeezed into five small rooms of the adobe building where Bent and his family lived. | 117A Bent St. | 505/758–2376 | $1 | Daily 10–5.

Kit Carson Home and Museum. Kit Carson bought this low-slung 12-room adobe home in 1843 as a wedding gift for his wife, Josefa Jaramillo, the daughter of a powerful, politically influential Spanish family. Three of the museum's rooms are furnished as they were when the Carson family lived here. The rest of the museum is devoted to gun and mountain-man exhibits, such as rugged leather clothing and Kit's own Spencer carbine rifle with its beaded leather carrying case, and early Taos antiques, artifacts, and manuscripts. | Kit Carson Rd. | 505/758–0505 | $5 (or use Kit Carson Historic Museums of Taos joint ticket) | Apr.–Oct., daily 9–5; call for winter hrs.

Kit Carson Memorial Park. The noted pioneer is buried in the park that bears his name. His grave is marked with a *cerquita,* a spiked wrought-iron rectangular fence used to outline and protect burial sites. Also interred here is Mabel Dodge Luhan, the pioneering patron of the early Taos art scene. | Paseo del Pueblo Norte at Civic Plaza Dr. | 505/758–8234 | Free | Late May–early Sept., daily 8–8; early Sept.–late May, daily 8–5.

La Hacienda de los Martínez. Spare and fortlike, this adobe structure built between 1804 and 1827 on the bank of the Rio Pueblo served as a community refuge during Comanche and Apache raids. Its thick walls, which have few windows, surround two central courtyards. Owned by Don Antonio Severino Martínez, a farmer and trader, the hacienda was the final stop along

El Camino Real. The restored period rooms here contain textiles, foods, and crafts of the early 19th century. There's a working blacksmith shop, and weavers create beautiful textiles on reconstructed period looms. | Ranchitos Rd. (Rte. 240) | 505/758–1000 | $5 (or use Kit Carson Historic Museums of Taos joint ticket) | Apr.–Oct., daily 9–5; Nov.–Mar., daily 10–4.

Ranchos de Taos. A few minutes' drive south of the center of Taos, this village still retains some of its rural atmosphere despite the highway traffic passing through. It was settled by Spaniards in 1716.

The Spanish Mission–style **San Francisco de Asís Church** (Rte. 68, 500 yards south of Rte. 518, Ranch de Taos | 505/758–2754 | $2) was erected in the 18th century as a spiritual and physical refuge from raiding Apache, Ute, and Comanche. The earthy, clean lines of the exterior walls and supporting bulwarks have inspired generations of painters and photographers.

Taos Plaza. The Spanish settlement of Taos consisted of two plazas: the first Plaza, at the heart of the town, became a thriving business district for the early colony, and a walled residential plaza was constructed a few hundred yards behind. As authorized by a special act of Congress, the American flag flies in the center of the Plaza day and night in recognition of Kit Carson's heroic stand protecting the settlement from Confederate sympathizers during the Civil War. | Kit Carson Rd. between Paseo del Pueblo Sur and Camino de la Placita.

Taos Pueblo. For nearly 1,000 years the mud-and-straw adobe walls of Taos Pueblo have sheltered Tiwa-speaking Native Americans. The pueblo today appears much as it did when the first Spanish explorers arrived in New Mexico in 1540. The adobe walls glistening with mica caused the conquistadores to believe they had discovered one of the fabled Seven Cities of Gold. Even after 400 years of Spanish and Anglo presence in Taos, inside the pueblo the traditional Native American way of life has endured. Tribal custom allows no electricity or running water in the two main buildings, where varying numbers (usually fewer than 100) of Taos Native Americans live full-time. The pueblo Church of San Geronimo, or St. Jerome, the patron saint of Taos Pueblo, was completed in 1850 to replace the one destroyed by the U.S. Army in 1847 during the Mexican-American War. You can take a guided tour by appointment. The pueblo closes for funerals, religious ceremonies, for a 2-month "quiet time" in late winter or early spring, and for the last part of August. It's best to call ahead before visiting to make sure guests are welcome. | About 5 mi north of Taos Plaza via Paseo del Pueblo Norte, then follow signs | 505/758–1028 | www.taospueblo.com | Tourist fees $10; still-camera permit $10 (note: cameras that may look commercial, such as those with telephoto lenses, might be denied a permit); video-camera permit $20 | Apr.–Nov., daily 8–4; Oct.–Mar., daily 8:30–4.

NORTH DAKOTA

———◆———

hippewa, Mandan, Hidatsa, Arikara, Sioux-Yanktonai, Hunkpapa, Sisseton, Wahpeton, and other tribes lived in North Dakota when the first non–Native American visitor—explorer Pierre La Verendrye—arrived from Canada in 1738. La Verendrye's visit initiated a fur-trading era that lasted more than 100 years; his sons, Chevalier and Louis Joseph, claimed the region for France in 1743. In the ensuing century the intermingling of mostly French fur traders and Chippewa women created a new people, the Métis, who tried unsuccessfully to establish their own nation.

Lewis and Clark entered what is now North Dakota from the south via the Missouri River in mid-October 1804. The "Mighty Mo" juts like a giant elbow into the southwestern section of the state and marks the eastern edge of the Rocky Mountain foothills. Lewis and Clark traveled north on the river for about two weeks and then wintered at Fort Mandan 2 mi east of what is now Washburn. Here the two explorers met Toussaint Charbonneau, a French-Canadian trader, and his wife Sacagawea (also spelled Sakajawea and Sakakawea), a Shoshone teenager.

The area now encompassed by the state of North Dakota is marked by the Red River on its eastern edge, where the rich farmland is so flat that the horizon is a long, unbroken line. To the west, the land gradually begins to show slopes and hills, small valleys, lakes, and prairie potholes. North Dakota beckoned as an agricultural promised land. When the Homestead Act was passed in 1862, settlement of the Dakota Territory began in earnest. Immigrants from overseas and emigrants from the east arrived in North Dakota on wagon trains and established homestead claims where they found land they liked. Several North Dakota towns are still largely populated with the second- and third-generation descendants of these pioneers.

Many of North Dakota's cities and towns were established when the railroad came through in 1872. As white settlers demanded more and more land for farming, reservations for Indians were set aside, then reduced; then portions were opened for settlement. In 1876 General George Custer and the 7th Cavalry, stationed near Bismarck, went in search of Native

Americans who refused to be confined to the reservations. The resulting annihilation at Little Big Horn in 1876 made names such as Custer, Crazy Horse, and Sitting Bull famous.

Between 1879 and 1886, more than 100,000 people—mostly Scandinavians and Germans—entered Dakota Territory. The U.S. Army relentlessly continued to track down North Dakota's Native Americans, and Sitting Bull finally surrendered at Fort Buford near Williston in 1881. He was killed at his home on the Standing Rock Indian Reservation in 1890, a year after North Dakota and South Dakota became states.

Homesteading claims and bonanza farms established North Dakota as an agricultural state, with ranching another primary activity. But in the far western part of the state, the terrain is rugged and very dry. Craggy ravines, tablelands, and gorges make up a badlands region, where most of the land remained untouched and untamed. President Theodore Roosevelt built a home and ranch out there, near the frontier town of Medora on the meadows of the Little Missouri grasslands. Today the area is preserved in Theodore Roosevelt National Park.

Throughout North Dakota, the spirit of the Old West lives on at old forts, re-enactments of fur trade rendezvous, museums filled with bits of history, chuck-wagon cook-outs, and wide-open spaces. About 26,000 Native Americans still live in the state, mainly on four reservations, and you can take in an Indian powwow and visit an Indian heritage center. Or you can float down the Missouri River in a replica 1800s canoe, eat a meal prepared over an open fire, and bed down under black, starry skies, much as the early explorers did.

Along the Mighty Mo

A DRIVING TOUR FROM BISMARCK TO MEDORA

▼▼▼

Distance: About 450 mi **Time:** 4 days
Breaks: Overnight in Bismarck, Williston, and Medora

This tour captures the fascinating story of the Missouri River, which served as the Old West's main highway for travel and commerce.

Spend your first morning at Fort Abraham Lincoln State Park south of **Mandan** on Route 1806. Within walking distance is the On-A-Slant Indian Village, lodges that were inhabited by Mandan Indians. In the afternoon, go to the Port of Bismarck on North River Road, Exit 157 off I-94, and take a ride on the Lewis and Clark Riverboat, a 1800s paddlewheeler. Drive back to **Bismarck** to tour Camp Hancock State Historical Site. Then head for the Capitol grounds, where you will find the North Dakota Heritage Center.

On your second morning, take U.S. 83, north of Bismarck for 35 mi to **Washburn.** Stop at the Lewis and Clark Interpretive Center at the junction of U.S. 83 and Route 200A. From the interpretive center, drive 1½ mi north to Fort Mandan. Then continue to Stanton, 20 mi west across the river, to the Knife River Indian Villages National Historic Site. Return to Washburn for lunch, and then follow U.S. 83 north for 67 mi. Turn west on U.S. 2 and drive 115 mi to **Williston,** to have dinner and stay overnight.

On your third morning, drive 22 mi southwest of Williston on Route 1804 to the Fort Buford State Historic Site. Then head 2 mi west to Fort Union Trading Post National Historic Site, located at the confluence of the Yellowstone and Missouri rivers. Continue south on Route 58 for 9 mi, turn east onto Route 200 for 20 mi, and then turn south onto U.S. 85. Along this 65-mi stretch of U.S. 85 you will enter a region of butte formations known as the badlands (called Mako Shika by the Sioux). Keep your eyes open for wildlife and continue to Belfield, then turn west onto I-94 and go 15 mi to **Medora.** Just before you enter Medora, stop at the Painted Canyon Overlook visitor center (Exit 32 off I-94) in Theodore Roosevelt National Park for a spectacular panoramic view of the North Dakota badlands. Once in town, go to the Harold Schafer Heritage Center and buy tickets for the Pitchfork Fondue dinner on the bluffs overlooking Medora.

NORTH DAKOTA TIME LINE

1794 René Jusseaume builds a fur-trading post near present-day Washburn along the Knife River.

1797 Alexander Henry Jr. starts a fur-trading post at Park River and moves it to Pembina in 1801. The post attracts the first white settlement in North Dakota.

1803 The United States buys the western half of the Mississippi River basin from France in the Louisiana Purchase.

1804 Meriwether Lewis and William Clark enter North Dakota and winter near the present town of Washburn. Their post, Fort Mandan, is visited by Native Americans.

1806 The Lewis and Clark Expedition passes through North Dakota on its way back to St. Louis.

1818 The 49th parallel becomes the boundary between the United States and lands claimed by Great Britain in Canda.

1862 Dakota Territory is opened for homesteading.

1868 A peace treaty grants the Sioux the lands west of the Missouri River in Dakota Territory.

1869 Fort Berthold Indian Reservation is established. The Sioux and Chippewa cede most of eastern North Dakota to the government.

1872 The Northern Pacific Railway is built from the Red River to Jamestown.

1876 The 7th Cavalry, led by General George A. Custer, leaves Fort Abraham Lincoln near Bismarck to join the expedition against the Sioux. It is defeated at the Little Big Horn River in Montana.

1882 The last great Indian buffalo hunt occurs. The Turtle Mountain Reservation is established.

1887 Standing Rock Indian Reservation is opened to homesteading.

1889 North Dakota becomes the 39th state.

1890 Ghost Dance activities among the Sioux cause panic among settlers. Sitting Bull is killed at Standing Rock Indian Reservation.

1903 Fort Lincoln, located south of Bismarck, is completed and garrisoned.

1905 Railroads lay 529⅓ mi of tracks across North Dakota.

Spend your fourth day in Theodore Roosevelt National Park and Medora. You have many options, and the Tourist Information Center can give you directions and information about all of them. Your choices include taking a horseback ride through the badlands, driving through the national park, touring the majestic Chateau de Mores, spending the afternoon walking the wooden boardwalks and shopping, and taking in the outdoor Medora Musical that evening. You can easily spend several more days in Medora.

BISMARCK

Founded by railroad magnates and first named Edwinton in 1872, North Dakota's capital city of Bismarck was renamed in 1873 for the Chancellor of Germany, Prince Otto von Bismarck, in hopes of attracting German investments in the railroad. By the time General George Custer arrived in 1874 at nearby Fort Abraham Lincoln, Bismarck was thriving as a transportation

NORTH DAKOTA

CANADA

MONTANA

MINNESOTA

SOUTH DAKOTA

Pembina
Cavalier
Grafton
Walhalla
Mountain
Belcourt
Bottineau
Rugby
Devils Lake
Grand Forks
Fargo
Wahpeton
Carrington
Jamestown
SHEYENNE NAT'L GRASSLAND
Minot
Washburn
Bismarck
Mandan
Fort Abraham Lincoln State Park
Stanton
New Town
Lake Sakakawea
THEODORE ROOSEVELT NAT'L PARK
Watford City
Belford
Dickinson
Williston
Fort Union National Historic Site
LITTLE MISSOURI NAT'L GRASSLAND
THEODORE ROOSEVELT NAT'L PARK
Medora
LITTLE MISSOURI NAT'L GRASSLAND
Bowman
CEDAR RIVER NAT'L GRASSLAND

81 81 32 5 281 29 281 13 2 52 200 94 83 31 200 6 21 23 1804 85 22 12 85 21 22

60 miles
90 km

N

town with the Northern Pacific Railway crossing the steamboat-laden Missouri River. North Dakota became a state in 1889, and Bismarck, which now has a population of about 55,500, was named its capital. *Contact Bismarck–Mandan Convention and Visitors Bureau | 1600 Burnt Boat Dr., 58503 | 701/222–4308 or 800/767–3555 | www.bismarck-mandancvb.org.*

Camp Hancock State Historic Site. Camp Hancock was established in 1872 to protect crews working on the Northern Pacific Railroad. The site has a museum inside the clapboard main building, one of Bismarck's oldest churches, and a Northern Pacific steam locomotive. | 101 W. Main Ave. | 701/328–2666 | www.state.nd.us/hist/sitelist.htm | Free | Mid-May–mid-Sept., Wed.–Sun. 1–5.

Lewis and Clark Riverboat. Travel the Missouri River in fine style on a replica paddlewheeler steamboat. You'll be following the path taken by Native Americans and trappers. A full bar and food are on board; breakfast, lunch, and dinner cruises are available upon request. | Port of Bismarck, N. River Rd., Exit 157 off I–94 | 701/255–4233 | $15–$35 | Mid-May–early Sept., daily at 2:30, 6, and 8:30.

North Dakota Heritage Center. The state's largest collection of historic artifacts is here. Wander through several rooms containing Native American–made tepees, pottery, and hunting instruments such as fish traps. The Era of Change exhibit depicts the Old West between 1738 and 1870 with models of frontier forts and a diorama of the Battle of Little Big Horn, while the settlement period (until about 1915) is represented with a frontier home, a large windmill, iron crosses from prairie cemeteries, and antique tractors and plows. A statue of Sacagawea and her infant, Jean-Baptist, stands in front of the Heritage Center. | 612 E. Boulevard Ave. | 701/328–2666 | www.discovernd.com/hist | Free | Weekdays 8–5, Sat. 9–5, Sun. 11–5.

✦ ON THE CALENDAR: Sept. **United Tribes International Powwow.** One of the largest powwows in North America, this weekend festival draws contestants for Native American dancing and singing. Traditional garb, native foods, and handmade crafts add to the colorful festivities. | 701/255–3285 or 701/222–4308.

BOTTINEAU
▼▼

This town 10 mi south of the Canadian border was established in 1884 by the Great Northern Railroad and named for Métis frontiersman and trapper Pierre Bottineau. The town is the southwestern gateway to the Turtle Mountains, an area first inhabited by the native Chippewa, then explored by European traders and trappers in the mid-1700s. The two cultures came together to form a new people, called the Métis. Before Bottineau became a railway station, it served as a stagecoach stop. *Contact Greater Bottineau Area Chamber of Commerce | 103 E. 11th St., 58318 | 800/735–6932 | www.bottineau.com.*

Bottineau County Historical Museum. A frontier school house, an old country church altar and furnishings, an antique doll collection, military uniforms and weapons, medical equipment from the county doctor's offices, and a large camera collection are among the items in this museum. | 519 Main St. | 701/228–2943 | Free | Late May–early Sept., weekends 1:30–4; early Sept.–late May, by appointment.

Turtle Mountain Chippewa Heritage Center. Native American pottery and art, tools used for hunting and eating, tepee furnishings, arrowheads, furs, and other clothes depict life in an earlier time. The art gallery and museum is on the Turtle Mountain Indian Reservation. | Rte. 5, Belcourt, 35 mi east of Bottineau | 701/477–6140 | Free | Weekdays 8–5, Sat. 10–3.

POWWOWS: APPRECIATING NATIVE AMERICAN HERITAGE

Drums roll, voices rise in chants, and dancers dip and sway in brightly colored costumes. It's powwow time, an event important to Native Americans for both spiritual and social reasons. Powwows are traditional festivals that celebrate tribal heritage. Powwows attract many curious onlookers; you may not understand all the rituals but you are bound to appreciate the cultural experience and the beauty of the dancing.

You can recognize most powwow grounds by their circular arbors, which provide shade. Don't hesitate to bring a lawn chair, stake your place, and settle in comfortably for the daylong experience. Every powwow begins with a Grand Entry and includes speeches and other events that precede the dancing. Between events, sample the fry bread sold by vendors.

Announcers at powwows use a style of speaking and cadence established generations ago. Interspersed with dancing competitions are *giftings,* ceremonies wherein an individual or family presents gifts, often star quilts, in honor of a loved one's memory, to celebrate a homecoming, or to acknowledge a new family member. In some cases, a new family member is someone adopted into the clan. Clan families may call a fellow clan member a sister, grandson, or cousin although the member may be a distant relative or not even related by blood.

Dancers at powwows are as varied as the colors you see. Men performing traditional dances wear costumes decorated with beads and quill work. Their dances tell the stories of great battles or hunts. Grass dancers appear in colorful, fringed costumes, and their graceful movements resemble grasses blowing in the prairie breezes. Men, women, and even very young children, some barely able to walk, participate in the twirling and tapping in fancy dance costumes. Dancers score points by showing off their style and regalia.

Native Americans welcome visitors to their powwow circle and believe there are no spectators. Everyone is part of the circle. When the announcer calls an intertribal dance, you are invited to join the dancers in the circle. Yes, you can wear your street clothes.

Powwows are held regularly in summer in all areas of the state. If you're interested in going to one, the likelihood is good that there will be one somewhere in North Dakota on a summer weekend.

✦ **ON THE CALENDAR: June Traditional Powwow.** Learn about traditional Native American customs and enjoy dancing and costumes at this powwow held in Dunseith, 18 mi east of Bottineau. | 701/477–0471.

Sept. Turtle Mountain Labor Day Powwow. Dancing competitions, fine costumery, and education in Native American heritage make this a worthwhile event to see in Belcourt. | 701/477–0471.

BOWMAN

▼▼

In 1907, brothers A.L. and W.O. Lowden hauled lumber from Dickinson to a point 70 mi southwest of present-day Bowman, where two large rock formations jutted out of the prairie. There, amidst mostly unclaimed land and a few ranches, the Lowdens set up a printing plant and established the Bowman County Pioneer newspaper. They figured they needed something to advertise in their paper, so they also set up a real estate business and began to sell lots in the area. Shortly thereafter the town of Twin Buttes was incorporated, and by 1910 the town's named had been changed to Bowman. Early settlers spent their time playing Norwegian whist (a card game similar to bridge) and speculating when the railroad would come through the town. *Contact Bowman Chamber of Commerce | 13½ E. Divide, 58623 | 701/523–5880 | www.bowmannd.com.*

Fort Dilts State Historic Site. More military cemetery than park, this site holds the graves of soldiers killed during a 16-day standoff between a Sioux war party and the cavalry and civilians riding Captain J. L. Fisk's immigrant train to Montana in 1864. The corraled travelers were rescued by troops from Fort Rice. | U.S. 12, 4 mi northeast of Rhame and about 35 mi west of Bowman | Free | Daily.

Pioneer Trails Regional Museum. The second-largest museum in the state, the Pioneer Trails Regional Museum contains 19th-century military uniforms, furs, washboards, dolls and toys, and equipment used on cattle ranches and farms. Old photographs help show you what life was like in early North Dakota. | 12 1st Ave. NE | 701/523–3600 | www.ptrm.org | Free | Call for hrs.

✦ ON THE CALENDAR: Feb. **Penfield's Old West Auction.** Hard-to-find homesteading-era antiques and old-time cowboy collectibles go up for bids at this all-day auction at the Bowman County Fairgrounds. | 701/523–3652.

HISTORIC LODGING
Logging Camp Ranch. This working cattle and bison ranch, on the Little Missouri River and in the state's only ponderosa pine forest, lies amid early Native American campgrounds, an eagle trapping pit, and an ancient rock quarry. General Custer and his cavalry camped here on August 23, 1874, on their way back to Fort Lincoln. The ranch was built in the early 1900s, and three other buildings moved onto the site are made of local pine and were built in the 1880s. The log cabins have electricity, wood stoves, and warm quilts but little else. Some refrigerators, microwaves, fishing, archery, hiking, horseback riding, horseshoes, cross-country skiing, some pets allowed. | 5705 151st Ave. SW, 58623 | 701/279–5501 | fax 701/279–6663 | www.loggingcampranch.com | 5 rooms with 2 shared baths, 3 cabins (2 with no bath) | $50 per person | MC, V.

DEVILS LAKE
▼▼

Devils Lake, on the banks of the largest natural body of water in North Dakota, was established in 1882 by Lieutenant H. M. Creel after his retirement from the army. The town originally was named Creel, but the name was changed by officials of the St. Paul, Minneapolis & Manitoba Railway, when a station was built nearby. Just south of Devils Lake is the 137,000-acre reservation of the Spirit Lake Sioux. *Contact Devils Lake Area Visitors Bureau Office | Box 879, 58301 | 701/662–4903 or 800/233–8048 | www.devilslakend.com.*

Fort Totten State Historic Site. Fort Totten was built in 1867 as a military post and today is known as the best-preserved military fort west of the Mississippi River. Cavalry and infantry units carried out police functions, and units from the 7th Cavalry were called to serve under General Custer in the 1876 Sioux Campaign, which called for the forced settlement of the Sioux onto reservations. You can visit the 17 original buildings, one of which serves as a bed-and-breakfast. | Rte. 57, 14 mi south of Devils Lake | 701/766–4441 | www.state.nd.us/hist | $4 | Mid-May–mid-Sept., daily 10–5.

The fort's **Cultural Center and Museum** (701/766–4415) displays such artifacts as arrowheads, peace pipes, traditional dress, and beautiful beadwork made by Native Americans, plus majestic taxidermied eagles. Dioramas show how the Sioux and Chippewa lived during the 18th and 19th centuries. The museum is on the Fort Totten Candeska Cikana Community College campus in Fort Totten State Park.

Head to the **Lake Region Pioneer Daughters Museum** (701/766–4346) to see frontier firearms, pioneer farming equipment, home furnishings, steamboat equipment, and period clothing. The museum is in one of the 17 original buildings in Fort Totten State Historic Site.

Heritage House/Sheriff's Residence. Originally a large jail, this Greco-style building was home to Ramsey County sheriffs and their families from 1910 to 1974. The museum concentrates on the settlement period, with country-store fixtures, toys, a complete dental office, school equipment, musical instruments, tools, and laundry aids, all from the 19th and early 20th centuries. | 416 6th St. | 701/662–3701 | Free | Late May–early Sept., Wed–Sun. 1–4; early Sept.–late May, by appointment.

Lake Region Heritage Center. Built in 1908, this neoclassic-style building complete with a widow's walk was originally a post office. Inside you'll find an old-fashioned dental office, doctor's office, law office, and judge's courtroom, as well as taxidermied native animals, a vintage car, and artifacts from an early church. | 502 4th St. | 701/662–3701 | Free | Weekdays 10–5.

HISTORIC LODGING

Totten Trail Historic Inn. This B&B is one of the 17 original buildings that remain on the Fort Totten State Historic Site. It first housed the captains' and lieutenants' quarters and later served as an apartment building for employees of the Indian Industrial Boarding School. Rooms are decorated with antique furniture, flowery quilts or comforters, and framed pictures. Lake, fishing, croquet, cross-country and downhill skiing, library, gift shop, game room, Internet, meeting rooms, airport shuttle, some pets allowed; no smoking, no room TVs. | Rte. 57, 14 mi south of Devils Lake, 58335 | 701/766–4874 | fax 701/766–2001 | www.tottentrailinn.com | 10 rooms | $80–$110 | MC, V | CP.

DICKINSON

▼▼▼

Andy Messersmith and his family were some of the first settlers in what was known as Pleasant Valley. The Great Northern Railroad, in preparation for an expansion west through the valley from Mandan, hired Messersmith in the late 1870s to build a small restaurant in the area, so that railroad workers, and eventually passengers, would have a place to stop for food. Homesteaders and prospective ranchers came in great numbers to settle in Pleasant Valley after the completion of railroad. The city was incorporated in the fall of 1880 and renamed Dickinson in honor of a New York railroad official. Agriculture and ranching fueled Dickinson into the early 1900s. Cowboys are still a familiar sight in this community of 16,000, where Dickinson State University has a national collegiate rodeo team. *Contact Dickinson Convention and Visitors' Bureau | Box 181, 58601 | 701/483–4988, 800/279–7391 | www. dickinsonnd.com.*

Joachim Regional Museum. Tools and equipment used by early ranchers and cowboys are part of the permanent collection; rotating exhibits focus on other aspects of the settlement period in southwest North Dakota. | 200 Museum Dr. | 701/465–6225 | www.dickinsoncvb. com | $6 | Late May–early Sept., daily 9–5.

Pioneer Machinery Museum. Pioneer farmers used the threshing machines, old-time tractors, horse-drawn plows, and other machinery on display here. | 200 Museum Dr. | 701/456–6225 | Free | Late May–early Sept., daily 9–5.

Prairie Outpost Park. A stone house built by German immigrants (most of whom emigrated to Russia before arriving in the United States), a *stabbur* (a tiny wooden Norwegian storehouse), a train depot and caboose, a post office, a general store, a church, and a school are among the 19th-century structures at this museum. | 200 Museum Dr. | 701/465–6225 | www. dickinsoncvb.com | Free | Park year-round; tours late May–early Sept., daily 9–5.

✦ ON THE CALENDAR: July **Taylor Horsefest.** Horse-drawn rigs, cowboy movies, cowboy poetry, and horseback riding are the focus during this annual event in Taylor, 10 mi east of Dickinson and 1 mi north of I–94. | 701/483–4988 or 800/279–7391.

FARGO

▼▼

As homesteaders brought farming to the area, the Red River valley earned its reputation as the "breadbasket of the world." Pioneers, largely from Scandinavia, arrived by the thousands in the 1870s. Fargo was founded in 1871 and named for William G. Fargo, one of the owners of the Wells-Fargo Express Company. *Contact Fargo-Moorhead Convention and Visitors Bureau | 2001 44th St. SW, 58103 | 701/282–3653 or 800/235–7654 | www.fargomoorhead.org.*

Bonanzaville. Forty buildings, including a sod house, a school, a church, and log homes, comprise this pioneer-era village. In some buildings costumed guides show how people in the late 1800s made butter, washed laundry, and accomplished other household and farm tasks. | 1351 W. Main Ave., West Fargo | 701/282–2822 or 800/700–5317 | www.bonanzaville.com | $6 | May and Sept.–Oct., weekdays 9–5; June–Aug. daily 9–6; Nov.–Apr., Mon. 12:30–5 or by appointment.

Stop by Bonanzaville's **Milligan Indian Museum** for a look at pottery, beadwork, and paintings. The Native American art collection is one of the largest in the Midwest.

✦ ON THE CALENDAR: Aug. **Pioneer Days at Bonanzaville.** Learn and perform the everyday skills and homespun arts of the pioneers during this two-day celebration in West Fargo. Costumed demonstrators dip candles, spin cloth, and thresh wheat. | 701/282–2822.

JAMESTOWN

▼▼

After the railroad passed through southern North Dakota in 1872, enough homesteaders, ranchers, farmers, and immigrants arrived in the area for politicians to create several new counties. Jamestown, incorporated in 1883, was made the county seat of Stutsman County. The town was settled mostly by Germans, many of whom emigrated to Russia before continuing on to North America. Today, Jamestown's herd of about 30 American bison lives in the prairies behind the National Buffalo Museum. You can't miss North Dakota's most famous bison, a 26-ft-high, 46-ft-long, 60-ton concrete sculpture, which stands on a hill between I–94 and U.S. 281 and is visible for miles. *Contact Jamestown Promotion and Tourism Center | 212 3rd Ave. NE, 58401 | 701/252–4835 or 800/222–4766 | www.jamestownnd.com.*

Fort Seward Military Post and Interpretive Center. From 1872 to 1877, this fort was used to protect Northern Pacific railroad workers. The foundations and basements are all that remain of the original structure, but you can visit the ongoing archaeological dig on premises. | 601 10th Ave. NW | 701/252–6844 | Free | Apr.–Oct., daily.

Frontier Village. This re-created frontier village has the oldest general store in the state, a one-room school house, a barbershop, and a church, among other buildings. | Louis L'Amour St. at 17th St. SE | 701/252–6307 | Free | Late May–early Sept., daily 9–9.

National Buffalo Museum. A 10,000-year-old skull, full-size buffalo mounts, and the original oil painting *Thundering Herd* by Bill Freeman illustrate the history and cultural importance of the American bison. | 500 17th St. SE | 701/252–8648 | www.ndtourism.com | Free | Late May–early Sept., daily 9–8; early Sept.–late May, daily 10–5.

Stutsman County Memorial Museum. Musical instruments, medical equipment, home furnishings, and pioneer and military clothing, all from the 19th and early 20th centuries, are part of the collection here. The museum is in a beautifully preserved, late-19th-century brick home. | 321 3rd Ave. SE | $5 | June–Sept., Mon.–Tues. and Thurs.–Sat. 1–5, Wed. and Sun. 2–5 and 7–9, or by appointment.

✦ ON THE CALENDAR: June **Fort Seward Wagon Train.** Canvas-topped box wagons jostle you about as you live the life of the traveling pioneer during this weeklong trip across the North Dakota countryside. Teams of draft horses or mules pull the wagons with an experienced teamster at the helm, so you just have to hang on. Chuckwagon meals are part of the fun. | 701/252–6844.
Historic Dining

MANDAN
▼▼

Mandan, across the Missouri River from Bismarck, was settled in 1872 when the Northern Pacific Railroad laid tracks through the area. The town changed names several times until 1878, when a railroad official settled on Mandan after the Mandan tribe that lived near the river bank. After the Northern Pacific Railroad completed a bridge from Bismarck across the Missouri River in 1882, Mandan's future was secured. *Contact Convention and Visitors Bureau | 1600 Burnt Boat Dr., 58503 | 701/222–4308 or 800/767–3555 | www.bismarck-mandancvb.org.*

Fort Abraham Lincoln State Park. Originally occupied by Mandan natives, fur traders, and trappers who plied the Missouri River, North Dakota's oldest state park got its start when President Theodore Roosevelt deeded 75 acres to the State Historical Society in 1907. Here you'll find General George Custer's restored home and the 7th Cavalry barracks and commissary. Guides dressed in period clothing take you back to 1876, the year before the 7th Cavalry rode to its destiny at the Little Bighorn. | Rte. 1806, 7 mi south of Mandan | 701/663–9571 | www.lewisandclarktrail.com | Free | Late May–early Sept., daily 9–7; early–late May and Sept., daily 9–5; Oct. and last 2 wks of Apr., daily 1–5.

The natural history museum and four reconstructed earth lodges in **On-A-Slant Indian Village** (Mid-Apr.–Oct., 9–7; spring and fall hrs vary) in Fort Lincoln State Park bring an ancient civilization to life. The restored earth homes are filled with artifacts and examples of how the agricultural-based Mandan tribe worked and played. Daily guided tours are available.

North Dakota State Railroad Museum. Most North Dakota towns were established when the railroad came through or near them. This 5-acre museum depicts railroad history with memorabilia, a mini-train, models, and photographs. | 3102 37th St. NW | 701/663–9322 | Free | Late May–early Sept., daily 1–5, or by appointment.

✦ ON THE CALENDAR: Aug. **American Legacy Expo.** Relive the days of the 7th Cavalry with displays, drills, Custer House tours, demonstrations of how the Mandan Indians lived, and entertainment during a weekend encampment at Fort Abraham Lincoln State Park. | 701/663–4758.

MEDORA

▼▼

Founded in 1883, this small frontier town is named for the American-born wife of the French Marquis de Mores, who dreamed of building a slaughterhouse empire on the prairie. The venture collapsed—leaving behind a 26-room mansion and a dwindling cowboy town in the heart of the badlands. *Contact Harold Schafer Heritage Center | 335 4th St., 58645 | 701/ 623–4444 or 800/633–6721 | www.medora.com. Theodore Roosevelt Medora Foundation | 500 Pacific Ave., 58645 | 701/623–4444 or 800/633–6721 | www.medora.com.*

Billings County Courthouse Museum. The story of early Medora is told through an extensive collection of military and Old West firearms, regional and Ukrainian immigrant art, and Native American artifacts. | 475 4th St. | 701/623–4829 | $2 | Late May–early Sept., daily 9–5.

Chateau De Mores State Historic Site. The French nobleman for whom the chateau is named erected this 26-room mansion in 1883 with his wife, Medora. De Mores owned a meat-packing plant and encouraged cattle ranchers to settle in the area. The couple hosted extravagant hunting parties and even entertained Theodore Roosevelt during his Dakota ranching days, but they never fully realized their cattle empire. Eventually their business ventures failed and the De Moreses returned to France. The chateau has been restored, and interpretive tours are offered in summer. About 1 mi from the chateau is De Mores Memorial Park, wherein stands a lone brick chimney, all that remains of the meat-packing plant. | 1 Chateau La. | 701/623–4355 | fax 701/623–4921 | $5 | Mid-May–mid-Sept., daily 8:30–6:30; mid-Sept.–mid-May, by appointment.

A replica of the stage coach operated by the Marquis de Mores leaves the chateau daily on the half hour from mid-May to early September for a 20-minute interpretive ride. The **Medora-Deadwood Overland Stage Line** (701/872–3192 | $10) follows the river bank to the outbuildings of this historic site.

Harold Schafer Heritage Center. Western art and other memorabilia fill this center named after the creator of the Theodore Roosevelt Foundation. Schafer led the effort to restore Medora's 19th- and early 20th-century properties. | Rte. 10, ½ mi southwest of Medora | 701/623–4355 | www.medora.com | Free | Late May–early Sept., daily 10–6.

Medora Doll House. Antique dolls and toys fill almost every inch of this small house, built by the Marquis de Mores in 1884 and listed on the National Register of Historic Places. | 485 Broadway | 701/623–4444 or 800/633–6721 | fax 701/623–4494 | www.medora.org | $3 | Late May–early Sept., daily 10–6.

Museum of the Badlands. Native American tools as well as clothing and wax figures of Medora's early citizens, including Theodore Roosevelt and the Marquis de Mores, depict frontier days. | 195 3rd Ave. | 701/225–5151 or 800/633–6721 | www.medora.com | $4 | Late May–early Sept., daily 10–7.

Theodore Roosevelt National Park. Two distinctly different units, the North and South, comprise this savage, untamed land in North Dakota's beautiful badlands. Evidence of early history is everywhere, from tepee rings to wildlife and marks left by early settlers and ranchers. The South Unit is off I–94 at Exits 24, 27, and 32 (the Painted Canyon Overlook). The North Unit is off U.S. 85. | Box 7, 58645-0007 | 701/842–2333 North Unit; 701/623–4466 South Unit | www.medora.com | $10 per vehicle | Daily.

Often referred to as the third unit of Teddy Roosevelt National Park, the 218-acre **Elkhorn Ranch** (35 mi north of South Unit visitor center) is the land Roosevelt purchased in 1883 and where he often retreated. Today there are no buildings here, although foundation blocks outline the original house and outbuildings. You do not need a permit to trek through the land, but you are required to check with the South Unit visitor center about road and river-fording conditions before you go.

THEODORE ROOSEVELT NATIONAL PARK

Theodore Roosevelt once wrote: "I would not have been President, had it not been for my experience in North Dakota."

Roosevelt first stepped off the train in North Dakota in the fall of 1883, 18 years before he became president. He was 24 years old and eager to shoot his first bison. Roosevelt was so impressed with the beauty of the region that within two weeks he had purchased the Maltese Cross open-range cattle ranch, and the following year he returned to buy the Elkhorn ranch. Both are now a part of the 70,000-acre national park that bears his name.

The nation's 26th president returned to the ranches and his Maltese Cross log cabin many times throughout his life—once to mourn the deaths of his wife and mother, another time to write *Hunting Trips of a Ranchman*. During his time in western North Dakota, Roosevelt witnessed firsthand the destruction of the grasslands and the devastation of many species of animals due to hunting and overgrazing. Hating to see the nation's natural resources over-exploited, Roosevelt became an advocate for conservation. He established the U.S. Forest Service and over time created five national parks, 150 national forests, 51 bird reserves, and four game preserves.

Theodore Roosevelt National Park was established in 1947, almost 30 years after Roosevelt's death, to commemorate the president whose conservation efforts were first inspired by North Dakota. The park is divided into South and North units, through both of which winds the Little Missouri River. Both units are inhabited by plenty of bison, deer, antelope, coyote, prairie dogs, wild horses, and golden eagles, and both have peaks with exceptional views of the canyons, caprocks, petrified forests, and other bizarre geological formations that make up the badlands.

Drive along the South Unit's 36-mi scenic loop, which takes you past several overlooks, nature trails, prairie-dog towns, the Little Missouri River, and a petrified forest. The terrain, shaped by wind, rain, erosion, fire, and the meandering Little Missouri River, remains much the same as that which greeted Teddy Roosevelt more than a century ago and inspired him to write: "Nothing could be more lonely and nothing more beautiful than the view at nightfall across the prairies to these huge hill masses, when the lengthening shadows had at last merged into one and the faint after-glow of the red sunset filled the west."

Next door to the South Unit visitor center sits Theodore Roosevelt's summer home, the **Maltese Cross Ranch Cabin** (South Unit entrance, Exits 24 and 27 off I–94). The cabin's sturdy ponderosa pine logs had to be floated down the Little Missouri River from Montana. Inside the cabin are Roosevelt's original writing table and rocking chair, as well as other traditional period furnishings. You can tour the cabin year-round. Interpretive tours are held on the half hour every day June–September.

✦ ON THE CALENDAR: June–Aug. **Pitchfork Fondue.** From the top of the bluffs overlooking Medora at Tjaden Terrace, you'll enjoy rib-eye steaks cooked the cowboy way, on the end of a pitchfork. | 701/623–4444 or 800/633–6721.

June–early Sept. **Medora Musical.** This celebrated and long-lived show, which pays tribute to the Old West and its most colorful characters, is held nightly in the 2,900-seat Burning Hills Amphitheater. As you take in the western music, yodeling, and dancing on stage, you can see the badlands all around. Admission is $21. | 701/623–4444 or 800/633–6721.

Dec. **Old-fashioned Cowboy Christmas.** A cowboy jamboree, interpretive history demonstrations, cowboy poetry, storytelling, and a lighting ceremony pack a western punch into a Christmas festival. | 701/623–4190.

HISTORIC LODGING

Rough Riders Hotel Medora Getaway. Theodore Roosevelt frequented this 1884 hotel in downtown Medora and gave a speech from the balcony during a presidential campaign. Rooms are decorated in early 20th-century style, with brass beds, patchwork quilts, and red-velvet drapes. Buffalo ribs are on the menu in the dining room ($16–$26). Restaurant, cable TV. | 301 3rd Ave., 58645 | 701/623–4444 or 800/633–6721 | fax 701/623–4494 | www.medora. com | 9 rooms | $89–$120 | MC, V.

MINOT

▼▼▼

Prairie roses, buffalo, and other wildlife was all Ole Sundre saw when he stopped beside the Souris River in the winter of 1884 and decided to build a homestead. About 40 other settlers, many from Scandinavia, joined Sundre along the banks of the river by the time the railroad came through and Minot was established in 1886. The town was named for a Great Northern Railway director Henry D. Minot, who was killed in a train wreck. In the late 1800s and early 1900s, Minot grew so rapidly that it was nicknamed North Dakota's "Magic City." *Contact Minot Convention and Visitors Bureau | 1020 S. Broadway, 58702 | 701/857–8206 or 800/624– 2626 | www.visitminot.org.*

Railroad Museum. Railroads helped establish most North Dakota towns, and you can catch a glimpse of those early railroad days at this museum. Railroaders' clothing and train parts are on display. Afterward, take a miniature-train ride through Roosevelt Park and Zoo ($2). | 19 1st St. SE | 701/852–7091 | Free | May–Aug., weekdays 10–4, Sat. 1–4.

Ward County Historical Society Museum and Pioneer Village. Here you can see preserved and restored 19th-century buildings, such as a log cabin and a one-room school house, plus early home furnishings and automobiles. | 2005 Burdick Expressway E | 701/839–0785 | $2 | May– Sept., Tues.–Sun. 10–6, or by appointment.

✦ ON THE CALENDAR: July **North Dakota State Fair.** Volunteers set up a mock frontier encampment for the nine days of this fair, reenacting the lifestyle of fur traders in the 1800s. Livestock shows and a rodeo are among the fair's events. | 701/852–3247.

Oct. **Wild West Hostfest.** Watch the state's largest indoor rodeo, eat at a pitchfork fondue, and go to a cowboy-style church service with Preacher Paul on Sunday morning. | 701/852–2368.

PEMBINA

▼▼▼

Pembina was established by the Chippewa and Métis people in 1797. Several groups of Native Americans—the Ojibwe, Dacotah, Assiniboine, and Cree—each lived here at one time, hunting buffalo and gathering wild berries. Because of its proximity to the Canadian border, Pembina played an important role in the fur trade. *Contact Pembina State Museum | Exit 215 off I–29, 58271 | 701/825–6840 | www.state.nd.us/hist.*

Gingras Trading Post State Historic Site. Listed on the National Register of Historic Places, these hand-hewn log buildings are the restored home and trading post of Métis fur trader Antoine B. Gingras, who moved into the area in the 1840s. The buildings are among the oldest standing structures built by the children of Native Americans and European immigrants in North Dakota. | 12882 129th Ave. NE, Walhalla, 30 mi west of Pembina | 701/549– 2775 | www.state.nd.us/hist | Free | Mid-May–mid-Sept., daily 10–5.

Pembina County Historical Museum. Pioneer farm machinery and rotating exhibits show what early agriculture was like here. There's also a research library. | Division and Main Sts., Cavalier, 30 mi southwest of Pembina | 701/265–4941 | Free | Late May–early Sept., daily 1–5.

Pembina State Museum. Ride an elevator to the top of this museum's 85-ft-high observation tower for a spectacular view of the surrounding countryside. The Red River oxcart and other objects related to Pembina's fur-trade industry, the Native Americans and Euro-Native American settlers, agriculture and the transportation networks of the 1800s in northeast North Dakota are among the exhibits in the 1,000-square-ft gallery. | Exit 215 off I–29 | 701/825–6840 | www.state.nd.us/hist | Free | Mid-May–mid-Sept., Mon.–Sat. 9–6, Sun. 1–6; mid-Sept.–mid-May, Mon.–Sat. 9–5, Sun. 1–5.

Pioneer Heritage Museum. Visit an 18th-century church, sit a spell in a log cabin, and learn about the lives and achievements of the area's first settlers at this museum in Icelandic State Park. | Rte. 5, 5 mi west of Cavalier, 35 mi southwest of Pembina | 701/265–4561 | Free | Daily.

◆ ON THE CALENDAR: June **Rendezvous Festival.** Visit a buck skinner's encampment and enjoy crafts from the 18th century along with other festivities at Icelandic State Park. | 701/265–4561.

HISTORIC LODGING

221 Melsted Place. This three-story 1910 Victorian house has hardwood floors and rooms filled with antiques. Icelandic president Olafur Grimsson chose it as his official accommodations for his visit to North Dakota in 1999. Enjoy massage therapy in the spa, croquet by torchlight, and dinner by candlelight. A phone and cable TV are available in the living room. Dining room, spa, Internet; no A/C, no room phones, no room TVs, no kids under 12. | 8735 130th Ave. NE, Mountain 58262, 60 mi west of Pembina | 701/993–8257 or 888/993–8957 | fax 701/993–8257 | www.melstedplace.com | 4 rooms with shared bath | $80–$120 | MC, V | BP.

RUGBY

▼▼▼

The Rugby area was settled by homesteaders in the early 1880s. After the Great Northern Railroad established a station there in 1886, many of the pre-existing houses and stores were hauled across the railroad tracks to what became downtown Rugby. The first business erected there was a general store owned by C.F. Anderson and Nels Jacobson. In August 1886 trains began stopping at Rugby Junction in the evening as well as during the day, prompting a reporter at the Pierce County Tribune to write that the station town's "hum and bustle of life might be compared with the Union Depot of St. Paul." Rugby Junction was incorporated as a village in 1897 and, after several years, came simply to be called Rugby. The town, which was named by a railroad official for Rugby, England, is at the geographical center of North America. *Contact Greater Rugby Area Convention and Visitors Bureau | 224 U.S. 2 SW, 58368 | 701/776–5846 | www.rugbynorthdakota.com.*

Dale and Martha Hawk Museum. An 1890 threshing machine, a buggy, and a rare Hackney auto plow that still works are among about 100 vehicles and 300 antiques on this former 19th-century farm. There is also a one-room schoolhouse and a general store. | Off Rte. 17, Wolford, 33 mi northeast of Rugby | 701/583–2381 | $3 | Apr.–mid-Oct., daily 9–7; mid-Oct.–Mar., by appointment only.

Geographical Center and Prairie Village Museum. Impeccably preserved buildings in this village transport you back in time to the 19th century. A 21-ft-high granite pyramid marks the geographical center of North America. | U.S. 2 at Rte. 3 | 701/776–6414 | $5 | May–Sept., Mon.–Sat. 8–7, Sun. 1–7.

Victorian Dress Museum. From fashions worn by affluent women to prairie school teachers' garments, the articles of clothing in this museum are replicas based on photographs and illustrations in 19th- and early 20th-century family albums and books. | 312 2nd Ave. SW | 701/776–2189 | $5 | Weekdays 3–5.

✦ ON THE CALENDAR: June **Dale and Martha Hawk Antique Threshing Show.** Threshing machines from the past chug into action to demonstrate harvesting. Reenactors churn butter and perform other tasks as they were done before there was electricity and running water. | 701/583–2381.

Aug. Village Fair. Watch demonstrators prepare meals in a wooden cook cart, do laundry with old-time washboards, and perform blacksmith tasks at the Prairie Village Museum. There's live music in the church and saloon, where people gather to dance the old-time way. | 701/776–6414.

WAHPETON
▼▼

Native American tribes first called the town Chahinkapa, which means "End of the Woods" in Sioux, before they changed the name to Wahpeton, which means "Leaf Village." On the Red River across from Minnesota, Wahpeton was settled by immigrants who found the surrounding valley ideal for growing wheat, sunflowers, sugar beets, and corn. When the Northern Pacific Railroad went bankrupt during the economic crash of 1873, Wahpeton became one of the North Dakota communities where thousands of acres of railroad land was turned into giant spreads known as bonanza farms. *Contact Wahpeton Area Chamber of Commerce | 118 6th St. N, 58075 | 701/642–8744 or 800/892–6673 | www.wahpchamber.com.*

Bagg Bonanza Farm. J. F. Downing, an attorney and businessman from Erie, Pennsylvania, established the mainly wheat-producing farm in the 1870s on more than 9,000 acres of land purchased from the financially insecure Northern Pacific Railroad. His nephew, F. A. Bagg, worked on the farm for $20 a month until he became the farm superintendent in 1887. When Downing died, Bagg inherited some of the farm's holdings and began his own bonanza farm. The site is now run by the Bagg Bonanza Farm Historic Preservation Society. Nine of the original 21 buildings have been restored, and guided tours are available. | Rte. 13, 10 mi west of Wahpeton | 701/274–8989 | $3.50 | Late May–early Sept., Fri. noon–5, weekends noon–6.

Fort Abercrombie State Historic Site. The first fort in North Dakota that the government established to be permanent (most forts were built as temporary outposts), Fort Abercrombie was erected in 1858 to protect steamboats and wagons traveling along the Red River. The fort was the only post in the area besieged by Sioux warriors—for more than six weeks—during the Dakota Conflict of 1862. You can see an original building and museum, plus reconstructed blockade houses. | Rte. 44 off I–29, 10 mi north of Wahpeton | 701/553–8513 | www.state.nd.us/hist | Free; museum $3 | Mid-May–mid-Sept., Wed.–Sun. 8–5.

Richland County Historical Museum. Rosemeade pottery manufactured in Wahpeton, the world's largest registration book, 19th-century needlework, and other items reflect pioneer life in southeastern North Dakota. | 11 7th Ave. N | 701/642–3075 | www.wahpchamber.com | Free | Late May–early Sept., Tues., Thurs., and Sun. 1–4.

HISTORIC LODGING

Adams Fairview Bed and Breakfast and Bonanza Farm. Built in the 1880s, this house and six other original buildings were once part of a bonanza farm. The house, originally the Adams summer home, has been maintained in the turn-of-the-20th-century style. Dining room; no A/C, no phones, no TV in some rooms, no smoking. | 17170 82nd St. SE, 58075 | 701/274–8262 | www.ndbba.com | 3 rooms with shared bath, 1 suite | $50–$70 | Closed Oct.–Apr. | No credit cards | BP.

WASHBURN

▼▼

Lewis and Clark spent the winter of 1804–05 at Fort Mandan, 2 mi west of Washburn. Part of the Lewis and Clark National Historic Trail, Washburn (population 1,500) sits on the Missouri River and was a major stopping place for fur traders and explorers following the river west. *Contact City of Washburn | 907 Main Ave., 58577 | 701/462–8558 | www.washburnnd.com.*

Birdwoman Missouri River Adventures. Travel down the Missouri River in a replica 19th-century canoe with guides dressed in period clothing. Learn about the Lewis and Clark expedition as you experience what it was like. The guides cook meals over an open fire, and nights are spent in tepees. Half-day to multiday trips are available. | Box 59, 58577 | 701/462–3367 | www.birdwoman.com | $40–$250 | Late May–early Sept., by appointment.

Fort Clark Trading Post. Fort Clark contains the archaeological remains of a large earth-lodge village, cemetery, and two fur-trade posts. You may take a self-guided tour through the grounds. | Rte. 200A, 12½ mi west of Washburn | 701/462–8535 | Free | Daily.

Fort Mandan. Lewis and Clark spent the longest portion of their journey of exploration at Fort Mandan, where they set up their headquarters for the winter of 1804–05. Some 40 members of the Corps of Discovery helped to build the fort and dig out six canoes that they later used to continue the trip up the Missouri River. Lewis and Clark named the fort after their hospitable neighbors, the Mandan Indians, who taught expedition members how to stay alive during the bitter winter. Today you can visit a perfect replica of Fort Mandan, built from rough logs like the original. Rooms contain reproduction bunks, buffalo robes, tools, dried vegetables, and a blacksmith's workshop, like they did when the Corps lived there. Costumed interpreters are on site June–August daily. | McLean County Rte. 17, 1.5 mi west of the Lewis and Clark Interpretive Center at the junction of U.S. 83 and Rte. 200A | 701/462–8535 or 877/462–8535 | www.fortmandan.com | Free | Grounds, daily; buildings, June–Sept., daily 9–5; Oct.–May, call for hrs.

Knife River Indian Villages National Historic Site. This site preserves the ruins of Hidatsa and Mandan villages near Fort Mandan, including a village where Sacagawea lived. The prairie is dotted with hundreds of depressions that mark where the earth lodges used to stand. | Rte. 200A, Stanton, 19½ mi west of Washburn | 701/745–3309 | www.nps.gov/knri | Free | Late May–early Sept., daily 8–6; early Sept.–late May, daily 8–4:30.

Lewis and Clark Interpretive Center. The hand-built, 36-ft canoe here is a replica of the 16 canoes Lewis and Clark built during the winter they spent in the area. Also on display are buffalo-skin robes, a baby cradle like the one Sacagawea used to carry her son on her back, dioramas of native life, and watercolor prints by Karl Bodmer, a Swiss artist who visited the Knife River native villages with German prince Maximilian in 1833–34. Mandan flute music plays in the background. | U.S. 83 at Rte. 200A | 701/462–8535 | www.fortmandan.com | $5 | Late May–early Sept., daily 9–7; early Sept.–late May, daily 9–5.

McLean County Historical Society Museum. Buffalo-hide coats, antique typewriters, journals from the 1800s, and re-created 19th-century doctors' offices, living rooms, and an old printer's shop are among the attractions. | Main St. | 701/462–8535 | Free | Late May–early Sept., daily.

✦ ON THE CALENDAR: July **Northern Plains Indian Culture Fest.** Music, dancing, and traditional native cooking are part of this festival at the Knife River Indian Villages near Stanton. | 701/745–3309.

HISTORIC LODGING
Knife River Ranch. Ride horseback across rugged land where tepee rings are still visible, canoe down Knife River like trappers and Native Americans did, and then settle down for a deep sleep in the bunkhouse or cabins of this working ranch set in an isolated valley. A hanging bridge built by farm hands in the early 1900s provides passage across the river to the horse barns. Cabins have wood floors, handmade quilts, and front porches overlooking the river. There are no private baths. Packages include up to three meals daily. Dining room, refrigerators, horseback riding, horseshoes, cross-country skiing; no A/C, no room phones, no smoking. | 1700 Rte. 5, Golden Valley 58541 | 701/983–4290 | fax 701/983–4295 | www.kniferiverranch.com | 5 cabins, 1 bunkhouse | $55 | MC, V. *Contact McKenzie County Tourism | Box 699, 58854 | 800/701–2804 | www.4eyes.net.*

WILLISTON
▼▼

In 1887 the Great Northern Railroad built a station at the confluence of the Missouri and Yellowstone rivers, where Lewis and Clark camped, and called it Little Muddy. Visiting a year later, the president of the company renamed it in honor of a friend. Agricultural settlers found the soil to their liking and turned from ranching to wheat farming. *Contact Williston Convention and Visitors Bureau | 10 Main St., 58801 | 701/774–9041 or 800/615–9041 | www.willistonndtourism.com.*

Buffalo Trails Museum. In seven buildings you will find antiques, geospheres, and fossils, but the most unusual items are the dentist's office, sickroom, and parlor. | Rte. 42, Epping, 22 mi northeast of Williston | 701/859–4361 | $2 | June–Aug., Mon.–Sat. 9–5, Sun. 1:30–5:30; Sept.–Oct., Sun. 1:30–5:30, or by appointment.

Fort Buford State Historic Site. Chief Joseph and Sitting Bull were once detained at this fort. Now you can walk among the original buildings, including the officer's quarters, where an educational center provides information on the rivers, and the flora and fauna of the region. | Rte. 1804, 21 mi southwest of Williston | 701/572–9034 | $4 | Mid-May–mid-Sept., daily 10–6.

Fort Union Trading Post National Historic Site. One of the largest trading posts on the upper Missouri River, Fort Union had walls 18 ft high and cornerstone bastions. Today the partly reconstructed white-clapboard fort contains a bookstore and a museum with clothing and accessories from the fur-trading era. Replicas of trade goods like buffalo hides and beaver furs are sold in the Indian Trade House. | Rte. 1804, 24 mi southwest of Williston | 701/572–9083 | www.nps.gov/fous | Free | May–Sept., daily 8–8; Oct.–Apr., daily 9–5:30.

Frontier Museum. See what living in the 1800s was like when you visit a furnished log cabin and a two-story pioneer home here. To get there, take Route 24 out of Williston; then turn north on U.S. 85 and look for signs past Spring Lake Park. | Off U.S. 85, 5 mi east of Williston | 701/572–9751 | Free | Late May–early Sept., daily 9:30–6.

Lewis and Clark Trail Museum. Each room of this former school house is devoted to one facet of local history. You'll find school furniture and books, home furnishings, and antique cars among the exhibits. | U.S. 85, Alexander, 35 mi south of Williston | 701/828–3595 | $2 | Late May–early Sept., Mon.–Sat. 9–5, Sun. 1–5.

✦ ON THE CALENDAR: June **Fort Union Trading Post Rendezvous.** Witness reenactments of all kinds of activities related to the fur trade, all to the sound of bagpipes and fiddles, at this event at Fort Union. Antique weapons and tools are on display. | 701/572–9083.

July **Fort Buford 6th Infantry State Historical Encampment.** Military ceremonies, drills, and black-powder firing demonstrations evoke Fort Buford's most spirited years, 1866–1895. | 701/572–9034.

OKLAHOMA

One of the youngest states in the Union, Oklahoma was one of the last outposts of the American frontier. Its name comes from the Choctaw words *Okla* and *humma*, which translate to "people" and "red," respectively. Spanish conquistador Francisco Vásquez de Coronado was the first European to visit the area, in 1541, when he crossed the state's Panhandle in search of the legendary Seven Golden Cities of Cibola. Later, Spanish and French trappers encountered nomadic Plains tribes, who traversed western Oklahoma to follow the buffalo. In 1719, French trader Bernard de La Harpe established a post among the Caddoan-speaking Wichita along the Red River in eastern Oklahoma, and traded guns, ammunition, tools, cloth, and paint for furs. Oklahoma was a Spanish territory from 1763 until 1800, when France gained control. However, French hegemony was short-lived; in 1803, the area now known as Oklahoma became a part of the United States through the Louisiana Purchase.

In 1825, Congress designated Oklahoma as Indian Territory. The Choctaw, Chickasaw, Cherokee, Muskogee-Creek, and Seminole—known as the Five Tribes—were forced to resettle west of Arkansas in one of the most ignominious chapters of American history. On their way to Indian Territory, a full third of the 15,000-member Cherokee Nation died, and their journey came to be known as The Trail of Tears. But in spite of the circumstances of their removal, the tribes flourished in Indian Territory, establishing farms, cotton plantations, schools, and churches and creating the state's first legislatures and law enforcement agencies. Four of the tribes' 19th-century capitols are still standing, as well as numerous homes and schools.

Fearing raids by the nomadic Plains tribes in the western part of the territory, the Five Tribes negotiated treaties requiring the federal government to build a string of forts inside Indian Territory. At the outbreak of the Civil War, the Five Tribes were pressured to swear allegiance to the Confederacy. Although they did so, large numbers of Cherokee, Creek, and Seminole supported the Union. This created much friction within the tribes as they fought against each other. By war's end, the devastation to Indian Territory was immense.

Families, homes, and towns were destroyed. The federal government claimed that the tribes had voided their treaties by declaring war against the United States, and stripped them of thousands of acres of land in western Oklahoma. Over the next two decades, dozens of tribes and remnants of tribes were moved from other parts of the United States to Indian Territory as the westward expansion of the white population continued to intensify hard feelings between settlers and Native Americans.

In the aftermath of the Civil War, lawlessness overtook the areas near Oklahoma's borders with Kansas and Missouri. Outlaws like Jesse James, Belle Starr, the Youngers, and the Daltons found that Indian Territory made an ideal hideout after robbing banks and trains or stealing horses. Federal marshals were few, land was plentiful, and the outlaws often befriended the Indians.

Land, however, was becoming a coveted commodity, and homesteaders lobbied to open up land within Indian Territory, setting their sights on a 2-million-acre tract that was not assigned to any specific tribe. In 1889, President Benjamin Harrison signed a proclamation opening the "unassigned lands" to settlement, and central Oklahoma was claimed by home-steaders in a one-day, frantic race for land on April 22, 1889. This infamous land run and the ones that followed led to many towns' being settled literally overnight. People who partic-ipated in the first land run were called "eighty-niners." Eighty-niners who crossed the borders before the official opening were called "Sooners."

In 1890 Congress created Oklahoma Territory, and over the next decade the federal government continued to make more land available to homesteaders by breaking up tribal lands into individual farms for Native Americans. Among the settlers were many African-Amer-icans who had traveled to Indian Territory as slaves on the Trail of Tears or as Buffalo Soldiers at the frontier forts, cowboy drovers herding cattle, and gunfighters. A large number of African-Americans also settled here during the land runs. More all-black towns were created in Oklahoma than in the rest of the country. In 1905, the residents of Indian Territory asked to join the Union as a separate Indian state that would be called Sequoyah, a request that Congress rejected. Instead, Indian Territory and Oklahoma Territory were joined together, and Oklahoma became a state in 1907.

Few visitors to Oklahoma leave without remarking on the friendliness of the people, who blend southern hospitality with the openness found in the West. Many an out-of-state visitor driving the western plains has been mystified by the number of total strangers who wave hello. "Oklahomans are what other people think Americans are like," Will Rogers said about his native state in the 1920s. "Oklahoma is the heart, it's the vital organ of our national existence."

The Chisholm Trail

A DRIVING TOUR FROM THE TEXAS BORDER TO ENID

▼▼

Distance: 183 mi   **Time:** 3 days
Breaks: You can find food and lodging in Duncan, El Reno, and Enid, the largest towns near the Old Chisholm Trail.

The cattle drives of the late 1800s gave birth to one of the Old West's most enduring icons, the cowboy. Grass and water were usually plentiful on the Chisholm Trail, named after a part-Cherokee trader, Jesse Chisholm. Today, U.S. 81, which closely follows the old cattle trail, is known as the Chisholm Trail Historic Route. If you want to stop at all of its approx-imately 400 trail markers, allow yourself more time than is estimated for this tour.

The cattle came from many places in Texas, but millions of head of Texas Longhorn crossed the Red River into Oklahoma near a small town known as Terral. Twenty miles north on U.S. 81 to the junction with U.S. 70 is the first of several museums dedicated to the Chisholm

OKLAHOMA TIME LINE

1541 Francisco Vásquez de Coronado crosses western Oklahoma looking for the Seven Cities of Cibola.

1719 French trader Bernard de La Harpe makes trading alliances with Caddoan tribes near the Red River.

1803 The Louisiana Purchase transfers Oklahoma from France to the United States.

1805 The Kiowa move from the northern plains to Oklahoma.

1820 The Choctaw become the first of the five eastern tribes forced to relocate to Indian Territory.

1830 President Andrew Jackson signs the Indian Removal Act, creating Indian Territory.

1842 The Seminoles are the last of the Five Tribes to relocate to Indian Territory.

1861 The Five Tribes are forced into an alliance with the Confederacy during the Civil War.

1866 Reconstruction treaties cede the tribes' western lands to the federal government.

1867 The Treaty of Medicine Lodge creates reservations in western Oklahoma for the Cheyenne, Arapaho, Kiowa, and Comanche. Longhorn cattle begin moving north along the Chisholm Trail.

1874 Fort Sill is established in southwestern Oklahoma as a base of operations for the Indian Wars.

1889 Central Oklahoma is opened to non-Indian settlement with a land run on April 22.

1890 The Organic Act creates Oklahoma Territory.

1891–92 Indian reservations of the Iowa, Sac and Fox Nation, Pottawatomie, Shawnee, Cheyenne, and Arapaho are opened for settlement.

1893 The Cherokee Outlet is opened to non-Indian settlement; 100,000 people race to claim 50,000 homesteads.

1894 Chiricahua Apache tribal members, including Geronimo, are imprisoned at Fort Sill.

1897 The first commercial oil well in Oklahoma is drilled in Bartlesville by Frank Phillips.

1904 The Red Fork oil field is discovered at the Creek settlement Tulsey Town—later Tulsa.

1906 The last of the land openings (Kaw and Osage lands) occurs.

1907 Indian Territory and Oklahoma Territory are joined to create Oklahoma, the 46th state; tribal governments are abolished.

Trail, in **Waurika.** Cowboys often let their herds graze for a day or so in the plentiful pasture land here. Continuing on U.S. 81, you can still see the trail ruts 8 mi north at Monument Hill. A granite marker called the Chisholm Trail Lookout Point marks this spot 2½ mi east of Addington. Continue on U.S. 81 for 26 mi to **Duncan,** where you can get a comprehensive look at how the Chisholm Trail developed and endured, at the Chisholm Trail Heritage Center. The Chisholm Train went through the frontier town of Marlow, 10 mi north, where the five Marlow brothers had their famous shoot-out. Overnight in Duncan.

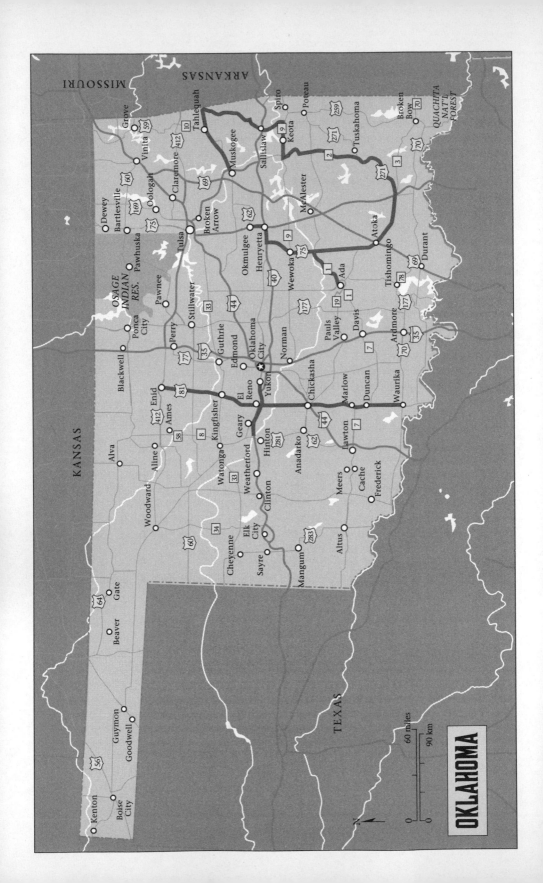

OKLAHOMA

One of the longest segments of your journey will start from Duncan north on U.S. 81 for approximately 70 mi. Head east on I–40 to Yukon, where there is another watering hole and more Chisholm Trail markers. Take Route 66 west for 13 mi to **El Reno,** where you can stop for a meal or visit nearby Fort Reno. There's plenty to do if you want to stop for the day. If you're willing to go a little out of your way, you might want to pay your respects to the namesake of the king of cattle trails. The Jesse Chisholm Gravesite is approximately 20 mi west of El Reno on I–40, then north on U.S. 281. Between the towns of Geary and Greenfield, Jesse's grave is on a hill overlooking the North Canadian River. Reconnect with U.S. 81 and travel toward Kingfisher, a stop on the Pony Express. Stop at the Chisholm Trail Museum and find out more about the trail and Kingfisher. The last part of your Chisholm Trail drive introduces you to the Cherokee Strip. **Enid** is 38 mi north of U.S. 81 on U.S. 64. Across the street from the Museum of the Cherokee Strip is Government Springs Park, a once popular water stop on the trail. From here, the drovers took the cattle first to Caldwell, Kansas, and later to Abilene. If you take a minute to stop where the tall grass seems to go on forever, you can imagine a sea of cattle traveling up the Chisholm Trail.

The Five Tribes

A DRIVING TOUR FROM MUSKOGEE TO OKMULGEE

▼▼▼

Distance: 446 mi   **Time:** 3–4 days
Breaks: Eastern Oklahoma, where the Five Tribes relocated, is primarily a rural area. Larger towns like Tahlequah, Sallisaw, and Durant offer a few choices for lodging and dining.

One of the saddest facts of American history is the treatment that Native Americans received at the hands of Europeans and Euro-Americans. Many tribes, like those of the southeastern United States, were peaceful farmers. Yet when white settlers wanted the land, tribes such as the Cherokee, Choctaw, Creek, Chickasaw, and Seminole were forcibly removed to Indian Territory. This tour will allow you to glimpse how five very different tribes made the best of an extremely difficult situation. The Five Tribes have been called the "Five Civilized Tribes" for their ability to adapt to white ways. But they have also managed to preserve many of their traditions. If you're traveling during the summer, check at each location about powwows that might be held. Many powwows are intertribal and open to the public. Note: Do not photograph or videotape any type of Native American ceremony without permission.

A good place to start learning about the Five Tribes is at the Five Civilized Tribes Museum in **Muskogee.** Next, take Route 10 east 31 mi to the Cherokee Nation's capitol in **Tahlequah.** The Cherokee Heritage Center documents the story of the Trail of Tears, and other points of interest bring the area's 19th-century history to life. Because there is so much to see in Tahlequah, it is also a logical place to stop for the night.

Start your second day traveling Route 82 south to I–40, then east for 49 mi to **Sallisaw,** where you can visit the 1829 log cabin that was the home of Cherokee linguist Sequoyah. Some of the old tribal capitals are no longer used for day-to-day business, but they are still open as museums and ceremonial sites. One example is the Choctaw Council House in Tuskahoma, about 102 mi from Sallisaw via U.S. 59 south, Route 9 west, and Route 2 south to U.S. 271. Picturesque Route 2 takes you past Wilburton on your way to U.S. 271. Travel east in U.S. 271 for a few miles and then follow the signs to Choctaw Council House. The Chickasaw Council House in Tishomingo is another 98 mi away via Route 43 west to U.S. 69 south to Route 22 west. Stop for the night in Tishomingo or the nearby community of **Durant.**

On day three, take U.S. 377 north from Tishomingo to Seminole and drive east on U.S. 270 or take U.S. 69 north from Durant to McAlester and drive west on U.S. 270 to the Seminole Nation Museum in Wewoka, 108 mi away. Afterwards, take Route 56 north to I–40 and go east to U.S. 75 north to **Okmulgee,** about 58 mi away, to visit the Muskogee Creek capitol and location of the Creek Council House.

ADA

▼▼

Settler Jeff Reed arrived at a crossroads in the Chickasaw Nation in 1890. He built a log cabin and store, and when he added a post office he named the newly formed town for his oldest daughter. Ranching, agriculture, and oil have long been its economic mainstays of this town on the plains south of the Canadian River. *Contact Ada Chamber of Commerce | 300 W. Main St., 74820 | 580/332–2506 | www.adachamber.com.*

Arbuckle Historical Museum. Housed in the former Santa Fe Deport, this museum displays photographs and artifacts relating to Chickasaw and pioneer history, including an old dress embellished with beads and coins, tomahawks and moccasins, and relics from now-vanished Fort Arbuckle, established in 1851 west of present-day Davis to protect the Chickasaws from the Plains tribes. | 12 Main St., Davis | 580/369–2518 | Free | Tues.–Sat. 10–4, Sun. 1–4.

Chickasaw Cultural Center. Guided tours here take you through Chickasaw culture dating from the 1500s, when the Chickasaw lived in Mississippi. The center houses such tribal artifacts as old court records, diaries of Chickasaw families, and a photo gallery showcasing past governors and council members of the tribe. Also on the center's grounds is an old two-story granite building that served as the tribal capital building; plans are to transform it into a museum. | 520 E. Arlington St. | 580/436–2603 | Free | Weekdays 9–5, Sat. by appointment.

✦ ON THE CALENDAR: Aug. **Western Heritage Week.** Townspeople dress western-style, and windows of local businesses are decorated in the western motif during this weeklong celebration. A parade includes local round-ups clubs, and a rodeo has barrel riders, bull riders, and calf roping. | 580/332–2506.

ALVA

▼▼

Alva became a farming community during the opening of the Cherokee Strip in 1893. Its ability to survive when other towns shut down came from its location as a stop on the Atchison, Topeka & Santa Fe Railroad from Kansas. Alva owes its name to Alva Adams, a railroad attorney who later became governor of Colorado. *Contact Alva Area Chamber of Commerce | 410 College Ave., 73717 | 580/327–1647 | www.alvaok.net.*

Cherokee Strip Museum. The museum describes life in the Cherokee Strip with 40 rooms of displays, including a pioneer drugstore and kitchen. | 901 14th St. | 580/327–2030 | Free | Weekends 2–5.

Sod House Museum. Marshall McCully built a two-room sod house in 1894, popular with homesteaders settling on the Cherokee Strip. Now the last remaining sod house in Oklahoma, it is preserved by the Oklahoma Historical Society as a museum with period furnishings. | Rte. 8, 40 mi south of Alva, Aline | 580/463–2441 | www.ok-history.mus.ok.us | Free | Tues.–Fri. 9–5, weekends 2–5.

✦ ON THE CALENDAR: Aug. **Freedom Rodeo and Old Cowhand Reunion.** One of the country's best rodeos can be found in the small town of Freedom, near Alva. The population (254) more than quadruples in size for the annual three-day rodeo. A local cowhand is honored every year. | 580/621–3276.

ANADARKO

▼▼▼

Anadarko started as an Indian agency in 1871 for the Wichitas and other tribes in the area. In 1901, a land lottery opened the area to settlers, and the town soon flourished. Today, seven tribes have their headquarters in a 30-mi radius. *Contact Anadarko Chamber of Commerce | 516 W. Kentucky Ave., Box 366, 73005 | 405/247–6651 | www.anadarko.org. Visitor Information Center | U.S. 62 E, Box 366, 73005 | 405/247–5555. Wichita and Affiliated Tribes | Box 729, 73005 | 405/247–2425 | www.wichita.nsn.us.*

Anadarko Philomathic Pioneer Museum. See a turn-of-the-20th-century physician's office plus other period Anadarko artifacts housed in a Rock Island depot. Antiques and railroad memorabilia donated by pioneer families make up most of the collection, although Indian artifacts are also included. | 311 E. Main St. | 405/247–3240 | Donations appreciated | Tues.–Sun. 1–5.

Anadarko Post Office Murals. Murals from the 1930s commissioned by members of the "Kiowa Five" (a group of local painters) depict life on the plains before the arrival of European settlers. | 120 S. 1st St. | 405/247–6461 | Free | Daily 7 AM–10 PM.

Indian City USA. Reproductions of villages of seven Indian tribes—Navajo, Chiricahua Apache, Wichita, Kiowa Winter Camp, Caddo, Pawnee, and Pueblo illustrate traditional Plains lifeways. The museum adjoining the gift shop displays historical Plains Indian clothing and beadwork. | 2 mi southeast of Anadarko on Rte. 8 | 405/247–5661 | www.indiancityusa.com | $7.50 | Daily 9–5.

National Hall of Fame for Famous American Indians. An outdoor park of bronze busts includes likenesses of Quanah Parker, Geronimo, Will Rogers, and Jim Thorpe. | 851 E. Central Blvd. | 405/247–5555 | Free | Mon.–Sat. 9–5, Sun. 1–5.

Southern Plains Indian Museum and Craft Center. The Oklahoma Indian Arts and Crafts Cooperative is an independent arts-and-crafts business and museum owned by Native American artists. Exhibits change throughout the year and include dolls and fans. | 715 E. Central Blvd. | 405/247–6221 | $3, free Sun. | June–Sept., Mon.–Sat. 9–5, Sun. 1–5; Oct.–May, Tues.–Sat. 9–5, Sun. 1–5.

✦ ON THE CALENDAR: Aug. **American Indian Exposition.** A weeklong celebration—the oldest Indian-owned and -operated fair in the world—is held each year at the Caddo County fairgrounds. Ceremonial dances, authentic food, and more are included. | 405/247–6651.

Aug. **Wichita Annual Dance.** This annual dance event brings Wichita, Keechi, Waco, and Wawakonie participants to Anadarko. | 405/247–2425.

HISTORIC LODGING
Wolf's Heaven Indian Encampment. Powwows, sweat lodge rituals, and more may be part of a stay at this tepee village for adults only. Fishing, hiking, horseback riding; no kids. | Rte. 1, Box 250, 73005 | 405/247–3000 | fax 405/247–3006 | $65 | No credit cards | FAP | Closed mid-Oct.–mid-May.

BARTLESVILLE

▼▼▼

Originally a Delaware trading post, Bartlesville was founded by Jacob H. Bartles in 1887, on the Caney River east of the Osage Hills. Transformed by the discovery of oil in 1894, the city has a downtown historic district that includes 48 buildings from the 1900–20 oil boom.

Bartlesville Area History Museum. A model of a one-room schoolhouse occupies a room in this museum on the fifth floor of the downtown City Center. Photographs and artifacts chronicle the lives of Bartlesville's early settlers and the town's ranching, oil, and Native American history. | 401 S. Johnstone Ave. | 918/338–4290 | Free | Tues.–Sat. 10–4.

Dewey Hotel Museum. "Jake" Bartles started building this Dewey landmark in 1899, and the town's first Sunday School classes were held here before the three-story, 28-room hotel was ready for occupancy in May 1900. Now a museum, the Victorian hotel displays period furnishings, including Jake's roll-top desk. | 801 N. Delaware St., Dewey | 918/534–0215 | $2 | Apr.–Oct., Tues.–Sat. 10–4, Sun. 1–4; tours by appointment.

Osage Tribal Museum. The oldest continuously operated tribal museum in the United States preserves Osage culture with photographs, Osage ribbon work and other regalia, and an exhibit about Osage cosmology. It's housed in the old Osage Agency, now the Osage Nation headquarters 25 mi southwest of Bartlesville. | 819 Grandview Ave., Pawhuska | 918/287–4622 | Free | Tues.–Sat. 10–5.

Prairie Song, I.T. A schoolhouse, homesteader's cabin, post office, trading post, jail, covered bridge, and cowboy line shack (a shelter built on a main cattle line to house cowboys on a long drive or in bad weather) make up this re-created 1800s pioneer village. | 402621 W. 1600 Rd., Dewey | 918/534–2662 | fax 918/534–3435 | $6 | Daily 9–5; guided tours Mon., Wed., and Fri. at 10 AM. Call for appointment.

Woolaroc Museum. Once the ranch of oil man Frank Phillips, this western museum–wildlife refuge is now home to bison and 40 other species. The drive-through wildlife preserve surrounds a museum packed with memorabilia of art and artifacts of the Southwest. | Rte. 123, about 12 mi southwest of Bartlesville | 918/336–0307 | www.woolaroc.org | $5 | Late May–early Sept., daily 10–5; early Sept.–late May, Tues.–Sun. 10–5.

✦ ON THE CALENDAR: Sept. **Indian Summer Festival.** Highlights of this event held in Bartlesville's Community Center include Native American art, an intertribal powwow, and children's games. | 918/337–2787.

BOISE CITY
▼▼

Boise (pronounced "boys") City stands east of the Cimarron Cut-Off of the Santa Fe Trail, which was a major westward route in the mid-1800s. Limited water, dangerous outlaws, and Plains Indians all were a threat along the trail. You can still see the wagon ruts worn into the trail by people traveling from Missouri to New Mexico. *Contact Cimarron County Chamber of Commerce | 6 Northeast Sq., 73933 | 580/544–3344.*

Autograph Rock. See the signatures that pioneers carved into this sandstone bluff as far back as the 1840s. This is the easternmost certified site on the Santa Fe Trail. Reservations are required as Autograph Rock sits on private property. | 580/544–3479 | Free | Call for reservations.

Cimarron County Heritage Center. Dinosaurs, American Indians, and cowboys are all part of northwestern Oklahoma's history. More Native American artifacts have been discovered in this county than anywhere else in the country. The Cimarron Heritage Center displays dinosaur fossils, Indian tools and pottery, plus remnants from the cattle trails. A special exhibit recounts the story of the Santa Fe Trail. | 1300 N. Cimarron Ave. | 580/544–3479 | Free | Mon.–Thurs. 10–noon and 1–4, Fri.–Sat. 1–4.

✦ ON THE CALENDAR: June **Santa Fe Trail Daze Celebration.** Dig for gold or join a fiddling contest. These are just some of the events held each year at the Boise City Santa Fe Trail Daze Celebration. | 580/544–3344.

HISTORIC DINING AND LODGING

The Hitching Post. Established in the early 1800s, this working ranch sits between high mesas near Black Mesa. Participate in cattle drives and calf branding, or take a ride in a circa-1882 stagecoach. The full array of ranch entertainment is available, from cookouts to campfire sing-alongs. Sleep in the B&B, the log house, or a trailer home. Hiking, horseback riding. | Rte. 325 west of Boise City, Kenton 73933 | 580/261–7413 | www.ccccok.org/hp | $45 | No credit cards | FAP.

Kenton Mercantile. Established in 1898, this café–gas station–general store–museum is the local gathering place for news, gossip, and hamburgers. The building was the site of an 1882 Studebaker wagon assembly plant. | 101 W. Main St., Kenton | 580/261–7447 | Free | May–Sept., daily 9–7; Oct.–Apr., hrs vary (call ahead).

CHEYENNE

▼▼

In the winter of 1868–69 the U.S. Army mounted a campaign to stop hostile action among the Cheyenne and Arapaho. One devastating result of the winter campaign was the Black Kettle Massacre, in which troops led by Lieutenant Colonel George Custer killed dozens of Cheyenne in a peaceful village. The California Trail later crossed through present-day Cheyenne where U.S. 283 and Route 47 now intersect. The Cheyenne Reservation opened for white settlement on April 19, 1892, at high noon, and the town of Cheyenne was quickly born. *Contact Cheyenne Chamber of Commerce | Box 57, 73628 | 580/497–3318 | www. rogermills.org.*

Black Kettle Museum. Black Kettle was a Cheyenne leader who in 1867 signed the Medicine Lodge Treaty with the U.S. government. A year later, however, Lieutenant Colonel George Custer advanced upon Black Kettle's peaceful village in the pre-dawn hours, killing 37 people and destroying food supplies for the winter. The museum recounts this event and outlines a history of the Cheyenne people. Artillery items, beadwork, and other Cheyenne-made items are exhibited. | 101 S. L. L. Males, at Rte. 47 and U.S. 283 | 580/497–3929 | Free | Mon.–Sat. 9–5, Sun. 1–5.

Pioneer Community Museum Complex. See what life was like in the late 1800s by taking a look at furnishings, clothing, and household items of the time. You can take a self-guided tour through the Roll One Room School House. The Kendall Log Cabin Home is an original log cabin from the early 1900s. | City Park, U.S. 283 S | 580/497–3318 | Free | May–Sept., Mon.–Sat. 9–5; Oct.–Apr., Wed.–Sat. 9–5.

Washita Battlefield NHS. This is the site of the Black Kettle Massacre. A ¾-mi trail leads from an overlook into the battlefield. Ranger-guided tours are conducted in the summer. | 2 mi west of Black Kettle Museum on Rte. 47A | 580/497–2742 | www.nps.gov/waba | Free | Daily dawn–dusk.

✦ ON THE CALENDAR: Sept. **Pioneer Days Celebration.** Held the first weekend after Labor Day each year, this early-settler celebration includes living-history displays and activities in Cheyenne's City Park. | 580/497–2106.

DUNCAN

▼▼

In 1892, William Duncan built a store along the Chisholm Trail, when he learned the Rock Island Railroad planned to extend its line into the area. Duncan quickly became a major town in southwestern Oklahoma. In downtown Duncan, granite sidewalk markers engraved with bits of town history tell more of the trail's tale. You can see traces of the Chisholm Trail at Monument Hill south of town. *Contact Duncan Convention and Tourism Bureau | 911 W. Walnut Ave., Box 981, 73533-4664 | 580/255–3644 or 800/787–7167 | www.duncanok.org.*

Chisholm Trail Heritage Center. Oklahoma's largest bronze statue, *On the Chisholm Trail,* sits outside the doors of the Heritage Center. The sculpture depicts a scene from the trail and is a good introduction to the history described inside. Interactive displays tell more of the story, including the mechanics of driving cattle. Talk to a life-size Animatronic Jesse Chisholm about his life. Staff also provides guided tours to Monument Hill by reservation. | 1000 N. 29th St. | 580/252–6692 or 800/782–7167 | www.onthechisholmtrail.com | Free; guided tour to Monument Hill $5 | Mon.–Sat. 10–5, Sun. 1–5.

Marlow Area Museum. Marlow, 13 mi north of Duncan, gained notoriety when the five Marlow brothers had a shoot-out with a mob over some stolen cattle from the Chisholm Trail. Some people say it was just a case of mistaken identity, but you can make up your own mind at this museum, which displays town artifacts and shows a special exhibit created by members of the Marlow family. Included is the original tombstone of three of the brothers: Alfred, Boon, and Lewellyn. | 127 W. Main St., Marlow | 580/658–2212 | Free | Call for hrs.

Redbud Park Creek Walk. As you walk around the creek, stop at the signboard with biographies and documents telling the stories of four of the five Marlow brothers. | W. Main St., Marlow | 580/658–2212 | Free | Daily.

Stephens County Historical Museum. In a vintage sandstone building that formerly served as a National Guard armory, the museum has exhibits ranging from a replica of an early oil well to Plains Indian artifacts to antique farm machinery. Vignettes illustrate various aspects of 19th- and early 20th-century local history. Photography of the county dating from 1892 traces the progress. | Fuqua Park, U.S. 81 and Beech Ave. | 580/252–0717 | Free | Tues. 1–5, Thurs.–Sat. 1–5.

✦ ON THE CALENDAR: Sept. **Outlaw Days.** Gunslinger and settler reenactors tell the story of Marlow's wilder days at Redbud Park. There is also music and a parade. | 580/658–2212.

DURANT

▼▼

Dixon Durant, a member of a French-named Choctaw family, founded this principal agricultural center in Oklahoma's Red River valley in 1872. The name Durant Junction was given the community by the Missouri-Kansas-Texas Railroad when it entered the Choctaw Nation that year. It was shortened to Durant 10 years later. Durant is the headquarters for the Choctaw Nation. *Contact Durant Chamber of Commerce | 215 N. 4th St., 74701-4354 | 580/924–0848. Durant Main Street | 323 W. Main St., 74701 | 580/924–1550. Lake Texoma Association | 1001 Texoma Park Rd., Durant 73439 | 580/564–2334.*

Chickasaw Council House. The Chickasaw tribe was the last of the five tribes to be relocated to Indian Territory. This Victorian Gothic granite building served as the third council house in 1898 until the tribal complex moved to Ada. A log cabin that served as the first

Chickasaw Council House from 1856 to 1858 is inside. Guided tours provide insight into the earlier days of the Chickasaw people. An oral history collection of tribal elders is also available for public viewing. | 200 N. Fisher, Tishomingo | 580/371–3351 | Free | Weekdays 8:30–5, Sat. by appointment.

Confederate Memorial Museum and Information Center. On the site of the state's only Confederate cemetery, this museum depicts the Battle of the Middle Boggy, in which federal troops engaged the First Choctaw and Chickasaw Cavalry, through staged scenes and such authentic artifacts as a cannon, battle flags, and uniforms. In addition to Civil War exhibits, the museum also displays Choctaw artifacts. This museum is 32 mi northeast of Durant in Atoka. | 258 N. U.S. 69 Atoka | 580/889–7192 | Free | Mon.–Sat. 9–4.

Fort Washita Historic Site. A fort was established here in 1842 to protect the Chickasaw and Choctaw tribes from Plains tribes and to supervise the traders, trappers, and other migrants who crossed Chickasaw land. Of the 100 buildings that once stood on the site, some reconstructed barracks, a former Indian agent's cabin, and scattered foundations remain. | 12 mi northwest of Durant, on Rte. 199. | 580/924–6502 | Free | Mon.–Sat. 9–5, Sun. 1–5.

Three Valley Museum. Named for the Blue, Red, and Washita River valleys, this museum is in the former Oklahoma Presbyterian College for Girls, established in 1909. The top two levels of the building house Choctaw history displays and artifacts. The basement museum has exhibits on the history of Durant and Bryan County, including an 1860 piano shipped up the Red River, an 1896 presidential campaign button for William J. Bryan (after whom the county is named), an 1812 cobbler's bench, and medical saddlebags from the 1890s. | 16th and Elm Sts. | 580/920–1907 | Free | Weekdays 2–4:30.

✦ ON THE CALENDAR: Apr. **Fur Trade Rendezvous.** Trappers and traders reenact an 1840s rendezvous at the Fort Washita Historic Site. | 580/924–6502.

ELK CITY
▼▼

Elk City gets its name from nearby Elk Creek, which in turn was named after an Indian chief, Elk River. The Great Western or Dodge City cattle trail passed nearby. Elk City became a town in 1901 when the Choctaw, Oklahoma & Gulf Railway passed through. *Contact Elk City Chamber of Commerce | 1016 Airport Blvd., Box 922, 73648-0972 | 580/225–0207 or 800/280–0207 | www.elkcitychamber.com.*

Farm and Ranch Museum. Explore the history of farming and ranching in western Oklahoma at this large complex. Tools and farming equipment from the 1800s to the present show how farming and ranching have evolved. | Behind Old Town Complex | 580/225–6266 | Included in admission for Old Town Complex | June–Aug., Mon.–Sat. 9–7, Sun. 1–5; Sept.–May, Mon.–Sat. 9–5, Sun. 2–5.

Mohawk Lodge Trading Post. Established in 1892 to sell Cheyenne-Arapaho beadwork, this trading post moved to its current location on Route 66 in 1942, and erected a canvas Plains-style tepee out front. Now Oklahoma's oldest Indian-goods store, it displays rows of brightly colored appliquéd dance shawls, handmade moccasins, Pendleton blankets, and strings of glass beads. Cheyenne women continue to supply leather goods and beadwork, resulting in the museum-quality collection that hangs on the wall. | 28 mi east of Elk City on Rte. 66 | 580/323–2360 | Free | Mon.–Sat. 9–5.

Old Town Complex. This complex includes the turn-of-the-20th-century Rock Bluff School, the Pioneer Chapel, and a physician's office. Pioneer life of the late 1800s is further depicted in a residence furnished with period objects, an opera house, a grist mill, and other early Elk City businesses. | 2717 W. 3rd St., Pioneer Rd. and U.S. 66 | 580/225–2207 | Combination ticket to all museums in complex $5 | Mon.–Sat. 9–5, Sun. 2–5.

HISTORIC LODGING

Standifer House. Built in the early 1900s, this brick Victorian once served as a hospital. Period furniture, polished hardwood floors, richly painted walls, and decorative columns and arches lend a traditional look to the inn. Rooms are lushly appointed in a variety of themes— western, Oriental, modern—and some have fireplaces, Jacuzzis, or balconies. Cable TV, in-room VCRs. | 1030 W. 7th St., 73648 | 580/225–3048 | www.standiferhouse.com | 10 suites | $104–$250 | No credit cards | BP.

EL RENO

▼▼

The "Reno" in El Reno refers to Fort Reno; the community was built around the 1870s frontier fort established to protect the Darlington Indian Agency. Reno City (as it was originally called) stood on the western boundary of the area opened in the 1889 Land Run. When a railroad line was built south of the fort in 1889, Reno City's buildings were moved south to the new site and the city of El Reno was founded. A snapshot of the town's history can be seen in the 108-by-18-ft El Reno Heritage Mural (Bickford and Woodson streets), which depicts characters such as Fort Reno soldiers and land run pioneers. *Contact El Reno Chamber of Commerce | 206 N. Bickford, Box 6733036, 73036 | 405/262–1188 or 877/935–7366. El Reno Convention and Visitors Bureau | Box 700, 73036 | 888/535–7366 | www.elreno.org.*

Canadian County Historical Museum. This museum is housed in an old Rock Island Railroad passenger depot and contains artifacts and photographs relating to area history, such as land runs, African-American Buffalo Soldiers, and the Cheyenne-Arapaho reservation period. The grounds include the restored Possum Hollow School, a barn filled with vintage machinery, and a restored two-story hotel. You can also see a log cabin used by General Phillip Sheridan. | 300 S. Grand St. | 405/262–5121 | Free | Wed.–Sat. 10–5, Sun. 1–5.

Chisholm Trail Museum. From the outside, the size of this museum 23 mi north of El Reno is deceptive. But indoors is a complete collection of every facet of Old West life that touched the town of Kingfisher, including the Chisholm Trail. One display focuses on barbed wire, which by 1877 shut down the cattle drives. Numerous pioneer artifacts are displayed along with a frontier village. In addition to a school, church, and bank, you can also visit a cabin belonging to the mother of the Dalton gang. | 605 Zellers Ave., Kingfisher | 405/375–5176 | Free | Tues.–Sat. 9–5, Sun. 1–5.

Chisholm Trail Watering Hole. In Yukon, 13 mi east of El Reno, you'll find this watering hole and more bits of the Chisholm Trail legend posted on markers. Yukon was settled first by Civil War veterans, then later by Czech immigrants. | 2200 S. Holly, Yukon | 405/354–8442 | Free | Daily, dawn–dusk.

Fort Reno. Fort Reno was established by General Phillip Sheridan in 1875 to protect settlers from Cheyenne and Arapaho raids. By the 1880s, fort personnel were needed to maintain law and order during the land runs. Some of the early fort buildings from the late 1800s are still standing and open to the public. The cemetery on the western boundary is the site of 187 pre-statehood graves. A small visitor center contains written material about Fort Reno. | 7207 W. Cheyenne St. | 405/262–5291 | www.fortreno.org | Free | Weekdays 10–5, weekends 10–4.

Jesse Chisholm Gravesite. The namesake of the most famous cattle trail was a part-Cherokee trader. Jesse Chisholm died at Left Hand Spring Camp in Geary in 1868. | 16 mi west of El Reno on I–40, then 5 mi north on U.S. 281, Geary | Free | Daily.

✦ ON THE CALENDAR: Apr. **'89ers Day.** Celebrate the land run that started it all, on the third Saturday of April. Living-history reenactments and old-time crafts are part of the fun. | 405/262–5121.

June **Chisholm Trail Festival Days.** Relive the days of the Chisholm Trail with reenactments, pioneer demonstrations, and a reconstruction of an Old West town in Yukon. | 405/354–3567.

Sept. **Tombstone Tales.** At the Fort Sill cemetery, reenactors tell of life in the latter half of the 1800s and include a few ghost stories. | 405/262–3987.

ENID
▼▼

Enid, founded on the day of the largest Oklahoma land run—the opening of the Cherokee Strip on September 16, 1893—is northwestern Oklahoma's largest town. No one is certain of the origins of the town name, but one story is that a railroad official wanted to name it after Enid, wife of Geraint in Tennyson's "Idylls of the King." A watering hole in what is now Government Springs Park was a busy stop along the Chisholm Trail. *Contact Great Enid Chamber of Commerce and Convention and Visitors Bureau | 210 Kenwood Blvd., Box 907, 73701 | 580/237–2494 or 888/229–2443 | www.enidchamber.com/ecvb. Sons and Daughters of the Cherokee Strip Pioneers | Box 465, 73702 | 580/237–1907.*

Humphrey Heritage Village. Next to the Museum of the Cherokee Strip, on the west side of Government Springs Park, this collection of settlement-era buildings includes the land office that handled claims during the land run of 1893. The restored Victorian Glidewell Home, a one-room schoolhouse, and Enid's oldest church are also on the grounds. | 509 S. 4th | 580/237–1907 | Free | Tues.–Sat.; call for hrs.

Museum of the Cherokee Strip. Run by the Oklahoma Historical Society, this museum documents all periods of northwestern Oklahoma history. Exhibits on the prehistory and Native American heritage of the Enid area, a display on the September 16, 1893, land run that established the city, and other artifacts and photographs tell the story of the Cherokee Strip. An animated robot named "Grandpa" tells what it was like to be a cowboy and stake a claim in the land run. Farm equipment, such as a wooden threshing machine and a water-drilling rig, are on view in a large tin barn. | 507 S. 4th St. | 580/237–1907 | Free | Tues.–Fri. 9–5, weekends 2–5.

Railroad Museum of Oklahoma. Preserved railway cars and memorabilia tell of the early railroad days. | 702 N. Washington | 580/233–3051 | Free | Tues.–Fri. 1–4, Sat. 9–1, Sun. 2–5.

✦ ON THE CALENDAR: Sept. **Cherokee Strip Days Celebration.** Held each year at the Museum of the Cherokee Strip, this celebration includes a reenactment of pioneers staking their claims during the Cherokee Strip Land Run. | 580/237–2494.

CHEROKEE STRIP RUN

Six-year-old Edith Joyce Davis stared up in awe at a horse hitched to a buckboard parked in front of her home in Arkansas City, Kansas. The hot wind was blowing through her uncombed red hair as her father and another man loaded the wagon with provisions, including food and a tarpaulin. Several hours later, they were in place with thousands of others at the Kansas border, waiting for a gunshot. That shot, at noon on September 16, 1893, started the biggest land rush in history, the Cherokee Strip Run.

Recalling that day 100 years later during a centenary celebration of the run, Davis said her father was not among those who staked a claim in the Strip (now northern Oklahoma). But he was among some 100,000 people, including 30,000 from Arkansas City, who rushed for free land. The Strip— also called the Cherokee Outlet—encompassed eight million acres purchased by the United States government from the Cherokee Nation in 1891, for $1.25 per acre. It was 226 miles long (from east to west) by 58 miles deep (north to south), and was to include seven new counties, each with a designated county seat.

Land seekers departed on the run from five Kansas border towns and four towns on the south border of the strip, in Indian Territory. Arkansas City was the major land rush departure point for southbound land seekers, while Stillwater and Orlando were major starting points south of the Strip. A carnival atmosphere prevailed in Stillwater in the days preceding the run. Land seekers on fast ponies practiced daily, as did young men who decided to make the run on bicycles. But when the dust settled after the great event, only a fraction of the participants ended up with land. New towns in the Strip, including Enid and Ponca City, were settled quickly. In the confusion after the run, Enid grew to 5,000 citizens within hours. Ponca opened its first school two months to the day after the run.

GUTHRIE

Founded during the 1889 Land Run in central Oklahoma, Guthrie was the capital of Oklahoma Territory before becoming Oklahoma's first state capital. A referendum later moved the capital to Oklahoma City in 1910. Today, more than 400 square blocks of Guthrie are listed on the National Register of Historic Places. *Contact Guthrie Convention and Visitors Bureau | 212 W. Oklahoma Ave., Box 995, 73044 | 405/282–1947 or 800/299–1889 | www.guthrieok.com.*

Guthrie Historic District. The largest urban district on the National Register of Historic Places, Guthrie's has 2,169 restored 19th-century Victorian buildings. The First Capitol Trolley gives narrated tours. | 2nd St. and Harrison Ave. | 405/282–1948 or 800/299–1889 | www. guthrieok.com | Tour $2 | Daily.

Oklahoma Frontier Drugstore Museum. Oklahoma Territory's first drugstore has been re-created, right down to its soda fountain and turn-of-the-20th-century apothecary jars. | 214 W. Oklahoma Ave. | 405/282–1895 | $2 donation requested | Tues.–Fri. 9–5, Sat. 10–4, Sun. 1–4.

Oklahoma Territorial Museum. Art, documents, and homesteading artifacts all illustrate the 1889 Land Run into central Oklahoma and the social and political history of the territorial era. The museum adjoins a restored 1902 Carnegie library building; Oklahoma's first governor was inaugurated on the library steps. | 406 E. Oklahoma Ave. | 405/282–1889 | Donations accepted | Tues.–Fri. 9–5, Sat. 10–4, Sun. 1–4.

State Capital Publishing Museum. This Territorial-days publishing office includes a printing press and equipment from the late 1800s. | 301 W. Harrison Ave. | 405/282–4123 | Free | Tues.–Fri. 9–5, Sat. 10–4, Sun. 1–4.

✦ ON THE CALENDAR: Apr. **'89er Celebration.** Nobody celebrates '89er Day quite like Guthrie, which goes all out as the former territorial capital. | 405/282–1947.

Nov. **Statehood Day Celebration.** Statehood days are relived at the Territorial Museum. Students from all over the state reenact life in Guthrie in 1907. | 405/282–1889.

Nov.–Dec. **Territorial Christmas Celebration.** Guthrie kicks off the holiday season with a Victorian walk, special tours, and a presentation of *A Territorial Christmas Carol.* | 405/282–1947.

HISTORIC DINING AND LODGING
Blue Belle Saloon. Steak. Oklahoma's oldest saloon serves up a good steak. Look for Tom Mix memorabilia; he tended bar here before heading off to Hollywood. | 224 W. Harrison | 405/260–2355 | Closed Sun. | $8–$14 | AE, D, DC, MC, V.

Harrison House. This 1893 Victorian inn stands in the middle of the historic district. Each room in the four buildings is named after a figure from history. Period furnishings adorn each room. | 124 W. Harrison, 73044 | 405/282–1000 or 800/375–1001 | 34 rooms | $100 | AE, D, DC, MC, V | BP.

GUYMON
▼▼

The Oklahoma panhandle was part of Texas until passage of the Organic Act of 1890, which combined the panhandle referred to as "No Man's Land" with that of Oklahoma Territory. A man by the name of Edward Guymon purchased land in anticipation of the arrival of a railroad line. When the railroad line extended south from Kansas in in the 1890s, the town of was named after him. *Contact Guymon Chamber of Commerce | 711 S.E. Rte. 3 (Rte. 5, Box 120), 73943 | 580/338–3376. Guymon Convention and Tourism | 219 N.W. 4th, 73942 | 580/338–5838 | www.guymonok.com.*

Gateway to the Panhandle Museum. Numerous collections document the Panhandle's history over the years. Artifacts include military items from the Civil War and farming equipment. The museum is 85 mi east of Guymon. | U.S. 64 W, Gate | 580/934–2004 | Free | Mon.–Sat. 1–6.

Jones and Plummer Trail Museum. Sixty-nine mi east of Guymon, see what a parlor, bank, general store, and barber shop looked like in No Man's Land. | S. Douglas St., county fairgrounds, Beaver | 580/625–4439 | Free | Wed.–Fri. 1–5:30, Sat. 1–5, Sun. 2:30–5.

No Man's Land Museum. Panhandle history—from prehistoric times through Dust Bowl days—is chronicled in four galleries. Native American and early pioneer artifacts are on display at this museum 10 mi southwest of Guymon. | 207 W. Sewell St., Panhandle State University, Goodwell | 580/349–2670 | Free | Tues.–Sat. 9–5.

✦ ON THE CALENDAR: May **Pioneer Days Celebration.** This celebration honors Panhandle pioneers and includes the largest Professional Rodeo Cowboys Association–sanctioned rodeo in the state, a parade, cookouts, trail rides, and square dancing. | 580/338–3376.

LAWTON

▼▼

Lawton was founded on August 6, 1901, when the Kiowa-Comanche Reservation was opened for white settlement by the drawing of lots. The community was settled in a single day. Nearby Fort Sill was established in 1869 by Major Philip Sheridan to control the Plains Indians. It continues to be an active Army base. *Contact Lawton/Fort Sill Chamber of Commerce and Industry | 629 Southwest C, 73501 | 580/355–3541 | www.lcci.org. Southwest Oklahoma Genealogical and Historical Society | Box 148, 73502–0148 | www.sirinet.net/~lgarris/swogs.*

Eagle Park. A complex of historical buildings was moved to this site 15 mi west of Lawton in the mid-1900s. Picket House, built by Buffalo Soldiers in the 1870s, and the late 1800s–Quanah Parker's Star House, with 14 white stars, are the most interesting sites. Noticing that the homes of U.S. frontier military generals could be identified by a painted star on the exterior, Comanche War Chief Quanah Parker decided his home warranted 14 white stars on the outside. | Rte. 115 and U.S. 62, Cache | 580/429–3238 | Free | Tours by appointment only.

Fort Sill Military Reservation. Fort Sill was established as an Indian fort to protect settlers from Plains Indians. Buffalo Soldiers were a major force in the development of the fort. The fort's original headquarters, Old Post Headquarters and Visitors Center, now serves as a museum office and resource library; next door is an 1875 stone building erected as a supply warehouse and later used as a barracks. Exhibits trace the history of the fort from its years as a base of operations for the Indian Wars through World War I. Southern Plains tribal history is also told through beadwork and clothing. A display of heavy artillery dating from 1600 to the present can be seen along the Cannon Walk. | 437 Quanah Rd. | 580/442–5123 | Free | Daily 8:30–4:30

    Apache Cemetery, east of the fort on Sheridan Road, is where many Apache prisoners such as Geronimo are buried. Many noted Indian leaders are buried on **Chief's Knoll,** a section of the Post Cemetery on Condon Road. Permanent residents include Kicking Bird, Satanta, and Quanah Parker and his mother, Cynthia Parker.

    Geronimo's Guardhouse (Bldg. 336, Randolph Rd. | 580/442–6570) is an 1873 stone structure that held Geronimo, the Chiricahua Apache warrior, on several occasions after the Apache band was brought to Fort Sill. The main floor and basement cells show photos, as well as weapons and other items belonging to the Comanche, Kiowa, and Apache tribes and to 19th-century cavalry and foot soldiers.

Mattie Beal Home. Mattie Beal was a 22-year-old telephone operator from Kansas when she drew the No. 2 ticket in the 1901 Kiowa-Comanche lottery, securing for herself the right to prime real estate. Beal and her husband built this 14-room Greek Revival home in 1908 and filled it with such details as stained-glass windows depicting the nearby Wichita Mountains. | 1006 S.W. 5th | 580/353–6884 | $2 | 2nd Sun. of month 1:30–4:30 and by appointment.

Medicine Park. Built around Medicine Creek, which the Kiowa and Comanche believed to have healing powers, Medicine Park was born in 1908. The resort was popular with politicians and criminals alike. All structures at this mountain retreat are built from melon-size granite cobblestone quarried in the nearby Wichita Mountains. The downtown area looks like a kind of cobblestone village. The Grand Hotel functioned until recently as the Old Plantation Restaurant. Although undergoing restoration, it's a picturesque community well worth a visit. | 6 mi east on I–44, then 6 mi west on Rte. 49 | 580/529–2825 | www.medicinepark.com | Free | Daily.

Museum of the Great Plains. The museum focuses on the cultural history of the southern Great Plains, with special emphasis on the Plains tribes. Equipment used by trappers and traders is shown alongside the gunfighters of the Old West. Part of the museum is a replica of Red River Trading Post, which operated in the 1830s and 1840s. | 601 Ferris | 580/581–3460 | www.museumgreatplains.org | $2 | Tues.–Sat. 10–5, Sun. 1–5.

✦ ON THE CALENDAR: May, Oct. **Encampment.** The Red River Trading Post hosts these spring and fall events in which living-history interpreters in period dress re-create activities that would occur at a wilderness outpost. | 580/581–3460.

July **Comanche Homecoming.** Comanche from all over the world come for the annual Homecoming celebration at Sulton Park in Walters. A powwow, dancing competitions, parade, and other activities take place in the weekend celebration. | 580/492–3822.

Sept. **Fort Sill Apache Annual Ceremonial.** The Fort Sill Apache and Mescalero Apache hold a fire dance in the Fort Sill Apache Tribal Complex in Apache. | 580/588–2314.

MANGUM
▼▼

The southwest corner of Oklahoma known as Old Greer County was made up of parts of four present Oklahoma counties. The area was claimed by 14 governments from 1669 until Oklahoma statehood. Mangum was the seat of Old Greer County. *Contact Mangum Chamber of Commerce | 222 W. Jefferson St., 73554 | 580/782–2444.*

Museum of the Western Prairie. The history of southwest Oklahoma from the Plains Indians who followed the buffalo to the cowboy driving cattle up the Western Trail is retold in this museum designed as a half-dugout. The Spanish and French influences from the 1700s are also shown. Originally opened in 1970, the museum, 25 mi southeast of Mangum, continues to expand and includes a blacksmith shop and working windmill on grounds. | 1100 Memorial Dr. Altus | 580/482–1044 | members.staroffice.com/www/muswestpr | Free (donations appreciated) | Tues.–Fri. 9–5, weekends 2–5.

Old Greer County Museum and Hall of Fame. A 1908 hospital building is now a museum that houses four floors of artifacts. A restored operating room, which was part of the original hospital, remains. The basement contains farming equipment including a horse-drawn plow and a variety of barbed wire used for fencing by pioneers. The first floor has period furnishings in the Indian Room and the Cowboy Room. On the second floor, pictures and items from turn-of-the-20th-century schools and businesses are on display. The third floor houses old doctors' offices. | 222 W. Jefferson | 580/782–2851 | Free | Tues.–Fri. 9–5, Sat. by appointment.

Peace on the Plains. A granite marker tells the story of the first Oklahoma meeting between the United States and Plains Indians to promote peace in 1834. | 222 W. Jefferson | 580/782–2851 | Free | Tues.–Fri. 9–5, Sat. by appointment.

✦ ON THE CALENDAR: July **Mangum Mounties Rodeo and Pioneer Reunion.** Enjoy an old-time fiddling contest and examples of pioneer life of the homesteaders. | 580/782–2444.

MUSKOGEE
▼▼

Just south of the confluence of the Verdigris, Arkansas, and Grand (Neosho) rivers, Muskogee became site of the 1874 "Union Agency," built to consolidate government services to the Five Civilized Tribes relocated to Oklahoma. It was at this agency that the first settlement in the Muskogee region started. When the Missouri-Kansas-Texas Railroad crossed the Arkansas, the town began to populate. Its first settlers were adventurous fortune seekers, who had waited in camp on the north bank of the river for the completion of the bridge. They rode the first train over, got off at the station, and began to build stores and houses on both sides of the track. Incorporated in 1898, the city has evolved into a major center for Native American history and culture. *Contact Greater Muskogee Area Chamber of Commerce | 230 W. Broadway, Suite 201 74401 | 918/682–2401 | fax 918/682–2403 | www.muskogee.org. Muskogee Convention and Tourism Bureau | 425 Boston St. 74401 | 918/684–6363 | www.muskogee.org. Muskogee Tourist Information Center | 2113 N. 32nd St., 74401 | 918/682–6751.*

Five Civilized Tribes Museum. Built in 1875, this imposing two-story sandstone building once served as the Union Indian Agency for the superintendency of the five civilized tribes. After it was used as a school and orphanage, dance hall, tea rooms, and offices for the American Legion, the building was converted to a museum in 1966. It contains maps, artifacts, photographs, and art work detailing the removals of the Five Tribes from the southeastern United States to Indian Territory, as well as displays on the culture of the Native Americans in the 19th century. | 1101 Honor Heights Dr. | 918/683–1701 | $2 | Mon.–Sat. 10–5, Sun. 1–5.

Fort Gibson Historic Site. In 1824, Colonel Matthew Arbuckle selected the site of this fort on the banks of the Grand (Neosho) River above the confluence of the Arkansas and Verdigris to suppress conflict between Osage warriors and the Cherokees and to protect settlers. The site 10 mi east of Muskogee includes a museum with uniforms, weapons, and tools from the 19th century; an 1845 army barracks constructed of stone masonry; and a reproduction of the original fort of log buildings (about one-third of original size). | 907 N. Garrison, on Rte. 80, Fort Gibson | 918/478–4088 | $3 | Apr.–Oct., Tues.–Sun. 10–5; Nov.–Mar., Thurs.–Sun. 10–5.

✦ ON THE CALENDAR: Mar. **Public Bake Day and 19th Century Dance Workshop.** Fort Gibson's original 19th-century brick ovens are fired up annually, and you're encouraged to cook your own dishes here. Nineteenth-century dance lessons are offered while you wait for your meal. | 918/478–4088.

NORMAN
▼▼▼

Oklahoma's third-largest city was settled in a single day during the 1889 Land Run. It takes its name from a railroad surveyor, Abner Norman. Norman is home to the University of Oklahoma, the second oldest institution (established in 1890) of higher learning in the state. The town later grew as a stop on the Atchison, Topeka & Santa Fe Railroad. *Contact Norman Convention and Visitors Bureau | 224. W. Gray, Suite 104, 73069 | 405/366–8095 or 800/767–7260 | www.visitnorman.com.*

Cleveland County Historical Museum. Housed in the Moore-Lindsay House, an 1899 Queen Anne–style residence, this museum is filled with period furniture and illustrates upper-middle class life in Oklahoma Territory. | 508 N. Peters Ave. | 405/321–0156 | Free | Weekdays 1–4 and by appointment.

Norman Historic Downtown. One of the first downtown historic districts placed on the National Register of Historic Places, Norman's downtown now houses shops, restaurants, and businesses. | 100 to 200 blocks of E. Main | 405/366–8095 | Free | Daily.

Sam Noble Museum of Natural History. The nation's largest university–based museum traces 300 million years of Oklahoma history. The Hall of People showcases Oklahoma's native population with special emphasis on historical Plains-tribes dress, beadwork, and tools. Examples of dwellings and a canoe are included. Similar exhibits on eastern Oklahoma tribes are in the works. | 2401 Chautauqua | 405/325–4712 | www.snomnh.ou.edu | $4 | Mon.–Sat. 10–5, Sun. 1–5.

Santa Fe Depot. This turn-of-the-20th-century depot was once a busy railroad stop. The renovated station now serves as a stop for the Heartland Flyer, a passenger train that travels through central Oklahoma into Texas. | 200 S. Jones | 405/366–5472 | Free | Daily.

OKLAHOMA CITY
▼▼▼

Oklahoma City was "born grown" on April 22, 1889, the date of the first Oklahoma land run. The rush began at noon, and by nightfall 10,000 tents were pitched near the Canadian River crossing of the railroad. The town's access to rail freight service helped it build meatpacking and other industries. The state capital was moved from Guthrie to Oklahoma City in 1910. *Contact Oklahoma City Convention and Visitors Bureau | 189 W. Sheridan, 73102 | 405/ 297–8912 or 800/225–5652 | www.visitokc.com.*

45th Infantry Division Museum. The military museum includes collections of firearms, artillery, cannons, and uniforms dating back to 1541. Special exhibits cover topics such as frontier forts of Oklahoma and the Indian Wars. | 2145 N.E. 36th St. | 405/424–5313 | www.45thdivisionmuseum.com | Free | Tues.–Fri. 9–4:15, Sat. 10–4:15, Sun. 1–4:15.

Harn Homestead and 1889er Museum. An original farmhouse built on a homestead claimed in the 1889 Land Run is now joined by a town house, two barns, a one-room school, and demonstration fields and gardens to illustrate daily life in territorial Oklahoma. | 313 N.E. 16th St. | 405/235–4058 | $3 | Sept.–July, Tues.–Sat. 10–3.

National Cowboy Hall of Fame and Western Heritage Center. It may be that no other museum describes the Old West as comprehensively as this one. Exhibits focus on the frontier, rodeo, art, and the cowboy. Learn about the many names for the cowboy and how his role evolved from the early 1800s to the present day. A hands-on building lets children dress up as cowboys. Don't forget to stop at Prosperity Junction, a frontier town from the 1890s. | 1700 N.E. 63rd St. | 405/478–2250 | www.nationalcowboymuseum.org | $8.50 | Daily 9–5.

Oklahoma Heritage Center. The former family residence of Judge Robert A. Hefner, a state Supreme Court justice, this 1917 mansion holds photographs, memorabilia, paintings, and bronze busts of Oklahomans inducted into the Oklahoma Hall of Fame. The adjacent Shepherd Oklahoma Heritage Library holds more than 10,000 books and periodicals related to Oklahoma history. | 201 N.W. 14th St. | 405/235–4458 | $3 | Mon.–Sat. 9–5. Sun. 1–5.

Overholser Mansion. This three-story French château–style mansion was built in 1903 by Henry Overholser, who came to Oklahoma Territory during the 1889 Land Run and became one of Oklahoma City's early civic leaders. The restored mansion has early 20th-century furnishings and stained-glass windows. | 405 N.W. 15th St. | 405/528–8485 | $3 | Tours on the hr Tues.–Sat. 10–5, Sun. 2–4.

Red Earth Indian Center. Part of Omniplex, a complex of five museums, Red Earth Indian Center houses kid-friendly exhibits—a stuffed bison, scale models of Indian dwellings, and a full-size tepee—on the nation's Native American heritage. The Omniplex presents special exhibits such as one on early Oklahoma statehood days, and another on the clothing of Oklahoma's First Ladies. The other Omniplex museums are a planetarium, an air and space museum, a science museum, and the International Photography Hall of Fame. | 2100 N.E. 52nd St. | 405/427–5461 | www.omniplex.org | $7.50 and up | Daily.

State Museum of History. The Oklahoma Historical Society's sizable museum covers every aspect of Oklahoma history, from area Indians to homesteading. Special exhibits have focused on the lives of such famous Oklahomans as Woody Guthrie and Wiley Post. A third-floor gallery traces the approximately 50 all-black communities that developed during

THE LAND RUNS

The white settlement of Oklahoma was unlike that of any other state. Many communities are settled gradually, but Oklahoma was literally settled in a single day. The federal government initially used Oklahoma as a resettlement area for Native Americans relocated from other areas by Indian Removal. Yet the white hunger for land was insatiable as Oklahoma became one of the last frontiers. Not yet settled by displaced Indians, two million acres in central Oklahoma became known as the Unassigned Lands after the Civil War. Congress encouraged President Benjamin Harrison to open the region for white settlement under the Homestead Act of 1862. That law allowed settlers to claim 160 acres of public land and receive title to it if they lived on and improved the claim for five years.

Farmers, tradesmen, capitalists, and politicians from the United States and abroad saw the opening of Oklahoma Territory as an opportunity to grab. Many thousands of people arrived in Oklahoma by horse, wagon, and train. These would-be land-owners gathered at the borders of the Unassigned Lands to wait for April 22, 1889. Settlers who snuck past the borders before the actual opening were called "Sooners," a name that has stuck to Oklahomans ever since. When the gunshot echoed at noon that day, settlers poured in to stake their claims. Tent cities went up, and Oklahoma City, Guthrie, Edmond, Kingfisher, Norman, Purcell, and other communities became instant cities.

Other land runs followed. When the northwestern Cherokee Strip opened in 1893, more than 100,000 people raced for 50,000 homesteads. The strong competition for land, coupled with the appearance of "instant" cities, earned some towns a reputation as wild and dangerous. Indeed, some towns held little more than saloons and houses of prostitution. Soldiers from Fort Reno were supposed to help maintain order, but the task was just too big. Government officials must have realized that the dynamics of huge land runs were causing problems. Later and smaller land openings in places like Lawton were organized around land lotteries. Today many communities celebrate the land runs that led to the settlement of Oklahoma.

Indian Territory and early statehood days. | 2100 N. Lincoln | 405/522–2491 | www.okhistory.mus.ok.us | Free | Mon.–Sat. 8–5.

✦ ON THE CALENDAR: May **Chuckwagon Gathering and Children's Cowboy Festival.** Meals are prepared and served from authentic 1900s chuck wagons by chefs from across the West in this Memorial Day weekend celebration. Live music is performed at the National Cowboy Hall of Fame, and there are a number of hands-on activities for kids. | 405/478–5228.

June **Red Earth Native American Cultural Festival.** Native American dancers come from all over North America to participate in competitive dancing held at the Myriad Convention Center. Art shows, a parade, and storytellers are included. | 405/427–5228.

HISTORIC DINING AND LODGING

Cattlemen's Steak House. Steak. Oklahoma City's oldest restaurant, established in 1910, takes pride in serving real cowboy food, whether it's a huge steak or calves' brains and eggs. Photos and drawings of working and movie cowboys sit alongside old photos of the stockyards. | 1309 S. Agnew | 405/947–1484 | $12–$20 | AE, MC, V.

The Grandison. As the downtown Oklahoma City business district grew, many early homes were razed for office buildings or parking lots. The Grandison at Maney Park is an exception. This 1904 Victorian home was built by one of the city's original settlers. Some rooms are decorated in the Victorian style. Some in-room hot tubs, massage; no room TVs. | 1200

N. Shartel, 73103 | 405/232–8778 or 800/240–INNS | www.bbonline.com/ok/grandison | 9 rooms | $95–$145 | AE, D, MC, V | BP.

OKMULGEE

▼▼▼

In the Creek language, Okmulgee means "bubbling water." This town has been headquarters for the Creek Nation since 1868. In the late 1800s, Okmulgee sprang up around the Creek Council House, the tribal house of government for the Muscogee (Creek) Nation. Trading posts, banks, and stores were established. Oil was discovered in the early 1900s. Within the next few decades, many of the largest buildings in downtown Okmulgee were built. Okmulgee is known for oil and oilmen, and their magnificent mansions still remain. Many are now restored and renovated for a new generation of residents. *Contact Okmulgee Tourism Development Program | 112 N. Morton Ave., 74447 | 918/756–6172 | www.tourokmulgee.com.*

Creek Council House Museum. The Creek legislature met in this handsome sandstone building from 1878 until Oklahoma statehood in 1907. The building has been impeccably restored and displays Creek artifacts, including a 1765 treaty made between a Creek chief and a British agent, and a piece of 16th-century Spanish chain mail carried over the Creek Trail of Tears. | 106 W. 6th St. | 918/756–2324 | Free | Tues.–Sat. 10–4:30.

Seminole Nation Museum. Artifacts from early Seminoles in Oklahoma are displayed in this museum 58 mi southwest of Okmulgee. There are also exhibits about the Freedmen, a group of African-Americans who moved to Oklahoma with the Seminole and became members of the tribe after the Civil War. | 524 S. Wewoka, Wewoka | 405/257–5580 | Free | Feb.–Dec., weekdays 10–5, weekends 1–5.

✦ ON THE CALENDAR: June **Creek Festival and Rodeo.** This event includes horse and bull riding, arts and crafts, and live entertainment. | 918/756–8700.

PAULS VALLEY

▼▼▼

Smith Paul, a North Carolina native, first spotted this site on a wagon-train trip to California. Paul moved with the Chickasaw tribe from northwestern Mississippi to Indian Territory in 1837. He settled in the Washita River valley a decade later. The settlement at first was known as Smith Paul's Valley. The railroad arrived in 1899, when the town was founded and its name subsequently shortened to Pauls Valley. *Contact Pauls Valley Chamber of Commerce | 112 E. Paul Ave., 73075 | 405/238–6491 | www.paulsvalley.com.*

Murray-Lindsay Mansion. Irish immigrant Frank Murray and his wife, Alzira Murray, a member of the Choctaw Nation, lived in this three-story home. The Murrays' 20,000-acre ranch so dominated the area at one time that circuit judges held court on their front lawn. The 1879 home has been restored and holds family photos and artifacts, including a 187-piece teapot collection. | 2 mi south of Lindsay on Rte. 76 | 405/756–2121 | By appointment.

Santa Fe Depot Museum. The 1905 wooden building that housed the Pauls Valley stop on the Atchison, Topeka & Santa Fe Railroad is today part of a railway museum. The museum contains antique railroad memorabilia and an authentic 1901 Atchison, Topeka & Santa Fe steam locomotive engine and caboose. Maps of walking and driving tours of the brick streets of downtown Pauls Valley are available at the depot. | 204 S. Santa Fe | 405/238–2244 | Free | Mon.–Tues. 10–4, Wed.–Sat. 11–4, Sun. 1:30–4.

Washita Valley Museum. Displays include photographs and artifacts depicting local history and the pioneers who settled the Washita River valley. | 1100 N. Ash St. | 405/238–3048 | Free | Wed.–Sat. 11–4, Sun. 1–4.

PAWNEE
▼▼▼

The former site of the Pawnee Agency and headquarters of the modern Pawnee tribe, Pawnee originated as a trading post. It was made the site of the Pawnee Agency in 1876, when the tribe was removed from its Nebraska home to present-day Oklahoma. In 1893, when the Pawnees accepted allotments, the rest of their land was opened for settlement and the town began to develop. *Contact Pawnee Chamber of Commerce | 608 Harrison St., 74058-2521 | 918/762–2108.*

Pawnee Bill Buffalo Ranch Site. This is the former home and ranch of Gordon "Pawnee Bill" Lillie, who operated a Pawnee trading post and founded Pawnee Bill's Wild West Show (reminiscent of Buffalo Bill's famous act). Now it's part museum, part refuge (buffalo graze in the pasture), and part entertainment venue. Reenactments of the original show are held regularly in summer. | U.S. 64, ½ mi west of Pawnee | 918/762–2513 | Free | Tues.–Sat. 10–5, Sun.– Mon. 1–4.

Pawnee County Historical Museum. The history of Pawnee County is told through such ghost-town artifacts as post-office boxes, photographs, and old newspaper clippings. Other museum displays include photographs of Pawnee County veterans and memorabilia including their uniforms and medals, artifacts, and other memorabilia. | 513 6th St. | 918/762–4681 | Free | Mon.–Sat. 10–2.

✦ ON THE CALENDAR: June **Pawnee Bill Wild West Show.** This historically accurate reenactment of the Pawnee Bill Wild West Show features cowboys, mock stage hold-ups, and Native American dancing. | 918/762–2108.

PERRY
▼▼▼

The Cherokee Outlet was established in the northwestern part of Indian Territory as an outlet for the Cherokee tribe to have a "perpetual outlet west." After the Civil War, the western section was given to the Osage, Kaw, Ponca, Pawnee, Nez Perce, Otoe-Missouria, and Tonkawa for settlement. The Cherokee tribe rented the eastern section to cattlemen for grazing. The 57-mi-wide strip was a wild place frequented by the Doolin Gang. More than 100,000 people took part in the Cherokee Strip land run on September 16, 1893. Perry, founded on the opening day of the run, was assured its future by a train station 1 mi south of the city. *Contact Perry Chamber of Commerce | 300 6th St., Box 426, 73077 | 580/336–3522 | www.perryok.org.*

Cherokee Strip Museum. This 5-acre museum complex traces the history of the Cherokee Outlet from prehistoric times to its sale to the federal government by the Cherokee Nation, and its opening to settlers in a 1893 land run. Documents, photographs, and early pioneer artifacts tell the story, and there are living-history programs in an 1895 one-room schoolhouse called Rose Hill. An early 20th-century attorney's office and a photo display on the Otoe-Missouria Indians, who came to the area in 1881, are also here. | 2617 W. Fir | 580/336–2405 | www.cherokee-strip-museum.org | Free | Tues.–Fri. 9–5, Sat. 10–4.

"If Buildings Could Talk" Tour. This historic walking tour traces the history of Perry from the Cherokee Strip land run onward. | Perry Square | 580/336–4684 | Free | By appointment.

◆ ON THE CALENDAR: May **Rural Heritage Festival.** Reenactors, living arts demonstrations, one-room school sessions, maypole dances, food, and old-time music re-create the Perry area's rural past. | 580/336–2405.

Sept. **Cherokee Strip Celebration.** Since 1893, the city of Perry has celebrated the opening of the Cherokee Strip. Events include a parade, the Noble County Fair, a rodeo, plus gunfighters and horseshoe-throwing contests. | 580/336–2405.

PONCA CITY
▼▼▼

Opened to settlement in the 1893 Cherokee Strip Land Run, Ponca City blends a ranching-culture heritage, the influences of five Native American tribes, and a legacy of art and architecture built with oil money. The tallgrass and shortgrass prairies fold into one another in the area. Oil production began before 1909 in fields developed in the Ponca Indian reservation south of the city. Oil was largely responsible for Ponca City's growth, most of which occurred between 1915 and 1940. *Contact Ponca City Visitor Information Center | 10th St. and Grand Ave., 74601 | 866/763–8092, 580/763–8092 | www.poncacitytourism.com.*

Marland's Grand Home. This stucco mansion was the first Ponca City home of E. W. Marland, an oil man and former governor. On the lower level of the mansion are exhibits from the 101 Ranch, including a player piano and grandfather clock from the ranch's White House, along with a selection of spurs and saddles. There is also an exhibit on Lucille Mulhall, a trick rider in the 101 Wild West Show. Additional collections include Plains Indian artifacts. | 10th St. and Grand Ave. | 580/767–0427 | $3 | Tues.–Sat. 10–5.

North Central Oklahoma Wild West Tours. Custom-made tours of Ponca City-area communities highlight historic homes, prairie preserve areas, and gardens. Call to arrange an itinerary and fee. | 800/700–3928.

Pioneer Woman Statue and Museum. The life of 19th-century pioneer women is honored with a 17-ft bronze statue. The museum houses authentic work tools used by 19th-century women, as well as the clothing they wore and their handiwork. Museum artisans work on 100-year-old looms, on which they weave rag rugs and dish towels. Also on display are a pump organ that came west by covered wagon, farm implements, old sewing machines, dolls, and quilts. The museum's "Wall of Fame" pictures Oklahoma women who have made significant contributions in various professions and occupations. | 701 Monument Rd. | 580/765–6108 | $3 | Tues.–Sat. 9–5, Sun. 1–9.

Top of Oklahoma Museum. Housed in this museum 20 mi northwest of Ponca City are displays of the pioneer history of the Cherokee Outlet. You can see a buggy, saddles, farm implements, and sample bedroom, living room, dining room, and kitchen from a typical house of the early 1900s. The building was built in 1912 as a community building, and it was called the Electric Pavilion because it was the first building in town to have electricity. | 303 S. Main St., Blackwell | 580/363–0209 | Free | Mon.–Sat. 10–5, Sun. 1–5.

POTEAU
▼▼▼

Built in a river valley, Poteau was founded in 1887 and named for a nearby river. Coal and lumber have sustained the town's economy. *Contact Poteau Chamber of Commerce | 201 S. Broadway St., 74953-3319 | 918/647–9178 | fax 918/647–4099.*

Kerr Museum. Housed in a carport next to the former home of Oklahoma governor and U. S. senator Robert S. Kerr, this museum depicts the development of eastern Oklahoma from prehistoric times, including the Spiro Mounds culture, the Choctaw Indians, and 19th-century pioneers. Exhibits include a Civil War surgical kit with a bone saw, rifles, pistols, 19th-century quilts and saddles, children's dolls, tops, marbles, and tea sets. | 23009 Kerr Mansion Rd. | 918/647–8221 | $1 | Weekdays 9–5, weekends 1–5.

Peter Conser Historic House Site. This is the restored 1894 home of Peter Conser, who served as a captain of the Choctaw Lighthorseman, an elite law-enforcement corps that patrolled Indian Territory in the 19th century. Inside the two-story frame house are period furniture, an original woodstove in the kitchen, an old piano and phonograph, and family photographs. | Conser Rd., 3 mi west of U.S. 59 | 918/653–2493 | Free | Wed.–Sat. 10–5, Sun. 1–5.

Spiro Historical Society Museum. Antique business machines, a blacksmith shop, and household items illustrate life in the late 1800s and early 1900s in the Ouachita Mountains. Other exhibits focus on prehistoric Native American culture, the settlement of the Choctaw Nation, the Civil War, and the Iron Horse. The museum is 17 mi north of Poteau. | 216 S. Main St., Spiro | 918/962–2708 or 918/962–3344 | Free | Wed.–Thurs. 9–4, Fri. 9–3:30, or by appointment.

SALLISAW
▼▼

Sallisaw began as a trading post along the military road linking Fort Gibson to Fort Smith in Arkansas Territory. French trappers named the place "Salaison," which means "salt provision" or "salt meat," because of large salt deposits nearby. Originally, the Sallisaw post office was established on September 29, 1873, but the office with that name was moved 15 mi south in 1888. The name of the former Sallisaw was changed to Mays on June 7, 1888. On December 8, 1888, the name of the post office (at present-day Sallisaw) was changed back to Sallisaw. *Contact Sallisaw Chamber of Commerce | 111 N. Elm St., 74955 | 918/775–2558.*

Choctaw Council House. Originally from Mississippi, the Choctaw became the first of the five tribes to be removed to Oklahoma after the Indian Removal Act of 1830 passed. Tuskahoma became the Choctaw Capitol shortly thereafter and served as the tribal headquarters until 1978 when it was moved to Durant. The Council House now serves as a museum with early Choctaw artifacts such as clothing, historical documents, and photographs. The council grounds are still occasionally used for ceremonial purposes such as the annual Choctaw Labor Day festival. | Council House Road Tuskahoma | 918/569–4465 | Free | Weekdays 8–4.

Overstreet-Kerr Living History Farm. Once the residence of Indian Territory settlers, the farm includes a restored 1895 home and plantings of old strains of grains, vegetables, and livestock that were used by the Choctaw in the late 19th century. | U.S. 59, Keota, 10 mi south of Sallisaw | 918/966–3396 | $3 | Fri.–Sat. 10–4.

Sequoyah's Home. Cherokee linguist Sequoyah built this one-room cabin after he moved to Indian Territory from Tennessee in 1829. Sequoyah invented the 85-character Cherokee alphabet, which allowed the tribe to write in their language and teach it more easily. The cabin holds exhibits on the Cherokee alphabet and Cherokee culture. Artifacts include grinding stones to make corn meal, household implements, farm implements, and salt tubs. | Route 101, 10 mi northeast of Sallisaw | 918/775–2413 | Free | Tues.–Fri. 9–5, weekends 2–5.

STILLWATER

▼▼

"Sooners," settlers who traveled illegally into federal lands in Oklahoma Territory to push for the opening of central Oklahoma to homesteaders, made the first organized attempt to establish a town near present-day Stillwater in 1884. The Sooners were repeatedly evicted, and this town of 39,000 was (legally) founded immediately after the 1889 Land Run. *Contact Stillwater Convention and Visitors Bureau | 409 S. Main St., 74074 | 405/743–3697 or 800/991–6717 | fax 405/372–0765 | www.come2stillwater.com.*

Oklahoma Museum of Higher Education. "Old Central," Oklahoma State University's oldest building, has been restored to its 1894 appearance and includes historic photographs and re-created rooms from a variety of state higher-education institutions. | Between Hester St. and Knoblock Ave., on the OSU campus | 405/744–2828 | Free | Tues.–Fri. 9–5, Sat. 10–4.

Washington Irving Trail Museum. This small museum traces the route writer Washington Irving took through the area in 1832. You'll also learn about early Oklahoma lawmen and outlaws, the first battle of the Civil War in Indian Territory, Boomer leader David L. Payne, and the beginnings of country music. | Mehan Rd., 6 mi east of Stillwater on Rte. 51 | 405/624–9130 | www.cowboy.net/non-profit/irving | Free | Wed.–Sat. 10–5, Sun. 1–5, or by appointment.

TAHLEQUAH

▼▼

Tahlequah's Cherokee history is one of its defining characteristics—major street names downtown appear in both English and Cherokee. The Cherokee Nation established its capital here just west of the Illinois River in 1839. The town was platted in 1843 but only consisted of a council ground with a large shed in the middle and a camping site for the delegates of the 18 tribes that regularly attended council meetings. A permanent capitol was completed on the site in 1869. In 1907, when Indian Territory and Oklahoma Territory were joined to become the state of Oklahoma, the Cherokee Capitol became the Cherokee County Court House. *Contact Tahlequah Area Chamber of Commerce/Tourism Council | 123 E. Delaware St., 74464 | 800/456–4860 or 918/456–3742.*

Cherokee Capitol Building. The historic square in downtown Tahlequah has been a meeting place for the Cherokee tribe since its arrival in Indian Territory; the redbrick capitol was built in 1870 and houses the judicial branch of the modern Cherokee Nation. | 101 S. Muskogee Ave. | 918/456–0671 | Free | Weekdays 9–5, when court is in session.

Cherokee Heritage Center. This 44-acre wooded site includes the Cherokee National Museum, which chronicles the history of the Cherokee Nation from the time of the Trail of Tears to the present. It includes Tsa-La-Gi Ancient Village, a living-history installation illustrating Cherokee life before European contact. Costumed tribal members demonstrate basket weaving, pottery, stickball games, and other Cherokee traditions. You can also take a self-guided tour of the Adams Corner Rural Village, a re-created pioneer village from the 1800s. A walking trail around the Heritage Center grounds identifies trees and plants used in traditional Cherokee medicine. If you are visiting in the summer, be sure to take in the "Trail of Tears" drama inside the Heritage Center. | Willis Rd. | 918/456–6007 or 888/999–6007 | www.cherokeeheritage.org | $8.50 | Feb.–Dec., Mon.–Sat. 10–5, Sun. 1–5.

George Murrell Home. The antebellum home of Minerva Murell, niece of Cherokee principal chief John Ross, was the only one of the family homes to escape destruction by troops led by Confederate general Stand Watie. He was a Cherokee and enemy of Ross, who sided with the Union forces. Inside the 1845 house are original furnishings, a library with videos and exhibits,

TRAIL OF TEARS

"I will not go to war for you, John Ross. It's too damned late." Ross, the Cherokee chief, would never forget President Andrew Jackson's raspy response after his final appeal to "Old Hickory" to respect the tribe's land rights in Georgia. By signing into law the Indian Removal Act in 1830, Jackson was codifying what already was well under way—the removal of Native American tribes from the eastern United States. The Indians were to give up their eastern lands in exchange for land in the wilderness west of the Mississippi. Termed "voluntary," the removals mostly were not.

Many Indians of the "Five Civilized Tribes" didn't want to leave their towns and rural settlements in the East. That was the case with the Cherokees who followed Ross. They stayed put while Ross, the son of a Scottish father and part-Cherokee mother, worked to secure his tribe's land rights. Nevertheless, by 1838, federal and state authorities had determined it was time for them to go. That year, an estimated 17,000 Cherokees were rounded up by U.S. soldiers under General Winfield Scott, and forced to evacuate. They had to leave behind homes and property, and many were hurried into line with nothing except the clothes they had on, according to a magazine report.

Though he had opposed the relocation, Ross accepted a government appointment as superintendent of removal and subsistence. The Cherokee traveled in wagons, on horses, and on foot and were marched like an army during a summer drought that extended into autumn. Many died from famine. Some survivors perished later, during an icy-cold winter. Ross's wife, Quatie, a full-bloodied Cherokee, was one of the victims, dying of pneumonia in Little Rock, Arkansas. About a quarter of the Cherokee Nation died on the Trail of Tears.

Soon after arriving in Indian Territory in the northeastern section of present-day Oklahoma, Ross became chief of the new United Cherokee Nation, a position he held until 1866. Ever the diplomat, Ross worked for the unification of a number of tribes, not just the Cherokee. In 1843, he presided over a council at Tahlequah, headquarters of the Cherokee Nation, that was attended by 18 tribes. They signed an agreement to respect the rights of each tribe and promote the general welfare.

and period artifacts. A self-guided 1-mi nature trail leads through a bird sanctuary behind the mansion. | 3 mi south of Tahlequah on Rte. 82, 1 mi east on Murrell Rd. | 918/456–2751 | Free | Apr.–early Sept., Wed.–Sat. 10–5, Sun. 1–5; early Sept.–Mar., hrs vary (call ahead).

✦ ON THE CALENDAR: June–Sept. **Trail of Tears Drama.** A mostly Native American cast portrays experiences of the Cherokees in the 1800s during the removal of Native Americans from their land in the southeastern United States and their long, hard journey to Oklahoma. The performances are held outdoors at the Cherokee Heritage Center, Thursday–Saturday evenings, through Labor Day weekend. Admission is $15. | 888/999–6007.

Sept. **Cherokee National Holiday.** This annual gathering of the Cherokee Nation includes a rodeo, powwow, gospel singing, Cherokee language and culture workshops, children's activities, and Cherokee crafts booths with demonstrations. | 918/456–0671.

TULSA
▼▼

Originally a Creek crossroads, Tulsa was known as "Tulsey Town," tulsey being a variation on the Creek word *tallasi,* for "town." Oklahoma's second-largest city was incorporated in

1898 northeast of the Arkansas River, 16 years after the Frisco Railroad was extended to the city from Vinita. The discovery of oil in the nearby Red Fork field in 1901 soon transformed Tulsa into the "Oil Capital of the World." There was so much oil beneath the city that workers once accidentally struck oil at a petroleum exposition at the fairgrounds while demonstrating a new piece of equipment. *Contact Tulsa Historical Society | 2445 S. Peoria, 74114 | 918/712–9484. Tulsa Metro Chamber of Commerce | 616 S. Boston Ave., 74119 | 918/585–1201 | www.tulsachamber.com.*

Black Settlers: The Search for the Promised Land. Oklahoma State University–Tulsa is the permanent home of this photographic exhibit and documentary project that chronicles the migration of black settlers to Oklahoma and their contributions to Tulsa. | 700 N. Greenwood Ave., North Hall 151 (B.S. Roberts Room) | 918/583–6494 | www.osu-tulsa.okstate.edu | Free | Weekdays 7 AM–10 PM, weekends 7–6.

Creek Council Oak Tree. This site of the 1830s Creek encampment marks the beginnings of "Tulsey Town." The council met at an ancient oak tree from the time they arrived in the area from Alabama, until 1898. Along with elections and tribal business, ceremonial dances were held on the square. The site has an oak tree planted in the 1850s, plus and ethno-botanical plant display. | 18th St. and Cheyenne Ave. | Free | Daily.

Gilcrease Museum. Its collection, dedicated to western art and Americana, includes paintings by such artists as Frederic Remington and Charles Russell, as well as Native American art and artifacts. | 1400 Gilcrease Museum Rd. | 918/596–2700 or 888/655–2278 | $5 suggested donation | Tues.–Sun. 10–4.

Sunbelt Railroad Museum. The history of American and Oklahoma railroads is the focus of this museum. Displays include a working telegraph station. | 1323 E. 5th | 918/584–3777 | Free | Sat. 10–4.

✦ ON THE CALENDAR: Aug. **Tulsa Powwow.** Members of more than 50 tribes compete in evening dance competitions. Native American art, crafts, and foods enrich the experience. It's held in Tulsa's Expo Square at 21st and Yale. | 918/744–1113.

VINITA
▼▼▼

Vinita was founded in 1871 where the Frisco and Missouri-Kansas-Texas railroads crossed. A town founder, Colonel Elias Boudinot, named Vinita for an unrequited love, artist Vinnie Ream, who created the sculpture of Abraham Lincoln in the Capitol in Washington, D.C. In the 20th century the town became a stop along Route 66. Wilson Avenue, Vinita's main thoroughfare, follows the path of the old road through downtown. *Contact Vinita Chamber of Commerce | 125 S. Scraper St., 74301 | 918/256–7133 | www.vinita.com.*

Cabin Creek Civil War Battle Site. Confederate president Jefferson Davis termed the Battle of Cabin Creek (September 19, 1864) "the most complete battle" in the Civil War. Every three years in October, the battle is reenacted near the actual battle site. You can visit the battlefield and see the monument there | U.S. 60 west to 4400 Rd. road south, turn left onto 350 Rd. | 918/256–7133 | Free | Daily.

Eastern Trails Museum. Browse amid photographs and artifacts relating to railroads, pioneer settlements, and the Civil War battle of Cabin Creek in this museum. It provides maps for a self-guided walking tour of 38 historic buildings and homes. | 215 W. Illinois Ave. | 918/256–2115 | Free | Mon.–Sat. 1:30–4.

Har-Ber Village. You'll see more than 100 historic cabins and buildings in this reconstructed 19th-century frontier town, including a chapel, newspaper office, law office, and jail. All are filled with such pioneer artifacts as cooking utensils, tools, furniture, clothing. | 4404 W. 20th St., Grove | 918/786–6446 | Free | Mar.–Nov., Mon.–Sat. 9–6, Sun. 11–6.

WATONGA
▼▼▼

Founded in 1892, this town on the Canadian River is named after Arapaho chief Wa-ton-gle, which translates to Black Coyote. The canyons north of town were used as a Cheyenne winter camp in the 19th century. Watonga was part of the Wichita-Caddo Reservation, opened for white settlement by lottery on April 8, 1901. *Contact Watonga Chamber of Commerce | Box 537, 73772 | 580/623–5452 | www.watonga.com/chamber.*

Roman Nose State Park. The canyons north of town are named for Henry Caruthers Roman Nose, a Southern Cheyenne chief. Members of the Cheyenne tribe once used the natural springs—known as the "Spring of Everlasting Waters"—and canyons of this park for a winter camp. Notorious outlaw gangs such as the Black-Yeagers, the Daltons, and the Doolins used the canyon as a hideout. | Rte. 1, 6 mi northwest of Watonga | 580/623–7281 or 800/892–8690 | Free | Daily.

T. B. Ferguson Home. This restored three-story house belonged to Thomas Benton Ferguson, territorial newspaper editor and publisher, who arrived with his printing press in a covered wagon after the 1892 Land Run. President Teddy Roosevelt appointed Ferguson the sixth Oklahoma territorial governor. Ferguson served from 1901 to 1906, preparing Oklahoma for statehood the following year. An 1870 cavalry remount station and the old Watonga city jail stand in the home's backyard. The home includes period furnishings the Ferguson family brought to Oklahoma. | 519–521 N. Weigel St. | 580/623–5585 | Free | Tues.–Fri. 9–5, weekends 1–5.

✦ ON THE CALENDAR: Feb. **Bitter Creek Frontier Daze.** Roman Nose Resort Park near Watonga hosts a living-history reenactment of the 1830–90 time period, featuring Plains Indians, fur trappers, U.S. cavalry, outlaws, and homesteaders. | 580/623–7281.

HISTORIC DINING
Noble House Restaurant. American. This restored 1912 hotel has been converted to a family-style restaurant that serves such Oklahoma specialties as fried catfish and country fried steak. | 112 N. Noble | 580/623–2559 | $7–$12 | AE, D, MC, V.

WAURIKA
▼▼▼

In the late 1800s Waurika, 20 mi north of the Red River border between Texas and Oklahoma, was a stopping place and popular grazing spot for herds of cattle being driven up the Chisholm Trail. The town was founded in 1907 and later became a rail center. *Contact Waurika Chamber of Commerce | 120 W. Broadway, Box 366, 73573 | 580/228–2081 | www.waurika.net.*

Chisholm Trail Historical Museum. See a full-size covered wagon and photograph depicting the history of the Chisholm Trail, which funneled millions of head of cattle through Indian Territory in the decades following the Civil War. Exhibits include information about Delaware-born trader Jesse Chisholm, who popularized the trail, and the daily life of cattle drovers.

The Pioneer Room includes a full-size covered wagon. | U.S. 70 and U.S. 81 | 580/228–2166 | Free | Thurs.–Sat. 10–4, Sun. 1–4; closed 1st Sun. of month.

Greater Southwest Historical Museum. This sprawling museum 50 mi east of Waurika houses a 19th-century log cabin and staged versions of a general store, medical and dental offices, and barber shop using artifacts from the late 1800s and early 1900. In a separate wing is a military exhibit with uniforms, medals, photographs, and maps. | 35 Sunset Dr. Ardmore | 580/226–3857 | Free | Tues.–Sat. 10–5, Sun. 1–5.

Rock Island Depot/Library. This restored 1912 railroad-ticket office with Italian marble floors displays railroad memorabilia and artifacts and serves as a public library. | 98 Meridian St. | 580/228–2575 | Donations appreciated | Mon., Wed., and Fri. 9–4:30; Tues. and Thurs. 9–7; Sat. 9–noon.

✦ ON THE CALENDAR: June **Chisholm Trail Celebration.** Outdoor living-history exhibits depict life along the Chisholm Trail. Native American dances, storytelling, a beef brisket dinner, an outdoor melodrama, and western music are part of this event held at the Chisholm Trail Museum. | 580/228–2166.

WOODWARD
▼▼

Established during the Cherokee Strip Land Run of 1893, this tough frontier town saw more than one gunfight on its streets. One of Woodward's most famous residents was frontier lawyer and gunfighter Temple Houston, a son of Texas soldier and politician Sam Houston. Nearby Fort Supply was an important early cavalry outpost on the Western Cattle Trail. *Contact Woodward Chamber of Commerce | 1006 Oklahoma Ave., Box 1026, 73802 | 580/256–7411 | www. woodwardok.com.*

Historic Fort Supply. Lieutenant Colonel George Custer used this 1868 supply camp as his base when he set out for the Cheyenne village of Black Kettle. Five buildings dating from 1870 to 1892 still remain. The 1892 guardhouse holds a small museum. | 14 mi north of city on U.S. 270 | 580/766–3767 | Free | Mon.–Sat. 9–5.

Plains Indians and Pioneers Museum. The murals inside the front door of the museum transport you back to the Old West, and inside are Native American and pioneer history exhibits. Artifacts ranging from Cheyenne beadwork to pioneer household items in a pioneer-town vignette are displayed along with excerpts from old journals and vintage newspaper clippings. Another display tracks the decline of buffalo. The curator has extensive information about frontier lawyer and gunfighter Temple Houston. | 2009 Williams Ave. | 580/256–6136 | Free | Tues.–Sat. 10–5, Sun. 1–4.

✦ ON THE CALENDAR: Oct. **Fort Supply Cavalry Days.** This celebration of the history of northwest Oklahoma features living-history reenactments. | 580/256–7411.

Oct. **Boiling Springs Indian Expo.** This Native American fair includes a powwow, arts, and crafts. Native American dancers from across Oklahoma take part in a competition. The Indian Expo is held in conjunction with Fort Supply Cavalry Days. | 580/256–7411.

OREGON

———◆◆◇———

With more than 96,000 square mi of mountainous foothills and scorched deserts all but unchanged over the centuries, Oregon is a true-to-life slice of the Old West. The state was once the domain of hundreds of different Native American tribes, who probably came from somewhere in Asia around 10,000 years ago and migrated down the Pacific coast or east along the Columbia River. Artifacts have been found near Klamath Lakes and the Great Basin, both important areas to the early tribes for their abundance of water and game. Even today, it's easy to picture Indian settlements scattered along the serene riverbanks and tucked into the wide, placid valleys.

Oregon's rugged, rocky coast, where many an explorer first touched North American land, is still strewn with the shipwrecks of those who didn't survive. European explorers arrived in the mid-1500s, when Juan Rodriguéz Cabrillo of Portugal sighted the Oregon coast while searching for a shortcut to the Atlantic Ocean. Notables who made a stopover in Oregon over the next three centuries included Sir Francis Drake, Captain James Cook, and George Vancouver. Trade routes were established between 1792, when American Captain Robert Gray sailed into the Columbia River from the Pacific, and the early 1800s, when British army Lieutenant William Broughton pushed even farther to the Columbia Gorge. In 1805, after a 19-month expedition across North America, William Clark and Meriwether Lewis reached the mouth of the Columbia River from the East. Their route blazed the way for the thousands of pioneers who would reach the Northwest by foot and wagon. But before settlers flooded into the area along the Oregon Trail, fur trading was king and and trading posts such as John Jacob Astor's place in Astoria, established in 1811, popped up around the area.

British entrepreneurs, particularly Dr. John McLoughlin, the "Father of Oregon," took the lead in the region during this time. In 1825, McLoughlin established the Hudson Bay Company headquarters at Fort Vancouver, and in 1827 he built the Northwest's first sawmill. His successes in business helped attract more than 300,000 pioneers from the East, mostly farmers and traders, who followed the rugged Oregon Trail between 1841 and 1861.

Thousands of settlers arrived after the territory became a state in 1859 and prospectors discovered gold in the late 1860s. Some struck it rich and moved into the rapidly expanding new towns in the eastern mountains and along the coast; some failed to find riches and quit to become farmhands or miners; and some brainstormed their own innovative routes to profit. Among the Northwest businesses that sprang up at the time was salmon-canning, started in Astoria in 1864, and cheese-making, founded in Tillamook at the turn of the 20th century.

Pioneers who took the 2,170-mi Oregon Trail—which winds through Missouri, Kansas, Nebraska, Wyoming, and Idaho—entered Oregon by crossing the Snake River at Fort Boise (near Nyssa) in the southeast corner. This route soon became a well-used pathway to the Pacific Coast for gold seekers, fur traders, missionaries, and eastern emigrants. Today, the route can still be followed by car, foot, horse, or mountain bike in many places. Signs, historical markers, and old wagon-wheel ruts mark the route. Along the trail are more than 235 historic sites, former encampments, graves, and way stations used by the thousands of pioneers who made the five-month sojourn to the Northwest. Some ended their travels in the quickly growing towns of Baker City and Pendleton, while others continued westward toward The Dalles and Oregon City, where the trail ends.

A southern route of the Oregon Trail, known as the Applegate Trail, was blazed in 1846 as an alternate route through the territory. The three Applegate brothers, who traversed the original Oregon Trail in 1843, lost two of their sons and their uncle while rafting the Columbia River rapids outside of The Dalles. After settling in the Willamette Valley, they formed the South Road Expedition to find a safer route west, eventually traveling through Corvallis, Eugene, Ashland, and Greensprings Mountain all the way to Humboldt, Nevada.

Although many settlers eventually moved to the burgeoning cities of Portland, Eugene, and Salem, which were linked by rail to the East by the end of the 1800s, there are still many places throughout Oregon that keep alive the spirit of the Old West. Nearly every town has at least one museum or historic place commemorating the lives of local settlers, Native American tribes, and events in regional history. After all, the Old West really isn't that old—it's been barely two centuries since Lewis and Clark first arrived at the Columbia River, so most artifacts and buildings are well preserved. A week or two in Oregon will give you the chance to explore a fascinating era of American history.

The Willamette Valley

A DRIVING TOUR FROM PORTLAND TO EUGENE
▼▼

Distance: 114 mi   **Time:** 4 days
Breaks: Overnight in Oregon City and Albany

The lushly fertile Willamette Valley, watered by the Willamette River and flanked by the Cascade Range on the east and the Coast Range on the west, was the Eden that beckoned to the first pioneers who headed west to Oregon. Reports of the valley's beauty and bounty inspired thousands upon thousands to make the arduous journey along the Oregon Trail toward this promised land. Many of the emigrants ended up elsewhere, but the Willamette Valley remained a symbol of the new life hoped for by the pioneers. This driving tour takes you through the heart of the valley that captured the imagination of so many people who decided to come west.

Start your trip in **Portland,** where the Willamette River drains into the Columbia River. Spend a day discovering the remnants of Portland's frontier era, at the James F. Bybee House and Howell Territorial Park and at the Oregon History Center. For a look all the way back to the beginning, venture out with Lewis and Clark Columbia River Tours. At the end of the day, drive 5 mi east on I–84 and 12 mi south on I–205 to Oregon City for dinner and a good night's sleep.

There's lots to see in **Oregon City,** which was the terminus of the Oregon Trail, so get an

OREGON TIME LINE

1543 An expedition of Spanish explorers led by Juan Rodriguéz Cabrillo sails from Acapulco and reaches the Rogue River.

1603 Martin d'Aguilar sails along the Oregon coast and sights what is later named the Columbia River.

1788 Robert Gray becomes the first white American and Markus Lopius the first black American to set foot on Oregon soil.

1792 Gray sights the Columbia River and names it after his ship.

1805 Explorers Meriwether Lewis and William Clark arrive at the mouth of the Columbia River.

1811 John Jacob Astor's fur traders establish a trading post on the site of present-day Astoria.

1814 Jane Barnes is the first white woman to arrive in the Pacific Northwest.

1827 Dr. John McLoughlin builds the first sawmill in the Pacific Northwest.

1829 Oregon City incorporates, the first Pacific Coast town to do so.

1833 Timber is first shipped from Oregon, headed for China.

1841 The first of more than 300,000 pioneers traverses the Oregon Trail.

1848 Oregon Territory is established.

1851 Portland is incorporated.

1859 Oregon becomes the 33rd state.

1861 Henry Griffin discovers gold near the Powder River.

1863 Fort Klamath military post is established.

1877 The Nez Perce War begins.

1878 The Bannock Indian War takes place.

1891 The Sumpter Valley Railroad narrow-gauge line connects Baker City to Prairie City.

1902 Crater Lake is designated a National Park.

early start on day two. A good place to begin your exploration is the End of the Oregon Trail Interpretive Center, where you can learn all about the pioneer conduit that brought so many settlers to the Willamette Valley. At Old Aurora Colony Museum, Baker Cabin Historic Site and Pioneer Church, and Foster Farm, glimpse the lifeways of the earliest citizens of Oregon City. Spend another night in Oregon City.

On your third morning, take in a couple more Oregon City sights: Visit McLoughlin House National Historic Site to see where the "Father of Oregon" lived, and stop at the Rose Museum for a look at territorial politics. Next, drive 8 mi south on I–205 and 29 mi south on I–5 to **Salem,** the state capital. Here, three 1840s pioneer homes at Mission Mill Village reveal what life was like for the earliest Oregon settlers, and Willamette University, founded in 1842, demonstrates their dreams for the future. Finish your day by driving 20 mi south on I–5 to **Albany,** which has one of Oregon's largest collections of historic architecture. Stroll some of the 80-square-block historic district or take in an historical dinner theater show before retiring for the evening.

Day four starts with a visit to Albany's Monteith House Museum and the Linn County

Historical Museum/Brownsville Depot. Next, head 40 mi south on I–5, through the upper-most Willamette Valley, to **Eugene.** At the Lane County Historical Museum there, you can take a look at artifacts of the Oregon Trail and learn more about the early settlements that grew up near the end of the trail.

The Old Days
Along the Coast

A DRIVING TOUR FROM ASTORIA TO GOLD BEACH

▼▼

Distance: 305 mi   **Time:** 3 days
Breaks: Overnight in Astoria and Newport

With the 1792 arrival of American merchant-ship captain Robert Gray, a thriving sea-borne fur trade appeared along the Oregon coast. Fishing also became a major industry, as well as shipping. In contrast to the Spanish colonists of the southwest, the mining prospectors of the Rockies, and the sodbusters of the Great Plains, coastal Oregonians of the 19th century built their lives around the sea. A drive down the Oregon coast will show you a whole differ-ent side of the Old West—one that has to do with sailing vessels rather than covered wagons, with salmon rather than longhorns.

Your tour starts at the mouth of the Columbia River in **Astoria,** one of the oldest cities west of the Rockies. This is where Lewis and Clark first saw the Pacific Ocean, and where New York fur baron John Jacob Astor set up the trading operation that made him rich. The major events in the town's history are recorded on the Astoria Column. The Lewis and Clark expedition spent an unhappy winter here, a period that's documented at Fort Clatsop National Memorial and at the Salt Works. The Columbia River Maritime Museum traces the shipping history of the area, and Flavel House displays the kind of wealth accumulated by local shipping tycoons. Overnight here.

On your second day, drive 63 mi south on U.S. 101, climbing the side of Neahkahnie Mountain and skirting Tillamook Bay. When you reach **Tillamook,** stop in at the Pioneer Museum. South of the downtown area, off 3rd Street, turn onto Three Capes Loop, a spec-tacularly scenic, winding byway that leads to Cape Meares Lighthouse (about 10 mi west of Tillamook), built in 1890. Another 25 mi on the loop takes you along rugged shoreline to Pacific City, where you'll get back on U.S. 101. About 34 mi south of Pacific City (and 5 mi south of Depoe Bay) on U.S. 101, Otter Crest Loop branches off the highway to take you along cliff tops past Cape Foulweather (named by Captain James Cook in 1778) and the Devil's Punchbowl. You'll rejoin U.S. 101 near Yaquina Head, where you can see Yaquina Head Light-house, built in 1872 and still in operation. Another 5 mi south on U.S. 101 brings you to **Newport.** At Yaquina Bay State Park you can see the 1871 Yaquina Bay Lighthouse and its displays on maritime history and the history of the lighthouse. To absorb the mood of seaside Oregon past and present, stroll the streets of the Bayfront area, grab a seafood dinner, and fall asleep to the sound of buoy bells and foghorns.

Day three starts with a 95-mi drive south on U.S. 101 to **Coos Bay.** Along the way, stop at the 1857 Umpqua River Lighthouse and the museum next door. Once you reach Coos Bay, a visit to the Coos County Historical Society Museum will bring you up to speed on the early history of the area. Have lunch in Coos Bay and head south on U.S. 101; after about 15 mi (near Blandon), the highway enters a particularly scenic stretch that will continue to the end of your tour. About 50 mi south of Coos Bay you will reach Cape Blanco Light Station, where you can take a fascinating tour. Get back onto U.S. 101 for a lovely 35-mi drive to **Gold Beach.** At the Curry County Historical Museum you can see everything from an exhibit on the early salmon industry to a display of musical instruments played by local pioneers.

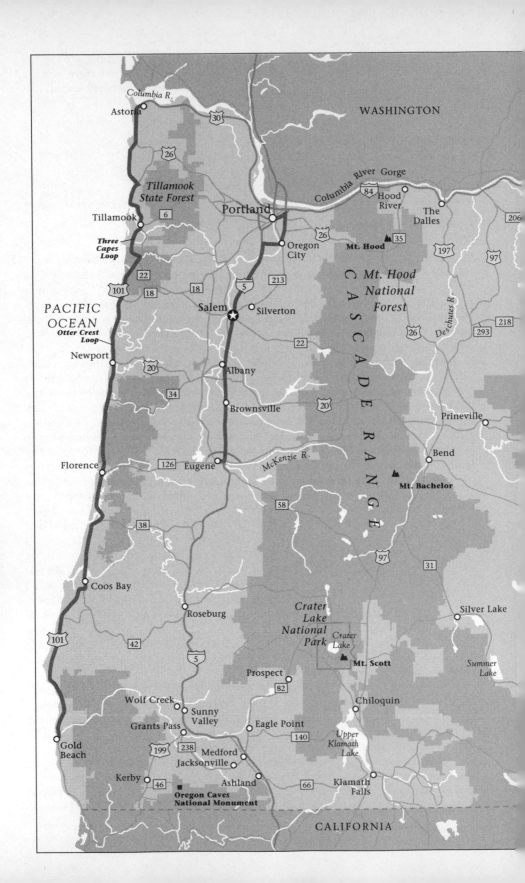

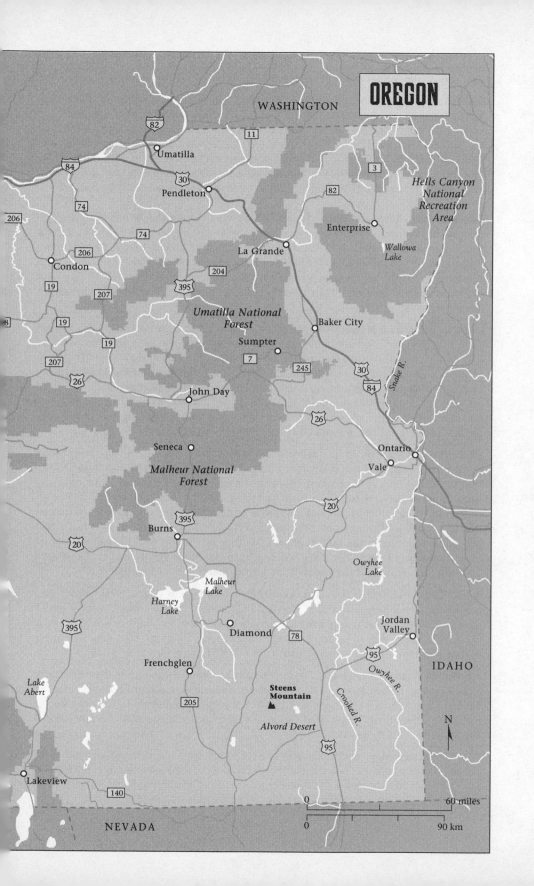

ALBANY

▼▼

For an immersion in Victorian architecture, this is the town to visit. Named by Thomas and Walter Monteith after their hometown in New York State, Albany has one of the largest and most varied collections of historic buildings in Oregon. An 80-square-block area is listed on the National Register of Historic Places. *Contact Albany Area Chamber of Commerce | 435 1st Ave. W, 97321 | 541/926–5617 or 800/526–2256 | www.albanyvisitors.com. Albany Visitors Association | 300 2nd Ave. SW | 541/928–0911 or 800/526–2256 | www.albanyvisitors.com. Linn County Historical Society | 1132 30th Pl. SW, Albany 97321 | 541/926–4680 | www.linnhistorical.com.*

Flinn's Heritage Tours and Dinner Theater. Experience turn-of-the-20th-century Oregon domesticity firsthand, on a tour of historic homes, pioneer cemeteries, covered bridges, ghost towns, and other features of the Albany area's past. Or step back in time at Flinn's Dinner Theater, where you can watch living history re-enactments, old-time vaudeville shows, and a pioneer Christmas story. Flinn's also operates a tea parlor where servers in period dress pour high tea in an 1887 building. | 222 1st Ave. W | 541/928–5008 or 800/636–5008 | www.flinns. com | Prices vary.

Linn County Historical Museum/Brownsville Depot. You'll find some noteworthy pioneer-era exhibits at this small museum, housed in an 1890 railroad depot in the town of Brownsville. Included is a covered wagon that arrived in 1865 after a trek along the Oregon Trail from Missouri. Consider the Brownsville Walking Tour. Just pick one of myriad maps showing Brownsville's historic buildings and homes at the museum. Most businesses in this town 17 mi south of Albany on I–5 operate out of buildings from the late 1800s, and a high per-capita rate of historic homes makes it easy to look back to the town's founding days in the early 1850s. | 101 Park Ave., Brownsville | 541/466–3390 | Free | Mon.–Sat. 11–4, Sun. 1–5.

Monteith House Museum. The first frame house in Albany, Monteith House was built in 1849 by brothers Walter and Thomas Monteith. The pair had traveled by ox team over the Oregon Trail two years earlier and purchased 320 acres of land along the Willamette River for a mere $400. Thus was born the town of Albany. The house has been fully restored and filled with period furnishings and historic photos. It's widely thought to be the most authentic restoration of a Pacific Northwest pioneer-era home. You can pick up a Monteith Historic District Landscape Tour map at the Visitors Association if you'd like to take a self-guided walking tour of the area. | 518 2nd Ave. SW | 800/526–2256 | www.albanyvisitors.com | Donation | Mid-June–mid-Sept., Wed.–Sat. noon–4; mid-Sept.–mid-June, by appointment.

♦ ON THE CALENDAR: June **Linn County Pioneer Picnic.** The picnic is the state's oldest continuing community festival, and has been held every year since 1887. There is a horse-shoe tournament, horse riding, a flower show, loggers' jamboree, children's parade, 1800s period costumes, a quilt show, and a Saturday-night dance. The picnic takes place in Pioneer Park in Brownsville (17 mi south of Albany off I–5). | 541/466–5311.

July **Historic Interior Homes Tours.** Carefully restored to showcase their 19th-century beauty and efficiency, the homes on this tour provide for a worthwhile afternoon. Held on the last weekend in July from 11 to 5, the event includes live entertainment, horse-drawn wagon rides, and refreshments. Tickets ($10) are available from the Albany Visitors Association. | 541/928–0911 or 800/526–2256.

Dec. **Christmas Parlour Tour.** This is your chance to see several wonderfully restored 19th-century Victorian homes dressed up in their holiday best. Costumed carolers and vendors add to the period festivities of this tour, offered on the second Sunday of December from 2 to 7. Tickets ($10) are available from the Albany Visitors Association. | 541/928–0911 or 800/526–2256.

ASTORIA

▼▼▼

Astoria is one of the oldest cities west of the Rockies. The town draws its name from New York businessman John Jacob Astor, who sent two expeditions to the region to establish the American Fur Company in 1808. Since that time, it has been a seaport, a cannery town, and a logging and fishing community. *Contact Astoria-Warrenton Area Chamber of Commerce | 111 W. Marine Dr., 97103-0176 | 503/325–6311 | www.oldoregon.com.*

Astoria Column. This monument, constructed atop 600-ft-high Coxcomb Hill, offers 14 chronologically arranged scenes of crucial historic events. As you ascend the 165 stairs winding around the 125-ft-high monolith sculpture, you will find murals depicting pre-17th century native wilderness, Captain Robert Gray's discovery of the Columbia River in 1792, the arrival of the Lewis and Clark expedition in 1805, the building of Fort Astoria, and several other milestones. The view from the top is astounding—you'll see the Astoria Bridge, the Pacific Ocean, the mouth of the Columbia River, Youngs Bay, various lakes, the shores of Washington State, the peaks of Mount St. Helens and Mount Rainier, and Saddle Mountain. | From U.S. 30 downtown take 16th St. south 1 mi to top of Coxcomb Hill | Free | Daily 9–dusk.

Columbia River Maritime Museum. This fascinating museum tells the story of the mighty Columbia, the river named by Captain Robert Gray in 1792. See, hear, and feel why they call the river the "Graveyard of the Pacific." The personal belongings of the ill-fated passengers of the 2,000 ships that have foundered here since 1811 are on view. | 1792 Marine Dr., at 17th St. | 503/325–2323 | www.crmm.org | $8 | Daily 9:30–5.

Flavel House. This prim and proper Victorian-era mansion was built between 1884 and 1886 and has six fireplaces and a fine library. Furnished in the Victorian style, the house reflects the tastes of shipping tycoon Captain George Flavel, a well-known and respected Columbia river pilot and entrepreneur. It it said that Flavel would get his river traffic reports by standing at the windows in the fourth-floor cupola. | 441 8th St., at Duane St. | 503/325–2203 | www.clatsophistoricalsociety.org | $5 | May–Sept., daily 10–5; Oct.–Apr., daily 11–4.

Fort Clatsop National Memorial. "Ocean in view! O! The joy!" recorded William Clark, standing on a spit of land south of present-day Astoria in the fall of 1805. Fort Clatsop is a faithful replica of the log stockade depicted in Clark's journal and utilized by the 33-member Lewis and Clark expedition as a winter encampment. Rooms are furnished with period hand-made leather clothing and artifacts. Park rangers, who dress in period garb during the summer and perform such early 19th-century tasks as making fire with flint and steel, lend an air of authenticity, as does the damp and lonely mood of the fort itself. | Fort Clatsop Loop Rd. (5 mi south of Astoria; from U.S. 101 cross Youngs Bay Bridge, turn east on Alt. U.S. 101, and follow signs) | 503/861–2471 | www.nps.gov.focl | $5 per vehicle | Mid-June–early Sept., daily 8–6; early Sept.–mid-June, daily 8–5.

Fort Stevens State Park. The park was once the site of a Clatsop Indian settlement, according to the writings of explorer William Clark. The park, 6 mi southwest of Astoria, has a museum of U.S. military history, a blacksmith shop, a replica of an Indian longhouse, Civil War–era cannon and rifle demonstrations daily, and guided tours. The corroded skeleton of the *Peter Iredale,* a turn-of-the-20th-century English four-master ship, protrudes from the sand just west of the Fort Stevens campground, a stark testament to the temperamental nature of the Pacific. | 1675 N.W. Peter Iredale Rd. | 503/861–1671 or 800/551–6949 | www.prd.state.or.us | $3 per vehicle | May–Oct., daily 10–6; Nov.–Apr., daily 10–4.

Salt Works. This stone camp is a memorial to the draining labors of members of Lewis and Clark's Corps of Discovery. The sight recognizes the endless work of explorers in 1805 as they continuously hauled up ocean water to campfires to boil it down for salt. From December 28 to February 21, 1806, the Salt Works operated continuously. | U.S. 101 to Seaside. Turn west on Ave. G and follow green signs to South Beach Dr. and Lewis and Clark Way | 503/861–2471 Ext. 214 | www.nps.gov/focl/salt.htm.

✦ ON THE CALENDAR: Aug. **Astoria Regatta Festival.** This maritime festival began in 1894 and is the oldest of its kind in the Northwest. Watch for the "Shanghaied in Astoria" melodrama and for the historic ships, which sometimes include replicas from the 17th and 18th centuries, that often arrive for the festival. It's held the second weekend in August along the Astoria Waterfront, with related events at other locations. | 503/325–6311.

BAKER CITY

▼▼▼

This town's claim to fame were its abundant surrounding goldfields. The Oregon Trail stretches through the midst of the rugged terrain surrounding the city, and pioneers trekking through Baker Valley in the mid-1800s had their first glimpse of Oregon Territory from here. When gold was discovered, travelers congregated here in hopes of gathering riches, and the settlement soon became a mining town. Colonel J. S. Ruckel, owner of a now-defunct gold-stamp mill along the banks of the Powder River, named the settlement Baker City in the 1860s. *Contact Baker County Chamber of Commerce | 490 Campbell St., 97814 | 541/523–5855 | www.visitbaker.com.*

National Historic Oregon Trail Interpretive Center. For immersion into pioneer life, this museum should be at the top of your list. The realistic, 100-ft-long pioneer train lets you join the 300,000 hardy travelers who headed west between 1841 and 1861 on the 2,000-mi journey from Missouri to the Columbia River. Wear comfortable walking shoes so you can follow the 4-mi round-trip trail, which winds through the surrounding terrain along the original ruts left by pioneer wagons. The center's indoor and outdoor theaters present plays, movies, and multimedia presentations relevant to events on the Oregon Trail. | Rte. 86 E, east of I–84 | 541/523–1843 | www.or.blm.gov/nhotic | $10 per vehicle | Apr.–Oct., daily 9–6; Nov.–Mar., daily 9–4.

Oregon Trail Regional Museum. Exhibits on gold mining, regional archaeology, and cowboy life fill this museum. Pore over the unusual pioneer implements, and check out the old-time vehicles—including a covered wagon and a firefighting wagon. | 2490 Grove St., at Campbell St. | 541/523–9308 | $3.50 | Mid-Apr.–Oct., daily 9–5; Nov.–mid-Apr., by appointment.

Sumpter Valley Railroad. Gold diggers rode this 1891 steam railway along the narrow-gauge line between Baker City and Prairie City. Today, the antique open-air cars wind through 5 mi of sculpted mountains where you'll have wildlife sightings aplenty—just keep an eye out for (mock) train robbers! The DeWitt Museum, which exhibits old railway photos and memorabilia, is housed inside the depot. | Rte. 7, Sumpter, 25 mi southwest of Baker City | 800/523–1235 | www.svry.com | Train $9 | Railroad late May–Sept., weekends; museum Thurs.–Sat. 10–3.

U.S. Bank. Gold coins, gold leaf, pea gold, crystallized gold, gold nuggets, and more show off the region's finds and creations during Old West times. The pride of the collection is the 6¾-pound Armstrong Nugget, found on June 19, 1913, in Grant County. | 2000 Main St. | 541/523–7791 or 800/872–2657 | www.usbank.com | Free | Mon.–Thurs. 10–5. Fri. 10–6.

✦ ON THE CALENDAR: July **Miners' Jubilee.** All of Baker City gathers for this raucous celebration, which includes a fierce old-time fiddling competition and gold-panning contests. | 541/523–5855.

GHOST TOWNS OF EASTERN OREGON

Dusty, windswept streets and ramshackle clapboard buildings occupy many ghost towns in eastern Oregon. Each settlement has its own story and is open for exploring year-round—plus, they're convenient to reach, given that many are within an hour's drive of Baker City. Here you can immerse yourself in pioneer times.

Along Route 7 heading east from Baker City, the closest ghost town is Auburn, established on Blue Canyon Creek in 1862. Supposedly the site of the first gold rush in eastern Oregon, the town quickly declined after prospectors moved on to other gold finds in the mid-1860s.

One of the best-known ghost towns is Sumpter, established in 1862 by settlers who intended to farm the rich countryside. Gold prospectors took over after gold was discovered nearby, and mining, dredging, and logging soon became major industries. The land and riverbanks became eroded, ruining any farming potential, and many settlers moved on after the early 1900s. Newer buildings, a museum, and rail depot were later added to attract tourists, who often outnumber the town's meager population of under 200.

Northeast of Sumpter is Bourne, a town originally called Cracker, which was later renamed after Senator Johnathon Bourne. There's just one long main street, framed by cliffs that prevented the town from growing any direction but sideways. Although a flood in 1937 washed away most of the residences, many of the original buildings—including the 1895 post office—still remain.

Whitney was the main depot station on the 80-mi, narrow-gauge Sumpter Valley Railroad. At its peak, the town housed 14 rail crews, as well as 75 people who worked at the sawmill to supply lumber for the gold-mining camps. When the mill burned down in 1918, settlers left to find other prospects. Many of the original buildings remain, including several cabins, a farmhouse, and the mill.

South of The Dalles, Shaniko is one of the West's most attractive ghost towns, complete with all the original buildings but with added tourist facilities. Built in 1898, the settlement began as a simple rail depot for moving wool from the surrounding sheep ranches to the processing facilities in The Dalles. You can take a walking tour past the old sheep pastures, a barn full of antique cars, a water tower, the schoolhouse, and the chapel—where more than 300 weddings are performed each summer.

July **Pioneer Heritage Festival.** On the last Saturday of the month, the Oregon Trail Interpretive Center presents a daylong festival of living history, which includes goldsmiths, trappers, and artisans demonstrating their crafts in period costume. Pioneer recipes and children's games make this a great family event. | 541/523–1843.

HISTORIC DINING AND LODGING

Geiser Grand Hotel. Built in 1889 to house lucky pioneers who struck it rich during the peak gold-rush days, this National Historic Landmark hotel still drips with Old West poshness. Guest rooms have crystal chandeliers, antiques, luxury bathrooms, and 10-ft windows with views of either the town's historic district or of the distant, snow-covered mountains. Relax in the enormous Palm Court beneath a suspended stained-glass ceiling, or dine on the city's finest American and Italian fare in the Swan restaurant. Restaurant, room service, cable TV, in-room data ports, in-room VCRs, gym, hair salon, bar, library, laundry service, concierge, business services, meeting room, free parking; no-smoking floor. | 1996 Main St., 97814 | 541/523–1889 or 888/434–7374 | fax 541/523–1800 | www.geisergrand.com | 30 rooms | $79–$209 | AE, D, MC, V | BP.

BEND

▾▾

Nestled between the snow-capped Cascades and the winding Deschutes River, Bend was orig-inally a timber mill town named for Farewell Bend, the last curve of the river. Today, with around 35,000 people—many of whom came for an outdoor-oriented vacation and decided to stay—Bend is Oregon's largest city east of the Cascades. *Contact Bend Chamber/Visitor and Convention Bureau |63085 N. U.S. 97, 97701 |541/382–3221 |www.bendchamber.org. Crook County Historical Society | 246 N. Main St., Prineville, 97754 | 541/447–3715.*

A. R. Bowman Memorial Museum. The original structure at this location was a wooden, one-story drugstore built in 1883. The stone replacement, built in 1910, was a bank for many years. Today you can walk through the first-floor Hall of History, amid original bank fixtures, to view black-and-white photos and pioneer implements that highlight the town of Prineville's booming days as the cattle-ranching and logging center of Crook County. On the second floor are walk-through displays, including a post office, general store, and lending library. The Wright Cabin and Ranchers' Memorial on-site lets you experience the past first-hand as you walk among the stuff of pioneer life. | 246 N. Main St., Prineville, northeast of Bend | 503/447–3715 | www.bowmanmuseum.org | $1 suggested donation | Feb.–Dec., Tues.–Fri. 10–5, Sat. 11–4.

Deschutes Historical Museum. The name honors a local Indian tribe, and some exhibits focus on local native artifacts. Photos of the original town and the surrounding settlements offer a glimpse of pioneer life in the Old West. Give your kids a fun dose of the way it used to be by making them sit in the old schoolroom for a mock lesson. | 129 N.W. Idaho | 541/389–1813 | Free | Tues.–Sat. 10–4:30.

High Desert Museum. This 150-acre complex, which traces the lives and legends of North-west pioneers, miners, and cowboys, is one of the best in the state. Walk-through dioramas—including a stone-age Indian campsite, a pioneer wagon camp, a mine, and a settler's cabin—are full of artifacts that capture the character of each era. | 59800 S. U.S. 97, 3½ mi south of Bend | 541/382–4754 | www.highdesert.org | $7.75 | Daily 9–5.

HISTORIC LODGING

Lara House Bed & Breakfast Inn. In the midst of Bend's historic district and just a two-block stroll from downtown, this bright, comfortable 1910 Craftsman-style home provides pleas-ant views of Drake Park from beneath high eaves. Cozy, sunny second-floor rooms with seat-ing areas and private baths are done in period furnishings, with soft pastel accents. Breakfast, served on lace tablecloths in the dining room, is included, as are snacks at the daily after-noon guest get-togethers. Dining room, library, laundry service, free parking; no-smoking. | 640 N.W. Congress St., 97701 | 800/766–4064 | fax 541/388–4064 | www.larahouse.com | 6 rooms | $95–$150 | AE, D, DC, MC, V | BP.

Sather House Bed & Breakfast Inn. The star of Bend's "Historic Homes Tour" brochure, this Colonial Revival home has been a prominent listing in the town's premier residential neigh-borhood since 1911. Guest quarters have floral accents and hand-sewn quilts and are furnished with such period antiques as a picket-fence headboard and a 1910 clawfoot tub. A well-prepared breakfast is served in the formal dining room. Dining room, library, recre-ation room, laundry service, free parking; no-smoking rooms. | 7 N.W. Tumalo, 97701 | 541/338–1065 | fax 541/330–0591 | www.satherhouse.com | 4 rooms | $88–$126 | D, MC, V | BP.

BURNS

▼▼

A cowboy town from the start, and still a compact settlement of just 3,000 residents, Burns is the gathering spot for those who live amid the grasslands of Harney County. The area doesn't see many visitors, other than those intent on outdoor pursuits in the nearby Steens Mountains or the Malheur National Wildlife Refuge, 30 mi to the south. This section of the state is ideal for exploring landscapes and towns that are nearly unchanged from pioneer days. *Contact Harney County Chamber of Commerce | 76 E. Washington St., 97720 | 541/573–2636 | www.harneycounty.com.*

Harney County Historical Museum. Housed in a former brewery, this compact museum traces the county's history through photos and knickknacks. Handmade quilts and other crafts adorn the walls and displays, so you can see the time and care put into decorating the homes of the times. Just for fun, imagine trying to throw a dinner party using only the implements in the turn-of-the-20th-century kitchen exhibit. | 18 W. D St. | 541/573–5618 | Free | May–Oct., Tues.–Sat. 9–5.

Pete French Round Barn. Cattle baron Pete French Diamond, one of Oregon's most prominent early ranchers, once owned more than a dozen ranches covering almost 1.5 million acres that supported 45,000-plus cattle. His unusual Round Barn, built in 1883, was 100 ft in diameter with a 60-ft lava-rock corral inside and was used to train horses during the winter. To get to the barn, drive 43 mi south of Burns on Rte. 205, then about 15 mi east on the road to Diamond. | Diamond Station, Frenchglen | No phone | Donation | Daily 8–4.

✦ ON THE CALENDAR: Sept. **Harney County Rodeo and Fair.** This family-style rodeo is held at the county's cowboy showgrounds. Spanning the week after Labor Day, it draws close to 30,000 people, both local and out-of-state, who come to see the animal exhibits, handmade crafts, carnival rides, and bucking-bronco competitions. | 541/573–6852.

HISTORIC LODGING

Ponderosa Cattle Company Guest Ranch. This 120,000-acre spread, built in 1860, is the definition of a true Northwest cattle ranch. The owners take pride in their rustic accommodations and basic activity format: sleep, eat, and ranch—which here includes riding along with the cowboys to rope, herd, and brand the herd of more than 4,000. Eight log cabins have three rooms each with private baths, and no phones, TVs, or cellular service keeps things quiet at night. The main lodge, complete with a library, stone fireplace, and bar, is great for relaxing after a hard day's work. Sate your appetite with hearty, home-cooked ranch-style meals. The ranch is in Seneca, 45 mi north of Burns on U.S. 395. Dining room, hiking, horseback riding, bar, library, recreation room, shop, laundry service, travel services, free parking; no kids under 18, no room TVs. | U.S. 395, Seneca, 97873 | 541/542–2403 or 800/331–0102 | fax 541/542–2713 | www.ponderosa-ranch.com | 24 rooms | $775–$875 for 3-day package, $1,350–$1,600 for 6-day package | AE, D, DC, MC, V | FAP.

Steens Mountain Resort. This elegant resort is housed in a two-story dance hall, moved from a nearby ghost town and combined with the home of Frenchglen's first schoolteacher. The place is pure Northwest, with Native American artifacts, black-and-white photos, and works by regional artists. A wide cedar deck connects second-floor bedrooms that overlook Steens Mountain and Blitzen Valley. Located 60 mi south of Burns on Route 205, the hotel is the base for the area's only wilderness guide service, so plan time for plenty of hiking and learning about the area's history. Dining room, room service, hiking, library, recreation room, laundry service, travel services, free parking; no room TVs. | Rte. 205, Frenchglen, 97736 | 541/493–2738 | fax 541/493–2835 | 2 rooms | $135–$150 | AE, D, MC, V | FAP.

COOS BAY

▼▼

Originally named Marshfield, Coos Bay has been synonymous with boat traffic since the early 1800s. In those days a mosquito fleet of small boats, ferries, and stern-wheelers ferried people and services up and down the coast daily. In the 1850s, logging, coal mining, agriculture, and ship building bolstered Coos Bay development. *Contact Bay Area Chamber of Commerce | 50 E. Central, Coos Bay 97420 | 800/824–8486 | www.oregonsbayareachamber.com.*

Coos County Historical Society Museum. In this small, homespun museum are exhibits on life in Coos County from Native American times to the early 20th century. A butter churn, wood stove, and other items from a pioneer kitchen; a piano and other furnishings from a family doctor's parlor; and baskets, a canoe, and other Native American artifacts are among the assortment of objects on display. | 1220 Sherman Ave. | 541/756–6320 | www.cooshistory. org | $2 | Tues.–Sat. 10–4.

Marshfield Sun Printing Museum. This five-sided building contains all of the printing equipment used by the *Sun* newspaper, a weekly that began publication in 1891 and continued until 1944. The museum also exhibits photographs of early Marshfield and river transportation. Call the Coos Bay Chamber of Commerce for tour information. | 1049 N. Front St. | 800/824–8486.

Umpqua River Lighthouse. Some of the highest sand dunes in the country are found in the 50-acre Umpqua Lighthouse Park. The first lighthouse here, built on the dunes at the mouth of the Umpqua River in 1857, lasted only four years before it toppled over in a storm. It took local residents 33 years to build another one. The Douglas County Coastal Visitors Center, adjacent to the lighthouse, offers a brief history of Douglas County. | Umpqua Hwy. north of Coos Bay off U.S. 101 | 541/271–4118 | Donation | Lighthouse May–Sept., Wed.–Sat. 10–4, Sun. 1–4.

EUGENE

▼▼

The first white settler to take up residence in what is now Eugene was Eugene Franklin Skinner, who built his cabin in 1846. The home served as a general trading post and was authorized as a post office in 1850. Skinner, along with Judge David Risdon, are credited with platting and recording Eugene City in 1852. In its early days, heavy winter rains reduced the town to a mud slick, earning it the nickname Skinner's Mud Hole. Thankfully, the town was replatted on higher ground in 1853. Settlers and industry came hand in hand to Eugene. A flour mill, woolen mill, and saw mill were soon established along the banks of the Willamette River, and by 1859 there were upwards of 500 people in the city. Imagine a settlement town served by two bookstores, two printing offices, three doctors, nine dry-goods stores, two hotels, and several other key services associated with much older cities to get a picture of this well-heeled pioneer town. *Contact Lane County Convention and Visitors Association | 115 Olive St., between 7th and 8th Aves. | 800/547–5445 | www.visitlanecounty.org.*

Lane County Historical Museum. An endpoint for many emigrants of the Oregon Trail, Lane County played an important role in national and Northwest history. The county-museum collections represent the area's history, dating from the 1840s, in commerce, architecture, entertainment, and more. Exhibits include period rooms and vehicles, implements from early mill and other key trades, memorabilia from the Oregon Trail and early settlements, and historic photographs. | 740 W. 13th Ave. | 541/682–4239 | $2 | Wed.–Fri. 10–4, Sat. noon–4; archives by appointment.

University of Oregon. The true heart of Eugene lies southeast of the city center at its university, founded in 1876. Several fine buildings can be seen on the 250-acre campus; Deady Hall (1877) is one of the university's first buildings. Look for bronze sculptures by Alexander Proctor, *Pioneer* and *Pioneer Mother,* dedicated to the men and women who settled Oregon Territory. | Main entrance: Agate St. and Franklin Blvd. | Free | Daily.

Bohemia Mining District. This is a great place to experience the mid-19th century gold rush. In the Bohemia Mountains east of the town of Cottage Grove, prospectors found gold in 1863. The strike wasn't huge, but gold mining in the area continues to this day. (Check with the Cottage Grove Ranger Station before visiting so you don't trespass on any active mining claims.) Bohemia City is now a ghost town, and there are covered bridges and abandoned mines sprinkled through the hills. | 78405 Cedar Park Rd., 21 mi south of Eugene on I-5, then 40 mi east of Cottage Grove | 541/942–5591 | Free | Daily.

In the town of Cottage Grove, the **Cottage Grove Historical Museum** (Birch and H St. | 541/942–3963) has exhibits about the Bohemia Mining District.

✦ ON THE CALENDAR: July **Bohemia Mining Days Celebration.** A celebration of Old West Oregon kicks off when the Grand Miner's Parade marches down Cottage Grove's Main Street, the only road in the world paved in gold. A gold-panning championship, a simulated shoot-out, and a Native American powwow hosted by the Confederated Tribes Rogue Table and Associated Tribes make July the time to visit Cottage Grove. | 541/942–5501 | www. cottagegrove.org.

GOLD BEACH
▾▾

Gold Beach was christened with a name that reflects the glittering precious metal found in its sands. The town was one of the first in Oregon to be affected by the gold rush as the fervor moved up from California, just 37 mi south. The mighty glittering grains were discovered in the sand near the mouth of the Rogue River in 1853. At the time, rough and rugged prospectors poured into the area and set up sluice boxes first on the beach and later up and down the rivers and streams of the area. *Contact Gold Beach Chamber of Commerce | 29279 Ellensburg Ave., No. 3, 97444 | 541/247–7526 or 800/525–2334 | www. harborside.com/gb.*

Cape Blanco Light Station. With its 59-ft tower, this isolated lighthouse, first lit on December 20, 1870, holds at least four Oregon records: it is the oldest continuously operating light, the most westerly, the highest above the sea (245 ft), and was overseen by Oregon's first woman keeper, Mable E. Bretherton, who signed on in 1903. The tour takes you to the keepers' workroom and up 64 steps to the lantern room, where the famed Parisian Fresnel lens resides. Also in the park is the Hughes House. Built in 1898, the Hughes ranch is a testament to the 38 years of hard work and toil of Irishman Patrick Hughes and his wife. Over the years, the Hugheses' ranch grew to 2,000 acres and employed up to 14 ranch hands to produce some of the finest butter available in the West. Special Christmas open houses are held in mid-December. | North off U.S. 101 | 541/332–6774 state park; 541/332–2750 lighthouse | Free | Park daily dawn–dusk; lighthouse Apr.–Oct., Thurs.–Mon. 10–3:30.

Curry County Historical Museum. The museum houses rare and curious artifacts dating back to the mid-19th century. The "R. D. Hume, Salmon King" exhibit looks back at the Gold Beach entrepreneur who caught and packaged salmon in the region while publishing the *Radium,* a local newspaper. The "Day in the Life" exhibit about pioneer settlers contains authentic artifacts from woodstoves to musical instruments. The museum also offers an interesting display of early hospital machines and medical instruments from the old Curry General

Hospital. | Alice Wakeman Memorial Bldg., 29410 S. Ellensburg Ave. | 541/247–6113 | www.curryhistory.com | Tues.–Sat. 10–4.

Rogue River Mail Boat Trips. The mail-boat company has provided continuous postal service ever since it started by meeting the communication needs of remote settlers and miners living in the wilderness of the Rogue River canyon. The service allowed settlers to send and receive letters and packages, often from distant relatives. You can ride along on its 64-, 80-, or 104-mi trips along the Rogue River. Keep an eye out for bears. | Mail Boat Dock, U.S. 101, 37 mi north of California-Oregon border | 541/247–7033 or 800/458–3511 | www.mailboat.com | $34–$75 | May–Oct., daily; call for hrs.

GRANTS PASS

▼▼

The first settlers in the area named their postal stop Grant in honor of Union general Ulysses S. Grant. As it turned out, there was already a Grant, Oregon, so the town decided to take the name Grant's Pass. Over time the apostrophe fell out of use by the locals. The arrival of the Southern Pacific Railroad in 1883 put Grants Pass on the map as the terminus. A railroad depot was built along the tracks right in the center of what is now 6th Street. Southern Oregonians from the Medford-Jacksonville area had to come here to catch the train or ship goods. Many took up residence in the growing town because of the depot. *Contact Grants Pass/Josephine County Chamber of Commerce | 1995 N.W. Vine St., 97526 | 541/476–7717 | www.grantspasschamber.org. Grants Pass Visitors and Convention Bureau | 1995 N.W. Vine St.,, 97526 | 541/476–5510 | www.visitgrantspass.org. Josephine County Historical Society | 508 SW Fifth St., Grants Pass, 97526 | 541/479–7827 | www.webtrail.com/jchs/index.html.*

Applegate Trail Interpretive Center. This center celebrates those who traveled the southern route of the Oregon Trail, known as the Applegate Trail. The trail was laid by brothers Jesse and Lindsey Applegate after they both lost their sons on the wild Columbia River portion of the Oregon Trail. The Applegates swore they'd find a safer route to the Willamette Valley. Exhibits focus on gold mining, the impact of the stagecoach in the region, a visit from President Rutherford Hayes in 1878, and the influence of the railroad. Antique cabins and reconstructed wagons give the museum its life-size feel. The relocated log town-hall building is also on the property. | 500 Sunny Valley Loop Sunny Valley, 14 mi north of Grants Pass | 541/472–8548 or 888/411–1846 | www.rogueweb.com/interpretive | Donations accepted | Mid-Mar.–mid-Nov., daily 10-5, mid-Nov–mid-Mar. Wed.–Sun. 10-5.

Indian Mary Park. On the banks of the Rogue River, Indian Mary Park was established in 1884, when President Grover Cleveland signed legislation making the area the smallest Indian reservation in the United States. The reservation was created as thanks to Umpqua Joe, a local Indian who in 1855 warned settlers of a pending massacre by other local Indians. The park, named for Joe's daughter, offers many points of historic interest chronicling Indian battles, gold-mining efforts of early settlers, and evidence of Chinese labor camps, all highlighted by historical markers. | 10 mi west of I–5 at Exit 61 (follow Merlin-Galice Rd. west to park) | 541/474–5285 | www.co.josephine.or.us/parks | $5 overnight parking, camping varies | Year-round.

Kerbyville Museum. Dedicated to documenting area Native American and pioneer history, the Kerbyville Museum is showcased in an 1871 home that is listed on the National Register of Historic Places. If you have ever wondered about your own pioneer or mining heritage, the museum's research library may help you locate ancestors. Kids'll love the taxidermy exhibited here. Kerby is 27 mi southwest of Grants Pass on Route 199. | 24195 Redwood Hwy., Kerby | 541/592–5252 | $3 | Mid-May–mid-Sept., Mon.–Sat. 10–5, Sun. noon–5; mid-Sept.–mid-May, by appointment only.

HISTORIC DINING AND LODGING

Wolf Creek Inn. Originally named the Six Bit House (a room went for 75¢), Wolf Creek Inn was built in 1883; it is the oldest continuously operated hotel in the Pacific Northwest. The inn, known throughout southern Oregon as a first-class traveler's hotel, served passengers making the 16-day stagecoach trip between Portland and San Francisco. Rooms are outfitted to resemble the inn's turn-of-the-20th-century accommodations, with wood or iron bedsteads and handmade quilts. In the rustic Wolf Creek Tavern ($10–$20), hearty country dishes such as herb-roasted chicken and grilled salmon are served. The inn is 20 mi north of Grants Pass at Exit 76 on I–5. Restaurant, no room phones, no room TVs, no pets, no smoking. | 100 Front St., Wolf Creek, 97497 | 541/866–2474 | fax 541/866–2692 | www.thewolfcreekinn.com | 8 rooms, 1 suite | $80–$107 | AE, MC, V | BP | Closed Mon.–Tues. Oct.–Apr.

JACKSONVILLE

▼▼▼

A historical showcase, the gold-rush town of Jacksonville was founded in the 1850s and is designated a National Historic Landmark Community. The main street here looks as if it were built for a western movie and has actually been used in a few. More than 90 original brick and wooden buildings, dating back to the 1850s, remain in town, offering an up-close glimpse of pioneer life. Summer is the best time to visit Jacksonville. Horse-drawn carriage rides, cable-car tours, and the renowned Peter Britt Music Festival are summer highlights. *Contact Jacksonville Chamber of Commerce | 185 N. Oregon St., 97530 | 541/899–8118 | www. jacksonvilleoregon.org.*

Butte Creek Mill. This 1872 water-powered flour gristmill is listed in the National Register of Historic Places and is still a working mill. The giant stones that were originally purchased from a quarry in France, shipped to California, and packed over the Sisiyous mountains by wagon, are still in use in the mill. If you're lucky you may just see a miller grinding the grains. | 402 Royal Ave. N, Eagle Point | 541/826–3531 | www.buttecreekmill.com | Free | Mon.–Sat. 9–5.

C. C. Beekman House. History comes alive as actors dressed in costumes of the period portray the banker C. C. Beekman and his family at this 1876 house. Take a close look at the original furnishings and other essentials of the mid-19th century wealthy. The house is situated on historic California Street in the center of Jacksonville. The street's colorful balustraded brick buildings have been wonderfully restored to their original grandeur and are just one of the many reasons the entire town of Jacksonville is registered as a National Historic Landmark. The Beekman Bank, established in 1863, is also open to the public. | 352 E. California St. | 541/773–6536 | $2 | Late May–early Sept., daily 1–5.

Children's Museum. This museum in the 1920 Jackson County Jail has hands-on exhibits of pioneer life and a great collection of antique toys. Young pioneers will love the Indian tepee and old-fashioned (circa 1890) store. | 206 N. 5th St. | 541/773–6536 | www.sohs.org | $3 | Wed.–Sat. 10–5, Sun. noon–5.

Gin Lin Mining Trail. Once gold fever claimed California, it was only a matter of time before prospectors came clamoring to the Siskiyou Mountains of southern Oregon. This very informative interpretive trail winds for nearly a mile through a mining site dating from the 1850s. Start your tour at Applegate Ranger District. | 6941 Upper Applegate Rd. | 541/899–3800.

Jacksonville Museum of Southern Oregon History. Inside the old Jackson County Courthouse, you'll find the Jacksonville Museum and its intriguing gold rush–era artifacts. The "Miner, Baker, Furniture Maker" exhibit lays out the area's history in terms of its industrial development. "History in the Making" follows the footsteps of early residents who experienced some of the historic milestones of Jackson County, including the first doctor to serve the region, brave pioneers, and Chinese sojourners who arrived with the gold rush. | 206 N. 5th St. | 541/773–6536 | $3 for each museum, Pass for both $7 | Late May–Sept., daily 11–5; Oct.–late May, Tues.–Sun. 11–5.

✦ ON THE CALENDAR: Dec. **Jacksonville Victorian Christmas.** Get a real taste of Christmas in the 19th century at the Jacksonville Victorian Christmas celebration, offering horse-drawn wagons, tree lighting, caroling, historic characters in period dress, and visits from St. Nicholas. The celebration begins with a Grand Parade and tree lighting the first Friday in December. Activities continue at different locations in the city throughout December. | 541/899–8118 or 541/899–1001 | www.jacksonvilleoregon.org.

KLAMATH FALLS

▼▼

The city has deep pioneer roots, as travelers across the Oregon plains often paused here to collect water at Klamath Lake, the largest freshwater lake in the state. Finding year-round sunshine, they concluded the climate wasn't bad either, and it wasn't long before hundreds of settlers were calling the area home. *Contact Klamath County Department of Tourism and Visitors Center | 507 Main St., 97601 | 800/445–6728 | www.klamathcounty.net.*

Collier Memorial State Park and Logging Museum. At this logging site, you'll find an old cabin housing 1880s lumbering implements such as axes, splints, and saws. | 46000 U.S. 97, Chiloquin, 30 mi north of Klamath Falls | 541/783–2471 | www.collierloggingmuseum.org | Free | May–Oct., daily 8–8; Nov.–Apr., daily 8–4.

Fort Klamath Museum and Park. This 8-acre site includes the original buildings from the area's 1863 frontier military post. Constructed to protect pioneers from Indian attack, the fort today houses old-fashioned tools and cookware, uniforms, and tribal costumes and jewelry. | Rte. 62 44 mi north of Klamath Falls | 541/381–2230 | Donation requested | June–early Sept., daily 10–6.

Klamath County Museum. The Klamath Basin has yielded all sorts of archaeological finds, many of which you'll find at this museum. Fossils, tribal tools, pioneer clothing and cookware, and regional wildlife are thoroughly covered. In summer a replica street trolley runs between this museum and the Baldwin Hotel Museum. | 1451 Main St. | 541/883–4208 | $2 | Early Sept.–late May, Tues.–Sat. 8–4:30; late May–early Sept., Tues.–Sat. 9–5:30.

Senator George Baldwin Hotel Museum. Guided tours of this small museum focus on regional history, including historic photographs of local life. In summer a replica street trolley runs between this museum and the Klamath County Museum. | 31 Main St. | 541/883–4207 or 541/883–4208 | www.kchs.org | $4 | June–Sept., Tues.–Sat. 9–4.

HISTORIC DINING AND LODGING

Prospect Historical Hotel. This famous stagecoach stop has housed travelers and explorers since 1872. The owners don't like to name-drop about previous guests, but they do have antiques-filled, period-style guest rooms named for Zane Grey, Jack London, and Teddy Roosevelt. A newer motel unit in back has some kitchenettes and accepts pets. The Dinner House restaurant (open seasonally for dinner only) serves pasta, seafood, and European fare. Restaurant, dining room, some kitchenettes, library, laundry service, free parking, some pets allowed. | 391 Mill Creek Dr., Prospect, 30 mi northwest of Klamath Falls, 97536 | 541/560–3664 or 800/944–6490 | fax 541/560–3825 | www.prospecthotel.com | 23 rooms, 1 suite | $80–$145 | D, DC, MC, V | BP.

NEWPORT

▼▼▼

One of the largest commercial fishing fleets on the Oregon coast operates out of the historic bayfront of Newport. The area's abundance of seafood, most notably Dungeness crab, has been famous since the mid-1800s, when the Yaquina Bay oyster beds were first discovered. Lighthouses, which you can tour along with neighboring tide pools, dot the coastal area along U.S. 101 and at Yaquina Head. *Contact Greater Newport Chamber of Commerce | 555 S. W. Coast Hwy., 97365 | 541/265–8801 or 800/262–7844 | www.newportnet.com.*

Yaquina Bay State Park. Located at the north end of Yaquina Bay near its outlet to the Pacific, this park contains a lighthouse built in 1871. The Yaquina Bay lighthouse was once used as a Coast Guard Lifeboat Station. It's been restored to its original appearance and includes 19th-century furnishings and an interpretive exhibit. | U.S. 101 S, north end of Yaquina Bridge in Newport | 541/867–7451 | Donation | Late May–Sept., daily 11–5; Oct.–late May, daily noon–4.

Yaquina Head Lighthouse. The tallest lighthouse on the Oregon coast is the 93-ft Yaquina Head Lighthouse, built in 1872. The lighthouse is now part of the Yaquina Head Outstanding Natural Area, whose history is well represented in the nearby Interpretive Center. The center mounts exhibits on seabirds and marine and intertidal life and captures the human history of this coastal jewel. You'll see the wheelhouse of an old ship and a full-scale replica of the lighthouse lantern. A re-creation of the rocky island and its inhabitants helps you picture the rich history of Yaquina Head. | 5 mi north of Newport | 541/574–3146 | $10 per vehicle, plus $1 per passenger | Daily dawn–dusk.

OREGON CITY

▼▼▼

The first incorporated city west of the Rocky Mountains and the first capital of Oregon's territorial government in 1848, this was the destination for thousands of pioneer families who traveled the Oregon Trail in hopes of settling on the western frontier. Several of Oregon's prominent early residents built homes in Oregon City on the Willamette River's east bank, including the "Father of Oregon," Dr. John McLoughlin. Dozens of historic homes, churches, and other buildings have been restored and offer tours into times past. *Contact Oregon City Chamber of Commerce | 1810 Washington St., Box 226, 97045 | 503/656–1619 | www.oregoncity.org.*

Baker Cabin Historic Site and Pioneer Church. This 3-acre historic site marks the spot where stone mason Horace Baker and his wife, Jane, built their house in 1856. The two-story cabin was created out of 12-inch square-hewn logs without any nails or pegs. It is the only cantilevered log cabin in Oregon. The little white Pioneer Church also located here was built in 1895 by German immigrants. | Take Exit 12A off I–205 east of Oregon City; site is 5 mi east of exit in Upper Logan area | 503/631–8274 | www.bakercabin.org | Free | Grounds daily, dawn–dusk; cabin open summer only, dates and hours vary.

End of the Oregon Trail Interpretive Center. This exceptional center is on land first claimed by George Abernethy, merchant, miller, and first governor of Oregon County. Abernethy was revered for allowing emigrants from the East to park their wagons, graze their oxen, and set up camp on a meadow behind his house. The interpretive center now stands in the same spot that many of those pioneers called the end of the Oregon Trail. Special docents, or Trail Guides, makes this the best place in Oregon to get the big picture of Oregon's pioneer history from the arrival of the first fur traders to the arrival of the railroad. The center offers daily showings of "The Spirit Lives On!," a multimedia presentation using special effects, panoramic screens, and quotes from Oregon Trail diaries to enrich the telling of a truly epic story. | 1726 Washington St. | 503/657–9336 | www.endoftheoregontrail.org | $6.50 | Center hrs and show times vary seasonally; call to confirm.

Foster Farm. The farm here was built in the late 1840s by Philip Foster, one of Oregon's earliest settlers and the first treasurer of the provisional government. Foster funded pioneer Sam Barlow's construction of the Barlow Road, the road that brought emigrants from The Dalles, over treacherous Mount Hood and into the Willamette Valley, allowing them to avoid travel along the deadly Columbia River. The farm, situated on 640 acres in Eagle Creek at the end of the Barlow Road, was remembered as a place of welcome warmth in many diaries of emigrants coming off of Mount Hood. The homestead appears much as it was at the turn of the 20th century. The frame house has been preserved, and it is shaded by the oldest lilac in Oregon. You can tour the farm's original blacksmith shop, an 1860s barn, and an apple orchard, planted with what are now considered antique or heirloom apples. | Take Exit 12A off I–205 and follow signs to Rte. 224. Turn north on Rte. 211 and look for signs to farm at Eagle Creek, east of Oregon City | 503/630–5051 or 503/637–6324 | Free | Mid-June–Aug., Fri.–Sun. 11–4; Sept., weekends 11–4.

McLoughlin House National Historic Site. Dr. John McLoughlin, who crossed the Rockies in 1824 and established Fort Vancouver in 1825, claimed land in Oregon City for the Hudson Bay Company in 1829. When he retired in 1845 he bought back a portion of the land to build an elegant home near Willamette Falls. McLoughlin and his family lived there until his death in 1857, but industrial development along the falls waterway led to the home's relocation to Center Street in 1909. The home and furnishings of the man the region's legislature called the Father of Oregon have been fully restored to their mid-19th century grandeur. | 713 Center St. | 503/656–5146 | www.mcloughlinhouse.org | $4 | Feb.–Dec., Tues.–Sat. 10–4, Sun. 1–4.

Old Aurora Colony Museum. In 1856 a group of German immigrants, followers of Dr. Wilhelm Keil, purchased land alongside Pudding River to create a Christian community. Keil was a charismatic Prussian tailor, self-styled physician, and preacher who had arrived in the United States in 1831. The Keil colonists worked hard and lived simply, much like the Shakers. At its height, the colony owned 13,000 acres and had more than 600 members. It was known far and wide for its hospitality, farms, orchards, and music. The colony was disbanded in 1883 but some of the simple homes remain, and a museum offers a taste of Old West communal living. | 503/678–5754 | www.auroracolonymuseum.com | $3.50 | Mid-Oct.–mid-Apr., Fri.–Sat. 10–4, Sun. noon–4; mid-Apr.–mid-Oct., Tues.–Sat. 10–4, Sun. noon–4.

The Rose Farm Museum. William and Louisa Holmes and their children completed their home in 1847, one of the first in Oregon City. The home's second-floor ballroom was the ipso facto social, legislative, and entertainment center of the region. In fact, it is the only known building in which both provisional and territorial legislatures met. The name Rose Farm came from Louisa's love and nurturing of early mission roses. Period furnishings, historical documents from early legislative activities, and the famous roses are worth the visit. | Holmes La. at Rilance St. | 503/656–5146 or 503/245–0588 | www.mcloughlinhouse.org/rosefarm.html | Free | Apr.–Oct., Sun. 1–4.

PENDLETON

▼▼

Pendleton—with its rich pioneer heritage, its museums, and its Oregon Trail sites—is a major stop on any Old West itinerary. Buildings such as the Pendleton Wooden Mills, the Shamrock Card Room, Hop Sing's Chinese Laundry, and the Cozy Room bordello are now part of the city's famous Underground tour. The region's biggest event, the Pendleton Round-

Up, was launched in 1910 by a group of eastern Oregon farmers and has been held every September since to celebrate the harvest and show off Pendleton's fine livestock and produce. *Contact Pendleton Chamber of Commerce/Visitors Bureau | 501 S. Main, 97801 | 541/276–7411 or 800/547–8911 | www.pendleton-oregon.org.*

Oregon Trail Interpretive Park. Shaded pine paths lead to remnants of the historic pioneer route at this serene outdoor museum. A paved trail with information panels is easy enough for the whole family to walk, and there's a forest trailhead if you want to walk farther. There is a picnic area if you want to bring lunch. | Blue Mountain Crossing La Grande, I–84 Exit 248 | 800/848–9669 | $3 | Daily 9–5.

Pendleton Underground Tour. Experience life in 19th-century Pendleton on this colorful 90-minute tour. You'll first head into a subterranean labyrinth of gambling rooms, opium dens, and cramped Chinese laborers' quarters—remnants of the days when the town had no fewer than 32 saloons and 18 brothels—followed by a visit to Madame Stella Darby's bordello. Call for information and tour schedules; reservations are strongly recommended. | 37 S.W. Emigrant Ave. | 541/276–0730 or 800/226–6398 | www.pendletonundergroundtours.com | $10 | Mon.–Sat. 9–5.

Round-Up Hall of Fame Museum. Wander amid a broad selection of photographs, costumes, saddles, guns, and other rodeo memorabilia to get a feel for the region's main event, the Pendleton Rodeo. The pictures tell some great stories in one shot—look for the Rodeo Queens and the Happy Canyon Princesses (all Native American). Don't miss War Paint, the stuffed championship bronco. | Round-Up Grounds, 1205 S.W. Court Ave., near S.W. 12th St. | 541/278–0815 | Free | May–Oct., daily 10–5; Nov.–Apr., by appointment.

Umatilla County Historical Society Museum. Housed in a 1909 railway depot, this museum depicts the lives and times of Pendleton residents through photos, publications, and other memorabilia. The fascinating exhibits show the different events and legacies of the farmers, loggers, ranchers, missionaries, explorers and others who made the town their home. | 108 S.W. Frazer Ave. | 541/276–0012 | $2 | Tues.–Sat. 10–4.

✦ ON THE CALENDAR: July **Oregon Trail Days.** Locals never miss this traditional celebration of pioneer heritage, held in La Grande, 53 mi south of Pendleton on I–84. Tour a replica pioneer camp, make old-time crafts, and sample the buffalo barbecue. Don't miss the feisty old-time fiddlers contest, where you'll hear lively tunes from the 19th century. | 541/963–8588; 800/848–9969 visitor information | www.oregontraildays.com.

Sept. **Pendleton Round-Up.** More than 50,000 rodeo performers and fans take over town for four days during this annual event. You can watch wild-horse races, sample local barbecues, cheer for parades, listen to country bands, and participate in milking contests. Budget for the souvenirs you'll inevitably buy as you stroll between the beadwork and crafts stands along Main Street and Court Avenue. If you'd like to stay in town, make your reservations well in advance—this (along with Cheyenne Frontier Days in Wyoming) is one of the top two rodeos in the United States. | 541/276–2553 or 800/457–6336 | www.pendletonroundup.com.

HISTORIC DINING AND LODGING

Foley Station. American/Casual. The historic Foley Building in La Grande houses this popular restaurant, part of a structure that dates from Oregon Trail days. The hubbub of the casual, busy dining room echoes between the booths, brick walls, and high ceilings, but you can have quieter conversations outdoors on summer days. Northwest cuisine with an international flair includes entrées like Northeast Oregon Painted Hills beef and Santa Fe spice-crusted Alaskan sockeye salmon. | 1011 Adams Ave., La Grande | 541/963–7473 | $18–$23 | Closed Mon.–Tues. No lunch Wed. | MC, V.

Working Girls Hotel. Yes, this 1890s hotel was once a bordello (and also a boardinghouse)—so this is your chance to say you spent the night at a cathouse. Antiques fill the rooms, which have soaring 18-ft ceilings, period furnishings, and polished wood floors. The helpful staff is extremely knowledgeable about the history of the hotel and historic things to do and see around town. Dining room, recreation room, laundry service, free parking. | 17 S.W. Emigrant Ave., 97801 | 541/276–0730 or 800/226–6398 | fax 541/276–0665 | 5 rooms without bath | Closed Nov.–May | $40–60 | D, MC, V | BP.

PORTLAND
▼▼▼

In 1843, Tennessee native William Overton and Massachusetts lawyer Asa Lovejoy beached their canoe on the banks of the Willamette River. Overton saw great potential for the timber-rich land encircled by mountains, and he borrowed 25¢ from Lovejoy to file a claim to the 640-acre site he called The Clearing. Soon bored with clearing trees and building roads, however, Overton sold his half to Francis Pettygrove. Lovejoy and Pettygrove began debating what to name their new township, with Lovejoy advocating for his native Boston and Pettygrove determined to name it for his hometown. Two coin tosses out of three declared Pettygrove the winner, and Portland took the name of his Maine hometown.

The first art museum in the Pacific Northwest, Portland Art Museum, opened here in 1892 and the city has been recognized as a regional cultural center ever since. The town's many historic districts reflect every aspect of life in pioneer Oregon. *Contact Portland Oregon Visitor Information and Services Center | 715 S.W. Morrison | 503/275–8355 or 877/678–5263 | www.travelportland.com | Weekdays 8:30–5:30, weekends 10–4.*

Glazed Terra-Cotta National Historic District. Around the turn of the 20th century terra cotta was often used in construction because of its availability and low cost; it could also be easily molded into the decorative details that were popular at the time. Elaborate lions' heads, griffins, floral displays, and other classical motifs adorn the rooflines of the district's many buildings that date from the late 1890s to the mid-1910s. Get ready to stroll—this historic district is best seen on foot. | S.W. 5th and S.W. 6th Aves. between S.W. Oak and S.W. Yamhill Sts.

Historic Skidmore District. Part of Old Town, claimed by William Overton and Asa Lovejoy in 1843, Historic Skidmore District encompasses some 21 city blocks. The district has many of Portland's most significant historic buildings, including such landmark treasures as the New Market Theater, designed in 1872 by architects Piper and Burton. Look for the Skidmore Fountain on Southwest Ankeny Street at Southwest Naito Parkway. This unusually graceful fountain was built in 1888. Citizens once quenched their thirst from the spouting lions' heads below, and horses drank from the granite troughs at the base of the fountain. Take in this district by foot; traffic makes it difficult by car. | Bounded by N.W. 3rd St. and N.W. Naito Pkwy. and by N.W. Davis and S.W. Oak Sts.

James F. Bybee House. This 19th-century classical revival house and grounds offer a wonderful glimpse at Sauvie Island's culture and development from 1850 to 1875. An agricultural museum on the property displays pioneer equipment and shops, and the Pioneer Orchard has more than a hundred apple-tree varieties. Bybee House is in Howell Territorial Park, 14 mi northwest of downtown Portland via I–405 north to U.S. 30 west (N.W. St. Helens Road); turn onto N.W. Sauvie Island Road and look for the signs. | 13901 N.W. Howell Park Rd. | 503/222–1741 | www.ohs.org | Summer weekends only; call for times.

Lewis and Clark Columbia River Tours. Take a half-day, full-day, or multi-day cruise into history. The company's catamaran vessels take you down the mighty Columbia Gorge or gentle Willamette River following the routes used by early explorers and Oregon pioneers. Tour leaders are informed and insightful and armed with an enthusiasm for history. Reservations are required; departure times and dates vary. Tour launch locations vary. | 2719 N. Hayden Island Rd. | 888/464–1805 | www.lewisandclarkcruisetours.com | $44–$1,199.

Nob Hill. Many of Portland's founding families, among them Francis Pettygrove, who bought much of what is now downtown Portland for $50 in 1844, have lived in this neighborhood. View the fine restoration and furnishings of the historic homes in this neighborhood. Some homes are open to the public; call the Portland Oregon Visitors Association (503/275–8355) for tour information. | Bounded by N.W. 17th Ave. and N.W. 24th Ave. and by Kearney and Davis Sts.

Old Church. Erected in 1882, the Old Church is one of Portland's oldest, most beloved structures as well as a prime example of Carpenter Gothic architecture. Tall spires and original stained-glass windows enhance its exterior of rough-cut lumber. The acoustically resonant church hosts free classical concerts at noon each Wednesday. | 1422 S.W. 11th Ave. | 503/222–2031 | www.oldchurch.org | Free | Weekdays 11–3, Sat. by appointment.

Oregon History Center. Impressive eight-story-high trompe l'oeil murals of Lewis and Clark and the Oregon Trail cover two sides of this downtown museum, which follows the state's story from prehistoric times to the present. The bookstore is a good source for maps and publications on Pacific Northwest history. | 1200 S.W. Park Ave. | 503/222–1741 | www.ohs.org | $6.

Oregon Maritime Center and Museum. For a solid review of Northwest maritime history, starting with early trader vessels, come to this museum. The stern-wheel tugboat *Portland* on exhibit was built in 1947, but it represents the bygone era of pioneer river travel before the railroads came along. The admission fee includes entrance aboard the last operating stern-wheel steam tug in the United States, which is docked across the street. | 113 S.W. Naito Pkwy. | 503/224–7724 | www.oregonmaritimemuseum.org | $4 | Late May–early Sept., Fri.–Sun. 11–4; early Sept.–late May, Thurs.–Sun. 11–4.

Portland Police Historical Museum. Portland has had a police force since the mid-1800s, and this little museum does a good job of giving you the highlights. You'll find strange weapons from the past, old uniforms, badges, and more. The Rogues Gallery puts you face to face with Old Portland's old-fashioned bad guys. | 1111 S.W. 2nd Ave., 16th floor | 503/823–0019 | Free | Mon.–Thurs. 10–3.

Yamhill National Historic District. Many examples of 19th-century cast-iron architecture have been preserved within this district's six square blocks. Because the cast-iron facade helped support the main structure, these buildings traditionally did not need big, heavy walls to bear the weight; the interior spaces could therefore be larger and more open. | Bounded by S.W. Naito Pkwy. and S.W. 3rd Ave. and by S.W. Morrison and S.W. Taylor Sts.

SALEM

▼▼

Some say Salem got its name from an anglicization of the Jewish greeting "shalom," others claim it was named for the East Coast town made famous by witch trials, and there are still other stories about Salem's name. Originally, the town was referred to as Chemeketa, a Calapooya Indian name meaning "place of rest," but it was apparently renamed by missionaries. Preceded by trappers and farmers, Methodist missionaries settled here in 1834 to minister to Native Americans. The missionaries established the first academic institution west of the Rockies in 1842, now known as Willamette University. Salem became the capital when Oregon achieved statehood in 1859. *Contact Marion County Historical Society | 260 12th St. SE, Salem 97301 | 541/364–2128 | fax 541/391–5356 | www.open.org/mchs. Salem Convention and Visitors Association | 1313 Mill St. SE, 97301 | 503/581–4325 or 800/874–7012 | www.scva.org.*

Bush House Museum/Bush's Pasture Park. This 1878 Italianate mansion was built by Asahel Bush II, founder of the *Salem Statesman* newspaper. The thousands of original furnishings and mid-19th century modern conveniences reflect his love of beauty and utility. Wallpapers were imported from France; lighting fixtures were powered by Tirrill's Gas Machine; and each of the 10 fireplaces in the home was cut in a distinctive style from imported Italian marble. Although the house has fireplaces, a central heating system was installed in the house when it was built. The 1877 wood-burning kitchen stove, built by inmates of the state penitentiary, is still used in winter. The house and gardens, covering 90 acres, are on the National Register of Historic Places. | Bush's Pasture Park, 600 Mission St. SE | 503/363–4714 | $3 | Oct.–Apr., Tues.–Sun. 2–5; May–Sept., Tues.–Sun. noon–4:30.

Court-Chemeketa Historic District. Take a 1-mi stroll and view 117 historic homes of many architectural styles. Among them are many homes built by Salem's founders; they can be identified by historical markers. | 1 mi along Court and Chemeketa Sts. | 503/581–4325.

Marion County Historical Society Museum. Exhibits in the museum depict life in Marion County over the years. Healthcare in the 19th century, boarding houses, and farming are among the subjects of the displays here. | 260 12th St. SE | 503/364–2128 | www.marionhistory.org | $3 | Tues.–Fri. noon–4.

Mission Mill Village. The Thomas Kay Woolen Mill Museum complex (circa 1889), complete with working waterwheels and millstream, looks as if the workers have just stepped away for a lunch break. Teasel gigging, napper flock bins, and the patented Furber double-acting napper are but a few of the machines and processes on display. The Jason Lee House, the John D. Boon Home, and the Methodist Parsonage are also part of the village. There is nothing grandiose about these early pioneer homes, the oldest frame structures in the Northwest, but they reveal a great deal about domestic life in the wilds of Oregon in the 1840s. | Museum complex, 1313 Mill St. SE | 503/585–7012 | www.missionmill.org | $6 including tour | Wed.–Fri. noon–4, Sat. 10–4 | Guided tours of houses and woolen mill museum leave from mill's admission booth every hr on the hr.

Willamette University. Behind the Capitol, across State Street but half a world away, are the brick buildings and grounds of Willamette University, founded in 1842 and the oldest college in the West. Tall, prim Waller Hall, built in 1841, is one of the oldest buildings in the Pacific Northwest. | Information Desk, Putnam University Center, Mill St. | 503/370–6300 | Weekdays 9–5.

THE DALLES

▼▼

French explorers christened this area *dalle,* or flagstone, for the effect created by a series of rapids here. It's now the seat of Wasco County and the trading center of north-central Oregon, but its historic buildings and museums give it a small-town Old West aura, even today. The Dalles first gained fame as the settlement that split the Oregon Trail. From here, pioneers could choose either to continue down the Columbia River or tackle Mount Hood to reach the Willamette Valley. The latter route was blazed by Samuel K. Barlow and Joel Palmer, who arrived at The Dalles in 1845 and decided to head southwest through the mountains rather than follow the river. The men made it past the timberline of Mount Hood just before the first snowfall and sighted a possible route to Summit Meadow below. They opened a toll road along the trail in 1846, and for more than 70 years afterward pioneers traversed this gap to reach Oregon City and points beyond. *Contact The Dalles Chamber of Commerce | 404 W. 2nd St., 97058 | 541/296–2231 or 800/255–3385 | www.thedalleschamber.com.*

Fort Dalles Museum. Housed in the 1856 Fort Dalles Surgeon's Quarters, this museum exhibits the clothing, furniture, and household items of the region's early settlers. Be sure to visit the Anderson House museum across the street, which also has pioneer artifacts. | 15th and Garrison Sts. | 541/296–4547 | $3 (includes Fort Dalles and Anderson House) | Daily 10–5.

Gilliam County Historical Society's Depot Museum. Have fun learning local history at this outdoor museum. You can explore an 1884 log cabin and a 1905 rail depot, among other buildings. The museum is about 60 mi southeast of The Dalles via Route 206. | Gilliam County Fairgrounds, Condon | 541/384–4233 | $2.50 | May–Sept., Wed.–Sun. 1–5.

Wasco County Courthouse. This 1880s building houses outstanding exhibits that illustrate, through drawings, journal excerpts, pioneer artifacts, and photos, the trials and tribulations of those who traveled the Oregon Trail. | 410 W. 2nd Pl. | 541/296–4798 | Free (donation suggested) | Mon.–Tues. and Fri.–Sat. 11–3.

TILLAMOOK

▼▼

What is now Tillamook County and the town of Tillamook entered American history books on August 14, 1788, when American captain Robert Gray and his sloop *Lady Washington* anchored in Tillamook Bay. He wasn't the first white man to set foot on the Oregon coast, however. A few years earlier, English trader and explorer John Meares had sailed into the muddy bay, which he called Quick Sand Bay. When Gray arrived, he believed he had found the Great River of the West. The Columbia River, it turns out, was miles north. In 1853, Tillamook became the 12th county in Oregon to be organized. The county and city were named after the Tillamook Indians, who occupied the areas around the Tillamook and Nehalem bays. *Contact Tillamook Chamber of Commerce | 3705 U.S. 101 N, 97141 | 503/842–7525 | www.tillamookchamber.org.*

Cape Meares Lighthouse. In Cape Meares State Park, on the northern tip of the Three Capes Loop, this restored lighthouse was built in 1890 and provides a sweeping view over the cliff to the caves and sea-lion rookery on the rocks below. Cape Meares was named for English navigator John Meares, who voyaged along this coast in 1788. A fur trader, Meares was on his way to Alaska. | Three Capes Loop, 10 mi west of Tillamook | 800/551–6949 | Free | Park daily dawn–dusk. Lighthouse May–Sept., daily 11–4; Mar.–Apr. and Oct., weekends 11–4.

Pioneer Museum. In Tillamook's 1905 county courthouse, this museum has an intriguing mix of Native American, pioneer, logging, and natural-history exhibits. There's the replica of the stump house once occupied by Joseph Champion, Tillamook's first white settler, who stayed on after his whale boat landed in the area in 1851. The Children's Room is filled with reproductions of toys and musical instruments dating back to the pioneers, and the Quilt Room displays items from the home of Webley Hauxhurst. Mr. Hauxhurst was a signer of the petition asking Congress to make Oregon Country a territory in 1837. Tillamook Indian basketry and artifacts, aged medical instruments, and the last stagecoach to make the mail run from Tillamook to Yamhill, in 1911, are on display. | 2106 2nd St. | 503/842–4553 | $2 | May–Sept., Mon.–Sat. 8:30–5, Sun. 12:30–5; Oct.–Apr. closed Mon.

VALE

▼▼

Where Vale now lies, pioneers traveling the Oregon Trail crossed the Malheur River, often camping for a few days to rest and do their laundry in the hot springs. White settlers lived here as early as 1813, but conflicts with Native American locals prevented a permanent settlement from taking hold until the 1860s. In 1864 Jonathan Keeney built here, and a few years later Louis Rhinehart, the "Father of Vale," bought out Keeney. Vale's first school opened in 1887 and the town incorporated in 1889. Contact: Vale Chamber of Commerce | Box 661, 97918 | 541/473–3800 | www.valeoregon.org.

Oregon Trail Murals. Walk through historic Vale, a main stop on the Oregon Trail, to view 23 larger-than-life painted murals depicting pioneer life during the migration west. Scenes run from "The New Arrivals" and "First Set of Shoes" to "Castor Oil: The Cure-All" and "Death on the Trail." Metal cut-out murals mark each of the four entrances to town. Contact Wilcox Horse and Buggy (www.wilcoxhorsebuggy.com) for a tour of the murals by horse-drawn Victorian carriage. | Box 631 | 541/473–3333 | www.valeoregonmurals.com | Free | Daily.

Stone House Museum. Built as a way station for pioneers who crossed the river from Idaho, this 1872 structure is a highlight along the Oregon Trail. It served as an inn, a Pony Express station, and a residence for wealthy pioneer families. The Stone House was also a meeting place for General Howard and Sarah Winnamucca, two famous figures in the Bannock Indian wars. | 255 Main St. S | 541/473–2070 | Donation | Mar.–Oct., Tues.–Sat. 12:30–4.

HISTORIC LODGING

Farewell Bend State Recreation Area. Spend the night in an authentic covered wagon or Native American tepee and test your outdoor skills at this historic park on the banks of the Snake River's Brownlee Reservoir. Pioneers on the Oregon Trail rested here before traveling inland on their way to Oregon City. Historic markers and interpretive displays dot the camp and trails, and you can follow wagon ruts cutting through the countryside. The full-service RV and tent campgrounds include several covered wagon and tepee accommodations. Basketball, hiking, volleyball, beach, dock, boating, waterskiing, fishing, shop. | Off I–84, 42 mi north of Vale | 541/869–2365 or 800/551–6949 | 3 covered wagons, 4 tepees, 2 cabins | $12–$64 | AE, D, MC, V | EP.

Sears & Roebuck Home. This impressive Victorian residence, built in 1900, is actually a kit home built from plans ordered from an early Sears & Roebuck catalog. The towering mansion is decorated with lively floral wallpaper, brass light fixtures, handmade quilts, and other period antiques. Sportsmen and cowboys are particularly welcome—you're even invited to bring your own horse, and retriever. Dining room, library, laundry service, kennel; no room TVs. | 484 N. 10th St. 97918 | 541/473–9636 | www.searshomebb.com | 5 rooms | $50–$85 | AE, D, DC, MC, V | BP.

SOUTH DAKOTA

—◆—

ver succeeding centuries, the land that is South Dakota has been home to enormous dinosaurs, woolly mammoths, giant short-faced bears, Paleolithic peoples, herds of buffalo so vast they darkened the prairie to the horizon, more than a half-dozen Native American nations, explorers, missionaries, U.S. cavalry units, gunslingers, mule skinners, and madams.

South Dakota's first people followed herds of buffalo to the plains. From these mostly nomadic peoples descended the Arikara, Lakota Sioux, and Yankton tribes that the first European explorers and trappers met in the 1600s and 1700s. French explorers François and Joseph La Verendrye were the first white explorers to document a visit to what is now South Dakota. The brothers left an inscribed lead plate claiming the region for French King Louis XV on the banks of the Missouri River in 1743; the plate wasn't discovered until 1913.

In 1803, the United States purchased the Louisiana Territory and Lewis and Clark embarked on their journey to explore the West. When they passed through South Dakota, they discovered a land rich with waist-high prairie grasses and black with enormous buffalo herds. It was also in South Dakota that they first met Native Americans: a Sioux tribe camped between the present-day towns of Vermillion and Yankton.

Learning of the beaver-rich lands in the West, the intrepid trader Manuel Lisa traced the Lewis and Clark expedition's route in 1807. Other traders and trappers followed suit, and within two years a lively fur trade flourished along the entire Missouri River. Trading posts and military forts were built, and pioneer settlements developed, leading to a clash with indigenous cultures. As battles and skirmishes between Native Americans and emigrants grew ever more violent in the mid-19th century, the government drafted the 1868 Fort Laramie Treaty to establish a border between Indian country and land that could be settled peacefully. Native Americans kept 60 million acres west of the Missouri River—covering the western half of present-day South Dakota and reaching south into Nebraska, west into Wyoming, and north into North Dakota.

Despite the treaty, Anglo-Americans continued pressing west, and in 1870 the Northern Pacific Railroad began to expand into Sioux territory. The federal government winked at the illegal maneuver, but it could not ignore the gold rush of 1874–76, which began when Lieutenant Colonel George Custer's men discovered gold in the Black Hills. The news brought thousands of miners and other emigrants into Native American territory. In 1876, the Congress-backed Maypenny Commission coerced a few Sioux tribal leaders to give up the Black Hills. The remainder of the 19th century saw an influx of homesteaders and the relocation of Native Americans to reservations. By 1912 most of the gold had been mined from the Black Hills, but the towns had taken hold as settlers turned from mining to other industries, such as timber, tourism, and farming.

An exploration of South Dakota's history yields one conclusion: a great deal of blood, sweat, and tears flowed through the prairie grasses and ponderosa pines to create this rough-and-tumble state. With virtually every step, you can follow the footprints of a thousand faceless Native Americans, pioneers, prospectors, and miners who variously sought fortune, fame, or mere subsistence in this often unforgiving land. In much of the state you can see 100 mi to the horizon and retrace 100 years in a day. At Bear Butte, Wounded Knee, and a hundred other sites revered by Native Americans, you can come to understand the plight of the region's first inhabitants. And in frontier forts, simple sod shanties, and Victorian mansions, you can see how the first settlers lived.

For a relatively young state, South Dakota has risen with surprising grace and energy to the occasion of preserving its rich and colorful past. Its revived mining towns, long and lonesome highways, far-reaching prairies, and tree-filled mountains all recall a bygone era in America. And in evidence everywhere is the spark of individuality that helped settle the West, tame the raging rivers, and harness the land with horse, pick, and plow.

The Black Hills and the Badlands
A DRIVING TOUR FROM DEADWOOD TO WALL

▼▼

Distance: 300 mi   **Time:** 4 days
Breaks: Stay in Deadwood, Custer, and Hot Springs, each of them a vibrant town with a colorful Old West history.

This tour travels through the Black Hills from north to south, passing some of the nation's best-known memorials and ending in the state's gorgeous, eerie badlands.

Established in 1876 as a gold camp, historic **Deadwood** has never ceased to celebrate its past. Begin your tour here with a visit to the Adams House Museum and the Adams House, a restored Victorian home. Then climb Boot Hill to see the graves of some of the wildest characters in the Old West at Mount Moriah Cemetery. Have lunch in town; then head 3 mi southwest on U.S. 85 to Deadwood's sister city, **Lead,** another mining community born in the Black Hills gold-rush frenzy of the late 19th century. Visit the Homestake Visitor Center and Black Hills Mining Museum to learn more about the ethnic origins of the town's settlers and the history of gold mining from the 19th century until today. Drive back to Deadwood in time for the evening reenactment of the shooting of Wild Bill on Main Street. Then have a look and maybe a drink at Old Style Saloon No. 10 and dinner at the Deadwood Social Club upstairs. Stay the night in one of Deadwood's 19th-century hotels.

On day two, head south from Deadwood along U.S. 385 toward Hill City, 45 mi away. There you can have lunch and take a step back in time aboard an 1880 train operated by the Black Hills Central Railroad. In the afternoon, go south on U.S. 385 to Crazy Horse Memorial to see the enormous carving and Native American artifacts in the Indian Museum of North America. Dine and stay in **Custer** or one of Custer State Park's mountain lodges.

Begin day three with a driving tour of Custer State Park to see the landscape and wildlife that native people and pioneers encountered in past centuries. Then travel south via Route 87 to make either the 10 AM or 11:30 AM cave tour at Wind Cave National Park, which has

SOUTH DAKOTA TIME LINE

1743 Frenchmen François and Joseph La Verendrye leave an inscribed lead plate on a Missouri River bluff near present-day Fort Pierre, claiming the surrounding region for their king, Louis XV.

1790 Jacques d'Église and Joseph Garreau, French-Canadians in the employ of the Spanish, venture into Dakota to trade furs.

1803 The French-owned Louisiana Territory is purchased by President Thomas Jefferson.

1804 Meriwether Lewis, William Clark, and a crew of 29 set out to follow the Missouri River to its headwaters.

1807 Spanish explorer and entrepreneur Manuel Lisa leaves for the upper Missouri valley to trade with the Indians.

1822 The Rocky Mountain Fur Company starts to send trading parties, including Wild West legends Jedediah Smith, Jim Bridger, and Hugh Glass, into present-day South Dakota.

1831 The *Yellowstone* becomes the first steamboat to paddle its way up the Missouri River, reaching Fort Tecumseh (later Fort Pierre). The first permanent white settlement in South Dakota is established at Fort Pierre Chouteau.

1851 The Fort Laramie Treaty allots 60 million acres to the Sioux and establishes tribal borders.

1858 The U.S. negotiates a treaty with the Yankton Sioux for the purchase of 14 million acres between the Big Sioux and Missouri rivers for 12¢ an acre. Norwegians begin to establish claims near the Vermillion and James rivers.

1861 Congress establishes Dakota Territory. Yankton is named territorial capital.

1862 U.S. Congress passes the Homestead Act, opening up millions of acres to homesteaders. In the Dakota Territory, 160-acre parcels sell for about $18 each.

1868 A new Fort Laramie Treaty establishes the Great Sioux Reservation, granting the tribes all rights to land in the Dakota Territory west of the Missouri River to the Bighorns of western Wyoming.

1870 The Northern Pacific Railroad begins laying tracks through the Powder River country west of the Black Hills, in obvious violation of the 1868 Fort Laramie Treaty.

1874 George A. Custer, whom the Sioux called "Yellow Hair," leads 10 cavalry and 2 infantry companies on the first white expedition into the Black Hills. They discover gold there.

1875 All Sioux bands are ordered to report to reservation agencies by January 31, 1876.

1876 Hundreds of miners and merchants descend on the Black Hills.

1877 The Manypenny Commission forces the Sioux to relinquish the Black Hills. Crazy Horse and 1,100 followers surrender to authorities at the Red Cloud Agency on May 6. Crazy Horse dies after receiving a fatal wound from a soldier's bayonet while in military custody.

1880 The "Great Dakota Boom" begins in earnest with the influx of Bohemians, Germans, Swedes, Finns, Poles, and Swiss.

1889 South Dakota becomes the nation's 40th state on November 2.

1890 Native American policemen and special government agents attempt to arrest Sitting Bull at his encampment. They kill 14 people, including Sitting Bull.

the world's seventh-longest cave, discovered in 1881. Picnic in the park or have lunch in **Hot Springs,** 6 mi farther south on U.S. 385. Later, in the tradition of 1890s visitors to therapeutic springs, take a swim at Evans Plunge. Stay the night in Hot Springs.

Day four takes you east via U.S. 18 to **Pine Ridge** on the Pine Ridge Indian Reservation. Visit Wounded Knee Historical Site before continuing east on U.S. 18 and then north via Routes 27 and 44 through Badlands National Park.

CUSTER

▼▼▼

When Custer was settled in August 1875, it was in violation of the Fort Laramie Treaties of 1851 and 1868, which reserved Black Hills land for the Great Sioux Nation. Regardless of the laws, settlers—many of them miners in search of gold—flocked to the Black Hills, and some laid claims in the valley where General Custer camped and first found gold. The next summer, when new gold mines opened at the burgeoning ramshackle camps of Lead and Deadwood, most of Custer's townspeople headed north. A few hundred stayed on, however, to continue working their claims, running their stores, and harvesting the abundant timber in the region. The town flourished in the 20th century with the advent of tourism in the Black Hills. *Contact Custer Area Chamber of Commerce & Visitors Bureau | 615 Washington St., 57730 | 605/673–2244 or 800/992–9818 | www.custersd.com.*

Crazy Horse Memorial. The colossal carving-in-progress depicts Lakota leader Crazy Horse atop his steed. At the memorial's base is the Indian Museum of North America, which houses one of the most impressive collections of Plains Indian artifacts in the country, including beautiful leather and beaded clothing, artwork, and turn-of-the-20th-century photographs. | Ave. of the Chiefs, 5 mi north of Custer on U.S. 385 | 605/673–4681 | www.crazyhorse.org | $9 per person or $19 per vehicle | June–Aug., daily 7 AM–9 PM; Sept.–May, daily 8–4:30.

Custer County Courthouse Museum. One of the earliest brick buildings in the Black Hills, this 1881 courthouse served as the Custer County courthouse for 92 years. Now a museum, it houses a rock and mineral collection; antique mining tools, including a sluice box and a rocker; and the region's premier exhibit on General Custer's 1874 Black Hills expedition. You'll also also find an 1875 log cabin, one of the earliest built in the Black Hills. | 411 Mount Rushmore Rd. | 605/673–2443 | Free | June–Aug., Mon.–Sat. 9–9, Sun. 1–9; Sept., call for hrs.

Custer State Park. Looking out on undisturbed forests, pre-Cambrian granite spires, and free-roaming bison, you'll have no trouble imagining what Native Americans and early settlers saw on this land in the 19th century. The park has 73,000 acres of scenic beauty, with exceptional drives and nature trails. You can visit a replica of the Gordon party stockade, a log fort built by the first settlers in the valley in 1874, and walk along the banks of French Creek, where Custer's expedition discovered gold. Stay in one of the park's remarkable lodges. | U.S. 16A | 605/255–4515 | www.custerstatepark.info | $5 per person or $12 per vehicle | Year-round.

HISTORIC DINING AND LODGING

Custer State Park Lodges. Though they do not date from the 1800s, three of the four lodges in Custer State Park provide an authentic Western experience. At the Blue Bell Lodge and Resort, whose log lodge was built in the 1920s, you can stay in one of the 29 log cabins with fireplace. Hayrides, trail rides, and cookouts are part of the entertainment. The State Game Lodge and Resort offers the park's 7 most elegant rooms, in a stone-and-wood lodge built in 1920 and now on the National Register of Historic Places. There are also 40 motel-style rooms and 33 pine-shaded cabins. The main lodge at Sylvan Lake Resort, built in 1937 after the original 1895 hotel burned, overlooks pristine Sylvan Lake and Harney Peak; it has 35 guest rooms. Thirty-one rustic cabins, some with fireplaces, are scattered along the cliff and in the forest. Each of the lodges houses a restaurant where such specialities as trout, pheas-

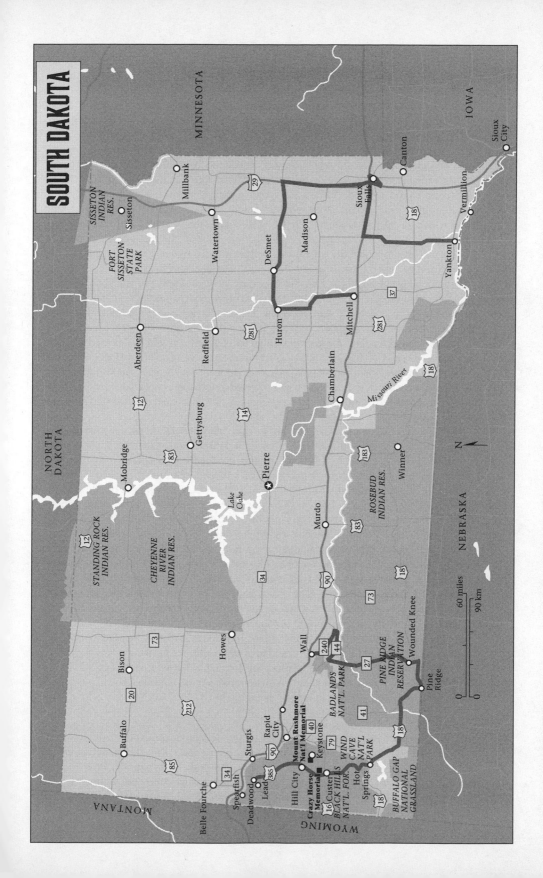

THE LAST GOLD RUSH OF THE WEST

In the summer of 1874, Civil War General George Armstrong Custer and nearly 1,000 men set out from Fort Abraham Lincoln near present-day Bismarck, North Dakota, to explore the Black Hills. The expedition, which included cavalry units, wagon teams, cartographers, photographers, and newsmen, found a well-timbered, well-watered range of peaks and valleys teaming with wildlife and carpeted with wildflowers and trees. In late July, the expedition set up camp on the banks of French Creek in the southern Black Hills. Soldiers rested in the tall meadow grasses and feasted on venison in a spot their leader named Golden Valley. "This valley presents a most wonderful and beautiful aspect, the like of which has never been seen," Custer wrote to the War Department in one of many dispatches. As Custer wrote a report to his superiors, Horatio N. Ross, a civilian prospector who had accompanied the expedition, rushed into his tent and spilled gold dust on a clean sheet of paper. Custer quickly changed the emphasis of his report.

News quickly spread to the civilized world of a new gold strike in the West. Pleased with the golden success of his foray into the wilderness and its attendant publicity, Custer ordered his camp struck and set out on the 500-mi journey back to his post. The dust had hardly settled behind Custer's horses before a party of gold-seekers set out for the Black Hills from Sioux City, Iowa, even though the U.S. government had not yet opened the region to settlers. The Gordon party, which spearheaded the Black Hills gold rush, included 24 men, a boy, and a woman. After two months on the trail, the Gordon party arrived at Custer's former camp and hastily erected a stockade as protection against hostile Native Americans and the elements. A replica of the stockade stands on the same ground today near the shores of Stockade Lake.

The Gordon party worked the gravel of French Creek all fall and winter with moderate success. Then, in the spring of 1876, they were discovered by a detachment of troops and herded to Fort Laramie. By this time, however, gold-seeking scavengers from throughout the West were descending on the Black Hills. Soldiers attempted to uphold the treaty rights of the Native Americans, but there were too many people hell-bent on filling their pockets with gold dust to keep them all out. Exasperated, the government finally threw up its hands and, while not officially sanctioning entry into the Black Hills, did less to prevent the encroachment. President Ulysses S. Grant established the Maypenny Commission to meet with the Sioux about land rights. Many Sioux leaders signed an agreement relinquishing their rights to the United States that fall, and the agreement was ratified by Congress in February 1877, unleashing another settlement rush in the Black Hills.

Two miles above Custer's old camp, the village of Custer took shape as a rag-tag collection of tents, covered wagons, log shacks, grazing horses and oxen, and boisterous men each intent on discovering his own El Dorado. A cave in the granite above the town, still visible, served as the community's post office. In August 1875, the insurgents laid out the town in streets and lots, and mining claims were numbered up and down the creek. In the spring of 1876, Custer's population had swelled to between eight and ten thousand. Then when news of a new gold strike in Deadwood Gulch reached them, most men left almost overnight. Custer's boom was over.

ant, buffalo, and steaks are served. The restaurants at State Game Lodge and Sylvan Lake Resort are closed October–mid-May. 3 restaurants, picnic areas, some kitchenettes, cable TV, lake, beach, boating, hiking, horseback riding, playground, 3 bars, laundry facilities; no a/c in some rooms, no phones in some rooms | 42 lodge rooms, 40 motel rooms, 93 cabins | Custer State Park, 57730 | 800/658-3530 | fax 605/255-4706 | www.custerresorts.com | $95–$243 lodge rooms, $106–$151 motel rooms, $86–$370 cabins | AE, D, MC, V.

DEADWOOD

▼▼▼

Once known as the wildest and woolliest gold camp in the West, Deadwood has been tamed a bit since it was founded in the 1870s by a wave of miners, mule skinners, and madams. The town's original residents sought the new El Dorado in gold-filled Deadwood Gulch, where gold production totaled well over $1 billion (in today's dollars) during 125 years of mining activity. Since the 1990s more than $150 million has been invested in restoration and preservation projects in the mile-high community, earning the whole town the designation National Historic Landmark. As you come into town, you are greeted by ornate Victorian facades, brick streets, and 19th-century-style lampposts. *Contact Deadwood Area Chamber of Commerce & Visitors Bureau | 735 Main St., 57732 | 605/578–1876 or 800/999–1876 | www.deadwood.org. Deadwood Historic Preservation Commission | 108 Sherman St., 57732 | 605/578–2082.*

Adams House Museum. The restored 1892 Adams House recounts the tragedies and triumphs of two of the community's founding families, the Franklins and the Adamses. The house is decorated with the original furnishings and wall coverings of the two families. See the cookies Mary Adams left in the pantry when she closed the house and moved to California in 1936. | 22 Van Buren St. | 605/578–3724 | www.adamsmuseumandhouse.org | $4 | May–Sept., Mon.–Sat. 9–7, Sun. noon–5; Oct.–Dec. and Feb.–Apr., Tues.–Sat. 10–4, Sun. noon–4.

Adams Museum. A gift to the city from Mr. W. E. Adams, this museum has three floors of displays, including the first locomotive used in the Black Hills, photos of the town's early days, a two-headed calf, a firearms collection, and the largest gold nugget ever discovered in the Black Hills. | 54 Sherman St. | 605/578–1714 | www.adamsmuseumandhouse.org | Donations accepted | May–Sept., Mon.–Sat. 9–7, Sun. noon–5; Oct.–Dec. and Feb.–Apr., Tues.–Sat. 10–4, Sun. noon–4.

Boot Hill Tours. Leave the driving to someone else for an hour on this narrated bus tour of Deadwood and Mount Moriah. The starting point is on Main St. near the Bodega Bar. | 11 Jackson St. | 605/722–3758 | fax 605/722-3090 | www.deadwood.net/boothill | $6.

Broken Boot Gold Mine. Join guides on a journey into a late-19th-century underground gold mine and pan for gold. If nothing else, you'll receive a souvenir stock certificate. | Upper Main St. (U.S. 14A) | 605/578–9997 | $4.50; gold panning $4.50 extra | May–Aug., daily 8–5:30; Sept., daily 9–4:30.

Deadwood Public Library. Founded in 1895 by the Round Table Club, a ladies' literary group, the Deadwood Public Library has an impressive store of genealogical and local history resources. | 435 Williams St. | 605/578–2821 | dwdlib.sdln.net | Free | Mon.–Wed. 10–8, Thurs.–Fri. 10–5, Sat. noon–4.

Mount Moriah Cemetery. This cemetery is the final resting place of such Wild West notables as Wild Bill Hickok, Calamity Jane Canary, and Potato Creek Johnny. You can pick up a brochure with some interesting tales and a walking map with gravesite locations. The classic "Boot Hill" has a panoramic view of the town and the once gold-filled gulch. | Top of Lincoln St. | 605/578–1087 | $1 | Late May–early Sept., daily 7 AM–8 PM; early Sept.–end of Sept., daily 9–5.

Original Deadwood Tour. This is an entertaining and informative hour-long bus tour of Deadwood and Mount Moriah Cemetery. | 677 Main St. | 605/578–2091 | fax 605/578–1092 | www.originaldeadwoodtour.com | $7.75.

✦ ON THE CALENDAR: May–Sept. **The Shooting of Wild Bill Hickok.** A reenactment of one of Deadwood's most infamous events takes place four times a day outside Old Style Saloon No. 10, probably the only museum in the world with a bar. | 605/578–3346.

THE SHERIFF AND THE PRESIDENT

One of Deadwood's most revered characters was also its first sheriff, Seth Bullock. Born to a British major and his Scottish wife in 1849 in the tiny village of Sandwich, Ontario, Bullock moved to Montana Territory at age 18 and ran for the territorial legislature at age 20. He was defeated that first time but elected a year later, serving in the 1871 and 1872 sessions. During his time in office Bullock introduced legislation calling on the U. S. Congress to set aside Yellowstone as the first national park in the United States. The resolution was adopted, and Yellowstone National Park was established March 1, 1872.

In 1873, Bullock was elected sheriff of Montana Territory and, in addition to his law enforcement duties, he served as chief engineer of the Helena Fire Department, became an auctioneer, and dabbled in the hardware business. In 1876, Bullock joined his partner, Sol Star, and followed the gold rush to Deadwood, Dakota Territory. Their hardware venture was an unmitigated success, and Bullock was soon elected treasurer of the Board of Health and Street Commissioners, organized to battle a looming smallpox epidemic.

A few months after Wild Bill Hickok was gunned down in a Main Street saloon, Bullock was appointed the first sheriff of Deadwood. Quiet and capable, Bullock quickly anointed several fearless deputies and with little fanfare, gun smoke, or graft, law and order had settled on the gold-filled gulch. With the roughest cowboys relegated to jail cells, shallow graves, and outbound stages, Bullock began concentrating on ranching and raising Thoroughbred horses while continuing to serve as Deputy United States Marshal.

During the Spanish-American War, Bullock volunteered for active service and was named captain of a troop of "Grigsby's Rough Riders," so-named in honor of the famous "Rough Riders" (1st U.S. Volunteer Cavalry) commanded by Theodore Roosevelt. The outfit never saw combat, patiently sitting out the war in a Louisiana training camp.

Later, on Bullock's rangeland near present-day Belle Fourche, the lawman shared beans and coffee over the tailgate of a chuckwagon with the newly elected Vice President Theodore Roosevelt. Sharing a love for the West, cattle and hunting, the two quickly became friends, and Roosevelt had Bullock appointed the first Forest Supervisor of the Black Hills Reserve.

In 1905, President Roosevelt appointed Bullock United States Marshal for South Dakota. (He was reappointed in 1909 by President Taft and continued for a year under President Wilson.) Roosevelt's death in January 1919 dealt a blow to Bullock, who himself was sick, but by mid-February Bullock was engaged in one last act of devotion to his famous friend. With the assistance of the Society of Black Hills Pioneers, he raised and dedicated a monument to Roosevelt on Sheep Mountain near Deadwood. The peak was renamed Mt. Roosevelt, and the tower, constructed of native Black Hills stone, became the first memorial to Theodore Roosevelt. Bullock died just two months later at age 70.

Today you can hike a trail (off U.S. 85, 2 mi west of Deadwood) to the monument and gaze out at the hills and rangeland loved by Deadwood's first sheriff and one of America's great presidents.

June **Wild Bill Days.** This weekend festival includes the World Fast-Draw Championships, gun spinning, parades, historic reenactments, a battle of the bands, kids' games, vendors, and big-name entertainment. | 605/578–1876 or 800/999–1876.

July **Days of '76.** Five days of PRCA rodeo performances, two 3-mi historical parades with vintage carriages and coaches, street dances, and a western arts-and-crafts festival make this one of the best events in the region. | 605/578–1876 or 800/999–1876.

HISTORIC DINING AND LODGING

1903's Dining Room. American. In the Franklin Hotel, which has hosted numerous U.S. presidents, dignitaries, and stars such as John Wayne, this Victorian dining room serves charbroiled steaks, buffalo, and trout. | 700 Main St. | 605/578–2241 | $8–$18 | AE, MC, V.

Deadwood Social Club. Italian. With deftly prepared Black Angus beef and one of South Dakota's best wine selections, this restaurant in the 1904 Levinson building is one of the most popular in town. You'll also find numerous chicken, seafood, and pasta dishes on the menu. Photographs of some of the legendary figures who helped establish Deadwood's well-deserved reputation, including Wild Bill Hickok, Calamity Jane Canary, Potato Creek Johnny, Deadwood Dick, and Poker Alice Tubbs, decorate the walls. Downstairs is the Old Style Saloon No. 10, with nightly live entertainment, sawdust on the floor, Wild Bill's death chair, and hundreds of photographs and artifacts tied to the town's rough and storied past. | 657 Main St. | 605/578–3346 or 800/952–9398 | Closed Mon. | $8–$18 | AE, MC, V.

Bullock Hotel. The tall windows in this 1895 hotel overlook Deadwood's historic district. Rooms are furnished with Victorian reproductions and firm, contemporary beds. The first floor, where you'll find the casino, has high ceilings and brass-and-crystal chandeliers. Restaurant, cable TV, gym. | 633 Main St., 57732 | 605/578–1745 or 800/336–1876 | fax 605/578–1382 | www.heartofdeadwood.com/bullock | 28 rooms | $99–$179 | AE, D, MC, V.

DESMET

▼▼

Fans of the *Little House* children's books may want to visit the town where author Laura Ingalls Wilder lived for 15 years. The Ingalls family moved to DeSmet in 1879, when Laura was 12, and lived first in a surveyor's house, next in a shanty, then in a farmhouse, and finally in town. *Contact Glacial Lakes and Prairies Association | Box 244, Watertown 57201 | 605/886–7305 or 800/244–8860. Laura Ingalls Wilder Memorial Society | Box 426, DeSmet 57231 | 605/854–3383 | www.liwms.com.*

Hazel L. Meyer Memorial Library. Here you can see several of DeSmet native Harvey Dunn's oil paintings depicting pioneer life in South Dakota. | 102 1st St. NE | 605/854–3842.

Laura Ingalls Wilder Memorial Site. A stone marker sits on the unchanged acre of land where the Ingalls family used to live. The five cottonwood trees were planted by Charles "Pa" Ingalls in honor of each of his girls. | U.S. 14, 1 mi southeast of DeSmet | 605/854–3383 or 800/880–3383 | Free.

Surveyors' House and Ingalls Town Home. The homes are open to the public and contain period furnishings and belongings of the Ingalls and Wilder families. The Surveyors' House, the oldest building in DeSmet, is described in Laura Ingalls Wilder's book *By the Shores of Silver Lake*. Charles Ingalls built the town home in 1887. | Surveyors' House, 103 Olivet Ave.; Ingalls Town Home, 210 3rd St. SW | 605/854–3383 or 800/880–3383 | www.liwms.com | $6 | June–Aug., daily 9–5:30; Sept.–Oct. and Apr.–May, Mon.–Sat. 9–3:30; Nov.–Mar., weekdays 9–3:30.

✦ ON THE CALENDAR: June–July **Laura Ingalls Wilder Pageant.** During the last weekend of June and the first two weekends of July, actors re-create scenes from the pioneering days of DeSmet. A pageant based on the life of Laura Ingalls Wilder is presented outdoors each night near the plot of land where the Ingalls family lived. | 605/692–2108.

BADLANDS NATIONAL PARK

The Lakota called the stark, rugged, and very dry country that makes up southwestern South Dakota *"mako sica,"* or "land bad." French trappers, who were the first Europeans to enter the region, called it *"les mauvaises terres a traverser,"* or "bad lands to travel across." So stark and isolated are the chiseled spires, ragged ridge lines, and deep ravines of South Dakota's badlands, that Lieutenant Colonel George Custer once described the area as "hell with the fires burned out." While a bit more accessible and host to considerably more life than the depths of the underworld, the landscape of the badlands is easily the strangest in the state. Ruthlessly ravaged over ages by wind and rain, the 380 square mi of wild terrain continue to erode and evolve, sometimes visibly changing shape in a few days.

Despite harsh conditions, a community of prairie creatures, from bison and bald eagles to rattlesnakes and pronghorn antelope, thrives on the untamed territory. Fossil evidence shows that mammals have roamed the area for more than 35 million years. In fact, there are more Oligocene fossil deposits in the badlands than anywhere else in the world. Within the ancient rock formations, paleontologists have detected the evolution of such mammals as horses, cats, sheep, rhinoceroses, and pigs, plus traces of various birds and reptiles.

For the best overview of the badlands, stop by the Ben Reifel Visitor Center at Cedar Pass, 9 mi south of I–90 on Route 240, in Badlands National Park (605/433–5361 | www. nps.gov/badl). At Journey Overlook, about 7 mi northwest of Ben Reifel Visitor Center, you can see Bigfoot Pass, where Sioux chief Big Foot and his band traveled through the badlands on their way to that fateful day at Wounded Knee, December 29, 1890.

HILL CITY

▼▼▼

In February 1876, Hill City became the second city founded in the Black Hills, less than two years after General Custer's expedition discovered gold in the nearby creeks. With a sawmill, two stores, a hotel, and a small mine that provided decent returns, the town prospered. Miners and their families continued to arrive, although there were few claims left by 1877. Many of Hill City's residents, like Custer's, moved to Deadwood and Lead in the late 1870s, as those towns' larger mines yielded more gold. Then, in 1883, tin was discovered in Hill City, and the Harney Peak Tin Mining Co. began operating there, employing about 3,000 workers. The demand for tin eventually dropped off, and again Hill City's growth subsided. Today Hill City is the gateway to Mount Rushmore National Memorial. *Contact Hill City Area Chamber of Commerce | Box 253, 57745 | 605/574–2368 or 800/888–1798 | www.hillcitysd.com.*

Black Hills Central Railroad. You step back in time when you board this antique steam locomotive for a ride through South Dakota's backcountry. The two-hour trip takes you through the Black Hills from Hill City to Keystone. Reservations are essential. | Hill City Depot, Railroad Ave. | 605/574–2222 | www.1880train.com | $18 | Mid-May–early Oct., four daily departures; call for schedule.

Wade's Gold Mill. Pan for gold and see some of the equipment used in a 19th-century mine. There's a stamp mill powered by a steam engine, a modern placer mill, and an extensive collection of historic photographs. | 12401 Deerfield Rd. | 605/574–2680 | $8; panning $5 extra | Late May–early Sept., daily 9–6.

✦ **ON THE CALENDAR:** Late May–early Sept. **Bank Robbery and Shoot Out.** Western characters stage a demonstration in front of City Hall, then stroll down Main Street and defend the town in a shoot-out with desperadoes every Monday, Thursday, and Friday at 7 PM. | 605/574–2368.

HOT SPRINGS

▼▼

For more than a century before settlers entered the area that is present-day Hot Springs, the Sioux and Cheyenne tribes fought for control of the natural warm-water springs that have since given the town its name. According to local legend, one of their battles took place on a peak now called Battle Mountain. Following the miners who came to the Black Hills during the gold rush of the 1870s, farmers and ranchers settled and founded Hot Springs in 1879. In 1890 a group of ambitious entrepreneurs decided to turn the town into a health spa. Leading the pack was Fred Evans, who built Evans Plunge over many of the springs. After the railroad arrived in 1891, trainloads of visitors disembarked at the Hot Springs depot intent on soaking in the healing waters. For nearly 20 years the town prospered as a vacation and health center. It was during this period of wealth and growth that residents constructed many of the stately standstone buildings you can still see today along River Street and Chicago Avenue in the historic district. By 1914, visitation to Hot Springs had seriously declined in part because doctors were less likely to recommend mineral baths as a cure for ailments. *Contact Hot Springs Area Chamber of Commerce | 801 S. 6th St., 57747 | 605/745–4140 or 800/325–6991 | www.hotsprings-sd.com.*

Black Hills Wild Horse Sanctuary. See one of the symbols of the West at this 11,000-acre wild horse preserve. Two-hour guided bus tours take you among the American Mustangs running freely on short-grass prairies. Ancient Native American petroglyphs are also on site. You can travel up the spectacular grand canyon of the Cheyenne River in a horse-drawn wagon for a chuckwagon cook-out on the prairie. | Rte. 71, 12 mi south of Hot Springs | 605/745–5955 | Bus tour $20, dinner $35 | Bus tours May–Sept., Mon.–Sat.; dinners June–Aug., Tues., Thurs., and Sat.

Evans Plunge. Fred Evans constructed buildings over the water of Hot Springs in 1890, and Evans Plunge has been in operation ever since. Today there are large and small indoor and outdoor geothermal pools and three water slides. | 1145 N. River St. | 605/745–5165 | www.evansplunge.com | $8 | Daily 5:30 AM–9 PM.

Hot Springs Historic District. In 1890, a group of ambitious entrepreneurs decided to create a health spa around the "healing waters" of Hot Springs. Aided by the arrival of the railroad in 1891 and the construction of many beautiful sandstone buildings, they succeeded, and the town thrived around the spa for two decades. Today, buildings from that era form the community's historic district, which includes homes, resort hotels, sanatoriums, and commercial buildings erected between 1890 and 1915. | Chicago Ave. and River St. | 800/325–6991 | www.hotsprings-sd.com | Free.

Wind Cave National Park. Discovered by Tom and Jesse Bingham in 1881, Wind Cave was named for the strong currents of air that blow in and out of the entrance. In the late 1880s and through the 1890s, a young man named Alvin McDonald explored about 9 mi of the cave and recorded his findings in a diary. During that time, many of the cave's passageways were given names such as Lincoln's Fireplace, Dante's Inferno, and Fat Woman's Misery. Alvin and his father led a few guided tours into the cave, and word of the beautiful interior reached an entrepreneur named John Stabler in 1891. Stabler bought an interest in the cave and began to publicize it as a tourist attraction, intending to offer tours and build a hotel nearby. The government took control of the cave in 1900, however, and the national park was established in 1903. Today, cave tours let you see examples of unusual and beautiful geological formations with such names as button popcorn, starburs, Christmas trees, frostwork, nail quartz, helicite bushes, and gypsum flowers. Above ground, a 28,000-acre wildlife preserve protects bison, pronghorn, prairie dogs, and other animals. | U.S. 385, 7 mi north of Hot Springs | 605/745–4600 | www.nps.gov/wica | Tours $6–$20 | Daily 8–4:30.

✦ ON THE CALENDAR: Sept. **Badger Clark Hometown Cowboy Poetry Gathering.** Cowboy musicians and poets join for jam sessions and a cowboy show. Admission is $8. | 800/325–6991.

LEAD
▼▼▼

Lead (pronounced leed) was founded in 1876 by miners who rushed across the Dakota prairie when the U.S. Army opened the Black Hills to gold prospectors. Four prospectors originally claimed and mined Lead's mineral-rich gulch, but they quickly sold out to a group of rich Californians (among them mining magnate George Hearst) who brought in the machinery necessary for large-scale ore mining in 1877. Almost immediately, the town population swelled with immigrant miners from Italy, the United Kingdom, and Scandinavia, and distinct ethnic neighborhoods were built on the steep mountain slopes of the gulch. At the turn of the 20th century, Lead was one of the most populous towns in South Dakota. When it ceased operating in December 2001, the Homestake Gold Mine had been the longest continuously operating gold mine in the world. Major restoration projects on Main Street include the $7 million renovation of the 1914 Homestake Opera House. *Contact Lead Area Chamber of Commerce | 309 W. Main St., Suite A, 57754 | 605/584–1100 | www.leadmethere.org.*

Black Hills Mining Museum. Learn the history of Black Hills mining through life-size models, videos, gold-panning, and guided tours through a simulated mine. | 323 W. Main St. | 605/584–1605 | www.mining-museum.blackhills.com | $4.25 | Mid-May—Sept., daily 9–5; Oct.–mid-May, Tues.–Sat. 9–4:30.

Homestake Gold Mine Surface Tours and Visitor Center. You may tour the surface workings of one of the oldest continuously operating mines in the world. You'll view giant hoists, ore crushing and processing, and the huge Open Cut surface mine. | 160 W. Main St. | 605/584–3110 or 888/701–0164 | www.homestaketour.com | $5.25 | Visitor center weekdays 9–5; weekends 10–5; tours May–Sept., daily 8:30–3:30.

HISTORIC DINING AND LODGING
Stampmill Restaurant & Inn. A dark-wood and brick interior, with a large fireplace in the restaurant, makes the rooms in this 1892 building especially intimate. Photos trace the history of Lead and the mines. Rooms have Victorian furnishings, feather beds, and windows that look out on historic Main Street and the massive Open Cut. In the restaurant ($7–$17), you might try the Black Angus steaks or the French onion soup. Restaurant, cable TV, cross-country skiing. | 305 W. Main St., 57754 | 605/584–1984 | 2 suites | $70–$99 | D, MC, V.

MITCHELL
▼▼▼

As is the case with virtually every South Dakota town east of the Black Hills, Mitchell was founded when the railroad came through (in 1879). Immigrant sodbusters were enticed to settle here by overly optimistic promotional materials produced by railroad and land companies. Mitchell remains a farming community. *Contact Mitchell Convention and Visitors Bureau | 601 N. Main St., 57301 | 605/996–6223 or 866/273–2676 | www.cornpalace.org.*

Corn Palace. This fanciful structure, built in 1892 to encourage settlement and prove the richness of eastern South Dakota soil, is topped by gaily painted Moorish-style domes and covered with multicolored corn, grain, and grass. Inside is an exhibition hall built to showcase the state's agricultural production. The exterior designs—murals and decorations of corn and illustrations of life on the Dakota prairie—are changed annually. | 604 N. Main St. | 605/996–5031 or 866/273–2676 | Free | May–Sept., daily 8 AM–9 PM; Oct.–Apr., weekdays 8–5.

Middle Border Museum of American Indian and Pioneer Life. The seven buildings that form this museum include the Case Art Gallery, an 1885 schoolhouse, a 1909 country church, a 1900 train depot, and a restored 1886 Italianate home. On display are more than 100,000 artifacts, including Native American tools, weapons, and leather and beaded clothing; and Victorian toys, furnishings, and clothing; plus artwork by Oscar Howe, Harvey Dunn, and others. | 1311 S. Duff St. | 605/996–2122 | $3 | May–Sept., Mon.–Sat. 10–5, Sun. 1–4; Oct.–Dec. and Mar.–Apr., Tues.–Sat. 10–4, Sun. 1–4; Jan.–Feb., by appointment only.

PINE RIDGE
▼▼

Founded in 1877 as an Indian agency for Chief Red Cloud and his band of followers, Pine Ridge is the location of the Oglala Sioux tribe's headquarters and the main settlement in Pine Ridge Indian Reservation, south of Badlands National Park. *Contact Oglala Sioux Tribe | Box 87, Oglala 57764 | 605/867–1024.*

Red Cloud Indian School Heritage Art Museum. Exquisite star quilts and works by artists representing 30 tribes fill the galleries. | 100 Mission Dr. | 605/867–5491 | Free | Weekdays 8–4:30, Sat. 9–4:30.

Wounded Knee Battlefield Site. In the late 19th century, tensions mounted dramatically between the U.S. military and Native American tribes who resisted government orders to retreat to reservations. After learning about the death of Sioux spiritual leader Sitting Bull on December 15, 1890, Sioux Chief Big Foot and his followers broke camp on the shores of the Cheyenne River and moved south toward Pine Ridge, where the chief hoped to meet Red Cloud, another Lakota leader. As the 350 men, women, and children in the band approached Wounded Knee they moved slowly, for the cold and 150-mi trek had taken its toll. On December 28, Major Samuel Whitside and about 200 members of the Seventh Cavalry caught up with the band and escorted them into camp along Wounded Knee Creek. Whitside and his officers made plans to disarm the band and detain the warriors in the morning. As the sun rose, the army surrounded the Indian camp, which had hoisted a white flag as a sign of peace. The Indians were ordered to give up their weapons, but when only a few guns were surrendered, the officers began searching tepees. This alarmed the Indians and in the commotion, a shot was fired. Soldiers responded with a barrage of bullets, and in minutes about 200 Sioux and 30 soldiers were dead. A solitary stone obelisk commemorates the site of the massacre, considered to be the last major conflict between the U.S. military and Native Americans. | 12 mi northwest of Pine Ridge, along U.S. 18.

✦ ON THE CALENDAR: Aug. **Oglala Nation Powwow and Rodeo.** If you get the chance to visit the Pine Ridge Reservation when this traditional powwow and rodeo takes place, don't miss it. The Oglala Sioux tribe hosts the dancing, competitions, and merriment at the Powwow Grounds on the west side of Pine Ridge. | 605/867–5821.

SIOUX FALLS

Sioux Falls has long been considered a prime piece of real estate. Evidence suggests prehistoric people lived beside the falls for which the city is named, and later Native Americans also were known to migrate through the area and hold trade meetings near the falls. From the early 1800s through the 1850s, white trappers, traders, and military men passed by and saw the falls, but a settlement was not established until 1856, when the Western Town Company purchased a 320-acre lot for a song. Company investors planned to resell the land in smaller pieces to settlers, who were just beginning to immigrate west. The Dakota Land Company joined in the venture, and by the early 1860s the camp started to look like a real town. After the Minnesota Uprising of 1862, however, when hostilities between immigrants and the Santee Indians reached boiling point, the town was deserted, and it remained empty for nearly a decade. Finally, in the early 1870s some of the town's first residents, as well as new homesteaders and farmers, returned to Sioux Falls. By 1890, the city's population exceeded 10,000. An infestation of grasshoppers slowed growth around the turn of the 20th century, but the town remained stable and is today South Dakota's largest city. *Contact Minnehaha County Historical Society | 200 W. Sixth St., 57104 | 605/334–7762. Sioux Falls Chamber of Commerce, and Convention and Visitors Bureau | 200 N. Phillips Ave., Suite 102, 57104 | 605/336–1620 or 800/333–2072 | www.siouxfallscvb.com.*

Old Courthouse Museum. A massive Romanesque structure, the courthouse was built in 1890 of a native red stone called Sioux quartzite. Its interior is embellished with 16 murals painted in 1915. The museum hosts special events and activities throughout the year, including the Almost Forgotten Crafts program, which reanimates sheep shearing, tin smithing, and weaving in spring. In the fall, a buffalo feed is capped with regional talent performing Native American and ethnic dancing. | 200 W. 6th St. | 605/367–4210 | Free | Mon.–Sat. 9–5, Sun. 1–5.

Pettigrew Home and Museum. This beautiful 1889 Queen Anne–style building was purchased in 1911 by South Dakota's first full-term U.S. senator, Richard F. Pettigrew. Upon his death in 1926, he donated the house and its contents to the people of Sioux Falls. A visit lets you see the former senator's original period furnishings, including detailed gorgeous silk damask wall coverings and beautiful jeweled glass windows, as well as Native American and natural-history exhibits. | 131 N. Duluth Ave. | 605/367–7097 | Donations accepted | Mon.–Sat. 9–5, Sun. noon–5.

✦ ON THE CALENDAR: Sept. **Northern Plains Tribal Arts Show.** This two-day show brings together the works of more than 100 tribal artists throughout the Midwest and West, plus Native American dance, music, and storytelling. | 605/334–4060.

SISSETON

Joseph N. Nicollet mapped the vast region to the northeast of present-day Sisseton in the 1830s, opening the way for settlers to cross the territory. Following a period of conflict and violence between area Native Americans and early settlers, the U.S. military built Fort Wadsworth in 1864. In 1876 the fort was renamed Fort Sisseton after a local tribe, and it continued to serve its purpose of keeping the peace between natives and immigrants. Finally, the town of Sisseton was founded on April 15, 1892, followed by an influx of settlers seeking to stake claims on land newly opened by the government. Sisseton's population today reflects the community's Norwegian immigrant and Native American heritage. *Contact Sisseton Area Chamber of Commerce | Box 221, 57262 | 605/698–7261.*

Fort Sisseton State Park. Seventeen original and reconstructed buildings fill the grounds of this Civil War–era fort, originally called Fort Wadsworth. The fort was built in 1864 in response to the Minnesota Uprising of 1862, which left 800 white men, women, and children dead in southern Minnesota, Dakota Territory, and northern Iowa, at the hands of the Santee Sioux, who violently protested a government order confining them to small reservations. Thanks to reconstruction work by the Works Progress Administration in the 1930s, the fort remains one of the best-preserved military posts in the United States. It is 30 mi west and 5 mi south of Sisseton along Routes 10 and 25, respectively. | 11545 Northside Dr., Lake City | 605/448–5701 | $3 per person or $5 per vehicle | Grounds year-round; visitor center June–Aug., daily 8–5.

Joseph N. Nicollet Tower and Interpretive Center. The center's 75-ft-tall observation tower overlooks three states and a dozen communities. Inside is a great map, showing the vast area between the Mississippi and Missouri rivers, created by the French cartographer Joseph N. Nicollet in 1839. You'll also find original works of art depicting the history of the area and an interpretive film that explores the region's plains and prairies. | Rte. 10, 3½ mi west of Sisseton | 605/698–7672 | Free | Late May–early Sept., daily 10–5.

Sica Hollow State Park. This park 15 mi northwest of Sisseton preserves the favored campsites of the Dakota Indian bands that once roamed the Great Plains. Great numbers of white-tailed deer, wild turkeys, marmots, beavers, minks, raccoons, and songbirds are protected here. A 3-mi road winds through ravines and along wooded hillsides, but the best way to experience the park is to hike the Trail of Spirits, a National Recreational Trail. | 11545 Northside Dr., Lake City | 605/698–7261 | $3 per person or $5 per vehicle.

✦ ON THE CALENDAR: June **Fort Sisseton Historical Festival.** Arts and crafts, Native American cultural demonstrations, old-time fiddlers, square dancing, cowboy poetry, a military costume ball, cavalry and infantry drills, and muzzle-loader shoots are all part of this event in Fort Sisseton State Park. | 605/448–5701.

YANKTON
▼▼▼

Founded in 1859 by fur trappers and traders plying the Missouri River, the original capital of Dakota Territory stands on the banks of the Missouri River. Yankton was a major destination for settlers, who mainly arrived by riverboat after the passing of the Homestead Act of 1862. When the Dakota Southern Railroad passed through the state in 1873, Yankton lost importance as a port city. Shortly after South Dakota gained statehood in 1889, the more centrally located Pierre was chosen over Yankton as the state capital. Historic homes hint at a heritage steeped in riverboats and railroads, frontier forts and the fur trade. *Contact Yankton Area Chamber of Commerce | 218 W 4th St., 57078 | 605/665–3636 | www.yanktonsd.com.*

Dakota Territorial Capitol. Built in 1989 and housed in Riverside Park, this structure is a replica of the original Dakota Territory Capitol building, which was built in 1862. Much attention to detail was placed upon the doors, windows, and woodwork in order to mimic construction of the original building. | Levy and Douglas Sts. | 605/668–5231 | www.yanktonsd.com | Free | Tours by appointment only.

Dakota Territorial Museum. Sioux artifacts and steamboat displays trace the history of the region and the first settlement in Dakota Territory. In one exhibit, you can see the musical instruments and papers of Felix Vinatieri, an Italian-born musician who immigrated to Dakota Territory in 1869. Vinatieri joined General Custer's Seventh Calvary as bandmaster in 1873, but was not among those who traveled to Little Big Horn. Historic buildings on the museum grounds include the Great Northern Depot, the Territorial Council building, and a working blacksmith shop, all of which date back to the late 1800s and early 1900s. | 610 Summit Ave. | 605/665–3898 | $2 | Late May–early Sept., Tues.–Sat. 10–5, Sun. noon–4; early Sept.–late May, weekdays 10–5, Sun. by appointment.

Spirit Mound. On a hot August day in 1804, Lewis and Clark and other members of the Corps of Discovery walked to the top of this hill, which was rumored to be inhabited by 18-inch-tall warriors. The explorers noted a flock of swallows feeding on the mound and a splendid view of the surrounding prairie, but not a warrior did they see. Today you can hike to the top to enjoy the same view. | Off Rte. 19, 7 mi north of Vermillion.

✦ ON THE CALENDAR: June **Czech Days.** Tiny Tabor (20 mi east of Yankton) celebrates the old country and its rich Czech heritage with polka music, traditional dance featuring 130 performers in native costume, and a parade. You may also watch how a popular Czech pastry, the kolache, is made. | 605/463–2476.

Aug. **Yankton Riverboat Days.** This three-day celebration of the town's ties to the Missouri River includes food booths, a beer tent, free live entertainment, fireworks, parades, hot-air balloon rides, car shows, antique tractor pulls, paintball and golf tourneys, and a summer arts festival with more than 100 artists. The event attracts more than 100,000 people to Riverside Park on the banks of the Missouri River. | 605/665–3636.

TEXAS

≕◆≔

The story of early Texas is one of colonists and conquerors. The Spanish, French, Mexicans, Americans, and, of course, Texan revolutionaries all flew flags over Texas at one time or another—some more than once. But before the European explorers arrived, it was the Apache, Caddo, Tonkawa, Karankawa, and Cohailtecan tribes who lived here. The name Texas is said to come from *tejas,* a word similar to the Caddo word for "friend" and the root of the Mexican name for the tribe.

The story of the Old West in Texas begins with the first Spanish immigrants who arrived in the 16th century. In 1519, Alonso Alvarez de Pineda mapped the Texan coastline, and in 1528 another Spaniard, Cabeza de Vaca, was shipwrecked on what is today Galveston Island. Eventually, Vaca ventured west and south through the southern interior of Texas to Mexico City, the seat of the Spanish colonial government. In 1540, Francisco Vásquez de Coronado took 1,000 men on a trek across the southwestern United States. Tales of a fabled city of gold led Coronado to the north-central plains of Texas, but in 1542 he was forced to give up and return to Mexico City empty-handed.

Permanent European settlement in Texas began in the 1600s with the construction of forts and missions; the first, Mission Nuestra Senora del Carmen, was built near El Paso in 1681. In 1685 Frenchman Robert Cavelier de La Salle led four ships (filled with close to 200 colonists) to settle at the mouth of the Mississippi River, but the explorer missed his mark, and only two of the four landed safely at Matagorda Bay. There La Salle oversaw the construction of Fort St. Louis, where he raised the French flag and claimed Texas for France. Two years later, La Salle's men murdered him and by 1689 the fort was abandoned. In 1691, Spanish rulers in Mexico took control of Texas and began to construct a great network of Catholic missions, including the 1718 Mission San Antonio de Valero (later renamed the Alamo).

On August 8, 1812, Spanish rule in Texas was threatened when 130 Americans, Texans, and Mexicans of the Gutierrez-Magee expedition rebelled. Skirmishes lasted until 1813 when in-fighting and rebel deaths spelled an end to the uprising. Further revolts in Spanish-Mexican territory culminated in the August 24, 1821, treaty granting Mexican independence, and a third flag was raised over Texas lands.

Early Spanish, and then Mexican, policy encouraged settlement by U.S. immigrants, and in 1822 Stephen F. Austin, the "Father of Texas," obtained a land grant that allowed 300 families to settle in an area near the Brazos River. Growing tensions between Mexico and the United States, however, led Mexico to pass laws in 1830 curbing the flow U.S. immigration into Texas. The fight between Texans and Mexicans at Velasco foreshadowed the Texas revolution. On October 1, 1832, and April 1, 1833, Texan delegates met at conventions to draft resolutions to be presented to the Mexican government for the reform of tariff and immigration laws. Stephen F. Austin took the petition to Mexico City, where he was imprisoned on unspecified charges in 1834. Scrap metal expelled from a canon at Gonzales became the first shot of the Texas Revolution, on October 2, 1835.

Several Texan victories preceded the drafting of the Texas Declaration of Independence, signed on March 2, 1836. The 54 convention delegates gathered at Washington-on-the-Brazos, drafted a constitution, formed an interim government, and elected Sam Houston as president, before they were forced to flee advancing Mexican troops. While the convention was in session, the Alamo in San Antonio had been besieged. The siege ended three days later with the bombardment and storming of the mission. All 189 of the Texan fighters were killed, but a few women and children were released to spread the tale. On March 27, Colonel James Fannin and 342 Texans had surrendered in a battle near Goliad. They were relocated to a nearby fort and, instead of being imprisoned, they were massacred. "Remember Goliad!" joined the battle cry of "Remember the Alamo!" and on April 21 Texans under Sam Houston soundly defeated Mexican general Antonio Lopez de Santa Anna's forces at the Battle of San Jacinto, finally winning independence.

The Republic of Texas encompassed far more territory than the state does today, but the boundaries were continually in dispute. Arguments about the western edge—whether it included part of the lucrative Santa Fe trail or not—led the republic's second president, Lamar Mirabeau, to authorize a settlement expedition to the area. Mexican forces confronted the 300 men, who were taken prisoner and marched all the way to Mexico City. Texas remained independent until, at its own request, it was annexed by the United States as the 28th state in December 1845. Southern border disputes ignited the Mexican-American War, the first battle of which was fought at Palo Alto near Brownsville in May of 1846. The U.S.-Mexican boundary was established as the Rio Grande, ending fighting on that front. Then in the Compromise of 1850, the state of Texas gave up one-third of its northern and western land to other U.S. states.

The next territorial conflict came when state representatives voted in favor of Southern secession from the Union on February 1, 1861. Opposed to secession, Governor Sam Houston retired to his farm. Of the close to 90,000 Texans that served the Confederacy during the Civil War, two-thirds of them spent their time in the Southwest—defending settlements against hostile Apache and other tribes, fighting Union invasions, or participating in moves to expand control into New Mexico and Arizona. One such attempt was made by General H. H. Sibley, whose men marched from San Antonio to Santa Fe from January to March 1862. Battle successes were few, and they were forced to retreat after their supply train was captured.

The main Union offensive in Texas was a naval one directed at the coastline. During the Battle of Galveston, October 4, 1862, the Union captured the port. A counteroffensive on New Year's Day 1863 returned the island to Confederate control, though the Union maintained a blockade throughout the war. The Union had some success in South Texas, but in the last battle of the war, John S. Ford's unit defeated Union soldiers near Brownsville on May 13, 1865. From captured soldiers Ford learned that Confederate troops had surrendered all across the South, including General Lee at Appomattox, a month before.

Union soldiers poured into Texas to maintain order after the war. A decline in the price of cotton, and attempts to diversify the economy during reconstruction, led to the development of the cattle industry in the west. Texas was readmitted to the Union on March 30, 1870, and Old Glory flew again, but reconstruction continued for four more years. The largest cattle drive of the period moved 700,000 head of cattle to Kansas City in the spring of 1871.

In the late 1800s, Texas's population gravitated to urban areas and the economy improved. Czech, German, and Italian immigrants entered through Galveston Island and took up residence in Hill Country and beyond. James S. Hogg was elected as the first native-born Texan governor in 1891, running on a program of reform for big business. Things really began looking up when, on January 10, 1910, a new source of income gushed forth from Spindletop. Soon oil derricks would dot the fields and the industry would dominate the state's economy.

Today the Old West experience typically associated with Texas—ranches and oil, saloons and dust—is still especially evident in the western part of the state and in the Panhandle Plains, places etched with canyons, mesas, spires, gulches, arroyos, rivers, and unending horizons.

The Panhandle and the Plains

A DRIVING TOUR FROM AMARILLO TO SAN ANGELO

▼▼▼

Distance: 215 mi   **Time:** 4 days
Breaks: Stay in Amarillo, Lubbock, and Abilene.

This tour leads you from an authentic cowtown to a superbly restored cavalry fort, passing exquisite, lonely, rugged scenery along the way.

Pack a picnic lunch and start your trip with a morning visit to Palo Duro Canyon State Park, 20 mi southeast of **Amarillo.** In the afternoon, head to the Panhandle-Plains Historical Museum in Canyon or to the American Quarter Horse Heritage Center and Museum in Amarillo. If it's Tuesday, peek into Amarillo's weekly livestock auction. Stay the night in Amarillo, or camp in Palo Duro Canyon State Park, where you can see the evening musical extravaganza *TEXAS!,* performed on the canyon floor against a 600-ft cliff.

On your second day, visit the Panhandle-Plains Historical Museum in Canyon if you didn't do so the day before; then head south on I–27 for a two-hour drive to **Lubbock,** where you can visit the renovated period buildings at the Ranching Heritage Center and see the Lubbock Lake Landmark State Historic Park.

Get an early start on day three to drive the 160 mi east on U.S. 84 for **Abilene.** Here you can see the beautiful, lonely ruins at Fort Phantom Hill and wander around Buffalo Gap, a onetime trading post that is now an authentic (if re-created) pioneer village.

On your fourth morning, head 90 mi southwest on U.S. 277 to **San Angelo** to explore the national historic landmark that is Fort Concho, thought to be the best preserved of all pioneer cavalry forts.

The Big Bend of the Rio Grande

A DRIVING TOUR FROM FORT STOCKTON TO DEL RIO

▼▼▼

Distance: 185 mi   **Time:** 5 days
Breaks: Stay in Fort Stockton, the Fort Davis area, Big Bend National Park, and Del Rio.

View the beautiful landscape that early pioneers shared with Native Americans as you journey through Big Bend National Park and over the Rio Grande at Lake Amistad. Stops at a frontier outpost and the oldest winery in Texas let you see how human history developed in southwestern Texas.

TEXAS TIME LINE

1519 Alonso Alvarez de Pineda, a Spanish adventurer, is the first European to reach Texas. He explores and maps the coastline.

1528 Spanish explorer Alvar Nunez Cabeza de Vaca is shipwrecked on Galveston Island. After trading in the region for about six years, he explores the Texas interior on his way to Mexico.

1540 Francisco Vásquez de Coronado leads a two-year expedition into northwestern Texas in search of fabled cities of gold.

1681 Mission Nuestra Senora del Carmen is founded near El Paso to convert the Tigua Indians.

1685 French explorer Robert Cavelier La Salle arrives in Matagorda Bay and establishes Fort St. Louis, claiming Texas for France.

1689 On April 22, Mexican explorer Alonso de León reaches Fort St. Louis on an expedition planned to reestablish Spanish presence in Texas. He finds the fort abandoned.

1691 Texas becomes a Spanish province.

1716 Spain begins to build many more Catholic missions in Texas, including those that would be the foundation for the towns of San Antonio, Goliad, and Nacogdoches. Construction continues until around 1789.

1718 Mission San Antonio de Valero (the Alamo) is founded.

1731 Canary Islanders arrive in San Antonio de Bexar to establish the first civilian municipality.

1812 The Gutierrez-Magee expedition, consisting of about 130 men from Louisiana, Texas, and Mexico, crosses the Sabine River heading west in a rebel movement against Spanish rule in Texas.

1819 The Florida Purchase Treaty is signed, relinquishing the U.S. claim to Texas.

1820 Moses Austin, with son Stephen F., receives permission from the Spanish government to bring 300 colonists to Texas.

1821 Mexico declares its independence from Spain and gains control of Texas.

1823 Stephen F. Austin acquires a grant from the Mexican government for a colony already settled on the Brazos River.

1830 Relations between Texans and the Mexican government reach a new low when Mexico passes a law to curb further immigration into Texas by settlers from the United States.

1832 Texans and Mexicans fight the Battle of Velasco. A convention of Texan rebels draws proposals for the reform of Mexico's policies on tariffs and immigration.

1835 Texans repulse a detachment of Mexican cavalry at the Battle of Gonzales, beginning the Texas Revolution.

1836 The Texas Declaration of Independence is signed on March 2; Sam Houston is elected the first president of the Republic of Texas. On March 6, Texans are overwhelmed by the Mexican army after a siege at the Battle of the Alamo. On March 27, Colonel James Fannin and 342 Texans are executed at Goliad under General Santa Anna's orders. On April 21, Sam Houston leads the Texan victory against Santa Anna at the Battle of San Jacinto.

1839 The Texas Congress first meets in Austin, the frontier site selected for the capital of the Republic.

1845 On December 29, U.S. president James Polk follows through on a campaign platform promising to annex Texas and signs legislation making Texas the 28th state of the United States.

1846 The Mexican-American War ignites as a result of disputes over Texas boundaries. The outcome of the war fixes the boundary at the Rio Grande.

1853 The first state capitol is built in Austin.

1861 On February 1, Texas secedes from the Union following a 171-to-6 vote by the Secession Convention. Governor Sam Houston is one of those opposed to secession.

1863 After several weeks of Union occupation, Texan Confederates win back control of Galveston Island for the remainder of the Civil War.

1865 The last land engagement of the Civil War is fought in May, at the Battle of Palmito Ranch in South Texas, more than a month after General Lee's surrender at Appomattox, Virginia. Texas slaves are freed.

1866 The abundance of longhorn cattle in South Texas and the return of Confederate soldiers mark the beginning of the era of Texas cattle drives to northern markets.

1870 The United States Congress readmits Texas into the Union on March 30.

1898 Theodore Roosevelt recruits and trains his Rough Riders in San Antonio.

1900 Galveston is hit by hurricane; 6,000 residents are killed.

1901 "Black gold" is discovered at the Spindletop oil field near Beaumont.

Spend your first day exploring **Fort Stockton**'s historic district. You'll discover a marvelous orientation to the Big Bend region in the Annie Riggs Memorial Museum.

On your second day, travel west on I–10, then south on Route 17 toward Fort Davis National Historic Site, an 1854 frontier post bearing the rich heritage of the Ninth Cavalry, a regiment of African-Americans known as the Buffalo Soldiers. Spend the night in one of the many historic lodgings in the area.

Use your third and fourth days to visit **Big Bend National Park.** Gather food, water, camping, and picnic supplies, and head almost due south on Route 118. Allow yourself plenty of time to hike and drive through this immense park and bring lots of extra film.

On your fifth morning, exit Big Bend via U.S. 385, and turn east at its junction with U.S. 90 toward **Del Rio.** Stop in Langtry for lunch. There you'll find the Judge Roy Bean Visitor Center. Driving southeast on U.S. 90 to Del Rio, you'll cross the exquisitely blue Lake Amistad on a 6-mi-long dam. Once in Del Rio, visit Val Verde Winery, the state's oldest, begun by Italian immigrant Frank Qualia in 1883 and the only such operation to survive Prohibition.

The Republic Trail

A DRIVING TOUR FROM NACOGDOCHES TO GOLIAD

▼▼▼

Distance: 313 mi   **Time:** 3 days
Breaks: Stay in Nacogdoches and Brenham.

Discover the heritage of Texas as you explore the world of the Texan revolutionaries from the oldest town in Texas to the site of the tragic Goliad massacre.

Start your exploration of the Republic of Texas period deep in the Piney Woods town of **Nacogdoches,** generally believed to be the oldest town in Texas. The Old Stone Fort is an exact replica of a 1779 stone house that served as a fort and a prison, as well as government headquarters during several attempts to found a republic. Nine flags have flown over the fort, including three from failed republics, and it's the site where Davy Crockett, Sam Houston, and Thomas Rusk were administered the oath of allegiance to Mexico. Also in Nacogdoches, the Sterne-Hoya House operates as a memorial library and museum of Texas history.

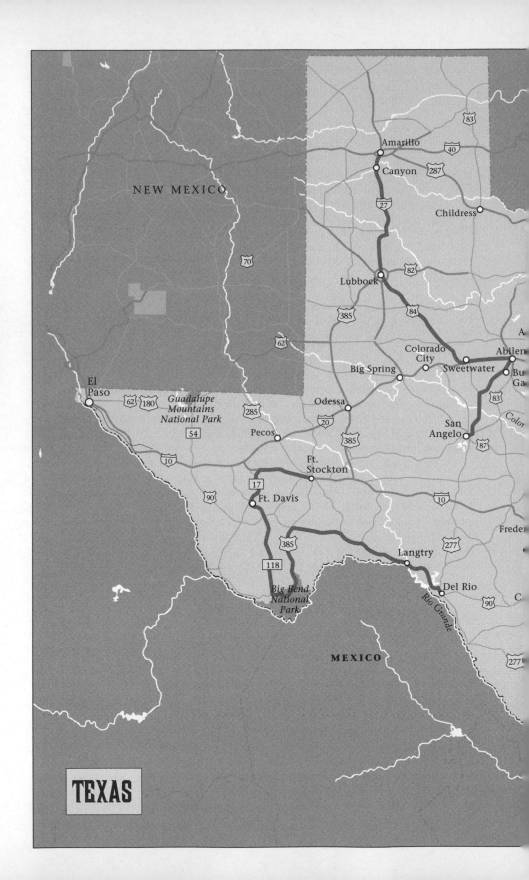

OKLAHOMA

Oklahoma
City

ARKANSAS

Wichita
Falls
82
82
281
Jacksboro
380
287
Sherman
Denison
Bonham
Texarkana
59
30
Jefferson
Lake
Caddo
Ft. Worth
Dallas
Albany
180
377
20
Waxahachie
20
Tyler
Jonesville
Abilene
Buffalo
Gap
35
Corsicana
Nacogdoches
LOUISIANA
83
Comanche
67
31
59
Colorado R.
377
67
Waco
21
94
Lufkin
96
281
Temple
77
Burnet
Huntsville
71
30
45
59
Austin
36
Washington
Beaumont
Round
Top
90
Fredericksburg
290
Brenham
Houston
90
Comfort
New
Braunfels
San Marcos
La
Grange
290
San
Felipe
10
Baytown
10
Port
Arthur
Castroville
San
Antonio
77A
Gonzales
77
La Porte
Galveston
Angelton
35
183
59
37
Goliad
Victoria
277
35
59
Corpus Christi
359
285
Laredo
Kingsville

N

83
77

0   100 miles
0   100 km

Brownsville

On your second day, follow U.S. 59 south to Lufkin, where you'll pick up Route 94 through national forest lands to **Huntsville.** At the Sam Houston Memorial Museum Complex you'll discover a 15-acre spread, two homes, a law office, and possessions, all of which belonged to the Texas hero. From Huntsville, drive southwest on Routes 30 and 90 to Washington, site of Washington-on-the-Brazos State Historical Park. Here the Texas Declaration of Independence was signed in 1836, as was the Republic's new constitution. An excellent museum tells the story. Spend the night in nearby **Brenham.**

On your third day, drive west on U.S. 290, then south on U.S. 77 to Monument Hill and Kreische Brewery State Historical Park in La Grange. On Monument Hill, you can see the grand tower that honors the Texan soldiers who were massacred at Salado Creek in 1842, plus a beautiful view over the Colorado River. From La Grange, follow U.S. 77 south to Victoria, where you'll pick up U.S. 59 south to **Goliad.** Here lies the most fought-over Spanish fort in Texas and, many will argue, the true birthplace of Texas. The Presidio La Bahia, established in 1749, is the site where Colonel James Walker Fannin and 341 Texas volunteers were held captive before being marched out and shot under the orders of Mexican general Santa Anna. The death toll was twice that of the battle at the Alamo.

ABILENE

▼▼

Abilene was already populated by ranchers and cowboys when the Texas & Pacific Railroad laid tracks through it in 1881, turning the small cow town into the transportation hub of West Texas. Two years later Abilene (named for Abilene, Kansas) was incorporated and named Taylor County seat. Although the city has a long history as a cattle-producing area, the livestock industry yielded to oil when wells were discovered here in the early 1900s. The nearby ruins of Fort Phantom recall frontier days and cavalry heroism as well as the struggles between settlers and the Comanche and Apache people. Downtown, the historic district's restored turn-of-the-20th-century buildings are now occupied by galleries and museums. *Contact Abilene Convention and Visitors Bureau | 1101 N. 1st St., Abilene 79601 | 915/676–2556 or 800/ 727–7704 | fax 915/676–1630 | www.abilene.com/visitors.*

Albany and Fort Griffin. Albany, the Shackelford County seat, 35 mi northeast of Abilene, is worth a detour to see the ornate 1883 courthouse and the jail. At the corner of Main and 1st, find the Georgia Monument, erected to honor the battalion from Georgia who fought for Texas independence, many of whom were massacred at Goliad. Wander 15 mi north of Albany to the ruins of Fort Griffin, surrounded by rolling, scrubby state park lands along the Brazos River. Admire the grazing longhorns, part of the official state herd, and check out the meticulously restored buildings amidst the ruins. Historical markers and exhibits note the fort's establishment in 1867 and the six companies that lived here; the site was also known as "the wickedest place on earth," thanks to the parade of gamblers and outlaws who reportedly killed a person a day during the roughest days of the 1870s. Ask the chamber of commerce for information. | Central Railroad at Main | 915/762–2525 | Free.

Buffalo Gap Historic Village. Twenty buildings from the region's frontier days, including the Old Taylor County Courthouse, a country store, a blacksmith shop, and a bank, make up this historical village 12 mi south of Abilene. A short video screened in the visitor center introduces you to the area's history, including how the Buffalo Gap lost the title of county seat to Abilene in 1881. | 133 N. William St., Buffalo Gap 79508 | 915/572–3365 or 915/572– 5211 | $5 | Mon.–Sat. 10–6, Sun. noon–6.

Fort Phantom Hill and Lake. Fort Phantom was constructed in 1851 to ward off attacks by Native Americans but was abandoned by the Army in 1854 and burned shortly thereafter. A stone commissary, guardhouse, powder magazine, and a dozen cactus-studded stone chimneys mark the site one soldier is said to have called a "barren waste." The ruins, 14 mi north of Abilene, once housed five companies of infantry. | Rte. 600 | 915/677–1309 | www. fortphantom.org | Free | Daily dawn–dusk.

Grace Museum. In a 1909 former railroad hotel, this cultural center houses three museums. Of Old West interest is the History Museum, which displays original Texas & Pacific Railroad coal bins and train whistles; turn-of-the-20th-century photographs; and reconstructed period kitchens and living rooms with appliances and furniture from the 1910s. | 102 Cypress St. | 915/673–4587 | www.thegracemuseum.org | $4 | Tues.–Sat. 10–5.

✦ ON THE CALENDAR: June **Fort Griffin Fandangle.** Hundreds of townfolk come together to reenact a story about West Texas settlers and Native Americans. The show is set to music and takes place under the stars. | 915/762–2525.

HISTORIC DINING AND LODGING

Fort Griffin General Merchandise. Steak. Beautifully prepared Black Angus steak, prime rib, and rack of lamb are on the menu at this comfortable roadside restaurant. Seafood lovers can order the fried shrimp or fish of the day. Oil lamps on the tables, rough wood walls, and bare cement floors add to the period feel of the building, built in 1907. | 517 U.S. 180, Albany | 915/ 762–3034 | Closed Sun.–Mon. | $16–$25 | MC, V.

Stasney's Cook Ranch. In 1897, Matilda "Dude" Nail Cook and her husband, W. I., purchased most of the land this ranch is on today. For 30 years they raised cattle, until an oil field was discovered on the property, bringing the Cooks' wealth to last a lifetime. Stay in the Cooks' original, sprawling, white ranch house or in one of two cabins that are replicas of the officers' quarters at nearby Fort Concho and Fort Griffin. The ranch-style cabins are made of native limestone and furnished with cow-hide rugs, early photographs of Fort Griffin and Fort Concho, and, in one case, a replica of an officer's uniform in a shadow box. Various meal plans are available. Dining room, some kitchenettes, mountain bikes, laundry service, Internet; no phones in some rooms, no TV in some rooms, no smoking. | U.S. 283 Box 1826, Albany, 76430, 35 mi northeast of Abilene | 915/762–2313 or 888/762–2999 | www.stasney. com | 1 ranch house, 10 cabins | $625 ranch house, $125–$175 cabins | MC, V | CP.

AMARILLO
▼▼▼

Some early houses gleamed with newly applied, bright yellow paint after the name of this central Texas Panhandle city changed from Oneida to Amarillo (Spanish for "yellow"), when it was designated a railroad stop in the late 1800s. Amarillo first was recognizable as a settlement in 1888, when support services and workers were needed to maintain a massive stockyard holding livestock destined for railroad cars. Amarillo has also became a gateway to the nation's second largest canyon, Palo Duro Canyon State Park, the site of the last major battle with Comanche Indians. *Contact Amarillo Convention and Visitor Council | 1000 S. Polk St., 79101 | 806/374–1497 or 800/692–1338 | www.amarillo-cvb.org.*

American Quarter Horse Heritage Center and Museum. Devoted to the quarter horse, considered the first breed native to the United States, this expansive museum contains the world's largest equine registry, as well as numerous exhibits, hands-on displays, and videos. Exhibits explain the development of the quarter-horse breed for cattle herding and its early origins as a short-distance race horse. | 2601 I–40 E | 806/376–5181 | fax 806/376–1005 | www.aqha. com/horse/museum | $4 | Mar.–Oct., Mon.–Sat. 9–5, Sun. noon–5; Nov.–Feb., Mon.–Sat. 9–5.

Carson County Square House Museum. Recounting the history of the Panhandle, this local history museum houses exhibits detailing stories of the region's early Native American inhabitants, cattle ranches, and the arrival of the railroad. | Rte. 207 and 5th St., 25 mi northeast of Amarillo in Panhandle | 806/537–3524 | fax 806/537–5628 | www.squarehousemuseum.org | Free | Mon.–Sat. 9–5, Sun. 1–5.

Palo Duro Canyon State Park. On the high plains 12 mi east of the Panhandle town of Canyon is the site of the last great battle between the U.S. and the Comanche. Truly a Texas-size wonder, this natural chasm stretches 120 mi wide. Among its rock spires and precipitous cliffs is an outdoor amphitheater where the historical drama *TEXAS!* is presented every summer, June–August. | 11450 Park Rd. 5, Canyon 79015 | 806/488–2227 | www.tpwd.state.tx.us/park/paloduro | Day-use $3, primitive camping $9, camping with electrical hook-up $12, pageant performance (depends on section) $5–$23.

Panhandle-Plains Historical Museum. A re-created saloon and blacksmith shop are among exhibits in Pioneer Town, one of several demonstrating Old West lifestyles in the late 1800s. Guns, saddles and other artifacts are also displayed; traveling exhibits highlight items such as the development and design of cowboy boots. | 2503 Fourth Ave. Canyon 79015, 16 mi south of Amarillo off I-27 | 806/651–2244 | www.panhandleplains.org | $4 | June–Aug., Mon.–Sat. 9–6, Sun. 1–6; Sept.–May, Mon.–Sat. 9–5. Sun. 1–6.

✦ ON THE CALENDAR: Apr.–Oct. **Cowboy Morning Breakfast.** A cowboy-style breakfast, cooked and enjoyed outdoors, is held at the Figure 3 Ranch in Palo Duro Canyon near Amarillo, reached via a 20-minute ride on mule-drawn wagons. Following breakfast, cowboys show off their skills with some roping, riding, and branding. Evening steak dinners are also available. | 800/658–2613.

June **Cowboy and World Championship Chuckwagon Roundup.** The Texas Panhandle's cowboy culture is illustrated in cattle drives, trade shows, cowboy poetry, and competitions among chuck-wagon cooks during annual festivities at Amarillo's Tri-State Fairgrounds. | 806/376–7767.

June–Aug. *TEXAS!* **Musical Drama.** This spectacular pageant within an outdoor canyon amphitheater at Palo Duro Canyon State Park near Amarillo tells the powerful story of the settlement of the Texas Panhandle. The 80-member cast, sometimes on horseback, performs amid special effects such as simulated thunder and lightning. | 806/655–2181.

ANGELTON
▼▼

Angelton is one of eleven small towns near the mouth of the Brazos River, where in 1821 Stephen F. Austin landed to plat out a new colony. Hoping to establish an ally in the area, the Spanish government had granted Austin enough land for 300 families, who were to immigrate there from the United States. Austin planned to build cabins and plant crops in preparation for the families' arrival, but he soon learned that Mexico had gained independence from Spain. Instead of building, Austin set out for San Antonio and Mexico City to get confirmation of the land grant from provincial and national authorities. In the meantime, the families started to arrive. The settlement grew slowly but surely, and in 1824 a Mexican land grant was issued. Although a few U.S. settlers were known to have entered Texas before 1821, the Brazos River settlement was considered the core of a new Texas. Clashes with the native Karankawan Indians were inevitable, as the tribe did not believe in personal property. Nearby Columbia served as the first capital of the Republic of Texas from October 1836 to March 1837 and later was hometown of the first native-born governor of Texas, James S. Hogg. Hurricanes and time have taken a toll on local landmarks, and few have survived. *Contact Southern Brazoria County Visitors and Convention Bureau | 1239 W. Rte. 332, Klute 77531 | 979/265–2505 or 800/938–4853 | www.tourist-info.org.*

Brazoria County Historical Museum. Illustrations and commentary on interpretive panels discuss Texas's colonial period (1821–50), including Stephen F. Austin, the original colony, the native Karankawans, the battles of the Texas Revolution, and the founding of the Republic of Texas. Original letters of the settlers offer a glimpse into the hardships of the time. | 100 E. Cedar St., Angleton | 979/864–1208 | www.bchm.org | By donation | Weekdays 9–5, Sat. 9–3.

Varner-Hogg Plantation State Historical Park. The former home of the first native-born governor of Texas, James S. Hogg, the 1830s Varner-Hogg Plantation was one of Austin's original 300 plots of land. Tour the home to see period pieces, including elaborately carved and upholstered sofas, a tall secretary with glass-enclosed book shelves, and a large quilt collection (on display in the fall). | 1702 N. 13th St., East Columbia | 979/345–4656 | www.tpwd.state.tx. us/park/varner | $4 | Wed.–Sat. 9–11 and 1–4, Sun. 1–4.

AUSTIN
▼▼

In 1838, Mirabeau B. Lamar, the second president of the Republic of Texas, proposed that the committee searching for a new site for the capital consider the small, remote town of Waterloo, on a bend in the Colorado River. Lamar had admired the area, which previously had been the Lipan-Apache home range, when he was there on a buffalo hunt. Building a grand capital was part of Lamar's campaign to create the illusion of a greater Republic of Texas, thereby distracting constituents from the republic's problems with Native American raids and its hostile southern neighbor, Mexico. By 1839, the government had moved and construction on the capitol building was under way. *Contact Austin Convention and Visitors Bureau | 201 E. 2nd St., 78701 | 512/474–5171 or 800/926–2282 | www.austintexas.org.*

Austin Carriage Service. Let a magnificent Percheron draft horse pull you in a reproduction 19th-century carriage on a one-hour tour of downtown Austin, the capitol grounds and Governor's Mansion, and the Bremond Block Historic District. | 203 San Jacinto St. | 512/243–0044 | www.austincarriage.com | $80 per hr | Weekends 10–4.

Austin History Center. This center is a repository for what seems like every conceivable newspaper clipping, photograph, and book related to Austin's past and present. Look around, then pick up brochures for self-guided walking tours of old neighborhoods. | 810 Guadalupe St. | 512/974–7480 | www.cityofaustin.org/library/ahc | Free | Mon.–Thurs. 9–9, Sat. 10–6, Sun. noon–6.

Calaboose African-American History Museum. Docents take you through exhibits on the Buffalo Soldiers and the cotton era, in the 1873 Hays County Jail. | 200 Martin Luther King Dr., San Marcos, 25 mi south of Austin | 512/393–8421 or 512/353–0124 | $3 | By appointment.

Camp Mabry Texas Military Forces Museum. Battle dioramas, weaponry, maps, flags, and uniforms chronicle the state's military history. | 2200 W. 35th St. | 512/406–6967 | Free | Wed.– Sun. 10–4.

Governor's Mansion. Since the 1860s Texas governors have resided in the mansion, which has an impressive collection of 19th-century American furnishings. You'll see a tall, four-poster mahogany bed purchased during Sam Houston's administration circa 1860, plus handmade quilts embroidered with historical scenes and natural Texas motifs like bluebonnets. | 1010 Colorado St. | 512/463–5516 | Free | Weekdays 10–5; tours Mon.–Thurs. 10–noon.

Pioneer Farm. Experience life on a working 1880s farm complete with animals such as pigs and horses, crops such as corn and cotton, and chores such as sausage making, butter churning, and cotton picking. Costumed docents help you try out the chores and explore the two homes, barns, and outbuildings. | 11418 Sprinkle Cut-Off Rd. | 512/837–1215 | $3 | June–Aug., Mon.–Thurs. 9:30–1, Sun. 1–5; Sept.–May, Mon.–Wed. 9:30–1, Sun. 1–5.

Republic of Texas Museum. The Daughters of the Republic of Texas curate a collection of military and household artifacts commemorating pioneers' way of life and the 10 years of the Republic. Step into a complete period kitchen with an wood-fired stove, pie cupboards, flour bins, and wooden utensils. | 510 Anderson La. | 512/339–1997 | $2 | Weekdays 10–4.

State Cemetery. Here lie the grave sites of Stephen F. Austin, the Father of Texas; various signers of the Texas Declaration of Independence; 11 governors; and numerous Texas Rangers and Confederate soldiers. Statuary by artist Elisabet Ney adorns the grounds. | E. 7th and Comal Sts. | 512/463–0605 | www.cemetery.state.tx.us | Free | Daily 8–5.

Texas State Capitol. When the old state capitol building burned in 1881, it cleared the way for this domed structure designed by Elijah E. Myers and reminiscent of the Washington Capitol—only taller, of course. Tours of the interior highlight the architectural and decorative details: the cupola, wainscotting, stained-glass panels, and numerous paintings of Texas Revolution scenes. Twenty-two acres of grounds contain monuments to the heroes of the Alamo and to Confederate soldiers. | 1100 Congress Ave. | 512/463–0063 | Free | Weekdays 8:30–4:30, weekends 9:30–4:30.

Treaty Oak. The only survivor of a grove known as the Council Oaks, this past-its-prime tree got its name because it's believed (though there's no proof) that under these trees in the 1840s Stephen F. Austin signed the first boundary agreement between native locals and the area's white settlers. | Baylor and W. 5th Sts. | No phone | Free | Daily.

✦ ON THE CALENDAR: June **Hyde Park Historic Homes Tour.** The grande Victorian dames of Austin's first subdivision open their doors to the public on Father's Day. | 512/452–4139.

Nov. **Muster Day.** Scenes of the Texas Revolution and other military events are reenacted at Camp Mabry, plus there's a parade of military armor, aircraft displays, helicopter demonstrations, and exhibits on the Buffalo Soldiers. | 512/465–5059.

HISTORIC DINING AND LODGING

Paggi House. American. Robert E. Lee is rumored to have stayed in this 1845 stage-coach stop, which later was owned by Michael Paggi, the entrepreneur who introduced ice making to Austin in the 1870s. Ask for the farm-raised redfish topped with lump crab meat and beurre blanc, like the regulars do. | 200 Lee Barton Dr. | 512/478–1121 | Reservations essential | Closed Sun. No lunch weekends. | $19–$29 | AE, D, DC, MC, V.

Scholz Garten. American/Casual. German-inspired beer gardens with Sunday afternoon concerts were an inseparable part of immigrants' social life in the 19th century. August Scholz took over one of the existing establishments and in 1872 expanded, moving Scholz Garten to the current location. Today you can still watch live music on outdoor stages while you eat sausage and hoist a mug. | 1607 San Jacinto St. | 512/474–1958 | $4–$9 | AE, D, DC, MC, V.

Driskill Hotel. This hotel has hosted governors' balls and visiting dignitaries—imagine the tales it could tell about political wheelings and dealings—since 1886, when cattle baron Jesse Driskill had it built. Choose between Victorian-style rooms in the Driskill Tower, added circa 1929, and rooms in the original hotel, which have high ceilings, some antiques, and black-marble baths. Restaurant, café, room service, in-room safes, cable TV with movies, gym, massage, bar, laundry service, concierge, Internet, business services, meeting rooms; no smoking rooms. | 604 Brazos St., 78701 | 512/474–5911 | fax 512/474–2214 | www.driskillhotel.com | 188 rooms | $215–$290 | AE, D, DC, MC, V.

BEAUMONT

▼▼▼

In 1835, land prospector Henry Millard purchased a tract near a Spanish and French trading post in order to subdivide it into a small town. Growth was slow until oil started gushing forth from Spindletop Hill at the rate of approximately 100,000 barrels per day in January 1910. Beaumont's population jumped from 9,000 to 30,000 within the year. *Contact Beaumont Convention and Visitors Bureau | 801 Main St., 77701 | 409/880–3749 or 800/392–4401 | www.beaumontcvb.com.*

Sabine Pass Battleground State Historical Park. A monument honors Confederate troops that repelled a Union attack in 1863 at this supply-line site 15 mi south of Port Arthur. | Rte. 87, Port Arthur, 20 mi southeast of Beaumont | 409/971–2451 | www.tpwd.state.tx.us/park/sabine | $2 | Daily dawn–dusk.

Spindletop/Gladys City Boomtown Museum. See what Beaumont was like after the first Texas oil gusher was struck in 1910. Walk through a town of original and reproduction wood buildings, such as a fully stocked blacksmith shop, a photo studio, a post office, an oil-and-gas office, and a wooden oil derrick field. | Lamar University, University Dr. and U.S. 69 | 409/835–0823 | hal.lamar.edu/~psce/gladys.html | $2.50 | Tues.–Sun. 1–5.

BIG BEND NATIONAL PARK

▼▼▼

Early visitors had mixed reactions to the unending desolation and beauty of Big Bend, which Spanish explorers dubbed El Despoblado (the unpopulated place). One French writer in 1885 complained that the land gave him a feeling of "supreme melancholy." A strategic crossroads for thousands of years, the park has witnessed a parade of Comanche, Apache, Spanish conquistadores, U.S. soldiers, Mexican revolutionaries, and many others. Big Bend National Park itself spans more than 800,000 acres across desert plains and mountains, appearing much as it did hundreds of years ago, without even a fence post to mar the view. *Contact Big Bend National Park | U.S. 385 and Rte. 118, 145 mi south of Fort Stockton, 79834 | 915/477–2251 | www.nps.gov/bibe.*

Castolon Historic District. Lingering adobe buildings are what's left of early 20th-century farming settlement of Castolon. The La Harmonia Company Store operates from one of the buildings, selling commodities such as milk and household goods to customers on both sides of the border. The Alvino House (built 1901) at Castolon is the oldest known adobe structure in the park. | Southwest side of park, at end of Ross Maxwell Scenic Dr. | 915/477–2222 store | Park $10 | Store 10–6 daily (closed for lunch, usually 1–1:30).

Hallie's Hall of Fame Museum. Hallie Stillwell was a local pioneer, teacher, and rancher. Her namesake museum includes mementos of Hallie's life such as her old .38-caliber Colt revolver, and other relics of West Texas frontier life. To enter the museum go next door to the general store and obtain the key. | Rte. 2627, 6 mi east of Big Bend National Park | 915/376–2244 | www.our-town.com/stillwell/welcome.html | Donation accepted | Daily 7 AM–8:30 PM.

HISTORIC LODGING

Lajitas Resort. Once a cavalry outpost built to protect residents from Mexican bandito Pancho Villa, this revived ghost town is now an Old West–style resort alongside the Rio Grande. In the Calvary Post lodge, styled after an old cavalry post, rooms adorned with rustic wooden furnishings face a shaded courtyard. Rooms in the Badlands Hotel, decorated to reproduce the feeling of an Old West hostelry, occupy the second floor of the stores along Main Street in Old

THE LAST OF THE LONGHORNS

The massive spread of horns on a once common, scrappy breed of cattle known as the Texas longhorn became almost symbolic of the state itself in the late 1800s and early 1900s. In the late 19th century, all of the nation's cattle—estimated at about 60 million—were believed to have at least some Texas longhorn blood. Because of these vast numbers, beef was served on many dinner tables as an alternative to wild game. But as European and other cattle breeds such as the Hereford and Angus were introduced into American herds, the longhorn (directly descended from early Spanish stock) was almost bred out of existence. The longhorn's distinctive characteristics began to disappear as ranchers deliberately created hybrids to attain the best characteristics of all the different breeds—in particular, a gentler and heavier replacement for the sometimes cantankerous, lean longhorn. Beginning in 1948, the state's few remaining longhorns were rounded up and collected together to begin a breeding program aimed at restoring and preserving the famous longhorn. Since then, the Texas Legislature has established officially protected longhorn herds, which can be viewed in various state parks including Palo Duro Canyon and Big Bend Ranch. Numbers of longhorns from pure stock are today estimated at about 250,000.

Town Lajitas. The Officers Quarters replicates accommodations in the original officers' quarters of Fort Davis. All the amenities plus extra luxury touches are furnished. A frontier boardwalk has specialty shops where you can buy baked goods, coffee, and souvenirs. The western-style Ocotillo Restaurant sometimes serves exotic menu items—including armadillo and rattlesnake. Restaurant, bar, dining room, some kitchenettes, some minibars, some microwaves, some refrigerators, some in-room hot tubs, cable TV, pool, 3 ponds, golf, tennis court, horseback riding, boating, laundry facilities, pets allowed (fee). | Rte. 170, 25 mi west of Big Bend National Park entrance, Lajitas 79852 | 915/424–3471 | www.lajitas.com/accommodations.html | 89 rooms, 26 condos, 2 suites, 1 house | $125–$195 | AE, D, DC, MC, V.

BRENHAM

▼▼

A predominantly German population settled here to farm in the 1820s and '30s, and immigration continued until the Civil War. On March 1, 1836, Texas Republic delegates gathered at nearby Washington-on-the-Brazos for a meeting that would culminate in the signing of the Texas Declaration of Independence. Brenham was incorporated in 1844. *Contact Brenham/Washington County Convention and Visitors Bureau | 314 S. Austin St., 77833 | 979/836-3695 | www.brenhamtexas.com.*

Monument Hill and Kreische Brewery State Historical Park. Buried here are Texans who died in two conflicts, the Dawson Massacre and the Mier Expedition, involving the opposing forces of Mexico and the Republic of Texas. On September 18, 1842, 36 volunteer militiamen led by Captain Nicholas Dawson were killed in an attack by Mexican forces at Salgado Creek. Texans mounted a punitive campaign that led them to Mier, Mexico, where they were forced to surrender and march toward Mexico City. They escaped but were recaptured, and every 10th man was executed. Later the remains of both groups were recovered and buried in a tomb with a monument. A visitor center tells of the battles fought by the men interred here. Also on site is one of Texas's first breweries and the home of the German immigrant who started it. | Off U.S. 77 on Rte. 92, 35 mi southwest of Brenham, La Grange | 979/968–5658 | www.tpwd.state.tx.us/park/monument | $2 | Daily 8–5; brewery tours weekends at 2 and 3:30.

Stephen F. Austin State Historical Park. Two days a week you can tour a replica of Stephen F. Austin's cabin and a general store, among other pioneer buildings. | Rte. 1458 and Park Rd. 38, 35 mi southeast of Brenham, San Felipe | 979/885–3613 | www.tpwd.state.tx.us/park/sfa | $3 | Park daily 8 AM–10 PM; tours weekends at 1.

Washington-on-the-Brazos State Historical Park. Explore the Star of the Republic Museum, 10,000-square-ft visitor center, and replica of Independence Hall to learn about the 59 men who gathered in March 1836 to sign the Texas Declaration of Independence. Military uniforms and weaponry, maps, and video presentations focus on the history and development of the fledgling republic. The Barrington Living History Farm includes a replica of a homestead belonging to Anson Jones, the fourth and last president of the Republic of Texas. For more in-depth information, a 90-minute tour starts at the visitor center. | 23200 Park Rd. 12, 14 mi northeast of Brenham | 979/878–2214 | www.birthplaceoftexas.com | Visitor center and grounds free, Independence Hall $4, Star of the Republic Museum $2, Barrington Living History Farm $4; combination ticket $7 | Visitor center and buildings daily 10–5 (last tour at 3), grounds daily 8–dusk.

Winedale Historical Center. The 215-acre complex contains a large collection of pioneer homes, stables, storage barns, and workshops, plus a research center, a nature trail, and a picnic area. Tour homes furnished with period antiques and stenciled ceilings, which recall the German culture of the area. | 3841 Rte. 2714, 25 mi southwest of Brenham, Round Top | 979/278–3530 | www.cah.utexas.edu/divisions/winedale | $3 | Weekdays 8–5, Sat. 10–5, Sun. noon–5.

✦ ON THE CALENDAR: Mar. **Texas Independence Day Celebration.** See battle reenactments, hear musical performances, and take a special tour as part of the weekend-long celebration at Washington-on-the-Brazos State Historical Park. | 979/878–2461.

HISTORIC LODGING

Mariposa Ranch. Several early buildings, including an 1820s long cabin, an 1836 Greek Revival home, and a circa-1900 farm house, were moved to this ranch by owner Charles Chamberlain, a lifelong Republic of Texas history buff, and his wife, Johnna. The ranch and cabins are decorated with saddles, Lone Star quilts, and wood and iron furniture. The ranch is 10 mi north of downtown Brenham, off U.S. 36, near Little Rocky Creek, where Sam Houston was baptized. Cable TV, in-room VCRs; no smoking. | 8904 Mariposa La., 77833 | 979/836–4737 | fax 979/836–2565 | www.mariposaranch.com | 5 rooms, 2 suites, 4 cabins | $85–$205 | AE, MC, V | BP.

BROWNSVILLE

▼▼▼

The southernmost city in Texas evolved from Fort Brown. To defend the United State's new southern boundary, General Zachary Taylor and his troops began construction of the fort in 1846. Although Texas had declared its independence in 1836, Mexico never recognized that claim. When the United States annexed the Republic as the 28th state in 1845 and began to build Fort Brown, the activity there was viewed as an act of war by Mexico, sparking the Mexican-American War. The first battle was fought in May 1846 at nearby Palo Alto. A peace treaty signed in February of 1848 set the border at the Rio Grande, and by then speculators Charles Stillman and Samuel Belden had purchased enough land to map out a town site of 4,676 acres. In December of that year, they formed the Brownsville Town Company and began selling lots for as much as $1,500. *Contact Brownsville Convention and Visitors Bureau | Box 4697, 650 Rte. 802, 78523 | 956/546–3721 | www.brownsville.org.*

Palo Alto Battlefield National Historic Site. Soldiers fought the first battle of the Mexican-American War in this grassy field on May 8, 1846. A short walking trail takes you by a few informational markers on-site. Check out the visitor center (1623 Central Blvd.) in downtown Brownsville to learn the story of the war through interpretive signs and displays of weapons, ammunition, maps, and other artifacts. | Rte. 1847 and Rte. 511, off U.S. 77, 5 mi north of Brownsville | 956/541–2785 | www.nps.gov/paal | Free | Weekdays 8:30–4:30.

Stillman House Museum. This one-story house of bricks made from local river sand was built in the 1850s by Charles Stillman, the founder of Brownsville. Furnishings, documents, maps, clothing, and other artifacts from the period contemporary to Stillman (1835–1880) are on display. | 1305 E. Washington St. | 956/541–5560 | $2 | Weekdays 10–noon and 2–5, Sun. 3–5.

BURNET
▼▼▼

Burnet developed around former Fort Croghan in the mid-1800s. The fort was built in 1842 by U.S. Dragoons, mounted infantrymen whose job was to defend white settlers' land against Native Americans. Later, Texas Rangers were sent to the fort by the federal government. A settlement called Hamilton Valley grew on the banks of Hamilton Creek 3 mi from the fort, and the town was founded in 1849. Stock-raising and farming formed the basis of the early economy. Although Fort Croghan was abandoned in 1855 and residents endured several conflicts with area Native Americans, the town survived and was renamed in 1858 after David G. Burnet, the provisional president of the Republic of Texas. By 1860, Burnet County had 2,480 residents, and county farmers were managing large cattle and hog herds as well as producing an abundance of corn and wheat. A railroad was built to connect Burnet to Austin in 1882, when pink stone quarried in Granite Mountain was needed for the construction of the grand state capitol. *Contact Burnet Chamber of Commerce | 703 Buchanan Dr., 78611 | 512/756–4297 | www.burnetchamber.org.*

Fort Croghan. In operation from 1842 to 1854, the fort was one of several established to protect the region between the Rio Grande and Trinity River from attacks by Native Americans. Guided and self-guided tours cover the fort plus a one-room schoolhouse, stage-coach shop, blacksmith shop, powder house, and several cabins. Exhibits in the museum include early pioneer clothing, yolks for oxen, branding irons, and different kinds of barbed wire. | 703 Buchanan Dr. (entrance on Rte. 29) | 512/756–8281 | Free | Apr.–Aug., Thurs.–Sat. 10–5.

Longhorn Cavern State Park. This dry cavern has few formations but plenty of history. In the early 20th century, a wealthy rancher's daughter named Mariel King was kidnapped by a band of Comanche and brought to this cave, where she was tied up as the Comanche chief prepared to negotiate for her ransom. Several hours later, three Texas Rangers came down on ropes through one of the ceiling entrances. Legend has it that the echo of their gunfire reverberated so much that the Comanche thought they were outnumbered and fled. The cave also is rumored to be where outlaw Sam Bass buried a stash of stolen treasure in the 1870s. The guided tour is nonstrenuous, with wide, well-lit trails through the huge limestone rooms. | Park Rd. 4 off U.S. 281, 11 mi southwest of Burnet | 830/598–2283 or 877/441–2283 | www.longhorncaverns.com | $10.95 | Weekdays 10–4, weekends 10–5.

Llano. Settled on the lovely, spring-fed Llano River in 1855, this town about 30 mi west of Burnet has a well-restored downtown historic district with 1860s buildings occupied by shops and offices. The county museum, on the north side of the Llano River on Route 16, is in a drugstore built in 1922. Inside, you'll see selected pieces of furniture from the late 1880s, including chairs from an old hotel and a table that was once in the now submerged Heath

Mine. Pick up visitor information at the chamber of commerce. | 700 Bessemer St., off Rte. 16 | 915/247–5354 | www.llanochamber.org.

Mason. A cattle-ranching town with German heritage, Mason was settled when Fort Mason was built in 1851 on a hilltop that afforded a good view of advancing Comanches. The post's best-known soldier was Lieutenant Colonel Robert E. Lee. Although the sandstone fort was dismantled in 1869, the stone was salvaged and used to build local Mason businesses and homes. Around 15 years ago, the fort was rebuilt on its original site. You'll see reconstructed officers' quarters with typical 1850s furnishings and photographs from Mason's early day. In the town center is the county courthouse, an 1870s schoolhouse that houses the county museum, and the beautiful 1880s Seaquist Home. | U.S. 87, 65 mi west of Burnet | 915/347–5758 | www.masontxcoc.com.

HISTORICAL DINING AND LODGING

Badu House. Built in 1891 as the First National Bank of Llano, this inn is listed on the National Register of Historic Places and is a Texas Historical Landmark. Within the sturdy brick exterior with its granite checkerboard trim, past the doors inset with stained glass, a grand oak staircase leads you to six bedrooms and a two-bedroom suite, all furnished with antiques. | 601 Bessemer St., Llano 78643 | 915/247–1207 | www.baduhouse.com | 6 rooms, 1 suite | $70–$100 | MC, V | BP.

COMFORT

▼▼▼

Germanic immigrants (including Alsatians and Czechs) settled many small Hill Country towns in the mid-1800s. Comfort is typical of these villages. More than 120 buildings from the 19th and early 20th centuries survive and today house antiques shops, restaurants, and B&Bs instead of feed, dry-goods, and grocery stores. Original residents decided against naming the town "Gemütlichkeit," meaning peace, serenity, comfort, and happiness. *Contact Comfort Chamber of Commerce | 7th and High Sts., 78013 | 830/995–3131 | www.comfort-texas.com.*

Ingenhuett Store. Fourth- and fifth-generation family members run this general store, which was built in 1880 by Peter J. Ingenhuett. It's one of the oldest continuously operated stores in Texas. Photos of the family ancestors and Comfort's early days are on display inside. | 834 High St. | 830/995–2149 | Free | Weekdays 8–5:30, Sat. 8–4:30.

Treue der Union Monument. During the Civil War many German immigrants who didn't approve of slavery were burned out of their farms. When 35 tried to defect to Mexico they were caught by Confederates and killed, and their bodies were left unburied. The remains were eventually returned to Comfort, where the *True to the Union* monument, the only one honoring the Union south of the Mason-Dixon line, was dedicated in 1866. | High St., adjacent to Comfort High School | No phone | Free | Daily.

DALLAS

▼▼▼

Founded in 1841 on the Trinity River, Dallas was a trading post that boomed once the Houston & Texas Central Railroad brought the train through in 1872. The city's founder, John Neely Bryan, a lawyer from Tennessee, envisioned Dallas as a major Trinity River port, and indeed it emerged as an important shipping point and economic force in the mid-19th century. European immigrants, ex-Confederates, and midwesterners of all trades settled the town. The first State Fair of Texas was held here in 1886 and the Federal Reserve Bank arrived in

1914. Contact Dallas Convention and Visitors Bureau | 325 N. St. Paul St., Suite 700, 75201 | 214/571–1000 or 800/232–5527 | www.visitdallas.com. Dallas Historical Society | 3939 Grand Ave., 75201 | 214/421–4500 | www.dallashistory.org.

Dallas Historical Society/Hall of State. Built for the Texas Centennial Exposition and now housing the Dallas Historical Society, the Hall of State's murals, statues, and artifacts tell the story of Texas from the 1500s to 1936. Collections include a watch belonging to Colonel James Fannin, the commander of Texas forces at the 1835 Battle of Goliad, and a medal belonging to Santa Anna, former president of Mexico, along with Sam Houston's handwritten account of the Battle of San Jacinto. The G. B. Dealey Library—named after the Dallas Historical Society's founder—holds more than 3 million historic documents. | 3939 Grand Ave., Fair Park | 214/421–4500 | Free | Tues.–Sat. 9–5, Sun. 1–5.

John Neely Bryan Cabin. This one-room cedar log cabin was built shortly after John Neely Bryan founded the settlement of Dallas in 1841. Floods washed away his first log cabin, which was built on the east banks of Trinity River. This is believed to be his third cabin. | 600 block of Elm St., Dealey Plaza area | 214/653–6653 | www.dallascounty.org | Free | Daily.

Old City Park. Immediately south of downtown, this 13-acre village depicts life in northern Texas between 1840 and 1910. A living-history farm includes animals and costumed residents busy with chores. Artisans are sometimes on hand to demonstrate candle making, weaving, and printing. Volunteers give guided tours of most of the 40 structures, which include a blacksmith shop, lawyer's office, bank, print shop, and log cabins, all from the 19th or early 20th century. | 1717 Gano St., one block south of the farmers' market | 214/421–5141 | www.oldcitypark.org | $7 | Tues.–Sat. 10–4, Sun. noon–4.

Old Red Courthouse. An 1892 Romanesque building of red sandstone, the many-turreted courthouse is one of the city's oldest surviving structures and a familiar landmark. A renovation slated for completion in January 2004 will restore the building's interior to its original Victorian style and create a space for a museum dedicated to the history of Dallas County. | Main and Houston Sts., Dealey Plaza area | 214/653–6653.

Pioneer Plaza. Celebrating the legendary cattle drives of the Old West, three bronze cowboys herd 70 longhorn steers, each weighing 1,000 lbs., on this grassy 4-acre park. Sculptor Robert Summer's interpretation of life on the old Shawnee Trail is said to be the largest bronze sculpture in the world. In Pioneer Cemetery, you'll find the graves of prominent pioneers and settlers, such as James W. Latimer, an early newspaper man, and Juliette Fowler, who founded the Juliette Fowler Home for orphans in 1870s. Statues by Elisabet Ney dot the grounds. | 650 S. Griffin St., downtown | 214/653–6653 | Free | Daily.

HISTORIC DINING

Brent Place. American/Casual. In an 1876 farmhouse decorated with antiques, this restaurant makes you feel right at home with country pot roast and garlic-mashed potatoes. You can also get more sophisticated fare like a pecan-and-chicken-salad sandwich with champagne grapes on a croissant, as well as Gulf crab cakes with baby greens in a whole-grain mustard vinaigrette. | 1717 Gano St., Old City Park | 214/421–3057 | $7–$12 | No dinner | MC, V.

DEL RIO

▼▼

A quirky character named Judge Roy Bean became known as the "law west of the Pecos" following Del Rio's formal establishment with the opening of a post office in 1883. Bean named his saloon the Jersey Lilly, in honor of an English actress he much admired (her name was Lillie Langtry). Bean is buried in the town where his odd interpretations of justice made him an Old West legend and the stuff of Hollywood films. *Contact Del Rio Chamber of Commerce | 1915 Ave. F, 78840 | 830/775–3551 or 800/889–8149 | www.drchamber.com.*

Judge Roy Bean Visitor Center. Inside the center, enjoy the preserved historic saloon, courtroom, billiard hall, and opera house where Bean measured out his six-shooter justice. A six-part diorama, loaded with sound, details his memorable career; the center's exterior is now landscaped with a noteworthy cactus garden. The center is 60 mi northwest of Del Rio in the town of Langtry. | Torres Ave., off Rte. 25 Loop, Langtry | 915/291–3340 | Free | 8–5.

Val Verde Winery. Founded in 1883 by Italian immigrant Frank Qualia, this is the oldest bonded winery in Texas and even survived Prohibition. Try a taste of the past in the house specialty, Don Luis Tawny Port, an aromatic, sweet red dessert wine. | 100 Qualia Dr. | 830/775–9714. | Free. | Mon.–Sat. 10–5.

Whitehead Memorial Museum. On 2½ acres containing open-air exhibits, you can soak up the spirit of the Old West era in Del Rio and Val Verde County. Among the 20 sites is the Perry Mercantile Building, built in 1871. The building has original native rock structure and wooden doors and includes displays such as the original water trough used by stage-coach horses and pack animals. The museum site is where Judge Roy Bean meted out his own peculiar brand of justice within the walls of his own saloon—the Jersey Lilly (misspelled by a sign painter). Bean's grave is also on site. | 1308 S. Main St. | 830/774–7568. | www.whitehead-museum.com | $4 | Tues.–Sat. 9–4:30, Sun. 1–5.

DENISON
▼▼▼

Born as a stop on the Butterfield Overland Mail Route in 1858, this Grayson County town is just 5 mi shy of the Red River. In the late 1800s, Denison became an important stop for several rail lines. Extensive historic restoration has revived the town where Dwight D. Eisenhower was born in 1890. *Contact Denison Area Chamber of Commerce and Visitor Center | 313 W. Woodard St., Denison 75020 | 903/465–1551 | www.denisontx.com.*

Fannin County Museum of History. A restored turn-of-the-20th-century Texas & Pacific Railroad depot houses this museum, which takes up one full city block between Main and Center streets in Bonham, about 30 mi east of Denison. Highlights of the museum include Native American artifacts, such as wood tools and beaded leather clothing; framed land grants from the 1880s, when Texas "gave away" land to populate the territory; late-Victorian clothing, including nine antique wedding gowns, dating back to 1858; a turn-of-the-20th-century ball gown; and a collection of 19th-century hand-made furniture. | 1 Main St., Bonham | 903/583–8042 | Donations accepted. | Apr.–early Sept., Tues.–Sat. 10–4; early Sept.–Mar., Tues.–Sat. noon–4.

Fort Inglish Village. This village in Bonham contains a replica of Fort Inglish, which was built in 1837 to defend Texas territory against Native Americans. The fort is surrounded by a stockade, and the village also has an authentic 1849 cabin. | Chinner St. and Rte. 56, Bonham | 903/640–2228 | Free | Apr.–Aug., Tues.–Fri. 10–4, Sat. 1–4.

Grayson County Frontier Village. Take a tour of this re-created 19th-century village to see structures built between 1840 and 1900, including a log school house, a jail, and homes with period furnishings. | Loy Lake Rd. exit off U.S. 75 | 903/463–2487 | Free | Apr.–Sept., Wed.–Sun. 1–4.

Red River Historical Museum. The town of Sherman, about 12 mi south of Denison, was named for Texas Republic general Sidney Sherman, who first said "Remember the Alamo!" and led the Battle of San Jacinto. In this former Carnegie Library, built in 1914 as a public library, you can see thousands of historic photographs, including 43 prints by western photographer Erwin E. Smith, born in 1886 in Honeygrove, Texas, and famous for his images of the American cowboy. Also on display are such artifacts as 19th-century furniture from Glen Eden Cotton Plantation, as well as a lock of hair from Sophia Porter, who owned and ran the plantation and is rumored to have swum across the Red River to alert Confederate forces that Yankee troops were in the area. | 301 S. Walnut St., Sherman 75090 | 903/893–7623 | www.texoma.net/rrhms | Donations accepted. | Tues.–Fri. 10–4, Sat. 1–5.

EL PASO

▼▼

In April 1598, Spanish explorer Don Juan de Oñate dubbed the entire Rio Grande valley "Paso del Rio del Norte" ("the pass through the river of the north")—from which El Paso derives its name. Because the area served as a crossroads for Spanish travelers accessing colonies in northern frontiers of New Mexico, the region thrived as a trade center. This fertile agriculture valley also once was noted for its vineyards and wine. Mexico's independence from Spain in 1821 ended more than two centuries of Spanish occupation in the area. Following the Mexican-American War, in 1848, the U.S.–Mexico boundary drawn along the Rio Grande divided the settlement of Franklin (renamed El Paso a year later) from the neighboring Mexican community eventually to be known as Juárez. El Paso was a major stopping point on the way west during the California gold rush. Today El Paso is most strongly associated with Anglo-America's Old West tales of cattle drives and gunfighters. *Contact El Paso Convention & Visitors Bureau | 1 Civic Center Plaza, 79901 | 915/534–0600 or 800/351–6024 | www.elpasocvb. com. El Paso County Historical Society | Box 28, 79940 | No phone | www.elpasohistory.com.*

Concordia Cemetery. North of I–10, this cemetery (once a ranch belonging to an early settler) is the final resting place of many Chinese laborers who helped build the railroad westward in the 19th century. Among the graves, which were once segregated by ethnicity, religion, and status, is the burial site of John Wesley Hardin, a Texas outlaw who claimed to have killed 40 people. | Gateway North and U.S. 54 | Free | Daily.

El Paso Museum of Art. Collections here date back to the 13th century. You'll find striking religious art in the Spanish Viceroyal and Mexican folk *retablos* room. | One Arts Festival Plaza | 915/532–1707 | www.elpasoartmuseum.org | Free. | Tues.–Sat. 9–5, Sun. noon–5.

El Paso Museum of History. Life-size dioramas depict the people of El Paso, past and present: Indians, Spanish explorers, cowboys, and cavalrymen. | 12901 Gateway West | 915/858–1928 | www.ci.el-paso.tx.us/mohistory.htm | Free | Tues.–Sat. 9–4:50, Sun. 1–4:50.

Fort Bliss Replica Museum. Established as an outpost to guard against Native American attack in 1848, this site was later used by Confederate soldiers. The museum is a reconstruction of the original fort and includes reproductions of an old woodworking shop and wagon house. | Building 5051, Pershing and Pleasonton Rds. | 915/568–4518 | www.bliss.army.mil | Free | Daily 9–4:30.

Magoffin Home State Historical Park. Early El Paso pioneer Joseph Magoffin erected his Territorial-style adobe homestead (now near downtown El Paso) in 1875. The home's traditional design includes thick adobe walls and an enclosed patio. Belongings of Magoffin and family, include paintings and furniture such as an imposing 13-ft-tall half-canopy bed with rose-color silk upholstery. The bed is part of a five-piece bedroom set purchased at the 1884 World's Fair in New Orleans. | 1120 Magoffin St. (follow signs off I–10; westbound traffic takes Cotton St. exit, eastbound traffic takes Downtown exit to Kansas St.) | 915/533–5147 | $2 | Daily 9–4.

Mission Trail. The nation's oldest continually active Spanish missions are found in historic districts of the lower Rio Grande valley just southwest of El Paso. A guided tour includes stops at Mission Ysleta, Socorro Mission, and Presidio Chapel San Elceario. If you want to look on your own, take the Zaragoza exit off I–10 just east of El Paso southwest for 4 mi, and then turn south onto Socorro Road and follow the mission trail signs. | Mission Trail Association, 1 Civic Center Plaza | 915/544–0061 or 800/259–6284 | www.missiontrail.com.

Ysleta del Sur Pueblo. As the oldest ethnic group in Texas, Tigua Indians established this settlement in 1681 after they fled in what is now northern New Mexico. At the cultural center, you'll find historical and cultural displays along with items for sale such as Tigua pottery, jewelry, and art. | 305 Yaya Lane (off Socorro Rd., take Zaragoza exit off I–10 just east of El Paso southwest for 4 mi and then turn south onto Socorro Rd.) | 915/859–7913 | Cultural center Tues.–Fri. 9–4, weekends 9–5.

✦ **ON THE CALENDAR:** June–Aug. **Viva El Paso!** A celebration of the El Paso region's history and legendary characters through music, dance, and drama takes place at the outdoor McKelligon Canyon Amphitheater in the Franklin Mountains. (Take I–10 east to U.S. 54 north to the Fred Wilson Road exit; turn left on Fred Wilson Road and left on Alabama Street to the entrance on McKelligon Canyon Road). | 915/565–6900 or 800/915–8482.

HISTORIC LODGING

Camino Real Hotel. This towering redbrick downtown hotel is listed on the National Register of Historic Places. The jewel of the hotel is the high-ceiling Dome Bar, surrounded by marble and beneath a 1912 Tiffany stained-glass dome of rich blues. In the days when the hotel was the Hotel Paseo del Norte, cattlemen filled the bar with smoke as they cut their deals. Although the hotel itself is a landmark, its rooms are refurbished and have ample space and contemporary furnishings with extra flourishes such as floral arrangements. 2 restaurants, coffee shop, room service, cable TV, pool, sauna, gym, meeting rooms, airport shuttle, parking, some pets allowed (fee). | 101 S. El Paso St., 79901 | 915/534–3000 or 800/769–4300 | fax 915/534–3024 | www.caminoreal.com | 359 rooms | $99–$104 | AE, D, DC, MC, V.

FORT STOCKTON

▼▼▼

Fort Stockton is a designated Texas Main Street city and has refurbished many storefronts to their original appearance, with some adobe buildings dating from the 19th century. Buildings such as the 1884 jail and the Grey Mule Saloon recall the days when Fort Stockton was a frontier army post, originally established in 1859. *Contact Fort Stockton Chamber of Commerce Visitor Center | 1000 Railroad Ave., 79735 | 915/336–2264 or 800/334–8525 | www. fortstocktontx.com.*

Annie Riggs Memorial Museum. Built in 1899, this hotel turned museum is filled with local history exhibits such as an original cast-iron bed (ordered from Sears for $6.75), branding irons, antique carriages, and period costumes fill rooms alongside pieces like a desk where a sheriff was sitting when he was shot. The hotel's original owner, Annie Riggs, had strict guest rules that prohibited, among other indiscretions, spitting on the floor. | 301 S. Main St. | 915/336–2167 | $2 | Mon.–Sat. 10–5, Sun. 1:30–5.

Fort Davis National Historic Site. Ninety miles southwest of Fort Stockton, the community of Fort Davis originated as a U.S. Army post in the mid-1800s. Fully and partially restored buildings on 474 acres of the fort site include exhibits such as depictions of early lives of African-American cavalry troops known as Buffalo Soldiers. The buildings include a bunkhouse and officers' quarters, furnished with authentic period pieces. | Box 1379, Rtes. 17 and 118,

Fort Davis | 915/426–3224 | www.nps.gov/foda | $3 | Late May–early Sept., daily 8–6; early Sept.–late May, daily 8–5.

Historic Fort Stockton. The original and reconstructed buildings from the 1858 fort include officers' quarters, a guardhouse, and a jail. | 300 E. 3rd St. (off U.S. 290) | 915/336–2400 | $2 | Mon.–Sat. 10–5, Sun. 1–5.

West of the Pecos Museum and Park. For a glimpse of what life was like in the 1880s, stop by this former saloon turned museum. Inside, a chuck box used for cattle drives and saddles are among artifacts from area ranches. In the courtyard out back are horse-drawn buggies and wagons, as well as the grave of gunfighter Clay Allison. The museum is in Pecos, 53 mi northwest of Fort Stockton via U.S. 285. | 120 E. 1st St., at Cedar St., Pecos | 915/445–5076 | $4 | Sept.–May, Tues.–Sat. 9–5; May–Aug., weekdays 9–6, Sat. 9–5, Sun. 1–4.

✦ ON THE CALENDAR: Feb. **Texas Cowboy Poetry Gathering.** Dances, poetry and cultural displays reflecting the true West ranching life are on the Sul Ross University campus and in its Museum of the Big Bend, in Alpine (65 mi southwest of Fort Stockton). | 915/837–2326.

HISTORIC DINING AND LODGING
The Hotel Limpia. Restoration of a 1912 hotel constructed from native pink limestone of the Davis Mountains provides a cozy retreat amid Victorian furnishings (an earlier hotel was built on this site in 1884). You can cool off in a courtyard garden, where rocking chairs help lull you into the peace of mind of a slower-paced world from almost a century ago. The restaurant serves homestyle cooking, such as savory buttermilk biscuits. Restaurant, 2 shops, no room TV, no room phone, pets allowed (fee), no smoking. | 100 Main St., Fort Davis 79734 | 800/ 662–5517 | fax 915/426–3983 | www.hotellimpia.com | 39 rooms | $89–$120 | AE, D, MC, V.

FORT WORTH
▼▼▼

Cattle ranchers and farmers began to settle the area around present-day Fort Worth in the 1830s, and in 1849 a military fort was built to protect the settlers from attacks by Native Americans. The outpost was then one of the westernmost forts of the American frontier and is still famous for being the town "where the West begins," a phrase that has appeared on the masthead of the *Star-Telegram* since the 1840s. The notion is said to have come from a peace treaty that allowed Native Americans use of the area west of Fort Worth.

The starting point of the Chisholm Trail—the famous cattle-drive highway between Texas and Kansas—Fort Worth was a favorite hangout for cowboys, soldiers, merchants of every trade, and outlaws like the Sundance Kid. Its reputation for rowdiness didn't depreciate after the railroad came through in 1876, when its value as a livestock shipping center beefed up even further. It's no wonder Fort Worth's contemporary nickname is Cowtown and its downtown and historic district fairly brims with authentic cowboy culture. Mounted police wear cowboy hats, rodeos and livestock shows are weekly events, and there's a daily cattle drive to boot. *Contact Fort Worth Convention and Visitors Bureau | 415 Throckmorton St., Sundance Square, 76102 | 817/336–8791 or 800/433–5747 | www.fortworth.com. Tarrant County Historical Commission | 100 E. Weatherford St., Downtown, 76196 | 817/884–3272.*

Cattle Raiser's Museum. This museum has the largest collection of documented branding irons in the world—16,000 to be exact. It also has a collection of spurs by famous spur makers, plus maps and historical documents on the Chisholm Trail and the Good Night Trail. Special exhibits distinguish black cowboys. | 1301 W. 7th St., northwest of Downtown | 817/332– 8551 | $3 | Mon.–Sat. 10–5, Sun. 1–5.

Fort Worth Stockyards National Historic District. Fort Worth's stockyards were what made the city the fastest-growing boomtown of the Old West. Cowboys driving their herds to northern markets always here, and the cattle that filled Exchange Avenue, called the "Wall Street of the West," were traded in the Livestock Exchange like the stock of companies is traded on the New York Stock Exchange today. The stockyards were also the biggest hog and sheep marketing center in the Southwest. One of Cowtown's crowning glories, the superbly restored 19th-century neighborhood still has its original brick-and-stucco warehouses, saloons, shops, hotels, and cattle offices. Today you can walk along the wooden sidewalks and brick streets and see saddle makers and antiques stores, saloons and cafés, a vintage train station, and, of course, cowboys on horseback. Weather permitting, the Fort Worth Herd, pure-bred Texas longhorn cattle, are driven through the Stockyards every day between March 15 and November 15. | Between Main St. and Packers Ave., and N.W. 28th St. in the north and N.E. 23rd St. in the south | 817/624–4741 | www.fortworth.com | Free | Daily.

The **Cowtown Coliseum** (121 E. Exchange Ave. | 817/625–1025 or 888/269–8696 | www.stockyardsrodeo.com | $9) was built in 1908 and held the world's first indoor rodeo. It still hosts rodeos every Friday and Saturday night, as well as traditional Wild West shows on summer weekends. The box office is open daily 9–5.

Artifacts such as turn-of-the-20th-century saddles and office furniture document the history of the cattle business in the **Stockyards Museum** (Livestock Exchange building, 131 E. Exchange Ave. | 817/625–5087 | Free). The museum is open Monday–Saturday 10–5.

Tarantula Train (140 E. Exchange Ave. | 817/625–7245 or 888/952–5717 | www.tarantulatrain. com | $22 round-trip) offers a nostalgic ride aboard 1920s railroad cars pulled by locomotives built in the 1890s. Ride through historic Forth Worth to Gravepine and back again. Open-air cars are popular in spring and fall. The train's unusual moniker is a reference to an 1873 railroad map that looked like a crazy spider, with Fort Worth at its center and proposed rail lines stemming out in all directions. Rides are on Saturday 10–2 and Sunday 1–5.

Granbury. Granbury's 19th-century courthouse square was the first in Texas to be listed on the National Register of Historic Places and has served as a blueprint for restoration efforts across the state. The country town is the seat of Hood County. A popular opera house, numerous antiques shops, a historic inn, and several good restaurants occupy the beautifully preserved buildings that line the square. The old jail has a small museum, and Wagon Yard antiques isn't shy about displaying some 100 reproduction 19th-century guns. | U.S. 377, 30 mi southwest of Fort Worth | 817/573–5548 or 800/950–2212 | www.granburytx.com.

Grapevine. Named for the wild mustang grapes that grew throughout the area, this town was settled in 1844 by the Peters colony, a group of Missourians who all bore the last name Peters. In the well-restored downtown area, you'll find numerous wineries, boutiques, and restaurants, most in original period buildings, plus the restored Palace Theater home of the Grapevine Opry Country Music Review. Sam Houston once visited Grapevine to sign the Bird's Fort Treaty on behalf of the Republic of Texas. The treaty divided a prairie among settlers and Native Americans. The train depot, where the Tarantula Train stops, is at the south end of town. Stop by Grapevine Visitor Information in the Heritage Center for self-guided walking tour brochures, maps, and suggestions. | Rte. 114, 20 mi northeast of Fort Worth | 817/410–3185 | www.grapevinetexasusa.com.

Log Cabin Village. Historical interpreters and craftspeople bring pioneer heritage to life at this living-history museum. Seven 19th-century log cabins from different parts of Texas stand on 2½ wooded acres in Historic Forest Park. | 2100 Log Cabin Village La. adjacent to Forth Worth Zoo | 817/926–5881 | www.logcabinvillage.org | $2 | Tues.–Fri. 9–5, Sat. 10–5, Sun. 1–5.

National Cowgirl Museum and Hall of Fame. The only museum in the world honoring women of the American West, this exceptional museum celebrates the "pluck and spirit" of more than 400 cowgirls and pioneers, including Annie Oakley, considered one of the greatest sharpshooters of all time. Among the more than 2,000 artifacts, you will find Oakley's riding habit and the 12-gauge shotgun given to her by Buffalo Bill, plus a collection of the serial dime novels that were popular in the late 1800s. | 1720 Gendy St., Cultural District | 817/336–4475 | fax 817/336–2470 | www.cowgirl.net | $6 | Tues. 10–8, Wed.–Sat. 10–5, Sun. noon–5.

Sundance Square. In the late 19th century downtown Fort Worth became so notorious for attracting and harboring deviants and lawbreakers that it was widely called Hell's Half Acre. In fact, sometime around 1898, outlaws Harry Longbaugh, aka the Sundance Kid, and Robert Leroy Parker, aka Butch Cassidy, hid out in the neighborhood, which was renamed Sundance Square in 1985 (and replatted a little to the south and east). The 20-block area of redbrick streets has some of Fort Worth's oldest buildings—built between 1885 and 1910— and is one of Texas's liveliest shopping-and-entertainment neighborhoods. | Between 1st and 5th streets, and between Jones St. to the east and Throckmorton St. to the west, Downtown | 817/339–7777 | www.sundancesquare.com | Free | Daily.

The **Sid Richardson Collection of Western Art** (309 Main St. | 817/332–6554 or 888/332–6554 | www.sidrmuseum.org | Free) is made up of oil paintings by western artists such as Frederic Remington (1861–1909) and Charles Russell (1864–1926). The museum and gift shop are wheelchair accessible and open daily.

HISTORIC LODGING

Stockyards Hotel. Rising three stories over the busy corner of Exchange Avenue and Main Street, this handsome hotel was built in 1906 by Colonel Thomas Marion Thannisch, one of northern Fort Worth's early developers. Native American–style comforters, horse-shoe and spur decorations, oil lanterns, and Victorian furniture give the rooms and public spaces an authentic Old West aura. Restaurant, in-room data ports, some refrigerators, dry cleaning, some pets allowed (fee). | 109 E. Exchange Ave., the Stockyards, 76106 | 817/625–6427 | www.stockyardshotel.com | 52 rooms | $169–$375 AE, D, MC, V.

Nutt House Hotel. This 1893 limestone beauty on Granbury's courthouse square has rooms and suites filled with period antiques. Downstairs is the enormously popular Nutt House restaurant, where celebrity chef Grady Spears wows the masses with his cowboy cuisine. Restaurant, fans, cable TV. | 119 E. Bridge St., 76048 | 817/279–1207 or 888/678–0813 | www.nutt-hotel.com | 7 suites | $150–$175 | AE, MC, V | BP.

GALVESTON
▼▼

Spanish explorer Cabeza de Vaca was stranded here among the Karankawa Indians in the 1500s. Centuries later, pirate Jean Lafitte used the island as a base. But it wasn't until 1837 when Galveston was made an official U.S. port of entry that the town was really established. Tens of thousands of immigrants from Europe came through on the way to the Hill Country, or to the gold fields of California. Many of the first public buildings in Texas, including a post office, bank, and hotel, were built here, but most were destroyed in the Great Storm of 1900. *Contact Galveston Island Convention and Visitors Bureau | 2428 Seawall Blvd., 77550 | 409/763–4311 or 800/351–4236 | www.galvestoncvb.com. Heritage Visitors Center | Aston Villa, 2328 Broadway, 77550 | 409/762–3933 | www.galvestonhistory.org.*

Pier 21 Theater. Watch as the Great Storm of 1900 comes to life in a multimedia presentation with archival drawings and accounts from survivors' diaries. Also playing is a film about the exploits of pirate Jean Lafitte. | Pier 21 | 409/763–8808 | www.galvestonhistory.org/plc-pier21.htm | $3.50 | Sun.–Thurs. 11–6, Fri.–Sat. 11–8.

Texas Seaport Museum. Aboard the 1877 tall ship *Elissa* numerous detailed interpretive signs provide information about the shipping trade in the 1800s, including *Elissa*'s routes and the cargos she once carried into Galveston port. Inside the museum building, you can view personal possessions and read about the different ethnic groups who immigrated through this port

THE GREAT STORM

Floodwaters on the barrier island of Galveston (which protects Galveston Bay from the Gulf of Mexico) began to rise as early as dawn on September 8, 1900. Long before storm chasers and satellite tracking systems, Galveston residents went about their business with little idea that a hurricane was approaching. A meteorologist, noting unusually high seas that morning, rode his horse up and down the beach urging sunbathers to move to higher ground. By 8 PM there was a 15-ft storm surge, and the Gulf of Mexico and Galveston Bay had merged into one. The few houses that remained standing on Galveston Island themselves became islands. People moved to second stories and then to rooftops. Howling winds and human screams pierced the darkness as debris swirled in the air and water.

That night 6,000 to 8,000 of the town's 37,000 residents died. Winds reached an estimated 150 mph. When dawn rose again, whole sections of Galveston were missing. Photographs of the wreckage show piles of what looks like wood kindling.

Galveston began to recover almost immediately, and the most pressing concern became disposal of the dead. A mass burial at sea was thwarted as the bodies rolled back ashore with the incoming tide. The military came in to prevent looting, and men on the street were recruited to recover the corpses and build a funeral pyre. Telegraph and water services were restored within a week, telephone and electrical within three. The city council voted to raise the island from its maximum elevation of 9 ft to 17 ft, beginning with a new seawall to be built on the gulf side, sloping down 1 ft for every 1,500 ft toward the bay. Buildings were raised on jacks, and by 1911 the project was completed. Newspaper accounts at the time said that not one family and not one building was left untouched by the Great Storm, and it remains the deadliest natural disaster in U.S. history.

town. You can search a database to find out when your own ancestors docked. | Pier 21 | 409/763–1877 | www.tsm-elissa.org | $6 | Daily 10–5.

✦ ON THE CALENDAR: May **Galveston Historic Homes Tour.** The first two weekends in May you can tour privately owned homes dating from the 1800s. Tickets ($20) include admission to several of the island's house museums and are available from the Heritage Visitors Center (2328 Broadway). | 409/765–7834.

HISTORIC LODGING

The Tremont House. Sam Houston presented his last speech at this hotel, Confederate then Union soldiers bunked here, and Great Storm victims took refuge under the Tremont House's roof. Period reproductions and Victorian-pattern wallpapers decorate the rooms. Restaurant, room service, cable TV, golf privileges, bar, meeting rooms; no-smoking rooms. | 2300 Ship's Mechanic Row, 77550 | 409/763–0300 | fax 409/763–1539 | www.galveston.com/thetremonthouse | 119 rooms | $99–$150 | AE, D, DC, MC, V.

GOLIAD

▼▼

To protect passage along the San Antonio River to the gulf, Spaniards moved Mission Espiritu Santo and a fort, Presidio La Bahia, here in 1749. In 1835, Texas colonists made a bid for independence from Mexico by taking over the Presidio. The next year Texan commander James Fannin surrendered his forces to Mexican general Jose Urrea when caught in retreat at the Battle of Coleto outside town. After being imprisoned at the Presidio, the 342 Texan soldiers were executed by Mexican general Antonio Lopez de Santa Anna, who later would become a dictator of Mexico. His cruelty in war made him the most hated enemy of Texas. "Remember Goliad!" soon became a Texas war cry alongside "Remember the Alamo!"

After Texas won independence, Goliad was largely deserted. A land grant in 1844 was the beginning of today's town site, but it wasn't until 1885 when the railroad arrived that the population started to grow in earnest. Cotton was the primary crop for local farmers, and in 1904 the town had two gins. *Contact Goliad County Chamber of Commerce | 25 S. Market St., 77963 | 361/645–3563 | www.goliad.org.*

Fannin Battleground Historic Site. Models of the battle ground, historical markers, and views from an observation tower explain the March 20, 1835, Battle of Coleto, in which Colonel Fannin surrendered to Mexican forces. | U.S. 59, 14 mi west of town | 361/645–3752 | www.tpwd.state.tx.us/park/fannin | $1 | Daily 8–5.

Goliad State Historical Park. Tour the restored Espiritu Santo de Zuniga, plus a small museum and the birthplace of General Ignacio Zaragoza, a Mexican general who defeated the French in the 1860s. Spinning, weaving, and pottery-making demonstrations are often held on weekends. | 108 Park Rd. 6 | 361/645–3405 | www.tpwd.state.tx.us/park/goliad | $2 | Daily 8–noon and 1–5.

Presidio La Bahia. This was the most fought-over Spanish fort in Texas and, many will argue, the true birthplace of Texas. The 1749 fort was where Colonel Fannin and 341 Texas volunteer soldiers were held captive before they were marched out and shot under the orders of Mexican general Santa Anna. A flag emblazoned with a bloody arm wielding a saber is flown here in remembrance, and artifacts in the museum and barracks illustrate the revolution. Today the structure is the oldest restored fort in the West. | U.S. 183, 2 mi south of town | 361/645–3752 | $3 | Weekdays 9–5, Sat. 10–4.

✦ ON THE CALENDAR: Mar. **Goliad Massacre Reenactment.** Events leading up to the occupation of Fort Defiance by Colonel Fannin, and his army's subsequent surrender, are re-created at Presidio La Bahia. | 361/645–3752.

HISTORIC LODGING
The Quarters. When the tourists go home for the day, you are left all alone in the centuries-old Presidio La Bahia. The priests of the fort used to sleep in what is now a spartan, unheated two-bedroom apartment with two queen beds. Hauntings have been reported in the courtyard, the quadrangle, the chapel—and the living quarters. No a/c, no room phones, no room TVs, no smoking. | U.S. 183, 2 mi south of town | 361/645–3752 | 1 apartment | $150 | No credit cards.

GONZALES
▼▼

The first shot in the Texas Revolution rang out when Mexican general Santa Anna tried to retrieve a cannon that had been given to the town of Gonzales for protection against Native American raids. On October 2, 1835, residents hoisted a banner with a crude drawing of the cannon and the slogan "Come and Take It!" The only ammunition left was scrap metal lying about, but it was gathered, stuffed in the barrel, and fired. Toward the end of the war in early 1836 General Sam Houston was in Gonzales when he learned about the fall of the Alamo. From here he rallied troops and marched on to defeat Santa Anna at the Battle of San Jacinto.

After Texas won the war, the area first surveyed by James Kerr as the Gonzales townsite in 1825 was still the westernmost point in Anglo-American settlement. It took until 1837 for the county and town to be incorporated officially into the new Republic. In the 1850s,

German and Czech farmers settled here, and by 1880 the town had a grist mill and a cotton gin to serve the area industries. *Contact Gonzales Chamber of Commerce and Agriculture | 414 St. Lawrence St., 78629 | 830/672–6532 | www.gonzalestexas.com.*

Gonzales Memorial Museum. This museum honors the soldiers who fought in the opening battle of the Texas Revolution in 1835. Highlights include the cannon that fired first and the original town charter, printed in 1841. | 414 Smith St. | 830/672–6350 | Donations accepted | Tues.–Sat. 10–noon and 1–5, Sun. 1–5.

Gonzales Pioneer Village. Eleven 19th-century buildings, including a single-room log cabin, 1870 church, broom factory, and smokehouse, are part of this village. Volunteers demonstrate how to make horseshoes and thread brooms, among other tasks. | 183 Business St. | 830/672–2157 | $2.50 | Sept.–May, Sat. 10–5, Sun. 1–5; June–Aug., Fri. 10–4, Sat. 10–5, Sun. 1–5.

✦ ON THE CALENDAR: Oct. **Come and Take It Days.** On the first weekend of the month, this reenactment of the skirmish that started the Texas Revolution, at Pioneer Village, is fueled by food booths, games, and music. | 830/672–6532.

HOUSTON
▼▼▼

Augustus and John Allen, two brothers from New York, founded Houston in 1836, naming the town for General Sam Houston, the hero of the battle of San Jacinto. The area's rich farmland guaranteed Houston's early success, and as local cotton production increased, the city became a major trade center. Railroads built in the mid-1800s were used to transport locally produced cotton, timber, and cattle north and west. Steamships from the port of Galveston navigated the Buffalo Bayou until the Houston Ship Channel was constructed in the early 1900s. By the time of the Civil War, Houston was the undisputed commercial center of southeast Texas. The 1901 discovery of petroleum in East Texas's Spindletop oil field further fueled Houston's growth as oil refineries sprung up around the ship channel. *Contact Greater Houston Convention and Visitors Bureau | 901 Bagby Ave., Suite 100, 77002 | 713/437–5200 or 800/365–7575 | www.houston-spacecityusa.com. Greater Houston Preservation Alliance | 712 Main St., 77002 | 713/216–5000 | www.ghpa.org.*

Antioch Missionary Baptist Church. Houston's oldest African-American Baptist congregation, founded in 1866 for emancipated slaves, worships in this sandstone-and-marble church surrounded by the downtown area's modern skyscrapers. The church was built between 1875 and 1879, and you can still see an original cornerstone, though the structure was expanded in 1895 and 1936. | 500 Clay Ave., downtown | 713/652–0738 | Free | Daily.

Bayou Bend Collection. Bayou Bend is the former home of Ima Hogg, daughter of Texas governor James Hogg and granddaughter of Joseph Hogg, who helped to write the Texas Constitution. Ms. Hogg's former furnishings and ornaments, plus additional pieces collected by the museum, are on display in magnificently styled period rooms. Part of the Museum of Fine Arts, Bayou Bend contains one of the finest existing collections of American decorative arts from 1620 to 1870, as well as an impressive 14-acre garden. | 1 Westcott St., River Oaks area | 713/639–7750 | www.bayoubend.uh.edu | $10 | House weekends 1–5; tours Tues.–Fri. 10–11:30 and 1–2:45, Sat. 10–11:15 Gardens Tues.–Sun. 10–5, tours Tues.–Sun. 10 and 11.

Lynchburg Ferry. After the Battle of San Jacinto, the Lynchburg Ferry transported wounded soldiers from the battlefield to the nearby town of Lynchburg. You can ride the ferry, which has operated continuously since 1822, across the mouth of the San Jacinto River, 20 mi east of Houston. The ride lasts 7–10 minutes, and the ferry operates around the clock. | Between

San Jacinto Battleground State Historic Park and Lynchburg Landing, Baytown | 281/424–3521 | Free | Daily.

Sam Houston Park. This park holds eight of the city's oldest buildings, including an 1823 cedar log cabin; the Kellum-Noble house, Houston's oldest surviving brick house, which still stands in its original location; a home once owned by William Marsh Rice; and the Yates House, built by a freed slave in 1870. All the buildings are restored, and several contain original period furnishings. | 1100 Bagby St., downtown, 77002 | 713/655–1912 | www.heritagesociety.org | $6 | Mon.–Sat. 10–4, Sun. 1–4.

San Jacinto Battleground State Historic Park. The San Jacinto monument, a 570-ft-tall limestone tower, stands over the battle site where the Republic of Texas won its independence from Mexico in 1836. Inside the pedestal, a museum exhibits paintings and artifacts, such as military uniforms, maps, and medals, relating to the history of Texas from the 15th century to the present. | 3523 Battleground Rd., on Rte.134, La Porte, 20 mi east of Houston | 281/479–2421 | www.sanjacinto-museum.org | Museum free, observation floor $3, battleship $5 | Daily 9–6.

✦ ON THE CALENDAR: Jan.–Dec. **Greater Houston Preservation Alliance Walking Tours.** Walking tours of historic sites within the city limits are held the fourth Sunday of the month at 2 PM. Call or check the Web site for tour departure points. | 713/216–5000 | www.ghpa.org.

Apr. **Reenactment of the Battle of San Jacinto.** The definitive battle for Texas's freedom, which occurred on April 21, 1836, between the Texans, led by Sam Houston, and the Mexicans, led by Santa Anna, is reenacted in period dress at the San Jacinto Monument in La Porte. | 281/479–2421.

Dec. **Candlelight Tour.** Take a yuletide candlelight tour of Sam Houston Park's historic homes, complete with refreshments and period music. | 713/665–1912.

HUNTSVILLE
▼▼▼

Hunstville began as trading post where Native Americans and early settlers came together to exchange goods. The trading post's founder, Pleasant Gray, came to Texas in the early 1830s to appropriate some of the so-called "free land" that the federal government was granting to emigrants in order to populate the area. The town is named after Gray's hometown, Huntsville, Alabama, and was officially chartered under the Republic of Texas in 1845 and the State of Texas in 1852. In 1844, Republic of Texas president Sam Houston retired to an estate just outside of town. A 77-ft-high likeness of Houston stands out on I-45. *Contact Huntsville Chamber of Commerce | Box 538, 77342 | 936/295–8113 or 800/289–0389 | www.chamber.huntsville.tx.us.*

Oakwood Cemetery. The burial site of Sam Houston and other famous Texans, Oakwood also has graves of pioneers and Union and Confederate soldiers. Self-guided-tour brochures are available at the chamber of commerce. | 9th St. at Ave. I | 936/295–8113 | Free | Daily.

Sam Houston Memorial Museum Complex. In the Woodland Home, the residence Sam Houston built himself, you can see Houston's leopard-skin vest, two of his walking sticks, a brace of his dueling pistols and General Santa Anna's saddle, plus interpretive panels on the history of the home. The Steamboat House is the home where Sam Houston died in 1863. Its original furnishings remain. In the Exhibit Hall, you can see Native American clothing and baskets as well as pioneer pistols and rifles from the late 1800s. In the main museum, there are reproductions of original documents on the secession and annexation of Texas. A short orientation film on Sam Houston can be viewed at a separate education center. | 1836 Sam Houston Ave. | 936/294–1832 | www.samhouston.org | Free | Tues.–Sun. 9–4:30.

JEFFERSON

▼▼

Jefferson developed as a port city on the Big Cypress Bayou, which linked northeastern Texas with Shreveport, Louisiana, and the Red River. By 1840 it was the second-largest port in Texas and known as the gateway to the Southwest. After the Civil War, the Corps of Engineers blew up the Red River log jam, which had kept up the water level in the Jefferson bayou, and the bayou started to drain out. Steamboat traffic slowed down until, in 1920, it came to a full stop.

When J. Gould proposed in the late 1860s that railroads run through Jefferson, locals voted against it, fearing that the railroad would damage the steamboat industry. J. Gould then went to Dallas, which had a population of 400 people at that time, and expanded his railroad there. After the bayou went dry, many settlers, who no longer had a way to transport their cotton and timber, moved to neighboring cities. Only a few farms and ranches survived. Today, Jefferson's lively downtown historic district is tucked beneath tall pines and moss-draped cypresses. Combine your visit to Jefferson with a drive to Marshall, 16 mi south, to see the richest examples of 19th-century heritage in northeastern Texas. *Contact Jefferson Chamber of Commerce | 118 N. Vale St., 75657 | 903/665–2672 | www.jefferson-texas.com.*

Jefferson Historical Society Museum. A tea set belonging to a czar of Russia, Confederate flags and money, Caddo Indian artifacts, and original documents signed by Sam Houston are among the hundreds of objects that fill four floors of exhibits from Jefferson's steamboat era. | 223 W. Austin St., 75657 | 903/665–2775 | $3 | Daily 9:30–5.

Jefferson Riverboat Landing and Depot. Guides recount Jefferson's steamboat-era history on one-hour boat tours that depart from here. | U.S. 59 and Cypress River Bridge | 903/665–2222 | www.historicjefferson.com/bayoutours | $6.50 | Daily 10, noon, and 2.

Marshall. Founded in 1841, Marshall quickly became the seventh-largest city in Texas. Its rapid growth was due largely to the Texas & Pacific Railroad, which came through in 1872, bringing railroad employees, builders, skilled craftsmen, and other settlers. The cotton industry all but vanished when Caddo Lake started to drain and steamship traffic declined after 1873. The three-square-block downtown Ginocchio National Historic District includes the 1896 Ginocchio Hotel, the 1912 T&P Depot, and the 1879 Allen House. The county courthouse, built in 1901, is listed on the National Register of Historic Places and is both a Texas Historical Landmark and a State Archaeological Landmark. | U.S. 59 and I–20 | www.marshalltxchamber.com.

In the Ginocchio Hotel, the **Harrison County Historical Museum** (707 N. Washington | 903/938–2680 | free) displays Caddoan arrowheads and pottery, Civil War memorabilia, and other historical items. The museum is open Tuesday–Saturday 10–4.

✦ ON THE CALENDAR: May **Historical Pilgrimage.** Tours of Jefferson's historic homes are led by docents in period dress, and a Victorian murder-mystery melodrama is performed. | 903/665–2672.

Dec. **Christmas Candlelight Tour.** Historic homes in Jefferson are opened for public tours to view holiday decorations. | 903/665–2672.

HISTORIC LODGING

Excelsior House. In continuous business since 1858, the Excelsior is Texas's second-oldest hotel and Jefferson's most-prized landmark. During the town's steamboat age, the Excelsior hosted such esteemed guests as Ulysses S. Grant in 1888 and Rutherford B. Hayes in 1878. Crystal chandeliers, Italian marble mantels, elegant period furniture, and paintings in heavy baroque frames all conspire to bring you back in time to a world of exclusive wealth in a burgeoning nation. Each room is differently decorated with antiques. Cable TV; no smok-

THE REIGN OF KING RANCH

Often referred to as the birthplace of the American cattle industry, King Ranch is still run by descendants of its founder, Captain Richard King. Born in New York City, King worked on steamboats in Alabama before he made his way to Brownsville in 1847 to serve in the Mexican-American War. As a steamboat captain he transported U.S. troops and supplies and afterward went on to co-own a steamboat company that dominated the Rio Grande for decades. As his wealth grew, he also formed a partnership to create a cattle operation centered 124 mi north of Brownsville on the Santa Gertrudis Creek. After King married Henrietta Chamberlain, Robert E. Lee (a close friend), suggested the current site for the home ranch. King hired almost all the residents of a Mexican village to help him create a hacienda system and to teach him the *vaquero* (cowboy) traditions. *Los kinenos* (the descendants of the original foremen) still play key roles in operations.

King was in Mexico chasing cattle rustlers when Brownsville was taken by Union troops during the Civil War. From Mexico his operation continued to run blockades to provide supplies for Confederate troops. King himself did not return to the ranch until he received a full presidential pardon in 1865. With his wartime profits, he began to rebuild and expand the ranch. King and onetime steamboat partner Mifflin Kennedy overhauled the ranching industry, initiating fencing, cattle drives to the north, and scientific breeding. The last paid off when the Santa Gertrudis breed of cattle, part Brahman bull and part British shorthorn, became the first of only two new breeds ever established in the United States. The other breed, the Santa Cruz, was also developed and established on King Ranch.

King's descendants went on to breed championship Thoroughbred and quarter horses. His legacy today is a privately held multinational corporation with interests in the transportation and energy industries, large-scale farming and processing (citrus crops, cotton, and grain in Texas, Florida, and Brazil), and other endeavors (hunting leases, retail developments, and conservation projects). Oh, and King Ranch is still one of the largest ranching operations in the world—covering 1,300 square mi, the kingdom is bigger than the state of Rhode Island.

ing. | 211 W. Austin St., 75657 | 903/665–2513 or 800/490–7270 | fax 903/665–9389 | www.theexcelsiorhouse.com | 15 rooms | $85–$119 | AE, D, MC, V | BP.

McKay House. One of the oldest bed-and-breakfasts in the South, this Greek Revival home was built in 1851 in the Quality Hill section of Jefferson's historic district. The rooms are fully restored with Victorian furnishings; most have either a wood- or coal-burning fireplace. You are invited to use the inn's Victorian nightgowns and nightshirts. The regionally famous gentleman's breakfast may include orange French toast and baked or fried apples. In-room data ports, laundry service, Internet, some pets allowed; no room TVs, no smoking. | 306 E. Delta St., 75657 | 903/665–7322 or 800/468–2627 | fax 903/665–8551 | www.mckayhouse.com | 7 rooms | $89–$169 | AE, D, MC, V | BP.

KINGSVILLE

King Ranch began in the 1850s when Richard King and a few partners acquired a land grant for a livestock ranch. King continued to acquire land through the 1800s (it is one of the largest ranches in the world today). By 1900 there was a growing need for a railroad to connect nearby Corpus Christi and Brownsville. Heiress Henrietta King, owning most of the land between the two cities, donated part of King Ranch for the rail line and part for a townsite named after her husband. Streets were laid out and, in 1904, lots were sold. Most of the residents were still railroad employees well into the 1910s and '20s. *Contact Kingsville Convention and Visitors Bureau | 1501 N. U.S. 77, 78363 | 361/592–8516 or 800/333–5032 | www.kingsvilletexas.com.*

King Ranch. This bastion of the Old West's cattle kingdom traces its origins to 1853, when it was founded by Captain Richard King, who made his fortune in the steamboat trade on the Rio Grande. Enjoy a guided tour of the working ranch in an air-conditioned bus, or watch a free video on its history at the visitor center. | Rte. 141, 1½ mi west of town | 361/592–8055 | www.king-ranch.com | Tour $7 | Mon.–Sat. 10–4, Sun. 1–5.

King Ranch Museum. Antique carriages, saddles, and guns, plus videos and photo essays, provide you with a look at ranch history. | 405 N. 6th St. | 361/595–1881 | $4 | Mon.–Sat. 10–4, Sun. 1–5.

King Ranch Saddle Shop. Operating from the John B. Ragland Mercantile Company Building downtown, this store carries on the tradition of saddlemaking begun after the Civil War. Early saddles are on display, and you can buy purses, bags, luggage, and belts. | 201 E. Kleberg | 361/595–1881.

LUBBOCK
▼▼▼

Named after Texas Ranger Colonel Thomas S. Lubbock (also a brother of a past state Texas governor), this farming and ranching settlement sprouted in 1891 and became a marketing center. The Santa Fe Railroad's arrival in 1909 sealed Lubbock's destiny as a thriving city in the Panhandle's south plains, dubbed Llano Estacado (Staked Plains) by early Spanish explorers. *Contact Lubbock Chamber of Commerce Convention and Visitor's Bureau | 1301 Broadway, Suite 200, 79401 | 806/747–5232 or 800/692–4035 | www.lubbocklegends.org.*

Ranching Heritage Center. The center includes 35 relocated period buildings, ranging from ranch homes to bunkhouses. The buildings along with exhibits such as a branding-iron collection and views of architectural innovations aimed at survival—such as gun ports—help depict the history of the Panhandle and its role in ranching. | 3121 4th St., 79409 | 806/742–0498 | www.ttu.edu/ranchingheritagecenter | Free | Mon.–Sat. 10–5, Sun. 1–5.

NACOGDOCHES
▼▼▼

Caddo Indians lived alone in the area around present-day Nacogdoches (pronounces Nack-uh-*doh*-chez) until a Spanish mission was established there in 1716. Many hold that Nacogdoches is the oldest town in Texas, a claim that is disputed because the settlement was deserted for several years in the mid-1700s after the mission closed down. The site was resettled in 1779 by Spanish traders led by Antonio Gil Y'Barbo, who oversaw the construction of a stone trading post. The fort was the site of at least three insurgencies; while six flags have flown over Texas, nine have flown over Nacogdoches. *Contact Nacogdoches Convention and Visitors Bureau | 200 E. Main St., 75963 | 936/564–7351 or 888/653–3788 | www.visitnacogdoches.org.*

Millard's Crossing Historic Village. You are invited to travel back in time to the 19th century and imagine what it was like when water was pulled out of wells in pails, plows were operated manually, and people used turkey-quill pens to write. A collection of restored 19th-century structures includes an 1830s cabin, an 1840s house, an 1843 chapel, and a 1900 parsonage. All are filled with period furnishings open for guided tours. | 6020 North St., off U.S. 59 | 936/564–6631 | $3 | Mon.–Sat. 9–4, Sun. 1–4.

Mission Tejas State Historical Park. A replica of the first mission built in East Texas, in 1690, stands in this park between the towns of Crockett and Alton. | Rte. 21 to Park Rd. 44 | 936/687–2394 | fax 936/687–3623 | www.tpwd.state.tx.us | $2 | Daily 8 AM–10 PM.

Sterne-Hoya Home. Adolphus Sterne, an early Nacogdoches resident who was active in the founding of the Republic of Texas, built this home in 1828. It's the site where Sam Houston was baptized a Roman Catholic in 1833, as dictated by Mexican law. Joseph van der Hoya, who once lived in the house and tutored Sterne's children, bought the house from Sterne's widow in 1869. The Hoya family and descendants continued to live in the house until 1941, eventually donating it to the city in 1958. | 211 S. Lanana St. | 936/560–5426 | Free | Mon.–Sat. 9–noon and 2–5.

Stone Fort Museum. This museum is in a replica of Nacogdoches founder Antonio Gil Y'Barbo's 18th-century stone trading post. The original structure was torn down in 1902, and the replica is on the campus of Stephen F. Austin State University. Changing exhibits focus on Texas history, art, and culture. In the collection is a sword rumored to have been owned by Y'Barbo and a shot glass from the Stone Fort Saloon. | Clark and Griffith Blvds. | 936/468–2408 | fax 936/468–7084 | Free | Tues.–Sat. 9–5, Sun. 1–5.

Texas State Railroad State Park. Steam locomotives from 1901 carry you between the towns of Rusk and Palestine through piney woods, across 30 bridges, and into depots built to recall the heyday of steam-powered travel. The 51-mi round-trip journey takes three hours, and you can catch a short film on the history of the railway in Rusk. Peak season is in late March and early April, when flowering dogwoods dot the landscape, and in November, when the woods are alive with autumn colors. Reservations recommended year-round. | Palestine Train Depot, 2 mi east of Palestone on U.S. 84, 65 mi northwest of Nacogdoches | 903/683–2561 | fax 903/683–5634 | $15 round-trip, $10 one-way | Mar.–Nov., weekends at 11.

✦ ON THE CALENDAR: Dec. **Victorian Christmas Train Ride.** Servers dressed in Victorian-style outfits dish out waffles, hot apple cider, lemonade, and cookies aboard a steam-powered train during a two-hour nighttime ride from Palestine halfway to Rusk and back. | 903/723–3014 or 800/659–3484.

HISTORIC LODGING

Llano Grande Plantation. Three 19th-century houses stand on this 700-acre forested plantation 6 mi south of the Nacogdoches courthouse. The Tol Barrett House, made of heavy native-pine timbers in the 1840s, was named for the oilman credited with having drilled the first oil-producing well west of the Mississippi River. The 1850 Sparks House is classic East Texas dogtrot—a term used to describe houses with a center passage that promoted easy ventilation. The 1855 Simpson House is a small, elegant plantation home that was built for Victor Jefferson Simpson. Rooms in all three homes are furnished with fine antiques, including an 1855 grand piano and a sideboard that belonged to Charles S. Taylor, one of the men who signed the Texas Declaration of Independence. Breakfast includes homemade bread and jam, fresh fruit, and venison sausage. Kitchenette, some pets allowed; no room phones, no TV in some rooms, no children under 12, no smoking. | 433 Phillips Rd. 75964 | 936/569–1249 or 800/505–9868 | www.llanogrande.com | 3 houses | $95–$125 | No credit cards | BP.

SAN ANGELO

▼▼▼

San Angelo grew around Fort Concho, which was built in 1867 to protect settlers moving west following the end of the Civil War. The city flourished as a center for agriculture and trade—boosted, naturally, by the arrival of the Santa Fe Railroad in 1888. *Contact San Angelo Convention and Visitors Bureau | 500 Rio Concho Dr., 76903 | 915/655–4136 | www.sanangelo-tx.com. Historic San Angelo Inc. | Box 350, 76902 | 915/653–4291 | www.historicsanangelo.org.*

Fort Concho National Historic Landmark. This former military post, active from 1867 to 1889, is one of the best-preserved forts in the state. You can tour the 23 buildings that once were part of the fort; exhibits contain uniforms, weapons, and furnishings dating to the site's early days. | 630 S. Oakes | 915/657–4444 | www.fortconcho.com | $2 | Tues.–Sat. 10–5, Sun. 1–5.

Miss Hattie's Bordello Museum. After 50 years as a "gentleman's social center," this former bordello was shut down by the Texas Rangers in 1946. Miss Hattie was the hostess who oversaw a bevy of accommodating ladies at the once bawdy establishment. Now, after restoration, the 10 bedrooms look as they did in the property's heyday. If you eat at Miss Hattie's Cafe and Saloon you can get into the museum for half price. | 18½ E. Concho Ave. | 915/653–0570 | www.misshatties.com | $5 | Hour-long tours Thurs.–Sat. at 1, 2, 3, or 4, or by appointment.

Railway Museum of San Angelo. Thanks to a restoration project in the late 1990s, San Angelo opened one of its earliest depots as a museum to help chronicle the arrival of the Santa Fe Railroad in 1888. Box cars, locomotives, dioramas, and scale models are among exhibits outdoors and inside the two-story building. | 703 S. Chadbourne St. | 915/486–2140 | www.railwaymuseumsanangelo.homestead.com | $3 | June–Aug., weekdays 1–5, Sat. 10–5; Sept.–May, Sat. 10–4.

HISTORIC DINING

Miss Hattie's Cafe & Saloon. American/Casual. Although the flourishes and flowers are all in fun (and in keeping with the theme of the nearby Miss Hattie's Bordello Museum), this restaurant originally was an old bank building. Antiques help set the mood here as you ponder the not-so-discreet visits that soldiers from old Fort Concho once made to Miss Hattie's gals in the quarters now occupied by the museum. The menu is varied, from sandwiches to steaks. | 26 E. Concho Ave. | 915/653–0570 | Closed Sun. | $12–$15 | AE, D, MC, V.

SAN ANTONIO

▼▼▼

The Spanish built the presidio San Antonio de Béxar in 1718. The same year, Spanish priest Antonio Olivares founded the Mission San Antonio de Valero, which was later renamed the Alamo, in the watery area Native Americans called *yanaguana* ("refreshing" or "clear waters"). A string of other area missions followed in the years before 1789. After Mexico gained independence from Spain in 1810, San Antonio was the chief Mexican stronghold in Texas and had the largest Mexican population in the state well into the 1900s.

The town is probably best known as the site of the Battle of the Alamo, where 189 Texan soldiers fighting for independence went up against superior Mexican forces numbering as many as 2,000 men. The siege ended in the death of all 189 Texans. After Texas won its independence, urban development was rapid: government buildings and hospitals were built, utility lines laid, streets paved. By 1880 the town was wired for telephones and had a new power plant, and by 1900 it had recovered from war loses and had the largest population in the state. *Contact San Antonio Visitors Information Center | 317 Alamo Plaza, 78205 | 210/207–6748 | www.sanantoniocvb.com.*

Alamo. A repository of Texas history, the Alamo is also a monument to the 189 volunteers who died there in 1836 during a 13-day siege by the notoriously cruel Mexican general Santa Anna. Today the historic chapel and barracks contain the guns and paraphernalia used by William Travis, Davy Crockett, James Bowie, and other Texas heroes. Illustrated on a courtyard wall is the history of the Mission San Antonio de Valero, as the Alamo was originally called. | 300 Alamo Plaza | 210/225–1391 | www.thealamo.org | Free | Mon.–Sat. 9–5:30, Sun. 10–5:30.

Casa Navarro State Historical Site. Legislator and signer of the Texas Declaration of Independence, José Antonio Navarro lived in this home. Tours of the home and exhibits examine the Mexican heritage of the region as well as Navarro's personal contribution to state history. | 228 S. Laredo St. | 210/226–4801 | www.tpwd.state.tx.us/park/jose | $2 | Wed.–Sun. 10–4.

Fort Sam Houston Museum and National Historic Landmark. This army base dating back to 1870 retains its original buildings, including barracks and offices, most of which are not open to the public. You can see army uniforms at the museum. | 1210 Stanley Rd. | 210/221–1886 | Free | Wed.–Sun. 10–4.

Guenther House. Shortly after Hilmer Guenther built the Pioneer Flour Mill to grind local grain in 1860, he started construction on this home adjacent to the mill. The house-museum—filled with Victorian furniture, some belonging to the Guenthers—welcomes self-guided tours. In season, it's decorated with elaborate Victorian Christmas garlands and ornaments. A mini-mill museum, a gift shop, and a cheerful restaurant are also on-site. | 205 E. Guenther St. | 210/227–1061 | www.guentherhouse.com | Free | Mon.–Sat. 8–4, Sun. 8–3.

Pioneer, Trail Drivers, and Texas Rangers Memorial Museum. Sheriffs' badges, saddlebags, cattlemen's tools, and other artifacts, plus educational signs, tell the story of cattle drives and the Texas Rangers on the frontier. | Brackenridge Park, 3805 Broadway | 210/822–9011 | $2 | Mon.–Sat. 11–4, Sun. noon–4.

San Antonio Missions National Park. Except for the Alamo, all of San Antonio's 18th-century Spanish missions constitute this national park. All are active parish churches. Mission Trail starts at the Alamo and continues 9 mi along the San Antonio River past the others. | Park Headquarters, 2202 Roosevelt Ave. | 210/534–8833 | www.nps.gov/saan | Free | Daily 9–5.

The largest, and best-known, mission outside the Alamo is the **Mission San José** (6701 San José Dr. | 210/922–0543 | www.sanjosemission.com), built in 1720. An outer wall, Native American dwellings, granary, water mill, and workshops have been restored. Watch a 20-minute video on mission history at the on-site national park visitor center. A noteworthy ceiling fresco in the library of the **Mission Concepción** (807 Mission Rd. | 210/534–1540), built in 1731, shows God as a mestizo. Much preservation work is yet to be done.

Mission San Juan Capistrano (9102 Graf Rd. | 210/534–0794), built in 1731, has Romanesque arches and a serene chapel.

You can still see segments of the Arab-inspired aqueduct, part of the missions' famous *acequia* (water management system), on the grounds of the remote **Mission San Francisco de Espada** (10040 Espada Rd. | 210/627–2021), built in 1731.

Spanish Governor's Palace. Masonry key-hole doors characterize the Spanish colonial style of this one-story government building finished in 1749. It served as the seat of Spanish power in Texas, and is where Stephen F. Austin went to request the first 300 land grants for Anglo settlers. Period Spanish pieces furnish the museum today. | 105 Plaza de Armas | 210/224–0601 | $1.50 | Mon.–Sat. 9–5, Sun. 10–5.

✦ ON THE CALENDAR: Mar. **Remembering the Alamo Weekend.** Educational exhibits and living history reenactments at 300 Alamo Plaza on the first weekend of the month portray those involved in both sides of the Battle of the Alamo. | 210/978–8100.

HISTORIC LODGING

Menger Hotel. Legend has it that William Menger built this hotel in 1859 to accommodate patrons of his brewery. Guests have included Teddy Roosevelt, Mae West, Ulysses S. Grant, and ranching magnate Richard King, who died here in 1885. The two-story lobby colonnade is filled with antiques. Rooms are all decorated differently, but neoclassical lines predominate. Restaurant, cable TV, pool, hot tub, gym, spa, bar, concierge, meeting rooms; no smoking rooms. | 204 Alamo Plaza, 78205 | 210/223–4361 | fax 210/228–0022 | www.historicmenger.com | 350 rooms | $119–$215 | AE, D, DC, MC, V.

Landmark Inn State Historic Site Bed and Breakfast. The first floor of this inn was built as a general store circa 1849. In 1853 a new owner expanded the building to become a stagecoach stop, post office, and basic lodging. A few years later, the gristmill and cotton gin were built on the grounds. With the addition of a second story, the main building became a hotel in 1863. Hardwood floors and wood furniture complete the small, simple rooms. Breakfast can be served in bed for a small fee. No room phones, no room TVs, no smoking. | 402 E. Florence St., 20 mi east of San Antonio, Castroville 78009 | 830/931–2133 | www.tpwd.state.tx.us/park/landmark | 8 rooms, 3 with bath | $50–$55 | D, MC, V | BP.

SWEETWATER

▼▼

The town's name originated with the Kiowa Indians, who identified the site as a source of extraordinarily fresh-tasting water. One of the first establishments was a dugout store catering to buffalo hunters who moved into the area after the Civil War. Sweetwater's first post office (known as Blue Goose) was opened in 1879. *Contact Sweetwater Chamber of Commerce | 810 E. Broadway, Sweetwater 79556 | 915/235–5488 or 800/658–6757 | www.sweetwatertexas.org.*

City-County Pioneer Museum. Housed in a 1906 residence of an early pioneer, this museum houses such relics as an old buggy, a fire truck, and a barber's chair. | 610 E. 3rd St. | 915/235–8547 | Free | Tues.–Sat. 1–5.

Heart of West Texas Museum. On display 25 mi west of Sweetwater are skeletal remains of an extinct bison that was a forerunner of modern-era buffalo found in herds that once roamed West Texas plains. Kiowa resistance to Anglo-American settlers who moved into the area also is documented. Barbed-wire exhibits and antique games represent the early life of settlers. | 340 E. 3rd St., Colorado City | 915/728–8285 | www.coloradocity.net/museumheartofwesttexas | Free | Tues.–Sat. 10–5.

Sweetwater Historic District. Listed on the National Register of Historic Places, Sweetwater's downtown area has about 50 buildings of note, the oldest dating from 1875. | Bounded by 1st and 5th Sts. and by Ash St. and the Texas & Pacific Railroad tracks.

WACO

▼▼

Situated at the confluence of the Brazos and Bosque rivers, Waco takes its name from the Hueco (pronounced *Way*-co) Indians—related to the Wichita—who lived on the area's rich, fertile land. Although Spanish explorers had identified this site in 1542, more than 300 years elapsed before permanent settlement began. After the Civil War, ranchers and cowboys settled along the Chisholm Trail, which crossed the Brazos River into what is now Waco. The city was incorporated on August 29, 1856. Waco became a major trade center with the 1870 completion of a 474-ft suspension bridge across the Brazos River. *Contact Waco Convention and Visitors Bureau | 100 Washington Ave., 76702 | 254/750–5810 or 800/321–9226 | www.wacocvb.com.*

Billy the Kid Museum. Texas is a land of tall tales, and this museum is is dedicated to one Texan's claim that he was gunfighter Billy the Kid. History holds that the Kid was born William Bonney and was shot dead at the age of 21 in New Mexico's Lincoln County War (1878–81). But Bill Roberts lived to the age of 90 insisting that he was the famous gunfighter. Decide for yourself. Convincing stories and so-called evidence are gathered here, 68 mi northwest of Waco. | 105 Pecan St., Hico | 254/796–4004 | $3 | Mon.–Sat. 11–4, Sun. 1–5.

Czech Heritage Museum. Czechs played an important role in settling central Texas, and their contribution is remembered in this museum, where you can see traditional Czech clothing, a 1549 Bible, handmade quilts and a handmade dulcimer, and more than 18,000 Czech language books dating back to the 1600s. | 520 N. Main St., Temple, 35 mi south of Waco | 254/773–1575 | Free | Weekdays 8–noon and 1–5.

Old Fort Parker Historic Site. This site is where pioneer Cynthia Ann Parker was kidnapped by Native Americans at the age of nine. She later became the mother of Quanah Parker, the Native American leader. | Off U.S. 14, Park Rd. 35 | 254/729–5253 | $2 | Daily.

Suspension Bridge and River Walk. Designed by the New York firm of engineers that later oversaw the construction of the Brooklyn Bridge, this is one of the earliest suspension bridges in America, and for a time it was the longest single-span suspension bridge west of the Mississippi. Completed in 1870 with a span of 470 ft, it supplied the cowboys and cattle following the Chisholm Trail, with the only means of crossing the Brazos River with wagons. Open today to foot traffic, the bridge offers splendid views of the scenic Brazos River. | Washington Ave. and University Parks Dr. | 254/750–5810 or 800/321–9226 | Free | Daily.

Texas Ranger Hall of Fame and Museum. On the banks of the Brazos River, this museum invites you to see guns of every description, including the rare Colt Patterson and Colt Walker, used by the Texas Rangers, a corps of mounted military men founded by Stephen F. Austin to defend the Texas frontier against Native Americans, Mexicans, and other enemy forces. The Rangers had the reputation of lone lawmen who always got their man. Dioramas and films recount the history of the Rangers. | 100 Texas Ranger Trail, off I–35 | 254/750–8630 | www.texasranger.org | $5 | Daily 9–5.

✦ ON THE CALENDAR: Dec. **Christmas at the Fort.** This holiday event takes place the second weekend in December and includes tours of Old Fort Parker by docents in pre-1840 period clothing. | 254/729–3894.

WAXAHACHIE
▼▼

The first settlers emigrated to the plains 90 mi south of Dallas in the 1840s, and Waxahachie (pronounced Wacks-uh-*hatch*-ee) was founded in 1871. The town's name came from a local Native American tribe's word for either "cow" or "buffalo creek." After the railroad came through in 1879, the population boomed. In the 1890s, cowboys and ranchers from all over Texas passed through Waxahachie on the Chisholm Trail. Numerous restored turn-of-the-20th-century buildings survive in downtown and residential Waxahachie. *Contact Waxahachie Chamber of Commerce | 102 YMCA Dr., 75165 | 972/937–2390 | www.waxacofc.com.*

Ellis County Courthouse. Built in 1895 for the then outrageous price of $150,000, this is one of the most impressive courthouses in Texas. Italian artisans were hired to complete the elaborate carvings on the pink granite–and–sandstone exterior. Look up to see original copper gutters. | 1201 N. U.S. 77 | 972/923–5000 | Free | Weekdays 8–5.

Ellis County Museum. In a restored 19th-century building on the town square, this museum recounts local history through clothing and quilts dating back to the 1870s, cotton sample boxes used to judge the quality of cotton, and reproductions of original photos of cotton wagons, yards, and mills. | 201 S. College St. | 972/937–0681 | Donations accepted | Mon.–Sat. 10–5, Sun. noon–4.

Robert S. Reading Indian Artifact Collection. The more than 48,000 arrowheads here are part of what's considered one of the finest Native American artifact collections in the Southwest. | Navarro College Library, Rte. 31 (3200 W. 7th Ave.), Corsicana | 903/875–7442 | www.nav.cc.tx.us | Free | Mon.–Thurs. 8 AM–9 PM, Fri. 8–5, Sun. 5 PM–8 PM.

WICHITA FALLS

▼▼

This town takes its name from the Wichita Choctaw word *weachitoh,* meaning "big arbor," a reference to the grass-thatched arbors used by the Wichitas in their villages. Three different tribes—the Comanche, Apache, and Wichita—lived in the area until the 1830s. Farmers and cattle barons were drawn to the area in the 1860s by the vast expanses of prairies. Legends tell that the original 640 acres on which the town was founded were won by John A. Scott in a poker game. Wichita Falls became an agricultural hub when the Fort Worth & Denver Railroad came to town. The real boom, however, came at the turn of the 20th century with the discovery of oil in the Burk Burnett suburb. *Contact Wichita Falls Convention and Visitors Bureau | 1000 5th St., 76301 | 940/716–5500 or 800/799–6732 | www.wichitafalls.org.*

Fort Richardson State Historical Park. Fifty-eight miles south of Wichita Falls, this 540-acre park includes a historic area where you can see the original stone Old Post Hospital, a magazine depot, the remains of a guard house, a morgue, and a bakery, as well as what is reputed to be one of the oldest standing soft-wood officers quarters in the United States. The fort was built in the 1860s to protect settlers against Native American attacks. The interpretive center is housed in a replica of the officers' barracks and has exhibits on local cultural and natural history. | On U.S. 281 in Jacksboro | 940/567–3506 | fax 940/567–5488 | www.tpwd.state.tx.us | $2 | Daily; winter hrs vary.

Historic Doan's Adobe House. The oldest building in Wilbarger County, this house was constructed in 1881 for Mr. and Mrs. Corwin Doan and family. It is on the Western Trail's cattle crossing over the Red River, where thousands of cattle passed annually on the way north to the Kansas cattle markets. The one-room house is furnished as it might have been in the heyday of the cattle drives. | Follow signs from U.S. 283 N | 940/552–2564 or 800/687–3137 | Free | Call for hrs.

Red River Valley Museum. This museum in Vernon displays exhibits on ranching, as well as local artwork and Native American artifacts such as arrowheads, weapons, tools, and pottery. An enormous canvas mural depicts W. T. Waggoner Ranch history. The Waggoner Ranch, founded by the Waggoner family in the 1850s, is one of the largest ranches in the world. | 4600 College Dr. | 940/553–1848 | Free | Tues.–Sun. 1–5.

✦ ON THE CALENDAR: June **Texas Ranch Roundup.** Many working ranches compete in different categories, such as riding, roping, and ranch tasks, at the Wichita County Mounted Patrol Arena and the J. S. Bridwell Arena. | 940/322–0771.

UTAH

—◆—

Vast sections of Utah were blank spots on the map until the late 1800s. The Great Salt Lake, the deep canyons of the Green and Colorado rivers, and the West Desert created deadly hazards that travelers preferred to bypass; as a result few people traveled through the region. But eventually, explorers, fur trappers, immigrants, Mormons, railroaders, homesteaders, miners, and ranchers all came to Utah. Their stories became part of Utah's colorful history, but many of those stories are hair-raising tales of danger and hardship.

Before 1847, Utah's history was somewhat similar to that of other western territories. The ancient Fremont people and the ancestral Puebloan people had lived here and then moved on. Ute, Navajo, Paiute, Gosiute, and Shoshone Indians had worked out complex land use and trade patterns. Spanish expeditions had passed through the central and southern areas in attempts to establish a trade route from the pueblos of New Mexico to the Spanish settlements of California. These early incursions left behind a trail used by Mexican, Native American, and other groups. Fur-trapping mountain men had gathered in the far northern valleys each year to trade furs for provisions and to socialize at rendezvous. Emigrant parties had passed through on their way to California. Several regions had been settled, mostly by mountain men who had grown fond of Utah and tired of wandering.

On July 24, 1847, a small band of Mormons led by Brigham Young first saw the valley of the Great Salt Lake. When the party emerged from the Wasatch Mountains through Emigration Canyon, Young cast his gaze over the vast land and declared to his followers: "This is the place." After months of traveling across the Great Plains, the Mormons, too, had grown tired of wandering, and the prospect of settling down overrode any misgivings they might have had about raising houses, crops, and children in the desolate valley below.

From that day on, the history of Utah and the history of the Mormon Church would be tightly entwined, making Utah unique in the Old West. The members of the relatively new Church of Jesus Christ of Latter-day Saints (LDS) had migrated west to escape religious intolerance. Each time they had tried to make a home in the eastern United States, their unusual practices—especially polygamy—had raised the ire of "Gentile" (non-Mormon) neighbors and officials, who had forced them to move on. After being run out of Nauvoo, Illinois, they had headed west, determined to find a deserted place that no one else wanted, where they could practice their religion openly and without restrictions or reprisals.

When the Mormons arrived in the Salt Lake Valley, it was part of Mexico. Beyond the control of the U.S. government, and so far from the capital of Mexico that it is likely no Mexican had yet seen the Great Salt Lake, the Mormons felt safe. While his followers built shelters and planted crops, Brigham Young drew plans for a city to house the Saints. Salt Lake City was to be the hub of Zion, the Mormon promised land—a vast empire that was to encompass much of the western United States from the Rockies to the Pacific Ocean. The place would be governed by the Mormon leader, with no separation of church and state. Young's plans for an empire were revised a bit when, in 1848, the treaty of Guadalupe Hidalgo gave control of Utah to the United States. Young proposed an expansive State of Deseret plan to the U.S. government in 1850. The government dismissed his grandiose Deseret, created a much smaller Utah Territory, and set up a civil government in the territory. That government was ignored by the Mormons and was basically powerless, but its presence established the right of Americans—including Mormons—to live in Utah.

Mormons began to make Utah their own. In 1852, church leaders conceded publicly what everyone already knew—that their followers practiced polygamy—and Mormons began living the principle openly. Their history of persecution had convinced them they would survive only if they were independent of the Gentile world, so they set up cooperative communities to provide all the necessities of life. Pioneers settled far-flung parts of Utah Territory to stake a claim to the land, even though Native Americans already lived there. Conflicts between settlers and Native Americans over land use escalated into the Walker War, during which people on both sides were killed, including several members of the federal government's Fremont surveying expedition. The deaths, especially those of the survey team, prompted the United States to force Native Americans off lands that Mormon settlers desired. The Indians were relegated to reservations in less desirable areas of the state.

To further strengthen the Mormon grip on Utah, missionaries traveled across the Atlantic Ocean to convert land-starved Europeans and convince them to move to the promised land. Many converts spent all their money on passage to the United States and were too poor to buy the expensive wagons and teams commonly used for the overland journey from Missouri to Utah. Undeterred, they hit upon the idea of using wooden handcarts. In 1856, a new wave of pioneers began heading for Zion: poor Mormons who, propelled by their own two feet, pushed and pulled their belongings across the plains in handcarts.

However, the Mormon vision of a religiously homogeneous promised land was not to be. In part, the dream was doomed by Mormons' own ingrained fear of persecution and their bitterness about past treatment at the hand of Gentiles. Their defensiveness erupted in violence in 1857, when Mormons and their accomplices ambushed a party of non-Mormon emigrants traveling through Utah Territory. More than 120 people, many of them women and children, were murdered on their way to California in the Mountain Meadows Massacre. Fearing a possible uprising, President James Buchanan sent federal troops to Utah. A few years later, when pre–Civil War unrest was sweeping the country, Mormon leaders spoke out a bit too gleefully about the possible demise of the Northern government, which they blamed for forcing them out of the East. To head off a potential secession by Utah Territory, troops were sent again.

The soldiers were only the first trickle of Gentiles who would soon flood into Utah. Because the Mormons didn't revolt or secede, the troops had little to do, so in their spare time they explored Utah's mountains. When the soldiers discovered gold, silver, and copper, Mormon leaders cautioned their followers not to develop the mineral strikes because the possibility of instant wealth would draw more outsiders to Zion. But the federal troops kept digging ore, and mining fever struck Utah in the early 1860s. Miners of all nationalities, cultures, and religions swarmed into the territory, diversifying the population and establishing the rowdy tent cities of Park City, Alta, and Eureka.

Economic and scientific progress continued to link Utah ever more closely to the rest of the United States. The Pony Express mail route crossed the territory, followed by overland telegraph lines, which were joined near Tooele. In 1869, the tracks of the Union Pacific and Central Pacific railroads met in Promontory, uniting the nation coast to coast by rail. Utah was no longer isolated from the rest of the United States. Mormon leaders, recognizing that their isolationist attempts had failed, began to use their new connections to the outside world to bring in much-needed capital to fund the continued growth of Zion. In the end, the Mormons decided that if they couldn't fight the Gentiles, they would join them.

Only one step remained for Utah Territory to enter mainstream America: statehood. Other territories had gained that status, but Utah's petitions for statehood were denied time after time. The problem was polygamy. Many federal lawmakers did not see the practice of polygamy as an exercise in religious freedom; rather, they saw it as a violation of the basic principles upon which the nation was founded. Both sides of the polygamy debate were adamant: the Mormons continued to take plural wives, and the U.S. government continued to send Mormon men to prison for marrying more than one woman at a time. It seemed that only an act of God could solve the problem, and according to Mormon history, that's exactly what happened. In 1890, Wilford Woodruff—the new president of the Mormon church and thus a living prophet in the eyes of the faithful—declared that he had received a revelation from God that Mormons should no longer practice polygamy. The resulting change in church policy paved the way to statehood, which Utah was granted in 1896.

Statehood attracted more settlers, both Mormon and non-Mormon, to Utah, and the economy began to grow along with the population. The wild beauty of Utah's landscape soon attracted the attention of conservationists, too. Between 1908 and 1910, the federal government passed legislation creating Zion Canyon, Natural Bridge, and Rainbow Bridge national monuments. Since then, almost 75% of Utah's dramatic landscape has been preserved as public lands, open to everyone.

Padres and Pioneers

A DRIVING TOUR FROM SPANISH FORK TO ST. GEORGE

▼▼▼

Distance: 364 mi   **Time:** 4 days
Breaks: Manti and Marysvale have historic inns, making them excellent choices for overnight stays.

Although the various routes through the heart of Utah were first used by Native Americans, most are named for travelers who came later. The path Franciscan fathers explored in 1775 is called the Old Spanish Trail, and several connected trails that Mormon pioneers followed through central Utah are known collectively as the Heritage Loop. This tour, which follows sections of the Old Spanish Trail and the Heritage Loop, is long on driving, but it will give you a good idea of the diverse landscape—mountain ranges, red rock canyons, dry lake beds, deserts, valleys, and narrow ravines—that these padres and pioneers (and at least one notorious outlaw) saw on their travels.

From **Provo,** take I-15 south 8 mi to Spanish Fork; then turn east on U.S. 6 and follow it 14 mi to the junction with U.S. 89. This stretch of U.S. 6, part of the Old Spanish Trail, traverses the canyon that Franciscan explorers passed through in 1776. Turn south on U.S. 89; you are now on the Heritage Loop, a series of connected trails used by Mormon pioneers. Follow U.S. 89 south for 30 mi to Fairview and spend a few hours at the Fairview Museum. Head south again on U.S. 89 for 6 mi through the Sanpete Valley and stop for lunch in Mt. Pleasant, which has many restored buildings from pioneer days. An 11-mi side loop, Route 117, leads to Spring City. Take the self-guided walking and driving tour of this town; the whole place is listed on the National Register of Historic Places. Continue on Rte. 117 back to U.S. 89, then turn south and follow the Heritage Loop again for 17 mi to **Manti.** This is a good place to stop for the night; try the Manti House Inn.

UTAH TIME LINE

1600S Utes acquire horses from the Spanish through trade.

1765 Spanish explorer Juan Maria Antonio de Rivera travels through a small section of southeastern Utah.

1776 Franciscan fathers Francisco Atanasio Dominguez and Francisco Silvestre Velez de Escalante explore northeastern and central Utah. Their route becomes part of the Old Spanish Trail.

1780S Utah's section of the Old Spanish Trail becomes a major trade route for Spanish, Mexican, and Native American groups.

1820S Mountain men and fur trappers explore most of Utah's rivers and valleys.

1821 Mexico claims a large region of the Southwest, including the area that is now Utah.

1824 Mountain man Jim Bridger is the first non-native to see the Great Salt Lake.

1832 Antoine Robidoux sets up a trading post in the Uinta Basin.

1841 The Bartleson-Bidwell Party is the first immigrant group to cross Utah.

1843 Members of the Fremont expedition explore Utah.

1844 Miles Goodyear establishes Fort Buenaventura, the first town in Utah, on the site of present-day Ogden.

1847 Brigham Young and the first group of Mormon pioneers arrive in the Salt Lake Valley.

1848 The treaty of Guadalupe Hidalgo ends the Mexican War, giving the United States title to much of the Southwest, including Utah.

1849 Mormons form a government and Brigham Young proposes the creation of a State of Deseret, encompassing much of the area between the Rockies and the Pacific Ocean.

1850 As part of the Missouri Compromise, Utah is given territorial status. Utah, derived from a Spanish name for the Ute Indians, is chosen as the name for the new territory.

1852 The Mormon Church officially acknowledges that the practice of polygamy is part of its religion.

1853–1854 The expansion of settlers into Native American lands in central Utah leads to the Walker War.

1856 Mormon pioneers begin using handcarts to cross the plains, opening up settlement opportunities for families too poor to buy wagons and teams.

1857 More than 120 non-Mormon settlers are killed by Mormons and their accomplices in the Mountain Meadows Massacre. President James Buchanan sends troops to Utah Territory.

1860–1861 The Pony Express route crosses the central section of Utah's West Desert.

1861 President Lincoln sets aside almost 2 million acres in the Uinta Basin for Utes.

1863 More than 250 Shoshone Indians are killed by the military near Logan in the Bear River Massacre.

1863–1869 Ute resistance to relocation results in skirmishes and the Black Hawk War, but Utes finally move to the Uinta Basin reservation.

1869 The Union Pacific and Central Pacific railroads meet at Promontory, Utah, completing the Transcontinental Railroad and uniting the nation by rail.

1869 John Wesley Powell makes his first expedition on the Green and Colorado rivers.

1877 Brigham Young dies and Wilford Woodruff assumes leadership of the Mormon Church.

1885 President Chester Arthur adds the land south of the San Juan River, in southeastern Utah, to the Navajo Reservation.

1890 Wilford Woodruff issues a statement forbidding the practice of polygamy.

1896 Utah becomes the 45th state.

1897 Ute lands in the Uinta Basin are taken back and opened to white settlement.

1900 An explosion in the Winter Quarters Mine in Scofield kills 200 coal miners, leading to the organization of labor unions in the state.

1908–1910 The Zion Canyon, Natural Bridge, and Rainbow Bridge areas are set aside as national monuments.

On the morning of your second day, check out the Mormon Temple across the street from the Manti House Inn before hitting the trail again. Continue on the U.S. 89 Heritage Loop, 29 mi south of Manti to Salina. From Salina on, this driving tour follows, as closely as possible, the Old Spanish Trail. Stay on U.S. 89, drive south for 18 mi to **Richfield,** and spend the afternoon visiting the Piute County Courthouse and exploring the museum collections in the Ramsay House. Then continue south on U.S. 89 for 11 mi to **Marysvale,** a convenient stopping place for the night. The Old Pine Inn has been in operation since the 1800s, and both Zane Grey and Butch Cassidy stayed here.

Begin your third day back on the Old Spanish Trail with a visit to the home of one of the Old West's most notorious outlaws—Butch Cassidy. Cassidy lived, as a child, in Circleville, 21 mi south of Marysvale on U.S. 89; his family's cabin is 2 mi south of town on the right-hand side of the road. Continue south on U.S. 89 for 15 mi to the junction with Route 20; turn west, drive over the mountains to the junction with I–15, and take the interstate south for 18 mi to Parowan. There are several cafés in town where you can stop for lunch before visiting the Rock Church Museum. Hop on I–15 again and drive 19 mi south to **Cedar City.** Pass the rest of the afternoon visiting the Iron Mission State Park Museum at the north end of town, and spend the night.

On the morning of your fourth day, pick up a picnic lunch at one of the delis in Cedar City and drive west on Route 56 for 30 mi to Newcastle. There's a Spanish Trail marker at the edge of town; look for it on the left as you pass. Continue on Route 56 for 6 mi to the junction with Route 18. Take that route south for 21 mi to the site of the Mountain Meadows Massacre; a stone monument marks the location, which is a peaceful, and beautiful, place for a picnic. Follow the road for another 30 mi to **St. George** and spend the rest of the afternoon touring the homes of Brigham Young and Jacob Hamblin. If you're staying overnight, consider the Seven Wives Inn.

Beyond the Golden Spike

A DRIVING TOUR FROM PROMONTORY TO SALT LAKE CITY

▼▼

Distance: 109 mi   **Time:** 4 days
Breaks: The railroad history and numerous lodgings of Ogden and Park City make them appealing places to spend the night.

Utah, where the Transcontinental Railroad was completed, has a special place in railroad history. Likewise, trains have an important place in the history of Utah, much as they did in other western states. This tour takes you to back in time to explore Utah's railroad heritage. The high point is a ride through the Wasatch Mountains on a train pulled by an old steam locomotive.

Start outside Promontory at the Golden Spike National Historic Site, the place where the Transcontinental Railroad was finished in 1869. Bring a lunch and some water, and plan on spending at least half a day on the exhibits, films, and auto tours. Drive 25 mi east on Route 83 and take a spin through Historic Corinne City, the old section of Corinne that became a ghost town when the railroad passed it by. Many original buildings remain; some have been restored. Next, continue east 6 mi on Route 83 to **Brigham City** and wander through the restored Brigham City Train Depot. Then visit the Brigham City Museum-Gallery to see exhibits on the railroad history of the area. Head south on Main Street, which becomes U. S. 89, nicknamed "The Fruit Way" in honor of the many orchards and farm stands along the road. Stop at the Maddox Ranch House, 2 mi south of Brigham City, for an authentic western supper; then drive 23 mi to **Ogden** to spend the night.

On the second day, spend the morning at the Utah State Railroad Museum in Ogden's Union Station. Next to the depot in the historic railroad district, stroll along 25th Street, which is lined with a series of restored buildings now filled with shops. This is a good place to have lunch. After a break, take I–84 east and I–80 west to **Park City** (56 mi). Visit the Park City Museum's exhibits about the town's mining and railroad history. Spend the night in town; the Washington School Inn is a good lodging choice, and you have lots of dining choices.

Plan on spending most of the third day riding the Heber Valley Historic Railroad and viewing exhibits at the railroad's station in Heber City, 20 mi south of Park City on U.S. 40. Choose a trip powered by a steam locomotive for a real Old West feel, and try to take one of the longer rides. Spend the night in Orem, 28 mi south of Heber City on U.S. 189.

Begin your fourth day with a visit to the Orem Heritage Museum and be sure to visit the model railroad exhibit. Then drive 40 mi north to **Salt Lake City** on I–15, taking the 600 South exit and following 400 West to the Rio Grande Depot. The Utah State Historical Society is housed here, and it's easy to spend hours viewing exhibits and searching for tidbits of railroad history in the user-friendly archives, which are open to the public. If you're staying in the city for the night, consider the Brigham Street Inn.

BEAVER

White settlement of the Beaver Valley started in 1856, when Mormon pioneers built an outpost here. Two years later, the population of Beaver was boosted by an influx of Mormon families returning from San Bernardino, California. They had been called home by Brigham Young to bolster the Mormon presence in Utah during the pre–Civil War period of Mormon conflict with the U.S. government. Beaver was a major center for agriculture and ranching. Mercantile and other retail businesses also prospered as the town established itself as the main supply station for prospectors combing the nearby Tushar Mountains for ore. The U.S. military built Fort Cameron, a military barracks, in 1873 along the north side of the Beaver River near town. In 1886, the town grew even larger when residents of nearby Circleville abandoned their town in the wake of an episode of the Black Hawk Indian War called the Circleville Massacre. They feared retribution from the Piute after townsmen savagely massacred a group of Piute Indians. Today, more than 300 structures from the 19th century, ranging from basalt rock houses to log cabins, still stand in Beaver. One of those is the birthplace of notorious outlaw Butch Cassidy, who was born Robert Leroy Parker in Beaver in 1866. That house, at 300 West 355 South, is privately owned, but you can drive by for a look at the exterior. *Contact Beaver County Travel Council | 40 S. Main St., Beaver 84713 | 435/438–2975.*

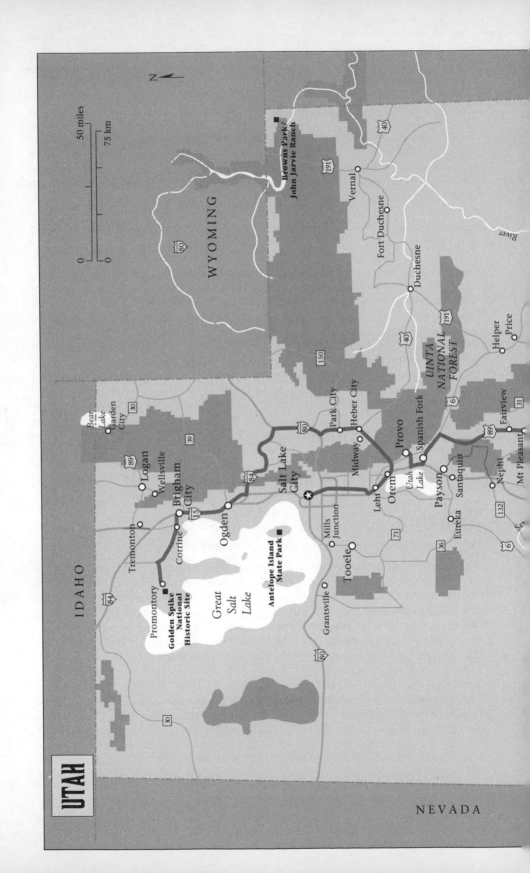

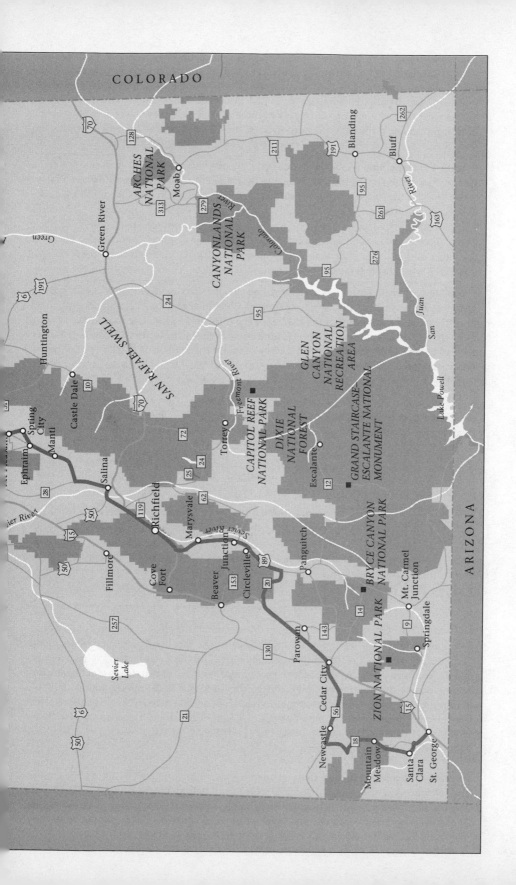

Beaver Historic District. More than 100 pioneer-era homes still stand in Beaver, many of them on the National Register of Historic Places. Their architecture is as varied as the lives led by the town's early residents: old log cabins, one-story stuccoed adobes built in the 1860s, and houses of black basalt, pink tufa, or ruddy brick, built in the 1870s and 1880s. All are private homes and not open for tours, but a walk or drive around town is well worth it. You can get more information at the Beaver County Travel Council office in the County Courthouse on Main Street. | 435/438–2975 or 435/438–2808 | www.dced.state.ut.us/history.

Cove Fort Historic Site. Many historians believe Cove Fort is the most perfectly preserved pioneer fort in the West; it is the only remaining 19th-century fort built by Mormons. Raised in 1867–1877, the fort was a popular resting stop along the main route from Salt Lake City to southern California. Twenty-four miles north of Beaver (near the junction of I–15 and I–70), the fort has been restored to its original appearance and houses a telegraph office, stage depot, pioneer kitchen, and bedrooms, all with period furnishings. You can also see barns and other outbuildings, such as a working blacksmith shop. | 1 Pioneer Dr., Cove Fort | 435/438–5547 | Free | Daily 8 AM–dusk.

Frisco Ghost Town. When the Horn Silver Mine at Old Frisco opened in 1800, Frisco quickly grew into a thriving community of 4,000. Horn Silver proved to be one of the richest mines in history, but a cave-in forced the closing of the mine in 1885. At the time of the cave-in, more than $54 million in ore had been plumbed from the mine. Without access to the silver, most of Frisco's residents abandoned the town. Spend the better part of a day exploring the many remaining stone and wooden structures and absorbing the bonanza era's aura of adventure. Don't miss the old cemetery and the five beehive-shape charcoal kilns. | Rte. 21, 45 mi northwest of Beaver | Free.

Old Beaver County Courthouse. Built in 1882 and rebuilt after an 1889 fire, the three-story brick building with a center pavilion topped by clock tower is known for its dungeon-like basement, which once served as a jail. The old courthouse is now a museum with a large collection of pioneer tools and other antiques, such as a uniform from the Beaver Mormon militia, most donated by descendants of the original pioneer families. | 90 E. Center St. | 435/438–2808 | Free | June–early Sept., Tues.–Sat. 11–5.

✦ ON THE CALENDAR: July **Pioneer Days.** Horse races, a parade with more than 100 floats, and contests (including a tricycle race for children) all celebrate the state's settlement by Mormon pioneers in 1847. | 435/438–2975.

BLANDING

▼▼▼

The Navajo once called this place "Sagebrush" because of the area's abundance of that quintessential western plant. Pioneers started settling along the base of the Abajo and Henry mountains in 1897. Some of the stone buildings they raised still stand, and the town has a number of excellent museums that document the past. Little evidence of Blanding's ranching history is immediately evident in town, but some cowboy line shacks can still be found along old trails through the deep canyons nearby. Thousands of ancient Pueblo ruins are scattered across the surrounding mesa top. *Contact San Juan County Community Development and Visitor Services | 117 S. Main St., Monticello 84535 | 435/587–3235 or 800/574–4386 | fax 435/587–2425 | www.canyonlands-utah.com.*

The Nations of the Four Corners Cultural Center. This center, operated by Utah State University, celebrates the Ute, Navajo, Hispanic, and early Anglo pioneer cultures that have coexisted in southeastern Utah through the centuries. Folk-art presentations, guided tours, demonstrations of cultural arts and crafts, concerts, and workshops highlighting these cultures are regularly presented at this visitor center and museum. A ½-mi trail leads from the center through the grounds to replicas of structures representing each culture: a Navajo hogan, Ute tepee, Spanish colonial–style hacienda, and pioneer log cabin. There's also an observation tower overlooking the grounds, with views of Utah's famous red rock canyon-lands. | 707 W. 500 S | 435/678–2072 | Free | Mon.–Sat. dawn–dusk.

✦ ON THE CALENDAR: Sept. **Bear Dance.** Traditional Ute ceremonial dances, contests of skill, games, and cooking demonstrations at White Mesa Ute Reservation fill a three-day cele-bration held Labor Day weekend. | 435/678–3397.

Sept. **Four Corners Indian Arts Festival.** Native American arts and crafts, traditional tribal music and dancing, and demonstrations of ancient Indian crafts such as flute making and kachina carving fill this two-day event at Edge of the Cedars State Park. The festival draws the finest artists from the Navajo, Hopi, and Ute tribes, who compete for the Native Amer-ican Arts Awards. | 660 W. 400 N | 435/678–2238 | www.parks.state.ut.us | $5 per vehicle | Daily 9–5.

BLUFF
▼▼▼

To the Mormon emigrant party that first passed through the famous "Hole in the Rock," Bluff must have looked like paradise. Their arduous six-month journey ended here in 1880, and the settlers immediately set about building a ranching and farming community along the San Juan River. Crop fields and orchards encircled the new pioneer fort and village, which included a church, school, and general store. But farming along the river was difficult, and in the spring of 1884, a flood destroyed so many homes and damaged farmland so badly that it drove some of the settlers out. Those who stayed took up ranching and formed the "Bluff Pool," a livestock cooperative that allowed them to compete with larger cattle outfits, and Bluff relied on ranching well into the 20th century. In the town's center stand the sand-stone-block homes of the first Mormon settlers. *Contact San Juan County Community Devel-opment and Visitor Services | 117 S. Main St., Monticello 84535 | 435/587–3235 or 800/574–4386 | fax 435/587–2425 | www.bluff-utah.org.*

Bluff Walking Tour. Pick up the free "Historic Bluff by Bicycle and on Foot" brochure at any business in town, and then take a walk through the era it describes. Most of the original homes from the 1880 townsite of Bluff City are part of the Bluff Historic District. In a dozen or so blocks are 42 historic structures, most built between about 1890 and 1905. On a windswept hill above town, gravestones bear the names of many of the town's first fami-lies. | www.bluff-utah.org | Free | Daily.

✦ ON THE CALENDAR: Aug. **Navajo Fair and Rodeo.** The people of the reservation wind up the summer with two days of traditional Navajo song and dance, food, crafts, and rodeo, all at the Bluff fairgrounds. | 435/672–2309.

HISTORIC LODGING
Pioneer House Inn. Pioneers James B. and Anna M. Decker built this two-story Victorian-style adobe homestead in 1898. Part of the original Hole in the Rock Expedition, the Deckers were among the first Mormon settlers in the area. Legend has it that some of their 11 children helped make the adobe bricks from which the home was built. In what is now the town's historic district, Pioneer House has been restored to its original appearance; all its rooms are suites. Hosts Thomas Rice and Kelly McAndrews can rattle off details of the town's history and nearby sites like tour guides. That's because they are: Through their company, Bluff Expe-ditions, the pair, both archaeologists, offer backcountry hiking and river trips exploring the

THE HOLE IN THE ROCK EXPEDITION

In November 1879, a group of 250 men, women, and children with 83 wagons and more than 1,000 head of livestock embarked on one of the most arduous journeys in the history of the Mormon colonization of Utah. Along the way, they spent six weeks in the freezing heart of winter blasting a road through a canyon wall to reach the Colorado River, 1,200 ft below. This "hole in the rock" would allow them to shorten the west–east emigrant and supply trail by hundreds of miles.

Called by church leaders to settle the eastern part of the state, the Hole in the Rock Expedition, as it came to be known, gathered at Forty Mile Spring south of the ranching town of Escalante. Expedition leaders were determined to blaze a new, shorter trail across the Colorado River, and early scouting groups had reported the discovery of a "hole in the rock," a narrow crevice in the west rim of Glen Canyon above the banks of the Colorado.

Two weeks into their journey, the group reached the mesa overlooking the Colorado River Gorge. While the women and children struggled through winter in camp at a nearby spring, the men spent six weeks opening up a narrow slit at the top of a sheer sandstone canyon wall. Equipped with pickaxes, shovels, and a small supply of blasting powder, they widened the crevice to permit the passage of wagons and leveled the descent through the crevice as much as possible, cutting away a 40-ft drop-off and removing huge boulders. Near the bottom of the graded crevice, they had to devise a way to traverse the rest of the sheer drop to the canyon floor. They drilled holes into the north wall of the crack at 2-ft intervals, drove in oak stakes, and constructed a pathway atop the stakes using logs, brush, fill dirt, and rocks. This "crib" road would support the outside wagon wheels while the inside wheels hugged the rock along a treacherous decline.

On January 26, 1880, the wagons clattered through the "Hole in the Rock." Anxious animals pulled them one at a time to the brink of the crevice. The wagons' rear wheels were rough-locked with large chains, ropes were attached to the rear axles, and the wagons were pushed against the backsides of the animals, inching them slowly forward until the weight of the wagon physically forced them over the edge of the precipice and onto the makeshift trail. Men, women, boys, and animals pulled against the ropes tied to the wagons to slow the descent. The scene was repeated all day long and into evening until all the wagons reached the canyon floor, and the livestock and pioneer families then picked their way down on foot. A crude ferry was built to take the party across the river to the eastern bank. Young cattle drovers guided the livestock through the river to safety.

After another three months of grueling struggle through dense piñon forests and across rock so slippery that they had to carve footholds for their horses, the pioneers arrived at what is now the town of Bluff. Hole in the Rock emigrant Charles Redd later described the arrival: "As they rested in exhaustion from the last intensive strain, for the first time they began to see themselves for what they were; weary, worn-out, galled, both teams and men. For so long they had walked and slept and eaten and lived on sloping, uneven ground that the thought of level bottom-land was extremely sweet." Amazingly, none in the group died, and two babies were born along the way. Much of the trail they blazed is still visible today, mostly across rough four-wheel-drive terrain. The Hole in the Rock Trail is listed on the National Register of Historic Places.

cultural and natural history of the area. Kitchenettes, hot tub, meeting rooms; no smoking. | 189 N. 300 E 84512 | 435/672–2446 or 888/637–2582 | fax 435/672–2446 | www.pioneerhouseinn.com | 5 suites | $56–$125 | MC, V | BP.

BRIGHAM CITY

▼▼

Brigham City, first settled in 1851, became a premier example of a Mormon cooperative community. The hundreds of faithful who lived here were encouraged by church leader Brigham Young to produce all the necessities of life—food, fuel, furniture, and basic material goods—so they would be independent of the outside world. The experiment in communalism was a success, but only as long as the citizens were willing to work hard at their assigned jobs and to give up the niceties of life—china, imported fabrics, fine firearms, and other goods they had been accustomed to in their European and eastern hometowns. The experiment became less appealing after 1869, when the two branches of the Transcontinental Railroad met just west of Brigham City, creating a permanent commercial link between Mormons and the rest of the United States. Easy access to outside goods, and the canny understanding that the railroad also opened up lucrative markets across the country for Utah goods, led to the gradual abandonment of Mormon communalism. *Contact Bear River Valley Chamber of Commerce | Box 100, Tremonton 84337 | 435/257–7585 | www.bearriverchamber.com. Brigham City Chamber of Commerce | 6 N. Main St., Box 458, 84302 | 435/723–3931 | www.bcareachamber.com.*

Anderson Wagon Museum. The largest private collection of wagons in the West is maintained by Mr. Anderson, who has spent his life studying the role of wagons in western history. Mr. Anderson enjoys sharing his knowledge, so plan on spending a few hours looking and listening. | 8790 W. Rte. 102, Tremonton | 435/854–3760 | Free | Tours by appointment.

Brigham City Museum-Gallery. Documents and artifacts from the city's early settlement and Mormon cooperative periods are the focus of this museum, which also has displays on the railroad and agricultural history of the Bear River valley. A gallery houses regional art collections and hosts regional and national touring shows. | 24 N. 300 W | 801/723–6769 | Free | Tues.–Fri. 11–6, Sat. 1–5.

Brigham City Train Depot. Railroad tools and implements, an authentic turn-of-the-20th-century train-ticket office, and a telegraph office are highlights of this restored 1906 depot building. | 833 W. Forest St. | 435/723–2989 | www.boxelder.org/tourism/historical/depot | Free | Thurs.–Sat. 1–5.

Golden Spike National Historic Site. The Union Pacific and Central Pacific railroads met here at Promontory Summit on May 10, 1869, when a golden spike was driven to complete the Transcontinental Railroad. You can stop in at the visitor center, tour the site by car, and see vintage locomotives. Reenactments of the driving of the golden spike are held on weekends in the spring and summer. | Rte. 83, 32 mi west of Brigham City | 435/471–2209 | www.nps.gov/gosp/home | $7 per vehicle | June–Aug., daily 8–4:30; Sept.–May, daily 8–6.

Historic Corinne City. Corinne was founded by non-Mormons—or "Gentiles," as they say in Utah. Sited on the provisional route of the Transcontinental Railroad, the town saw its future snatched away when Mormons lobbied successfully to reroute the railroad to bypass Corinne. Without the railroad's economic stimulus, most inhabitants moved away, leaving behind a ghost town. Many of the original buildings are still standing, and another city named Corinne later sprouted near the ghost town. | 8 mi west of Brigham City on Rte. 83, Corinne | 435/744–2442 | www.ghosttowns.com/states/ut/corinne | Free | Daily.

◆ **ON THE CALENDAR: May Driving of the Golden Spike.** Held each year on May 10 at Promontory Summit, this festival commemorates the 1869 linking of the Atlantic and Pacific coasts by railroad. Reenactments of the driving of the golden spike are performed at the National Historic Site, which is 30 mi west of Brigham City off Route 83. | 435/471–2209.

June **Western Heritage Festival.** Costumed Old West characters, Dutch-oven dinners, train and wagon rides, and a frontier town built for the occasion draw crowds to Tremonton, 19 mi northwest of Brigham City on I–15. | 435/257–2625 or 435/257–7585.

Aug. **Railroaders Festival.** Boiler stoking, rail walking, and hand-car racing test participants' skills at this festival, held at the Golden Spike National Historic Site. | 435/471–2209.

CAPITOL REEF NATIONAL PARK

▼▼

In the 1870s, Mormon missions sprang up in the valleys surrounding what is now one of Utah's most scenic national parks. Expeditions led by Major John Wesley Powell explored the region, and a quasi-military Mormon posse is said to have chased a band of Ute Indians, who had terrorized settlements to the north and west, through the canyons and mountains in 1866. But it was not until the 1880s that settlers established a town and planted orchards in this verdant corridor along the Fremont River. The site is now protected within Capitol Reef National Park, along with miles of spectacular red-rock landscape. *Contact Capitol Reef National Park /Rte. 24, Torrey 84775 /435/425–3791 /fax 435/425–3026 /www.nps.gov.care Capitol Reef Country /Box 7, Teasdale 84773 /800/858–7951 /www.xmission.com/~capreef.*

Capitol Gorge. Take a 2-mi round-trip hike to reach the two historic sites in this canyon. The canyon wall known as the Pioneer Register bears names and dates scratched into the stone by emigrants who passed this way as far back as the 1870s. Just beyond the next curve, sunk into a small mesa, are naturally formed pools known as the Tanks, where early settlers reportedly swam and bathed. | Off Scenic Dr., 9 mi south of the visitor center | Daily.

Fruita. In a desert oasis watered by the Fremont River, Mormon settlers who arrived in the 1880s planted hundreds of fruit trees. They named their town Junction, later changing the name to Fruita as their orchards prospered. A few of Fruita's old buildings have been preserved, including a blacksmith's shop, a hay barn, and the Gifford family farmhouse, which is now a museum operated by the Capitol Reef Natural History Association. Take a tour of the restored and refurnished home and surrounding outbuildings; on the farmstead grounds, watch and participate in typical pioneer activities such as felting and soap making. At the one-room schoolhouse, built in the 1890s and used until the 1940s, you can peer through the windows while listening to an oral history recorded by one of the school's 1930s teachers. The Gifford home's former kitchen has been converted into a shop that sells handmade reproductions of frontier utensils and household tools. You can buy flour sifters, butter churns, candles, crockery, and other typical Mormon pioneer items, all crafted by local artisans. The original pioneer orchards are now maintained by the National Park Service, and if you visit in season, you can pick fruit. | Scenic Dr., less than 1 mi from the visitor center | 435/425–3791 | Daily 11–5.

CEDAR CITY

▼▼

Rich iron-ore deposits drew Mormon leader Brigham Young's attention to this area, and he ordered that an LDS mission be established here. Originally named Little Muddy, the settlement became Coal Creek for a time before its present name stuck. The first iron works and foundry, opened in 1851, operated for only eight years because of problems with the furnace, flooding, and hostility between settlers and Native Americans. When the foundry closed, residents turned to farming, ranching, and agriculture for their livelihood, and Cedar City grew into a thriving community. The town's pioneer heritage is evident in a one-block stretch of downtown where many shop owners have restored historic buildings to their original western style. *Contact Iron County Travel Council | 581 N. Main St., Box 1007, Cedar City 84721 | 435/586–5124 or 800/354–4849 | fax 435/586–4022 | www.scenicsouthernutah.com.*

Daughters of the Utah Pioneers Museum. Displays of artifacts like an old trundle sewing machine, antique four-poster bed, photographs of old Cedar City and some of the community's pioneer families, plus clothing, quilts, and wagon wheels offer a glimpse into the daily lives of Iron County pioneers. The museum is inside the Iron County Visitors Center. | 582 N. Main St. | 435/586–4484 | Free | Weekdays 1–4.

Iron Mission State Park Museum. The museum chronicles the development of the iron industry in this area. Displays include carriages (including one bullet-scarred stagecoach that ran between southwestern Utah communities in the days of Butch Cassidy), tools, equipment, and other artifacts from the iron mines. A log cabin built in 1851—the oldest standing home in southern Utah—and a huge collection of wooden wagon wheels and farm equipment are located outside. Watch local artisans demonstrate pioneer crafts, and examine a working printing press. | 635 N. Main St. | 435/586–9290 | www.scenicsouthernutah. com | $5 | Daily.

Old Iron Town Ruins. On a well-graded dirt road about 5 mi west of Route 56, an 1800s beehive charcoal oven and other ruins mark the site of Iron County's second major attempt at iron manufacturing, which was made in the 1870s. To the north, tailings from the many iron pits on Iron Mountain are still visible. Driving the road to the site is not recommended in winter. | 25 mi west of Cedar City on Rte. 56 to mile marker 41 | 435/586–1112.

Parowan Heritage Park. On January 8, 1850, Parley P. Pratt and his scouting party erected a flagpole on a hill and dedicated Parowan as the starting place for Mormon colonization of southern Utah. Parowan supported and supplied the Mormon families that would later establish missions throughout the southern part of the state. You can see the original flagpole in this park built on the site of Pratt's first camp, 19 mi north of Cedar City via I–15. Monuments and historical markers related to the community's pioneer heritage are scattered throughout the park. | 300 S. Main St., Parowan | 435/477–8190 | www.parowan.org.

Rock Church Museum. Modeled after the Salt Lake City Tabernacle, Parowan's Rock Church was completed in 1867. Now a museum operated by the Daughters of the Utah Pioneers, it stands in the center of the town square. | Main St., between Center St. and 100 South St. | 435/477–3331 or 435/477–3549 | www.parowan.org | Free | By appointment.

✦ ON THE CALENDAR: June **Canyon Country Western Arts Festival.** Leatherworking, blacksmithing, and other western crafts demonstrations, combined with traditional cowboy poetry and music, bring the heritage of the Old West to life on the campus of Southern Utah University. | 435/586–4484 | www.westernartsfestival.org.

June **Paiute Restoration Gathering and Powwow.** Traditional Paiute music, a parade, and a powwow are part of this tribal gathering held annually in various locations on Paiute tribal lands. | dced.utah.gov/indian/today/paiute.htm | 435/586–1112.

June **Quilt Walk Festival.** During the bitter winter of 1864, Panguitch residents were freezing and starving. A group of men from the settlement set out over the mountains to fetch provisions from the town of Parowan, 40 mi away. When they hit waist-deep snow drifts they were forced to abandon their oxen. Town legend says the men, frustrated and ready to turn back, laid a quilt on the snow and knelt to pray. Soon they realized the quilt had kept them from sinking into the snow. Spreading quilts before them as they walked, leapfrog style, the men traveled to Parowan and back, returning with provisions that saved the lives of their families and friends. This three-day festival commemorates the event through dinner theater in which the story is acted out, quilting classes, a tour of pioneer homes in Panguitch, crafts shows, and a cowboy action shoot. | 435/676–8585 | www.panguitch.org.

FILLMORE

When U.S. president Millard Fillmore appointed Brigham Young governor of the newly created Utah Territory in 1850, Young sought to establish a capital city in a central location. He chose a site in the center of Utah Territory and, to honor the president, named the county Millard and the capital city Fillmore. Young envisioned Fillmore as the hub of an imaginary wagon wheel, with cities located along geographical spokes radiating out from the capital. But the territorial statehouse—the south wing of what was supposed to be a large, domed capitol building—had barely been completed when, in 1858, territorial legislators and newly appointed governor Alfred Cummings deemed it impractical to locate the capital city 150 mi south of the territory's major population center, Salt Lake City. The capital was moved to Salt Lake City that year. The lone south-wing statehouse was the only portion of the capitol building ever completed. Fillmore still takes great pride in its heritage as Utah's first capital and in its graceful statehouse. *Contact Millard County Tourism | 80 N. Main St., Delta 84624 | 435/864–4316 or 800/864–0345 | www.millardcounty.com.*

Territorial Statehouse State Park. The old statehouse and surrounding property became Utah's first state park in 1957. Visit its museum to see 1850s photographs of local families during Fillmore's brief history as territorial capital. Housewares, furniture, clothing, doll collections, and other relics from the territorial period (1850–1896) are also displayed. The park-like grounds contain a rose garden, picnic areas, and other historic buildings from pioneer times—which are open to park visitors. | 50 W. Capitol Ave. | 435/743–5316 | http://parks/state.ut.us | $5 per vehicle | Late May–early Sept., Mon.–Sat. 8–8, Sun. 9–6; early Sept.–late May, Mon.–Sat. 9–6.

✦ ON THE CALENDAR: Aug.–Sept. **Utah Western Heritage Week.** At this weeklong celebration of cowboy and western culture you can ride with a wagon train and remuda from Kanab to Fillmore. Watch a real rodeo and listen to cowboy poetry and music at various locations, including the Fillmore fairgrounds and the town of Delta. | 801/376–2258, 435/743–4470, or 800/864–0345 | www.utahwesternheritagefoundation.org.

Sept. **Old Capitol Arts and Living History Festival.** Demonstrations of pioneer crafts, such as wool carding and rug weaving, and exhibits of local arts and crafts are just two of the attractions of this two-day festival. You can watch living-history demonstrations of hide tanning, archery, blacksmithing, and other 19th-century mountain-man skills. Live music, children's pioneer games, and tours of the statehouse take place at Territorial Statehouse State Park. | 435/743–5316 or 800/864–0345.

GREEN RIVER

At a centuries-old river crossing along the Old Spanish Trail, the city of Green River is named for the river that runs through the middle of town. The town was first settled in 1878, when Blake Station, a stop on the overland mail route between Salina, Utah, and Ouray, Colorado, opened. In 1883, the completion of the Denver & Rio Grande Western Railway established Green River as a main shipping point for livestock and mining equipment and supplies. Cowboys, sheepherders, and prospectors from Book Cliffs and the San Rafael Desert traveled to town for provisions. Green River gained a reputation as a wild western town thanks to its location along the "outlaw trail" between Robbers Roost and Browns Park, known hideouts for infamous figures like Butch Cassidy and the Sundance Kid. *Contact Castle Country Travel Region | 90 N. 100 E, No. 2, Price 84501 | 435/637–3009 or 800/842–0789 | fax 435/637–7010 | www.castlecountry.com.*

John Wesley Powell River History Museum. Major John Wesley Powell passed through the Green River area during his exploration of the Colorado River and its largest tributary, the Green River. The Green River trip was his last major river expedition in the continental United States. A series of interactive displays in the museum tracks the Powell Party's arduous, dangerous 1869 journey. A wax figure of the one-armed explorer is seated in a model of the wooden flat-bottom boat he used in his river quests. The center also houses works of art depicting 19th-century explorations of the West, and the River Runner's Hall of Fame, a tribute to those who have followed in Powell's wake. | 885 E. Main St. | 435/564–3427 | $2 | June–Sept., daily 8–8; Oct.–May, daily 9–5.

Sego Canyon Rock Art Panels. Alongside ancient petroglyphs, 19th-century Ute drawings cover large rock panels in this spectacular canyon setting. Distinctive for their large anthropomorphic figures, and for horses, buffalo, and shields painted with red and white pigment, these rare drawings are some of the finest Ute pictographs in the region. The panels are 3½ mi off I–70 on a maintained gravel road. | 25 mi east of Green River on I–70 to Exit 185 | www.exploreutah.com/explore/fun-rr.htm.

LOGAN
▼▼

Before the 1820s, bands of Shoshone lived in Cache Valley, where Logan now stands. The valley became a favorite haunt for mountain men, who held rendezvous in the area and stashed, or "cached," bundles of furs here when they were traveling. Mormon pioneers created the permanent settlement of Logan in 1859, but the town didn't become prominent until 1890, when it was chosen as the site for Utah's land-grant agricultural college, now called Utah State University. *Contact Cache Valley Tourist Council | 160 N. Main St., 84321 | 435/752–2161 or 800/882–4433 | www.tourcachevalley.com.*

American West Heritage Center. A 1917 living-history farm, a re-created pioneer site, a mountain-man exhibit, a military display, and an authentic Shoshone encampment are part of this center, which focuses on life in northern Utah from 1820 to 1920. Docents dressed in period clothing demonstrate such tasks as sheepshearing and quilting. The center is located 8 mi south of Logan. | 4025 S. U.S. 89/91, Wellsville | 435/245–6050 or 800/225–3378 | www.americanwestcenter.org | $3–$5 | Late May–early Sept., Mon.–Sat. 10–5.

Bear Lake State Park. Here, 40 mi northeast of Logan on the south shore of Bear Lake, mountain men gathered for their annual rendezvous in 1827 and 1828. Their meeting place, Rendezvous Beach, now has interpretive signs about the gatherings, along with a day-use picnic area. Each September at Rendezvous Beach, a Mountain Man Rendezvous includes period cooking demonstrations, story-telling, cannon and rifle competitions, and a Native American encampment. | Rte. 30, Garden City | 435/946–3343 | www.utah.com/stateparks/bear_lake.htm | $5 | Daily.

Cache Museum/Daughters of the Utah Pioneers. In the same building as a well-stocked visitor information center, this small museum has mountain-man displays and musical instruments, furniture, clothing, and a large collection of personal journals from the 1850s to the early 1900s. | 160 N. Main St. | 435/752–5139 or 435/753–1635 | Free | June–Aug., Tues.–Sat. 10–4.

Logan Tabernacle. It took Mormon settlers 13 years to build this tabernacle (they completed it in 1878), which hosted church and community meetings during Logan's early days. You can search for information about your family history at the genealogical research facility or take a tour of the building. | 100 N. Main St. | 435/755–5598 | Free | Weekdays.

✦ ON THE CALENDAR: May **Old Ephraim's Mountain Man Rendezvous.** At this reenactment of an 1820s rendezvous, held in Wellsville Canyon 15 mi southwest of Logan, period costumes are all the rage for both participants and spectators, and lively games test hatchet, knife, and black-powder skills. It is one of the West's best mountain-man gatherings. | 435/792–3329.

July **Festival of the American West.** Traditional crafts demonstrations, historical games, western music and dancing, reenactments of mountain-man gatherings, and a Shoshone encampment are highlights of this annual celebration. | 800/225–3378.

HISTORIC DINING

Bluebird. American/Casual. Stop by this café to admire the early 1900s architectural details and to enjoy an ice cream treat at the original marble-counter soda fountain. Many of the photographs and artifacts used to decorate the Bluebird are from the 1800s, and a multi-wall mural in one dining area includes scenes from every period in Cache Valley history. Chocolates handcrafted with the Bluebird's turn-of-the-20th-century techniques and equipment are also available. | 19 N. Main St. | 435/752–3155 | $7–$15 | AE, D, MC, V.

MANTI

▼▼

Manti was one of the first five towns incorporated in Brigham Young's State of Deseret. The town is located in Utah's "Little Denmark," a string of rural villages—including Fairview and Mt. Pleasant—along U.S. 89 in the fertile Sanpete Valley. At one time, most of the inhabitants of this area were Mormon converts from Denmark, Sweden, or Norway, and the Scandinavian influence is apparent in architectural styles and in present-day celebrations. Pride in a shared cultural heritage has encouraged Sanpete Valley residents to preserve original buildings and grounds, making this area the most authentic example of Utah's settlement period. *Contact Sanpete County Chamber of Commerce | Box 59, Ephraim 84627 | 435/283–4321 or 800/283–4346 | www.sanpetecounty.org. Sanpete County Heritage Highway Information Center/Little Denmark Heritage Tours | U.S. 89 at Mt. Pleasant City Park, Mt. Pleasant 84647 | 435/462–2502 | www.heritageproducts.utah.org/tour/little_denmark.*

Ephraim Pioneer Memorial Park. Seven miles northeast of Manti, you can see genuine pioneer cabins, the site where a peace treaty was signed with Native Americans at the end of the Black Hawk War, and a house built in the late 1800s that now serves as a museum for local artifacts. Tours led by a local historian are available by advance request. | 46 W. 100 N, Ephraim | 435/283–6835 | Free | Park daily; tours by appointment only.

Fairview Museum. Old West miniature carvings, a local history archives, and a full-scale replica of a Columbian mammoth make this one of Utah's most interesting small-town museums. It's in Fairview, 28 mi northeast of Manti. Ask for a booklet with directions for a self-guided tour of local sites associated with the Black Hawk War. | 85 N. 100 E, Fairview | 435/427–9216 | www.sanpete.com/fairviewmuseum | Free | Mon.–Sat. 10–5.

Manti Temple. The Manti Temple has been called "the crowning achievement of 19th-century Mormon architecture." The temple was constructed of oolitic limestone by Mormon converts who brought their stone masonry skills over from Europe. Although the temple is open only to Mormons, non-Mormons can stroll about the grounds. | 500 N. Main St. | 435/835–2291 | www.sanpete.com/mantitemple.

Native Wines. Pears and apples from the original trees planted by Sanpete Valley pioneers are used in the wines and meads created by these vintners 22 mi northeast of Manti. They follow a wine-making process almost identical to that used by settlers during the late 1800s. Tours of the winery, conducted each Saturday, include wine tastings, and several dozen varieties of wines and meads are available for sale. | 72 S. 500 W, Mt. Pleasant | 435/462–9261 | Free | Sat. 11–3.

Spring City Historic Building Tour. The entire town of Spring City is listed on the National Register of Historic Places, so when you visit you might get an eerie but pleasant feeling of stepping back in time. Many buildings are studios for artists and craftspeople, who exhibit their works in meticulously restored parlors where Mormon pioneer ladies once served afternoon tea. Tours inside Spring City's historic buildings are offered each May, but you can take a self-guided tour of the town any time to see them from the outside. Ask for a brochure at any business in town. | 22 mi north of Manti off U.S. 89, Spring City | 435/462–2708 | www.heritageproducts.utah.org/tour.

✦ ON THE CALENDAR: May **Scandinavian Heritage Festival.** Ephraim celebrates the Scandinavians who settled the town in the late 1800s, at a festival that includes authentic Scandinavian food, music, and dancing, and displays of Old World crafts. | 435/283–6654.

May **Spring City Heritage Days.** Once each year, visitors are invited inside 15 to 20 of the finest old buildings in Spring City. Many of the buildings date from the late 1800s to the early 1900s, and most have undergone extensive restoration. | 435/462–2708.

HISTORIC LODGING

Manti House Inn. Presidents of the Mormon church stayed in this 1880 building when they visited the Manti Temple across the street. Antiques decorate the bedrooms and the elegant dining room, where a full breakfast is served. Dining room, cable TV, in-room VCRs, some in-room hot tubs; no-smoking rooms. | 401 N. Main St., 84642 | 435/835–0161 or 800/835–7512 | www.sanpete.com/manti_house | 5 rooms, 1 suite | $69–$129 | MC, V | BP.

MARYSVALE

▼▼

By 1865, a year after its founding, Marysvale was home to 16 Mormon families who had moved there with the intent to farm. But in 1866, troubles with the Ute Indians during the Black Hawk War forced the settlers to abandon the town. In 1868, after the conflict ended, prospectors and settlers arrived in droves to scour the nearby Tuscher Mountain range for deep pockets of gold, silver, and other valuable metals. A year later, two prospectors found waterfalls, gold, and the remains of an old mining operation, probably Spanish in origin, and the Bullion Canyon gold rush began. Mining camps sprang up in the mountains surrounding Marysvale, and the town traded on the miners' needs for supplies and mercantile goods and continued to flourish as a mining community into the early 1900s. Many of the old mines can still be seen outside town. *Contact Marysvale Chamber of Commerce | www.marysvale.org.*

Butch Cassidy's Boyhood Home. Notorious outlaw and beloved folk hero Robert Leroy Parker—alias Butch Cassidy—grew up near Circleville, a small town south of Marysvale, and the log cabin in which he was raised is worth a brief stop. Born in Beaver, Utah, on Friday, April 13, 1866, he was the first of 13 children. He gained notoriety as a bank and train robber and cattle rustler but was kindly regarded by many who considered him to be the Robin Hood of the western frontier. Cassidy and his Wild Bunch, including the Sundance Kid, were famed for their elusive escapes along the Outlaw Trail, a series of meandering paths and hideouts between Mexico and Montana. The two-room log cabin where Cassidy spent his youth is weathered and worn, but it still stands on the old homestead once owned by his parents. The cabin is now privately owned, but you may stop and explore the immediate grounds. | 20 mi south of Marysvale on U.S. 89.

Canyon of Gold Driving Tour. Visit a half-dozen old mines along the along a 2½-mi route that begins in Bullion Canyon west of Marysvale. A brochure available at the trailhead interprets 10 historic mining features that you will encounter along the way. Miner's Park, an easy ¼-mi trail that winds around interpretive displays of authentic mining equipment used in the late 1800s, is a highlight of the tour. | Tour begins at the Fishlake National Forest Boundary at Buillion Canyon, about 5 mi west of Marysvale off U.S. 89 | Free; donation for brochure | Daily.

HISTORIC LODGING
Moore's Old Pine Inn. Utah's oldest hotel, originally the Pines Hotel, was built in 1882. Pages from that year's issues of the *New York Times* are still glued to the rafters, and many of the ponderosa pines that shade it today are older than the hotel. Legend has it that author Zane Grey wrote *Riders of the Purple Sage* while staying at the Pines Hotel, and outlaw Butch Cassidy rested here from time to time. Owners Randy and Katie Moore took over the inn in 1994 and completely restored it to its authentic Victorian pioneer style. The four rooms share two large baths with showers and claw-foot tubs and sinks that are original to the hotel. The suites are decorated with historic photos, gold-mining tools, and handmade quilts. Two three-room cabins nestled on the banks of the Buillion River are also available. Some kitchenettes; no smoking. | 60 S. State St., 84750 | 435/326–4565 or 800/887–4565 | www.marysvale.org/pine-Inn.html | 4 rooms, 3 suites, 2 cabins | $50–$100 | DC, MC, V | BP.

MOAB
▼▼

Although Spanish explorers led by Juan Maria Antonio de Rivera ventured through the area in 1765, few whites appear to have visited the Moab region before the 1850s. In the early 1800s, travelers along the Old Spanish Trail passed through following the same route that U.S. 191 follows today. Then, in 1855, at the behest of Mormon leaders, a group of 41 men set out to establish the Elk Mountain Mission, where the city of Moab now stands. They were driven out by Indian attacks six months later, and permanent settlers did not return to the valley until the late 1870s. At first a ranching and farming community, Moab became a mining mecca and garnered a rich history as a boom and bust town. In the 1800s, Moab was a hangout for Butch Cassidy's Wild Bunch and other outlaw gangs. *Contact Moab Area Travel Council | Main and Center Sts., Box 550, Moab 84532 | 435/259–1370 or 800/635–6622 | www.discovermoab.com.*

Dan O'Laurie Canyon Country Museum. A tribute to Moab in its many incarnations, this museum displays artifacts of early European and Euro-American forays into southeastern Utah. Among the items on display are a map of the Old Spanish Trail, railroad artifacts, a reproduction of a Moab kitchen circa 1907, and blacksmithing tools. There is also an impressive exhibit of Ute Indian sandals, baskets, and pottery. | 118 E. Center St. | 435/259–7985 | $2 | Apr.–Oct., Mon.–Sat. 1–8; Nov.–Mar., Mon.–Thurs. 3–7, Fri.–Sat. 1–7.

Daughters of the Utah Pioneers Meeting Hall. Built in 1888, this adobe building was the first Latter-day Saints church in Moab; the bell tower and bell give away the building's original use. Now listed on the National Register of Historic Places and used as a meeting place for the Grand County chapter of the Daughters of the Utah Pioneers, the structure has been restored using authentic materials, including tongue-in-groove ceiling board. Inside are portraits of the area's pioneer families, and out back is a cabin built in the 1880s by Randolph Stewart, the first LDS bishop for Moab, for his first wife, Marietta. The cabin was moved to site in the 1990s. | 45 E. 200 N | 435/259–5225 | Wed. 2–4, or by appointment.

Dead Horse Point State Park. Now part of one of Utah's most scenic state parks, Dead Horse Point was used by cowboys in the 1800s as a natural corral for wild mustangs. Wranglers herded the horses onto a promontory that projects out into the canyons below and closed them in behind a 50-ft-high fence built at the neck of the peninsula. According to legend, the point takes its name from a herd of animals that died there after being abandoned in the corral. Elsewhere in the park are a modern visitor center and museum with historic photographs and interpretive exhibits detailing the park's history and the geology of the area. | 34 mi from Moab at end of Rte. 313 | 435/259–2614 | http://parks.state.ut.us | $6 per vehicle | Daily 8–6.

John Shafer Home. Constructed in 1884, this adobe farmhouse is possibly the oldest residence still standing in the county. It was built by John H. Shafer, who moved to the area in 1880 and ran a cattle operation in the La Sal Mountains. In the 1890s, Shafer advanced the money to build the county's first schoolhouse and pay its teachers. Local lore has it that he refused to accept interest on the loan, and he was dubbed the "father of Grand County Education." The adobe home now houses the non-profit Youth Garden Project and is a meeting place for community organizations. | 608 S. 400 E, at Grand County High School | Youth Garden Project, 435/259–2326.

Wolfe Ranch. When Civil War veteran John Wesley Wolfe completed his one-room cabin in 1907, he likely did not imagine that it would stand into the 21st century. Wolfe's 100-acre spread, where the rancher and his family lived a hardscrabble, isolated existence, is now part of Arches National Park. You can peek inside the small log cabin and step into the cool air of the nearby root cellar, which have both been restored. The buildings, now part of a National Historic Site, stand at the beginning of Delicate Arch Trail. | Arches National Park, N. U.S. 191 | 435/719–2299 or 435/259–2200 | www.nps.gov/arch | Park $10 per vehicle | Daily.

HISTORIC LODGING

Cali Cochita Bed and Breakfast. One of the first homes built in Moab, this late-1800s adobe has been restored to its classic Victorian style by owners David and Kim Boger. A rare example of the adobe construction that proliferated in 19th-century Moab, the inn is located in the heart of town, two blocks from Main Street shops and restaurants. Down comforters, plush robes, and hair dryers lend a touch of luxury to smallish rooms decorated with country style. In-room VCRs, hot tub; no smoking. | 110 S. 200 E, 84532 | 435/259–4961 or 888/429–8112 | fax 435/259–4964 | www.moabdreaminn.com | 3 rooms, 1 suite, 1 cottage | $89–$150 | AE, MC, V | BP.

NEPHI

▼▼

Nephi has been a resting place for travelers along Utah's main north–south route since explorers established that route as the Old Spanish Trail. The town was founded in 1851 as a ranching community, but the 1869 discovery of gold in the nearby mountains brought thousands of miners to the area. A huge tent city sprang up in the Eureka mining district, and Nephi became a supply station for the prospectors. When the mining boom ended in the late 1800s, both Nephi and Eureka regained their sleepy, small-town status. *Contact Juab Travel Council | 4 S. Main St., Box 71, 84648 | 435/623–5203 | www.juabtravel.com. Panoramaland Travel Region | Box 427, 84648 | 800/748–4361.*

Chieftain Museum. Life-size replicas of an 1800s school room, a pioneer cabin, a blacksmith shop, and a mining site are housed in this large and well-maintained museum, in the imposing 1903 Santaquin Schoolhouse. | 100 S. 100 W, Santaquin | 435/754–3910 or 435/754–3958 | www.ulct.org/santaquin/museum.shtml | Free | June–Aug., Fri.–Sat. 10–4.

Peteetneet Academy and Museum. Built in 1901 as the area's first multi-classroom elementary school, this adobe-and-redbrick building now houses galleries filled with exhibits on local, Utah, and military history. It is 27 mi northeast of Nephi. | 10 S. Peteetneet Blvd., Payson | 801/465–9427 | www.peteetneetacademy.homestead.com | Free | Weekdays 10–4.

Tintic Mining Museum. Call ahead for an appointment to see Old Eureka City Hall's exhibits on the settlement, mining, and railroad history of the Eureka area, and local newspapers dating back to 1902. You can also pick up information on self-guided tours of Eureka's historic buildings and mine sites. | 41 mi northwest of Nephi on U.S. 6, Eureka | 435/433–6842 | www. juabtravel.com/eureka.htm | Free | By appointment.

✦ ON THE CALENDAR: June **Iceland Days.** The first immigrants from Iceland—Mormon converts—arrived in Utah in 1855, and by 1877 a large group had settled in the Utah Valley. This celebration of the area's Icelandic heritage has been held in Spanish Fork (33 mi north of Nephi) for more than 100 years and includes traditional Icelandic music, food, and games. | 801/798–8352.

Aug. **Tintic Silver Festival.** During this festival in Eureka, you can take tours of the town's mining museum and historic homes and watch demonstrations on the operation of railroad and mining equipment. | 435/433–6824.

OGDEN
▼▼

The oldest town in Utah, Ogden was founded by mountain man Miles Goodyear, who settled here with his family in the early 1840s. Mormons, who arrived in the Salt Lake Valley in 1847 hoping they would have the area completely to themselves, were uncomfortable with a non-Mormon settlement so close to theirs, and they paid Goodyear almost $2,000—a fortune at that time—to leave the area. But all attempts to isolate Ogden from non-Mormon influences came to naught in 1869, when the town became a hub for the Transcontinental Railroad. *Contact Ogden and Weber Convention and Visitors Bureau | 2501 Wall Ave., 84401 | 801/627–8288 or 866/867–8824 | www.ogdencvb.org. Ogden-Weber Chamber of Commerce | 2393 Washington Blvd., Suite 400, 84401 | 801/621–8300 or 888/621–8306 | www.echamber.cc.*

Fort Buenaventura State Park. Replicas of the stockade, trading post, and cabins that Miles Goodyear built in the early 1840s are explained during tours led by guides in period costumes. | 2450 A Ave. | 801/621–4808 | $5 per vehicle | June–Sept., daily 8–8; Oct.–May, daily 8–5.

Miles Goodyear Cabin and Museum. The original cabin built by Miles Goodyear when he settled here in the early 1840s stands on this site, along with a museum that displays photos of local families and events, household goods dating from the mid-1800s, and household and farming antiques. | 2148 Grant Ave. | 801/393–4460 | www.utahmuseums.org/dup/dup.html | Free | Late May–early Sept., Mon.–Sat. 9–5.

Union Station. Incorporating elements of the original 1870s train depot, which was partially destroyed by fire, this impressive Spanish Revival structure built in the early 1900s houses

MORMON PROPHESY AND THE CIVIL WAR

No battles were fought in Mormon-controlled Utah during the Civil War, but members of the new religion felt they would be deeply affected by the conflict—and in a most surprising way.

As tensions rose between the North and South, the position that Utah Territory would take in any resulting conflict was unclear. The most powerful man in the territory—Mormon leader Brigham Young—had neither condemned nor condoned slavery, although he had allowed Southern converts who emigrated to Utah to keep their slaves. Also, Utahns had fought to keep intruders out of the territory, acting as if their lands were separate from the rest of the United States, and Mormon leaders had made speeches about how "godless" and corrupt the federal government had become. These seemed like the words and actions of Southern sympathizers, or even secessionists, and the federal government sent troops to Utah Territory to keep the Mormons in line and to show the restless Southern states what would happen to them if they broke with the Union. Yet Brigham Young professed a love for the United States Constitution and for a whole America. His patriotism made the South nervous.

Young refused to take a stand for the North or for the South because he felt no great attachment to either side. In fact, he believed he knew the outcome of the Civil War long before the first shot was fired. Joseph Smith, founder of the Mormon Church and a prophet in the eyes of his followers, had preached that God would tear apart the United States because it had become wicked. After the destruction of the nation, Smith claimed, the newly humbled people would give up their sinful ways and become Mormons, and then God would make the nation whole again. When the Civil War began, Young was sure Smith's prophesy was coming true. All he had to do was wait until the war ended to take his place as the leader of a re-created America, which would be founded on the Constitution and on Mormon beliefs.

As the Civil War began to wind down and the North began to triumph, speeches condemning the federal government became less frequent in Utah Territory. A new spin was put on the Mormon stance: the nation had been torn apart, just as Joseph Smith had prophesied, and now, Mormons thought, it would surely be more humble and more in tune with God's will. Hopes rose that a less arrogant America would be more tolerant of Mormons. Thus Utahns reacted to the end of the Civil War in the same way people across much of the country reacted—with hope that peace would herald the beginning of a better and more tolerant age.

---

three museums. | 25th St. and Wall Ave. | 801/629–8444 | Combined ticket to all three museums $3 | Mon.–Sat. 10–6, Sun. 11–3.

The **Browning Firearms Museum** showcases the Browning company's high-quality guns, which were the firearms of choice in the Old West and have been built in Utah since 1880. Historical documents about the creation of such famous firearms as Colts, Remingtons, and Winchesters are part of the collection, along with some of the original models and working prototypes of these weapons.

At the **Browning-Kimball Car Museum,** almost 60 unique restored cars are on display, including a single-cylinder 1901 Oldsmobile and a Cadillac that weighs 3 tons.

The **Utah State Railroad Museum** has well-documented exhibits that explain all phases of Utah's railroad history through displays and interpretive signs that appeal to both adults and children. The high point of the museum is an outdoor exhibit of several dozen restored train cars, engines, and cabooses that date from the late 1800s to the mid-1900s.

✦ **ON THE CALENDAR:** Apr. **Rendezvous.** Traders at this event, held over Easter weekend at Fort Buenaventura, are required to dress in authentic pre-1840s costumes, and any goods they sell must be similar to those sold at the original mountain-man rendezvous of the 1820s and '30s. | 801/394–7607.

July **Railroaders Festival.** Reenactments of the Transcontinental Railroad's completion, talks by railroad historians, and exhibits of miniature trains make this festival, held at Union Station, popular with rail buffs. | 800/255–8824.

HISTORIC DINING
Shooting Star Saloon. Welcome to the oldest saloon in Utah, in operation since the 1880s. The menu is simple—beer and burgers—and the frontier origins of the place show in the rough-hewn beams, the scarred bar, and the taxidermied animal heads on the walls. | 7350 E. 200 S., Huntsville 17 mi from Ogden via Rte. 39 | 801/745–2002 | $4–$8 | No credit cards.

PARK CITY
▼▼

Park City was a quiet ranching community until the 1860s, when the discovery of silver and gold brought a huge and rowdy population to town. Dozens of saloons and bordellos earned Park City the nickname "Sin City." A fire destroyed many of the town's buildings in 1898; this, combined with declining mining fortunes in the early 1900s, caused most of the residents to pack up and leave. Park City hit its second vein of "gold" when skiing became popular; it is now Utah's premier ski resort town. *Contact Heber Valley Chamber of Commerce | 475 N. Main St., 84032 | 435/654–3666 | www.hebervalleycc.org. Park City Chamber of Commerce/Convention and Visitors Bureau | Box 1630, 84060 | 435/649–6100 or 800/453–1360 | www.parkcityinfo. com. Park City Historical Society | Box 555, 84060 | 435/649–6104 | www.parkcityhistory.org.*

Heber Valley Historic Railroad. Following a line that first ran in 1899, vintage trains take you on nostalgic trips of various lengths through beautiful Provo Canyon. Each open-air and coach car from the late 1800s and early 1900s has been carefully restored, and two of the engines from that time period—No. 618 and No. 1907—are steam-powered locomotives. Trains leave from Heber City, 17 mi south of Park City. | 450 S. 600 W St., Heber City | 435/654–5601 | www.hebervalleyrr.org | $12 and up | Daily 10–5.

Park City Historical Society. The society offers historian-led day-long hikes around Park City and the Wasatch Mountains. Most of the tours, which focus on mining, railroad, or architectural history, begin in town; some include transportation to more distant locations. You must be a member to participate in the tours, but it's easy to join in advance over the Internet: membership is $25 for one person or $50 for a family. | Box 555, 84060 | 435/649–6104 | www.parkcityhistory.org.

Park City Museum. One of the best small museums in Utah is housed in Park City's old Territorial Jail. Life-size replicas of train cars that served the area, displays that focus on the town's devastating 1898 fire, and mining exhibits are highlights. All are accompanied by meticulous documentation that make mining history, and the history of mining towns, come alive. | 528 Main St. | 435/649–6104 | www.parkcityhistory.org/museum/museum.htm | Free | Mon.–Sat. 10–7, Sun. noon–6.

✦ **ON THE CALENDAR:** June **Historic Home Tour.** More than a dozen restored 19th-century homes in the historic section of Park City are opened to the public by their owners during this popular event, which includes food and beverages provided by some of the best eateries in this resort area. The tour is self-guided, but advanced registration is required. | 435/649–6104.

Aug. **Swiss Days.** Music, dancing, displays of local artifacts, and reenactments of daily life in the pioneer period honor the Swiss who founded Midway, 12 mi south of Park City, in 1866. | 435/654–3666.

HISTORIC LODGING

Johnson Mill Bed & Breakfast. The waterfall that turned giant grinding stones in the 1800s still flows beside the old mill, which now serves as a cozy inn. Implements used at the mill decorate guest rooms and the dining room, where a full breakfast is served. All rooms have fireplaces and jetted tubs. Dining room, microwaves, refrigerators, in-room VCRs with movies, pond, outdoor hot tub, boating, fishing, recreation room, meeting rooms; no smoking. | 100 Johnson Mill Rd., Midway 84049 | 435/654–4333 or 888/272–0030 | fax 435/657–1454 | www.johnsonmill.com | 5 rooms | $125–$165 | AE, D, MC, V | BP.

Washington School Inn. This 1889 stone building served as one of Park City's school houses until 1985. Now the inn's vaulted ceilings, cherry wainscoting, and Victorian-era furnishings recall the town's early years. Some of the individually decorated guest rooms have four-poster canopy beds. A full breakfast is served in the dining room. Dining room, gym, hot tub, sauna, laundry facilities; no-smoking rooms. | 543 Park Ave., Box 536, 84060 | 435/649–3800 or 800/824–1672 | fax 435/649–3802 | www.washingtonschoolinn.com | 12 rooms, 3 suites | $145–$310 | AE, D, DC, MC, V | BP.

PRICE

▼▼

The Price area was first settled in 1877 when fur trappers, who had passed through nearby mountains in their search for beaver and other animals, decided to return to the area to do some ranching. However, the community didn't thrive until a new kind of wealth was discovered in the mountains—coal. Railroad tracks were laid in the valley in 1883 to bring miners from around the world to dig the black mineral and to carry the coal out to markets across the country. The workers also took up residence in Helper, just north of Price. Coal continues to provide the economic base for many towns in the area, including Castle Dale, which is located 20 mi south of Price on a route that was used by Spanish explorers and traders as early as 1598. *Contact Castle Country Travel Region/Carbon County Visitors Bureau | 90 N. 100 E, 84501 | 435/637–3009 or 800/842–0789 | www.castlecountry.com. Emery County Chamber of Commerce | 410 E. Main St., 84513 | 435/381–2547 | www.emerycounty.com.*

Emery County Archives. Gathered here for display are ranching and mining tools, artifacts from several Native American tribes, and government documents from the early years of Castle Dale. | 935 N. Center St., Castle Dale | 435/381–2671 | www.emerycounty.com/archives | Free | Weekdays 10–4.

Museum of the San Rafael. Interpretive displays on the area's ancient Puebloan and Fremont Indian cultures, reproductions of local Native American rock art, and artifacts from Emery County's settlement period are housed in this museum in Castle Dale. | 64 N. 100 E, Castle Dale | 435/381–5252 | Free | Weekdays 10–4, Sat. noon–4.

Nine Mile Canyon. Several of the ranch houses, now in ruins, along this 40-mi route were once way stations for travelers through the Old West. You can also see more than a thousand rock art and habitation sites from the Fremont Indian culture. The last 25 mi of the 37-mi road is maintained gravel. | 7½ mi east of Price on U.S. 6, then north on Nine Mile Canyon Rd. | 435/636–3600 | www.utah.com/playgrounds/nine_mile.htm | Free | Daily.

Western Mining and Railroad Museum. Located in the Old Helper Hotel in the town's National Historic District, this museum mounts displays on mining in Castle Country, shows paintings of local scenes from the Depression era, maintains an archive room of interest to mining and railroading enthusiasts, and has an outdoor exhibit of trains and mining equipment from Helper's Old West days. | 296 S. Main St., Helper | 435/472–3009 | www.wmrrm. org | $2 | May–Sept., Mon.–Sat. 10–6; Oct.–Apr., Tues.–Sat. 11–4.

✦ ON THE CALENDAR: May **Utah Prehistory and Heritage Week.** Music, games, ethnic food, and tours of the College of Eastern Utah Prehistoric Museum and of historic buildings commemorate the area's unique past. Everything from dinosaurs to ancient Pueblo cultures, and from the many local Native American groups to the miners who settled here when the railroad came to town, are incorporated in the event. | 435/637–5060 or 800/842–0789.

July **Castle Valley Pageant.** Covered wagons rumble into Castle Dale during this annual reenactment of the arrival of Mormon pioneers in Castle Valley, south of Price, in the late 1870s. Tepees, mud-and-straw huts, and log cabins are set up in town for the pageant, and traditional Old West meals make this a popular event. | 435/384–2642.

PROVO

▼▼

The Utah Valley was a busy place long before Provo was founded. Several bands of Native Americans lived or hunted in the area, Spanish explorers passed through in 1775, traders from several countries used the explorers' trail to bring goods here and to capture slaves to sell in Mexico, and fur trappers spent winter seasons in the surrounding mountains. With so many groups competing for the area's resources, conflicts were inevitable. The conflicts became more intense when Mormons settled Provo in 1851 and then began claiming land in other parts of the valley, land that had always been used by Native Americans. Several battles were fought here between Mormon settlers and Native American groups during the Walker and Black Hawk wars; the re-created fort in Provo's historic district is evidence of the pioneers' efforts to defend their homes and maintain their control of the area. *Contact Mountainland Association of Governments | 586 E. 800 N, Orem 84097 | 801/229–3800 | www. mountainland.org/travel. Utah County Convention and Visitors Bureau | 100 E. Center St., Suite 3200, 84606 | 801/370–8390 or 800/222–8824 | www.utahvalley.org/cvb. Provo City | 55 N. University Ave., Suite 215, 84601 | 801/852–6161 | www.provo.org.*

John Hutchings Museum. Native American arrowheads, clothing, and pottery; pioneer plows, wagons, and other farm equipment; dishes, furniture, and other household items from the 1800s; and military items, including guns and uniforms, are housed in this family-run museum 16 mi northeast of Provo. | 685 N. Center St., Lehi | 801/768–7180 | www.utahvalley. org/visguide/attracts/hutchings.htm | $2 | Mon.–Sat. 9:30–5:30.

Museum of Peoples and Cultures. Housed at Brigham Young University, a school founded by the Mormon church in 1875, this museum 5 mi north of Provo has periodic exhibits focusing on Utah's many Native American tribes. Clothing, pottery, rugs, weapons, and agricultural tools of the original inhabitants of the West are often on display. | 700 N. 100 E | 801/ 378–6112 | www.fhss.byu.edu/anthro/mopc/main.htm | Free | Weekdays 9–5.

Orem Heritage Museum. The centerpiece of this museum, 5 mi north of Provo, is a model railroad that travels through a huge diorama of the Orem area as it was in the early 1900s. You can also see collections of Native American and pioneer artifacts, including clothes, household goods, tools and weapons, and agricultural equipment. | 745 S. State St., Orem | 801/ 225–2569 | www.utahvalley.org/visguide/attracts/heritage.htm | Free | Weekdays 10–4.

Pioneer Village. Re-created here is a fort built by Mormon settlers in the mid-1800s to protect the community during conflicts with the several Native American tribes that had traditionally hunted and planted in this area. The cabins and shops have been furnished with period antiques, and costumed volunteers explain what life was like for the first settlers in the mid-1800s. | 500 W. 600 N | 801/377–7078 | www.provo.org/parks/pioneer/pioneer.htm | Free | June–Aug., weekdays 2–5.

HISTORIC LODGING

Hines Mansion Bed & Breakfast. Much of the original woodwork, brick, and stained glass has been left intact in this 1896 mansion, originally owned by one of the wealthiest residents of Provo. Rooms are decorated with period furniture and antique household items, and they have two-person Jacuzzis and lots of light. A full breakfast is served in the dining room. Dining room, cable TV, in-room VCRs; no smoking. | 383 W. 100 S, 84606 | 801/374–8400 or 800/428–5636 | fax 801/374–0823 | www.hinesmansion.com | 9 rooms | $99–$199 | AE, D, DC, MC, V | BP.

RICHFIELD

▼▼

Mountain man Jedediah S. Smith and travelers along the Old Spanish Trail crossed through the area now known as Sevier County in the early 1800s, long before Mormons settled the region. Those pioneers arrived in 1864 and named their town for the fertile soil they discovered here. After three of its residents were killed by Indians during the Black Hawk War in 1865, the settlement was evacuated for nearly four years. But the settlers returned, and Richfield is still a ranching and farming community. *Contact Panoramaland Travel Region | 4 S. Main St., Box 71, Nephi 84648 | 435/623–5203 or 800/748–4361. Sevier County Travel Council | 220 N. 600 West St., 84701 | 435/896–8898 or 800/662–8898.*

Kimberly Ghost Town. Only the building foundations of this once thriving turn-of-the-20th-century mining town remain. Once considered the queen of Utah gold mines, the Kimberly was worked by more than 300 miners at its peak around the turn of the 20th century. After the mine closed in 1907, the town began a slow decline and was deserted by 1947. In the flat rocks you can still see openings that led to storage spaces and mines. The drive 7 mi up a mountain along a dirt road can be a bit rough, but it offers nice vistas. | West of Richfield via I–70 to Exit 17, then left on first dirt road | 435/896–8898 | Free | Daily.

Ramsay House. Built in 1850 by Ralph Ramsay, a renowned wood sculptor who helped create the facade of the famous Mormon Tabernacle pipe organ, the Ramsay home has been restored and is now a museum displaying period furniture and family memorabilia. It also serves as a repository for more than 200 oral histories gathered from Utah pioneer families and preserved for use by historians and scholars. | 11550 Clear Creek Canyon Rd. | 435/896–8898 | $5 | Daily 9–sunset.

SALT LAKE CITY

▼▼

On July 24, 1847, Mormon leader Brigham Young gazed across the valley of the Great Salt Lake and reportedly announced to his weary followers, "This is the place." Young chose to settle here because it was, at the time, under the control of Mexico rather than the U.S. government, which the Mormons blamed for much of their persecution. Also, the area had few permanent settlements and an adequate supply of water and building materials, and it offered a protected location, with the high Wasatch Mountains on the east side and a vast desert on the west.

Within hours of arriving, the pioneers began planting crops and diverting water for irrigation, and within days Young drew up plans for a large city. Salt Lake City was to be the hub of the Mormon's promised land, a vast empire stretching from the Rocky Mountains to the southern California coast. Although the area that eventually became the state of Utah was much smaller than Young originally planned, Salt Lake City became much grander than anything he could have imagined. Thousands of Mormon believers flocked to the city from around the world to live near their church president, who is also a living prophet according to Mormon doctrine, and to worship in their newly built temple. In the 1860s, income from railroads and mines created a wealthy class of industrialists who built mansions near the city's downtown area and whose businesses brought thousands of workers—most of whom were not Mormon—to Utah Territory. By the time Utah became a state in 1896, Salt Lake had become a diverse and thriving city. *Contact Downtown Alliance | 238 S. Main St., 84101 | 801/359–5118 | www.downtownslc.org. Salt Lake Chamber | 175 E. 400 S, 6th floor, 84111 | 801/ 364–3631 | www.saltlakechamber.org. Salt Lake Convention and Visitors Bureau | 90 S. West Temple, 84101 | 801/521–2822 or 800/541–4955 | www.saltlake.org.*

Alta Historical Society Museum. Almost $3 million in silver was extracted from mines in the mountain town of Alta, and to transport the ore a unique railroad was created in 1875: Mules hauled empty train cars up the canyon to the mines, and gravity pulled the ore-laden cars back down to the Salt Lake Valley below. This museum in the Alta Library/Community Center (28 mi from downtown Salt Lake) houses mining tools, ski equipment used by the miners, and interpretive displays about mining. | Little Cottonwood Canyon Rd. (Rte. 210) | 801/ 742–3522 | www.altahistory.org | Free | Nov.–Apr., Mon., Wed., and Fri. 6 PM–9 PM.

Beehive House and Lion House. Constructed in 1854, Beehive House was Brigham Young's home and is now a National Historic Landmark. Many furnishings are original, and one of the informative tours through the house will give you an authentic glimpse of an upper-class polygamist household in the late 1800s. Young built Lion House next door to house his 27 wives and 56 children; it is not open for tours. | 67 E. South Temple St. | 801/240–2672 | www.lds.org/placestovisit | Free | Mon.–Sat. 9:30–4:30, Sun. 10–1.

City and County Building. The original Mormon settlers circled their wagons on this site for their first night in the Salt Lake Valley. Forty-seven years later, this massive stone building, with ornate details common to the Romanesque Revival style, was completed. When Utah achieved statehood in 1896, the building served as the state capitol for 19 years (until the current capitol was constructed on a hill above the city). The interior of the building is open to the public during weekday business hours, and hundreds of trees, including species from around the world, make the grounds a cool and shady place for a downtown picnic. | State St. between 400 and 500 South Sts.

Fort Douglas. The United States government established this military post in 1862 to keep Mormon-dominated Utah Territory—which was rebellious for its own reasons—from siding with the Confederates during the Civil War. At one point in the 1860s, about 20% of all U. S. troops were stationed in Utah, and many of them were housed at Fort Douglas at some time during their tour of duty. The well-preserved buildings are excellent examples of military architecture in the 1800s, and a small museum preserves the fort's history. | East side of Wasatch Blvd. at 300 South | 801/581–1710 | www.fortdouglas.org | Grounds daily dawn–dusk, museum Tues.–Sat. noon–4.

Innsbrook Tours. Usually led by retired history professors, these day tours take you through Salt Lake City, to the Great Salt Lake, and to the Bingham Canyon Copper Mine. Some tours include half-day cruises on the Great Salt Lake. | 3353 S. Main St., Suite 804 | 801/534–1001 | fax 801/531–1922 | www.saltlakecityutah.org/sightseeingtours.htm | $17–$39 per person.

Museum of Church History and Art. Artifacts and works of art related to Mormon history—including belongings of church leaders Joseph Smith and Brigham Young—are housed in this large museum. Coins and scrip used as standard currency in Utah Territory during the 1800s, and examples of quilting, embroidery, and other handwork, are popular displays. | 45 N. West Temple St. | 801/240–4615 | www.lds.org/museum | Free | Weekdays 9–9, weekends 10–7.

Pioneer Memorial Museum. Four floors of exhibits, many related to Mormon pioneers, make this museum one of the most extensive collections of settlement-era relics in the West. Clothing, household furnishings, tools, wagons, carriages, and farm machinery are displayed. | 300 N. Main St. | 801/538–1050 | www.northernutah.com/mayflower/dup | Free | Mon.–Sat. 9–5.

Red Butte Garden and Arboretum. Follow the trails through 25 acres of gardens to see the landscape of the West much as it looked to early explorers, mountain men, and pioneers. The plants here were gathered from the grounds of nearby Fort Douglas, where they were protected for more than a century. As an active military base, the fort was closed to the public, allowing hundreds of acres of land to remain pristine. | Enter on Wakara Way east of Foothill Dr. | 801/585–0556 | www.redbutte.utah.edu | $5 | May–Sept., Mon.–Sat. 9–8, Sun. 9–5; Oct.–Apr., Tues.–Sun. 10–5.

Rio Grande Depot/Utah State Historical Society Museum. This 1910 depot was built to compete with the showy Union Pacific Railroad Depot three blocks north. It houses the state's historical society, a research archive, and a museum with rotating exhibits on various aspects of the history of Utah and of the West, including the history of this depot. | 300 S. Rio Grande St. | 801/533–3500 | www.history.utah.gov/services/exriograndedepot.html | Free | Weekdays 8–5, Sat. 10–3.

Temple Square. In the center of downtown Salt Lake City is Temple Square, a complex that contains some of the Mormon church's most important structures. The Mormon Temple, which took 40 years to build (it was completed in the 1880s), has walls that are 16 ft thick at the base and is used for marriages, baptisms, and other religious functions. Although the temple is open only to Mormons, non-Mormons can take tours of the 1882 Assembly Hall, which is used for large meetings, and of the Tabernacle, built in the 1860s, which is the home of the world-renowned Mormon Tabernacle Choir. You can learn more about Temple Square and Mormon history and practices at one of the two on-site visitor centers. | 50 W. North Temple St. | 801/240–2534 | www.lds.org/placestovisit/location | Free | Daily 9–9.

This Is the Place Heritage Park. Old Deseret Village, a representation of a typical 1800s Mormon community in Utah Territory, is the main draw of this park. Volunteers dressed in clothing of the type worn in the 1800s work both in original period buildings and in reproductions of period buildings to show visitors what life was like in Mormon pioneer days. Artisans and craftspeople demonstrate frontier skills. Elsewhere in the park, carriage rides and daily events are offered, and a monument depicts Brigham Young, Mormon settlers, representatives of several Native American tribes, explorers, and mountain men. | 2601 Sunnyside Ave. | 801/582–1847 | www.thisistheplace.org | Park free, village $6 | Park daily, dawn–dusk; village late May–early Sept., daily 10–5.

✦ ON THE CALENDAR: July **"Days of '47" Celebration.** Festivities are held statewide to celebrate the arrival of the first Mormon settlers in the Salt Lake Valley, on July 24, 1847. The activities in Salt Lake City are the most elaborate and draw the largest crowds. Among the events are a pioneer parade held downtown, a world-championship rodeo, and a lavish fireworks display. | 801/521–2822.

HISTORIC LODGING
Brigham Street Inn. Walter C. Lyne, whose wool brokerage business made him rich and who became one of Salt Lake City's most prominent early citizens, built this mansion in 1898. It stands on East South Temple, known informally now as the "Boulevard of Mansions." The mansion's original woodwork has been preserved throughout, along with unique curved glass windows in numerous alcoves. Most guest rooms have king-size beds and are decorated with

THE LEGENDARY GREAT SALT LAKE

Legends of an enormous body of water with an outlet to the Pacific Ocean drew explorers north from Mexico as early as the 1500s. By the 1700s, other legends—about piles of gold and mines full of jewels—had been proven false by Spanish explorers, but the lake legend endured. Following a source of water through the West's harsh desert, and traveling along a flat river bank instead of struggling over mountains, would make trade easier between New Mexico and the settlements springing up along California's coast. Perhaps goods could be shipped to the coast rather than hauled by mules, a trip the Spanish guessed (and they were right) would take months.

Franciscan fathers Francisco Atanasio Dominguez and Francisco Silvestre Velez de Escalante came close to finding Great Salt Lake in 1776, but they cut through the Wasatch Mountains too far to the south. They did blaze a major trade route through Utah, but there is no record of any travelers wandering far enough off the route to see the lake of legend. In 1804–1805, Lewis and Clark searched for a water route to the west coast, but their focus on the Columbia River gave them no reason to travel south of Idaho. They, too, missed the lake.

Mountain men had heard of the lake. Legend has it that an argument about the lake broke out at the alcohol-soaked 1824 rendezvous in northern Utah—the trappers couldn't agree whether the nearby Bear River flowed into the lake. Jim Bridger was chosen to settle the argument, some say because he was the youngest. For whatever reason, he was set adrift on the Bear River in a rickety bull boat and told to report his findings at a future rendezvous—if he survived.

Jim Bridger did survive, and he was able to report that the Bear River did flow into the Great Salt Lake. However, his travels and those of fellow mountain man Jedediah Smith indicated that the lake was landlocked. Plus it was no good for drinking. (With no rivers to drain the lake, water that flows in has no way out but to evaporate, leaving behind a highly concentrated solution of salts and minerals.) Even worse, the explorers found that travel around the lake was hampered by vast expanses of marshland, a muddy shoreline, and hundreds of square miles of salt flats that looked solid but were often little more than a thin crust over layers of muck.

With dreams of a fresh-water oasis and an easy route to the coast crushed, the legends of the lake changed. The lake became a place where monsters lurked in the water, giants rode elephant-like creatures on the islands, and the bottom periodically opened, swallowing everything nearby. The area became a place to avoid, or to pass by quickly, until 1847, when a legendary people crossed the plains to settle on its shore.

antique furniture and household items from the mansion's early days. Dining room. | 1135 E. South Temple, 84102 | 801/364–4461 or 800/417–4461 | fax 801/521–3201 | www. brighamstreetinn.citysearch.com | 9 rooms | $125–$185 | AE, D, DC, MC, V | CP.

ST. GEORGE

Believing the mild year-round climate would be perfectly suited to growing cotton, Brigham Young dispatched 309 LDS families to southwesternmost Utah in 1861 to found St. George. Their plan was to raise cotton and silkworms and to establish a textile industry, in order to make up for textile shortages resulting from the Civil War. The area was dubbed "Utah's Dixie," a name that stuck even after the war ended and the South could once again provide cotton to Utah. The settlers—many of them originally from southern states—found the desert climate preferable to northern Utah's snow, and they stayed on as farmers and ranchers. Crops included fruit, molasses, and grapes for wine that the pioneers sold to mining communities in Nevada and in Leeds, Utah. *Contact St. George Area Chamber of Commerce | 97 E. St. George Blvd., 84770 | 435/628–1658 | www.stgeorgechamber.com. Washington County Travel and Convention Bureau | 425 S. 700 East St., 84770 | 435/634–5747 or 800/869–6635 | fax 435/628–1619 | www.utahszionandbryce.com.*

Brigham Young's Winter Home. Mormon leader Brigham Young spent the last five winters of his life in the warm, sunny climate of St. George. Built of adobe on a sandstone and basalt foundation, his home has been carefully restored to its original condition. A portrait painted of Young during his lifetime hangs over one fireplace, and furnishings authentic to the time period have been donated by supporters who want the home preserved. You can take guided tours of the rooms. | 67 W. 200 N | 435/673–2517 or 435/673–5181 | www.infowest. com/utah/colorcountry/history/brigham.html | Free | Daily 9–dusk.

Jacob Hamblin House. Jacob Hamblin came to southwestern Utah in 1854 to serve as a Mormon missionary to the Paiute, Navajo, and Zuni Indians. Settling in Santa Clara, 5 mi northwest of St. George, he became best known among the Indian tribes not as a religious figure but as an even-handed negotiator between the tribes and Mormon settlers. Tour his sandstone home for a look at the life of a 19th-century Mormon missionary and for insight into the history of Utah's Dixie. | 3386 Santa Clara Dr., Santa Clara | 435/673–2161 or 435/673–5181 | www.infowest.com/utah/colorcountry/history/jhhome | Free | Daily 9–dusk.

Mountain Meadows Massacre Monument. On September 11, 1857, a wagon train passing through southwestern Utah on its way to California ended its journey prematurely and violently north of St. George. Unfortunately for the party, which was led by Alexander Fancher, they had come from Arkansas, where an LDS church official had recently been murdered and where church founder Joseph Smith and his brother Hyrum were killed in 1844. The local Mormons did not look charitably upon the emigrants. Perhaps as an act of "blood atonement," a group of Mormon militiamen from Iron County, aided by Paiute Indians, slaughtered more than 120 men, women, and children of the Fancher wagon train. Fancher and his entire family died. The bones of the victims were left exposed in the meadow for more than two years before U.S. Army soldiers buried them beneath a pile of stones topped with a cedar cross. John D. Lee, a Mormon leader in the area, was the only man convicted of any crime related to the massacre, by an all-Mormon jury in 1877. Lee was stripped of his church membership and his plural wives and was executed for the crime. (Curiously, the LDS Church posthumously reinstated Lee's church membership in 1961.) A new monument and surrounding rock wall were dedicated at Mountain Meadows in 1999. | About 35 mi north of St. George on Rte. 18 | www.mtn-meadows-assoc.com | Free | Daily.

Pine Valley Chapel. Most often described as a "ship built upside down" this two-story church is the oldest Mormon chapel still in use. It was supposedly designed and constructed by Ebenezer Bryce (Bryce Canyon's namesake), who had worked as a shipmaker in Australia. The chapel was made using only square iron nails and wooden pegs, techniques common to shipbuilding. The attic rafters are formed like ribs in the hull of a ship. Sunday services are still held in the church, and visitors are welcome to walk through and experience the architecture. | 40 mi north of St. George via Rte. 18, in Dixie National Forest | 435/673–3431 | Free | Daily 9–dusk.

St. George Temple. Completed in 1877, this red sandstone structure was a meeting place for both Mormons and other congregations. It is still in use today, and though you can't enter the temple unless you are Mormon, a visitor center next door offers spectacular views, and you can take a guided tour of the grounds. | 250 E. 400 S | 435/673–5181 | Free | Visitor center daily 9–9.

Tabernacle. Mormon settlers began work on this building in June 1863, just a few months after St. George was established. The building, built of sandstone and with a clock tower 140 ft tall, was dedicated by Brigham Young 13 years later. This is one of the best-preserved pioneer buildings in the entire state. It's still used for public meetings and programs for the entire community. | Main and Tabernacle Sts. | 435/628–4072 | Daily 9–6.

✦ ON THE CALENDAR: Sept. **Santa Clara Swiss Festival.** Mormon converts emigrated from Switzerland to southwestern Utah in 1861. The small town of Santa Clara celebrates its Swiss heritage with an array of events including historical displays, crafts and food booths, games, a parade, and a tour of historical homes. | 435/673–6712.

Sept. **Southern Utah Folklife Festival.** A three-day event highlights southern Utah's culture, traditional arts, and folkways with storytelling, a crafts market, saddle makers, quilting, cowboy poetry, music, and dance. | 435/673–6290.

HISTORIC LODGING

Green Gate Village. Step back in time in these restored pioneer homes dating to the 1860s. The inn takes its name from the green gates and fences that surrounded the homes of St. George's LDS leaders in the late 1800s. According to local legend, Mormon leader Brigham Young offered them green paint left over from painting the fences and gates of the St. George Temple, with the stipulation that they paint their own gates and fences with it. The last remaining original green gate is displayed in the inn's garden and served as a model for the gates now surrounding Green Gate Village. Behind the gates is a village of nine fully restored pioneer homes filled with antique furnishings and modern amenities. Many of the rooms have fireplaces and jetted tubs. Restaurant, in-room VCRs, pool, shop, meeting rooms; no smoking. | 76 W. Tabernacle, 84770 | 435/628–6999 or 800/350–6999 | fax 435/628–6989 | www.greengatevillage.com | 15 rooms | $85–$165 | AE, D, MC, V | BP.

Seven Wives Inn. After polygamy was outlawed by the U.S. government in 1882, polygamists sometimes hid in the attic of one of the three houses that now make up the inn. The inn is named for one of those polygamists, Benjamin F. Johnson, who really did have seven wives. Some early presidents of the Mormon church stayed in one of the other buildings. Today's inn, in St. George's historic district, occupies a small compound. You can stay in a room or the private cottage. Some of the rooms have a fireplace and jetted tub, and all have the old-fashioned charm of an elegant pioneer homestead. In-room VCRs, pool; no smoking. | 217 N. 100 W, 84770 | 435/628–3737 or 800/600–3737 | fax 435/628–5646 | www.sevenwivesinn.com | 10 rooms, 12 suites, 1 cottage | $75–$150 | AE, D, DC, MC, V | BP.

TOOELE
▼▼▼

The harsh desert climate and rough terrain of the Tooele area made it a place that most people—explorers, mountain men, non-Mormon immigrant parties, and Pony Express riders—passed through as quickly as possible. The first permanent settlements began to appear in the early 1850s, when the area was used by the Mormon Church as a place to graze cattle and to gather timber for construction in rapidly growing Salt Lake City. Mormon converts were sent by Brigham Young to oversee those operations. Telegraph lines strung from the east and west coasts met near Tooele in 1861, shutting down Pony Express service but opening up the town to the outside world. When silver, gold, and copper were discovered in the mountains outside of town in the 1860s, Tooele entered a boom period that lasted more than a century. *Contact Tooele County Chamber of Commerce | 201 N. Main St., Box 460, 84074 | 800/378–0690 | www.tooelechamber.com. Tooele County Travel and Tourism | 47 S. Main St., 84074 | 435/843–3198 | www.tooelechamber.com.*

Benson Grist Mill. This 1854 mill, one of the best examples of a 19th-century mill in Utah, is under ongoing renovation, but you can still take a tour through the building and see behind the scenes of the old milling industry. The cabin and blacksmith shop next to the mill are also open to visitors for tours. Special events, during which crafts of the 1800s are demonstrated, are scheduled throughout the year. | Rte. 138, 10 mi north of Tooele, Mills Junction | 435/882–7678 or 435/882-7137 | www.co.tooele.ut.us/ht05_bensonmill | Free | Late May–early Sept., Tues.–Sat. 10–4.

Camp Floyd/Stagecoach Inn State Park and Museum. From 1858 to 1861, Camp Floyd was a military post that housed 3,500 troops. The troops were sent to Utah after several bands of soldiers and non-Mormon settlers were attacked by Mormons, who feared that outsiders would take over their new home in the West. The military presence was supposed to stop an anticipated uprising by Mormons, but the Mormons never revolted and the soldiers ended up spending much of their time prospecting in the mountains near the encampment. Most of the soldiers were sent back East again in 1861, when the Civil War posed a bigger problem for the federal government. The Stagecoach Inn, now a small museum, was an overnight stop on the overland stage and Pony Express routes. | 30 mi southeast of Tooele on Rte. 73 | 801/768–8932 | http://parks.state.ut.us/parks/www1/camp.htm | $4 | Visitor center daily 9–5, closed Sun. mid-Oct.–Mar.

Donner-Reed Museum. The famously doomed Donner-Reed Party, a group of westward-bound emigrants who were stranded in the Sierra Nevada for one very long and hungry winter, took their first step toward their fate when they decided to follow the Hastings Cutoff of the California Trail. They departed the main trail at Fort Bridger, Wyoming, in the summer of 1846 and made their way across northern Utah along the new and untested route. At the Bonneville Salt Flats west of Tooele the party's wagons got bogged down in the salty sand and clay again and again, creating delays that ultimately caused the party to reach the Sierra Nevada passes too late in the season to cross. This museum, 11 mi northwest of Tooele, houses artifacts, many retrieved from the salt flats, that belonged to the Donner Party. | Cooley and Clark Sts., Grantsville | 435/884–3411 | Free | By appointment.

Tooele County Museum. The town's original train depot has been restored and now serves as a museum, with exhibits and displays that focus on the railroading, mining, and smeltering history of the area. Engines, a caboose, other train cars, and a replica of a mine shaft are the highlights. You can ride a small-scale train around the property. | Broadway and Vine St. | 435/882–2836 | www.co.tooele.ut.us/ht16_countymuseum | Free | Late May–early Sept., Sat. 1–4.

✦ ON THE CALENDAR: June **Pony Express Reenactment.** Horseback riders in authentic Pony Express costumes reenact the carrying of mail along Utah's section of the trail. The event, held at the old station in Simpson Springs (57 mi southwest of Tooele), also includes horseback rides, games, food, and music. | 800/378–0690.

VERNAL

▼▼

Vernal lies in the Uinta Basin, originally home to the ancient Fremont people. Spanish explorers surveyed the area in 1775, and mountain men made frequent trips through the valley in the early 1800s and set up at least one trading post. The Mormons thought about settling here in 1847 but decided the land was not fit for agriculture. When they checked the area again in the 1860s, they decided it was still no place to live. At their suggestion, President Abraham Lincoln set aside several million acres of the basin as an Indian reservation and moved members of Ute and other tribes here from their traditional lands in the Salt Lake and Utah Lake valleys. In the late 1800s and early 1900s, much of the Uinta Basin land that had been set aside as a reservation—including Vernal itself—was taken back by the U.S. government and opened to settlers from the East. Vernal, which became a cattle ranching community, is one of the few Utah towns founded by non-Mormons. However, it was the town's remote location—at the eastern edge of Utah, far from government authorities in Utah, Wyoming, and Colorado—not a lack of religion, that led to its early reputation as a wild and lawless place. Butch Cassidy was just one of the outlaws who found refuge in this unregulated corner of Utah. *Contact Dinosaurland Travel Board | 25 E. Main St., 84078 | 435/789–6932 or 800/477–5558 | www.dinoland.com. Ute Indians | Tribal Headquarters, Box 190, Fort Duchesne 84026 | 435/722–5141 | www.northernute.com. Vernal Chamber of Commerce | 134 W. Main St., 84078 | 435/789–1352 | www.vernalchamber.com.*

1877 Log Post Office and Store. This building, one of the few large log structures remaining in the region, served as Vernal's post office and general store for several decades. You can admire it from the outside while it undergoes careful restoration. | 1255 W. 2000 N.

Browns Park and the John Jarvie Ranch. Operated by the Bureau of Land Management (BLM), the John Jarvie Ranch includes several buildings constructed by Jarvie from 1880 to the early 1900s and is currently undergoing an extensive historic documentation process. Jarvie was a storekeeper, musician, and prospector whose even-handed treatment of customers earned him the respect of the area's ranchers and of the many outlaws who frequented the area. Butch Cassidy formed his Wild Bunch while living in Browns Park, and it was here that he met "Etta Place," or, as she was known in her home town, Ann Bassett. Although Jarvie tried to live in peace with all the area's residents and visitors, he was shot and killed during a dispute. The road into Browns Park can be rough during wet weather; be sure to call the BLM's Vernal office for current road conditions. | 65 mi northeast of Vernal on U.S. 191, then follow the signs to the ranch, Browns Park | 435/885–3307 | Free | May–Oct., daily 10–5.

Josie Morris Cabin/Dinosaur National Monument. Although most people visit this park to see dinosaur bones, it also offers an especially scenic drive that runs 6 mi east from the quarry to the cabin where Josie Morris lived. Josie was the sister of Ann Bassett, the "Etta Place" of Butch Cassidy legends. Ms. Morris was a rugged individualist who kept company with many of the fringe elements in this wild country. | 20 mi east of Vernal on Rte. 149 | 435/781–7700 quarry | www.nps.gov/dino | $10 per vehicle | Memorial Day–Labor Day, daily 8–7; early Sept.–late May, daily 8–4:30.

Ute Tribal Museum. This museum is on the Uintah and Ouray Indian Reservation. Although the collections and displays are not as polished as they might be in facilities that receive better funding, you will be able to view history through the eyes of a people whose story is often disregarded or told by outsiders. The museum is the kind of place where you can get a balanced perspective of the events that shaped the Old West. | 22 mi southwest of Vernal on U.S. 191, Fort Duchesne | 435/722–4992 or 435/722–5141 | www.northernute.com | Free | Call for hrs.

Western Heritage Museum. Inside this big, open building are collections of Fremont and Ute Indian artifacts, including baskets, water jugs, and bead-work pieces. Carriages, guns, saddles, farm implements, and children's toys from the Old West period are also on display. Local and regional historians have created documentation for the collections that allow the objects to tell the history of this area. | 302 E. 200 S | 435/789–7399 | Free | Weekdays 9–6, Sat. 10–2.

✦ ON THE CALENDAR: June–July **Outlaw Trail Festival.** Folk arts, a women's .22 rifle-shooting competition, guided horseback rides along outlaw trails, and a rodeo are among the main events of this Vernal festival. There is also a nightly performance of a musical based on Butch Cassidy's exploits in this corner of the state. | 435/789–6932 or 800/477–5558.

Aug. **Northern Ute Powwow.** Drumming, dancing, and singing competitions, a rodeo, and an arts-and-crafts fair take place at the Sundance Grounds in Neola, 28 mi west of Vernal on Route 121. | 435/722–5141 or 435/722–4598.

WASHINGTON

—◆—

When the Denny Party landed on Alki Beach and founded Seattle in 1851, it was timber that drew them and the waters of the Puget Sound that allowed them to get there. This is Washington's Old West story in a nutshell. The region's abundant natural resources—seemingly endless trees, rivers, and harbors—feature prominently throughout its history, distinguishing Washington from many other western states. Salmon, not buffalo, fed Washington's native inhabitants. Timber, not gold, made its first and biggest fortunes. Trade was its most significant commercial activity and remains so today. Notable battles were few, and notorious outlaws fewer still.

Human habitation in Washington may date back as far as 30,000 years, and archaeological evidence suggests that the people were able to live peaceably thanks to the area's abundant resources, especially the seemingly endless supply of salmon that returned each year to the Columbia River, the Snake River, and the Puget Sound's tributary rivers. Europeans first became interested in Washington for its natural resources, in particular otter and beaver, whose furs could be tranformed into profit. Spanish, Russian, and British seafarers explored the coast, and the Spanish claimed it in 1775. But Spain never acted on its claim.

In 1792, Robert Gray, an American seafarer representing a Boston fur company, came upon the mouth of the Columbia River, naming that great waterway after his ship, the *Columbia Rediviva*. That same year, Briton George Vancouver explored Puget Sound. Both men had been sent, in part, in response to Spanish forays into the area. In their initial explorations of the region, they sought the elusive Northwest Passage. Vancouver's party marveled at Puget Sound's immense trees, but neither he nor Gray fully realized the value of these forests.

The members of the Lewis and Clark expedition were the first Euro-Americans to traverse Washington by land. In 1805, they crossed much of the state on the north bank of the Columbia on their way to the Pacific. Blocked from the river's end by sheer cliffs, thick forests, and tempestuous weather, they ultimately retreated east and crossed the river to its southern shore to spend the winter near what is now Astoria, Oregon. Salmon, of course, was the mainstay of life along the Columbia, and the Corps of Discovery ate so much of it that they complained of it in their journals. After their brief visit, Washington escaped notice except by fur traders who established remote fur-trading forts, at Spokane in 1810, at Vancouver in 1821, and near Tacoma in 1833. The business-oriented fur traders who manned these outposts, bartering blankets and other trade goods for beaver skins, recognized they were in a land of extravagant natural resources, but these were not yet great lures for westward migration.

The first real non-native settlement was established in eastern Washington in 1837, when Marcus and Narcissa Whitman founded a mission at the foot of the Blue Mountains near present-day Walla Walla, helping to blaze the Oregon Trail along the way. Although the Whitmans' objective was religious conversion of the Indians, the missionaries brought unwelcome arrivals of another sort—diseases, largely measles, that decimated Native tribes. The Indians retaliated against the settlers in what has become known as the 1847 Whitman Massacre, which wiped out the mission and its inhabitants.

It wasn't until the Oregon Trail brought a steady stream of emigrants down the Snake and Columbia rivers in the 1840s that a few adventurous souls headed north into Puget Sound, rather than south into the Willamette Valley. There they found vast forests of Douglas fir, hemlock, and western red cedar, growing right up to the edge of a huge, deep natural harbor. In the 1850s numerous settlements sprang up along the many inlets and bays of the Puget Sound, including Seattle in 1851 and Tacoma in 1857. Virtually all were devoted to harvesting timber, which was shipped south along the Pacific coast to San Francisco's booming commercial districts. California had plenty of timber, but it was largely inaccessible. Clipper ships, carrying rocks as ballast, sailed north in search of more attainable wood. Seattle proved to be the best spot to anchor. There, the ships dumped the rocks they had brought north and replaced it with timber; today, a significant portion of the Seattle waterfront is composed of California rock.

While Seattle and other Washington cities pursued the logging dollar, the United States and Great Britain jockeyed for possession of the Northwest. One of the best-known conflicts in Washington history was part of this struggle. When the two nations partitioned the Northwest along the 49th parallel in 1846, north Puget Sound's San Juan Island was split in two. Small military forces from both sides continued to occupy the island for years, and in 1859 a British pig was caught grubbing around in an American settler's garden. When the pig was shot tempers flared, and both sides set up fortifications about 10 mi apart, ready for battle. But the famed Pig War was resolved by cooler heads without any further gunfire, and the island was given over to U.S. control.

A major turning point in Washington history came in 1897, when a steamer from Alaska docked in Seattle carrying a "ton of gold" from the Klondike. Seattle quickly became the major outfitter for gold rushers headed north to the Yukon, and the city's role as a trade center was established. Then in 1900, midwestern timberman Frederick Weyerhaeuser sat down in a Tacoma hotel and wrote a check for $1 million to buy 900,000 acres of prime timberland. The transition of Washington's economy, from pioneer lumbering, fishing, and farming to corporate enterprise had begun. By 1909, when Seattle hosted its first World's Fair (the Alaska-Yukon-Pacific Exposition, which drew almost 4 million visitors), Washington was no longer a frontier territory but a full-blown, 20th-century American state.

Logging Towns of the Puget Sound
A DRIVING TOUR FROM ABERDEEN TO BELLINGHAM
▼▼

Distance: 350 mi   **Time:** 4 days
Breaks: Overnight at Hoquiam's Castle Bed and Breakfast near Aberdeen for a taste of lumber tycoon-style living. Seattle has innumerable restaurants and inns. There are plenty of lodgings in the island town of Coupeville, some dating from the 19th century.

WASHINGTON TIME LINE

1792 Robert Gray explores the lower Columbia River. George Vancouver explores Puget Sound.

1805 Meriwether Lewis and William Clark traverse southern Washington along the Snake and Columbia rivers.

1810 The North West Company establishes Spokane House, a fur-trading post.

1821 Hudson Bay Company establishes Fort Vancouver.

1837 The Whitman Mission is established near Walla Walla.

1846 The U.S. and Great Britain divide the Northwest region along the 49th Parallel.

1847 The inhabitants of Whitman Mission are killed by Cayuse Indians.

1851 Settlers from the Denny Party found Seattle.

1872 The Northern Pacific Railroad chooses Tacoma as its western terminus.

1889 Washington is admitted as the 42nd state in the union. The Great Fire destroys 25 city blocks in Seattle.

1897 The first shipment of gold from the Klondike reaches Seattle.

1900 Frederick Weyerhaeuser buys 900,000 acres of Northwest timber.

1909 Seattle hosts a World's Fair, the Alaska-Yukon-Pacific Exposition.

Western Washington's heritage as a timber-cutting, -shipping, and -trading center is the focus of this tour, which takes you through the Puget Sound region to old-growth forests, logging museums, and towns built on lumbering. Along the way you will be treated to spectacular vistas of the sound and of Mount Rainier and the Olympic Mountains.

Make your way to **Aberdeen** to start your tour. Aberdeen once thrived as a timber-shipping port, and the Aberdeen Museum of History has photographs and other memorabilia of those days. If you're there in early September, pop up to Hoquiam 4 mi away for Logger's Playday, a celebration of the area's roots. Any time of year, spend a night at Hoquiam's Castle Bed and Breakfast, housed in the turn-of-the-20th-century home of a timber king.

From Aberdeen on your second day, drive 21 mi east on U.S. 12 and 21 mi east on Rte. 8, then 5 mi south on U.S. 101 and 29 mi north on I–5 to reach **Tacoma.** In Point Defiance Park, small stands of old-growth fir and hemlock are a reminder of the mighty forests that early settlers marveled at. Inside the park, Camp Six Logging Museum traces the early days of the western Washington timber industry, when two-man crews felled giants by hand and used steam donkeys to haul them to the mills. Six mi southeast of Point Defiance (follow Ruston Way to downtown Tacoma), the Washington State History Museum vividly depicts the development of the region's first industry. After lunch, drive 40 mi southeast of Tacoma on Route 7 to the little town of Elbe, where you can board Mount Rainier Scenic Railroad (June–September) for a trip through the forest on old logging trains. If you want to see the last major undisturbed old growth forest in the Puget Sound lowlands, skirt Mount Rainier (48 mi east on Route 706, 11 mi north on Route 123; portions of either may be closed by inclement weather) to reach Route 410 north. Follow Route 410 past Greenwater (22 mi) to Federation Forest State Park. A walk among the 250-ft firs and hemlocks makes time stand still. Continue on Route 410 about 30 mi to I–5, and head north 31 mi to downtown Seattle to have dinner and spend the night.

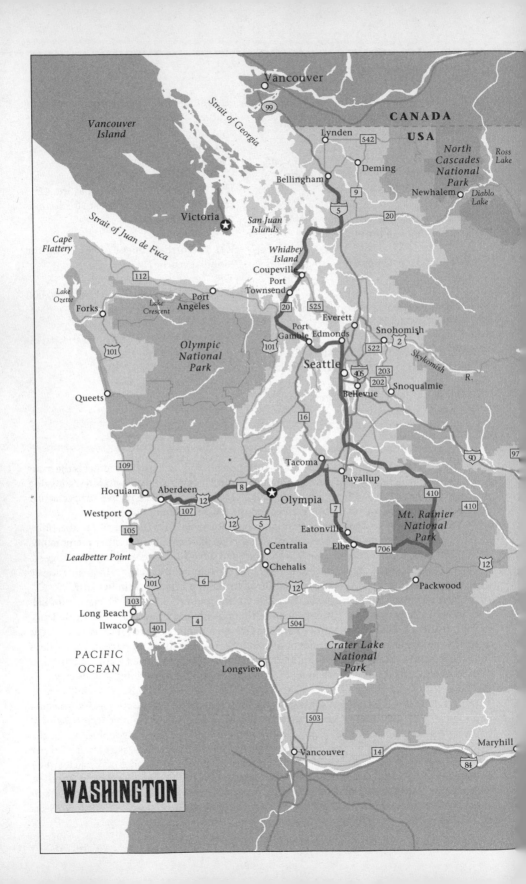

WASHINGTON

The morning of day three, take a peek at 19th-century **Seattle** in Pioneer Square. At 1st Avenue and Yesler Way is the site of one of the city's first sawmills and the original "skid row," where freshly cut trees slid down to the mill. Move on from Seattle, heading 12 mi north on I–5 and 5 mi west on Route 104 to the Edmonds–Kingston Ferry. Take the ferry to Kingston and drive 7 mi northwest on Route 104 to Port Gamble, 27 mi south of **Port Townsend.** At the Port Gamble Historic Museum, you can learn about the Pope and Talbot Timber Company, whose sawmills employed the town's people for many years. Next, drive 8 mi northwest on Route 104, 13 mi north on Route 19, and 5 mi north on Rte. 20N to the Whidbey Island–Port Townsend Ferry. When you get off the ferry, drive 4 mi north on South Engle Road into the town of **Coupeville.** Stop in at the Island County Historical Museum for a look back at the town's early industries, including logging, then stroll the streets to soak up the history first-hand. Overnight at one of Coupeville's Victorian bed-and-breakfasts.

Your fourth day takes you farther north, to the city of **Bellingham.** Drive 26 mi north of Coupeville on Route 20N, then 12 mi east on Route 20E and 23 mi north on I–5 to reach the historic downtown area. In the Syre Education Center at the Whatcom Museum of History and Art, take in the exhibits on logging. And if you're here in June, head 10 mi east of Bellingham to Deming to see the Deming Logging Show, a demonstration of traditional woodsmen's skills.

The Pioneer Palouse

A DRIVING TOUR FROM PASCO TO COLFAX

▼▼

Distance: 225 mi   **Time:** 2 days
Breaks: Dayton, with several small cafés and inns, is a good overnight stop.

The Palouse, the hilly countryside of southeast Washington, once nurtured native peoples such as the Nez Perce. It is named for a Nez Perce sub-group, the Palouse, who are credited with creating the Appaloosa horse. White settlers took over the land and turned it into the most productive wheat-growing region on earth, but not without a fight from the Indians. This trek is for anyone interested in frontier conflicts between settlers and Indians.

Begin in **Pasco,** at the Franklin County Historical Museum. Pioneer homesteading in the Palouse is the subject of some of the exhibits here. Near Pasco on U.S. 12, Sacajawea State Park overlooks the confluence of the Columbia and Snake rivers. Lewis and Clark camped here in 1805, and the interpretive center focuses on their relations with the local Native Americans. When you're through here, head for Walla Walla on U.S. 12, a distance of 48 mi. Along the way, about 16 mi southeast of Pasco, you will pass a stone marker commemorating Fort Walla Walla (an outpost of the Hudson Bay Company), and another about nine mi west of Walla Walla that marks the site of the Frenchtown Mission Church, named for the French-Canadian trappers who were the first whites to live in the area. Southwest of the second marker is the site of the 1855 Battle of Walla Walla, in which Walla Walla Indians lost a fight with white settlers. Continuing on U.S. 12 you will reach the Whitman Mission National Historic Site, about 5 mi west of Walla Walla proper. Exhibits here trace the history of the mission and of the Indian-missionary conflicts that led to the Whitman Massacre of 1847. In **Walla Walla,** the Fort Walla Walla Museum has an excellent collection of frontier farm equipment and a compound of restored pioneer buildings. Have a look around the town and then make your way 31 mi northeast via U.S. 12—this stretch is one of the most scenic routes in the Northwest—to **Dayton.** With 117 buildings listed on the National Register of Historic Places, Dayton is a snapshot of pioneer Palouse life. The Dayton Historic Depot illustrates the importance of the railroad to the area's settlement and early prosperity. Spend the night in Dayton, perhaps at the 1896 Weinhard Hotel.

On the second morning of your tour, drive 66 mi east on U.S. 12 to Clarkston. Three mi south of town in Asotin, the Asotin County Museum recounts the pioneer history of the area. From Clarkston, U.S. 195 will take you 47 mi north to **Colfax,** which likes to call itself the Heart of the Palouse. On U.S. 195, 16 mi north of town, stop at Steptoe Butte State Park. U.S. Army troops under the command of of Colonel E. J. Steptoe used the butte as a reconnaissance point during some of the last conflicts between the army and the Native Americans in eastern Washington. Another 11 mi north on U.S. 195 brings you to the town of Rosalia, location of the 1858 Indian victory over Steptoe. The Steptoe Battlefield Monument commemorates that event, which precipitated ruthless reprisals by the cavalry later that year, and the ultimate defeat of the Indians.

ABERDEEN

▼▼

This Grays Harbor town was settled in 1884, the same year its first sawmill was built. (It was only the third sawmill in the country at the time.) Named by Scottish settler James Stewart, Aberdeen was the very definition of a boomtown, growing quickly with the strength of its lumber industry. Despite a devastating fire that destroyed most of its original structures in 1903, the population of Aberdeen topped 12,000 in 1905. Today, it's a small town, not much bigger than it was in its pioneer days, living peacefully with its boomtown past. *Contact Grays Harbor Chamber of Commerce | 506 Duffy St., 98520 | 360/532–1924 | www.graysharbor.org.*

Aberdeen Museum of History. This pleasant small museum has a collection of canoes from local tribes, as well as a good display of historical photographs from Aberdeen's logging-shipping history. | 111 E. 3rd St. | 360/533–1976 | Donation | June–early Sept., Wed.–Sun. 11–4; early Sept.–May, weekends noon–4.

Grays Harbor Historical Seaport. Here you can see exhibits about shipbuilding and maritime history, but the centerpiece of the harbor is a reproduction of the 112-ft *Lady Washington,* which accompanied Captain Robert Gray's *Columbia Rediviva* on its first West Coast voyage. The ships traded with Washington coast Indians for furs, and the *Lady* took a load of furs to China while the *Columbia* went on to find the mouth of the Columbia River. When she's in port you can take a dockside tour of the *Lady* or climb aboard for a regularly scheduled day sail or a 1–2-week cruise. | 813 E. Heron St. | 360/532–8611 or 360/532–8612; 800/200-LADY | Harbor, free; day sail $105 | Harbor, daily; call ahead for ship tours and sailings.

✦ ON THE CALENDAR: Sept. **Logger's Playday.** People come from all over to participate in this festival honoring the area's logging roots. Held in Hoquiam (4 mi north of Aberdeen on U.S. 101) on the first Saturday after Labor Day, it hosts school bands, logging trucks, and Scottish pipe bands as they parade through downtown. At Grizzly Stadium you can see such old-time competitions as axe throwing, log rolling, and tree topping. | 360/532–9479.

HISTORIC LODGING
Hoquiam's Castle Bed and Breakfast. Located northwest of Aberdeen in Hoquiam, the grand former residence of timber baron Robert Lytle is one of the finest B&Bs in Washington State. This 10,000-square-ft Victorian-style mansion took Lytle three years to build, but it was worth the wait; the house is so well built it looks scarcely different from it did the day it was completed in 1900. Its five guest rooms are lushly appointed, with hand-woven rugs, antique wood furniture, and down comforters. Dining room; no kids under 12, no smoking. | 515 Chenault Ave., Hoquiam, 98550 | 360/533–2005 | www.hoquiamcastle.com | 5 rooms | $90–$140 | AE, D, MC, V | BP.

BELLINGHAM

▼▼▼

Modern-day Bellingham was once four small settlements—Whatcom, New Whatcom, Fairhaven, and Sehome—all situated along Bellingham Bay. The area bustled with nearly every industry Washington had to offer—fishing, farming, logging, and coal mines. Settlers poured into the four towns, which combined into one in 1903. Today, downtown Bellingham has numerous buildings from its pioneer days, most notably the turreted old city hall (1892), which now serves as the Whatcom Museum of History and Art. *Contact Bellingham/Whatcom County Convention and Visitors Bureau | 904 Potter St., 98226 | 800/487–2032 | www.bellingham.org.*

Lynden Pioneer Museum. This small museum has an eclectic collection of pioneer artifacts, including early 20th-century farm equipment, a full-scale representation of historic Lynden, and the largest public exhibition of horse-drawn Victorian Cabs west of the Mississippi— the most refined way of getting around town in frontier times. Lynden is 14 mi north of Bellingham. | 217 Front St., Lynden | 360/354–3675 | www.lyndenpioneermuseum.com | $3 | Sept.–May, Mon.–Sat. 10–4; June–Aug., Mon.–Sat. 10–5.

Old Fairhaven District. Old Fairhaven, south of downtown Bellingham at the beginning of Chuckanut Drive (Route 11), was an independent city until 1903. The beautifully restored 1890s redbrick buildings of the Old Fairhaven District, originally containing saloons, bunkhouses, barbershops, hay and feed stores, and dry-goods shops, have been converted to restaurants, taverns, galleries, and specialty boutiques. If you ignore the cars parked on the street, Harris Avenue looks much as it did in the late 1800s. | 12th St. and Harris Ave. | 360/676–6985 | www.cob.org | Free | Daily.

Whatcom Museum of History and Art. The Whatcom Museum is composed of an impressive four-building complex overlooking Whatcom Creek, Maritime Heritage Park, and Belling- ham Bay from a prominent bluff in downtown Bellingham. Its centerpiece is Bellingham's 1892 former city hall, a redbrick structure converted into a museum in 1940. Victorian cloth- ing, toys, games, and clocks are on display. The Syre Education Center has exhibits on Wash- ington's birds and logging history, and the Whatcom Children's Museum and Arco Exhibits building mount rotating exhibits. | 121 Prospect St. | 360/676–6981 | www.whatcommuseum. org | Free, children's museum $2.50 | Tues.–Sun. noon–5.

✦ ON THE CALENDAR: June **Deming Logging Show.** Loggers challenge each other in tradi- tional skill contests at this exhibition in Deming (10 mi east of Bellingham). Events include the Jill Ax throw, tree topping, obstacle pole sawing, and even a tug-of-war. Proceeds help loggers injured or maimed on the job and families of loggers killed in logging accidents. | 360/592–3051.

HISTORIC LODGING
North Garden Inn. This downtown B&B is in an 1897 Queen Anne Victorian house and is listed on the National Register of Historic Places. The rooms are comfortable and warm, and some afford a panoramic view of Bellingham Bay. A grand piano in the lobby adds to the inn's stately air. | 1014 N. Garden St., 98225 | 360/671–7828 or 800/922–6414 | www. northgardeninn.com/ngi | 10 rooms, 8 with bath | $50–$125 | AE, D, MC, V | BP.

CHEHALIS

▼▼▼

Originally called Saundersville—for settler Schuyler Saunders, who owned the land—the town of Chehalis (pronounced che-*hay*-liss) first established itself as a center for logging, mining, and agriculture when the railroad stopped in town in 1873. At the time, the nearby town of Claquato was the county seat. But with the establishment of the railroad in Chehalis, Claquato lost its title and Chehalis became the new seat of Lewis County. You can look back at the town's early days at a number of sites including the Claquato Church, circa 1857. *Contact Tourism Lewis County | 500 N.W. Chamber of Commerce Way, 98532 | 800/525–3323 | www.chamberway.com.*

Fort Borst/Joseph Borst Home. Constructed in 1856 to repel Indian raids—but never used in conflict—Fort Borst, also known as the Blockhouse, provided a home for farmer Joseph Borst and his family while their home was being built. Standing within a 100-acre park, the Borst Home is a Greek Revival mansion, built in 1857. You can tour the home and grounds, which are beautifully preserved. | Borst Park, 2500 Bryden Ave. W, Centralia, 6 mi north of Chehalis | 360/330–7688 | $2 | Late Nov.–late Dec. and late May–early Sept., weekends 1–4.

Historic Claquato Church. This pretty but austere white clapboard church, built in 1858, stands 2 mi west of Chehalis on Claquato Hill and is the oldest standing church in Washington State, still in its original location. The bell was cast in Boston in 1857, and the tower is capped with a unique wooden steeple shaped like a crown of thorns. | Claquato Hill | 360/740–1135 | Free | By appointment.

Lewis County Historical Museum. The former Burlington Northern Railroad Depot, built of brick in 1912, in the classic Mission style, houses this small museum dedicated to preserving the history and heritage of Lewis County. Rotating exhibits depict early pioneer life in the county, one of the first areas settled in the region and the oldest county in Washington State. Displays include a replica of a barber shop from the turn of the 20th century, a wood-burning stove from 1900, logging and farming tools, and a collection of Chehalis Indian art. | 599 N.W. Front Way | 360/748–0831 | www.lewiscountymuseum.org | $2 | Tues.–Sat. 9–5, Sun. 1–5.

✦ ON THE CALENDAR: July **Thunder Mountain Pro Rodeo/Cowlitz County Fair.** A traditional rodeo and carnival with live entertainment and children's activities takes place at the Cowlitz County Exposition Center. | 430 Washington St., Longview | 360/577–3121.

COLFAX
▼▼

Set along the Palouse River, Colfax calls itself the Heart of the Palouse. The Palouse branch of the Nez Perce tribe bred Appaloosa horses here before settlers transformed the land into the most productive wheat-growing area on earth. Centrally located in the area's hills, the town seems insulated from the tides of modern life. *Contact Colfax Chamber of Commerce | 117 S. Main St., 99111 | 509/397–3712.*

Asotin County Museum. A superb collection of branding irons is the highlight of this small museum in the county seat of Asotin. You'll also find a few late-19th century buildings moved here from nearby communities, including a blacksmith's forge set up in a log cabin. A half-dozen horse-drawn carriages and buckboards (the station wagons of the 19th century) are other remnants of frontier life in the Palouse. | 215 Filmore St., Asotin, 53 mi south of Colfax | 509/243–4659 | Free, donations accepted. | Mar.–Oct., Tues.–Sat. 1–5; Nov.–Feb., Sat. 1–5.

Steptoe Butte State Park. Steptoe Butte is named after Colonel Edward Steptoe, who used it as a reconnaissance point while fighting the Indians in the area. In 1858 Steptoe and most of his troops lost a battle and secretly snuck away at night. Historians believe this retreat was permitted by the Indians, whose method of warfare did not yet include annihilation. Long used by Indians, explorers, pioneers, and soldiers as a lookout, the top of the butte affords a spectacular view of the Palouse and the Blue Mountains, embracing hundreds of square miles. | Scholz Rd., 16 mi north of Colfax | 509/397–3712 | www.parks.wa.gov | Free | Daily 6–6.

COUPEVILLE

Washington's second-oldest town was settled by retiring sea captain Thomas Coupe in 1852. He joined Isaac Ebey, a farmer who had settled nearby in 1850. Ebey had become the leader of the local pioneers and a thorn in the side of the local Indians; he was slain by the Haidah tribe in 1857. In the town's early days, the residents of Coupeville built blockhouses, structures of heavy timbers used for defense, to withstand Indian raids. Many of these stand today. In fact, most of Coupeville's history remains: the town has the greatest number of historic structures in Washington. Walking through its narrow waterfront streets is like dreaming of the past. *Contact Central Whidbey Chamber of Commerce | Box 152, 302 N. Main St., 98239 | 360/678–5434 | www.islandweb.org/tourism.html.*

Ebey's Landing National Historic Reserve. The 25-square-mi Ebey's Landing reserve encompasses a sand and cobble beach, bluffs with dramatic views down the Strait of Juan de Fuca, two state parks, and several (privately held) pioneer farms homesteaded in the early 1850s—not to mention the town of Coupeville itself. The reserve, the first and largest of its kind, holds nearly 100 structures on the National Register of Historic Places, from Victorian times, among them private homes and stores and log battlements, or blockhouses, built to withstand Indian uprisings. Fort Casey State Park, set on a bluff overlooking the Strait of Juan de Fuca and the Port Townsend ferry landing, was one of three forts built in the 1890s to protect the entrance to Admiralty Inlet. The park has a small interpretive center in an 1890s lighthouse. | 2 mi west of Rte. 20 | 360/678–4636 | www.nps.gov/ebla | Day use free, campsites $11–$16 | Daily 8 AM–dusk.

Island County Historical Museum. This museum surveys the history of the island's fishing, timber, and agricultural industries. As nearly all of Coupeville is a museum, guides lead historical walking tours around town. The nearby Alexander Blockhouse, a timber watchtower and battlement, dates from the Puget Sound Indian War of 1855. Note the squared logs and dove-tailed joints of the corners—no overlapping log ends. Its function was basically that of a bunker—in case of attack, families would crowd inside. Fortunately, it never had to be used. | 908 N.W. Alexander St. | 360/678–3310 | $2 | May–Oct., daily 10–5; Nov.–Apr., Fri.–Mon. 11–4.

DAYTON

The tree-shaded county seat of Columbia County is the kind of untrammeled place many people conjure up when they imagine the best qualities of rural America. This tidy town has 117 buildings listed on the National Register of Historic Places, including the state's oldest railroad depot and courthouse, which testify to the importance early settlers placed on erecting buildings that symbolized their newfound prosperity. In this case, wheat was the economic engine—as it still is. *Contact Dayton Chamber of Commerce | Box 22, 166 E. Main St., 99328 | 800/882–6299 | www.historicdayton.com.*

Dayton Historic Depot. Built in 1881, this is Washington's oldest surviving railroad depot. It was built a few blocks from where it now stands but was moved to its current location in 1899 using horses and rolling logs. Today, it houses a museum with exhibits illustrating the history of Dayton and surrounding communities. | 222 Commercial St. | 509/382–2026 | $2 | Nov.–Mar., Tues.–Sat. 11–4; Apr.–Oct., Tues.–Sat. 10–5.

HISTORIC DINING AND LODGING

Weinhard Hotel. Once the Weinhard Lodgehall and Saloon, this lavishly renovated 1896 building is done up in full Victorian style, with plenty of red velvet, lush wallpaper, mahogany furniture, and glittering chandeliers. The 15 smallish rooms are furnished entirely in Victorian antiques. The Weinhard Café is famous in the region for its Northwest-style Continental cuisine, which relies heavily on fish, poultry, and local ingredients such as Walla Walla onions and Palouse grains. Restaurant, in-room data ports, cable TV, piano. | 235 E. Main St., 99328 | 509/382–4032 | fax 509/382–2640 | www.weinhard.com | 15 rooms | $75–$150 | DC, MC, V.

✦ ON THE CALENDAR: Sept. **Depot Festival.** Held on the third Saturday in September at the Dayton Historic Depot, this celebration of railroad history includes model railroad exhibits, railroad memorabilia and artifacts, and bumper car rides. | 509/382–2026.

Oct. **Historic Homes Tour.** On the second Sunday of October, the Dayton Historical Depot Society offers guided tours of some of the buildings listed on the National Register of Historic Places. Call for time and meeting place. Self-guided walking-tour maps of three national historic districts are available throughout the year at the Chamber of Commerce. | 509/382–2026 or 800/882–6299.

ILWACO
▼▼

Located at the mouth of the Columbia River, Ilwaco (pronounced il-WAH-koh) has been a fishing port for thousands of years, first as a village of the native Chinook tribe and, since about 1840, as an American settlement. Lewis and Clark camped here in November 1805—just a few days after William Clark famously sighted "this great Pacific Ocean"—before deciding to spend the winter across the river near present-day Astoria, Oregon. *Contact Long Beach Peninsula Visitor's Bureau | U.S. 101 and Rte. 103, Seaview (Box 562, Long Beach 98631) | 800/451–2542 | www.funbeach.com.*

Fort Canby State Park. This picturesque 1,700-acre state park, at the mouth of the Columbia River is rich with history. Fort Canby was constructed in 1863 to prevent Indian raids and was part of a buildup that saw military expenditures actually exceed the entire state budget in total cost. Some of its bunkers and batteries remain, but more impressive are the Cape Disappointment Lighthouse, constructed in 1856, and the North Head Lighthouse, constructed in 1898. The lighthouses, both open for tours, were constructed to counter a growing number of shipwrecks at Cape Disappointment, and running them wasn't easy—winds at North Head sometimes reach 120 mph. | Southwest of Ilwaco on U.S. 101 N | 360/902–8844 | Free; lighthouse tours $1 | Park Apr.–Oct., daily 6:30–10:30, Nov.–Mar., daily 6:30–4; call for lighthouse hrs.

The **Colbert House Museum** (Quaker Ave. SE at Lake St. | 360/642–8002 | $1 | Late May–Sept., Fri.–Sun. 10–4) preserves an 1840s National Register of Historic Places home and its contents. The Colbert family lived here for five generations.

On the Fort Canby grounds is the **Lewis and Clark Interpretive Center** ($2 | Daily 10–5), which examines the 8,000-mi journey of the two renowned explorers through paintings and murals.

Ilwaco Heritage Museum. The museum illustrates the history of southwestern Washington, beginning with the Native Americans and moving on to the influx of traders, missionaries, and pioneers. The museum also houses a model of the peninsula's clamshell railroad, a narrow-gauge train that transported passengers and mail along the beach from 1888 to 1930. Ground-up clam and oyster shells formed the rail bed on which the tracks were laid. | 115

THE FAST TRACK TO THE FUTURE

"Nothing a doing. Dull," wrote Levi Lathrop Smith, cofounder of what would become the city of Olympia, in the late 1840s. He wasn't alone in feeling alone, either. Early settlers in Washington Territory were largely isolated until the Northern Pacific Railroad reached the Pacific Northwest in 1883. A trip from the midwestern United States to Puget Sound used to take five months; the railroad pared the trip down to five days.

Washington, once accessible only by water or wagon, was about to catch up with the rest of the nation in a hurry. The flood of newcomers brought by the Northern Pacific line, drawn by the promise of farmland and fortunes to be made in coal and timber, caused the population of Washington to grow by 380% during the 1880s. Not even a mild depression late in the decade could slow down the growth—in 1897, news of a gold strike in the Canadian Yukon brought thousands more to the territory.

The Northern Pacific functioned not only as transportation, but as a recruiter of settlers. The company distributed pamphlets in English and several other European languages at stations along its line, touting Washington's "splendid opportunities for both labor and capital." By attracting Americans and immigrants alike, the railroad helped make Washington the culturally diverse state it is today.

Washington cities fought bitterly for train stations, and those that were fortunate enough to receive them prospered. Trains transported goods—timber, wheat, and more—as well as settlers, and in most railroad towns the train station became the city center. It's not surprising that many of these towns have preserved their train stations, some even converting them into museums.

S.E. Lake St., off U.S. 101 N | 360/642–3446 | $3 | May–Aug., Mon.–Sat. 9–5, Sun. noon–4; Sept.–Apr., Mon.–Sat. 10–4.

Oysterville. Founded by I. A. Clark and R. H. Espy in 1854, Oysterville was placed on the National Register of Historic Places in 1976. The town on the shores of Willapa Bay has a number of original buildings from the 1880s, including a church and a one-room schoolhouse. Take a walk through the village to get a feel for the town's origins. Once the county seat and a bustling oyster port, it is now a sleepy village. | North on Rte. 103, on the tip of Long Beach Peninsula | 360/642–2400 or 800/451–2542 | Free | Daily.

HISTORIC DINING
Milton York Restaurant. American. This establishment began making candy and chocolate in 1882 and has been a community mainstay ever since. The dinner menu includes seafood, steaks, and chicken, and the ice cream is homemade. The candy, made from recipes dating back to the turn of the 20th century, is a must-try. Breakfast is also served. | 107 S. Pacific St., Long Beach | 360/642–2352 | $13.50–$17 | MC, V.

OLYMPIA
▼▼

Olympia has been Washington's capital since 1853, almost four decades before Washington was admitted to the union as the 42nd state. It was designated a temporary capital by territorial governor Isaac Stevens, over other cities that wanted the honor. In the 1850s, because of its location at the very southern tip of Puget Sound, its maritime industry flourished and the city became the main port for distributing goods along the sound. When Washington became a state in 1889 the city flourished, adding amenities such as street cars, street lamps, and an opera house. Numerous buildings downtown are marked as historic landmarks. Self-guided walking-tour maps are available at the visitor center. *Contact State Capitol Visitor Information Center | Box 41020, 14th St. and S. Capitol Way, 98504 | 360/586–3460 | www.ci.olympia.wa.us.*

Bigelow House. This white clapboard house, built in the Carpenter Gothic style in 1854, originally belonged to local civic leader Daniel R. Bigelow and his wife, Ann E. White Bigelow. Both were avid supporters of the woman's suffrage movement, and in 1871 Susan B. Anthony dined here while passing through the area on one of her lecture tours. Today, members of the Bigelow family still live in the house, while the first floor is open to the public. Many of the home's original furnishings remain, including a Steinway piano from 1870. | 918 Glass Ave. NE, off East Bay Dr. | 360/753–1215 | $2 | Apr.–Oct., weekends 1–3; special tours by appointment.

HISTORIC LODGING

Swantown Inn. Antiques and lace ornament every room of this stylish Victorian inn. Built as a mansion in 1893, it has also served as a boarding house and, according to some, a brothel. Its rooms overlook landscaped lawns, gardens, and the capitol dome. No kids under 9, no room phones, no room TVs, no smoking. | 1431 11th Ave. SE, 98501 | 360/753–9123 | www. olywa.net/swantown | 4 rooms | $85–$125 | MC, V | BP.

OMAK

▼▼

Omak is a small mill and orchard town on the western boundary of the Colville Indian Reservation. When he visited the area at the turn of the 20th century, Ben F. Ross came to the conclusion that it would be a great place to grow apples, and he bought up the land. He brought his family here in 1901, built a house, and established a school district. Dividing 25 acres of his land into town plots, Ross quickly sold them to settlers and the town of Omak took root in 1907. *Contact Omak Visitor Information Center | 401 Omak Ave., 98841 | 509/826–4218 or 800/225–6625 | www.omakchronicle.com.*

Colville Indian Reservation. One of the largest Indian reservations in Washington, this was the final home of Nez Perce Chief Joseph, who fought a series of fierce battles with the U. S. Army in the 1870s. Banished from his native Wallowa Mountains, Chief Joseph lived on the Colville Reservation until his death in 1904. There's a memorial to him off Route 155 in the town of Nespelem, 36 mi southeast of Omak. Four blocks away (two east and two north) is his grave. You can drive through the reservation's undeveloped landscape, and except for a few highway signs, you'll feel like you've traveled back to pioneer days. | Rte. 155 southeast of Omak

On the southern border of the reservation, 54 mi southeast of Omak, the **Colville Confederated Tribes Museum and Gift Shop** has exhibits on traditional Northwest tribal ways, such as the salmon harvest. | 512 Meadway, Grand Coulee | 509/633–0751 | Free, donations accepted | Apr.–Dec., Mon.–Sat. 10–6.

Okanogan County Historical Museum. Historic items and displays of Okanogan pioneer life are exhibited here, including Old West buckboards, ranching and haying equipment, and local cattle brands. | 1410 2nd St., Okanogan, 4 mi southwest of Omak | 509/422–4272 | $2 | May–Sept., daily 10–4; Oct.–Apr., by appointment.

♦ ON THE CALENDAR: Aug. **Omak Stampede and World Famous Suicide Race.** Held on the second weekend in August at the Omak Stampede Arena, the 4-day rodeo is famous throughout the Northwest. In addition to cowboy competitions such as bronc riding, steer roping, and bulldogging, the festivities also include a western and Native American art show and numerous parades. In the hugely controversial Suicide Race, local Native American youths' ride their trained horses down a very steep slope across from the fairgrounds, then swim— or, if the tide is low, walk—across the Okanogan River. Horses are sometimes injured, but backers of the race argue that it honors traditional Native American contests. | $6–$15 | 509/ 826–1002 or 800/933–6625.

PASCO
▼▼

Tree-shaded Pasco, a college town and the county seat of Franklin County, is an oasis of green on the Columbia River. The neoclassic Franklin County Courthouse (1907) is worth a visit for its fine marble interior. Pasco, which started as a railroad switchyard, now has a busy container port from which barges carry wheat, fuel, hay, and other resources down the Columbia River to be shipped over the Pacific. *Contact Tri-Cities Visitor and Convention Bureau | 6951 W. Grandridge Blvd., Kennewick, 99336 | 800/254–5824 | www.visittri-cities.com.*

Franklin County Historical Museum. Once the Pasco Carnegie Library, built in 1910 as part of Andrew Carnegie's worldwide library construction program, this museum houses Native American artifacts such as salmon gaffs—the long poles Natives used to hook migrating salmon out of the Columbia—and hand-carved canoes. Exhibits on homesteading in the 19th century and the railroad are also of interest. | 305 N. 4th Ave. | 509/547–3714 | Free, donations accepted | Tues.–Sat. noon–4.

Sacajawea State Park. This day-use park, at the confluence of the Snake and Columbia rivers, occupies the site of Ainsworth, a railroad town that flourished from 1879 to 1884. The park is named for the Shoshone Indian woman who accompanied the Lewis and Clark expedition over the Rocky Mountains and down the Snake River in 1805. The 284-acre marine park includes one of the expedition's campsites, used by Lewis and Clark October 16–18, 1805. The interpretive center has information about the Lewis and Clark expedition and a large display of Native American tools. Check out the interpretive explanations of the interaction of the explorers with Native inhabitants. | 2503 Sacajawea Park Rd. | 509/545–2361 | Free | Late Mar.–late Oct., daily dawn–dusk.

PORT TOWNSEND
▼▼

Port Townsend was founded by settlers who thought the main connector to the Transcontinental Railroad would stop here. When the tracks stopped in Tacoma instead, Port Townsend, like Seattle, tried to build its own connecting railroad. The Hood Canal cliffs to the south, however, proved to be too formidable and the project was never carried out. This turned out to be a mixed blessing: since the railroad didn't come through here, the town didn't suffer the tumult and change that many of its neighbors did, and its Victorian past remains beautifully preserved to this day. *Contact Port Townsend Chamber of Commerce and Visitor Information Center | 2437 Sims Way, 98368 | 888/365–6978 | www.ptguide.com.*

Jefferson County Historical Museum. The 1892 City Hall building contains four floors of exhibits detailing Port Townsend's rich past. Originally, the building housed the police department, court room, city jail, and fire hall. Exhibits include a time line of the city from its first settlers to the present day; a look at the lives of Chinese immigrants who settled here; and artifacts from the Hoh, S'Klallam, and Chimacum tribes. | 210 Madison St. | 360/385–1003 | $2 donation | Mon.–Sat. 11–4, Sun. 1–4.

Port Gamble Historic Museum. The history of Port Gamble, a 19th-century mill town that looks like it was picked up in New England and plopped down, lock, stock, and barrel, on Puget Sound, is closely tied to the Pope and Talbot Timber Company, still in business today as Pope Resources. Pope and Talbot ran the town's two sawmills and was instrumental in preserving many of the town's historic structures. The Port Gamble Historic Museum focuses on the lives of the company's founders, with faithful re-creations of Captain William Talbot's ship quarters and A. J. Pope's office. | 1 Rainier Ave. Port Gamble, 27 mi south of Port Townsend | 360/297–8074 | fax 360/297–7455 | $2 | May–Oct., daily 10:30–5; Mar.–Apr. and Nov., weekdays by appointment.

Rothschild House. Built in 1858 by D. C. H. Rothschild, a local merchant, this simple home still has much of its original 1885 wallpaper and furnishings. Some items, including the piano in the parlor, a child's doll, and the china, are almost as old as the house—and other objects, such as the camphor wood cabinet in the guest bedroom, predate the house by several years. The house is surrounded by herb and flower gardens and overlooks Port Townsend Bay. | Jefferson and Taylor Sts. | 360/385–2722 | $2 | Apr.–mid-Oct., Wed.–Sun. 10–5; mid-Oct.–Mar., weekends 10–3.

HISTORIC DINING AND LODGING

The Belmont. Built in the 1880s as a tavern by saloon keeper George Sterming, this waterfront hotel and restaurant has high ceilings and views of the harbor and Port Townsend's only remaining 1880s waterfront restaurant, serving fresh seafood, steaks, and pastas. The guest rooms, cozy and elegant, have exposed brick walls and Victorian wallpaper and are handsomely furnished with antiques and replicas. Restaurant, bar; no a/c, no room TVs, no smoking. | 925 Water St., 98368 | 360/385–3007 | www.the-belmont.com | 4 rooms, 3 suites | $69–$109 | AE, D, DC, MC, V.

Palace Hotel. Located in the heart of downtown Port Townsend, this 1889 inn occupies the top two floors of the Captain Tibbals Building. A classic brick building, it was constructed for a retired sea captain, one of Port Townsend's most colorful residents. Built in the Richardson Romanesque style, the building is notable for arched windows that appear to extend for two stories, making it a beautiful example of Port Townsend's turn-of-the-20th-century architectural past. Over the years the building has housed many businesses, most notably a brothel from 1925 to 1933, and many of its tasteful Victorian rooms bear the names of the women that worked in them. Some refrigerators, cable TV, laundry facilities, pets allowed (fee); no a/c, no room phones. | 1004 Water St. | 360/385–0773 or 800/962–0741 | fax 360/385–2688 | www.olympus.net/palace | 17 rooms, 13 with bath | $65–$189 | AE, D, MC, V | CP.

PUYALLUP

▼▼

Puyallup (pronounced pyoo-*al*-lup) is one of western Washington's oldest towns. Ezra Meeker, the town's founder, came west on the Oregon Trail in 1852. Meeker is best remembered, however, for his return trip at the age of 76, when he drove an ox-drawn covered wagon back east to prod President Theodore Roosevelt into officially marking the Oregon Trail before its route was forgotten. To this day, Meeker is credited as the Champion of the Oregon Trail. *Contact Chamber of East Pierce County | 322 2nd St. SW, 98371 | 253/845–6755 | fax 253/848–6164 | www.puyallupchamber.com.*

Ezra Meeker Mansion. The mansion, completed in 1890 when Meeker was in his early 60s, is a 17-room Italianate Victorian house built for just two people. After Meeker presented his wife to Queen Victoria, she became enamored of affluent living and demanded a house of her husband, who agreed on the condition that she pay for it. Listed on the National Register of Historic Places, the house has been undergoing restoration since 1970, when it was acquired by the Ezra Meeker Historical Society. Volunteers hope eventually to restore the mansion to its 1891 condition. | 312 Spring St. | 253/848–1770 | www.meekermansion.org | $4 | Mar.–mid-Dec., Wed.–Sun. 1–4.

Pioneer Farm Museum. This is a museum devoted to educating people about daily pioneer life. You are invited to try activities such as grinding grain, milking cows and goats, and churning butter. Guided tours take an hour and a half and start every 20 minutes. | Rte. 7, off Ohop Valley Rd., Eatonville | 360/832–6300 | $6.50 | Mid-Mar.–mid-June and early Sept.–late Nov., weekends 11–5:30; mid-June–early Sept., daily 11–5:30.

SEATTLE
▾▾

Seattle's history is that of a true frontier town. Founded in the spring of 1851 by Illinois natives Arthur Denny, Carson Boren, and William Bell, Seattle grew from a modest cabin at Alki Point to a bustling lumber, canning, and port town inside of 20 years. The Native Americans who already occupied the land received the intruders with as much grace as they could muster. The chief of the Suquamish people, named Seattle, was so deeply respected that the American settlers, who had chased the natives off 2 million acres of their lands, named the city for him.

Much of Seattle's history is still visible along its streets despite the Indian War of 1855, the occasional freak snowstorm, and a devastating 1889 fire that consumed the town. The Pioneer Square district contains turn-of-the-20th-century structures above and below street level (a by-product of the 1899 fire), and many other historic buildings throughout the city stand shoulder-to-shoulder with modern Seattle. *Contact Seattle-King County Convention and Visitors Bureau | 800 Convention Pl., 98101 | 206/461–5800 | fax 206/461–3855 | www.seeseattle.org.*

Bill Speidel's Underground Tour. When Seattle was rebuilt after the Great Fire of 1889, the city fathers wisely decided to raise the level of the old downtown because it was so close to tidewater that sewers flowed backward during spring tides. But the old storefronts were not torn down—new ones were simply added at the new street level. This left a ghostly underground city of abandoned shop fronts intact. The underground tour takes you to the surviving parts of that lost city. | Ticket office and starting point: Doc Maynard's Tavern, 608 1st Ave. | 206/682–4646 or 888/608–6337 | www.undergroundtour.com | $8 | Daily 11–4.

Blackman's House Museum. In Snohomish, 35 mi northeast of Seattle, this 1878 Victorian mansion is filled with the odds and ends of local history—the kinds of furnishings, everyday objects, toys, and tools that make the antiques collector's heart skip a beat. If you've ever wondered how your ancestors lived, this is the place to find out. | 118 Ave. B, Snohomish | 360/568–5235 | June–Sept., daily noon–4; Mar.–May and Oct.–Dec., Wed.–Sun. noon–4 | $1.

Chief Seattle. Stoically watching the business and revelry in Seattle Center, a statue of Chief Seattle of the Duwamish tribe stands with his right arm raised in welcome. Seattle was among the first Native Americans to have contact with the white explorers who came to the region. He was viewed as a great leader and peacemaker by his fellow tribesmen and as a friendly contact by the white settlers. The sculpture was created by local artist James Wehn in 1912 and was dedicated by the chief's great-great granddaughter, Myrtle Loughery, on Founder's Day, November 13, 1912. | Intersection of 5th Ave., Denny Way, and Cedar St., near southeast corner of Seattle Center, Queen Anne.

Pioneer Square District. Pioneer Square is Seattle's oldest neighborhood and a lively hub of activity. It encompasses about 18 blocks and is chock-a-block with restaurants, shops, nightclubs, bars, and the city's largest concentration of art galleries. A glass-and-steel pergola on 1st Avenue and Yesler Way marks the site of the pier and sawmill owned by Henry Yesler, one of Seattle's first businessmen. The street known as Yesler Way today was actually the original Skid Row. In the 1880s timber logged in the hills was sent to the sawmill on a skid row made of small logs laid crossways and greased so that the freshly cut trees would slide down to the mill. The area grew into Seattle's first business center.

The Great Fire of 1889 destroyed many of the district's wood-frame buildings. The industrious residents and businesspeople rebuilt them with brick and mortar, and today many of these beautiful turn-of-the-20th-century redbrick buildings continue to line the streets. In 1897 and 1898, news of a gold strike in the Canadian Yukon brought hordes of gold-hungry miners to Seattle. They came to this port city to purchase their food, equipment, and ship tickets before heading north. In their wake the area became populated with saloons and brothels. Even with its modern-day amendments, Pioneer Square feels much as it did then—a bustling frontier metropolis, practically humming with optimism and purpose. | Roughly bounded by Alaskan Way S, Yesler Way, 4th Ave. S, and S. Royal Brougham Way.

Klondike Gold Rush National Historic Park. California may be synonymous with the gold rush of 1849, but Seattle experienced its own frenzy over the precious metal. The 1896 discovery of gold in northwestern Canada drew fortune seekers from around the country to Seattle, irrevocably changing its history. This museum illustrates the importance of the 1897–98 boom, when the city's small business district was forced to grow up to meet the needs of the Klondike rush. Audio and video presentations explain the adversities Northwest miners faced and introduce a few key historical figures. A gold-panning demonstration and a glimpse of the artifacts housed here, particularly photos of wizened miners and the cramped conditions they endured, make a visit memorable. | 117 S. Main St., at 1st Ave. S, Pioneer Square | 206/553–7220 | By donation | Daily 8–5.

SPOKANE

Spokane (pronounced spo-*can*) takes its name from the local Spokan tribe of Salish Indians. The word Spokan translates to "children of the sun," a fitting name for this sunny city of incredible trees, flowers, public gardens, and parks. Known as the Capital of the Inland Northwest, Spokane has been the cultural and financial center of eastern Washington since the 1870s.

Originally, Spokane was a native village located strategically near the roaring falls (which still flow at the town center) where salmon ascended in great numbers each autumn. Two small but key battles, the Battle of Spokane Plains and the Battle of Four Lakes, took place west of the present-day city in 1858. These fights, won by the U.S. cavalry, brought an end to Native American conflicts with settlers in the Columbia Basin.

Pioneers settled around the powerful falls in 1873, building a sawmill and bringing industry to the area. Several railroads arrived soon after, and in 1885, Spokane built the first hydroelectric plant west of the Mississippi, at the falls. The city soon became the transportation hub of eastern Washington. Downtown boomed after the fire of 1889, which destroyed more than half the city, and was followed by a massive rebuilding effort. The city grew rich from mining ventures in northeastern Washington and neighboring states and from shipping the wheat grown in the Palouse hills to the south. Today, Spokane is Washington's second largest city. For years, bridges and railroad trestles hid the great water falls at the town center, but they were cleared away in 1974 for the World's Fair. Today, they form the heart of downtown's Riverfront Park. *Contact Spokane Regional Convention and Visitors Bureau | 201 W. Main St., 99201 | 509/747–3230 or 888/SPOKANE | www.visitspokane.com.*

Fort Spokane. Don't expect any massive walls at this fort—the 1880–98 army post looks more like a college campus than a military establishment. The fort was established to ensure peace between settlers and Indians on the Colville Indian Reservation, located just across the Columbia River. Four of the original buildings remain for you to see. | 44150 District Office Lane N | 509/725–2715 | Free | Daily dawn–dusk.

Northwest Museum of Arts and Culture. Exhibits and collections here are divided among three disciplines—Regional History, Visual Art, and American Indian culture. None of the displays are permanent, but you will always find innovative exhibits, often the result of collaborations with other museums and historical societies, focused on the region's history and local Indian tribes. Check the Web site or call for a list of current exhibits and collections. The adjacent 1898 Campbell House surveys Spokane's mining-era past. Amasa Campbell, the original owner, was a miner who secured his fortune in the silver fields of Idaho. An interactive guided program leads you through the three-story Victorian. | 2316 W. 1st Ave., between Hemlock and Coeur d'Alene Sts. | 509/456–3931 | www.cheneycowles.org | $7; by donation first Fri. of month | Tues.–Sun. 11–5, Wed. 11–8.

Spokane House Interpretive Center. In the northern section of Riverside State Park, this center tells the story of the oldest building in Washington State. The region's first permanent white settlement was established in 1810 by two employees of the North West Company, a fur-trading concern. The first Spokane House was a small cabin, but when the North West Company acquired Fort Spokanfrom the Pacific Fur Company in 1813 they renamed the fort Spokane House. The company abandoned the post in 1825, when they had depleted the local waterways of furs. Displays in the interpretive center trace the history of fur-trading in the area, exhibit artifacts from Spokane House, and recount the archeological investigation of the site. | About 10 mi northwest of downtown Spokane via Rte. 291 (Nine Mile Rd.) | 509/465–5064 | www.riversidestatepark.org | Donation requested | Late May–early Sept., Thurs.–Mon. 10–6.

✦ ON THE CALENDAR: Aug. **Rendezvous.** Held in Colville for three days over the first weekend of August, this pioneer-theme festival draws as many as 5,000 people each year, who come to compete in numerous tournaments, browse through crafts booths, and enjoy free, live entertainment at Yep Kanum City Park (Elm and Hawthorne Sts.). Colville is 65 mi north of Spokane on U.S. 395. | 509/684–6312.

TACOMA
▼▼

Like many of Washington's harbor and coastal towns, Tacoma can trace its origins to a visit from European explorers Peter Puget and Captain George Vancouver in 1792. Their success encouraged the Hudson Bay Company to build Tacoma's first settlement, Fort Nisqually, here in 1833. The first permanent white settlers arrived in the early 1850s and established a sawmill in 1852. By offering the Northern Pacific Railroad land on Commencement Bay, Tacoma beat out Seattle to become the western terminus of the Northern Pacific in 1873, and its industries—flour, timber, and coal—more or less exploded. By 1892 Tacoma's population topped 50,000, and the town made a serious but ultimately unsuccessful effort to become the state capital. It was in Tacoma in 1900 that lumber baron Frederick Weyerhaeuser purchased 900,000 acres of prime timberland for $1 million. *Contact Tacoma-Pierce County Visitor and Convention Bureau | 1001 Pacific Ave., Suite 400, 98402 | 253/627–2836 or 800/272–2662 | fax 253/627–8783 | www.tpctourism.org or www.tourtacoma.org.*

Federation Forest State Park. Douglas fir, western hemlock, Sitka spruce, and western redcedarflourish in these 619 acres of protected old-growth forest. Here you can see the western Washington forest as the pioneers did, before lumber companies turned timber into one of the territory's primary industries. | Rte. 410, about 40 mi southeast of Tacoma | 360/663–2207 | Free | Daily 8–dusk; interpretive center May–Sept., Wed.–Sun. 9–4.

Job Carr Cabin Museum. A reconstruction of the cabin home of Commencement Bay's first settler, the Job Carr museum has photos and artifacts from Tacoma's early days. | 2350 N. 30th St. | 253/272–3500 | www.jobcarrmuseum.org | Free | Wed.–Sat. 1–4.

Mount Rainier Scenic Railroad. Beginning at Elbe, 40 mi southeast of Tacoma, late-19th-century locomotives take you through lush forests and over timber trestles, winding through 14 scenic miles at the base of Mount Rainier. Many of the engines were once loggers, pulling enormous loads of timber through the Washington wilderness, and no two look alike. | Rte. 7, Elbe | 888/783–2611 | $12 | June–Sept., weekends; trains leave at 11 AM, 1:15 PM, and 3:30 PM.

Point Defiance Park. In one of the largest urban parks in the United States, you will find several windows to Washington's frontier past. A tiny portion of the vast forests upon which Washington built its logging industry is preserved in stands of old-growth fir and hemlock in the park. The original forests of Puget Sound—giant trees whose boles could grow 10 ft thick and which could tower to 200 ft—must have seemed limitless to the earliest settlers. | N. 54th and N. Pearl Sts. | 253/305–1000 | www.metroparkstacoma.org | Free | Daily dawn–dusk.

Dedicated to preserving the steam era (1880s–1940s) of logging in western Washington, **Camp Six Logging Museum** (Five Mile Dr. | 253/752–0047 | www.camp-6-museum.org | Free) traces the history of the industry from the time of horse and ox teams through the time of steam-powered donkeys and railroads. On a forested 14-acre site in Point Defiance Park are bunk houses, bunk cars, and an operating replica of a logging railroad. Within the buildings are artifacts, photographs, and paintings, and outside are more than 500 tons of "fire-breathin', steam-spewin' iron beasts." You can take a logging train ride on the PDQ & K Railroad on weekends, April–September; the first departure is at noon. Outdoor exhibits are open every day from dawn until dusk; indoor exhibits are open April–October, Wednesday–Sunday and most holidays, generally 10–4 but later in summer.

The Hudson Bay Company outpost of **Fort Nisqually** (5400 N. Pearl St., No. 11 | 253/591–5339 | www.fortnisqually.org | $3), built in 1833 as a trade center, later became dependent on farming for its survival. It was never intended to be a military stronghold, which is probably why it still stands today in such a fine state of preservation. Scots, French Canadians, and even Hawaiians worked the fort and its grounds in its heyday, and today actors in period costume perform the same duties. The fort is open Memorial Day–Labor Day, daily 11–6, and the rest of the year Wednesday–Sunday 11–4.

Washington State History Museum. Washington's official history museum presents interactive exhibits and multimedia installations about the exploration and settlement of the state, divided into time periods by section. The "Frontier Towns and Railroad" section displays a cut-away recreation of a pioneer's covered wagon filled with Oregon Trail artifacts. The "Wageworkers Frontier" section re-creates the early days of Washington's mining and timber industries. Don't miss the Product Tree, an eccentric display made of reproductions of early 20th-century woodwork—dollhouses, chairs, caskets, and more. | 1911 Pacific Ave. | 253/272–3500 | $7 | Tues.–Wed. and Fri. 10–5, Thurs. 10–8, Sun. 1–5.

TOPPENISH
▼▼

Toppenish fancies itself a real-life cowboy and Indian town, with a touch of Old Mexico thrown in. The YakamaIndian Cultural Center at the southern edge of town has a museum that is well worth a visit, affording an evenhanded picture of traditional Native life and of the devastation that development has wrought on the natural resources of the Yakima Valley. The town's regionally famed murals (more than 50 in all, on the walls of virtually every downtown building) depict pioneer life and Toppenish history. *Contact Toppenish Chamber of Commerce | Box 28, 5A S. Toppenish Ave., 98948 | 509/865–3262 or 800/569–3982 | fax 509/865–3549 | www.toppenish.org.*

Fort Simcoe Historical State Park. Erected in 1856, these residential quarters of an old army fort near White Swan look more like a Victorian summer retreat than a military establishment—and indeed, soldiers quartered here saw little conflict since the "Indian Troubles" in the Northwest ended in the late 1850s. Exhibits focus on the history of local Yakama Indians and American settlers. | 5150 Fort Simcoe Rd. | 509/874–2372 | www.parks.wa.gov | Free, donations accepted | Apr.–Sept., daily 6:30 AM–dusk; Oct.–Mar., weekends 8 AM–dusk. Interpretive center Apr.–Sept. 9:30–4:30, Oct.–Mar. by appointment only.

Northern Pacific Railway Museum. The 1911 Northern Pacific Railroad Depot houses this small but richly stocked train buff's delight. Collections include china and linens from the golden age of rail travel in the late 19th century and signs and placards from the days when Toppenish was on the main line of the Northern Pacific Railroad. | 10 S. Asotin Ave. | 509/865–1911 | $2 | May–Oct., daily 10–5.

Yakama Nation Cultural Center. This Native American cultural center has a fascinating tribal museum, plus a gift shop, restaurant, theater, and a winter lodge used for meetings and banquets. The Yakama Nation is one of the country's largest and most powerful tribes. Its museum depicts traditional native life in marvelous detail and offers an impartial but not rosy perspective on the depletion of natural resources in the 20th century. | U.S. 97, 2 mi north of Toppenish | 509/865–2800.

✦ ON THE CALENDAR: May **Longhouse Powwow.** This annual powwow of Native American dancers from the United States and Canada is held on Mother's Day weekend at Satus, southeast of Toppenish on Route 22. The non-tribal public is welcome to attend. | 509/865–5121.

VANCOUVER
▼▼

The site of this now-sprawling river town was noticed in 1792 by a British explorer, Lieutenant William Broughton, who named it for his commander, Captain George Vancouver. Lewis and Clark camped here in 1806, and in 1825 Vancouver became the center of fur trade for the Hudson Bay Company and the base from which the British managed Oregon Territory. It soon became the frontier metropolis of the Pacific Northwest, dominating the fur trade for more than two decades. The U.S. Army built a fort on the bluff above the Hudson Bay post when Oregon Territory became part of the United States in 1846. Ulysses S. Grant, who would later become the 18th president of the United States, briefly served as quartermaster of Fort Vancouver. *Contact Greater Vancouver Chamber of Commerce | 404 E. 15th St., Suite 11, 98663 | 360/694–2588 | fax 360/693–8279 | www.vancouverusa.com.*

Clark County Historical Museum. This museum and interpretive center, housed in the former Carnegie Library building (built in 1909), has Chinook Indian artifacts, reproductions of an 1890 country store and 1900 doctor's office, and a Lewis and Clark reading room. | 1511 Main St. | 360/695–4681 | Free | Tues.–Sat. 11–4.

Fort Vancouver National Historic Site. This splendidly reconstructed fort, with squared-log buildings, an encircling palisade, and corner bastions, was first established by the Hudson Bay Company in 1825 and served as the western headquarters of the company's fur-trading operations. Park rangers dressed in period costume demonstrate various pioneer skills ranging from carpentry to baking to sewing. | 1501 E. Evergreen Blvd. | 360/696–7655 | www.nps.gov.fova/ | Free | Daily.

Officers' Row. One of Vancouver's treasures, Officers' Row is composed of 21 stately homes built between 1867 and 1906. Ulysses S. Grant lived in the 1849 log building now bearing his name when he was quartermaster of Vancouver Barracks from 1852 to 1853. Today, the Grant House displays historical artifacts and has a folk art center. You can also tour homes that once belonged to General George C. Marshall and General O. O. Howard. | 750 Anderson St. | 360/693–3103 | Free | Daily 9–5.

WALLA WALLA
▼▼

Founded in the 1850s on the site of a Nez Perce village, Walla Walla was Washington's first metropolis. As late as the 1880s, its population was larger than that of Seattle. Walla Walla occupies a lush green valley below the rugged Blue Mountains. It has a beautifully maintained (and partly restored) downtown, with many 19th- and early 20th-century residences, green parks, and the campus of Whitman College, Washington's oldest institution of higher learning, chartered in 1859. Often described as a transplanted New England town, Walla Walla illustrates the fervent desire of western pioneers to create tidy, prosperous towns that compared visually and economically with those back east. The nearby Whitman Mission was the site of the most infamous conflict between Native Americans and settlers in Northwest pioneer times. *Contact Walla Walla Valley Chamber of Commerce | Box 644, 29 E. Sumach, 99362 | 509/525–0850 or 877/998–4748 | www.wwchamber.com.*

Fort Walla Walla Museum. The Fort Walla Walla complex occupies the site of a former U.S. Army fort established in 1858. The grounds include 15 acres of park, a museum with 14 historic or reconstructed log buildings, and a new headquarters museum building. Exhibits include a 19th-century combine (harvesting machine) that was drawn by a team of 33 mules. | 755 Myra Rd., at Dalles Military Rd. west of Walla Walla | 509/525–7703 | www.fortwallawallamuseum.org | $6 | Apr.–Oct., daily 10–5.

Whitman Mission National Historic Site. In 1836, Dr. Marcus Whitman and his wife, Narcissa (one of the first two women to traverse what would become the Oregon Trail), established a Presbyterian mission for the Cayuse tribe at Waiilatpu ("place of the people of the rye grass"), 7 mi west of modern-day Walla Walla. The Waiilatpu Mission became an important station on the Oregon Trail. But tensions quickly arose between the missionaries and the Cayuse over land usage and cultural practices. In addition, a devastating measles outbreak in the fall of 1847 killed half of the Waiilatpu band of the Cayuse. Some of the Cayuse blamed these deaths on Dr. Whitman and retaliated by killing him, his wife, and 11 others. They also took 60 hostages, who were held at the site for about a month before the Hudson Bay Company paid a ransom to free them. The museum at the Whitman Mission National Historic Site includes a 10-minute introductory slide show, a model of what the mission looked like in 1847, life-size figures showing characters in period dress, and some of the Whitmans' belongings, including Marcus Whitman's Bible. In the surrounding park, you'll find the foundations of the mission buildings, the mass grave, and an 1897 monument to the Whitmans. | 328 Whitman Mission Rd. | 509/522–6360 or 509/529–2761 | www.nps.gov/whmi | Entrance fee varies | Daily.

✦ ON THE CALENDAR: June **Lewis and Clark Days.** Held at the Fort Walla Walla Museum, the festival includes demonstrations and reenactments of 19th-century frontier activities and events, including the Lewis and Clark expedition, 19th-century U.S. military encampments, and the battles at Steptoe Butte and Spokane Plains. | 509/525–7703.

YAKIMA

▼▼▼

Although it is the commercial and cultural capital of the Yakima Valley, the city of Yakima is located at the northwestern edge of the valley's agricultural heartland. Like so many other frontier towns, it was founded when the Northern Pacific Railroad brought its line through here in 1884, (bypassing nearby Union Gap). Surrounded by mountain ridges on three sides, some of which rise to 3,000 ft, and shielded from Pacific storms by the Cascades, Yakima is one of the balmiest cities in Washington. *Contact Yakima Valley Visitor and Convention Bureau | 10 N. 8th St., 98901 | 509/575–3010 or 800/221–0751 | fax 509/575–6252 | www. visityakima.com.*

Central Washington Agricultural Museum. Displays of antique farm machinery fill 20 large buildings at this unusual museum. A collection of hand tools, a relocated log cabin, and a windmill are a few of the highlights. You'll marvel at some of the huge machines, such as hay balers, that were drawn by horses in the late 19th century. | 4508 Main St., Union Gap | 509/457–8735 | Free, donations accepted | Daily 9–dusk; call beforehand for guided tour of interior.

Historic North Front Street. Yakima's old Northern Pacific Depot (1910) looks a bit like a California mission that got lost on a trip north. Across from the depot, Front Street is lined with turn-of-the-20th-century business buildings. Nearby you'll find St. Michael's Episcopal Church (E. Yakima and S. Naches Ave.), a tidy wood structure completed in 1889. In the depot is America's oldest brewpub, Grant's, one of the best spots in Washington State to grab a sandwich and a beer. Another favorite spot is the Barrel House, originally a saloon for local and transient cowboys transporting their cattle. | 509/248–2021 | Free | Daily.

Yakima Valley Museum. This museum contains a comprehensive collection of vehicles, ranging from the basic buckboards that were the station wagons of the 19th century to stagecoaches and antique automobiles. Also part of the museum is Orchard House, built in 1890, which is filled with authentic late-Victorian furnishings. | 2105 Tieton Dr. | 509/248–0747 | $5 | Tues.–Sun. 11–5.

✦ ON THE CALENDAR: Sept. **Ellensburg Rodeo.** The promoters of this four-day event, held each Labor Day weekend at the Kittitas County Fairgrounds (in Ellensburg, 36 mi north of Yakima), tout it as "the greatest show on dirt." Like most rodeos, it includes barrel racing, bull and bronc riding, and three events derived from real ranch work—calf roping, steer wrestling, and team roping. It is one of the four premier Northwest rodeos, drawing top professionals from the Columbia River Circuit. | 800/637–2444.

HISTORIC DINING AND LODGING

Birchfield Manor. On a perfectly flat plateau 2 mi outside Yakima, this inn is surrounded by fields and grazing cattle. The 1910 Old Manor House contains a well-regarded restaurant and five upstairs guest rooms. A newer cottage house provides every modern convenience. Rooms, each with a whirlpool tub, steam-sauna shower, and gas fireplace, have been designed for maximum privacy. Owner Brad Masset oversees the contemporary Northwest restaurant (reservations essential), whose menu changes seasonally but always includes valley produce. Restaurant, room service, some in-room hot tubs, minibars, pool. | 2018 Birchfield Rd., 98901 | 509/452–1960 | fax 509/452–2334 | www.birchfieldmanor.com | 11 rooms | AE, DC, MC, V | BP.

WYOMING

---

he first people to live in Wyoming were migrant hunters and gatherers who arrived about 25,000 years ago. When they first arrived in the region, Euro-American settlers met the descendants of those hunter-gatherers: the Comanche, Shoshone, Arapaho, Lakota, Cheyenne, Crow, Ute, and Blackfoot. The earliest recorded contact between white settlers and Native Americans in Wyoming came in 1807, when John Colter, a member of Lewis and Clark's Corps of Discovery, decided to go back west after the expedition reached the Mandan Villages in present-day North Dakota on the return trip. He made a circuitous route through northwestern Wyoming, seeing spouting geysers and sulfurous bubbling hot springs at a place later dubbed "Colter's Hell," just west of what is now Cody. Then he crisscrossed the Rocky Mountains, traveling into Jackson Hole and through land that is now protected by Grand Teton and Yellowstone national parks.

Other explorers followed Colter in 1811, with the biggest influx after 1822 when fur trappers started their quest for beaver in the West's clear mountain streams and rivers. Legendary mountain men like Jim Bridger, Thomas Fitzpatrick, Hugh Glass, David Jackson, William Pickney, Milton Sublette, and James Beckwourth were instrumental in the development of the West. These men explored throughout the region, leaving their names on many of the state's streams, mountains, and other physical features. The first mountain-man trade rendezvous took place in 1825 on the Black Fork of the Green River, southeast of the present city of Green River, Wyoming.

The explorers traveled paths they learned about from Native Americans, and they marked routes later followed by more than 500,000 emigrants headed toward Oregon, California, and Utah. During its 18-month existence, the Pony Express sent riders racing across Wyoming on the same corridor, linking East and West. The Pony Boys lost their jobs, however, when the transcontinental telegraph—built along the same overland corridor—began working in October 1861.

In 1849 Cherokee Indians crossed the southern portion of Wyoming, forging the Cherokee Trail as they headed toward California's gold fields. In 1865 wagons and stagecoaches started rolling across that landscape on the Overland Trail, established by the freighting firm of Ben Holladay. The Union Pacific Railroad was built along the route later that decade. As workers laid rail from east to west, a string of rowdy, lawless boomtowns sprang up; they became known as the hell-on-wheels towns, and included Cheyenne, Laramie City, Carbon, Benton, Rawlins, Rock Springs, Green River, Bear River City, Evanston, and several others. About half of these tent cities lived and died in short, dramatic episodes and are now only ghosts. The southern Wyoming region continued its legacy as a transportation corridor in 1913 when the Lincoln Highway—U.S. 30—was completed. Decades later I–80 would cut across the same portion of Wyoming, along most of the old Lincoln Route.

Except for Native Americans, few people lived permanently in Wyoming until the Union Pacific was established. But subsequent mineral discoveries—including coal in southern Wyoming and gold at South Pass—spurred growth, and Wyoming Territory was established on July 25, 1868. By the mid-1870s, cattlemen had brought Texas longhorns up the Texas Trail, the Goodnight-Loving Trail, and other routes to turn them loose on Wyoming's high-plains grassland. Sheep ranchers also began using the vast open spaces, creating conflicts over the range—some of which would continue through most of the 20th century. Homesteaders also staked claims, building homes and sometimes raising crops.

Increasing white settlement spelled the end of traditional ways of life for the Native Americans, some of whom fought violent battles with the U.S. Army, particularly in Wyoming's Powder River Basin. By 1880 the Native Americans had been forced onto reservations; and now only two Indian tribes are left—the Shoshone and Arapaho, who share Wind River Indian Reservation in central Wyoming. Homesteaders settled all over the territory, and Wyoming achieved statehood in July 1890. The rough ways of the frontier lingered, however, and in 1892 powerful cattlemen squared off against smaller livestock operators and homesteaders in a conflict over cattle range. The cattlemen hired an "army" and invaded Johnson County, only to be surrounded by townspeople. Subsequently, the U.S. Army rescued the cattlemen and their "invaders." Though charged with various crimes, including the deaths of two homesteaders, the cattlemen and their associates never went to trial.

Today a trip to Wyoming can be a journey into the past. There are still wide-open spaces, wild horses, and natural wonders in an untouched landscape. Railroads rumble across the prairie and cowboys chase cattle. The past has been preserved in historic sites like Fort Laramie and the Oregon-California-Mormon National Historic Trails, and in events like mountain-man rendezvous. Indians practice traditional dances and create traditional goods. You can walk the old trails, see the same vistas the pioneers saw, and face into the wind just as they did not so very long ago.

Trails Across Wyoming

A DRIVING TOUR FROM FORT LARAMIE TO FORT BRIDGER

▼▼▼

Distance: 469 mi   **Time: 3** days

Breaks: Plan to spend one night in Casper so you have plenty of time to see trail sites all along this route; then spend a second night in Atlantic City so you can experience the isolation emigrants felt when they neared South Pass.

Roughly 500,000 emigrants followed the Oregon-California-Mormon trails across Wyoming from 1841 to 1869, when the railroad was completed, making wagon-train travel no longer necessary. Wyoming has more miles of original trail still in existence than any other state along the routes, and much of it is on public lands run primarily by the Bureau of Land Management, so you have the opportunity to walk or drive actual trails and see the ruts left by the wheels of pioneer wagons.

WYOMING TIME LINE

1743 The Verendrye brothers are the first white men to visit Wyoming.

1803 The United States concludes the Louisiana Purchase, which includes Wyoming.

1807–08 John Colter explores Wyoming. He is the first European to lay eyes on the geyser basins of the Yellowstone ecosystem.

1811 Wilson Price Hunt's Astorians head east from Fort Astoria, crossing through Wyoming on a route that later becomes the Oregon Trail.

1825 The first trappers' rendezvous is held on Black Fork of the Green River.

1834 Wyoming's first permanent white settlement develops at Fort William near the confluence of the Laramie and North Platte rivers; it is eventually renamed Fort Laramie.

1843 Migration begins over the Oregon Trail.

1849 Gold seekers head to California over the California and Cherokee Trails.

1860–61 The Pony Express delivers the mail by horseback courier.

1865 Train travel shifts south from the Oregon-California-Mormon corridor to the Overland Trail in southern Wyoming.

1868 Wyoming Territory is established on July 25.

1869 On December 10 Wyoming grants women the right to vote, hold office, and serve on juries.

1870 Cowboys begin trailing cattle from Texas into and through Wyoming, beginning an industry that remains strong more than a century later.

1872 Congress designates Yellowstone as the first national park.

1880 Wealthy cattlemen form the Cactus Club in Cheyenne. It later becomes the Cheyenne Club, a base where anti-rustling activities are planned.

1886–87 A severe winter kills thousands of head of cattle. It becomes known as "The Great Die-Up."

1890 Wyoming becomes a state on July 10.

1892 A cattlemen's army invades Johnson County in an incident that becomes known as the Johnson County Invasion or Johnson County War.

1903 Shoshone National Forest, the nation's first, is created in northwestern Wyoming.

1906 Devils Tower becomes the first national monument.

Begin your trip on the eastern side of the state at **Fort Laramie,** a fur-trading post established by mountain men, which eventually became a major supply stop for emigrants. Travel west on U.S. 20/26 and then north on I–25 to **Casper,** stopping along the way at Register Cliff and the Guernsey ruts. In Casper visit the National Historic Trails Interpretive Center for an overview of the settlers' migration, tour Fort Caspar, and then see other trail sites in the area as time allows.

When you leave Casper on the second day of your tour, take a picnic lunch and head west on Route 220 toward **Rawlins,** stopping along the way at Independence Rock, where emigrants carved their names on the granite. Take a break at Handcart Ranch, where you can push or pull a handcart from the visitor center to Martin's Cove. Have lunch in the picnic

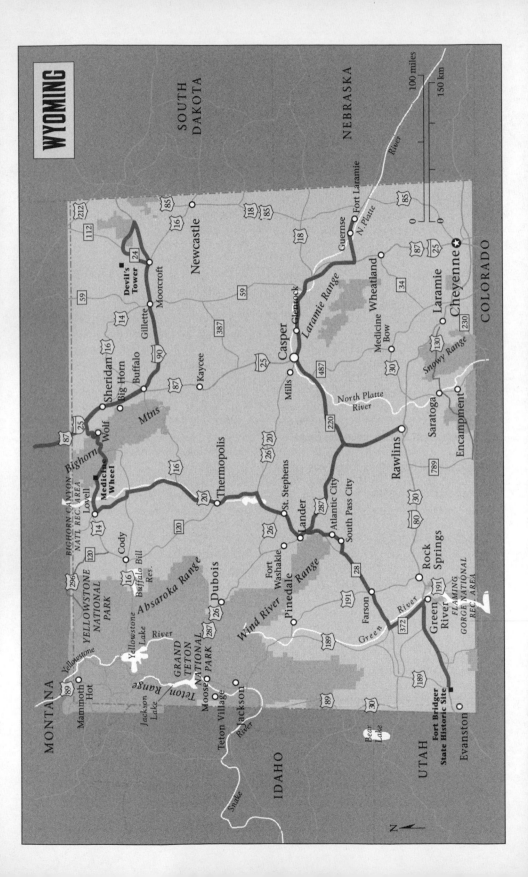

area by the visitor center; then turn north on U.S. 287 and follow the trail up the Sweetwater Valley before turning west on Route 28 to travel toward South Pass. (If you want to take dirt roads over South Pass, get road information and maps at the National Historic Trails Interpretive Center in Casper.) If you have time, take a side trip to South Pass City, where emigrants found gold in 1868. You'll need at least a couple of hours to visit the city. Have dinner and spend your second night in **Atlantic City.**

Begin your third day with a visit to South Pass City if you haven't been there yet. Then head toward South Pass, the route trail travelers took to get through the Rockies. There are a couple of markers at the pass itself, and an interpretive area west of the pass, just off Route 28. Then continue west to see trail sites along Route 28—the trail meanders both north and south of the highway all the way from South Pass, past present-day **Farson,** to the Green River. There are interpretive areas at many trail sites, with some right off the highway and others accessible by dirt road. Among the easily accessible sites are False Parting of the Ways, Simpson's Hollow, and Lombard Ferry. Just after you cross the Green River, turn south on Route 372, and then take I–80 west to Fort Bridger, near **Evanston.** This post, started in 1842 by mountain man Jim Bridger to serve the emigrant trade, was the second most important outfitting post for emigrants during the earliest years of trail travel.

American Indians, Basin to Basin
A DRIVING TOUR FROM BUFFALO TO LANDER
▼▼

Distance: 449 mi   **Time:** 3–4 days
Breaks: Plan to spend one night in Buffalo and another in Thermopolis, with a possible side trip to Cody.

For the Lakota, Cheyenne, and other tribes, the Powder River Basin of northeast Wyoming was sacred ground and their primary hunting territory. The Shoshone ranged in the Bighorn Basin, where they valued the healing waters of hot springs. Indians of the region fought vigorously to defend it from white settlers and the U.S. military in the mid-1800s. Finally defeated, the Shoshone and Arapahoe (former enemies settled in the Wind River Basin of central Wyoming, where they remain on a reservation today. This tour takes you to important Native American sites and places where the Indians fought the U.S. Army in an effort to preserve their traditional lifestyle.

Begin your trip at Devils Tower National Monument, 96 mi east of **Buffalo** on I–90. The 26 mi of Route 24 that you take north from the interstate to the monument is part of the path that Lieutenant Colonel George Armstrong Custer followed in 1874 as he explored the Black Hills of South Dakota and Wyoming. Spend the morning at Devils Tower, a site still sacred to Native Americans. From Devils Tower take U.S. 14 back to Sundance and then head west on I–90. Exit 12 mi north of Buffalo to visit Fort Phil Kearny and nearby battle sites such as the location of the Wagon Box Battle and the Fetterman Massacre. You can get directions at the fort to those and other battle sites. Spend the night in Buffalo.

On your second day pack a picnic lunch and take I–90 west past **Sheridan,** then follow U.S. 14A high into and across the Bighorn Mountains. Along the way, stop at the Medicine Wheel, a site sacred to all Northern Plains tribes but one whose origin is unknown. From the Medicine Wheel, continue west to Lovell, dropping down the hairpin turns of U.S. 14A on the west face of the Bighorn Mountains into the Bighorn Basin. In Lovell, turn south on U.S. 310 to U.S. 16/20 and follow that route south to **Thermopolis.** By nighttime you'll be tired and maybe even a bit sore from driving, so you'll appreciate a soak in the hot mineral waters that the Shoshone ceded to the government in 1896. These waters were always neutral ground for the various tribes. Spend the night in Thermopolis.

On your third day, take U.S. 20 south, then U.S. 26 west to **Lander.** Much of your route will be on the Wind River Indian Reservation, and you can learn more about the Shoshone and Arapaho tribes at cultural centers in and around Lander. Conclude your trip with a stay in the Lander area.

If you have the time and can add a day and about 100 mi to your journey between Sheridan to Thermopolis, take a side trip to **Cody** to visit the Plains Indian Museum at the Buffalo Bill Historical Center. The museum's interactive exhibits show what it was like in a Plains Indian lodge and demonstrates how Native Americans lived and traveled.

ATLANTIC CITY
▼▼

This town was formed in 1868 when gold miners flocked to the area to seek their fortune. Known for its red-light district, or "French" section, Atlantic City was the site of Wyoming Territory's first brewery. Once the gold boom petered out, the town was nearly deserted. It is now a near-ghost town, with only a few residents and a couple of tourist-oriented businesses. *Contact Wind River Visitor's Council | Box 1449, Riverton 82520 | 307/856–7566 or 800/ 645–6233 | www.wind-river.org.*

South Pass City State Historic Site. Now a ghost town, South Pass City was established during the South Pass Gold Rush of 1867. Close to a thousand people lived there, and it was known as one of the most progressive towns in the territory. The nation's first female judge was appointed in South Pass City in 1870. Then, in the early 1870s, the mining boom went bust, and by 1880 South Pass City was a bona fide ghost town. More than 15 of the original buildings have been restored, and a small museum displays old photographs and mining tools and equipment. At certain times during the summer you can try your hand at panning for gold in the cold stream that runs through town. | South Pass City Rd. off Rte. 28, 3 mi west of Atlantic City | 307/332–3684 | http://wyoparks.state.wy.us/south1.htm | $2 | Mid-May– early Sept., daily 9–5:30.

HISTORIC DINING AND LODGING
Atlantic City Mercantile. American. The town's original saloon, known as the Merc, still offers refreshment in a room that has seen its share of gold miners, perhaps an outlaw or two, and certainly some ruffians. When you step through the doors you'll feel as if you've walked directly into an episode of *Gunsmoke*. There are tin ceilings, a massive back bar (complete with a mirror that's been broken ever since a boomtown brawl), and an assortment of mismatched oak tables and chairs. At times a honky-tonk piano player is on hand. If you're here on the fourth Wednesday of the month, from November to May, try the seven-course Basque dinner. The rest of the time you'll find steak, chicken, seafood, and sandwiches in the restaurant ($15–$47). Accommodations are in the more contemporary A-frame cottages behind the Merc. Restaurant, kitchenettes, hiking, bar; no room TVs. | 100 E. Main St. | 307/ 332–5143 | fax 307/332–9376 | 4 cottages | $65 | D, MC, V.

Miner's Delight B&B. Rooms in the lodge are larger and have private bathrooms, but if you want to do things the way gold miners would have during the boom of the late 1860s, stay in the simple, rustic cabins. Each one has a small washstand with a bowl and a pitcher of water, and there are patchwork curtains and bed coverings. It's a short walk to the bathroom in the main lodge, which was built in 1895 as the town's hotel. Wherever you stay, you get a full breakfast. Dining room, picnic area; no-smoking rooms, no room phones, no room TVs. | 290 Atlantic City Rd., 82520 | 307/332–0248 or 888/292–0248 | www.holidayjunction. com/usa/wy/cwy0051.html | 3 lodge rooms, 5 cabins | $60–$75 | MC, V | BP.

BUFFALO

▼▼

Buffalo was established in 1879 following two different periods of conflict—from 1864 to 1868 and again in the years leading up to the Battle of the Little Bighorn in 1876—between the frontier army and the Northern Plains Indians. After the Native Americans retreated or were forced onto reservations, the region was settled quickly and grew into a profitable sheep-grazing and cattle-ranching area. In 1892, a group of Wyoming cattle barons staged what is known today as the Johnson County Invasion. The cattle barons hired a force of Texas gunmen to "clean out" rustlers, renegades, and small-ranch owners in the Buffalo area. In the 1890s and early 1900s, Butch Cassidy and other members of outlaw gangs periodically passed through the vicinity, particularly when attempting to elude a posse in Hole-in-the-Wall country, southwest of Buffalo. Buffalo settled down as an agricultural community in the early 1900s. *Contact Buffalo Chamber of Commerce | 55 N. Main St., 82834 | 307/684–5544 or 800/227–5122 | www.buffalowyo.com.*

Devils Tower National Monument. The first national monument authorized by Congress, Devil's Tower has been federally protected since 1906. Native American legend has it that the corrugated Devils Tower was formed when a tree stump turned into granite and grew taller to protect some stranded children from a clawing bear. This is a significant site for Native Americans, who often leave prayer bundles, which might be pieces of cloth, or native plants tied in cloth, around the monument. The bundles remain in place until the weather causes them to deteriorate. They are important religious offerings and should not be disturbed. You'll find 7 mi of hiking trails, a campground, a picnic area, and a visitor center. | 131 mi east of Buffalo via I–90 and U.S. 14 east, then 6 mi north on Rte. 24 | 307/467–5430 | www.nps. gov/deto | $8 | Visitor center early Apr.–late May and early Sept.–early Oct., daily 8:30–4:30; late May–early Sept., daily 8–8.

Fort Phil Kearny. The frontier army occupied this post from 1866 to 1868 to protect travelers heading to Montana's gold fields. The region became bitterly contested by the army and local Native Americans (primarily Lakota and Cheyenne). No original buildings remain at the state historic site (they were burned as soon as the military abandoned the fort in 1868), but the fort site is marked and the visitor center has good details. The stockade around the fort has been re-created. While you are here, ask for directions to the Wagon Box Battle and Fetterman Massacre sites. Outlaws routinely passed through this area in the 1800s trying to elude lawmen by slipping into Hole-in-the-Wall country, south of Buffalo and west of Kaycee. | 12 mi north of Buffalo on I–90 | 307/684–7629 or 307/777–7014 | www.philkearny. vcn.com | $2 | Mid-May–Sept., daily 8–6.

On December 21, 1866, Lieutenant William J. Fetterman and 80 soldiers rode from Fort Phil Kearny over Lodge Trail Ridge and to their deaths as Lakota Sioux, Northern Cheyenne, and Arapaho warriors led by Chiefs Red Cloud and Crazy Horse surrounded and attacked them. A stone monument marks the **Fetterman Massacre Site** (Off U.S. 87, 2 mi northwest of Fort Kearny).

In August 1866, frontier army soldiers gathering wood for Fort Kearny were engaged in battle with Lakota Sioux lead by Chief Red Cloud. The soldiers took refuge in a fortification made from the boxes of their wagons and although they were outnumbered successfully repelled the warriors, because they were equipped with Springfield repeating rifles. This was the first time the repeating rifles were used in a U.S. military–Native American battle. At the **Wagon Box Battle Site** (Rte. 193, 5 mi northwest of Fort Kearny), replica wagon boxes give you an idea of the corral where the soldiers took cover during the battle.

Jim Gatchell Memorial Museum. Native American moccasins, U.S. military weapons, and ranchers' branding irons are among the artifacts collected by a local druggist and displayed at this

THE COWBOY ON THE LICENSE PLATE

Ask an old-timer in Pinedale, Lander, Laramie, or Cheyenne who the cowboy is on the Wyoming license plate's bucking-horse symbol, and you'll probably get four different answers. Different regions of the state have favorite legends about the rider, each claiming the original model—Stub Farlow of Lander? Guy Holt of Cheyenne and Pinedale?—as its own. Artist Allen True, who created the cowboy, once said he had no particular rider in mind.

During World War I, George Ostrem, a member of the Wyoming National Guard serving in Germany, had a bucking horse and rider design painted on a bass drum. His 148th Field Artillery unit soon had the logo on its vehicles as well, and it became known as the Bucking Bronco Regiment from Wyoming. And which horse was the symbol modeled after? In the case of the Wyoming National Guard logo, the horse was Ostrem's own mount, Red Wing.

In 1921, the University of Wyoming first used a bucking horse and cowboy as a logo on its sports uniforms, with that design modeled after a 1903 photograph by UW professor B. C. Buffum, depicting Guy Holt riding Steamboat, widely regarded to be one of the five toughest bucking horses of all time. The state of Wyoming first put the bucking bronco on its license plate in 1936, and the trademarked symbol has been there ever since.

---

museum. There's also a sizable collection of old wagons. | 100 Fort St. | 307/684–9331 | www. jimgatchell.com | $4 | Mid-Apr.–Dec., daily 9–7.

Spiritrider Wagon Train Adventures. Beginning and ending your trip with a luxurious night at the Occidental Hotel or Willow Creek Ranch, take a three-day to two-week wagon trip through Hole-in-the-Wall country. Tours are led by Mikel Carmon, whose resume includes a seven-week wagon train journey on the Bozeman Trail from Fort Laramie to Virginia City, Montana. Assisting her are other veteran wagon train travelers, who make sure your experience is authentic. | 409 Trabing Rd. | 307/684–9397 | www.spiritrider-wagontrain.com | $320–$550 per person, per day.

✦ ON THE CALENDAR: June **Living History Days.** Costumed interpreters give presentations about frontier life at the Jim Gatchell Museum. | 307/684–9331.

Feb.–Mar. **History and Coffee.** Discussions about such historical topics as the Plains Indian Wars and the lives of early settlers take place once each month at the Jim Gatchell Museum. | 307/684–9331.

HISTORIC DINING AND LODGING

Occidental Hotel. Buffalo was barely a town when the Occidental opened for business in a tent in 1879. But the town grew rapidly and with it the hotel, which first moved into a log building and later the brick building that is still open for business today. Owen Wister spent time at the Occidental when he visited Wyoming in the late 1800s, and he immortalized the site in his novel *The Virginian*. Others who passed through its doors included Butch Cassidy, the Sundance Kid, Calamity Jane, and Buffalo Bill Cody. You can stay in a suite decorated with period furniture and patterned wallpaper, have a meal at the Creekside Cafe ($7–$10; open June–Sept., Mon.–Sat.) or in the Virginian Dining Room ($11–$25; no lunch Mon.–Sat.), or have a drink in the original turn-of-the-20th-century saloon. Take a moment to notice the elegant tin ceilings. 2 restaurants, in-room data ports, cable TV, some pets allowed; no room phones, no smoking. | 10 N. Main St. | 307/684–0451 hotel; 307/684–8989 saloon | fax 307/684–5880 | www.occidentalwyoming.com | 7 suites | $130–$175 | AE, D, MC, V | CP.

TA Ranch. In the Johnson County Invasion of 1892, cattlemen and their hired guns riding from the KC ranch, where they had killed cowboys Nate Champion and Nick Ray, turned back to the TA Ranch when they learned that armed men from the community were riding their way. The cattlemen took refuge at the TA and were soon pinned down by the local force. You can still see bullet holes in the ranch buildings. You'll get a horse to ride, all your meals, and a tour of the Powder River Basin. Ask about weeklong packages. Dining room, Internet; no-smoking rooms, no rooms TVs. | Rte. 196, 14 mi south of Buffalo (Box 313, Buffalo 82834) | 307/684–5833 | fax 307/684–5834 | www.taranch.com | 15 rooms | $165 per person | AE, D, MC, V | FAP.

Willow Creek Ranch at Hole-in-the-Wall. The only way to get to the actual Hole-in-the-Wall where outlaws slipped away from pursuing posses is by crossing private land owned by Hole-in-the-Wall Ranch. Fortunately, the ranch owners, Sammye and Gene Vieh, welcome guests who stay in a renovated bunkhouse that dates back almost to the time when Butch Cassidy and the Sundance Kid rode through. They also have a small cabin out on the range. Wagon train and trail rides are available. Dining room, hiking, horseback riding; no smoking, no room phones, no room TVs. | Willow Creek Rd., 35 mi southwest of Kaycee (Box 10, Kaycee 82639) | 307/738–2294 | fax 307/738–2264 | www.willowcreekranch.com | 4 room, 2 cabins | $900–$1,500 per week | No credit cards | FAP.

CASPER

▼▼

Casper can rightfully claim that it's one of the oldest permanent crossroads in the state. Native Americans regularly traded in the area, and the first white people to establish a winter home in Wyoming were probably Robert Stuart and his companions, who were headed east from Fort Astoria in 1811. Stuart and his fellow travelers identified the route that later became the Oregon-California-Mormon Trails. During almost all subsequent overland travel, people crossed the North Platte River near present-day Casper.

The town took its name from Lieutenant Caspar Collins, who, along with several companions, lost a fight with Sioux and Cheyenne warriors on July 26, 1865, as the soldiers rode from Platte Bridge Station (Fort Caspar) toward a wagon train that was being threatened. The warriors subsequently killed all the people in the train. The area near present-day Casper was originally a ferry crossing. Mormons built the first ferry there in 1847. Several bridges over the North Platte also were built in the region. In the late 1800s, homesteaders and ranchers developed the area, and by the early 1900s, oil had been discovered, attracting thousands of workers and securing Casper's future. *Contact Casper Chamber of Commerce | 500 N. Center St., 82601 | 307/234–5311 or 800/852–1889 | fax 307/265–2643 | www.trib.com/ads/casper. Casper Convention and Visitor's Bureau | 330 S. Center St., Suite 420, 82601 | 307/234–5362 or 800/ 852–1889 | fax 307/261–9928 | www.casperwyoming.info.*

Fort Caspar Historic Site. Early military history in the region is interpreted at Fort Caspar, which has replica buildings and a model of a ferry like those used by emigrants to cross the North Platte River. | 4001 Fort Caspar Rd. | 307/235–8462 | www.fortcasparwyoming.com | $2 | June–Aug., Mon.–Sat. 8–7, Sun. noon–5; May and Sept., Mon.–Sat. 8–5, Sun. noon–7; Oct.–Apr. museum only, weekdays 8–5, Sun. 1–4.

Fort Fetterman State Historic Site. This fort dates from 1867 and is named for Captain William J. Fetterman. There are two original buildings: a restored officer's quarters and an ordnance warehouse, plus an interpretive trail with signs describing the fort's role in 19th-century events. To get there from Caspar, take I–25 east for 45 mi, then take Exit 140 and go north on Route 93 for 7 mi. | Off Rte. 93, 7 mi north of Douglas | 307/358–2864 or 307/777–7629 | http://wyoparks.state.wy.us/fetter1.htm | $2 | Late May–early Sept., daily 9–6.

Historic Trails West. Travel the historic trails of the Casper area in specially designed Conestoga-style wagons and sleep in tepees or military-style tents. Your guide is Morris Carter, who used the wagons for a 1993 six-month traversal of the Oregon Trail from Independence, Missouri, to Independence, Oregon. Trips range from four hours to six days. | Box 428, Mills, 82644 | 307/266–4868 | fax 307/266–2746 | www.historictrailsexpeditions.com | $35 for 4 hours, $85 for 1 day, $895 for 5 days.

National Historic Trails Interpretive Center. Five major pioneer trails passed near or through Casper in the period 1843–70. The best known are the Oregon Trail and the Mormon Trail, both of which crossed the North Platte River near here. Through a series of films and interactive exhibits you will learn the early history of the trails and those who used them, from Native Americans to mountain men, missionaries, emigrants, and the Pony Express. You can climb into a wagon to see what it was like to cross the river, or learn about Mormon pioneers who traveled west with handcarts in 1856. | 1501 N. Poplar St. | 307/261–7700 | www.wy. blm.gov/nhtic | $6 | Apr.–Oct., daily 8–7; Nov.–Mar., Tues.–Sat. 9–4:30.

✦ ON THE CALENDAR: June **Fort Caspar Frontier Festival.** Living-history camps re-create Old West trades and activities, such as blacksmithing, gardening, and military drills, at Fort Caspar. | 307/235–8462.

CHEYENNE
▼▼

Cheyenne became a Wild West town overnight when the Union Pacific Railroad pushed its way over the landscape in 1867. The first permanent residents included six men and three women who established camp here on July 9 of that year. By the time the railroad crews arrived, the city was already a vibrant place with little order and less law. In early August, some of the town's residents organized a group of vigilantes to establish some type of control. Finally, toward mid-August, the military moved into Fort D. A. Russell and Camp Carlin, bringing a modicum of order to the raucous community.

Unlike some renegade railroad tent cities, which disappeared as the railroad tracks pushed farther west, Cheyenne established itself as a permanent city, becoming the territorial capital in 1868. Its wild beginnings gave way to respectability with the coming of the cattle barons, wealthy ranch owners who built fine homes—considered mansions in that era—on 17th Street, which became known as Cattle Barons Row. The cattle barons had a gathering place, initially called the Cactus Club and later the Cheyenne Club (but never the Cheyenne Social Club). It was at the Cheyenne Club that the cattlemen planned the 1892 invasion of Johnson County, also called the Johnson County War, to root out rustlers—lone cowboys who may or may not have been stealing the cattleman's cows out on the open range. Cheyenne became the state capital in 1890. Take a self-guided walking tour through the historic core of downtown Cheyenne to see such historic structures as the Union Pacific depot and the Tivoli Building. Pick up a downtown walking-tour leaflet at the visitors bureau. *Contact Cheyenne Area Convention and Visitors Bureau | 309 W. Lincolnway, 82001 | 307/778–3133 or 800/426–5009 | www.cheyenne.org.*

Cattle Barons Row. Many of the wealthy cattlemen's homes in Cheyenne were built on 17th Street and designed by George Rainsford, an architect trained in New York who came to Wyoming to raise horses. A stroll along 17th Street will take you past several of the large, prosperous-looking homes that remain. On the southwest corner of 17th Street and Russell Avenue is the home of William Sturgis, a founding member of the Cheyenne Club and co-owner of the Union Cattle Company. At 801 East 17th is the Freeborn House, once owned by the first cashier for the Wyoming Stock Growers State Bank. Colonel A. T. Babbitt, army

WOMAN SUFFRAGE

Wyoming's Territorial Legislature granted women the right to vote in a law that was enacted December 10, 1869. The law not only gave the state's female population the right to vote, but to serve on juries and to hold office. The act made Wyoming the first territory to grant women equal rights in the political domain. The following year, 70-year-old Louisa "Grandma" Swain cast the first ballot in Laramie. She was not the first woman in the nation to vote, as Utah Territory, which had also granted women the right to vote, held an election earlier, but Louisa Swain's home state would prove to lead the nation in woman suffrage in many other respects.

Wyoming was where the first all-female jury heard a case (in Laramie) and the first female justice of the peace was appointed (Esther Hobart Morris began serving at South Pass City in February 1870). In 1920, an all-woman town council, believed to be the first of its kind in the country, served in Jackson.

doctor, cattleman, and president of the Wyoming Stock Growers Association, lived at No. 719. No. 703 is known as Bachelor's Quarters and was the home of bachelor brothers Hubert and Arthur Tschmacher, and Frederick DeBillier and Richard Trimble, all of whom were founding members of the Cheyenne Club. The famous Cheyenne Club was also built on 17th Street in the early 1880s, but it was torn down in 1936. | 309 W. Lincolnway | 307/778–3133 or 800/426–5009 | Free | Daily.

Old West Museum. With more than 125 carriages and carts, this museum has an extensive exhibit on early modes of transportation in the Old West. You can also see thousands of artifacts, from cowboy gear to Native American regalia. The guided tours are geared toward children. | 4601 N. Carey Ave. | 307/778–7290 or 800/266–2696 | www.oldwestmuseum.org | $5 | Sept.–May, weekdays 9–5, Sat. 11–4; June–Aug., weekdays 9–7, weekends 10–5.

Wyoming State Museum. Native American leather and beaded clothing, a silver service from the ship *Wyoming,* and cowboy gear like saddles and bridles are among the exhibits in this museum. There is a special room for children and occasional speakers and programs. | 2301 Central Ave. | 307/777–7022 | fax 307/777–5375 | www.wyomingmuseum.state.wy.us | Free | Tues.–Sat. 9–4:30.

✦ ON THE CALENDAR: Sept. **Cheyenne Cowboy Symposium and Celebration.** A cowboy gear and trade show where you can buy anything from spurs to cowboy hats and boots is at the center of this Labor Day weekend event, which also includes plays, music, and traditional cowboy poetry. | 307/635–5788.

July **Cheyenne Frontier Days.** This is the cowboy state's premier cowboy event, held the last full week of July every year since 1897. Leading contenders in the Professional Rodeo Cowboys Association compete at Frontier Park, and there are many other activities, including chuck-wagon races. In the Indian village, Native Americans demonstrate flute making and playing and traditional crafts such as beadwork. Dancing and storytelling take place during the powwow. Call to reserve tickets ($10–$22). | 307/778–7222; 800/227–6336; 800/543–2339 in WY | www.cfdrodeo.com.

HISTORIC LODGING
Nagle Warren Mansion Bed & Breakfast. Built in 1888 for cattle baron Erasmus Nagle, this three-story Victorian mansion has gorgeous woodwork, ornate staircases, old-fashioned wallpaper, and lavish rooms decorated with antiques; some have gas fireplaces. A pointed

tower holds a peaceful sitting room with a view over town. In 1910 the Nagle mansion was the home of Francis E. Warren, who served as both governor of Wyoming and U.S. senator. Dining room, in-room data ports, gym, hot tub, library, piano, meeting rooms; no kids, no-smoking rooms. | 222 E. 17th St., 82001 | 307/637–3333 or 800/811–2610 | fax 307/638–6879 | www.naglewarrenmansion.com | 12 rooms | $98–$115 | AE, MC, V | BP.

Plains Hotel. Once a center for events in downtown Cheyenne, the 1911 Plains Hotel has Molesworth-style furnishings and carpets and wall coverings with an Arapaho motif. Rooms have copies of photos taken by J. E. Stimson, who worked as a photographer for the Union Pacific Railroad in the 1800s. The National Trust for Historic Preservation has designated the Plains Hotel a member of Historic Hotels of America. Restaurant, in-room data ports, cable TV; no-smoking rooms. | 1600 Central Ave., 82001 | 307/638–3311 | fax 307/635–2022 | www.theplainshotel.com | 99 rooms, 31 suites | $109 rooms, $129–$149 suites | AE, D, MC, V.

CODY

▼▼

After the approval of the 1894 Carey Land Act, which provided money to develop irrigation projects, northwestern Wyoming experienced substantial population growth. In 1896, Cody was founded and named for William F. "Buffalo Bill" Cody, Pony Express rider, army scout, and Wild West show entertainer. The town is the eastern gateway to Yellowstone National Park, but Cody has much to offer even without the country's oldest national park in its backyard. It is home to one of the finest museums in the West: the Buffalo Bill Historical Center. *Contact Cody Country Chamber of Commerce | 836 Sheridan Ave., 82414 | 307/587–2777 | fax 307/527–6228 | www.codychamber.org.*

Buffalo Bill Historical Center. The center, which has been called the Smithsonian of the West, houses five museums in one: the Whitney Gallery of Western Art, with works by traditional Western artists, including Charlie Russell and Frederic Remington; the Buffalo Bill Museum, with memorabilia such as clothing, guns, saddles, and show posters belonging or related to the scout and showman; the Plains Indian Museum, with art and artifacts of the Plains tribes; the Cody Firearms Museum, with the world's largest collection of American firearms; and the Draper Museum of Natural History. There are periodic programs and area tours, plus the McCraken Research Library. | 720 Sheridan Ave. | 307/587–4771 | www.bbhc.org | $15 (2 days) | Apr., daily 10–5; May, daily 8–8; June–mid-Sept., daily 7 AM–8 PM; mid-Sept.–Oct., daily 8–5; Nov.–Mar., Tues.–Sun. 10–3.

Trail Town. This collection of historic buildings from Wyoming's frontier days includes a cabin used by outlaws in Hole-in-the-Wall country. Among the famous folk buried in the Trail Town cemetery is Jeremiah "Liver Eating" Johnson, plus some other notorious characters. The buildings aren't fancy, and the displays are rustic, so you really get a feel for what an old western town was like. | 1831 Demaris Dr. | 307/587–5362 | www.nezperce.com/trltown.html | $4 | May–Sept., daily 8–8.

✦ ON THE CALENDAR: Apr. **Cowboy Songs and Range Ballads.** In this symposium, which has impromptu jam sessions as well as nightly concerts and educational programs, performers present the history of cowboy music and the ballads that range cowboys sang. | 307/587–4771.

June **Plains Indian Powwow.** Plains Indian fancy dancers, hoop dancers, traditional dancers, and jingle dancers from various tribes perform at the Buffalo Bill Historical Center and other venues in town. | 307/587–4771.

DINING AND LODGING

Irma Hotel. Named for Buffalo Bill's daughter, this hotel, part of which dates to 1902, retains a frontier charm with brass beds and oak or walnut bureaus in many rooms. The large restaurant ($8–$18) has an elaborate cherrywood bar and serves traditional American food from chicken-fried steak to prime rib. Stay in the hotel (which has 15 rooms) and not in the annex, which has 25 motel-style rooms. In summer, locals stage a gunfight on the porch Tuesday–Saturday at 7 PM. Restaurant, bar. | 1192 Sheridan Ave., 82414 | 307/587–4221 or 800/745–4762 | fax 307/587–1775 | www.irmahotel.com | 40 rooms | $71–$96 | AE, D, DC, MC, V.

ENCAMPMENT

▼▼▼

In 1838 trappers held a rendezvous near a stream flowing from the Sierra Madre range, calling the site Camp le Grande. The name stuck, and when copper miners struck it rich in 1897, the community that sprang up became Grand Encampment. But the copper boom went bust by 1910 and the town dropped the "Grand," even though it survived as an agricultural and logging center. *Contact Platte Valley Chamber of Commerce | Box 1095, Saratoga 82331 | 307/326–8855 | fax 307/326–8855 | www.saratogachamber.info.*

Grand Encampment Museum. This is Wyoming's best small-town museum, with turn-of-the-20th-century buildings including the Lake Creek stage station, Peryam homestead house, and Palace bakery and ice cream shop. There are three original towers from a 16-mi-long aerial tramway that transferred copper ore from the Ferris Haggarty mine (1897–1908) to the smelter near Grand Encampment. | 807 Barnett Ave. | 307/327–5308 | Free | June–Aug., Mon.–Sat. 10–5, Sun. 1–5.

✦ ON THE CALENDAR: June **Woodchopper's Jamboree and Rodeo.** Loggers test their skills at felling trees, handsawing, axe chopping, and power-saw log cutting while rodeo cowboys participate in traditional events. There's also a parade, barbecue, and melodrama. | 307/327–5558, 307/327–5576 (rodeo), or 800/592–4309.

Aug. **Sierra Madre Muzzleloaders Mountain Man Rendezvous.** The Sierra Madre Muzzleloaders hold their annual rendezvous on the Grand Encampment Museum grounds with events like a frying-pan throw and black-powder shooting. There is also a trader's row where you can see and buy mountain-man products like those from the era 1825–43, including black-powder guns and supplies, trade beads, and leather clothing. | 307/327–5308.

HISTORIC DINING AND LODGING

Old Depot Bed-and-Breakfast. Moved from its original location about a ½ mi away, the Encampment Railroad Depot no longer serves trains (the railroad pulled out of the community in 1974). Instead the depot welcomes road-weary travelers with three small rooms: the Western room has a pine-pole bed and porcelain sink, the Victorian room has a bay window and claw-foot tub, and the Southwestern room has a carpet with a Native American design, plus a Jacuzzi tub. Breakfast is served next door at the Bear Trap Cafe. Riverside adjoins Encampment to the north. Gym, outdoor hot tub; no room TVs, no smoking. | 201 N. 1st St., Riverside 82325 | 307/327–5277 or 800/619–6677 | www.oldedepot.com | 3 rooms | $80 | MC, V | BP.

Wolf Hotel. This 1893 hotel in Saratoga once served as a stop on the stage route from Walcott to Grand Encampment. Some rooms are tiny, while some suites have multiple rooms, plus nooks and crannies under gabled windows. All rooms are on the second and third floors, and there is no elevator. The restaurant ($8–$32) serves prime rib and other beef dishes, plus seafood, pasta, and chicken. Saratoga is 8 mi north of Encampment via Route 130, which turns into Route 230. Restaurant, cable TV, bar; no room phones, no smoking. | 101 E. Bridge St., Saratoga 82331 | 307/326–5525 | www.wolfhotel.com | 5 rooms, 4 suites | $47–$90 | AE, DC, MC, V.

EVANSTON

▼▼

Like other rowdy towns established as the Union Pacific laid track across southern Wyoming, Evanston started as a tent city in 1869. Among the rail workers were many Chinese, who built a Chinatown of shanties and tarpaper shacks north of the railroad tracks. The first major economic boom hit Evanston in 1900 when oil was found in the region. Through the years ranchers and farmers joined the railroad workers, miners, builders, and shop owners who first populated the town. *Contact Evanston Chamber of Commerce | 36 E. 10th St., 82931 | 307/ 783–0370 or 800/328–9708 | fax 307/789–4807 | www.etownchamber.com.*

Fort Bridger State Historic Site. Mountain man Jim Bridger and his partner Louis Vasquez established Fort Bridger in 1842 as a trading post on the emigrant route to California and Oregon. Mormons gained control of the fort by 1853 after they either purchased it or forced the original owners to leave—historians aren't sure which. As the U.S. Army approached during the Mormon War of 1857, the Mormons deserted the area and burned the original Bridger post. Fort Bridger then was rebuilt and occupied by the military until 1890. Many of the military-era buildings remain, and the trading post has been reconstructed. The fort has interpretive programs and living-history demonstrations during the summer. | Exit 34 off I–80, 34 mi east of Evanston | 307/782–3842 | http://wyoparks.state.wy.us/bridger1.htm | $5 | Grounds daily 8–sunset. Museum Apr. and Oct., weekends 9–4:30, May–Sept., daily 9–5:30. Bridger/Vasquez Trading Co. May–Sept., daily 9–5.

✦ ON THE CALENDAR: Aug. **Bear River Mountain Man Rendezvous.** Buckskinners set up camp for a rendezvous re-creation on Bear River in Bear River State Park, on the business loop of I–80. Events include shooting competitions and a traders' fair. | 800/328–9708.

Sept. **Fort Bridger Mountain Man Rendezvous.** Held on Labor Day weekend at the Fort Bridger State Historic Site, this is the largest gathering of buckskinners and traders in the region. Traders sell period items, and there's a Native American powwow. | 307/782–3842.

HISTORIC LODGING

Pine Gables Inn B&B. Pine Gables Inn was built in 1883, for A. V. Quinn, owner of the local lumber company and the man who started Evanston's first bank. In 1923, the Eastlake Victorian-style mansion was transformed into a guest house and now operates as a B&B. Some rooms have fireplaces and claw-foot tubs, and one room has a Jacuzzi. Ask for a low-numbered room on the back side of the house, where it is quieter. Dining room, library; no kids under 12, no smoking, no in-room TVs. | 1049 Center St., 82930 | 307/789–2069 or 800/ 789–2069 | www.cruising-america.com/pinegables | 4 rooms, 2 suites | $60–$85 rooms, $125– $135 suites | AE, MC, V | BP.

FARSON

▼▼

Emigrants headed to Oregon, gold seekers en route to California, and Mormons on their way to Zion (Utah) all passed near the site of this small town in the heart of Wyoming's Red Desert country. The trails they left behind are visible today. Farson was settled by farmers, and eventually ranchers, after the Seedskedee Irrigation Project of the early 1900s made the desert soil suitable for cultivation. *Contact Rock Springs Chamber of Commerce | 1897 Dewar Dr., Rock Springs 82901 | 307/362–3771 | fax 307/362–3838 | www.rockspringswyoming.net or www.tourwildwyoming.com.*

Oregon-California-Mormon Trail Segments. The best interpretive sites on the Oregon, Mormon, and California Trails in Wyoming are in the southwestern part of the state near Farson, where there are lots of easily accessible trail segments on public lands. The Bureau of Land Management in Rock Springs manages between 450 and 600 mi of the trails and, in cooperative projects, has placed interpretive signs at a number of trail locations, most of which can be reached by traveling Route 28 in the area east and west of Farson. The trails are marked and you can get maps and information from the bureau. | Bureau of Land Management, 280 U.S. 191 N, Rock Springs | 307/352–0256 | www.wy.blm.gov/rsfo/index.htm | Free | Weekdays 8–5.

False Parting of the Ways, 25 mi east of Farson on Route 28, is a point a few miles removed from the spot where travelers took different routes to Oregon and California.

At **Simpson's Hollow,** 20 mi west of Farson on Route 28, you can read interpretive signs about an 1857 attack by Mormon raiders on a government freight train. The attack is considered the only significant engagement of the so-called Mormon War of 1857.

Lombard Ferry, where Route 28 crosses the Green River west of Farson, has interpretive signs that describe how travelers crossed the river en route to Oregon or California.

FORT LARAMIE
▼▼▼

This small town (not to be confused with the city of Laramie) takes its name from the first permanent settlement in Wyoming, and what was possibly the most important U.S. military establishment of the 19th century, Fort Laramie. The town site was developed in 1834 as a fur trading post, known first as Fort William, then as Fort John. The military assumed control of it in 1849, changing the name to Fort Laramie. It was here that some of the most significant U.S. government–Native American treaties were written and signed. After the military abandoned the fort in 1890, the area depended on agricultural production as its primary industry. The town now is home to a couple hundred good people "and six soreheads" according to a sign on the main street. *Contact Goshen County Chamber | 350 W. 21st St., Torrington 82240 | 307/532–3879 | www.go-goshen.com.*

Fort Laramie National Historic Site. Fort Laramie is the most authentic historic site in Wyoming, in part because its original buildings are extremely well preserved, and also because four major periods in western history are represented inside its walls. Near the confluence of the Laramie and North Platte rivers, the fort began as a trading post, and it was an important provisioning point for travelers on the Oregon Trail in 1843, the Mormon Trail in 1847, and the California Trail in 1849, when it also became a military site. In 1851 the first treaty between the U.S. government and the Northern Plains Indians was negotiated near the fort, and in 1868 a second Fort Laramie treaty led to the end of the First Sioux War, also known as Red Cloud's War. Costumed interpreters reenact scenes of military life and talk about the fur trade, overland migration, and relations between settlers and Native Americans. | Goshen County Rd. 270, 3 mi west of Fort Laramie | 307/837–2221 | fax 307/837–2120 | www.nps.gov/fola | $2 | Daily 8 AM–dusk, visitor center 8–5.

Oregon Trail Ruts and Register Cliff. These ruts carved into sandstone above the North Platte River are among the most remarkable on the entire 2,000 mi Oregon Trail. The ruts are about 100 yards long and 3 ft deep in some places. Two miles east of the ruts, off Platte County Road, is Register Cliff, a sandstone bluff on which trail travelers carved their names during the period 1841–1869. A Pony Express marker is on the access road beside the North Platte River about ¼ mi from the cliff. | Platte County Rd. 34, 3 mi west of Guernsey | 307/532–3879 | Free.

✦ ON THE CALENDAR: July **Frontier Fourth of July.** Fort Laramie re-creates the Fourth of July frontier style with military parades, cannon firing, a period dance, and other events. | 307/837–2221.

GREEN RIVER
▼▼

This city is named for the river known to area Native Americans as the Seedskadee Agie and to early explorers as either the Rio Verde or Spanish River. In 1849 and 1850, Cherokee Indians left the area that is now Oklahoma and Arkansas to head to the gold fields in California, following the Santa Fe Trail to Bent's Old Fort in Colorado, then turning north along a route that became known as the Cherokee Trail. It entered eastern Wyoming near Laramie and continued west on a course roughly parallel to today's I–80, through the Green River area. The city was settled when the Union Pacific Railroad came through in 1869. In that same year and again in 1871, John Wesley Powell launched expeditions down the Green and Colorado rivers. Green River became the Sweetwater County seat in 1872 and remained an important railroad hub and division point. *Contact Green River Chamber of Commerce | 541 E. Flaming Gorge Way, Suite E, 82935 | 307/875–5711 or 800/354–6743 | fax 307/875–8993 | www.grchamber.com.*

Expedition Island. Foot paths on Expedition Island take you past monuments to John Wesley Powell's expeditions, which were launched from the island, and signs that describe the explorer's adventures. Along a walkway connecting the island with the city's Green Belt are signs with information about the Cherokee Trail, which crossed through the region in 1850. Take East 2nd South Street to South 2nd East Street, and follow it to a parking area beside the bridge to the island. | End of S. 2nd E. St. | 307/875–5711 or 800/354–6743 | Daily.

Overland Stage Station. One of the only remaining overland stage stations in Wyoming is also easy to find, since it is visible from I–80 and less than a mile from the exit at Point of Rocks. The station is on the route that also served the Cherokee Trail, and there are markers so you can walk a section of trail. | Off I–80 at Point of Rocks, 32 mi east of Green River | Daily.

JACKSON
▼▼

Visitors to this area often mistakenly refer to the seat of Teton County as Jackson Hole. Actually, the town is Jackson, while the mountain-ringed valley is Jackson Hole. Both get their name from mountain man David Jackson, who operated the Rocky Mountain Fur Company with his partners Jedediah Smith and William Sublette back in the late 1820s and early 1830s. The first homesteaders arrived in 1884, and the town of Jackson, originally called Marysville for its first postmaster, was incorporated in 1901. *Contact Jackson Hole Chamber of Commerce 532 N. Cache, Box 550 83001 | 307/733–3316 | fax 307/733–5585 | www.jacksonholechamber.com.*

Grand Teton National Park. A smaller park with a shorter history, Grand Teton might be dwarfed by its northern neighbor Yellowstone, but nothing overshadows peaks like these. The human history of the region started with Native American tribes who spent summers hunting in the area. Later, fur trappers came for the beaver in the cold mountain streams. Settlers arrived in the 1880s, claiming land under various provisions of the Homestead

Act. Grand Teton National Park was not established until 1929. | U.S. 26/89/191, 12 mi north of Jackson, Moose 83012 | 307/739–3300 or TTY 307733–2053 | www.nps.gov/grte | $20 per car, truck, or RV; $15 per motorcycle or snowmobile; $10 per person entering on foot or bicycle | Daily.

Menor's Ferry. The ferry on display is not the original, but it is a replica of the craft built by Bill Menor in the 1890s. You can ride the ferry across the Snake River to get an idea of how people crossed the river before there were bridges. Several cabins, including the home and store used by Bill Menor, who also operated the ferry, remain at the site. You can see a historic photo collection in one of the cabins and purchase souvenirs in the store. | ¼ mi north of Moose on Teton Park Rd. | Free | Daily 8–5.

Jackson Historical Society and Museum. You'll find ranch equipment, tools used by mountain men, and black-and-white photos of Jackson Hole in the early 20th century inside this small museum. | 105 Mercill Ave. | 307/733–9605 | Free | Daily.

✦ ON THE CALENDAR: May–Sept. **The Shootout.** Gunslingers stage daily shootouts in the town square between Memorial Day and Labor Day. Don't worry, the bullets aren't real. | 307/733–3316 or 800/782–0011.

HISTORIC DINING AND LODGING

Jedediah's House of Sourdough. American. In this 1910 Jackson residence, which has been turned into a friendly, noisy, elbow-knocking restaurant, you can get your fill of "sourjacks" (sourdough flapjacks) and biscuits and gravy. Burgers are mountain-man size, and dinner may include trout, barbecue chicken, or steak. | 135 E. Broadway Ave. | 307/733–5671 | $10–$18 | No dinner late Sept.–early May | AE, D, MC, V.

Moulton Ranch Cabins. From 1896 to 1907 homesteaders claimed land north of Blacktail Butte, with a view of the Tetons to the west and the Gros Ventre Range to the north. Among them was T. A. Moulton, who along with his sons claimed a 160-acre homestead and built a barn for the family livestock. Photographers have made the distinctive pitch-roofed Moulton Barn, with the Tetons in the background, famous; you can see the image all over Jackson and Wyoming. Some of the Moultons still own a small portion of the homestead in Grand Teton National Park, and have converted a few old ranch buildings, including the granary and bunkhouse, into fully appointed cabins. Three have small kitchens, one has only a bed and night stand, and all have handmade quilts and curtains. Photos of the area, and ranch and recreation gear like ropes and fishing poles, decorate the walls. Some kitchens, hiking; no room phones, no room TVs, no smoking. | Grand Teton National Park, Mormon Row, off Antelope Flats Rd. 2 mi north of Moose, Kelly 83404 | 307/733–3749 or 208/529–2354 | fax 307/733–1664 or 208/523–3161 | www.srv.net/~iblake/moulton/ | 5 cabins | $75–$135 | Closed Oct.–late May | MC, V.

LANDER

▼▼

Frederick West Lander engineered the first government-financed road built in Wyoming when he laid out a route from South Pass to Fort Hall, Idaho, in 1857. The crew that built the Lander Road spent the winter of 1857–58 camped in the Wind River valley along the Popo Agie (pronounced *po-po-sha*) River, building the area's first permanent house. Ranchers claimed homesteads near the town beginning in the 1860s. At the southwestern edge of the Wind River Indian Reservation and in the heart of country held dear by Shoshone chief Washakie and his people, Lander has always had a strong tie with the Native American community. *Contact Lander Chamber of Commerce | 160 N. 1st St., 82520 | 307/332–3892 or 800/433–0662 | fax 307/332–3893 | www.landerchamber.org. Wind River Visitor's Council | Box 1449, Riverton 82520 | 307/856–7566 or 800/645–6233 | www.wind-river.org.*

Arapaho Cultural Center Museum and Heritage Center. Beadwork, crafts, and clothing made by Arapaho tribal members from the mid-19th century through contemporary times make up the bulk of this museum's collection. | Off Rte. 137, St. Stephens, 24 mi east of Lander on Rtes. 789 and 138 | 307/332–3040 | Free; donations accepted | Weekdays 1–5, Sat. 1–4.

Shoshone Tribal Cultural Center. Photographs of the two most famous Shoshone, Chief Washakie and Sacagawea; early Native American clothing and weapons; and treaty maps showing the borders of the reservation and Native American-controlled lands prior to reservations are among the items displayed here. A small gift shop sells authentic contemporary Shoshone crafts and beadwork. The town of Fort Washakie is 15 mi northwest of Lander on U.S. 287. | 31 Black Cove Rd., Fort Washakie | 307/332–9106 or 307/332–3040 | www.wyshs.org/mus-shoshone.htm | Free; donations accepted | Weekdays 9–4.

✦ ON THE CALENDAR: May.**Yellow Calf Memorial Powwow.** Native American traditional dancing is a part of this annual powwow in Ethete. | 307/856–7566 or 800/433–0662.

June–Aug. **Native American Cultural Program.** Dancing and storytelling take place each Monday at 7 PM in Lander Jaycee Park. | 307/856–7566 or 800/433–0662.

June **Shoshone Indian Days.** A parade, rodeo, buffalo barbecue, and entertainment are part of this festival held at Fort Washakie. | 307/856–7566 or 800/433–0662.

LARAMIE

▼▼▼

Overland travelers started migrating through the Laramie Valley—named for trapper Jacques La Ramee—in 1849, when Cherokees from Oklahoma made their way to the California gold fields over a route that extended across Oklahoma, Kansas, Colorado, southern Wyoming, Utah, and Nevada. The Union Pacific Railroad arrived in the Laramie Valley in 1867, and Laramie City quickly became a busy railroad division headquarters and then a ranching center, a status it retains. *Contact Laramie Chamber of Commerce | 800 S. 3rd St., 82070 | 307/745–7339 or 800/445–5303 | fax 307/745–4624 | www.laramie-tourism.org. Albany County Tourism Board | 800 S. 3rd St., 82070 | 307/745–4195 or 800/445–5303 | fax 307/721–2926 | www.laramie-tourism.org.*

Wyoming Territorial Park. Laramie became the site of the Wyoming Territorial Prison in 1872. Until 1903, the prison was the region's federal and state penal facility, locking down Butch Cassidy and other infamous frontier outlaws. The park contains the restored prison with the original cells, a replica frontier town, and a 19th-century railroad display. You can see living-history demonstrations or catch dinner and a show at the Horse Barn Dinner Theater. | 975 Snowy Range Rd. | 307/745–6161 or 800/845–2287 | www.wyoprisonpark.org | Park $12, dinner theater $29.95 combination ticket $35.95 | Park late May–early Sept., daily 9–6; dinner theater June–Aug., Wed.–Sun. 6 PM.

✦ ON THE CALENDAR: Sept. **American Heritage Center Fall Symposium.** A different topic, from the history of education to water rights in the early 20th century, is chosen for discussion each year in this lecture series at the American Heritage Center. | 307/766–4114.

PINEDALE

▼▼▼

Trappers found the icy streams of the Green River watershed to be among the best places to capture beaver and even better for holding a summer rendezvous during the fur trading era of 1825–43. They held seven such meetings near what is now Pinedale. A short-lived fort built here in 1832 officially was called Fort Bonneville, after Captain Benjamin Bonneville,

LET'S RENDEZVOUS

In 1825 Andrew Henry met and traded with beaver trappers on the Black Fork of the Green River in what came to be known as the first mountain man rendezvous. For the next 18 years, trappers and traders, along with Native Americans and even a few missionaries, gathered annually to trade goods. The trappers sold or exchanged the furs they'd harvested during the previous winter for goods the traders had, such as weapons, ammunition, food, clothing, and other supplies they would need for another year of trapping beaver.

Though the first rendezvous was a quiet affair and simply an opportunity to exchange beaver pelts (called plews) for supplies, subsequent gatherings were raucous, with a lot of whiskey. At least seven rendezvous took place on the Upper Green River near present-day Pinedale; two took place on the Wind River near present-day Riverton; and one small rendezvous convened near present-day Encampment, on "Potter's Fork," a stream that became the Grand Encampment River.

The fur trade petered out by 1843 because many streams had been nearly emptied of beaver, and beaver hats had gone out of style, but the era of the mountain man has not been forgotten. Each summer, present-day buckskinners load up their tepees, put on their skins, and take their black-powder guns to a rendezvous held at or near some of the historic sites: Pinedale, Riverton, Encampment, and Fort Bridger. There they have shooting contests, throw axes and frying pans, or barter with traders for skins, beads, pots, or kettles.

---

but folks more commonly referred to it as Fort Nonsense, because the harsh winters on the upper Green made it utter nonsense to maintain a year-round fort in the area. In the later 1800s, the Pinedale area was settled by ranchers. The town is the seat of Sublette County, which doesn't have a single stoplight. *Contact Pinedale Chamber of Commerce | 32 E. Pine St., Box 176, 82941 | 307/367–2242 | fax 307/367–6830 | www.pinedaleonline.com.*

Museum of the Mountain Man. One of the top museums in Wyoming, this facility depicts the trapper heritage of the area with 19th-century guns, traps, and beaver pelts, some owned by Jim Bridger himself. Livestock brands burned into wood planks, cowboy gear, and old photos of local ranches illustrate the pioneer and ranching history of Sublette County. | 700 E. Hennick Rd. | 307/367–4101 or 877/686–6266 | fax 307/367–6768 | www.museumofthemountainman. com | $4 | May–Sept., daily 10–5; call for winter hrs.

✦ ON THE CALENDAR: July **Green River Rendezvous.** Buckskinners gather for a rendezvous at the town rodeo grounds in commemoration of the get-togethers the fur trappers staged between 1825 and 1843. There's a parade, crafts booths, black-powder demonstrations, a historical pageant, and rodeo. | 307/367–4101.

RAWLINS

One of the original hell-on-wheels towns that sprang up in the path of the Union Pacific, Rawlins was an important transportation center as early as 1868. Miners heading for the gold fields at South Pass City rode the railroad to Rawlins or points nearby, then went overland to the gold diggings. The town became a large sheep-raising center in the late 1800s and early 1900s. *Contact Rawlins-Carbon County Chamber of Commerce | 519 W. Cedar St., Box 1331, 82301 | 307/324–4111 or 800/228–3547 | fax 307/324–5078 | www.oldwestfun.com.*

Carbon County Museum. Here and only here you can see a pair of shoes made from the skin of Big Nose George Parrott. Parrott was an outlaw who was lynched in 1881 after he attempted to escape from the county jail, where he was being held awaiting execution for his role in the murder of two law enforcement officers, the first officers to die in the line of duty in Wyoming. After his death Parrott's body was used for "medical study," and he was ultimately skinned (which is how they made the shoes). | 904 W. Walnut St. | 307/328–2740 | www.wyshs.org/mus-carboncty.htm | Free | Oct.–Apr., Mon., Wed., and Sat. 1–5; May–Sept., weekdays 10–noon and 1–5; tours by appointment.

Handcart Ranch. The Oregon-California-Mormon Trails cross this ranch, which is particularly important to the Mormons because two groups of pioneers traveling with handcarts to Salt Lake City became stranded in the area by snowstorms in 1856. You can push one of 100 handcarts up the trail to get a feel for this mode of transportation. The carts are loaned free, on a first-come, first-served basis, until 3:30 PM. The Martin's Cove Visitor Center is operated by the Church of Jesus Christ of Latter-day Saints and has exhibits on the Sun family ranching operation, which took place from 1872 until 1997. | U.S. 287, 60 mi northeast of Rawlins | 307/328–2953 | www.handcart.com | Free | Mon.–Sat. 8–7.

Independence Rock State Historic Site. The Oregon, California, and Mormon Trails converged at this turtle-shape granite monolith beside the Sweetwater River. Trail travelers from the 1830s onward carved their names into the rock, and you can still see many of the inscriptions as you walk around the rock, or if you climb up on top of it. You are asked by the State Parks commission not to mark the rock or change markings already there. | U.S. 287, 62 mi northeast of Rawlins | 307/577–5150 | http://wyoparks.state.wy.us/irock1.htm | Free | Daily.

HISTORIC DINING AND LODGING

The Pantry. American. Once the home of a prominent Rawlins sheepman, this 1881 Victorian home was converted into a restaurant in 1985. You dine in one of three rooms amid antiques. Prime rib, steak, halibut, and salmon are on the regular menu, while dinner specials may include lasagna. All breads and desserts are homemade. | 221 W. Cedar St. | 307/324–7860 | $9–$22 | D, MC, V.

SHERIDAN
▼▼▼

In the 1870s some of Wyoming's first large herds of cattle were turned loose in the Sheridan area, which became a power center as members of the British nobility established ranches here. In 1882 John Loucks took a sheet of wrapping paper and on it drew a layout of the town, naming it after General Philip Sheridan, one of the officers under whom Loucks had served in the Civil War. The first buildings—wood, with false fronts—gave way to brick and stone structures, many of which remain along Main Street. Sheridan's roots in agriculture and ranching extended through the 19th century and well into the 20th century. *Contact Sheridan Convention and Visitors Bureau | Box 7155, 82801 | 888/596–6787 | fax 307/ 672–7321 | www.sheridanwyoming.org. Sheridan Chamber of Commerce | Box 707, 82801 | 307/ 672–2485 or 800/453–3650 | fax 307/672–7321 | www.sheridanwyomingchamber.org.*

Bradford Brinton Memorial. On the site of the former Quarter Circle A Ranch, this home is a fine example of an old Wyoming ranch house. William and Malcolm Moncrieffe—relatives of Queen Elizabeth—established the ranch and house in 1892 and sold it to Bradfort Brinton in 1923. The Brinton family didn't exactly rough it in the 20-room clapboard home, complete with libraries, fine furniture, and silver and china services. A reception gallery presents changing exhibits from the Brinton art collection, which includes pieces by such famous western artists as Charles M. Russell and Frederic Remington. Other ranch buildings hold displays of late-19th- and early 20th-century equipment and household items, such as milk pails and butter churns. The ranch is 3 mi west of Bighorn and 10 mi west of Sheridan via Route 335. | 239 Brinton Rd., Bighorn | 307/672–3173 | www.bradfordbrintonmemorial. com | $3 | Mid-May–early Sept., daily 9:30–5.

Don King's Museum/King's Saddlery and Ropes. In their factory, the King family makes ropes for cowboys of all sizes and abilities, and behind the store and workshop is a free museum with a collection of cowboy memorabilia, including some of the best and oldest examples of saddles and tack in the region, assembled by Don King himself. | 307/672–2702 or 800/ 443–8919 | 184 N. Main St. | Free | Mon.–Sat. 8–5.

Medicine Wheel. The origin of the Medicine Wheel is unknown, but the site has always been sacred to Native Americans of different tribes, and many continue to make regular pilgrimages to the site. The wheel, made of rocks arranged in the shape of a hub and spokes, is protected by a wire fence. Access to the site is restricted to foot travel via a 1½-mi road, except for individuals with physical disabilities, who are allowed to drive in from the highway. From the site at the top of the mountain, you can see the entire Bighorn Basin. | 70 mi west of Sheridan on U.S. 14A | 307/672–0751 | Free | Daily.

Pryor Mountain National Wild Horse Range. Little more than 30,000 acres, this wild horse range is the first of its kind in the United States. A system of roads—accessible only by four-wheel-drive vehicles—circles the primary wilderness study area and allows you to view the horses, believed to be descendants of the first Spanish horses introduced to North America in the 1600s. Coat colors such as grulla, blue roan, dun, and sabino indicate Spanish lineage, as do markings such as a dorsal stripe, zebra stripes on the legs, and a stripe over the withers. | 113 mi west of Sheridan, via U.S. 14A west and Rte. 37 north | 307/548–7030 or 307/548–2706 | www.lovellchamber.com/wildhorses.html | Free | Daily.

✦ ON THE CALENDAR: June–Sept. **Equestrian Events.** In the 1880s aristocratic cattle barons built Wyoming's first polo field. You can attend polo games every Sunday afternoon and sometimes see cowboys roping steers on the grassy field to the west of the polo grounds. | 307/672–2485 or 800/453–3650.

HISTORIC DINING AND LODGING
Eaton's Guest Ranch. If you want to visit the oldest active dude ranch in the West, head for Eaton's. In the 1880s, the owners started charging their friends who came from the East to visit them, and the dude ranch is still going strong. West of Sheridan on the edge of the Bighorn National Forest, it offers horseback riding, fishing, cookouts, and pack trips. You stay in a log cabins and eat in the main lodge. All your meals are included. You can expect big breakfasts of eggs, meat, potatoes, and biscuits or pancakes; sandwich lunches; and chicken, beef, fish, or pasta dinners. There's a three- to seven-day minimum stay, depending on the season. The town of Wolf is 18 mi west of Sheridan. Dining room, pool, fishing, hiking, horseback riding; no room TVs. | 270 Eaton's Ranch Rd., Wolf 82844 | 307/655–9285 or 800/210– 1049 | fax 307/655–9269 | www.eatonsranch.com | 51 cabins | $165 per person | Closed Oct.– May | D, MC, V | FAP.

Sheridan Inn. American. Buffalo Bill Cody once auditioned cowboys for his Wild West Show while sitting on the porch of this 1893 inn. There's no lodging, but you can still enjoy a good steak or chicken dinner inside. A graceful covered porch fronts the building, and 69 gables sprout all along the roof. On the National Register of Historic Places, the Sheridan lured the likes of Herbert Hoover, Will Rogers, and Ernest Hemingway. Cowboys no longer ride their horses into the bar. | 856 Broadway | 307/674–5440 | $12–$20 | AE, D, MC, V.

THERMOPOLIS

▼▼

The hot mineral springs and surrounding land in this area were considered neutral territory by the Native Americans—particularly the Shoshone, who ceded the ground to the government in 1896 in a "gift of the waters." The Shoshone presented the land with the stipulation that the springs should remain available for the free use of all people, which is still the case at the state bath house, though not at the now-private pools. With the departure of Native Americans to reservations, Thermopolis was settled by ranchers and incorporated in 1897. *Contact Thermopolis Chamber of Commerce | Box 768, 82443 | 307/864–3192 | fax 307/864–3192 | www.thermopolis.com.*

Hot Springs State Park. This park is on land that area Native Americans considered sacred ground because of its "healing waters." You can hike and bike on the trails, watch a buffalo herd, and soak indoors or out at the free hot mineral pools at the Wyoming State Bathhouse. There are also commercial swimming facilities ($8) in the park. | U.S. 20 | 307/864–2176 or 307/864–3765 | fax 307/864–3419 | http://wyoparks.state.wy.us/hot.htm | Free.

✦ ON THE CALENDAR: Aug. **Gift of the Waters Pageant.** The program, held in Hot Springs State Park, is a re-creation of Shoshone chief Washakie's ceding the land around the mineral springs to the federal government. | 307/864–3192.

Aug. **Outlaw Trail Ride.** Cowboys and cowgirls saddle up for a multiday ride into "outlaw country"—Hole-in-the-Wall—on a 100-mi, one-week trip. The cost is $650 per person if you bring your own horse, or you can lease one at an extra charge. | 307/864–2367 or 877/807–2367.

YELLOWSTONE NATIONAL PARK

▼▼

The remote region now encompassed by Yellowstone National Park was inhabited by humans as long as 10,000 years ago. By the time Euro-Americans arrived on the scene, the Shoshone were the predominant people of the area, though the harshness of the climate and landscape kept their numbers few. John Colter, formerly of the Lewis and Clark expedition, was the first white visitor to Yellowstone, in 1807–08. Trappers such as Jim Bridger followed, and reports of northwestern Wyoming's wonders began to make their way into print. Many of these were dismissed as being too fantastic to be true. Prospectors had a go at Yellowstone starting in the 1870s, but it proved far richer in scenic wonders than in precious metals. At the same time, Ferdinand V. Hayden of the U.S. Geological Survey led an official expedition of scientists, along with painter Thomas Moran and photographer William H. Jackson, into the area. The beauty depicted in Moran's watercolors and Jackson's photographs, and the findings detailed in Hayden's report to Congress, were so impressive that they inspired a movement to protect the wilderness of northwestern Wyoming. Yellowstone became the world's first national park in 1872. Some of the first people to visit the American West as tourists were attracted by Yellowstone, and the federal government learned its earliest lessons in national park management there. *Contact Yellowstone National Park | Box 168, Mammoth, 82190 | 307/344–7381 | fax 307/344–2005 | www.nps.gov/yell.*

Fort Yellowstone. In 1886, following 14 years of poor civilian management of Yellowstone National Park, the Cavalry was called in to take over. Thinking they would be there only a short time, the troops initially established Camp Sheridan, near the base of the Mammoth Terraces. Later they built Fort Yellowstone in the Mammoth area. You can still visit the original red-roofed buildings, which now serve as park offices and a visitor center. | North entrance, Mammoth area, 5 mi south of Gardiner, MT | 307/344–7381 | www.nps.gov/yell | Free | Daily.

HISTORIC DINING AND LODGING

Lake Yellowstone Hotel. When it opened in 1891, the Lake Yellowstone Hotel was typical of the hotels built by railroad companies for their passengers. Backed by the Northern Pacific Railroad, the hotel stood on the north end of Yellowstone Lake, where Indians and mountain men were known to have gathered for many years. A 1903 renovation gussied up the place with Ionic columns, balconies, and huge picture windows overlooking the lake. In the lobby of the pale yellow hotel, afternoon chamber music provides a refreshing reminder of old-style luxury tourism in the wilderness. Rooms have brass beds and solid pine furniture. In the large and simple dining room ($12–$30; reservations essential), try the prime rib prepared in a marinade of thyme, rosemary, and garlic. Restaurant, some in-room data ports, lake, boating, fishing, hiking, bar, lounge, piano, meeting rooms; no-smoking rooms, no room TVs. | Lake Village, off Grand Loop Rd. | 307/344–7311 | fax 307/344–7456 | www.travelyellowstone.com | 162 rooms, 1 suite | $165–$175 rooms, $412 suite | Closed Oct.–mid-May | AE, D, DC, MC, V.

Old Faithful Inn. Built on the former site of an earlier lodging called "The Shack," Old Faithful Inn was designed to reflect its natural surroundings. Around 40 workers, most of them railroad trestle builders, raised the hotel in the winter of 1903–1904. The rhyolite stone and tall, straight lodgepole pines used to construct the hotel were taken from the surrounding land, and trees twisted by disease became the ornamental railings and details of the interior. When completed, the 140-room inn became the standard by which future national parks lodges would be judged. It was expanded in 1915 and 1927 to its present size. Today you can lounge in front of the massive stone fireplace beneath the lobby's 65-ft ceiling, and look up at balconies that seem to disappear into the night sky. On those deep balconies you can play cards, scribble at a writing desk, or just relax above the hubbub. More expensive rooms face the Old Faithful geyser, but the rough wood-paneled rooms—which have sinks but no bathroom facilities (they're down the hall)—in the original building will take you back in time. The cavernous, rustic dining room ($11–$23, reservations essential) serves up inventive American fare. Restaurant, some in-room data ports, hiking, bar, piano; no-smoking rooms, no room TVs. | Grand Loop Rd. | 307/344–7311 | fax 307/344–7456 | www.travelyellowstone. com | 318 rooms, 79 with shared bath, 9 suites | $72 rooms without bath; $97–$172 rooms with bath; $351 suite | Closed mid-Oct.–early May | AE, D, DC, MC, V.

RESOURCES

The Old West

HISTORICAL AND TOURISM ORGANIZATIONS

Center of the American West. | University of Colorado, Campus Box 234, Boulder, CO 90309 | 303/492–4879 | fax 303/492–1671 | www.centerwest.org.

Chinese Historical Society of America. | 965 Clay St., San Francisco, CA 94108 | 415/391–1188 | www.chsa.org.

Lewis and Clark Heritage Trail Foundation. | Box 3434, Great Falls, MT 59403 | 888/701–3434 or 406/454–1234 | fax 406/771–9237 | www.lewisandclark.org.

National Cowboy Museum and Heritage Center. | 1700 N.E. 63rd St., Oklahoma City, OK 73111 | 405/478–2250 | fax 405/478–4714 | www.cowboyhalloffame.org.

National Pony Express Association. | Box 236, Pollock Pines, CA 95726 | www.xphomestation.com/frm-npea.html.

National Trust for Historic Preservation. | 1785 Massachusetts Ave. NW, Washington, DC 20036 | 202/588–6000 | www.nationaltrust.org.

Oregon-California Trails Association. | Box 1019, Independence, MO 64051–0519 | 888/811–6282 | octahqts@gvi.net.

Santa Fe Trails Association. | Santa Fe Trail Center, Rte. 3, Larned, KS 67550 | 620/285–2054 | fax 620/285–7491 | www.santafetrail.org.

Thomas Gilcrease Institute. | 1400 N. 25th, Tulsa, OK 74127 | 918/581–5311.

HISTORY TOURS AND PACKAGES

Elderhostel Adventures in Lifelong Learning. | 11 Ave. de Lafayette, Boston, MA 02111–1746 | 877/426–8056 | fax 617/426–0701 | www.elderhostel.org | 55-plus age group only.

Gadabout Tours. | 700 E. Tahquitz Canyon Way, Palm Springs, CA 92202 | 800/952–5068 or 760/325–5556 | fax 760/325–5127 | www.gadabouttours.com.

History America Tours. Join other history buffs on five-day to two-week tours with themes such as Historic Texas, Lewis and Clark, War on the Central Plains, and Trail of Tears. | Box 797687, Dallas, TX 75379 | 800/628–8542 or 972/713–7171 | fax 972/713–7173 | www.historyamerica.com.

Shebby Lee Tours. The operator specializes in Vanishing Trails expeditions, including a 15-night Lewis and Clark Trail tour that thoroughly covers the entire historic route. | Box 1032, Rapid City, SD 57709 | 800/888–8306 | fax 605/343–7558 | www.shebbyleetours.com.

Smithsonian Study Tours. | Box 23293, Washington, DC 20026–3293 | 877/338–8687 or 202/357–4700 | www.smithsonianstudytours.org.

Traveling America. This partner of the National Trust for Historic Preservation creates themed driving tours, including accommodations, customized maps, and tickets to attractions. | www.travelingamerica.com.

FURTHER READING

Ambrose, Stephen. *Undaunted Courage.* New York: Simon and Schuster, 1996.

Atherton, Lewis. *The Cattle Kings.* Lincoln: University of Nebraska Press, 1961.

Beckham, Steven Dow. *Lewis and Clark in Oregon Country: From the Rockies to the Pacific.* Traces the western portion of the famous duo's trail. Portland, OR: Graphic Arts Center, 2002.

Bird, Isabella. *A Lady's Life in the Rocky Mountains.* Sausalito: Comstock, 1960.

Boatman, Mary Ann, Willis Boatman, and Weldon Willis Rau. *Surviving the Oregon Trail, 1852.* Personal accounts of overland travelers to the Northwest. Seattle: University of Washington Press, 2001.

Brown, Dee. *The Gentle Tamers.* New York: Bantam, 1958.

Butruille, Susan G. *Women's Voices from the Oregon Trail: The Times That Tried Women's Souls and a Guide to Women's History Along the Oregon Trail.* Tackles life on the trail from a woman's point of view. Boise, ID: Tamarack Books, 1994.

Coffman, Lloyd W. *Blazing a Wagon Trail to Oregon: A Weekly Chronicle of the Great*

Migration of 1843. This step-by-step account highlights the smaller trials and tribulations along the journey west. Enterprise, OR: Echo Books, 1993.

Dary, David. *Buffalo Book: Full Saga of the American Animal.* Athens, OH: Swallow Press/University of Ohio Press, 1989.

De Voto, Bernard. *The Year of Decision, 1846.* Boston: Houghton Mifflin, Sentry Books, 1943.

Doerper, John. *Compass American Guides: Pacific Northwest,* 3rd ed. New York: Fodor's Travel Publications, 2002.

Drago, Harry Sinclair. *The Great Range Wars: Violence on the Grasslands.* Lincoln: University of Nebraska Press, Bison Books, 1985.

Dykstra, Robert. *The Cattle Towns.* New York: Knopf, 1968.

Emsden, Katharine N., ed. *Voices from the West: Life Along the Trail.* Various accounts of the hardy souls who braved the Oregon Trail. Carlisle, MA: Discovery Enterprises Ltd., 1997.

Fanselow, Julie. *The Traveler's Guide to the Oregon Trail.* A modern-day guide to the trail's most famous and worthy sights. Tempe, AZ: Falcon Press, 1992.

Fifer, Barbara. *Going Along with Lewis and Clark.* This kids' guide to the Lewis and Clark Trail offers lively discussions of harrowing adventures and is illustrated with historic photos and spirited art. Helena, MT: Farcountry Press, 2000.

___ **and Vicky Soderberg.** *Along the Trail with Lewis and Clark.* Historical highlights of the Corps of Discovery expedition's encounters include listings for current parks, camp-grounds, and recreational opportunities. Helena, MT: Farcountry Press, 2001.

Franzwa, Gregory M. *Maps of the Oregon Trail.* Handy guide to visiting the pioneer road. Tucson: The Patrice Press, 1990.

___. *The Oregon Trail Revisited.* Another look at attractions along the trail. Tucson: The Patrice Press, 1978.

Haines, Aubrey. *Historic Sites Along the Oregon Trail.* A comprehensive guide to historic markers, buildings, camps, and settlements. St. Louis, MO, 1981.

Haines, Francis. *The Buffalo: The Story of American Bison and Their Hunters from Prehistoric Times to the Present.* Norman: University of Oklahoma, 1970.

Hill, William E. *The Oregon Trail: Yesterday and Today.* Comparisons of how the trail has changed and been preserved since its original days. Caldwell: Caxton Printers, Ltd., 1989.

Holmes, Kenneth L., ed. *Covered Wagon Women: Diaries and Letters from the Western Trails.* The travails and celebrations of women who joined their families on the migration west. Lincoln: University of Nebraska Press, 1995.

Hutton, Paul Andrew. *Phil Sheridan and His Army.* Lincoln: University of Nebraska, 1985.

Josephy, Alvin. *500 Nations: An Illustrated History of North American Indians.* New York: Knopf, 1994.

Lavender, David. *The Santa Fe Trail.* New York: Holiday House, 1995.

___. *The Way to the Western Sea: Lewis and Clark Across the Continent.* Lincoln: University of Nebraska Press, 2001.

___. *Westward Vision: The Story of the Oregon Trail.* A detailed account of the history of the Oregon Trail. Lincoln: University of Nebraska Press, 1985.

Luchetti, Cathy, and Carol Olwell. *Women of the West.* New York: Orion Books, 1982.

Masterson, Martha Gay. *One Woman's West: Recollections of the Oregon Trail and Settling of the Northwest Country.* A colorful collection of memories specific to pioneer life in the Northwest. Eugene: Spencer Butte Press, 1990.

Mattes, Merrill. *The Great Platte River Road.* Lincoln: University of Nebraska Press, 1987.

Moeller, Bill, and Jan. *The Oregon Trail: A Photographic Journey.* Stunning, evocative photos capture the landscape. Missoula, MT: Mountain Press Publishing Co., 1999.

Moulton, Candy, and Ben Kern. *Wagon Wheels: A Contemporary Journey on the Oregon Trail.* A modern story of traveling the pioneer route. Glendo: High Plains Press, 1996.

Ronda, James P. *Lewis and Clark among the Indians.* Lincoln: University of Nebraska Press, Bison Books, 1988.

Sandoz, Mari. *Love Song to the Plains.* Lincoln: University of Nebraska Press, Bison Books, 1966.

Schlissel, Lillian. *Women's Diaries of the Westward Migration.* New York: Schocken Books, 1982.

Slatta, Richard W. *Comparing Cowboys and Frontiers.* Norman: University of Oklahoma Press, 1997.

Twain, Mark. *Roughing It.* Samuel Clemens' detailed and hilarious accounts of life in the Sierra foothills and in Nevada at the time of the gold rush in the early 1860s. New York: New American Library, 1994.

Unruh, John D., Jr. *The Plains Across: The Overland Emigrants and the Trans-Mississippi West, 1840–60.* A sweeping saga of how the pioneers traveled across the U.S. to reach the Northwest. Urbana: University of Illinois Press, 1993.

Utley, Robert M. *Frontier Regulars: The United States Army and the Indian, 1866–1891.* New York: McMillan, 1973.

___. *Frontiersmen in Blue: The United States Army and the Indian, 1848–1865.* Lincoln: University of Nebraska Press, 1981.

___. *The Indian Frontier of the American West.* Albuquerque: University of New Mexico, 1984.

Walker, Dale. *Pacific Destiny: The Three Century Journey to the Oregon Country.* New York: Forge Books, 2000.

Ward, Geoffrey. *The West.* Boston: Little, Brown, and Company, 1996.

Webb, Walter Prescott. *The Great Plains.* Boston: Ginn and Company, 1931.

Zimmerman, Nancy, ed. *Compass American Guides: The Southwest,* 3rd ed. New York: Fodor's Travel Publications, 2000.

Arizona

HISTORICAL AND TOURISM ORGANIZATIONS

Arizona Historical Society Central Arizona Division. | 1300 N. College Ave., Tempe 85281 | 480/929–0292 | fax 480/967–5450 | community.tempe.gov/ahs/frames.htm.

Arizona Historical Society Northern Arizona Division. | 2340 N. Fort Valley Rd., Flagstaff 86001 | 928/774–6272 | fax 928/774–1596 | www.infomagic.net/~ahsnad/index.html.

Arizona Historical Society Southern Arizona Division. | 949 E. 2nd St., Tucson 85719 | 520/628–5774 | fax 520/628–5695 | w3.arizona.edu/~azhist/museum.htm.

Arizona Office of Tourism. | 1110 W. Washington St., Suite 155, Phoenix 85007 | 602/364–3700 | fax 602/364–3701 | www.arizonaguide.com.

Arizona State Parks. | 1300 W. Washington St., Phoenix 85007 | 602/542–4174 | fax 602/542–4188 | www.azstateparks.com.

HISTORY TOURS AND PACKAGES

Kino Mission Tours. Professional historians take groups on three-day tours of Spanish colonial churches in Sonora (Mexico) and Arizona, which were originally founded by the Jesuit missionary Father Eusebio Francisco Kino in the late 17th and early 18th centuries. | Box 27823, Tucson 85726 | 520/628–1269 | www.smrc-missiontours.com.

FURTHER READING

Banks, Leo W., et al. *Days of Destiny: 20 Stories of Desperados and Lawmen and How Fate Changed Their Lives.* Vol. 1 in the Wild West Series. This collection chronicles the lives of some of the most colorful characters in the Old West. Phoenix: Arizona Highways Book Division, 1996.

___. *Manhunts and Massacres.* Vol. 2 in the Wild West Series. History writers tell the stories of Arizona's violent frontier. Phoenix: Arizona Highways Book Division, 1997.

___. *They Left Their Mark: Heroes and Rogues of Arizona History.* These are the stories of 16 individuals who have molded Arizona since the mid-16th century. Phoenix: Arizona Highways Book Division, 1997.

Bruns, Roger A. *Desert Honkeytonk: The Story of Tombstone's Bird Cage Theatre.* The story of the "wickedest night spot between Basin Street and the Barbary Coast" and the colorful characters that passed through its doors. Golden: Fulcrum Publishing, 2000.

Cheek, Lawrence W. *Compass American Guides: Arizona,* 5th ed. New York: Fodor's Travel Publications, 1999.

Goff, John S. *Arizona: An Illustrated History of the Grand Canyon State.* The colorful characters and legendary landscapes of the Old West come to life in words, drawings, and historic photographs. Northridge: Windsor Publications, 1988.

Hartmann, William K. *Desert Heart: Chronicles of the Sonoran Desert.* Photographic essays, historic writings, and little-known stories convey the cultural and natural history of the Sonoran Desert in this oversize book. Tucson: Fisher Books, 1989.

Lauer, Charles D. *Tales of Arizona Territory.* Stories of the ranchers, Indians, wagon trains, and outlaws of Arizona's frontier days. Phoenix: Golden West Publishers, 1995.

Schieffelin, Edward. *Destination Tombstone: Adventures of a Prospector.* The biography draws from the handwritten memoirs of Edward Schieffelin, who founded Tombstone in 1877. Mesa: Royal Spectrum Publishing, 1996.

Sheridan, Thomas E. *Arizona . . . A History.* This volume chronicles human history in Arizona, from the arrival of prehistoric Paleolithic hunters to the urbanization of Phoenix and Tucson after World War II. Tucson: University of Arizona Press, 1995.

Trimble, Marshall. *Roadside History of Arizona.* Take a spin along Arizona's thoroughfares in this volume of historic driving tours. Missoula, MT: Mountain Press Publishing Co., 1986.

California

HISTORICAL AND TOURISM ORGANIZATIONS

California Historical Society. | 678 Mission St., San Francisco 94105 | 415/357–1848 | www.californiahistoricalsociety.org.

California Mission Studies Association. | Box 3357, Bakersfield 93385 | www.ca-missions.org.

California State Archives. | 1020 O St., Sacramento 95814 | 916/653–7715 general information; 916/653–2246 reference desk | www.ss.ca.gov/archives/archives.htm or www.learncalifornia.org.

California Tourism. | 1102 Q St., Suite 6000, Sacramento, 95814 | 916/322–2881 | fax 916/322–3402 | www.visitcalifornia.com.

Historical Society of Southern California. | 200 E. Ave. 43, Los Angeles 90031 | 323/222–0546 | www.socalhistory.org.

Society of California Pioneers. | 300 4th St., San Francisco 94107 | 415/957–1849 | www.californiapioneers.org.

FURTHER READING

Austin, Mary. *Land of Little Rain.* In her 1903 classic, Austin offers a detailed account of the terrain between Death Valley and the High Sierra. Bedford, MA: Applewood Books, 2000.

Barker, Malcolm E. *San Francisco Memoirs, 1835–1851: Eyewitness Accounts of the Birth of a City.* Letters and journals give first-hand accounts of people visiting or living in San Francisco between 1835 and 1851. San Francisco: Londonborn Publications, 1994.

Brechin, Gray. *Imperial San Francisco: Urban Power, Earthly Ruin.* A mix of history, geography, and cultural criticism, this book shows how San Francisco became the center of a mining and agriculture empire. Berkeley: University of California Press, 1999.

Brewer, William. *Up and Down California in 1860–1864.* The journals of a 19th-century professor make an excellent source of pioneer California history. Berkeley: University of California Press, 1975.

Caughee, John, and LaRee. *Los Angeles: Biography of a City.* More than 100 essays from the past 200 years tell the story of how Los Angeles came to be. Berkeley: University of California Press, 1977.

Dana, Richard Henry, Jr. *Two Years Before the Mast.* Based on the author's 1834 experiences as a merchant sailor, the text provides his perspective on early San Diego history and the hardships of the mariner's life. New York: Signet Classic, 2002.

Doerper, John. *Compass American Guides: Coastal California,* 2nd ed. New York: Fodor's Travel Publications, 2000.

___. *Compass American Guides: Wine Country,* 3rd ed. New York: Fodor's Travel Publications, 2000.

Fogelson, Robert M., and Robert Fishman. *The Fragmented Metropolis: Los Angeles, 1850–1930.* An excellent primer on Los Angeles shows how the city grew from dusty outpost to budding megalopolis. Berkeley: University of California Press, 1993.

Harte, Bret. *The Luck of Roaring Camp and Other Sketches.* Essays and stories by a luminary of 19th-century literature evoke life during the gold rush. New York: Penguin Classics, 2001.

Holliday, J. S. *The World Rushed In: The California Gold Rush Experience.* New York: Simon and Schuster, 1981.

Jackson, Helen Hunt. *Ramona.* The 19th-century romantic novel, a steady seller for decades and still in print, sets the mood for a visit to Old Town San Diego. New York: Signet Classic, 2002.

Mullen, Frank. *The Donner Party Chronicles: A Day-by-Day Account of a Doomed Wagon Train,* 1846–47. This narrative of the ill-fated journey is filled with the intimate details of daily pioneer life. Reno: Nevada Humanities Committee, 1997.

Parr, Barry. *Compass American Guides: San Francisco,* 5th ed. New York: Fodor's Travel Publications, 1999.

Pittman, Ruth. *Roadside History of California.* A good general history of the state, this volume is organized by major roads. Missoula, MT: Mountain Press Publishing Co., 1996.

Steinbeck, John. *East of Eden.* Steinbeck's Nobel prize–winning novel of fraternal good and evil vividly describes the landscape and culture of the Salinas Valley at the turn of the 20th century. New York: Penguin Books, 1992.

Stewart, George Rippey. *Ordeal by Hunger.* Though newer works contradict some of the details in this 50-year-old telling of the Donner Party saga, this text has long been considered the definitive work on the topic. Boston: Houghton Mifflin, 1992.

Walker, Dale. *Bear Flag Rising.* New York: Forge Books, 2001.

Colorado

HISTORICAL AND TOURISM ORGANIZATIONS

Colorado Historical Society. | 1300 Broadway, Denver 80203 | 303/866–3682 | www.coloradohistory.org.

Colorado Tourism Office. | 1625 Broadway, Suite 1700, Denver 80202 | 800/COLORADO or 303/892–3885 | www.colorado.com.

HISTORY TOURS AND PACKAGES

Colorado Sightseer. Destinations on half- and full-day guided bus tours include historic Denver, gold-mining towns, Pike's Peak, and Buffalo Bill's Grave. | 6780 W. 84th Cir., Suite 60, Arvada 80003 | 303/423–8200 or 800/255–5105 | fax 303/423–9750 | www.coloradosightseer.com.

Gray Line of Denver. Gray Line Tours offers bus tours out of Denver and Colorado Springs. Denver-based tours include one to the Georgetown Loop Railroad and Idaho Springs. The Colorado Springs branch offers a half-day Pike's Peak tour. | Box 17527, Denver 80217 | 303/286–7052 or 800/348–6877 | www.coloradograyline.com.

Gray Line of Colorado Springs. | 3704 W. Colorado Ave., Colorado Springs 80904 | 719/633–9643 or 800/348–6877 | www.coloradograyline.com.

FURTHER READING

Collier, Joseph, and Grant. *Colorado: Yesterday and Today.* A photographic history that brings together images by 19th-century photographer Joseph Collier with retakes by his great-great-grandson, Grant Collier. Montrose, CO: Western Reflections, 2001.

Danilov, Victor J. *Colorado Museums and Historic Sites.* An extensive and invaluable guide to the state's historic sites and institutions, large and small. Boulder: University Press of Colorado, 2000.

Eberhart, Perry. *Ghosts of the Colorado Plains.* Focusing on the state's often overlooked eastern plains, this book explores the region's rich pioneer history. Athens, OH: Ohio University Press, 1996.

Fay, Abbott. *I Never Knew That About Colorado: A Quaint Volume of Forgotten Lore.* A collection of odd historical anecdotes. Montrose, CO: Western Reflections, 1997.

Jackson, William Henry, John Fielder, et al. *Colorado, 1870–2000.* Fielder re-photographs images first taken by Jackson in the early days of Colorado statehood. Photos are accompanied by essays from noted historians and environmental writers. Englewood, CO: Westcliffe Publishing, 1999.

Jocknick, Sidney. *Early Days on the Western Slope of Colorado.* Written in 1913 by a former prospector, rancher, farmer, and Indian Agency cook, this book is the definitive first-hand account of pioneer days on the western slope of the Rockies. Montrose, CO: Western Reflections, 1998.

Klusmire, Jon. *Compass American Guides: Colorado,* 6th ed. New York: Fodor's Travel Publications, 2002.

Michener, James A. *Centennial.* Historical fiction that offers great insight into the lives of the early trappers, traders, Indians, ranchers, miners, and even animals of Colorado. New York: Fawcett Books, 1994.

Noel, Thomas J., Paul F. Mahoney, and Richard E. Stevens. *Historical Atlas of Colorado.* The reference book includes numerous maps and essays covering all major topics of Colorado history. Norman: University of Oklahoma Press, 1994.

Ubbelohde, Carl, et al. *A Colorado History.* A competent and complete record of the state from pre-history to present. Boulder: Pruett Publishing Co., 2001.

Varney, Philip. *Ghost Towns of Colorado: Your Guide to Colorado's Historic Mining Camps and Ghost Towns.* A detailed guide to 90 mining camps and ghost towns with extensive maps, color photos, driving directions, and brief histories. Stillwater, MN: Voyageur Press, 1999.

Wolle, Muriel Sibell. *Stampede to Timberline: The Ghost Towns and Mining Camps of Colorado.* This nearly 600-page book provides an exhaustive history of 240 Colorado mining camps and includes sketches drawn on-site by the author. Athens, OH: Swallow Press/University of Ohio Press, 1991.

Idaho

HISTORICAL AND TOURISM ORGANIZATIONS

Idaho Division of Tourism. | 700 W. State St., Dept. C, Boise 83720 | 208/334–2470 or 800/635–7820 | www.visitid.orget.

Idaho Historical Society. | 450 N. 4th St., Boise 83702 | 208/334–3356 | fax 208/334–3198 | www.idahohistory.net.

Nez Perce Indian Tribe. | Box 365, Lapwai 83540 | 208/843–2253 | fax 208/843–7354 | www.nezperce.org.

Nez Perce National Historical Trail Foundation. | Box 1939, Lewiston 83501 | 435/655–3210 or 760/776–7608 | fax 435/655–3210 | www.fs.fed.us/npnht.

Shoshone-Bannock Indian Tribe. | Box 368, Fort Hall 83209 | 208/237–8433 or 800/806–9229 | www.sho-ban.com.

HISTORY TOURS AND PACKAGES

Clearwater Connections "Clarkie Express" Motorcoach. Explore Lewis and Clark expedition trails, river crossings, and campsites on a 24-passenger motorcoach. Tours run one to five days. | Lewiston | 208/926–7875 | www.lewisclarkidaho.com.

Independent Outfitters of Idaho. This is an organization of outfitters and guides who offer a variety of trips, from river excursions to Lewis and Clark treks to horse-packing outings. | Box 95, Boise 83701 | 800/494–9746 | www.ioga.org.

Triple "O" Outfitters. To relive part of Lewis and Clark's journey, take the seven-day horseback and hiking trip offered by this outfitter. You'll camp at some of the explorers' resting places. | Box 217, Pierce 83546 | 208/464–2349 | www.tripleo-outfitters.com.

FURTHER READING

Arrington, Leonard. *History of Idaho,* 2 vols. This is the best overall history of the state. Moscow: University of Idaho Press, 1995.

Conley, Cort. *Idaho for the Curious.* This book has details about everything in Idaho, but watch some of the directions, as they are incorrect. Cambridge, ID: Backeddy Books, 1982.

Derig, Betty. *Roadside History of Idaho.* Having this book along on your travels through Idaho is like having an expert historian and storyteller in your back seat. Missoula, MT: Mountain Press Publishing Co., 1996.

Gottberg, John. *Compass American Guides: Idaho,* 2nd ed. New York: Fodor's Travel Publications, 2001.

Robertson, R. G. *Idaho Echoes in Time.* A good reference book by a top writer and researcher. Caldwell, ID: Tamarack Books, 1998.

Kansas

HISTORICAL AND TOURISM ORGANIZATIONS

Kansas Department of Commerce and Housing, Department of Travel and Tourism. | 800/252–6727 | www.travelks.org.

Kansas Heritage Center. | 1000 N. 2nd Ave., Dodge City 67801 | 620/227–1616 | fax 620/227–1701 | www.ksheritage.org.

Kansas State Historical Society. | 6425 S.W. 6th Ave., Topeka 66615 | 785/272–8681 | fax 785/272–8682 | www.kshs.org.

HISTORY TOURS AND PACKAGES

Kansas Explorers Club. This organization seeks to inspire and educate people about Kansas and to encourage the exploration and appreciation of the state. The group sponsors periodic tours of different areas. | 978 Arapaho Rd., Inman 67546 | 620/585–2374 | fax 620/585–2217 | explorekansas.org.

FURTHER READING

Barry, Louise. *The Beginning of the West: Annals of the Kansas Gateway to the American West, 1540–1854.* Barry chronicles the Old West from the first European contact to the beginning of settlement. Topeka: Kansas State Historical Society, 1972.

Miller, Nyle H., and Joseph W. Snell. *Great Gunfighters of the Kansas Cowtowns, 1867–1886.* Lincoln: University of Nebraska Press, 1963.

___ **and Joseph W. Snell.** *Why the West Was Wild: A Contemporary Look at the Antics of Some Highly Publicized Kansas Cowtown Personalities.* This volume provides a fine look at some of Kansas's famous and infamous characters, such as John Brown, Buffalo Bill Cody, Wyatt Earp, Wild Bill Hickok, and Doc Holliday. Topeka: Kansas State Historical Society, 1963.

Miner, Craig. *Kansas: The History of the Sunflower State.* An updated textbook view of the state's history. Lawrence: University Press of Kansas, 2002.

Richmond, Robert W. *Kansas: A Land of Contrasts.* Richmond's volume is considered a standard general history of the state, from Native American habitation through the 1970s. St. Charles, MO: Forum Press, 1974.

Webb, Dave. *399 Kansas Characters.* A brief but good who's who of Kansas's colorful past. Dodge City: Kansas Heritage Center, 1992.

Zornow, William Frank. *Kansas: A History of the Jayhawk State.* A good standard text of the history of the state, though somewhat dated, as it has not been revised since the publication date. Norman: University of Oklahoma Press, 1957.

Montana

HISTORICAL AND TOURISM ORGANIZATIONS

Glacier Country. | Box 1035, Bigfork, 59900–1035 | 406/837–6211 or 800/338–5072 | www.glacier.visitmt.com.

Gold West Country. | 1155 Main St., Deer Lodge 59722 | 406/846–1943 or 800/879–1159 | www.goldwest.visitmt.com.

Montana Historical Society. | 225 N. Roberts, Helena 59620 | 406/444–2694 or 800/243–9900 | www.montanahistoricalsociety.org.

Russell Country. | Box 3166, Great Falls 59403 | 406/761–5036 or 800/527–5348 | www.russell.visitmt.com.

Travel Montana. | Box 200533, Helena 59620–0533 | 406/444–2654 or 800/847–4868 | www.visitmt.com.

Yellowstone Country. | 1822 W. Lincoln, Bozeman 59715 | 406/556–8680 or 800/736–5276 | www.yellowstone.visitmt.com.

HISTORY TOURS AND PACKAGES

Blackfeet Historical Sites. Minibus tours by former Tribal Cultural Officer Curly Bear Wagner go to several Blackfeet Nation history and heritage sites, including the Fight Site where Meriwether Lewis met the Blackfeet, the Lewis and Clark Trail Interpretive Center, buffalo jumps, and sacred sites. Half- and full-day tours and custom trips up to 14 days are available year-round. | Box 2038, Browning 59417 | 317/443–1450 or 406/338–2058 | fax 406/338–2084 | www.curlybear.org.

Montana Rockies Rail Tours. Tours operate along 500 mi of tracks of the original Northern Pacific Railroad from Livingston. Three- to seven-day rail and motorcoach tours cover Lewis and Clark routes, national parks, and scenic landscapes. Westbound trips begin in Bozeman, Livingston, and Billings. | 1055 Baldy Park Ave., Sandpoint, ID 83864 | 208/265–8618 or 800/519–7245 | fax 208/265–8619 | www.montanarailtours.com.

Swan River Tours. This tour operator specializes in bus tours to Montana ghost towns, historical mining towns, national parks, and Lewis and Clark sites. Tours start at $280 per day and include vehicle, entrance fees, interpretation, lodging, some meals, and more. | Box 1010, Condon 59826 | 406/754–2540 or 877/696–1666 | fax 406/754–2538 | www.swanrivertours.com.

FURTHER READING

Lucey, Donna. *Photographing Montana 1894–1928, The Life and Work of Evelyn Cameron.* Superb black-and-white photos of the eastern Montana ranching frontier, accompanied by anecdotal text. Helena, MT: Farcountry Press, 2001.

Malone, Michael, and Richard Roeder. *Montana: A History of Two Centuries*. Required reading for most Montana history courses, this definitive volume is at time dense yet fully views the state's vibrant history. Seattle: University of Washington Press, 1991.

Spritzer, Don. *Roadside History of Montana*. This academic and anecdotal account of Montana history offers an in-depth narrative of two centuries of events. Missoula, MT: Mountain Press Publishing Co., 1999.

Tirrell, Norma. *Compass American Guides: Montana,* 5th ed. New York: Fodor's Travel Publications, 2002.

Nebraska

HISTORICAL AND TOURISM ORGANIZATIONS

Nebraska State Genealogy Center. | 100 N. 16th St., Beatrice 68310 | 402/223–3584 | www.beatrice.lib.ne.us.

Nebraska State Historical Society. | Box 82554, 1500 R St., Lincoln 68501 | 402/471–4754 or 800/833–6747 | www.nebraskahistory.org.

Nebraska Travel and Tourism Division. | Box 94666, Lincoln 68509 | 402/471–3796 800/228–4307 | visitnebraska.org.

HISTORY TOURS AND PACKAGES

Allied Tours. This company specializes in Lewis and Clark tours ranging from 1 to 10 days in length. | 720 E. Norfolk Ave., Norfolk 68701 | 402/721–8730 or 800/721–8730 | fax 402/721–7967 | www.alliedtt.com.

Fun Tours. The "Get to Know Nebraska" tour offered each June includes Chadron, Fort Robinson, Chimney Rock, and several Pony Express stations throughout the state. | 4720 Baldwin, Lincoln 68504 | 402/466–1776 or 800/742–7717 | fax 402/466–1414 | www.funtoursne.com.

River Barge Excursion Lines. One of the tours run by this company follows the route Lewis and Clark took along the Missouri River from near Kansas City to Sioux City, with stops in Brownville, Nebraska City, Bellevue, and the Desoto National Wildlife Refuge. Storytellers and historians make the journey informative. Packages are for seven to nine days. | 201 Opelousas Ave., New Orleans, LA 70114 | 888/462–2743 | www.riverbarge.com.

Tumbleweed Tours. This small company customizes day-long tours along the Oregon Trail, where you will hear about ghost towns, vigilante justice, and the Pony Express. | 30371 Rd. 3035, Fairfield 68938 | 402/262–2276 | fax 402/726–2489.

FURTHER READING

Boye, Alan. *The Complete Roadside Guide to Nebraska*. This book covers all 93 counties of Nebraska, including folklore and listings of thousands of historical sites and museums. St. Johnsbury, VT: Saltillo Press, 1993.

Cather, Willa. *Oh, Pioneers!* The fictional story of one immigrant family and their friends who make a new life on the Nebraska prairie. Boston, New York: Houghton Mifflin, 1913.

Hickey, Donald R. *Nebraska Moments*. A series of vignettes portraying people, places, events, and institutions sum up the story of Nebraska. Lincoln: University of Nebraska Press, 1992.

Moulton, Candy. *Roadside History of Nebraska*. Arranged in five major geographical areas, the guide narrates the entire history of the state. Missoula, MT: Mountain Press Publishing Co., 1997.

Nebraska State Historical Society. *Nebraska: A Guide to the Cornhusker State*. From ethnic groups to ecology to art and literature, this reference covers it all. Lincoln: University of Nebraska Press, 1979.

Olson, James C., and Ronald C. Naugle. *History of Nebraska*. With emphasis on the Native American experience, the authors have covered many of the political and cultural movements in the history of the state. Lincoln: University of Nebraska Press, 1997.

Sandoz, Mari. *Cheyenne Autumn*. The true story of the Cheyenne incarceration at Fort Robinson in the fall and winter of 1879. New York: Avon Books, 1969.

Nevada

HISTORICAL AND TOURISM ORGANIZATIONS

Nevada Commission on Tourism. | 401 N. Carson St., Carson City 89701 | 800/NEVADA-8 | www.travelnevada.com.

Nevada State Historic Preservation Office. | 100 N. Stewart St., Carson City 89701 | 775/684–3448 | fax 775/684–3442.

FURTHER READING

Carlson, Helen S. *Nevada Place Names: A Geographical Dictionary*. An alphabetical listing of the history and folklore of the names on the map of Nevada. Reno: University of Nevada Press, 1974.

Castleman, Deke. *Compass American Guides: Nevada,* 1st ed. New York: Fodor's Travel Publications, 2000.

Glass, Mary Ellen, and Al. *Touring Nevada: A Historic and Scenic Guide*. The best guide book for travelers interested in the historical sights of Nevada. Reno: University of Nevada Press, 1983.

Hulse, James. *The Silver State*. A readable and thorough history textbook for high school students. Reno: University of Nevada Press, 1998.

Laxalt, Robert. *Nevada—A History*. A personal and lyrical rendering of Nevada history by the state's best-known and most beloved writer, founder of the University of Nevada Press. Reno: University of Nevada Press, 1977.

Moreno, Richard. *Roadside History of Nevada.* Offbeat stories of people and places from Nevada's past. Missoula, MT: Mountain Press Publishing Co., 2000.

Paher, Stan. *Nevada Ghost Towns and Mining Camps.* An epic reference of 668 Nevada ghost towns, as well as caves, hot springs, gem sites, and emigrant trails. Reno: Nevada Publications, 1974.

New Mexico

HISTORICAL AND TOURISM ORGANIZATIONS

Historical Society of New Mexico. | Box 1912, Santa Fe 87504 | www.hsnm.org.

Indian Pueblo Cultural Center. | Albuquerque 87102 | 505/843–7270 | www.indianpueblo.org.

New Mexico Department of Tourism. | 491 Old Santa Fe Trail, Santa Fe 87503 | 505/827–7400 or 800/545–2070 | fax 505/827–7402 | www.newmexico.org.

New Mexico Genealogical Society. | Box 8283, Albuquerque 87198 | www.nmgs.org.

New Mexico Steam Locomotive and Railroad Historical Society. | Box 27270, Albuquerque 87125 | 505/332–2926 | www.nmrhs.org.

Spanish Colonial Arts Society. | Box 5378, Santa Fe 87502 | 505/982–2226 | fax 505/982–4585 | www.spanishcolonial.org.

HISTORY TOURS AND PACKAGES

Around and About Tours. | 6716 Mesa Grande Ave., El Paso, TX 79912 | 915/833–2650 | www.aroundandabouttours.com.

Enchanted Lands Enterprises. Van tours vary from a few hours to a day and can also be customized. Standard tours include explorations of mountain villages and Indian Pueblos. Bicycle tours can be arranged. | Box 1222, Los Alamos 87544 | 505/661–8687 | www.enchantedlands.com.

Gray Line of Albuquerque. | 300 2nd St. SW, Albuquerque 87102 | 505/244–9258 or 866/242–2998 | www.grayline.com.

New Mexico Tour Guides Association. Finding professional tour guides can be tough in a state as sparsely populated as New Mexico. It's best to start your search by consulting this organization. Members are dedicated to high standards and can provide expertise in various topics, such as natural history and architecture. Most expect you to provide your own transportation on tours. | Box 2463, Santa Fe 87504 | 505/466–4877 | www.nmguides.com.

FURTHER READING

Billington, Monroe Lee. *New Mexico's Buffalo Soldiers: 1866–1900.* African-American troops known as Buffalo Soldiers were stationed in remote forts throughout New Mexico to protect settlers from outlaws and Indians. Boulder: University Press of Colorado, 1994.

Frank, Larry, et al. *A Land So Remote: Religious Art of New Mexico 1780–1907.* Artistic depictions of saints and other revered figures were (and still are) integral to New Mexico culture. Santa Fe: Red Crane Books, 2001.

Fugate, Francis L., and Roberta B. *Roadside History of New Mexico.* Entertaining anecdotes and old photographs and maps describe the historic sights you can see as you drive through New Mexico. Missoula, MT: Mountain Press Publishing Co., 1989.

Harbert, Nancy. *Compass American Guides: New Mexico,* 4th ed. New York: Fodor's Travel Publications, 2000.

Harris, Linda. *Ghost Towns Alive! Trips to New Mexico's Past.* A guide to both newly resurrected and long-dead towns, illustrated with contemporary and historical photographs. Albuquerque: University of New Mexico Press, 2003.

Hillerman, Tony. *The Great Taos Bank Robbery: And Other True Stories of the Southwest.* Best known for his fictional accounts of law enforcement on the Navajo Reservation, Hillerman reveals some nonfiction tidbits from New Mexico's past. New York: Harper Perennial, 2001.

Knaut, Andrew L. *The Pueblo Revolt of 1680: Conquest and Resistance in Seventeenth Century New Mexico.* The story of the short-lived victory of northern New Mexico's Pueblo Indians over the cruelties of early Spanish settlers. Norman: University of Oklahoma Press, 1998.

Larson, Carole. *Forgotten Frontier: The Story of Southeastern New Mexico.* This book details the lawless territorial period of a rugged region from 1850 to 1912. Albuquerque: University of New Mexico Press, 1993.

North Dakota

HISTORICAL AND TOURISM ORGANIZATIONS

North Dakota Indian Affairs Commission. | 600 E. Boulevard Ave., 1st floor, J Wing, Bismarck 58505 | www.health.state.nd.us/ndiac.

North Dakota Tourism Department. | 604 E. Boulevard Ave., Bismarck 58505 | 800/435–5663 | fax 701/328–4878 | www.ndtourism.com.

State Historical Society of North Dakota. | 612 E. Boulevard Ave., Bismarck 58505 | 701/328–2666 | fax 701/328–3710 | www.state.nd.us/hist.

FURTHER READING

Dill, C. L. *Early Peoples of North Dakota.* Written in an easy-to-understand manner, this book traces the settlement of North Dakota from 11,000 years ago to 1858, when the first U.S. Army fort was built. Bismarck: State Historical Society of North Dakota, 1990.

Heidenreich, Virginia. *The Fur Trade in North Dakota.* The impact of the fur trade on American Indian cultures in North Dakota from the 1730s to 1880s is captured in four well-written essays by various authors. Bismarck: State Historical Society of North Dakota, 1990.

Hollow, Robert C., and Herbert T. Hoover. *The Last Years of Sitting Bull.* The life of the Sioux chief, from the 1870s to his death in 1890, is the focus of this volume. Bismarck: State Historical Society of North Dakota, 1984.

North Dakota Historical Society. *Fort Buford and the Military Frontier on the Northern Plains, 1850–1900.* The story of the fort that protected non-native travelers along the Yellowstone and Missouri rivers during the Indian Wars culminates with the surrender of Sitting Bull at the fort. Bismarck: State Historical Society of North Dakota, 2001.

Reid, Russell. *Lewis and Clark in North Dakota.* Through entries in the journals of Lewis and Clark, this superb example of diligent research traces the team's trip along the Missouri River and its encounters with local people and cultures. Bismarck: State Historical Society of North Dakota, 2003.

Oklahoma

HISTORICAL AND TOURISM ORGANIZATIONS

Arkansas River Historical Society. | 5350 Cimarron Rd., Catoosa 74015 | 918/266–2291 | fax 918/266–7678 | www.tulsaweb. com/port/society.

Oklahoma State Historical Society. | 2100 N. Lincoln Blvd., Oklahoma City 73105 | 405/ 521–2491 | www.ok-history.mus.ok.us.

Oklahoma Tourism and Recreation Department, Travel and Tourism Division. | 500 Will Rogers Bldg., DA92, Oklahoma City 73105 | 405/521–3981 or 800/652–6552 | fax 405/521–3992 | tourism.state.ok.us.

Southwest Oklahoma Genealogical and Historical Society. | Box 148, Lawton 73502 | www.sirinet.net/~lgarris/swogs.

HISTORY TOURS AND PACKAGES

Territorial Tours Ltd. This company focuses on the frontier heritage of the central Oklahoma area. | 1636 S.W. 79th Terr., Oklahoma City 73159 | 405/681–6432 | fax 405/681–6442 | territorialtoursltd@earthlink.net.

FURTHER READING

Burton, Jeffrey. *Indian Territory and the United States, 1866–1906: Courts, Government, and the Movement for Oklahoma Statehood.* Norman: University of Oklahoma Press, 1995.

Fitzgerald, David. *Oklahoma II.* Portland, OR: Graphic Arts Center Publishing Co, 1984.

Fugate, Francis L. *Roadside History of Oklahoma.* Drive into the past with this guide to Oklahoma's history, from the Butterfield Overland Mail to the Chisholm Trail. Missoula, MT: Mountain Press Publishing Co., 1991.

Irving, Washington. *A Tour on the Prairies.* Norman: University of Oklahoma Press, 1985.

Jahoda, Gloria. *The Trail of Tears: The Story of the Indian Removals.* New York: Random House, 1995.

Wallis, Michael. *The Real Wild West: The 101 Ranch and the Creation of the American West.* New York: St. Martin's Press, 1999.

Zellner, William W., ed. *Oklahoma: The First Hundred Years.* Ada, OK: Galaxy Publications, 1988.

Oregon

HISTORICAL AND TOURISM ORGANIZATIONS

Oregon Coast Visitors Association. | 137 N.E. 1st St., Newport 97365 | 888/628–2101 | fax 541/265–2188 | www.visittheoregoncoast.com.

Oregon Historic Cemeteries Association. | Box 14279, Portland 97293 | 503/232–1643 | www. oregoncemeteries.org.

Oregon Historic Trails Project. | 1726 Washington St., Oregon City 97045 | 503/657–9336 | fax 503/557–8590 | www. endoftheoregontrail.org/oregontrails.

Oregon Historical Society. | 1200 S.W. Park Ave., Portland, 97203 | 503/222–1741 | www.ohs.org.

Oregon State Park Information Center. | 1115 Commercial St. NE, Salem 97301 | 800/551–6949 | www.oregonstateparks.org.

Oregon Tourism Commission, Tourism Division. | 775 Summer St. NE, Salem 97310 | 503/373–1270; 800/543–8838 in Oregon; 800/547–7842 | www.traveloregon.com.

Southern Oregon Historical Society. | 106 N. Central Ave., Medford 97501 | 541/773–6536 | fax 541/776–7994 | www.sohs.org.

Southern Oregon Visitors Association | 541/ 779–4691 | www.sova.org.

Willamette Valley Visitors Association | 541/ 750–0156 or 866/548–5018 | www. willamettevalley.org.

HISTORY TOURS AND PACKAGES

Rail Travel Center. One terrific journey offered by this international company is the weeklong Columbia River stern-wheeler cruise, which includes daily road trips to many of eastern Oregon's historic Old West towns. | 800/458–5394 | fax 802/389–4350 | www.railtravelcenter. com.

FURTHER READING

Gulick, Bill. *Roadside History of Oregon.* A handy reference for the road tripper, the guide describes sites along Lewis and Clark's route and the Oregon Trail and tells the story of Oregon. Missoula, MT: Mountain Press Publishing Co., 1991.

Jewell, Judy. *Compass American Guides: Oregon,* 4th ed. New York: Fodor's Travel Publications, 2002.

O'Donnell, Terence. *An Arrow in the Earth: General Joel Palmer and the Indians of Oregon.* The story of Joel Palmer, who led one of the largest Oregon Trail emigrations and established the Indian reservation system in Oregon. Portland: Oregon Historical Society, 1991.

South Dakota

HISTORICAL AND TOURISM ORGANIZATIONS

Black Hills, Badlands and Lakes Association. | 1851 Discovery Cir., Rapid City 57701 | 605/355–3600 | www.blackhillsbadlands.com.

Great Lakes of South Dakota Association. | Box 786, 320 E. Capitol Ave., Pierre 57501 | 605/224–4617 or 888/386–4617 | fax 605/224–9913 | www.sdgreatlakes.org.

Preserve South Dakota. | 215 W. Sioux Ave., Pierre 57501 | 605/945–0409.

Society of Black Hills Pioneers. | 735 State St., Spearfish 57783 | 605/722–0315.

South Dakota State Historical Society. | 900 Governors Dr., Pierre 57501 | 605/773–3458 | fax 605/773–6041 | www.sdhistory.org.

South Dakota Tourism. | 711 E. Wells Ave., Pierre 57501 | 605/773–3301 | fax 605/773–3256 | www.travelsd.com.

Southeast South Dakota Visitors Association. | 800 Mariner La., Suite 104, Yankton 57078 | 605/665–2435 or 888/353–7382 | fax 605/665–8776 | www.travelsd.com.

HISTORY TOURS AND PACKAGES

Black Hills Tourmaster. Take the Old West Experience tour, which includes Spearfish Canyon, Pactola Lake, and Deadwood and concludes with the Circle B Chuckwagon Supper and Show. | 210 Main St., Hill City 57745 | 605/574–2678 or 877/710–7600 | fax 605/574–2679 | www.blackhillstourmaster.com.

Gray Line of the Black Hills. Customized sightseeing tours of the Black Hills and surrounding areas are available for groups or individuals. | Box 1106, 1600 E. St. Patrick St., Rapid City 57709 | 605/342–4461 or 800/456–4461 | fax 605/341–5152 | www.blackhillsgrayline.com.

L&J Golden Circle Tours. Take a narrated, personalized seven-hour tour of Custer State Park, Sylvan Lake, Needles Highway, and other locations. | Box 454, Custer 57730 | 605/673–4349 or 877/811–4349 | fax 605/341–5152 | www.goldencircletours.com.

FURTHER READING

Griffith, Thomas D. *Compass American Guides: South Dakota, 2nd ed.* A comprehensive guide book exploring the history, evolution, and attractions of South Dakota. New York: Fodor's Travel Publications, 1998.

Hasselstrom, Linda. *Roadside History of South Dakota.* Learn about the roles that fur traders, homesteaders, politicians, ranchers, and farmers have played in South Dakota's history. Missoula, MT: Mountain Press Publishing Co., 1994.

Parker, Watson. *Gold in the Black Hills.* A well-researched account of the Black Hills gold rush of 1874–79. Norman: University of Oklahoma Press, 1966.

Parker, Watson. *Deadwood: The Golden Years.* This history captures the colorful 1875–1925 period in Deadwood, a prototypical American frontier and gold-rush town. Lincoln: University of Nebraska Press, 1981.

Texas

HISTORICAL AND TOURISM ORGANIZATIONS

East Texas Historical Association. | Box 6223, SFA Station, Nacogdoches 75962 | 936/468–2407 | leonardo.sfasu.edu/etha.

East Texas Tourism Association. | 421 N. Center St., Longview 75601 | 903/757–4444 | www.easttexasguide.com.

South Texas Historical Association. | Department of History, MSC No. 166, Texas A&M University-Kingsville, Kingsville, 78363 | 361/593–2776 | www.tamuk.edu/webuser/history/stha.html.

Texas Department of Tourism Development. | Box 12728, Austin 78711 | 512/462–9191, 800/888–8TEX, or 800/452–9292 | www.state.tx.us.

Texas Department of Transportation, Travel Division. | 150 E. Riverside Dr., Austin 78704 | 512/462–9191, 800/888–8TEX, or 800/452–9292 | www.traveltex.com.

Texas Historical Commission. | Box 12276, Austin 78711 | 512/463–6100 | www.thc.state.tx.us.

Texas Parks and Wildlife. | 4200 Smith School Rd., Austin 78744 | 800/792–1112 | www.tpwd.state.tx.us.

Texas State Historical Association. | 1 University Station, D0901, Austin 78712 | 512/471–1525 | www.tsha.utexas.edu.

West Texas Historical Association. | Box 41041, Texas Tech, Lubbock 79409 | 806/742–9076 | swco.ttu.edu/WestTexas.

FURTHER READING

Fehrenbach, T. R. *Lone Star: A History of Texas and the Texans.* New York: DaCapo Press, 2000.

Metz, Leon C. *Roadside History of Texas.* A glimpse of Texas history in points of interest along highways and back roads throughout the state. Missoula, MT: Mountain Press Publishing Co., 1994.

Reavis, Dick. *Compass American Guides: Texas,* 2nd ed. New York: Fodor's Travel Publications, 1997.

Tyler, Ron ed. *The New Handbook of Texas.* A complete encyclopedia of Texas. Austin: Texas State Historical Association, 1996.

Utley, Robert M. *Lone Star Justice: The First Century of the Texas Rangers.* New York: Oxford University Press, 2002.

Utah

HISTORICAL AND TOURISM ORGANIZATIONS

Daughters of the Utah Pioneers. | 300 N. Main St., Salt Lake City 84103 | 801/538–1050 | fax 801/538–1119 | www.daughtersofutahpioneers. com/dup.

Utah Division of Parks and Recreation. | 1594 W. North Temple St., Suite 116, Salt Lake City 84116 | 801/538–7220 | www.parks.state.ut.us.

Utah Museums Association. | Box 2077, Salt Lake City 84110 | 801/240–4649 | fax 801/240–5343 | www.utahmuseums.org.

Utah State Historical Society. | 300 S. Rio Grande, Salt Lake City 84101 | 801/533–3500 or 801/533–3501 | fax 801/533–3503 | www. history.utah.gov.

Utah Travel Council. | Council Hall, Capitol Hill, Salt Lake City 84114 | 801/538–1030 or 800/200–1160 | www.utah.com.

HISTORY TOURS AND PACKAGES

Bluff Expeditions. Guides trained in local history, Native American history, and archaeology lead tours by foot, bike, boat, ski, and van throughout southeastern Utah and the Four Corners area. Although the company offers several pre-scheduled tours, it enjoys customizing trips based on the interests of participants. | Box 219, Bluff 84512 | 435/672–2446 or 888/637–2582 | www. pioneerhouseinn.com.

Hondoo Rivers and Trails. Led by experts and local history buffs, tours of southern Utah focus on archaeology, prehistory, and history. You can choose from single and multi-day tours by vehicle, horse, raft, and foot. | Box 98, Torrey 84775 | 435/425–3519 or 800/332–2696 | fax 435/425–3548 | www.hondoo.com.

FURTHER READING

Bennett, Cynthia Larsen. *Roadside History of Utah.* In-depth histories of almost every town in Utah, including many that no longer exist. Missoula, MT: Mountain Press Publishing Co., 1999.

Cuch, Forrest, ed. *A History of Utah's American Indians.* Many of the essays in this book are written by Native Americans from Utah, giving the work a perspective that differs from much of the other historical writing about the state. Logan: Utah State University Press, 2000.

DeLafosse, Peter H., editor. *Trailing the Pioneers: A Guide to Utah's Emigrant Trails, 1829–1869.* Detailed accounts of the exploration and use of Utah's five most famous emigrant routes are included in this collection. Logan, UT: Utah State University Press, 1994.

McCormick, John S. *The Gathering Place: An Illustrated History of Salt Lake City.* The Salt Lake City area has been the center of population, political power, and religious authority in Utah since the region was settled, making this book an excellent resource for anyone interested in the history of both the city and the state. Salt Lake City: Signature Books, 2000.

Peterson, Charles S. *Utah: A Bicentennial History.* Although this book is written by one of Utah's leading historians, the lively and accessible language gives it the page-turning qualities of a good novel. New York: W. W. Norton and Company, 1977.

Russell, Osborne. *Journal of a Trapper: In the Rocky Mountains Between 1834 and 1843.* Osborne Russell was a mountain man who kept this journal during his fur-trapping travels and spent much of his time in the region that would become Utah. Santa Barbara, CA: The Narrative Press, 2001.

Stegner, Wallace. *Mormon Country.* These personal essays, created by one of the West's leading writers, focus on how the Mormon presence has made Utah's history unique among American states. Lincoln: University of Nebraska Press, 1982.

Tanner, Annie Clark. *Mormon Mother: An Autobiography.* Born into a Utah polygamist family in 1864, the author chronicles the ways of polygamy, the Mormon church, and the women of the Old West. Salt Lake City: University of Utah Press, 1983.

Topping, Gary, ed. *Great Salt Lake: An Anthology.* These essays focus on the exploration of the lake, its meaning to mountain men and pioneers, legends about creatures that inhabit the waters, and human use of the lake over the years. Logan: Utah State University Press, 2002.

Wharton, Tom and Gayen. *Compass American Guides: Utah,* 5th ed. New York: Fodor's Travel Publications, 2001.

Washington

HISTORICAL AND TOURISM ORGANIZATIONS

Washington State Historical Society. | 1911 Pacific Ave., Tacoma 98402 | 253/272–3500 | www.wshs.org.

Washington Tourism Division. | Box 42500, Olympia 98504 | 360/725–5050 or 800/544–1800 | www.tourism.wa.gov.

HISTORY TOURS AND PACKAGES

Pacific Northwest Journeys. The company creates detailed journeys with a specific focus—say, Old West or cowboy theme—in Washington, Oregon, and British Columbia. | 6016 Fauntleroy Way SW, Seattle 90136 | 206/935–9730 or 800/935–9730 | fax 206/935–1091 | www.pnwjourneys.com.

FURTHER READING

Brokenshire, Doug. *Washington State Place Names: From Alki to Yelm.* Learn the history of the places you visit by reading the story of how they got their name. Caldwell, ID: Caxton Press, 1993.

Doerper, John. *Compass American Guides: Washington,* 3rd ed. New York: Fodor's Travel Publications, 2002.

Ficken, Robert E. *The Forested Land: A History of Lumbering in Western Washington.* The history of the economic mainstay of western Washington is traced from 1850 to 1945. Seattle: University of Washington Press, 1987.

___ **and Charles P. Lewarne.** *Washington: A Centennial History.* Seattle: University of Washington Press, 1988.

Kirk, Ruth, and Carmela Alexander. *Exploring Washington's Past: A Road Guide to History,* revised ed. Seattle: University of Washington Press, 1996.

Lewarne, Charles Pierce. *Washington State,* 3rd ed. A high-school history textbook. Seattle: University of Washington Press, 2003.

McDonald, Rob, et al. *Washington for the Curious.* Organized by highway number and equipped with maps and a mileage chart, this guide describes the towns and cities of Washington, their origins and history. Fairfield, ID: Peak Media, 1997.

Pelz, Ruth. *Washington Story: A History of Our State.* Seattle: Seattle Public Schools, 1993.

Roe, Joann. *Ghost Camps and Boom Towns.* The fascinating story of the mining towns of the Pacific Northwest, illustrated. Bellingham: Montevista Press, 1995.

Swan, James Gilchrist. *The Northwest Coast: Or, Three Years' Residence in Washington Territory.* This reprint edition includes illustrations by Norman H. Clark. Seattle: University of Washington Press, 1992.

Wyoming

HISTORICAL AND TOURISM ORGANIZATIONS

American Heritage Center. | 2111 Willett Dr., Laramie 82071 | 307/766–4114 | www.uwyo.edu/ahc.

Wyoming Division of Tourism. | I–25 at College Dr., Dept. WY, Cheyenne 82002 | 307/777–7777 or 800/225–5996 | www.wyomingtourism.org.

Wyoming State Historical Society. | 1740H Dell Range Blvd., Cheyenne 82009 | No phone. | wyshs.org.

HISTORY TOURS AND PACKAGES

Grub Steak Expeditions and Tours. A former Yellowstone park ranger and retired teacher leads these personalized tours in northwestern Wyoming, including the Big Horn Basin and Yellowstone National Park. You can take half-, full-, or multi-day outings. | Box 1013, Cody 82414 | 307/527–6316 or 800/527–6316 | www.grubsteaktours.com.

Platte Valley Shuttles and Tours. The company runs tours of the Snowy Range and Battle Mountain scenic highways, statewide tours of the Oregon Trail, and custom tours covering all of Wyoming. | Box 1652, Saratoga 82331 | 307/326–5582 | www.plattevalleyshuttles.com.

Wagons Across Wyoming. Choose a four-hour tour in the Casper Area, a full-day trip on emigrant trails, or a two-day, one-night tour of the Powder River Basin. | Box 132, Daniel 82331 | 307/859–8629 or 307/733–3045 | www.wagonsacrosswyoming.com.

Your Ride/Adventures West. Take a five-day, four-night wagon train adventure along the Lander Cut-Off of the Oregon Trail. Trips are offered in July and August. | 2041 E. 21st St., Casper 82601 | 307/577–1226 | fax 307/577–1226 | www.usatouring.com/historical_tours.html.

FURTHER READING

Blevins, Winfred. *Roadside History of Yellowstone National Park.* Organized by park roads, the guide details the historical events that took place within the region now protected by the park. Missoula, MT: Mountain Press Publishing Co., 1991.

Burt, Nathaniel. *Compass American Guides: Wyoming,* 4th ed. New York: Fodor's Travel Publications, 2002.

Larson, T. A. *History of Wyoming,* 2nd ed. This standard work on Wyoming gives the best overview of the state's history from an academic viewpoint. Lincoln: University of Nebraska Press, 1978.

___. *Wyoming, A History.* Written by the "grandfather" of Wyoming history, this is an easy-to-digest overview of the state's history. New York: W. W. Norton and Company, 1984.

Moulton, Candy. *Roadside History of Wyoming.* As you travel through the state, you can look up the historic sights you see in this comprehensive and entertaining volume. Missoula, MT: Mountain Press Publishing Co., 1995.

Sodaro, Craig, and Randy Adams. *Frontier Spirit, The Story of Wyoming.* A good general history of the state. Boulder: Johnson Books, 1996.

Trenholm, Virginia Cole. *The Arapahoes, Our People*. The definitive history of the Arapaho Indians, one of the two tribes remaining in Wyoming. Norman: University of Oklahoma Press, 1970.

___ and Maurine Carley. *The Shoshones: Sentinels of the Rockies*. A comprehensive history of the Shoshone Indians, who were at one time led by the great chief Washakie. Norman: University of Oklahoma Press, 1964.

ABOUT OUR WRITERS

✦ Bison, wolves, and elk regularly roam through the Gardiner, Montana backyard of **Jean Arthur,** who wrote the Montana chapter. Arthur's award-winning books include *Timberline* and *A Century of Skiing on Mount Hood.* She won the 2002 Sports Story of the Year Award from the Society of Professional Journalists, for an article on ice boating.

✦ A descendant of pioneers who settled the city of Bellevue, Washington, **Cheryl Murfin Bond** contributed to the Oregon chapter. The Oregon native, who studied U.S. history at the University of Washington, has written extensively on Northwest travel for publications that include *Portland Parent* magazine. She is coauthor of *Lobster Press Kids' Guide to Exploring Seattle.*

✦ **Kate Boyes,** a contributor to the Utah chapter, was the assistant editor of *Western American Literature* for many years. Her essays and reviews appear in numerous journals and anthologies, including *Western Historical Quarterly.* A resident of Utah since 1982, she has taught writing at two universities there.

✦ Nevada has been **Deke Castleman's** beat since the 1980s. An American history major in college, he savors every bit of the Old West left in the rapidly changing Silver State, which he covered for this guide. In his three travel guides to Nevada he's spotlighted the state's heritage in hopes of helping to preserve the rich history that does remain.

✦ Former editor of *Canyon Legacy,* a Moab-based journal that covers the cultural and archaeological past of the Four Corners region, **Lisa Church** contributed to the Utah chapter. A lifetime fascination with the history and images of the Old West drew her to her present home in Moab, from which she writes about the people, places, and heritage of the West.

✦ Santa Fe resident and inveterate road-tripper **Andrew Collins,** a former Fodor's editor, has authored more than a dozen guidebooks, including *Fodor's Gay Guide to the USA.* A contributor to the New Mexico chapter, he writes regularly for a number of newspapers and magazines, including *Travel + Leisure.*

✦ **Lori Cumpston,** winner of many journalism awards, contributed to the Colorado chapter. She works full-time covering stories of the West for a variety of publications, and writes regularly for Fodor's. The Colorado native still lives in the state where she was born.

✦ From the Valley to the Panhandle and from the Piney Woods to El Paso, veteran Fodor's writer **Lisa Dunford** has logged thousands of miles exploring the presidios, missions, and battle sites of Texas. She makes her home in South Texas, which she covered for this guide.

✦ Arkansas City, Kansas was the main jumping-off point for the greatest of all Oklahoma land rushes—the Cherokee Strip Run of 1893—and is the birthplace and present home of Oklahoma contributor **Foss Farrar.** Farrar has worked as a journalist for the *Kansas City Kansan* in Kansas City, Kansas, for Primedia Business Magazines in Houston, and for other publications. He is now a reporter at the *Arkansas City Traveler.*

✦ **Karen Gibson,** one of Fodor's Oklahoma stalwarts, contributed to the Oklahoma chapter. Her special interest in Native Americans and all things Oklahoman (she's lived there since the mid-1970s) have resulted in countless travel features and educational writing on the state.

✦ Black Hills resident **Tom Griffith,** who has served as Director of Communications for the Mount Rushmore Preservation Fund, wrote the South Dakota chapter. In his busy career he has worked for newspapers in Arizona, Montana, and South Dakota and has written several books, including *America's Shrine of Democracy.*

✦ New Mexico and West Texas contributor **Marilyn Haddrill,** born, raised, and still living in New Mexico, grew up exploring the desert on horseback. As a newspaper correspondent and freelance journalist she has written features on the history of southern New Mexico and West Texas, such as the lost treasures of the Spanish conquistadores and the outlaw life of Billy the Kid.

✦ **Lisa Hamilton,** a California contributor, is a food and agriculture writer who spends her days on California's back roads, investigating the history of farming in the state.

✦ **Candi Helseth's** grandparents came from Norway and traveled by wagon train to North Dakota, where they established a homestead. The Helseth family still lives there, and our North Dakota writer grew up trail riding in the area. Trading in her saddle for a computer, she has written several histories for area cooperatives and has published stories on Lewis and Clark in *American Profile Magazine*, *North Dakota Living*, and *North Dakota Horizons*.

✦ A contributor to numerous Fodor's titles, **Diana Lambdin Meyer** learned how to "spin a mean yarn" at the knee of her grandfather, the family genealogist. A Nebraska native who now lives in Missouri, she wrote the Nebraska chapter.

✦ Arizona contributor **Carrie Miner** writes frequently for *Arizona Highways* magazine, digging up local folklore and historical tidbits.

✦ **Cynthia Mines,** a Kansas contributor, has published two books on Kansas history. Her articles on Kansas topics have also appeared in several newspapers and periodicals. She is publisher/editor of the monthly *Wichita Times* and *Travel Kansas,* an annual magazine.

✦ A writer and lawyer based in Houston, Texas contributor **Janet Moore** regularly writes about travel and cultural topics. While attending Georgetown University's School of Foreign Service, she was a member of the history honor society, Phi Alpha Theta.

✦ Wyoming resident **Candy Moulton,** the author of ten books about the American West, wrote the Introduction and the Idaho and Wyoming chapters. Her titles include *Everyday Life in the Wild West from 1840 to 1900* and *Everyday Life Among the American Indians from 1800 to 1900*. She edits the *Western Outlaw-Lawman History Association Journal* and *Roundup* magazine, the official publication of the Western Writers of America. She is presently writing a history of Colorado and three books about frontier and military sites in Wyoming, Colorado, and Nebraska. She has traveled extensively throughout the West writing for *Sunset, True West,* and many other publications.

✦ **June Naylor,** a sixth-generation Texan who contributed to the Texas chapter, has made a career of writing about the storied backroads of her state. One of her favorite places to visit is the Oak Grove Cemetery in Nacogdoches, where William Clark Jr., her great-great-great-great-great grandfather and a signer of the Texas Declaration of Independence, is buried.

✦ Managing editor of *Kansas Heritage* magazine and associate editor of *Kansas History: A Journal of the Central Plains,* **Susan S. Novak** contributed to the Kansas chapter. She has been on the staff of the Kansas State Historical Society since 1993.

✦ California contributor **Reed Parsell** is a travel writer for *The Sacramento Bee*. He also is the great-grandson of a 19th-century Indiana sheriff.

✦ **Patrick Regan** is a descendant of Colorado gold rush pioneers. A contributor to the Colorado chapter, he is the author of numerous nonfiction and illustrated books. When not working he can be found (or better yet, not found) exploring the backcountry trails and trout streams of southwestern Colorado.

✦ Ever since that first cross-country trip in the family station wagon, Oregon contributor **Holly S. Smith** has been exploring the Old West. A Washington resident, she's a contributing writer and editor for several Fodor's titles.

✦ From his San Francisco home, California contributor **John Andrew Vlahides** tours the Sierra Nevada and Central Coast by motorcycle. In his travels he investigates tales of the 19th-century westward migration to California, particularly the story of the Donner Party. An advice columnist, essayist, and former Clefs d'Or concierge, he is a Fodor's regular.

✦ Arizona contributors **Bob and Gloria Willis,** a husband-and-wife travel-writing and photography team, live in Scottsdale, Arizona. They are happiest camping and four-wheeling throughout Arizona in search of stories and pictures.

✦ A life-long history enthusiast, **Bobbi Zane** comes by her passion genetically. Her enthusiasm for the Old West was sparked when, as a young girl, she was given a biography of her relative Betty Zane, written by distant cousin Zane Grey. A contributor to the California chapter, she has visited and written about many of Grey's frontier haunts. She is a frequent contributor to Fodor's guides.

REGIONAL DIRECTORY

ARIZONA

Central Arizona
Camp Verde, *21, 25–26*
Jerome, *21, 32–33*
Prescott, *21, 38–39*
Wickenburg, *21, 47*

East-central Arizona
Show Low, *40–41*

North Central Arizona
Flagstaff, *27–28*
Grand Canyon National Park, *21, 29–31*
Page, *21, 36*
Williams, *48–50*
Winslow, *21, 50*

Northeastern Arizona
Holbrook, *21, 31*
Hopi Mesas, *15, 31–32*
Kayenta, *15, 33–34*
Tuba City, *15, 21, 43–44*
Window Rock, *15, 50*

Northwestern Arizona
Kingman, *34–35*

South-central Arizona
Apache Junction, *22*
Casa Grande, *26*
Florence, *28–29*
Mesa, *35*
Phoenix, *36–38*
Scottsdale, *39–40*

Southeastern Arizona
Bisbee, *22–25*
Douglas, *26–27*
Tombstone, *41–43*
Tubac, *20, 44–45*
Tucson, *20, 45–46*
Willcox, *47–48*

Southwestern Arizona
Yuma, *51–52*

CALIFORNIA

Central Coast
Paso Robles, *59, 81–82*
San Luis Obispo, *59, 97*
Santa Barbara, *59, 97–99*

Gold Country
Amador City, *58, 59–60*
Auburn, *58, 60–61*
Coloma, *58, 62–63*
Columbia, *58, 63*
Grass Valley, *58, 67–68*
Jackson, *58, 69*
Jamestown, *69–70*
Mariposa, *73–74*
Murphys, *58, 77–78*
Nevada City, *58, 78–79*
Placerville, *58, 82*
Sacramento, *58, 83–85*
Sonora, *58, 100*

Metro Los Angeles
Los Angeles, *58, 72–73*
San Juan Capistrano, *58, 96*

Monterey Bay
Carmel, *59, 61–62*
Monterey, *75–77*

Northern Coast
Eureka, *65–66*
Ferndale, *66*
Mendocino, *74–75*
Sonoma, *59, 99–100*

Northern Valley
Marysville, *74*
Oroville, *81*
Red Bluff, *83*
Weaverville, *103*

San Diego County
Anza-Borrego Desert State Park, *60*
Coronado, *64–65*
Escondido, *65*
Julian, *70–71*

Oceanside, *58, 80–81*
San Diego, *58, 85–89*

San Francisco Bay Area
Fremont, *66–67*
Oakland, *79–80*
San Francisco, *59, 89–95*
San Jose, *59, 95–96*
Santa Clara, *59, 99*

San Joaquin Valley
Hanford, *68*
Merced, *75*

Sierra Nevada
Lake Tahoe, *71–72*
Truckee, *100–103*
Yosemite National Park, *103–105*

COLORADO

Central Colorado
Colorado Springs, *112, 120–121*
Cripple Creek, *112, 124–125*

Eastern Plains
Burlington, *118*
La Junta, *112, 136*
Sterling, *114, 143–144*

High Rockies
Aspen, *115–116*
Breckenridge, *117–118*
Central City, *108, 119–120*
Fairplay, *112, 130*
Georgetown, *108, 131–132*
Glenwood Springs, *132–133*
Leadville, *108, 138–139*

North-central Colorado
Boulder, *116–117*
Denver, *108, 126–128*
Estes Park, *129–130*
Fort Collins, *130–131*
Golden, *133–134*
Greeley, *114, 135–136*

INDEX

NOTES

NOTES

NOTES

NOTES

Fodor's Key to the Guides

America's guidebook leader publishes guides for every kind of traveler. Check out our many series and find your perfect match.

Fodor's Gold Guides
America's favorite travel-guide series offers the most detailed insider reviews of hotels, restaurants, and attractions in all price ranges, plus great background information, smart tips, and useful maps.

Fodor's Road Guide USA
Big guides for a big country—the most comprehensive guides to America's roads, packed with places to stay, eat, and play across the U.S.A. Just right for road warriors, family vacationers, and cross-country trekkers.

COMPASS AMERICAN GUIDES
Stunning guides from top local writers and photographers, with gorgeous photos, literary excerpts, and colorful anecdotes. A must-have for culture mavens, history buffs, and new residents.

Fodor's CITYPACKS
Concise city coverage with a foldout map. The right choice for urban travelers who want everything under one cover.

Fodor's EXPLORING GUIDES
Hundreds of color photos bring your destination to life. Lively stories lend insight into the culture, history, and people.

Fodor's POCKET GUIDES
For travelers who need only the essentials. The best of Fodor's in pocket-size packages for just $9.95.

Fodor's To Go
Credit-card–size, magnetized color microguides that fit in the palm of your hand—perfect for "stealth" travelers or as gifts.

Fodor's FLASHMAPS
Every resident's map guide. 60 easy-to-follow maps of public transit, parks, museums, zip codes, and more.

Fodor's CITYGUIDES
Sourcebooks for living in the city: Thousands of in-the-know listings for restaurants, shops, sports, nightlife, and other city resources.

Fodor's AROUND THE CITY WITH KIDS
68 great ideas for family days, recommended by resident parents. Perfect for exploring in your own backyard or on the road.

Fodor's ESCAPES
Fill your trip with once-in-a-lifetime experiences, from ballooning in Chianti to overnighting in the Moroccan desert. These full-color dream books point the way.

Fodor's FYI
Get tips from the pros on planning the perfect trip. Learn how to pack, fly hassle-free, plan a honeymoon or cruise, stay healthy on the road, and travel with your baby.

Fodor's Languages for Travelers
Practice the local language before hitting the road. Available in phrase books, cassette sets, and CD sets.

Karen Brown's Guides
Engaging guides to the most charming inns and B&Bs in the U.S.A. and Europe, with easy-to-follow inn-to-inn itineraries.

Baedeker's Guides
Comprehensive guides, trusted since 1829, packed with A–Z reviews and star ratings.

At bookstores everywhere.　　　　www.fodors.com/books